Marine
Steam Engines
and Turbines

Marine Engineering Series

Marine Auxiliary Machinery
E. Souchotte, C.Eng., F.I.Mech.E., M.I.Mar.E.
David W. Smith, C.Eng., M.I.Mar.E.

Marine Diesel Engines
Edited by C. C. Pounder

Marine Electrical Practice
G. O. Watson, F.I.E.E., F.A.I.E.E., M.I.Mar.E.

Marine Steam Boilers
J. H. Milton, C.Eng., F.I.Mar.E., M.N.E.C.I.E.S.,
and R. M. Leach, C.Eng., M.I.Mech.E., F.I.Mar.E.

Marine Steam Engines and Turbines
S. C. McBirnie, C.Eng., M.I.Mech.E.

Marine Steam Engines and Turbines

S. C. McBIRNIE
C.Eng., M.I.Mech.E.

BUTTERWORTHS
London — Boston
Sydney — Wellington — Durban — Toronto

The Butterworth Group

United Kingdom   Butterworth & Co. (Publishers) Ltd
                  London: 88 Kingsway, WC2B 6AB

Australia   Butterworths Pty Ltd
             Sydney: 586 Pacific Highway, Chatswood, NSW 2067
             Also at Melbourne, Brisbane, Adelaide and Perth

Canada   Butterworth & Co. (Canada) Ltd
          Toronto: 2265 Midland Avenue, Scarborough, Ontario
          M1P 4S1

New Zealand   Butterworths of New Zealand Ltd
               Wellington: T & W Young Building, 77-85 Customhouse
               Quay, 1, CPO Box 472

South Africa   Butterworth & Co. (South Africa) (Pty) Ltd
                Durban: 152-154 Gale Street

USA   Butterworth (Publishers) Inc
       Boston: 10 Tower Office Park, Woburn, Mass. 01801

First published 1952 by George Newnes Ltd.
   reprinted 1955
Second edition 1961
   reprinted 1965
Third edition 1970
   reprinted 1975, 1976
Fourth edition 1980

© Butterworth & Co. (Publishers) Ltd., 1980

British Library Cataloguing in Publication Data
McBirnie, Samuel Clark
Marine steam engines and turbines.—4th ed.
1. Marine engines
I. Title
623.87'22   VM731   79-40053
ISBN 0-408-00387-1

Typeset by Reproduction Drawings Ltd, Sutton, Surrey.
Printed in England by Fletcher & Son Ltd., Norwich
and bound by Richard Clay (The Chaucer Press) Ltd, Bungay, Suffolk.

Preface

In preparing the present edition, the need to include new material and for a considerable amount of updating and amplifying made it obvious that if the length of the book was to be kept to a reasonable limit, some of the older material would have to be omitted or considerably reduced. The present rather moribund position of the reciprocating steam engine suggested that this was the obvious field in which to make the necessary economies. Consequently, and with no little regret, the chapters dealing solely with reciprocating engines have been omitted, and have been replaced by a single chapter consisting of the principles of operation, description of constructional details, and the main features of compounding.

Whatever the future may hold, there can be little doubt that fuel economics will continue to be no less stringent than at present. From this aspect, the chapter dealing with steam turbine theory has been amplified to emphasise the need for high thermal efficiency commensurate with moderate first cost and moderate dimensions, and with simplicity and reliability. The modern concept of defining a turbine stage by its U/C_0 and its degree of reaction—rather than by the former broad terms 'impulse' and 'reaction'—is illustrated. A new section has been added to this chapter dealing with the fundamental conditions imposed on astern turbines, and how the turbines are specified and designed to best meet these conditions. Typical calculations for a two-row velocity-compounded stage have also been added.

The chapter dealing with steam turbines has been updated where necessary to include some recent examples of modern turbines, with comparisons of type, efficiency and arrangement. A new section has been added to show how the approach to automatic centralised control affects the turbines themselves. The notes on turbine operation, maintenance and overhaul have been updated and amplified in the light of modern practice.

The chapter on condensers has been amplified to include the basis of choice, operation under varying conditions, and the effects of air in leakage, air cooling and air extraction.

Turbine reduction gearing has become of such interest and importance that it has been made the subject of a separate chapter, which attempts to explain the necessary fundamentals, and to illustrate these by some recent examples of traditional parallel-shaft gears and of epicyclic gears. Possible gear arrangements for direct-reversing and for contra-rotating propellers are illustrated in principle.

Chapter 12 which with the Rankine Cycle in practice has had a section added to show the losses of available energy due to irreversible heat transmission in the condenser and to irreversible expansion in the turbines. These two features are fundamental factors in the quest for high efficiency.

The chapter on future possibilities has been updated and amplified to deal briefly, but it is hoped, clearly, with combined steam and gas turbine cycles, turbines operating in conjunction with nuclear boilers, the supercritical steam cycle, and the binary vapour cycle.

SI units are used throughout, in conformity with the decision of governments and industry in general. The current examination requirements of the Department of Trade have been borne in mind.

It is with gratitude that I would like to thank the various firms, authorities and individuals listed in the Acknowledgements, whose most generous response to my request has provided numerous and excellent illustrations, drawings, photographs, technical and operating data, etc.

I also wish to acknowledge the assistance received from colleagues, former students and many others, too numerous to mention individually, whose co-operation has rendered this book possible. I venture to hope that a careful study of this edition will not only enable students to go forward with confidence to examinations, but will be of interest to both senior and junior engineers, and will be of some value for a future in which it seems more than possible that marine steam machinery could become of major importance.

S. C. McBirnie

Contents

Acknowledgements

The very rapidly-changing industrial conditions of the last ten years have resulted in firms changing their identity, and in some cases, regrettably, in their going out of business altogether. It has been proved quite impracticable to record accurately such changes; consequently if any of the undernoted firms has changed its identity, the author's acknowledgement and thanks are deemed to extend to the new identity.

The Institute of Marine Engineers for permission to use information and illustrations from papers read before the Institute by S. S. Cook, F. J. Cowlin, J. H. G. Monypenny, S. A. Smith, A. F. Veitch and T. B. Hutchison.

The Institution of Mechanical Engineers for permission to use information and illustrations from a paper read before the Institution by E. L. Denny.

The Marine Engineer and Naval Architect.

The Manchester Association of Engineers for permission to use information from a paper read before the Association by Gaunt and Wilkinson.

The Cambridge University Press for permission to use information from a paper on SI units by R. W. Haywood.

The American Society of Mechanical Engineers for information from a paper on turbine reduction gears.

Messrs. Edward Arnold (Publishers) Ltd. for information on SI steam tables and Mollier charts.

W. H. Allen, Sons & Co. Ltd., Pershore, Worcs.
Andrews and Cameron, Kirkintilloch.
Aspinall's Patent Governor Co., Liverpool.
W. & T. Avery Ltd., Birmingham.
Barclay Curle & Co. Ltd., Whiteinch, Glasgow.

ACKNOWLEDGEMENTS

Brown Bros. & Co., Rosebank Ironworks, Edinburgh.
Christiansen & Meyer, Hamburg, Germany.
Cockburns Ltd., Cardonald, Glasgow.
G.E.C. Turbine Generators Ltd, Industrial & Marine Steam
    Turbine Division, Manchester.
G.E.C. Marine and Industrial Gears Ltd., Rugby.
Alfred Holt & Co., Liverpool.
Lockwood & Carlisle Ltd., Eagle Foundry, Sheffield.
North Eastern Marine Engineering Co. Ltd., Wallsend-on-Tyne.
David Rowan & Co. Ltd., Marine Engineers, Glasgow.
Scotts' Shipbuilding & Engineering Co. Ltd., Greenock.
Alexander Stephen & Sons, Ltd., Linthouse, Glasgow.
United States Metallic Packing Co., Bradford.
Weir Pumps Ltd., Cathcart, Glasgow.
White's Marine Engineering Co. Ltd., Hebburn-on-Tyne.

Thanks are also due to the following individuals for their help and guidance in the preparation of this edition:

R. E. Burn.	W. W. Low.
R. F. Cheers.	G. G. Maclennan.
J. J. Cottrell.	D. G. Nicholas.
K . Cruickshank.	J. F. Robb.
B. McDonald Gawley.	G. H. Shannon.
A. E. Fothergill.	G. Tembey.
A. L. Hemsley.	B. G. Wood.
D. T. Howell.	D. E. Yates.
	I. T. Young.

1 Generation and properties of steam

Steam tables

All the information concerning the properties of steam in which we are interested is contained in the *Steam Tables*. These tables are the result of many years of international research and experiment, and the various steam tables at present in use in different countries will ultimately be superseded by the International Steam Tables.

For our purpose, an adequate and convenient version is the Students' Tables in SI units.*

Note on the SI unit of pressure

The definition of pressure is force per unit area. The SI units of force, the newton (N), and of area, the square metre (m^2) are quite fundamental, hence the fundamental unit of pressure is the newton per square metre (N/m^2), also called the pascal (Pa), i.e. $1.0 \text{ Pa} = 1.0 \text{ N/m}^2$.

The Pa, or the N/m^2 is inconveniently small, hence the megapascal (MPa) or the meganewton per square metre (MN/m^2) may be used instead, i.e.

$$1.0 \text{ MPa} = 1.0 \text{ MN/m}^2 = 10^6 \text{ Pa} = 10^6 \text{ N/m}^2$$

Industry as a whole, however, has not adopted 10^6 N/m^2 as the unit of pressure, but has adopted 10^5 N/m^2, which is called *1.0 Bar*. This unit of pressure appears to have been so chosen, and so named, only because 10^5 N/m^2 is the round figure nearest to standard atmospheric pressure. As we shall use bar as the unit of pressure throughout, it is important for the student to remember its definition.

Thermophysical Properties of Water Substance (Students' Tables in SI units) Edward Arnold, London.

1

The Students' Tables

In the Students' Tables, the unit of pressure given is the mega-pascal (MPa) and on each page there is printed a reminder that

$$1.0 \text{ MPa} = 10^6 \text{ N/m}^2 = 10.0 \text{ bar}$$

Also in the Students' Tables, the unit of specific volume is m^3/Mg. This is numerically the same as the unit dm^3/kg which we shall use, and again there is a reminder to this effect in the Students' Tables.

The Students' Tables consist of the following, i.e.

Table 1

This table gives only certain transport properties of saturated steam and water which are not involved in any of our investigations. We will not therefore make reference to Section 1 at all.

Table 2

This table gives the properties of saturated steam and water at various *saturation temperatures*. The saturation temperature is given in the extreme right hand column, which although headed θ/K, simply means °C, as explained on page 2 of the tables. The extreme left hand column, headed T/K is the saturation temperature in °C.abs.

Table 3

This table gives the properties of saturated steam and water at various *pressures*. The pressure in MPa, is given in the extreme left-hand column, and 1.0 MPa = 10.0 bar.

Note. The information given in Tables 2 and 3 is exactly the same. We would use Table 2 if we were given the saturation temperature, or Table 3 if we were given the pressure.

Table 4

This table gives the properties of superheated steam at various pressures and various total temperatures. The number of °C by which the total temperature exceeds the saturation temperature is called the *superheat range* or simply the *superheat* of the steam.

Note that in Tables 2, 3 and 4, all enthalpies given are above an arbitrary zero at 0°C, i.e. 1.0 kg of saturated water at 0°C is reckoned to have zero enthalpy.

GENERATION AND PROPERTIES OF STEAM

Steam is generated in a boiler at *constant pressure*, and all properties of steam are stated with reference to unit mass of steam at this constant pressure. The constant pressure at which any job works is chosen after consideration of many factors, the more important of which are discussed in Chapter 12.

Although boiler technique as such is outside the scope of this book, the following important point must be made at this stage. An engine or turbine makes a certain demand for steam from the boilers in kg/h. In order to maintain constant pressure, the boilers must be capable of evaporating water *at the same rate* as the engines are consuming steam. It will be readily appreciated that if the boilers are producing steam at a greater rate than the engines are consuming it, the pressure will rise, and if unchecked, will ultimately blow the boiler safety valves. On the other hand, if the engines are demanding more steam than the boilers are producing, the pressure will fall below design, and the power and efficiency of the installation will be significantly reduced in consequence. The boiler *firing rate* must be controlled to that which just maintains the design working pressure. The modern tendency is towards automatic control, and reference to this is made in *"Marine Auxiliary Machinery"*, a companion volume in the Marine Engineering Series.

Use of the SI Steam Tables

It is well known that water boils and forms steam at a temperature of 100.0°C, when the water and steam are at standard atmospheric pressure. If the water is heated under pressure, the temperature at which it boils is increased. If the pressure on the water is reduced, the temperature at which it boils is also reduced. For each particular *pressure*, there is therefore a definite *saturation temperature* at which, if heat is added, the water boils and forms steam, or if heat is removed, steam condenses and forms water. For example, from Table 2 for saturated steam and water, the extreme right-hand column headed θ/K is in fact the saturation temperature (°C), and from the column headed P_{sat}, we find the corresponding pressure; viz.

Saturation temperature = 100.0°C, Pressure = 0.101325 MPa
= 1.01325 bar

Saturation temperature = 200.0°C, Pressure = 1.555 MPa
= 15.55 bar

Saturation temperature = 50.0°C, Pressure = 0.01234 MPa
= 0.1234 bar

Note: pressures expressed in bar are *always absolute*. Standard atmospheric pressure = Pressure corresponding to a saturation temperature of 100.0°C,

Hence standard atmospheric pressure = 1.01325 bar

Let 1.0 kg of water at a pressure of 60.0 bar and temperature 0°C be evaporated into steam. Firstly, the steam tables, Table 3 shows that for a pressure p of 60.0 bar, the corresponding saturation temperature t_s is 275.56°C. The water therefore must be heated to 275.56°C and evaporated into steam at this temperature. The process may be considered in three distinct stages:

1. The water must be forced into the boiler against the boiler pressure. During this stage, the feed pump does work on the water, and this *feed pump work* is stored up in the water.
2. The water then receives heat such as causes its temperature to rise from 0°C to 275.56°C. This *sensible heat* is also stored up in the water.

   Hence when the 1.0 kg of water reaches the saturation temperature, the water contains heat equal to the feed pump work plus the sensible heat. This quantity formerly known as the liquid heat, is now known as the *specific enthalpy of the saturated liquid* and is tabulated in the steam tables in the column headed h_f.
3. Once the water reaches saturation temperature, further heating does not cause the temperature to rise further, but causes the water to change into steam at 275.56°C. If this heating is continued until the entire 1.0 kg of water is converted to steam, the heat received, formerly called the latent heat, now known as the *increment of enthalpy for evaporation*, is also stored up in the steam, and is tabulated in the steam tables in the column headed h_{fg}.

Under these circumstances, finally, we have 1.0 kg of dry, saturated steam whose total heat is the sum of the heat of the liquid and the heat of evaporation. The total heat is now known as the *specific enthalpy of the saturated vapour* and is tabulated in the steam tables in the column headed h_g.

Thus, we may restate in SI terms,

Specific enthalpy of the saturated vapour = Specific enthalpy of the liquid + increment of enthalpy for evaporation,

or in SI symbols,

$$h_g = h_f + h_{fg}$$

The units of enthalpy are kilojoules per kilogramme (kJ/kg).

1.0 kg of water at a particular pressure and saturation temperature occupies a certain volume in dm^3. This is called the *specific volume of the saturated liquid* and is tabulated in the steam tables in the column headed v_f. 1.0 kg of dry saturated steam at the same pressure and saturation temperature occupies a certain volume in dm^3. This is called the *specific volume of the saturated vapour* and is tabulated in the steam tables in the column headed v_g.

Wet steam

In the term "dry saturated steam", the word "dry" means that the entire 1.0 kg is steam, i.e. there is no water present in the steam, while the word "saturated" implies that the steam is at the same temperature as the water from which it was produced, i.e. the saturation temperature.

No boiler is of itself capable of producing completely dry steam—there is always, depending on the area of the boiler water surface, on the height of the steam space above the water surface, and on the violence of ebullition at the water surface, a proportion of water carried along with the steam in the form of very fine water particles. Thus, of the 1.0 kg of water, perhaps only 0.98 kg will be converted to steam, and the remaining 0.02 kg carried along as water in the steam. Both the steam and the water particles are of course at saturation temperature.

The fraction of the 1.0 kg which is steam is called the *dryness fraction*, denoted by q. Steam which is q dry contains only q of the tabulated increment of enthalpy for evaporation, so that for wet steam having a dryness fraction q,

Specific enthalpy of vapour = Specific enthalpy of saturated liquid + (q × increment of enthalpy for evaporation),

or in SI symbols
$$h = h_f + q\, h_{fg}$$
For steam which is q dry, only q kg has the specific volume of the saturated vapour, while $(1 - q)$ kg has the specific volume of the saturated liquid. Hence for steam which is q dry,

Specific volume of vapour =
(q × Specific volume of saturated vapour) + $(1 - q)$ (Specific volume of saturated liquid),

or in SI symbols $v = q.\, v_g + (1 - q)\, v_f$

The term $(1 - q).\, v_f$ is usually neglected, as it is very small compared with the term $q\, v_g$.

Superheated steam

If wet steam from the boiler steam space is passed through a superheater (a series of tubes extending across the hotter parts of the boiler furnace), the steam temperature is raised above the saturation temperature corresponding to the steam pressure. All water particles in the steam are first evaporated, and further heat is then added to the specific enthalpy of the saturated vapour. This additional heat is called the *increment of enthalpy for superheat*.

Thus, for superheated steam,

Specific enthalpy of superheated vapour = Specific enthalpy of saturated liquid + Increment of enthalpy for evaporation + Increment of enthalpy for superheat.

The specific enthalpy of superheated steam is read directly from Table 4.

As the superheated steam is produced, the three enthalpies are added in the above order. To return the superheated steam to its original water state, the three enthalpies must be removed in the reverse order. The latter fact is one which renders superheated steam so valuable in practice. An engine or turbine is a *heat engine*; i.e. its function is to convert heat into mechanical work, hence the mechanical work done is done at the expense of the heat energy (enthalpy) of the steam.

Thus as the steam passes through the engine or turbine its specific enthalpy diminishes progressively. If the steam is initially dry saturated or wet, the work done is done at the expense of the increment of enthalpy for evaporation, and the steam becomes progressively wetter throughout the cycle, resulting in considerable *wetness losses*. If however the steam is initially superheated, the work done by the steam is done first at the expense of the increment of enthalpy for super-heat, and if the initial superheat is high enough, a considerable part of the expansion in the engine or turbine takes place without affecting the increment of enthalpy for evaporation, and within this range, condensation and wetness cannot occur.

While steam is being superheated, the application of heat causes the special volume to increase. The specific volume of superheated steam is read from Table 4.

In the present chapter, we confine our excursion into the steam tables to those properties of steam required for im-mediate purposes, i.e. pressure, temperature, specific enthalpy and specific volume. Certain other properties appearing in the steam tables will be explained in later chapters, when dealing with thermodynamical theory.

Example

Using the Students' Steam Tables, SI units, find the satura-tion temperature, the specific enthalpy, and the specific volume of steam at a pressure of 60.0 bar under each of the following conditions:

1. Steam dry saturated
2. Steam 0.965 dry
3. Steam superheated to a temperature of 475.0°C

We are given the *pressure*, hence use Table 3.

1. Steam at 60.0 bar, dry saturated 60.0 bar = 6.0 MPa
From Table 3, column headed p, where $p = 6.0$

Saturation temperature, $t_s = 275.6°C$
Specific enthalpy of saturated vapour, $h_g = 2784.0$ kJ/kg
Specific volume of saturated vapour, $v_g = 32.42$ dm^3/kg

2. Steam at 60.0 bar, 0.965 dry   60.0 bar = 6.0 MPa
From Table 3, column headed p where p = 6.0

Saturation temperature t_s = 275.6°C
Specific enthalpy of vapour
$$h = h_f + q. h_{fg}$$
$$= 1214.0 + (0.965 \times 1570.0)$$
$$= 1214.0 + 1515.05$$
$$= 2729.05 \text{ kJ/kg.}$$

Specific volume of vapour
$$v = q. v_g + (1 - q). v_f$$
$$= (0.965 \times 32.42) + (0.035 \times 1.318)$$
$$= 31.285 + 0.046$$
$$= 31.331 \text{ dm}^3/\text{kg.}$$

3. Steam at 60.0 bar, 475.0°C   60.0 bar = 6.0 MPa
From Table 4, column headed p where p = 6.0

Specific enthalpy of superheated steam, h = 3363.0 kJ/kg
Specific volume of superheated steam, v = 54.39 dm^3/kg.

Arising from the foregoing steam table exercise, the student should note the following points.

(a) *External work done during evaporation and during super-heating*
Referring to Case 1, above, we read from Table 3 that the specific volume of the saturated liquid v_f = 1.318 dm^3/kg. This shows that during evaporation, there is a considerable increase in volume. If we imagine the evaporation to take place in a cylinder with a sliding piston loaded to a pressure of 60.0 bar as shown in Figure 1.1, then during evaporation,

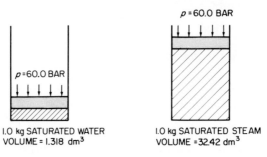

Figure 1.1 *External work done during evaporation*

the volume increases and drives the piston upwards against the constant pressure, thus doing work equal to

Pressure × Change in volume = 60.0 (32.42 − 1.318) = 1866.12 bar dm³, and since 1.0 bar dm³ = 0.1 kJ,

Work done = 1866.12 × 0.1 = 186.612 kJ/kg
This is called the *external work done during evaporation.*

In practice of course, evaporation takes place in a closed boiler of fixed volume, and the external work done during evaporation is therefore stored up in the steam as enthalpy, forming part of increment of enthalpy for evaporation. It is already included in the tabulated values of h_{fg} and h_g. The actual increase in volume can take place only when the steam encounters the sliding piston of a steam engine, or expands in the nozzles of a steam turbine. If we visualise a steam engine taking steam throughout the entire stroke, i.e. without any *expansion* of the steam, then such an engine uses only the external work done during evaporation, and does not use any of the *internal energy* of the steam, i.e. the inherent capability of the steam to expand (see Constant Volume Cycle, Chapter 9).

If the steam is wet, the external work done during evaporation is reduced since the increase in volume is less. If the steam is superheated, there is an increase of volume during superheating, hence the external work done during evaporation and superheating is greater than the external work done during evaporation of saturated steam.

(b) *Increase in specific volume due to superheating*
The specific volume of the superheated steam in case 3 is 54.39 dm³/kg compared with 32.42 dm³/kg for the saturated steam in case 1. Hence to fill a cylinder volume of say 100.0 dm³ requires only 100.0/54.39 = 1.84 kg of superheated steam compared with 100/32.42 = 3.09 kg of saturated steam—a reduction of 40.0 per cent.

(c) *Feed temperature*
The enthalpies given in the steam tables are based on an arbitrary zero at 0°C. This means that saturated water at 0°C is reckoned to have zero enthalpy, hence the enthalpies tabulated in the steam tables assume that the feed water enters

the boiler at 0°C. In practice, of course, the feed temperature is always greater than 0°C, hence the feed water passing into the boiler already has a significant enthalpy.

Thus although the boiler delivers steam having a specific enthalpy corresponding to the steam pressure and temperature at the superheater outlet, the steam does not receive all of this enthalpy in the boiler and superheater, but receives only

> Specific enthalpy at superheater output − Specific
> enthalpy of feed water entering boiler

This quantity is called the *nett specific enthalpy received above the feed*. Obviously, the higher the feed temperature, the less is the nett specific enthalpy received in the boiler, and the less the fuel required to generate 1.0 kg of steam. For example, consider steam at 60.0 bar, 475.0°C as in 3, but let the feed temperature be 150.0°C.

> From Table 4, specific enthalpy of steam at 60.0 bar,
>   475.0°C = 3363.0 kJ/kg
> From Table 1, specific enthalpy of feed water at
>   150.0°C =   632.2 kJ/kg
> ∴ Nett specific enthalpy received in boiler above the feed
>   = 2730.8 kJ/kg

(d) *Error due to neglecting $(1 - q) \cdot v_f$ in the specific volume of wet steam*
Referring to 2 above, if we neglect the term $(1 - q) \cdot v_f$, we get

> Specific volume of vapour, $v = q \cdot v_g = 0.965 \times 32.42 =$
>   31.285 dm^3/kg

This represents an error of 0.046 in 31.331, which is only 0.147 of 1.0 per cent. In practice it is usual to regard this magnitude of error as negligible, and to take $v = q \cdot v_g$.

(e) *Variation of steam properties*
Examination of the steam tables will show that for dry saturated steam, as the pressure p increases,

The saturation temperature t_s increases,
The specific enthalpy of the saturated liquid h_f increases,
The increment of enthalpy for evaporation h_{fg} diminishes,
The specific enthalpy of the saturated vapour h_g increases,
The specific volume of the saturated vapour v_g diminishes.

It is important to remember these, as it very often happens that we have to consider say a pressure which lies between two of the pressures appearing in the steam tables. This process, known as *interpolation*, is illustrated when dealing with certain numerical examples in succeeding chapters.

Specific enthalpy drop

Suppose the H.P. cylinder of a triple expansion engine to receive steam at 15.0 bar, 250°C at the rate of 7340.0 kg/h. The H.P. cylinder develops 403.0 kW by the indicator, and exhausts at 6.0 bar.

From the Steam Table 4, the specific enthalpy of the steam at supply h_1 = 2923.0 kJ/kg.

Now, since 1.0 W = 1.0 J/s, the work done in the cylinder is (403 × 3600) kJ/h.

To develop this work requires 7340 kg/h of steam, hence

$$\text{work done by the steam is } \frac{403.0 \times 3600}{7340} = 197.6 \text{ kJ/kg}$$

This work, known as the *specific enthalpy drop* is done at the expense of the specific enthalpy of the steam, hence the specific enthalpy of the steam leaving the H.P. cylinder at 6.0 bar is

h_2 = 2923.0 = 197.6 = 2725.4 kJ/kg.

Specific enthalpy drop is usually denoted by the symbol dh (see Figure 1.2).

By consulting Steam Table 3, we find that the specific enthalpy of dry saturated steam at 6.0 bar is 2756.0 kJ/kg, i.e. the specific enthalpy of the H.P. exhaust steam is *less* than if the exhaust steam were dry saturated. The conclusion

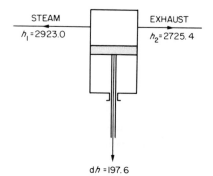

Figure 1.2 Enthalpy drop $dh = 197.6$

is that the steam has become *wet* during its expansion in the H.P. cylinder. We can find the dryness fraction at exhaust by equating the actual specific enthalpy to $h_f + q \cdot h_{fg}$, h_f and h_{fg} being read from Table 3 for a pressure of 6.0 bar, thus

$$h_2 \quad = h_f + q_2 \cdot h_{fg}$$
$$\therefore 2725.4 = 670.4 + 2086.0 \, q_2$$
$$\therefore q_2 \quad = \frac{2725.4 - 670.4}{2086.0}$$
$$\therefore q_2 \quad = \frac{2055.0}{2086.0}$$
$$\therefore q_2 \quad = 0.9851$$

Thus the steam becomes wet during expansion, work being done by the steam at the expense of its specific enthalpy. Subsequent expansion in the I.P. and L.P. cylinders will of course cause the steam to become progressively wetter.

If the initial steam temperature be increased, the steam can be maintained in a superheated condition during a greater part of its expansion, thus reducing wetness losses. For instance it is common practice with engines to arrange the initial superheat so that the steam remains in a superheated condition up to about half of the expansion in the I.P. cylinder.

Note:—The calculations and explanations given in this chapter are based on the Students' Steam Tables, SI units.

In certain other chapters, for greater accuracy, particularly where small differences are involved, the author has used the complete *U.K. Steam Tables in SI Units 1970*, (published by Edward Arnold Ltd., London) which may differ slightly from the Students' Tables.

2 Reciprocating engines

Principles of operation

The basic working parts of a reciprocating steam engine are shown in the simplified diagram in Figure 2.1. These consist of a cylinder, closed at top and bottom, in which slides a piston, the latter—by means of a piston rod passing through a steam-tight gland in the cylinder bottom—communicating its reciprocating motion to a crosshead. The reciprocating motion of the crosshead is converted into a revolving motion of the shaft by means of a connecting rod and crank.

The effort to produce the reciprocating motion of the piston is obtained by a slide valve alternately opening to steam and exhaust the passages (or ports) leading to the top and bottom ends of the cylinder. Basically, the slide valve is a hollow rectangular box without a bottom, arranged to slide up and down over the ends of the steam ports, the back of the valve being in communication with the steam supply, and the hollow interior of the valve with the exhaust.

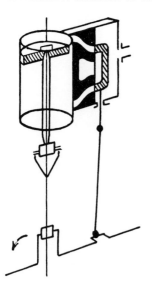

Figure 2.1 Simple double acting steam engine

As shown in Figure 2.1, the piston is at the top end of its stroke, and the slide valve in its mid-position, thus closing both the top and bottom cylinder ports. If the valve is moved downwards from its mid-position, steam will be admitted to the top end of the cylinder, and the bottom end will be opened to exhaust. If the valve is then moved upwards beyond its mid-position, the bottom end of the cylinder will be opened to steam and the top end to exhaust.

The necessary valve motion could be obtained by driving it by a small crank, set at right angles to, and preceding the main crank in the direction of rotation, in which case steam will begin to enter the top end of the cylinder when the piston begins its down-stroke, and will be cut off only when the piston reaches the end of the downstroke, i.e. steam would be admitted throughout the whole of the working stroke. The exhaust also, would be open throughout the whole of the return stroke.

In practice, the slide valve and its driving gear are considerably modified compared with the above simple conception. To save weakening the crankshaft, the slide valve is not driven by a crank, but by an eccentric, which is, in effect, a crank in which the crankpin diameter is made so large that it envelops the shaft diameter. Steam is not admitted to the cylinder during the full stroke, but only for a fraction of the stroke (called the cut-off fraction), the remainder of the stroke being completed by expansion of the steam, thus giving reduced steam consumption. To obtain this fractional cut-off, the steam edge of the slide valve is extended so that in the mid-position, it overlaps the edge of the steam port by an amount called the steam lap. The effect of this modification alone would be to cut off the steam supply earlier on the upstroke of the valve, and to admit steam later on the downstroke of the valve; the piston would therefore begin its stroke before the valve supplied steam. To overcome this, the position of the eccentric driving the valve is advanced beyond the 90° already shown to be basically necessary. The effect of this modification alone would be to give not only an earlier cut-off, but also a corresponding earlier point for opening to steam. A combination of these two modifications gives a generally satisfactory setting, i.e. steam lap is added to the valve and the eccentric is advanced. To ensure that the valve has opened slightly to steam when the piston begins its stroke, the steam edge of the valve at this instant is arranged to have uncovered

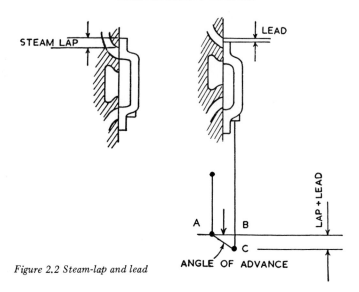

Figure 2.2 Steam-lap and lead

the steam port by a small amount called the lead. This requires a further slight increase in the angle of advance of the eccentric. These features are illustrated in Figure 2.2 from which it will be evident that

$$\text{Angle of advance} = \sin^{-1} \frac{\text{Steam Lap} + \text{Lead}}{\text{Half the Valve Travel}}$$

The valve is made to open to exhaust just before the end of the working stroke, and to close to exhaust some way before the end of the exhaust stroke. Some of the exhaust steam therefore remains behind and is compressed into the cylinder clearance volume, the rising pressure thus forming a "cushion" for the reciprocating masses as they are brought to rest before reversing the sense of their motion, so ensuring smooth running. The exhaust edges of the valve are given exhaust lap as necessary.

There are certain variations of the flat slide valve which are used, mainly to reduce the heavy steam pressure load on the back of the valve, and to obtain sufficient steam flow area with a reasonable size of valve. One such slide valve, Messrs Andrews and Cameron's Patent, is shown in Figure 2.3. Another type is shown in Figure 2.4 in which the cavities X are connected by ports to the outside of the valve.

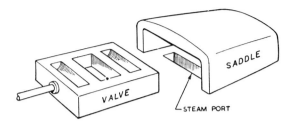

Figure 2.3 Double-opening balanced slide valve

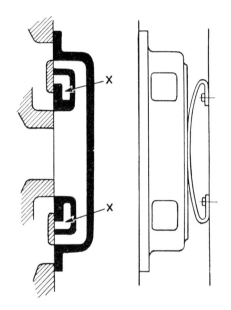

Figure 2.4 Double-ported slide valve

Instead of a flat slide valve, a cylindrical slide valve (piston valve) may be used, particularly where the steam pressure is high. So far as steam distribution is concerned, a piston valve acts exactly the same as an ordinary flat slide valve, but being cylindrical, it is pressure-balanced, and is therefore easier to move. Very often, with piston valves, the steam and exhaust cavities are reversed, i.e. the valve has "inside steam". This means that the valve spindle stuffing-box and gland are subjected only to the lower pressure and temperature of the exhaust steam. When a valve has inside steam, other things

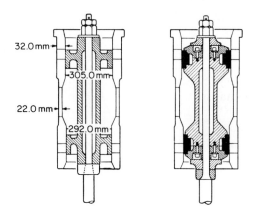

Figure 2.5 Piston valves
(left) solid piston valve, inside steam
(right) built up piston valve, with solid rings, inside steam

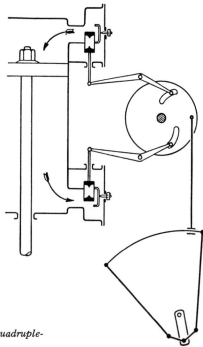

Figure 2.6 Andrews and Cameron quadruple-
opening valve gear

being equal, the position of the driving eccentric is 180° in advance of the position for outside steam, i.e. the eccentric follows the main crank by an angle of (90° minus the angle of advance.) Typical piston valves are illustrated in Figure 2.5.

The ordinary flat slide valve has four edges controlling steam and exhaust for top and bottom of the cylinder. In the Andrews and Cameron patent cam-operated system, each of these four edges is represented by one complete balanced slide valve each having four openings for the admission of steam or the expulsion of exhaust. It has the advantages of quick action, short ports (hence reduced clearance volume), and reduced load on the valve gear. The principle is illustrated in Figure 2.6.

When four separate steam and exhaust valves are used, they are sometimes made as balanced double-beat valves, generally called poppet valves. These valves, illustrated in Figure 2.7, are completely pressure-balanced, hence require very little power to operate. Sometimes only two poppet valves are used—one steam valve for each end of the cylinder—

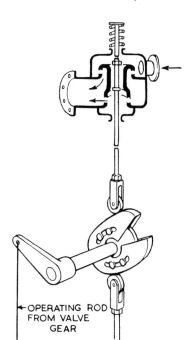

Figure 2.7 Arrangement of cam-operated poppet valve and gear

←OPERATING ROD
FROM VALVE
GEAR

the exhaust being controlled by the main piston uncovering
a ring of ports around the cylinder at the middle of its length.
Such an arrangement is called a uniflow engine—it is described and illustrated in chapter 7.

Whatever the type of valve used, some means must be
provided to enable the engine to be quickly reversed from
ahead to astern and vice versa. Reference to Figure 2.1 will
show that if the crankshaft is to revolve in the direction
opposite to that shown, then the position of the basic eccentric must be moved through 180°. One method of permitting
quick reversal therefore, is to provide the engine with two
eccentrics—one positioned for ahead, and the other for astern
running, and to arrange the valve driving gear so that either
the ahead or the astern eccentric may be made to operate the
valve at will. This type of valve gear, called the Stephenson
link motion, is widely used on marine engines; it is illustrated
in principle in Figure 2.8. By moving the curved link through

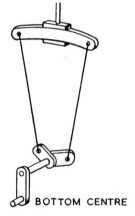

Figure 2.8 Principle of Stephenson link motion

BOTTOM CENTRE

the tumbling block, either the ahead or the astern eccentric
may be put in line with the valve spindle. If the link is placed
in any intermediate position (other than the mid-position),
the engine will run in the direction of that eccentric which is
nearest the valve spindle, but the influence of the other
eccentric will alter the steam distribution; in particular, it will
make the cut-off earlier than when in full gear.

Many engines, particularly of the later types, use a different
type of valve gear, requiring only one eccentric, and which
are lighter and have fewer working parts. Three such types,
called radial valve gears, are illustrated in Figure 2.9.

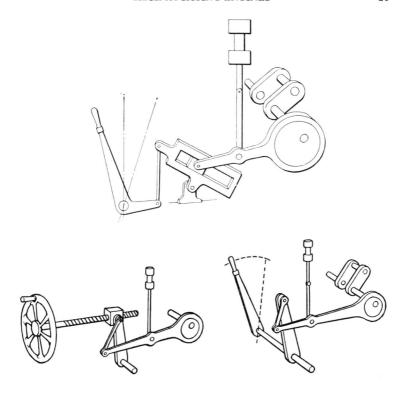

Figure 2.9 Radial valve gears

Constructional details

The constructional details of a typical marine reciprocating engine are simple, and if the engine is well designed and operated, very reliable.

The bedplate (Figure 2.10), is a rigid box structure, generally of cast iron, although fabricated steel has been used in some of the later designs. It forms the base for the engine columns, a support for the crankshaft, and is the means of attachment of the engine to the hull of the ship.

The main bearing shells may be either of the two types of which the bottom halves are shown in Figure 2.11. The flat-faced shell has the advantage that shims may be fitted under the shell to restore alignment; the other may be turned out for remetalling without lifting a section of the crankshaft. Bearing shells are of cast iron or cast steel lined with white metal. The top halves of the bearing shells are retained by a

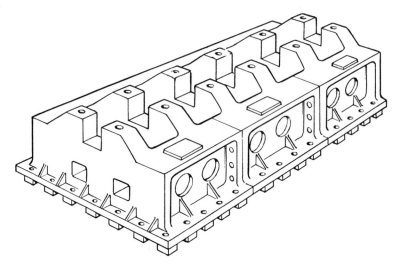

Figure 2.10 Construction of the bedplate, with the packing-chocks in position

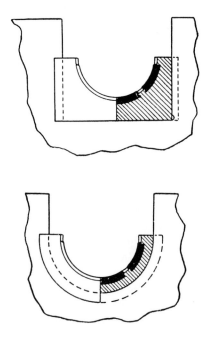

Figure 2.11 Two types of main-bearing shell

heavy steel bearing cover (or keep), fastened by bolts of the type shown in Figure 2.12.

The crankshaft is of forged steel and is usually built-up of sections such as shown in Figure 2.13. The crank webs are heat-shrunk on to the shaft and the crankpin, and are sometimes dowelled as well.

The engine columns are cast iron, and are of hollow rectangular section. They connect the engine cylinder(s) to the bedplate, and take the alternate tension and compression loads as the piston reciprocates. The columns also guide the engine

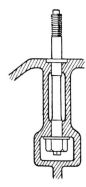

Figure 2.12 Method of fixing the main-bearing bolts

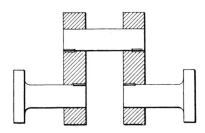

Figure 2.13 Section of crankshaft

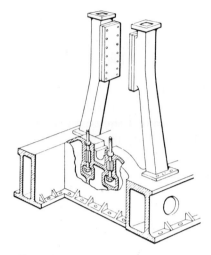

Figure 2.14 Arrangement of the columns connecting the cylinder castings and bedplate

crosshead in a straight vertical line, and take the side thrust produced by the horizontal component of the piston load acting at the crosshead. Suitable facings are cast on the columns for this purpose.

The arrangement of bedplate, columns, bearing shells and bolts is shown in Figure 2.14.

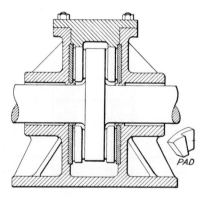

Figure 2.15 Typical thrust block of the Michell type

Immediately aft of the engine is placed the main thrust block, which transmits the forward (or aft) thrust of the propeller to the ship's structure. Thrust blocks are now in-

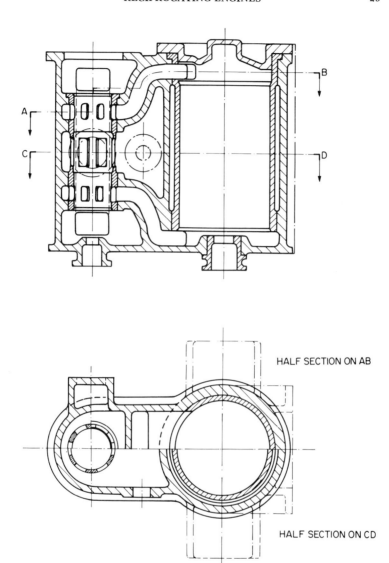

A

C

B

D

HALF SECTION ON AB

HALF SECTION ON CD

Figure 2.16 Cylinder and piston valve chamber

variably of the Michel type having a single collar on the shaft, with a ring of tilting thrust pads which allow the lubricating oil to form a high-pressure wedge between collar and pads such that the surfaces never actually come into physical contact (see Figure 2.15).

The cylinder castings are usually of cast iron, although cast steel has been used, and the valve chest is usually cast integral with the cylinder. For small engines having one, or two cylinders, the whole may be cast in one piece, but it is more likely that each cylinder will be cast separately, with flanges for bolting them together in the fore-and-aft direction. A typical cylinder and piston valve chamber is illustrated in Figure 2.16. The steam and exhaust ports must be of adequate cross-sectional area, and they should be as short and direct as is practically possible. The cylinder cover is shaped to conform with the piston shape so as to reduce clearance volume; all flat surfaces are externally ribbed for strength. Stuffing boxes are provided in the bottom of the cylinder and of the valve chamber, where the piston rod and valve spindle pass through. The stuffing boxes are packed with some form of special packing which ensures steam tightness while allowing free sliding of the rods.

The piston may be of cast iron or cast steel. A hollow cast iron piston such as is shown in Figure 2.17 is almost flat top and bottom and has internal radial ribs for strength. Figure 2.18 shows a solid cast steel piston which is made conical for strength and lightness. Either type has three main parts, viz. the piston body, the junk ring and the piston rings. The latter may be of the ordinary split-ring type, or one of the special types developed mainly for superheated steam. The top end of the piston rod fits into a cylindro-conical hole in the piston body and is secured by a nut.

The crosshead is a rectangular block of forged steel, with the two crosshead pins made integral with the block. The lower end of the piston rod fits exactly into the conical hole in the crosshead and is secured by a nut. The guide shoe (or slipper block), of cast iron or cast steel, is checked on to the crosshead block, and secured by steel setscrews. The sliding faces of the guide shoe are faced with white metal, usually in the form of horizontal strips cast into dovetails. The main sliding face slides on the ahead guide face, which is a rectangular cast iron pad, and is restrained on the other side by two cast iron clamping plates (which form the astern guide face).

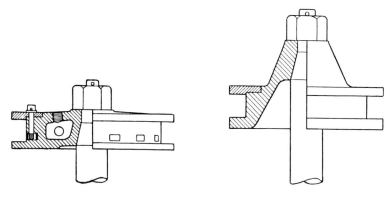

Figure 2.17 Hollow cast-iron piston   Figure 2.18 Solid cast steel conical piston

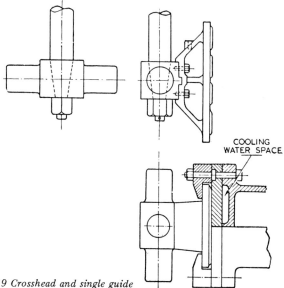

COOLING
WATER SPACE

Figure 2.19 Crosshead and single guide

The whole guide face assembly is fastened by collar bolts to a flange on the engine column. The hollow space in the column behind the ahead guide face is circulated with sea water to cool the sliding surfaces. Figure 2.19 illustrates this type, which is called a single guide crosshead or a slipper crosshead. Sometimes, mainly on large engines, double guides are used, i.e. having a guide shoe on both thwartship faces of the crosshead block—there are no astern bars as fitted on a single guide

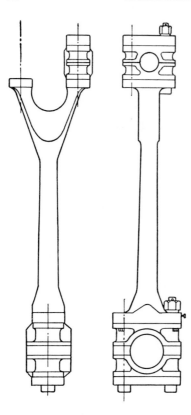

Figure 2.20 Connecting rod

crosshead. The double guide is strong and rigid, and gives
ample surface for prolonged astern running, but care has to
be exercised in adjusting the liners fitted between the abut-
ting faces.

The connecting rod, Figure 2.20, is the connecting link
between the crosshead pins and the crankpin, and its function
is to convert the reciprocating motion of the piston and
crosshead to the rotary motion of the crankshaft. The connecting rod is of forged steel, forked at the top end to allow
freedom of movement clear of the piston rod nut. The
length of the rod between the centres is about 4 to $4\frac{1}{2}$ times
the crank radius, and it is of ample dimensions to carry the
onerous duty imposed on it. The top and bottom end bushes
may be of brass or of cast steel, either being lined with white
metal. Heavy forged steel keeps hold the two halves of the
bushes together, and the whole is secured by the top and
bottom end bolts.

The eccentric sheaves are of cast iron or cast steel, and are split, as shown in Figure 2.21. The sheave is located on the shaft by a rectangular key, sunk partly into the shaft and partly into the sheave.

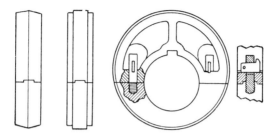

Figure 2.21 Eccentric sheaves

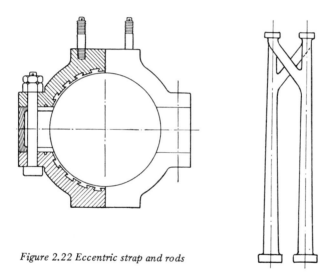

Figure 2.22 Eccentric strap and rods

The eccentric strap fits over the circumference of the sheave. It is of cast iron or cast steel, and is lined with white metal at the rubbing surface. The larger straps are made in four parts as shown in Figure 2.22, the assembly being reversible.

Assuming the engine to have Stephenson link motion, the ahead and astern eccentrics are fitted side by side on the crankshaft. The two eccentric rods, Figure 2.22, are of similar form to the connecting rod, and the top end brasses engage with pins projecting from, and forged solid with the reversing link, Figure 2.23. The link is usually built up of two curved

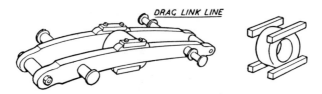

DRAG LINK LINE

Figure 2.23 Reversing link and block

forged steel bars bolted together at the ends, with distance pieces between, to allow space for the bars to pass over the saddle block as the link is moved over to reverse the engine. The cylindrical part in the middle of the saddle block forms a journal which works in the bush at the bottom end of the valve spindle, Figure 2.24. The latter is of forged steel, the upper half of the bottom end being either forged solid with the spindle, or mounted separately on a cone and secured by a cotter. The valve spindle is restrained to a vertical line by a guide bracket bolted to the underside of the cylinder casting, and passes through the valve spindle stuffing box into the valve chest, carrying the valve at its upper end.

At one side of the engine, the eccentric rod pins on the link are extended to form journals on which the drag links work. At their other end, the drag links engage with similar pins on the die block of the expansion lever, Figure 2.25. The die block can be variably, but positively, positioned in the slot of the expansion lever. The expansion lever of any one

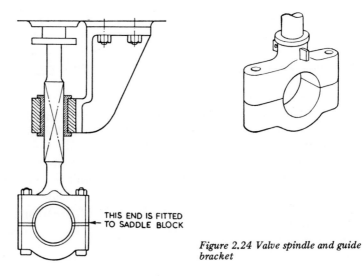

THIS END IS FITTED TO SADDLE BLOCK

Figure 2.24 Valve spindle and guide bracket

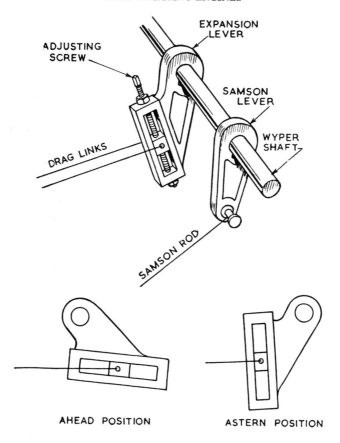

Figure 2.25 Wyper shaft and expansion levers

cylinder of an engine is used to vary the steam distribution in that cylinder alone. It is common practice to make the slot at an angle of about 30° to the expansion lever, so that any adjustment of the die block in the slot will have a very minor effect on steam distribution when going astern—full power is always immediately available when the engines are put astern. The expansion levers for all cylinders of an engine are keyed to a common wyper shaft running along the back of the engine, and the wyper shaft is rotated through that angle necessary to reverse the engine by the samson lever and samson rod, the latter being motivated by the hand gear, or by a reversing engine.

The primary steam supply to an engine is controlled by a stop valve, followed by a throttle valve—the former for start-

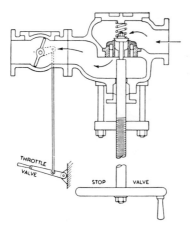

Figure 2.26 Main stop valve and throttle valve

ing, stopping and regulating in the ordinary way, and the latter for quickly controlling the engine as the propeller alternately comes out of the water and becomes resubmerged, during rough weather. A common arrangement is shown in Figure 2.26. The stop valve opens against the steam flow, and is provided with a small pilot valve, which opens first, thus pressure-balancing the main valve and allowing it to be opened easily. The stop valve is followed by a butterfly valve which can be opened and closed very quickly by the hand gear or the racing governor. Figure 2.27 shows the Cockburn-MacNicoll patent regulating throttle valve in which the functions of the stop and throttle valves are combined into one

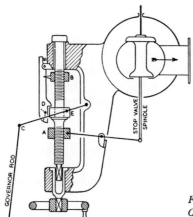

Figure 2.27 Simplified diagram of the Cockburn–MacNicoll regulating throttle valve

balanced double-beat valve. For ordinary purposes of regulation, the valve is operated by the handwheel, but this can be over-ridden at any time by the throttle gear. With either type of valve, in cases where the throttling is operated automatically by a governor, the latter is usually of the inertia type, mounted on one of the reciprocating parts of the engine.

In a multiple-expansion engine, only the first (high pressure) cylinder receives steam in the first instance when the stop valve is opened. If the H.P. engine happens to be standing on either of the dead centres, the engine will not start. Small auxiliary valves called impulse valves, or starting steam valves are provided, by which high pressure steam may be passed to one of the other cylinders for a short period, so allowing the engine to start. These valves are illustrated in Figure 2.28.

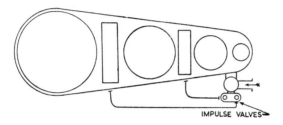

Figure 2.28 Impulse steam valves

To increase the range of expansion, the engine exhausts to a condenser in which the exhaust steam is condensed at a pressure well below atmospheric pressure. In the condenser, the steam is condensed by its coming into contact with a large number of tubes which are kept cold by having sea water circulated through them. The condensate is removed from the condenser bottom by a special type of reciprocating pump called a wet air pump, since it also removes air which leaks into the sub-atmospheric system, and which would otherwise raise the condenser pressure and reduce the overall efficiency. The condenser and the air pump are carried on brackets from the back columns of the engine, and the air pump, together with the bilge pump, sanitary pump, etc., are usually driven by a system of levers and links from one of the main engine crossheads. Figure 2.29 illustrates two types of wet air pump which are in common use.

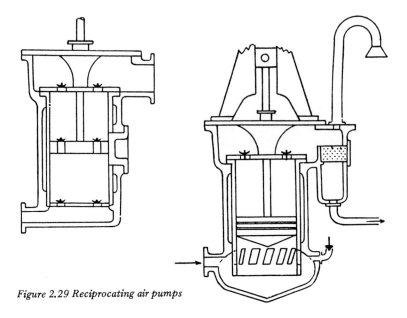

Figure 2.29 Reciprocating air pumps

Most of the engine parts briefly described in the foregoing may be clearly seen in their functional positions in Figures 7.3, 7.4, 7.5, 7.20 and 7.23 (see chapter 7).

Compounding

Single-cylinder engines are not used for marine purposes— invariably the engines are multiple-expansion, i.e. the total range of expansion of the steam from the boiler pressure to the condenser pressure is divided up into a number of stages, each stage having its own cylinder, the exhaust steam from the first cylinder passing into the second cylinder, and so on. Thus we have compound engines, having two stages of expansion, basically a high-pressure (H.P.) cylinder and a low-pressure (L.P.) cylinder; or we can have three stages of expansion, called a triple-expansion engine, having basically, a high pressure, an intermediate pressure (I.P.), and a low-pressure cylinder.

It will be immediately obvious that two or more cylinders will give a much more uniform turning moment on the crankshaft, and can be better balanced, thus giving smoother running. There are however some other features of compounding which we may examine briefly.

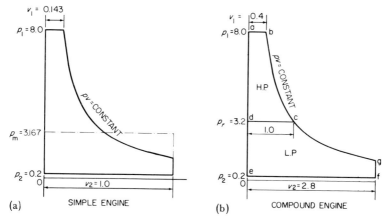

Figure 2.30 Simple engine and compound engine, each having the same conditions and the same total ratio of expansion

Figure 2.30(a) shows a hypothetical pressure-volume diagram for one end of a simple single-cylinder engine. This is in fact a graph of steam pressure on a base of piston stroke (the latter being proportional to volume). Clearance volume and all losses are neglected, and the steam after cut-off is assumed to expand hyperbolically. The mean piston velocity (i.e. 2 × stroke, m × rev/s) is assumed to be 2.5 m/s.

The ratio $v2/v1$ is called the ratio of expansion r, and in this case

$$r = \frac{1.0}{0.143} = 7.0$$

The mean effective pressure acting on the piston during one stroke,

$$p_m = p_1 \frac{(1 + \log_e r)}{r} - p_2$$

$$\therefore p_m = (8 \times 0.4209) - 0.2 = 3.167 \text{ bar}$$

The power kW, developed in a double-acting cylinder

= 100 × mean effective pressure, bar × cylinder area, m^2 × mean piston velocity, m/s

If the engine is to develop 750 kW, then

$$\text{Cylinder area required} = \frac{750}{100 \times 3.167 \times 2.5} = 0.946 \text{m}^2$$

$$\therefore \textit{Cylinder diameter} = \sqrt{\frac{4 \times 0.946}{\pi}} = 1.097 \text{ m}$$

Assuming the steam to be initially dry saturated, the maximum and minimum steam temperatures to which the cylinder is subjected are 170.4°C and 60.1°C. The cylinder metal will assume a temperature somewhere between these two, hence there will be an initial heat loss from steam to cylinder, causing quite a serious condensation loss. The greater the cylinder temperature range, the greater is the condensation loss.

As the piston begins its stroke and up to cut-off, it is subjected to full steam pressure on one side and to exhaust pressure on the other, hence

$$\text{Initial piston load} = \text{cylinder area } (p_1 - p_2) \times 10^5 =$$
$$0.946 \times 7.8 \times 10^5 = 7.38 \times 10^5 \text{ N}$$

The cylinder, columns, piston, rods and running gear must be designed to withstand this maximum force.

Suppose we now compound the engine, keeping the same total ratio of expansion as before viz., $r = 7.0$. Theoretically, when we compound the engine, all that is done is to divide the pv diagram into two parts by a horizontal line, the division being, in the first place, quite arbitrary (see Figure 2.30(b)).

Since the total ratio of expansion $r = 7.0$ as before, it follows that the final volume v_2 will be the same as before, hence the volume of the L.P. cylinder of a compound engine is the same as that of the single cylinder of the simple engine, having the same steam and exhaust pressures, same power and speed and same total ratio of expansion as the compound engine in question.

Thus, L.P. cylinder diameter = 1.097 m

In Figure 2.30(b), the length dc represents the total volume of the H.P. cylinder and the line ef the total volume of the L.P. cylinder, and the ratio

$$\frac{\text{L.P. volume}}{\text{H.P. volume}}$$

is called the cylinder ratio. Suppose we choose a cylinder ratio of 2.8.

The easiest way of dealing with compound engines is to always make the total volume of the H.P. cylinder equal to 1.0 unit, as in Figure 2.30(b). The total volume of the L.P. cylinder then has the same numerical value as the cylinder ratio (i.e. 2.8) and the initial volume

$$v_1 = \frac{2.8}{7} = 0.4,$$

which is the H.P. cut-off fraction.

Note that for a compound engine

$$\text{Total ratio of expansion} = \frac{\text{Cylinder ratio}}{\text{H.P. cut-off}}$$

Thus assuming the strokes to be equal:

$$\text{H.P. cylinder area} = \frac{\text{L.P. cylinder area}}{2.8}$$
$$= \frac{0.946}{2.8}$$
$$= 0.338 \text{ m}^2$$

$$\therefore \text{H.P. cylinder diameter} = \sqrt{\frac{4 \times 0.338}{\pi}} = 0.656 \text{ m}$$

Hence the two cylinders of the compound engine are 656.0 mm and 1097 mm diameter.

Since, during expansion, $p_1 v_1 = p_2 v_2$ etc, the L.P. receiver pressure

$$p_r = \frac{8.0 \times 0.4}{1.0} = 3.2 \text{ bar}$$

The H.P. exhaust steam should now be transferred to the L.P. cylinder without change in either pressure or volume. This means that ideally, the volume of the L.P. cylinder up

to the point of cut-off should be equal to the total volume of
the H.P. cylinder, i.e. L.P. cut-off = $1/2.8$ = 0.357. If the
L.P. cut-off is so arranged, steam expands usefully right down
to the receiver pressure in the H.P. cylinder, and that cylinder
is said to have complete expansion.

   To determine what proportions of the total engine power
are developed in the two cylinders and to find the initial
piston loads and the cylinder temperature ranges, refer to
Figure 2.30(b) and treat each cylinder in turn as a single
simple engine.

H.P. Cylinder

$$\text{Ratio of expansion } r = \frac{1.0}{0.4} = 2.5$$

$$p_{m_1} = p_1 \frac{(1 + \log_e r)}{r} - p_r$$

$$\therefore p_{m_1} = (8 \times 0.7666) - 3.2$$

$$\therefore p_{m_1} = 2.933 \text{ bar}$$

H.P. Power = $100 \times 2.933 \times 0.338 \times 2.5$ = 248.0 kW

H.P. Initial Piston Load = $0.338 (8.0 - 3.2) \times 10^5$ =
$$1.621 \times 10^5 \text{ N}$$

H.P. Cylinder Temperature Range = $170.4 - 135.8$ =
$$34.6°C$$

L.P. Cylinder

$$\text{Ratio of Expansion } r = \frac{2.8}{1.0} = 2.8$$

$$p_{m_2} = p_r \frac{(1 + \log_e r)}{r} - p_2$$

$$\therefore p_{m_2} = (3.2 \times 0.7249) - 0.2 = 2.12 \text{ bar}$$

L.P. Power = $100 \times 2.12 \times 0.946 \times 2.5$ = 502.0 kW

L.P. Initial Piston Load = $0.946 (3.2 - 0.2) \times 10^5$ =
$$2.837 \times 10^5 \text{ N}$$

L.P. Cylinder Temperature Range = $135.8 - 60.1$ =
$$75.7°C.$$

Note the total engine power $248.0 + 502.0$ = 750 kW.

The L.P. cylinder develops 2.03 times the H.P. power
The L.P. piston is loaded 1.75 times as heavily as the
H.P. piston.
The L.P. temperature range is 2.18 times the H.P.
temperature range.

To take full advantage of the compound engine, we must
render these much more nearly equal. Suppose we alter the
L.P. cut-off to 0.6. The L.P. cut-off volume therefore becomes
0.6 x 2.8 = 1.68, but the total volume of the H.P. cylinder
remains 1.0 as before, hence steam at a pressure of 3.2 bar,
and occupying a volume of 1.0 unit is transferred into the
L.P. cut-off volume of 1.68 units. There will therefore be a
free, or unresisted expansion of the steam from 3.2 bar to
some lower pressure in order to occupy the larger volume.

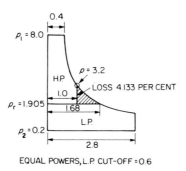

EQUAL POWERS, L.P. CUT-OFF = 0.6

*Figure 2.31 Combined indicator diagram showing the effects of altering the L.P.
cut-off*

Hence, referring to Figure 2.31, the new receiver pressure
will be

$$p_r = \frac{8.0 \times 0.4}{1.68} = 1.905 \text{ bar}$$

Individual calculations as before for the H.P. and L.P.
cylinders will now show that p_{m_1} = 4.228 bar; p_{m_2} = 1.527
bar, and that

Cylinder	H.P.	L.P.	Total
Power, kW	357.5	361.5	719.0
Initial piston load, N × 10⁻⁵	2.058	1.6125	
Temperature range, °C	51.7	58.6	

Thus by altering the L.P. cut-off to 0.6, we have brought the powers, initial piston loads and temperature ranges much more nearly equal, but at the expense of a loss of 31.0 kW in total engine power. This loss of pv diagram area is called the loss due to incomplete expansion in the H.P. cylinder. It must be made good by other means (see diagram factor).

In general, altering the H.P. cut-off alters the total engine power. Altering the L.P. cut-off alters the distribution of power between the cylinders, and may reduce the total engine power due to the creation of a loss due to incomplete expansion in the H.P. cylinder. Altering the L.P. cut-off also alters the initial piston loads and the temperature ranges.

It should be noted that there is also a loss due to incomplete expansion in the L.P. cylinder, but for a different reason. Were the steam to be expanded hyperbolically in the L.P. cylinder right down to the condenser pressure, the required volume of that cylinder would be so large as to be prohibitive in practice. By accepting some loss due to incomplete expansion, we can reduce very considerably the size of the L.P. cylinder (in this case, for example, from 16.0 to 2.8).

The initial piston loads of each of the two cylinders of the compound engine are of the order of 2.0×10^5 N, compared with 7.38×10^5 N for the single cylinder simple engine. The rods and running gear, etc., can therefore be made lighter. Each cylinder temperature range is of the order of 50.0 − 60.0°C compared with 110.3°C for the single-cylinder simple engine. The individual cylinder condensation losses will therefore be reduced, and a significant part of the H.P. cylinder condensation loss will be recovered in the L.P. cylinder; these features result in a considerable reduction in steam consumption.

In practice, the variation of steam pressure relative to the piston position during the steam and exhaust strokes of one end of an engine cylinder (i.e. the pv diagram) is recorded by an indicator, the principle of which is shown in Figure 2.32. In practice, the type of indicator instrument used is such that

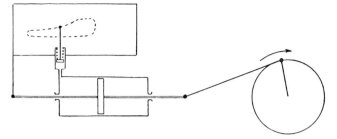

Figure 2.32 Principle of the indicator

both the travel of the main engine piston and of the indicator piston are drawn to a conveniently small scale. These indicator diagrams are used for calculating the power developed in the engine cylinder(s), and to detect faults due to deterioration, such as leaking valves or piston rings, wear-down of bearings, eccentrics, etc., or incorrect valve settings.

An example of well-formed indicator diagrams from both ends of one cylinder is shown in Figure 2.33, in which the line AL is the line of atmospheric pressure. Note also that the nett effective pressure on the engine piston at any point in the stroke is the pressure on one side minus the pressure on the other, i.e. at a distance x from top dead centre, the effective pressure on the piston is AB.

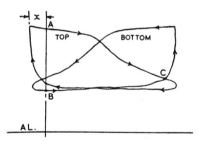

Figure 2.33 'Effective' pressure

Due to the various diagram losses, the area of the actual pv diagram, as obtained from the indicator is less than the area of the hypothetical pv diagram and the ratio

$$\frac{\text{actual diagram area}}{\text{hypothetical diagram area}}$$

is called the diagram factor. This means that, actual mean effective pressure = hypothetical mean effective pressure × diagram factor.

Thus, when calculating cylinder dimensions, the mean effective pressure calculated from

$$p_1 \frac{(1 + \log_\epsilon r)}{r} - p_2$$

must be multiplied by an estimated diagram factor. The exact diagram factor for any engine can be found only by taking indicator diagrams, from which the actual M.E.P. is found and compared with the hypothetical M.E.P. When dealing with compound engines, the H.P. and L.P. cylinder pv diagrams are combined, and an overall diagram factor applied to the total referred mean pressure.

In certain instances, where the L.P. cylinder of a compound engine would be inconveniently large, two L.P. cylinders in parallel are used, each being one half of the calculated area. This is known as a three-cylinder compound. Sometimes also, two H.P. cylinders in parallel and two L.P. cylinders in parallel are used. This is known as a four cylinder compound or a double compound.

By using a triple-expansion engine, i.e. one having three stages of expansion, the individual cylinder temperature ranges and the condensation and re-evaporation losses are further reduced, thus giving a further reduction in steam consumption. Generally, the cylinder areas of a triple-expansion engine are made approximately in geometric progression, i.e.,

$$\frac{\text{L.P. Area}}{\text{I.P. Area}} = \frac{\text{I.P. Area}}{\text{H.P. Area}}$$

This means that if the total cylinder ratio

$$\frac{\text{L.P. Area}}{\text{H.P. Area}} = R,$$

then the cylinder areas are in the proportion

H.P.	I.P.	L.P.
1.0	$\sqrt{R}$	R

The total ratio of expansion $r = \dfrac{\text{total cylinder ratio}}{\text{H.P. cut-off}}$

Again, the L.P. cylinder has the same total volume as the single cylinder of a simple engine having the same steam and exhaust pressures, same mean piston velocity and same total ratio of expansion as the triple. For the conditions shown in Figure 2.34.

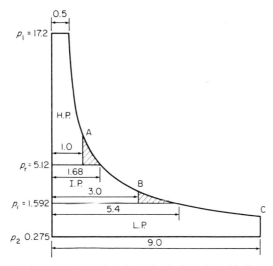

Figure 2.34 Triple-expansion engine—hypothetical combined indicator diagram

Total ratio of expansion $r = \dfrac{9.0}{0.5} = 18.0$, hence

Hypothetical referred mean pressure

$= 17.2 \left(\dfrac{1 + \log_e 18.0}{18.0} \right) - 0.275 = 3.444$ bar

An engine of this type could be expected to have an overall diagram factor of 0.65, hence actual referred mean pressure $= 3.444 \times 0.65 = 2.238$ bar.

If the engine has a stroke of 1.22 m, and is to develop 1865 kW at 1.167 rev/s then

L.P. Cylinder Area $= \dfrac{1865}{200 \times 2.238 \times 1.22 \times 1.167}$

$= 2.925$ m^2

∴ L.P. dia = 1.93 m

$$\text{H.P. Cylinder Area} = \frac{2.925}{9.0} = 0.325 \text{ m}^2$$

∴ H.P. dia = 0.643 m

$$\text{I.P. Cylinder Area} = \frac{2.925}{\sqrt{9}} = 0.975 \text{ m}^2$$

∴ I.P. dia = 1.114 m

If the I.P. and L.P. cut-offs are 0.56 and 0.6 respectively, then the receiver pressures and the approximate ratios of the powers, initial piston loads and cylinder temperature ranges may be calculated by the same methods as before, i.e.

Cylinder	H.P.	I.P.	L.P.
Ratio of powers	1.0	0.933	1.113
Ratio of initial piston loads	1.0	0.876	0.981
Ratio of temperature ranges	1.0	0.757	0.883

If the L.P. cylinder of a triple expansion engine is inconveniently large, it can be divided into two L.P. cylinders in parallel, each having one half of the calculated area. This results in a 4-cylinder triple.

If highly superheated steam can be used, then the advantage of reduced cylinder temperature range due to multiple expansion is not so significant. Steam is kept superheated or dry throughout the H.P. and I.P. cylinders, and only the L.P. cylinder suffers from condensation and wetness losses as well as a significant loss due to incomplete expansion. For this reason, the normal L.P. cylinder is sometimes omitted, and an exhaust turbine is fitted which is made sufficiently large as to develop the L.P. cylinder power as well as its own. When this is done, the normal H.P. and I.P. cylinders are each replaced by two cylinders of half the area, thus giving a double compound engine, i.e. two H.P. and two L.P. cylinders with four cranks. Examples of this type of combination engine are illustrated in chapter 7.

3 Steam turbines

The advantages of steam turbines are that they give a direct rotary motion and a more even torque on the propeller shaft. There is no internal mechanical friction, and therefore no internal lubrication is required; this is most important when using superheated steam, the use of which in a reciprocating engine necessitates lubricating oil. Oil is difficult to remove from the feed water and is detrimental to boilers.

The weight of engine is reduced for the power developed, especially with large powers. (The weight of a turbine engine per kilowatt is about one half of that of a reciprocating engine.)

Steam is expanded right down to the condenser pressure, giving a higher overall efficiency. The space occupied is less for turbines.

Disadvantages

There are disadvantages in that the condensing plant is larger and more expensive and requires greater auxiliary power due to the lower condenser pressure carried.

Special heat-resisting materials are required at the H.P. end for the rotor and casing if using high superheat.

A separate astern turbine is required which is mounted on the same spindle as the ahead turbine and results in a large *windage* loss, i.e., the astern blading *churns* the *dead* steam, and thus does work on the steam. This useless work has to be supplied by the ahead turbine. In addition, the astern disc or drum *rubs* on the dead steam, causing fluid friction, which represents another power loss. Disc friction and windage can, of course, be eliminated by providing astern turbines in casings entirely separate from the ahead turbine.

A reduction gear is required to allow the turbine to run at the high speed necessary for high efficiency, and the propeller at the comparatively slow speed for its best efficiency.

The main bearings of the rotor work under severe temperature conditions due to the conduction of heat from the inside of the turbine casing, and all bearings, including the thrust, have a comparatively high surface speed. The lubricating system is, of necessity, more complicated, and must be absolutely reliable.

More expert attention is required during warming-up, draining and shutting down, due to the liability of rotors and casings distorting.

Fundamental difference between reciprocating and turbine engine

The fundamental difference in principle between the reciprocating engine and turbine engine is that, in the reciprocating engine the velocity of the steam relative to the working parts (piston, etc.) is zero, while in the turbine engine the velocity of the steam relative to the working parts (blades, etc.) is very considerable, often of the order of 300 m/s. This simply means that the reciprocating engine uses pressure energy and the turbine uses velocity energy; or again, that in the reciprocating engine, work is done on the piston by the static pressure of the steam, while in the turbine work is done on the blades by the dynamic force of the steam.

Types of steam turbine

There are two main types of steam-turbine: the Impulse type and the Reaction type.

A simple impulse turbine consists of a ring of nozzles followed by a row of blades mounted on a wheel and facing the nozzles. The steam is expanded in the nozzles, and leaves in the form of high-velocity jets which impinge on the rotor blades. The latter deflect the steam-jets, causing a change in velocity and therefore a change of momentum. There is therefore a force applied to the blades which has a component in the direction of motion causing rotation of the wheel and a component at right angles to the direction of motion causing end thrust.

In an impulse turbine *the resultant end thrust is very small*. In a pure impulse stage all the pressure drop takes place in the fixed nozzles—there is no pressure drop across the blades.

A simple reaction stage consists of a ring of fixed blades acting as nozzles and followed by a row of similar blades mounted on the rotor. One-half of the stage-pressure drop takes place in the fixed blades, and the steam-jets enter the rotor blades in the same manner as an impulse stage. The rotor

Figure 3.1 Single-screw, double-reduction geared turbines with covers off (all impulse type)
H.P. turbine in front right, L.P. turbine at back right. First reduction pinions and wheels on left, second reduction pinions and main wheel in centre. Connecting pipes between H.P. and L.P. are clearly seen, with bellows expansion pieces and emergency connections for running H.P. or L.P. turbine alone

blades themselves act as moving nozzles and expand the steam over the remaining half of the stage-pressure drop. There is therefore a pressure drop across both the fixed and moving blades, resulting in *a considerable end thrust*.

In a reaction stage the velocity increases in the fixed blades and is reduced on entering the moving blades. The further expansion in the moving blades causes the velocity to again increase. This velocity is again reduced on leaving the moving blades. Although in practice the above is called a reaction stage, strictly speaking, it has only 50 per cent reaction.

Figure 3.1 shows a single-screw double-reduction geared impulse steam turbine installation designed and constructed by Scott's Shipbuilding and Engineering Co., Ltd., Greenock.

THE TURBINE ROTOR

The function of the rotor of a turbine is to transmit the effort of the steam load on the blades to the propeller shaft directly or through the pinion of the reduction gearing. When turbine

rotors, of the reaction type, were larger in diameter, for the
comparatively slow speed imposed by a direct drive, the rotor
was built up. The rotor spindles at each end were shrunk and
bolted to large cast-steel spider wheels, and wrapped round
the periphery of the spider wheels and riveted to them was a
forged-steel cylinder. Grooves were cut in the periphery of the
cylinder for reception of the blades.

As speeds increased and diameters were reduced, the spiders
were dispensed with, and the rotor was made in two main
parts instead of five. One part was in the form of an open-
ended cylinder, with spindle included as part of the forging.
The other part was a forging incorporating the other end of
the spindle and a disc-shaped part to form the closing end of
the rotor cylinder. The disc part of one was shrunk into the
cylindrical part of the other, and a few rivets at the joint completed the construction (Figure 3.2).

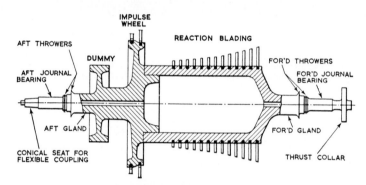

Figure 3.2 Drum rotor for impulse-reaction turbine

Smaller-diameter rotors (the H.P. rotor of a modern turbine
for a cargo vessel may be only about 400 mm diameter) are
solid forgings of high-quality steel with a hole about 50 mm
diameter bored axially through the spindle and rotor for the
entire length. This provides a means of inspection after the
rotor is completed and guards against internal flaws being
present, which might extend as fractures in later years. Grooves
are cut as before, in the periphery of the rotor, for the blades;
the type of groove depending on the method of fixture to be
employed. At one end or both ends of the rotor, depending on
the astern arrangement, there is a facing for the attachment of
a *dummy* piston. This dummy has brass or monel-metal rings

caulked into grooves in its periphery to form part of the labyrinth packing. It is bolted to the rotor end.

The rotor forging may be enlarged at the H.P. end to form a disc, integral with the rotor, to take two rows of impulse blades and, if the astern turbine is of the impulse type, a similar disc at the other end.

On the spindle, which may be about 150 mm diameter in way of the packed gland, there are raised circumferential rings which form part of the labyrinth gland packing. These rings may be part of the metal of the spindle, or they may be segments caulked into grooves. The rings or gland strips are made of brass for use with saturated steam or low-pressure steam and of monel metal for higher temperatures.

Next, along the spindle, there are again raised circumferential rings, the purpose of which is to throw oil which has leaked from the bearing away from the spindle, preventing it from mixing with the steam and reaching the boilers. Further along the spindle, fore and aft, the diameter is reduced in way of the bearing journals. Near one end, usually the forward end, the diameter is further reduced at a point where there is a collar about 300 mm diameter and 50 mm wide. This is the thrust collar, which is used to keep the rotor in its correct longitudinal position.

At the other extreme end, the spindle is tapered and threaded for a nut. This is for the attachment of the flexible coupling, where contact is made with the reduction-pinion spindle.

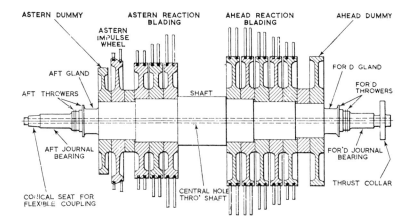

Figure 3.3 Built rotor for reaction turbine

Larger reaction-turbine rotors are built up by the method almost universally employed in impulse turbines. The spindle, which has journals, oil-thrower rings and thrust collar as in the type described, is stepped for the attachment of the forged-steel discs which carry the blades. These discs are keyed to the spindle and shrunk in place, or they are pressed on to the spindle by hydraulic pressure while hot to give a combination of force fit and shrink fit. Grooves are again cut in the periphery to take the blades and, in a reaction turbine, the sides of the discs abut one another until the outer appearance does not greatly differ from the drum type (Figure 3.3.)

In the impulse type, spaces must be left between the discs to make way for the diaphragms carrying the nozzles. As a

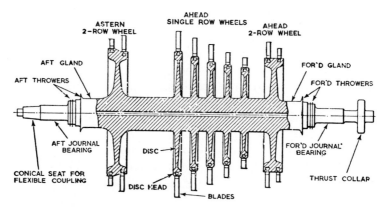

Figure 3.4 Solid rotor for impulse turbine

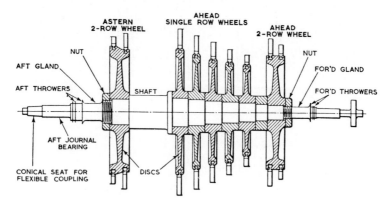

Figure 3.5 Built rotor for impulse turbine

Figure 3.6 H.P. ahead and astern turbine rotor

Figure 3.7 L.P. ahead and astern turbine rotor

safeguard against possible axial movement due to slackness in service, the whole group of discs is secured by a nut at one end. Figures 3.4 and 3.5 show sections of solid and built rotors respectively for impulse turbines and Figures 3.6 and 3.7 photographs of these.

Modern rotors are required to withstand high temperatures (up to 500°C) and are made of forged carbon-molybdenum or chrome-molybdenum steel.

TURBINE MAIN BEARINGS

The turbine main-bearing shells are made of gunmetal. They are in halves for ease of removal and adjustment, and are lined with good-quality white metal, dovetailed into the shells in the usual way. The bearing shell is $1\frac{1}{2}$ to twice as long as the shaft diameter. About 50 mm is left at either end uncovered by white metal. These parts at the ends of the bearing are called *rubbing strips*. The white-metalled surface of the bearing projects not more than 0.25 mm above the level of the strips. The arrangement represents one of the safety precautions in turbine work, in that, should the white metal ever wear down or be *run out* by overheating so that the shaft drops, allowing the journal to bear on the narrow gunmetal strips, a warning will be given by the smoke and noise which will ensue before the blade tips can make contact with the inside surface of the turbine casing and cause great damage.

Lubrication

No oil-grooves are cut in the white-metal surface of the bearing shells. The lubricating oil enters at the side, where the white metal is *washed away* to allow the oil access to a larger surface of the journal. It leaves the end of the bearing after travelling longitudinally under pressure from the pump and wedge action in the oil-clearance space. The clearance is much greater than in a corresponding bearing of a reciprocating engine, being about 0.5 mm. This allows the shaft or spindle to *float* while running, and provides a greater opening for the flow of the oil which performs the double role of lubricant and coolant. From the bearing ends, the oil returns to the sump. It must be remembered that, with superheated steam, the journal attains a high temperature by heat conduction alone, and a good flow of oil is required to keep the temperature from rising.

A small cock is fitted in the top of the bearing cover to provide a means of checking the flow of oil or to allow air to escape when starting up at any time when the cock is opened.

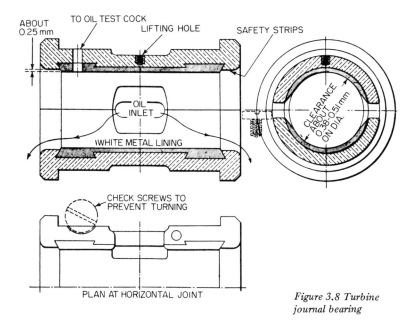

ABOUT 0.25 mm

TO OIL TEST COCK

LIFTING HOLE

SAFETY STRIPS

OIL INLET

WHITE METAL LINING

CLEARANCE ABOUT 0.38–0.51 mm ON DIA.

CHECK SCREWS TO PREVENT TURNING

PLAN AT HORIZONTAL JOINT

Figure 3.8 Turbine journal bearing

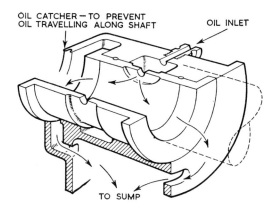

OIL CATCHER – TO PREVENT OIL TRAVELLING ALONG SHAFT

OIL INLET

TO SUMP

Figure 3.9 Path of oil in turbine journal bearing

The bent pipe attached to it discharges oil into a funnel. It is also useful for drawing off samples for testing the condition of the oil.

These bearing bushes are easily removed when the weight of the rotor is taken up. The turbine rotor, and with it the journal, need be lifted only a fraction of a millimetre to allow the bottom half to be pushed round the shaft and lifted out. This can be done without disturbing the sealing glands. Figures 3.8 and 3.9 illustrate the bearing construction and the path of the lubricating oil.

TURBINE BLADES AND BLADE FIXTURES

When a rotor is running at high speed there is a considerable centrifugal force set up, tending to pull the blades out of the grooves. A certain amount of vibration is set up due to variation of steam velocity at the blade, this effect being greater in an impulse turbine, where the nozzles extend for only part of the circumference, than in a reaction type, where the steam is evenly distributed over the whole circumference. These effects, combined with those of expansion and contraction, tend to loosen the blade at its fixing to the rotor, and a great many designs have been employed to secure the blade firmly in its groove and, at the same time, make the work of fitting the blades simple and effective. Figure 3.10 shows typical H.P. blades and Figure 3.11 shows several types of blade fixing.

The original turbine blades were of brass and made from strips. They were slightly curved with about 3 mm of the length at the tip thinned to about 0.075 mm thickness. There was a shaped brass root piece between the blades which was caulked in place radially. Each blade had to be inserted individually followed by a caulked root piece. The blading of a

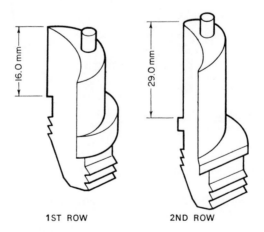

1ST ROW   2ND ROW

Figure 3.10 Typical H.P. blades of normal marine size

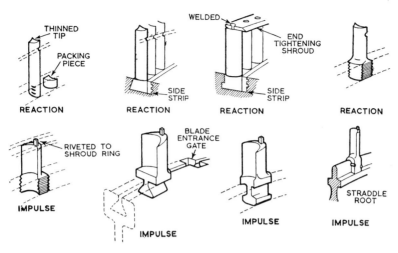

Figure 3.11 Turbine blade root fixings

large rotor was very slow by this method, and later types used blades which were built-up in segments of about fifty blades, secured and brazed to a common root piece. One edge of this root piece was machined at about 30 degrees to the vertical, while the other was vertical. The groove into which the segment fitted had one edge at 30 degrees, while the other edge was vertical and serrated. The root piece entered easily into the groove, and a side packing strip was caulked into the vertical space and into the serrations in the groove. This method is still used.

An alternative method is to have to root piece checked into the groove and secured by a side packing strip or to have individual blades with the root piece as an integral part and deep serrations on both sides. In this type of fixture no side packing strip is required, the blade being entered at an angle and twisted round, then caulked circumferentially.

The most common root shape for impulse turbines is the dove-tail. It fits into a groove of the same shape, and is entered through a *gate* or cut-away place in the groove and pushed round until all the blades but one are in position and caulked. The final blade has a specially shaped root piece and a side packing piece which is caulked into position, locking the blade in place.

In the *straddle* root type, the blade is shaped to straddle the circumference of the disc. The blades are secured by rivets which pass through the root and disc.

The search for the most suitable material for turbine blades has been continuous throughout the development. Some materials have a temperature limit, others have a tendency to harden and fracture, others corrode, and all are subject more or less to erosion, especially when water is present. Among the materials used are brass, phosphor bronze, manganese copper, monel metal, nickel steel and stainless iron which contains chromium. Figure 3.12 is a close-up view of a H.P. rotor, showing the blades.

Figure 3.12 H.P. rotor; close-up view showing blades
    The gradually increasing blade heights towards the exhaust end should be noted, and the expansion cuts in the shroud ring. Note also that the blade tangs pass through holes in the shroud ring and are riveted over on top. The finishing blades are clearly seen in the fourth and ninth stage wheels.

The properties required in modern turbine blades are very exacting due to the higher speeds and temperatures at which they operate. These are detailed in a paper to the Institute of Marine Engineers by J. H. G. Monypenny, F.Inst.P., thus: tensile and fatigue strength, toughness and ductility at the working temperature, resistance to corrosion and erosion (caused by priming of the boilers and the effects of chlorides and air while at rest), rate of expansion almost equal to that of the casing and rotor, easy to machine during manufacture and as light as possible to reduce centrifugal force.

Low tensile stainless iron is generally preferred to high tensile stainless iron on account of the superior fatigue-resisting qualities of the former material. The composition of low tensile stainless iron is as follows: carbon 0.1 per cent max., silicon 0.5 per cent max., manganese 0.5 per cent max., chromium 12.5–14.5 per cent, nickel 0.5 per cent max, sulphur 0.04 per cent, phosphorus 0.04 per cent max. The ultimate tensile strength is 45.0–60.0 kN/cm².

High tensile stainless iron has the same composition except that the carbon content is 0.14 per cent maximum, and the heat treatment is different. The ultimate tensile strength is 67.5 kN/cm².

Care must also be taken with the selection of blade materials where lacing wires have to be brazed in, as trouble may be experienced with intergranular penetration at the braze.

Figure 3.13 shows the blading of a rotor for double casing H.P. casing.

Figure 3.13 Blading rotor for double casing H.P. turbine

GLANDS

Where the rotor spindle or shaft passes through the turbine casing, some sort of packing must be provided just as the piston-rod of a reciprocating engine requires packing to pre-

vent steam escaping at the H.P. end, and to prevent air being
drawn in at the L.P. end. An ordinary stuffing-box and gland
with soft steam packing would seal the space between the
casing and the spindle, but the packing would wear away the
surface of the spindle and there would also be a friction loss.
Changes in temperature would cause expansion and contraction, sufficient to cause leakage, and this leakage would be
most undesirable at the L.P. end. The leakage at the L.P. end
is, of course, from the atmosphere into the turbine, due to
the pressure inside the turbine being lower than atmospheric.
When the condenser pressure is low it requires only a small
opening for leakage of air to make it impossible for the air-
pump to cope with it, with the result that the condenser
pressure increases. In a turbine installation an increase of
condenser pressure from say 0.035 bar to 0.07 bar results in
about 5.0 per cent loss of power and efficiency.

Carbon glands

In small turbines the glands may consist of two rings of a
carbon-composition material at each end. The rings are of
square section and in halves, with a garter spring holding the
two parts firmly together and pressing them lightly on the
surface of the spindle. This is called a *carbon gland*.

At higher pressure and powers the gland must be made
longer to prevent serious leakage. It is usually arranged in two
or three sections, e.g., four rings next the inside of the casing,
a space which is connected to the L.P. gland steam supply by
a pipe, then four rings at the outside position. On account of
the larger diameter of the spindle, these rings are made up of
four or six segments, secured as before with a garter spring
(Figure 3.14).

To minimise leakage, the radial clearance between the
shaft and the carbon ring when hot should be small—of the
order of 0.005 mm. Now the coefficient of linear expansion
of steel is greater than that of carbon, approximate values
being: carbon   0.0000072 mm/mm°C,   steel   0.0000108
mm/mm°C.

Therefore assuming a rise in temperature from cold of say
166.6°C, a steel shaft of 152.4 mm dia. when cold will expand
to 152.4 + (152.4 x 0.0000108 x 166.6) = 152.6742 mm dia.
when hot. To give a radial clearance of 0.005 mm when hot,
the bore of the carbon ring when hot must be 152.6742 +
0.01 = 152.6842 mm.

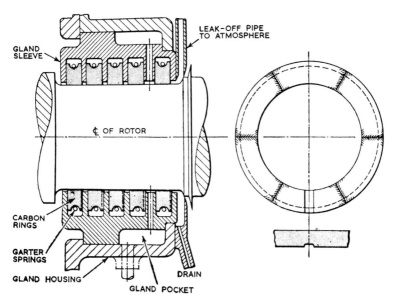

Figure 3.14 Carbon gland for turbines

Now, the hot diameter = cold diameter [1 + (coefficient of expansion × temperature rise)]

$$\therefore 152.6842 = \text{cold diameter} \left[1 + (0.0000072 \times 166.6)\right]$$

$$\therefore \text{cold diameter} = \frac{152.6842}{1.0011995} = 152.5103 \text{ mm}$$

Hence when cold, radial clearance between shaft and carbon ring

$$= \frac{152.5103 - 152.4}{2} = 0.05515 \text{ mm}$$

Because of the difference in working temperature at each turbine, separate dummies are provided for each end of each turbine, on which to fit the assembled carbon ring segments.

Labyrinth packing glands

There is also a type of gland packing called *labyrinth packing*. As the name implies, the steam is made to enter a labyrinth or maze of winding passages. These, in their simplest form,

consist of projecting rings or fins, half of the number being
attached to the casing, and the other half to the spindle. The
tips of the spindle fins project to within 0.5 mm of the inside
bore of the stuffing-box in the casing, and those projecting
from the stuffing-box towards the spindle project to within
0.5 mm of the surface of the spindle. These glands may, as in
the carbon type, be composed of two or three sections, and
are usually longer (Figure 3.15).

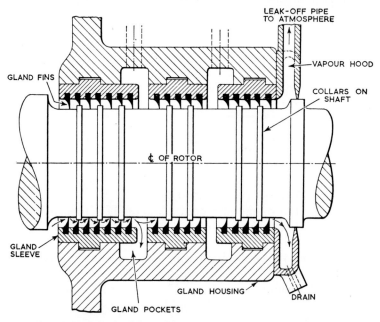

Figure 3.15 Labyrinth gland for turbines

H.P. steam entering the labyrinth box from the casing tends
to flow outwards towards the atmosphere and, while in
motion, it must pass through the 0.5 mm openings alternately
between casing and spindle. This results in throttling, and the
pressure of the steam drops at each fin until, at the space
between the two sections of packing, the pressure may have
dropped from an initial 20.0 bar to 1.3 bar. The outer set of
packing-rings reduce this pressure to very nearly atmospheric,
and very little leakage takes place. Formerly, it was common
practice to have labyrinth packing next to the casing and a
short box of carbon packing at the outside, Figures 3.16 and
3.17. Carbon glands are not now much used, modern marine
steam turbines generally having all-labyrinth glands.

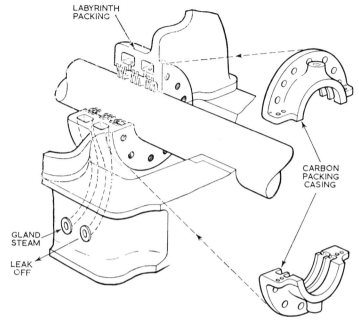

Figure 3.16 Combined labyrinth and carbon gland

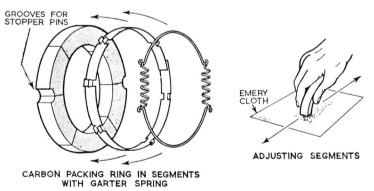

Figure 3.17 Carbon gland and springs

Gland steam system for simple turbine

Consider now a simple turbine in which the steam is expanded from a high pressure to exhaust at under atmospheric pressure. When the turbine is being warmed through before going on load, steam is admitted to the glands by opening the gland steam-control valve *A*, Figure 3.18. The low condenser pressure draws the steam into the casing.

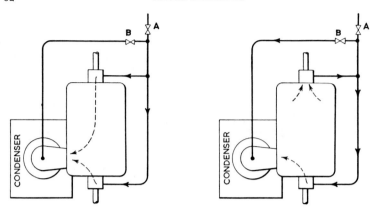

Figure 3.18 Gland steam system for simple turbine

Under running conditions, valve *A* is closed. The steam in the space between the two sets of packing in the H.P. gland, which may be, as stated, at about 1.3 bar, now passes through the connecting pipes to supply the L.P. gland, which requires steam at above atmospheric pressure filling the outer labyrinth spaces to prevent air being drawn into the casing and raising the pressure. Should the leakage from the H.P. end be insufficient to do this, the valve *A* may require to be eased to make up the deficiency; but should the leakage from the H.P. gland be in excess of that required to seal the L.P., then a valve *B*, which connects the gland steam-line to the condenser, may be opened to draw off the surplus. A pressure of 1.15 bar is usually sufficient to seal the L.P. gland.

Gland steam system for two-cylinder turbine

An arrangement of gland steam connections for a two-cylinder installation could be as shown in Figure 3.19. Valve *A* is in control of the supply of steam to the steam-collector or

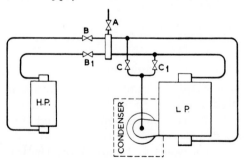

Figure 3.19 Gland steam system for two-cylinder turbine

steam-bottle. The steam to and from the H.P. glands may be controlled by separate valves, and the leak-off to the condenser from the forward- and after-end glands of the L.P. casing is controlled by valves on the respective pipe-lines.

When warming though the turbine, valves C and C_1 are closed, while A, B, B_1 are open. When running, A is closed and C, C_1 opened sufficiently to keep the gland steam-line pressure at 1.15–1.3 bar. B, B_1 are open.

Gland steam system for three-cylinder turbine

A possible arrangement for a turbine installation with H.P., M.P. and L.P. casings is as shown in Figure 3.20. The leak-off pipe is led to the exhaust-pipe opening from M.P. to L.P. turbine. This could be arranged to go to the condenser as shown in the simplified arrangement in the lower sketch, Figure 3.21.

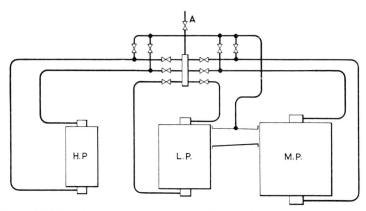

Figure 3.20 Gland steam systems for three-cylinder turbine

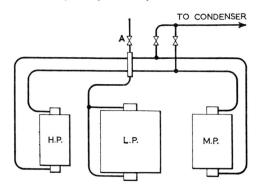

Figure 3.21 Simplified gland steam system for three-cylinder turbine

Note that the valves on the gland steam-bottle have been dispensed with. Valve *A* now controls the steam supply to all glands. Leak-off valves regulate the pressure when more steam is leaking from the H.P. glands than is required to seal the others.

The diagram in Figure 3.22 illustrates the gland steam arrangement in the old "Nestor" class of vessels in the Blue Funnel Line.

It will be observed that control of the pressures is at the hand of the engineer on duty at the panel of the manoeuvring cubicle; also that no vapour now escapes to the engine-room.

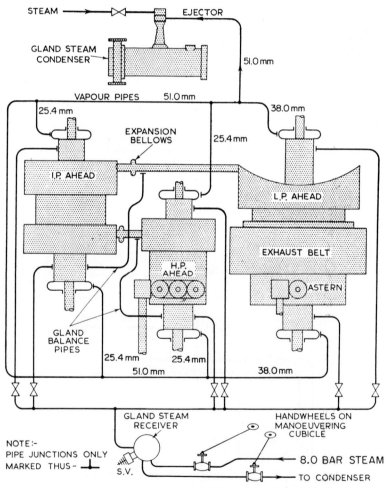

Figure 3.22 Gland steam arrangement in S.S. Nestor (Blue Funnel Line)

The vapour is drawn off by a steam ejector placed above the gland steam condenser. This arrangement prevents loss of water in the form of vapour, which is good for the boilers; prevents loss of heat energy, which is good for the general efficiency, and prevents that heat from raising the engine-room temperature, which is good for the engineer's comfort.

Note that faulty adjustment of the gland steam pressure during manoeuvring periods has at times allowed air to be absorbed by the condensate, causing increased condenser pressure at the time and eventual corrosion in water-tube boilers.

Gland steam pressure control is made very simple with the Cockburn–De Laval automatic gland steam seal regulator (Figure 3.23).

Tanks *A* and *B* are filled with water and connected by a hand-adjusted needle valve, the pressure in *B* compressing the bellows. This action raises the right-hand end of the floating lever against the pull of the spring, which at the same time raises the valve of the oil-relay cylinder. Oil under pressure now enters the cylinder, above the piston, forcing it down.

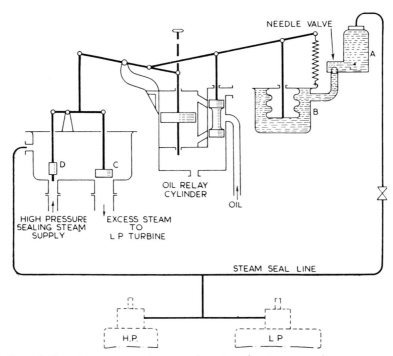

Figure 3.23 Cockburn–De Laval steam seal regulator (Cockburns Ltd.)

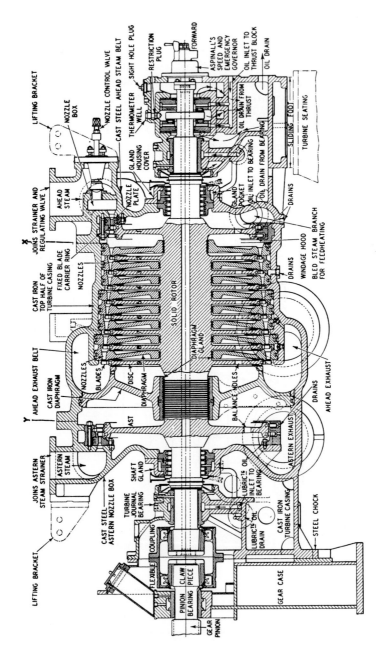

Figure 3.24 H.P. ahead and astern turbine

This has the effect, through the linkage, of opening valve *C* and closing *D* partly, so that the pressure in the steam seal line is reduced. At the same time the floating lever on its downward path has closed the oil relay valve. Should the pressure become too low in the steam seal line, the bellows will extend. Actions are now all reversed so that valve *D* is opened, admitting high-pressure steam while valve *C* closes. While maneouvring, the turbine may be at reduced or full power without any hand adjustment of gland steam pressure being required, except perhaps the needle valve between *A* and *B*, which is used for damping purposes only, i.e., to prevent *hunting*.

THE TURBINE CASING

The general construction of an impulse turbine casing may be seen in Figures 3.24 and 3.25 which show respectively a fore and aft section through a complete H.P. and L.P. ahead and astern turbine. The casing is made in four main parts:

1. *The Bottom Half*. If all nozzles are contained in the top, the bottom half is subjected only to steam at the wheelcase pressure and temperature, and is therefore of *cast iron*. The bottom half in this case extends from end to end and, reading from the forward end, contains the following sections (see also Figures 3.26 and 3.27):

(a) the thrust bearing housing;
(b) the forward journal bearing housing;
(c) the forward gland housing;
(d) the ahead turbine casing proper;
(e) the ahead exhaust belt;
(f) the astern turbine casing and exhaust belt;
(g) the aft gland housing;
(h) the aft journal bearing housing;
(i) the flexible coupling housing.

2. *The Ahead Nozzle Box*, which contains all the ahead nozzles, and is therefore subjected to steam at the boiler pressure and temperature. It is, in consequence, made of cast steel.

3. *Turbine Casing Cover*, which is not subjected to H.P., high-temperature steam, and is therefore of cast iron.

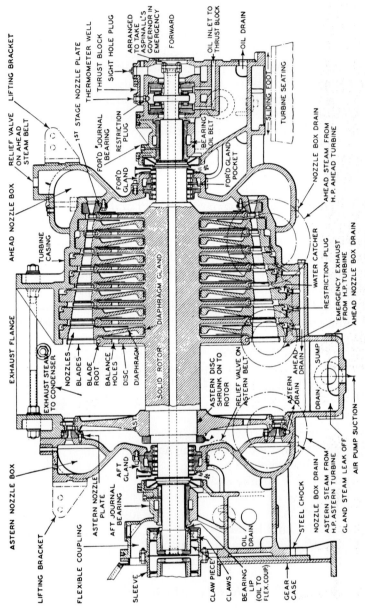

Figure 3.25 L.P. ahead and astern turbine

Figure 3.26 H.P. ahead and astern turbine casing, bottom half, with rotor removed showing the bearing housings, the gland pockets, with diaphragms and diaphragm glands. Note the windage hoods in the bottom half, and the diaphragm between ahead and astern sections. The top half lifting guide pillars are in position

Figure 3.27 H.P. turbine opened up; locking from aft end. The guide pillars and supporting columns for the top half are in position

4. *The Astern Nozzle Box* of cast steel, similar to the ahead nozzle box.

Items 2, 3 and 4 when bolted together at the vertical joints *X* and *Y* (Figure 3.24) may be regarded as the top half of the turbine casing.

All the stationary parts of a steam turbine, i.e., the casing, diaphragms, gland sleeves, etc., are split at the horizontal joint throughout the length. This enables the top half to be lifted completely clear of the bottom half and rotor (Figure 3.27).

When the top and bottom halves are bolted together at the horizontal joint, the various compartments in each half correspond.

Housings of thrust and journal bearings

In the illustration (Figure 3.24) a separate combined cover is fitted to the thrust and journal bearings at the forward end, and to the journal bearing and flexible coupling at the aft end. Separate covers are also fitted to the gland housings at each end.

The bearings, thrust block, glands and flexible coupling may therefore be opened up without disturbing the heavy turbine casing proper.

At the forward end, the thrust-bearing housing is bored to cylindrical form to receive the retaining rings and thrust pads. Holes are drilled through into the housing to conduct oil to the pads from the forced-lubrication supply. Oil passes over the thrust surfaces, drains into the bottom of the turbine casing and thence to the pump and cooler, for recirculation.

The thrust- and journal-bearing cover is provided with inspection plug, thermometer boss for oil temperature leaving bearing and a restriction plug to ensure that the oil pressure is maintained in way of the thrust collar.

The journal-bearing housing is also bored to cylindrical form to receive the bushes. Oil enters through a hole cast in the frame and passes into the oil belt surrounding the bush. The oil passes into the journal through slots in the brass, spreads along the shaft and drains to the bottom of the casing over the ends of the bush. A brass oil-scraper cleans oil off the shaft.

The forward end of the bottom half of the turbine casing rests on the turbine seating, the latter being part of the ship's structure. The turbine is not rigidly bolted to the seating here,

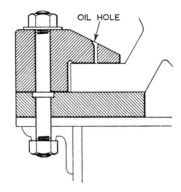

Figure 3.28 Sliding foot

but is held down by clamps forming a sliding foot (Figure 3.28) to allow for expansion.

A cavity is formed in the bottom half between the journal-bearing housing and the gland housing, by means of which oil escaping from the former and water escaping from the latter are conducted to the bilge.

A connection leads steam to or from the gland pocket, depending on the gland steam system.

Nozzles

Ahead steam enters the steam belt and passes through the nozzle control valve(s) to the nozzle box(es) and thence to the first-stage nozzles. The latter are formed in bronze or steel nozzle plates, bolted to the nozzle box. The nozzles may be machined from the solid, or they may be formed by casting steel partition plates into the nozzle plate casting.

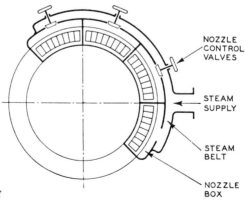

Figure 3.29 Nozzle grouping

In the present instance, the nozzles are divided into four groups with nozzle control valves as shown, each nozzle group having its own nozzle plate (Figure 3.29).

To minimise *pumping* and *windage* losses, that part of the blade annulus not covered by nozzles is screened by a hood. This hood takes the place of the fixed blades and their carrier ring.

Metals used

Not only do turbine materials have to withstand the stresses due to pressure and centrifugal force, but have to be suitable to withstand high temperatures. This is particularly important at the high-pressure end, where, in modern designs, pressures up to 60.0–70.0 bar and temperatures up to 480.0–535.0°C are now commonplace.

The application of the reheat cycle means that the I.P. turbine too could be subjected to similar temperatures at its high-pressure end. Pressures and temperatures in L.P. turbines are quite low, and generally do not require the use of special materials.

Formerly, cast iron was used for the stationary parts of steam turbines up to temperatures of 230.0°C, but its use has now become very limited, even in this temperature range, and in most modern designs has been replaced by fabricated steel.

Plain carbon steels may be used up to 400.0 or 425.0°C and may be of the electric furnace or acid open-hearth types, having carbon content not more than 0.25 per cent and manganese content not more than 0.9 per cent. Above 400.0–425.0°C, the phenomenon of *creep* is encountered, necessitating the use of special steels. Creep is a permanent plastic deformation which occurs when the material is under stress at high temperatures, and a creep-resisting material must meet the following requirement: the stress which will produce a creep deformation of 0.1 per cent in 100,000 working hours at 510°C must be not less than 4.65 kN/cm^2.

Thus, above 400.0°C molybdenum steel is used, and for temperatures of 480.0–510.0°C and above, molybdenum-vanadium steel is used, giving further improvement in creep properties. An average *molybdenum steel* has a composition: carbon 0.35 per cent max., silicon 0.25 per cent max., manganese 0.5–0.8 per cent, sulphur 0.04 per cent max., phosphorus 0.04 per cent max., molybdenum 0.5 per cent min., nickel 0.5 per cent max., chromium 0.5 per cent max.

An average *chrome-molybdenum* steel has a composition: carbon 0.2–0.35 per cent, chromium 2.8–3.5 per cent, molybdenum 0.45–0.8 per cent, nickel 0.5 per cent max., manganese 0.4–0.7 per cent, silicon 0.35 per cent max., sulphur 0.04 per cent max., phosphorus 0.04 per cent max. The creep-resisting properties of this steel are superior to those of molybdenum steel.

Diaphragms

The ahead turbine casing proper is bored to cylindrical form and *stepped* to receive the diaphragms. The latter consist of circular, cast-iron plates with a central circular hole through which the shaft passes. The periphery of the diaphragm fits into the grooves in the casing and has a ring of nozzles cast in (Figures 3.30 and 3.31).

The central role in the diaphragm is fitted with fins forming a diaphragm gland designed to reduce steam escaping from one stage to the next without passing through the nozzles and doing work on the blades. Two types of diaphragm gland are shown in Figure 3.32. Note that the H.P. turbine is fitted with a diaphragm between the ahead and astern stages (Figure 3.33) to prevent H.P. ahead exhaust steam passing to the L.P. astern turbine.

Figure 3.30 Typical half diaphragms, showing cast-in nozzle division plates, and diaphragm gland fins

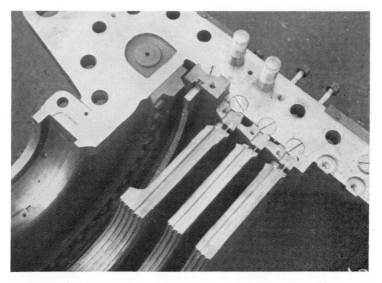

Figure 3.31 H.P. ahead turbine casing, part view of top half, showing three diaphragms in position with their locking screws. Each diaphragm is hooded in way of the rotor blades to minimise dead spaces and windage losses. Note the labyrinth fins in the diaphragm glands

Drain holes are provided at the bottom of any pockets in which water might lodge.

The aft end of the turbine casing is rigidly fixed to the gear-case bracket. The turbine casings are provided with the necessary branches to permit the H.P. turbine to exhaust direct to the condenser or the L.P. turbine to receive steam at reduced pressure from the main stop valve in case of emergency.

In the latter case, the Aspinall governor is taken off the H.P. and fitted to the L.P. turbine.

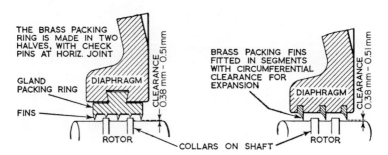

Figure 3.32 Diaphragm glands for impulse turbines

Figure 3.33 Half diaphragms between H.P. ahead and astern turbines

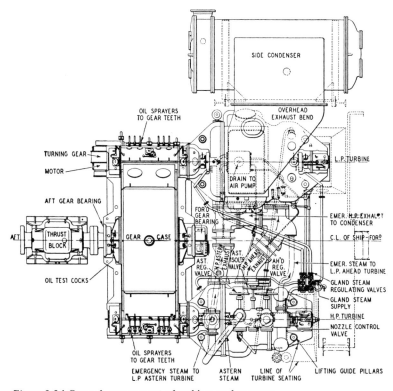

Figure 3.34 General arrangement of turbines and gearcase

Reaction tubing casings

While the foregoing remarks apply directly to the impulse turbines shown in Figures 3.24, 3.25 and 3.34, a reaction turbine casing is generally similar, but with rows of fixed blades instead of diaphragms and nozzles and with suitable modifications to accommodate dummies, etc. Figures 3.35 and 3.36 illustrate all-reaction H.P. and L.P. turbines with stepped casings such as might be fitted in an average cargo steamer.

Figure 3.37 illustrates an impulse-reaction H.P. turbine and Figure 3.38 a modern double-flow L.P. turbine with coned casing and drum rotor.

Figures 3.35–3.38 are taken from papers read to the Institue of Marine Engineers by S. S. Cook, F.R.S., and S. A. Smith, M.Sc.(Eng.). They are reproduced here by kind permission of the Institute.

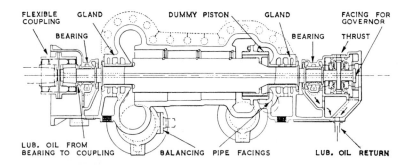

Figure 3.35 All-reaction H.P. turbine

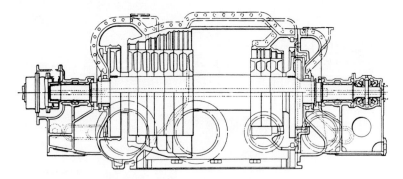

Figure 3.36 All-reaction L.P. turbine

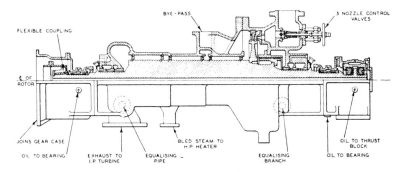

Figure 3.37 Impulse-reaction H.P. turbine

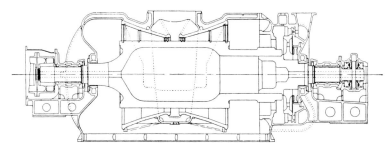

Figure 3.38 Double-flow L.P. turbine

Turbine casing, pipes and valve-chest drainage

In earlier steam turbines the H.P. drain, while manoeuvring, could be opened to the tank top just as with reciprocating engines. The purpose now in using steam traps for taking the water away to gland-steam condensers, the main feed tank and the condenser is to retain as much heat as possible to prevent loss of boiler water and to avoid excessive rise of temperature in the engine-room, which would occur if super-heated steam was released to the tank top.

It must never be possible for feed water to be sucked back into the turbine casing, and for this reason non-return valves and pipe loops are used.

Figure 3.39 shows the drainage lay-out and Figure 3.40 shows detail of the L.P. lower casing of a 5968 kW three-cylinder turbine installation.

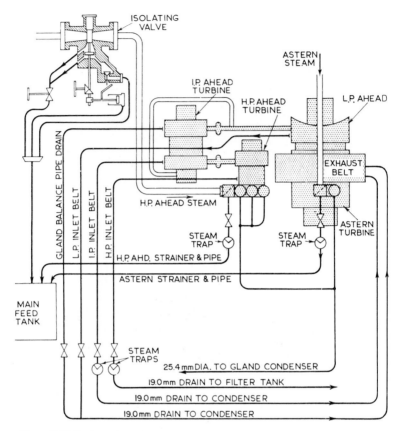

Figure 3.39 Drainage layout

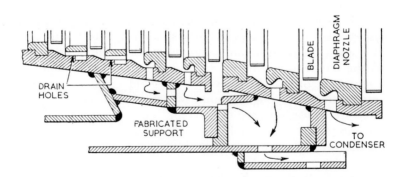

Figure 3.40 L.P. turbine ahead drainage from lower casing

Double-casing turbines

In a paper by E. L. Denny, B.Sc., read to the Institution of Mechanical Engineers on *Machinery for Cross-channel Passenger Ships*, the author gives for these ships: average full-power steaming per year, 1000 hours (i.e., little more than forty days); average full-power steaming per voyage, four hours.

Obviously, the conditions are very different from the ordinary cargo-ship, and with short runs of from two to six hours the turbine will spend a very small proportion of its useful life under steady temperature conditions. A robust simple turbine is obviously required, and the answer has been found in the single-cylinder, double-casing impulse turbine (Figure 3.41).

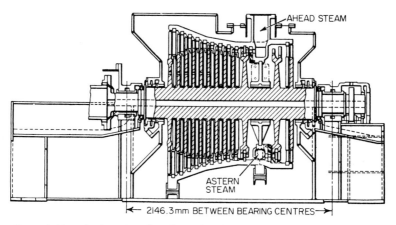

Figure 3.41 Basic plan of single-cylinder double-casing impulse turbine

It consists of a casing within a casing, the outer casing only having end-glands, so that the exhaust steam from the inner casing surrounds the inner casing and is confined by the outer casing.

In this way the outer casing temperature is always very slightly above the engine-room temperature and the casing does not require to be lagged. It may be constructed of welded mild steel.

Mr. Denny lists the following advantages:

> Lower first cost than ordinary design.
> Easy to inspect and maintain.

It has no cross-over pipes to produce heavy thrusts on
    the turbine.
A short time is required for warming through, and it can
    be shut down quickly.
Easy to operate for rapid manoeuvring.
The gland control requires only one setting for all powers
    of operation, as the glands are under sub-atmospheric
    pressure at all times.
Having the outer casing at sub-atmospheric pressure eliminates
    radiation loss under full power, as the casing temperature is
    the same as the saturation temperature of the exhaust
    steam. This also leads to a cool engine room.

Figure 3.42 Double-casing H.P. turbine

Figure 3.42 illustrates a double-casing turbine made by GEC
Turbine Generators Ltd., Rugby, by whose courtesy it is
included in this chapter. It clearly shows the sliding feet
supports of the inner casing within the outer casing.
    Figure 3.43 is a simplified sketch made from a drawing of
a marine double-casing turbine supplied by the same company.
The arrangement will be found interesting, with two astern

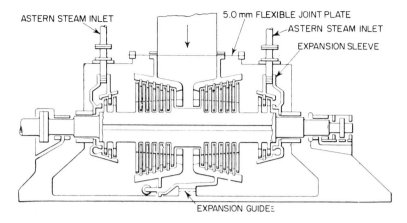

ASTERN STEAM INLET   5.0 mm FLEXIBLE JOINT PLATE
                          ASTERN STEAM INLET
                          EXPANSION SLEEVE

EXPANSION GUIDE

Figure 3.43 Double casing marine L.P. turbine

turbines, but the main purpose of the sketch is to show how the inner casing, which is supported by feet resting on the outer casing, is free to expand in relation to the astern steam inlet pipes, inlet-pipe for ahead steam and the outer casing.

EXPANSION ALLOWANCE IN ROTOR AND CASING

In all turbines allowance must be made for free expansion of rotor and casing, for both expand and contract with varying temperature.

The rotor is positioned by the thrust collar, usually placed at the forward end, and any expansion of the metal must take place from that collar towards the stern, i.e., towards the gearing.

Flexible coupling

If the rotor spindle was directly connected to the pinion, a heavy end load would be put on the helical teeth, because they, in turn, are kept in their position by the main thrust bearing on the intermediate propeller shafting. Complete freedom of movement in a longitudinal direction is afforded by fitting a *flexible coupling*, usually of the *claw* type (Figure 3.44). This coupling is not intended to make accurate alignments of the rotor spindle and pinion unnecessary, although any effect of mis-alignment may be minimised by its presence.

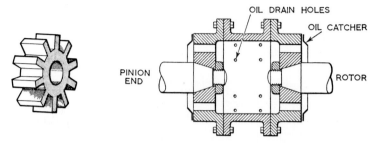

Figure 3.44 Flexible coupling, claw type

Its function is much the same as that of the ordinary muff coupling. The *muff* in this case has about twelve inwardly projecting teeth at each end, and it is made in two or three pieces with circumferential flanges securely bolted together. This is done for convenience in removal.

A boss with outwardly projecting teeth is secured to the turbine spindle end, the spindle being tapered and keyed to suit the boss, which is held in position by a large nut. A similar boss is fitted to the pinion spindle, the teeth engaging the teeth in the *muff* with a small working clearance of about 0.25 mm. The fore-and-aft movement permitted is about 9.5 mm. These claws take the full torque while running, and to avoid excessive wear they must be lubricated. This is generally accomplished by catching some oil coming from the main bearing and pinion bearing by a ring secured to the coupling. Centrifugal force carries the oil through the spaces between the teeth and projects it through small holes in the muff to drain away with the rest of the lubricating oil.

Sliding feet

The after flange of the turbine casing is secured to the seating, which may be a projection from the forward end of the gearcase. The forward end of the casing is made free to expand longitudinally by fitting *sliding feet* or some flexible fitting, which will allow end movement but no vertical or thwartship play. Sliding feet are similar to the guide-and-shoe arrangement for single guides in a reciprocating engine, as seen from Figure 3.28. Again, provision must be made for lubrication. A turbine casing was once fractured because the lubrication of the sliding feet had been neglected. They became firmly held with rust, preventing end movement and thereby putting a heavy stress on the casing.

A tell-tale pointer is sometimes fitted at the sliding feet to indicate the relative movement between the casing and the seating. The position of the pointer is used as a guide to the thorough warming up of the turbine before starting.

Gauging internal clearances

The relative longitudinal position of rotor and casing is of great importance because of the finer clearances, such as dummy clearance and tip clearance in an end-tightened arrangement of reaction turbines. The problem is to gauge the internal clearances without actually seeing them. This is done by pulling the rotor forward against the rings in question, preferably while the turbine is opened up in the first instance. The position of some mark on the rotor spindle, external to the casing, is then noted. The rotor is now moved endways until the dummy clearance is as required (about 0.5 mm) when the external mark is gauged relative to some fixed point on the turbine casing. When the turbine is assembled, the clearance, as indicated from these two marks, will also be the internal clearance.

The simplest arrangement is to have a machined collar on the spindle and a finger plate secured to the casting at the *gap* between the main bearing and the gland at the forward end. When the rotor is pulled hard up against the dummy rings, the clearance, taken with feelers, between the finger plate and the collar, may be 0.65 mm. When the rotor has been run back so that the feelers show a clearance of 1.15 mm, we know that *inside* the turbine the clearance at the dummy rings is as required. This method is not very convenient for gauging while the turbine is running.

Poker gauge

A *poker* gauge, i.e. a small-diameter rod with a collar at its end, is used by some makers. It may pass through the turbine casing, having a gland to keep it steam-tight, at a point where it can engage with the end of the dummy piston. As before, when the rotor is drawn forward, the clearance between the collar of the poker gauge and the casing is noted with feelers. The rotor is run back until the clearance, measured externally, shows that the internal clearance is 0.5 mm.

Naturally, the nearer to the internal clearance point that the external reading is taken, the more accurate will be the reading. The types mentioned have that advantage.

Some makers take the reading from the forward end of the rotor spindle, using a graduated wedge to take the clearance. This is most convenient, and in many shipping companies it is usual practice to record or *log* the dummy clearance each watch at sea.

LUBRICATING-OIL SYSTEM

All marine steam-turbine bearings, including the gearwheel and pinion bearings and teeth, are lubricated by oil under pressure.

A drain tank or sump in the double bottom of the ship contains about 2.25 m^3 gallons of lubricating oil. It is fitted with a float gauge, i.e., a float in the tank with a long rod attached which projects upwards into a slotted pipe. In the slot, a pointer, attached to the end of the rod, indicates to the engineer on watch, at a glance, how much oil is in the sump. There is also an air-vent pipe.

The lubricating-oil pumps—which are in duplicate, and are usually operated one at a time, the other being held as spare—draw the oil from the sump through a magnetic strainer and discharge it at about 2.75 bar. An air vessel on the discharge line prevents shocks (Figure 3.45). The oil then passes from the pump, through a tubular cooler in which sea-water passes through the tubes and the oil over the outer surface of the tubes. There are two coolers so that one can be in use while the other is being cleaned, or both may be required for cooling in hot climates where the sea temperature is high, 30.0°C or more. Another occasion on which both may be required is when the cooler tubes have become dirty.

Gravity tank

From the coolers, the oil is discharged to a gravity tank at the top of the engine-room. There are two gravity tanks, each capable of holding about 2.25 m^3. The oil enters at the top, and leaves through a valve in the bottom of the tank. The tanks also have pipe connections for filling from deck; for drainage of the contents to a *dirty oil* tank; vent pipes of the goose-neck type, with copper gauze covering the open end, and a float arrangement which operates a level indicator outside the tank as well as making contact with an electrical warning signal when the oil level falls to about half-way down the tank.

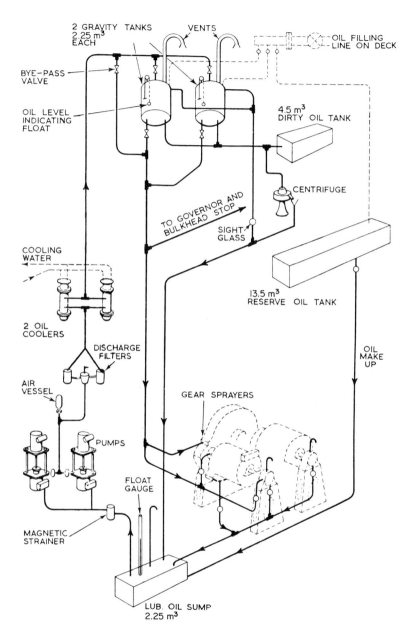

Figure 3.45 Forced lubrication system for turbines

Distribution

From the gravity tank, the oil falls by gravity (hence the name) to the distribution headers supplying the main bearings and gearing. The oil pipes vary in size, becoming smaller according to a reduction in flow required. The individual pipes to the bearings have shut-off valves and generally also some sort of flow indicator, operated by the flow of the oil acting on an impeller, the rotation of which is made visible through a glass and showing without doubt whether oil is flowing or not. It is the flow which is required, not pressure only.

On top of each bearing a pipe with a small cock attached is used to let air escape when priming and to test for flow or sample the oil. The oil enters the side or bottom of the bearings and passes out of each end to fall into a small sump and leaves by a pipe to join a return to the main drain tank. The overflow pipe has a sight glass about floor-plate level, and the speed of the lubricating-oil pump is regulated to allow a small overflow while the turbines are running at sea.

For a medium-sized vessel the quantity of oil in the system, including pipes, drain tank and gravity tank is from 4.5 to 9.0 m^3. The reserve tank may hold about 13.5 m^3. The make-up required due to vaporization and loss at the bearings varies a great deal, depending on the quality of the oil. A very good unit may require only 4.5 litres per day make-up, while others, using oil which is forming sludge, may require 25.0 litres or more per day.

Separator

An oil separator or centrifuge is incorporated in the system, receiving oil from the gravity tank and returning it, cleaned and with water removed, to the main drain tank. Three small-bore pipes from top, middle and bottom positions in the gravity tanks are led to small jets on a gauge board at the starting platform. These jets should show a steady flow while the pumps are running. Any water in the oil has the effect of breaking the continuity of the flow, the effect being so obvious that it may be used as a guide to the amount of water present in the oiling system. When the water content is excessive, the centrifuge is started up and kept running for a day or more until the flow from the jets is normal again.

Procedure at a terminal port

It is usual at a terminal port to shut the outlet to the turbine and gearing bearings from the gravity tank and open the valve to the *dirty oil* tank. The pumps are started up, and all the oil is discharged to the *dirty oil* tank. While the settling tanks are emptying, the external-level indicator should be checked and also the electric low-level alarm. While the main drain tank is empty it may be examined for signs of rust which forms on the steel plates due to the water present. This rust must be removed, as it may dislodge and be carried round the system to the bearings. Sludge lying in the bottom of the drain tank should be removed at the same time.

The lubricating-oil supply should be maintained while a turbine is cooling down. If the flow is stopped too quickly there is a danger of a varnish-like film being left on the bearing surface. The pump is generally kept running for three to four hours after *finished with engines*. On the other hand, while running, the temperature of the oil to the bearings should not be allowed to get too low. At low temperatures the oil becomes viscous and the rate of flow is reduced so that a bearing may become overheated and the white metal may run. A minimum of 24.0°C is common for the oil supply to the bearings. The pressure at the bearings is about 1.7 bar.

SAFETY DEVICES

The turbine rotor runs at high speed. Heat is transmitted by conduction from the steam along the spindle. The spindle in way of the bearing is therefore hot. It follows that any failure in the supply of lubricating oil (which must cool as well as lubricate) will be serious. It is usual for this reason to have some sort of device to give the alarm in case of failure and a valve which automatically shuts off the steam supply to the turbine.

Bulkhead stop valve

This valve is called the *bulkhead stop valve* and is situated between the boiler stop valve and the manoeuvring valves. In its simplest form it consists of a valve attached to a spindle, at the other end of which is a piston in a separate cylinder.

The piston is not intended to be steam-tight; it must allow steam to leak slowly past it. A small pipe connects the steam-supply side of the valve to the back of the piston.

In this pipe is a valve which is kept closed by the pressure of the lubricating oil on a small piston (Figure 3.46). There-fore, as long as there is sufficient oil pressure to keep the small valve closed, no steam can get to the back of the piston, so that when the regulating screw has been moved back and released the valve, steam flows past the valve to the turbine.

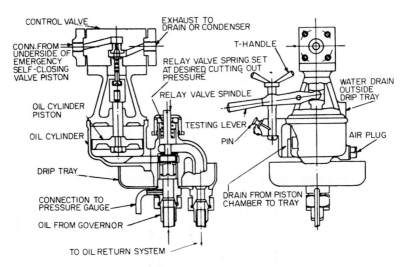

Figure 3.46 Oil operating cylinders (Cockburns Ltd.)
   The principle of operation is that of a needle valve held in the shut position by oil pressure on the cylinder piston. In the event of the oil pressure failing, the needles valve opens under the steam pressure to allow the steam to exhaust from the emergency valve piston. The relay valve on the oil cylinder is of the spring-loaded type, and can be set to lift at any required pressure. When the oil pressure in the forced-lubrication system fails, the relay valve operates and thus restricsts the passage of oil to the piston, the oil in the oil cylinder being discharged to the return system

Should the oil pressure fail, steam passes along the small pipe to the back of the piston, which is of sufficient area to give a force in excess of the steam load tending to open the valve. The valve therefore closes. It is also arranged that the valve will close when the turbine speed is excessive.

The bulkhead stop valve is made by Cockburns, Ltd., and the governing and emergency controls by Aspinall's Patent Governor Co.

Turbines are now also stopped if the rotor moves endways because of failure of the white metal in the thrust pads or if there is a serious increase of condenser pressure. When fittings for these duties are incorporated, the operation of the bulkhead stop valve is not as explained above.

In another type of Cockburn bulkhead stop valve (Figure 3.47) the back of the piston is opened to boiler steam pressure through a passage in the valve-chest casting. A supply valve in this passage is controlled by a lever, one end of which is engaged by a collar on the end of the regulating screw as that screw is moved to open the bulkhead stop valve. The supply valve is pushed inwards, and steam is admitted to the back of the valve. The first effect of this is to prevent the valve opening too quickly. A ball valve in the passage also prevents the return of steam and gives sufficient cushioning to ensure the gradual opening of the valve.

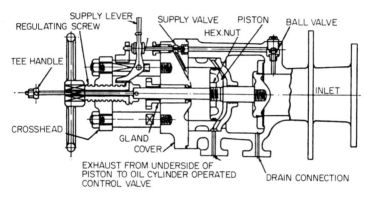

Figure 3.47 Valve opening against boiler steam (Cockburns Ltd.)
On moving back the regulating screw the collar on this screw has an inclined plane action on the supply valve lever, thus opening the supply valve which in turn admits steam to the piston. The accumulated steam applied to the top of this piston then leaks past the piston-rings and the valve opens.

As steam leaks past the piston, it reaches the control valve, which is closed when there is sufficient lubricating-oil pressure. Steam pressure therefore builds up on this side of the piston until it balances the load on the other side. The bulkhead valve is now free to open.

Should the oil pressure drop, the control valve opens and allows steam on the underside of the piston to escape to atmosphere. The steam load on the back of the piston now closes the valve sharply. Steam is, therefore, normally on both sides of the piston when the turbine is running, and if the underside steam is released to atmosphere, the valve shuts.

Condenser pressure control

The arrangement is most suitable for adapting to a condenser *high pressure* control and a *deck* control. The condenser control consists of a diaphragm in a casing, the top of which is connected by a pipe to the condenser (Figure 3.48). By suitable linkage, the absence of pressure on the top of the diaphragm keeps the valve closed. Increased condenser pressure acting on top of the diaphragm causes the valve to open and release the steam pressure on the underside of the bulkhead-valve piston as before. As shown in Figure 3.48, the turbines may be stopped from deck by simply opening a cock.

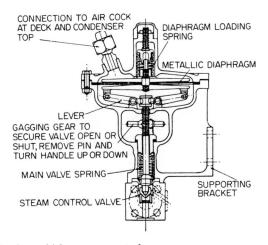

Figure 3.48 Condenser high pressure control.
    If the condenser pressure rises, the pressure of air, assisted by the disc-loading spring, deflects the metallic disc, and moves the lever, thus opening the steam-control valve. Steam is then allowed to exhaust from the underside of the emergency valve piston, causing the main valve to close down. This unit can be set to operate at a pre-determined pressure by adjusting the disc-loading spring.

By so doing, air pressure is allowed on top of the diaphragm, opening the valve and closing the bulkhead valve. Atmospheric pressure is quickly established in the condenser, and thus helps to bring the turbines to rest quicker.

On the lubricating-oil side of the control system, there is a valve at the level of the manoeuvring platform. By pulling a lever this valve opens and releases the oil pressure, so closing the bulkhead stop valve. It is useful to the engineer on watch as a means of stopping the main turbines quickly (Figure 3.49).

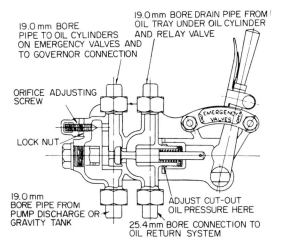

19.0 mm BORE
PIPE TO OIL CYLINDERS
ON EMERGENCY VALVES AND
TO GOVERNOR CONNECTION

19.0mm BORE DRAIN PIPE FROM
OIL TRAY UNDER OIL CYLINDER
AND RELAY VALVE

ORIFICE ADJUSTING
SCREW

LOCK NUT

19.0 mm
BORE PIPE FROM
PUMP DISCHARGE OR
GRAVITY TANK

ADJUST CUT-OUT
OIL PRESSURE HERE

25.4 mm BORE CONNECTION TO
OIL RETURN SYSTEM

Figure 3.49 Hand emergency control.
This control is fitted for the purpose of operating the emergency valve from the starting platform and from the deck, by means of the deck gear. An adjusting device is fitted so that a desired pressure, emergency control may be effected at any bearing, or at any point in the forced-lubrication control system. An adjustable orifice is provided on the discharge side of the hand control to limit the flow of oil to the governors and oil cylinder and to effect a quicker emergency control.

Excessive speed

When the revolutions of the turbine exceed the normal maximum, due to racing or in the extreme case of a broken propeller shaft or loss of a propeller, there is danger of complete breakdown. To avoid this, a centrifugal governor is fitted and arranged to close the bulkhead stop valve. The governor is normally fitted to the end of the H.P. turbine spindle.

In one type of Aspinall governor, two cylinders are arranged, bore in line, one on either side of the centre line. The end faces are ground so that the two form a valve and are pressed together by external springs. The outside surface of the cylinders is in communication with the lubricating-oil supply, while the inside is open to the oil return to the sump at atmospheric pressure.

When the speed becomes excessive, the cylinders separate due to centrifugal force and allow the oil to drain away, reducing the pressure in the lubricating-oil pipe under the oil-operating valve. This has the effect of closing the bulkhead stop valve as described before.

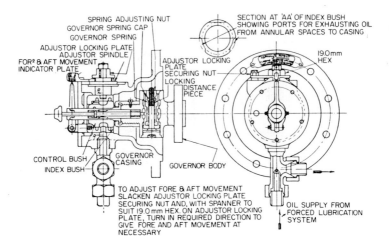

Figure 3.50 Emergency trip governor with fore-and-aft movement indicator and control
    The revolving head of this fitting is attached to the turbine rotor, the governor valve being of one piece and held in position by a spring. The valve is slightly unbalanced, and when the head is revolving, centrifugal force is set up which is counter-balanced by the spring. As the speed of the turbine approaches the predetermined revolutions, the centrifugal force tends to overcome the spring load, thereby adding further compression to the spring; on reaching full permitted revolutions, the valve flies out, the catch spindle contacts the landing, thus holding the valve in the set position. As the oil now has a discharge area of approximately ten times the area of the supply, the forced-lubrication pressure is dropped and the main valve then closes down.
    To reset the governor the catch spindle is pulled out, thus allowing the spring to return the valve to place. In order to alter the cutting speed it is only necessary to adjust the spring adjusting nut either up or down to raise or lower the speed.
    In addition, this governor also closes down the emergency system when any excessive end movement of the turbine rotor takes place

The illustrations give details of the safety arrangements. Note that the governor shown in Figures 3.50 and 3.51 and described is of the unbalanced-piston type. A diagram of the steam and governor connections is shown in Figure 3.52.

Cockburns 127 mm streamline parallel slide emergency isolating valve for ahead turbine

The action of the valve is as follows:

1. Normal opening and closing by direct hand-wheel operation.

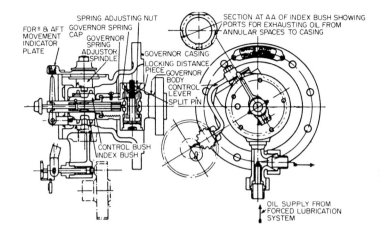

SPRING ADJUSTING NUT
FORE & AFT   GOVERNOR SPRING
MOVEMENT   CAP   GOVERNOR
INDICATOR   SPRING
PLATE   ADJUSTOR
                SPINDLE
SECTION AT A.A OF INDEX BUSH SHOWING
PORTS FOR EXHAUSTING OIL FROM
ANNULAR SPACES TO CASING
GOVERNOR CASING
LOCKING DISTANCE
PIECE GOVERNOR
BODY
CONTROL
LEVER
SPLIT PIN
CONTROL BUSH
INDEX BUSH
OIL SUPPLY FROM
FORCED LUBRICATION
SYSTEM

Figure 3.51 Emergency trip governor with fore-and-aft movement indicator and control, arranged for turbines with end-tightening gear
When the indicator is at the zero mark on the index, the control bush has a pre-determined overlap on each face relative to the index bush. If and when wear takes place on the turbine blocks, either in the fore and aft direction, the resultant movement is shown by the indicator lever, this movement being in the ratio of 4 to 1 with the actual movement. When the movement exceeds the overlap, the oil escapes, thus cutting out the system.
It should be noted that where end tightening is covered for in the governor, the effecting of the contacts does not alter the setting of the control bush, as the adjustment for both control and contact is synchronized.
If for any reason, the governor does not permit the index pointer to be brought into position by the adjusting screw, this adjustment may be carried out by the following simple procedure: the nut holding the control lever to the adjuster spindle should be slackened back and the lever lifted clear of the saw toothed serrations on this spindle. The spindle now clearing the control lever, the hand-wheel adjusting screw can now be rotated without imparting this movement to the other parts. When the adjusting screw nut has been moved sufficiently to give free screw in the required direction, the control lever should be replaced on the serrations and the nut hardened down. Any adjustment required to bring the pointer to the zero position can then be carried out

2. *Emergency Control.*—The main valve will shut automatically in the event of:

Overspeed
Axial movement of a main turbine rotor
Failure of lubricating oil pressure
Increase of condenser pressure
Operation of hand emergency control lever.

Details.—When the valve is open and closure is required, owing to one of the above causes, steam is admitted to the

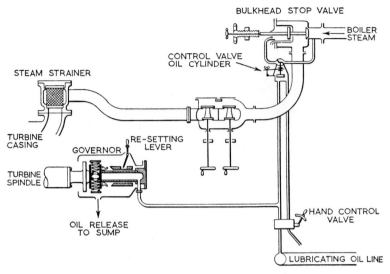

Figure 3.52 Diagram of turbine steam and governor connections

operating cylinder (supplied from the control valve on the oil operating cyclinder). Steam pressure then acting on the piston and its rod, attached to the emergency lever, pushes the lever over from *open* to *shut* position. An inclined plane on the emergency lever now comes in contact with the release-valve rod, thus opening the release valve and exhausting steam pressure from the underside of the main valve piston. The out-of-balance steam load now being on top of the piston and the catches on the screwed sleeve having been released from the catches on the emergency lever, the sleeve is free and, with the spindle, slides down a key in the dash-pot closing the valve.

In order to bring the gear back to normal position the hand-wheel is rotated in the direction to shut.

Details of the isolating valve are shown in Figures 3.53 and 3.54).

STEAM SUPPLY TO TURBINE

Steam is brought to the turbine through a steel pipe now generally of all-welded construction. Terminal flanges, where fitted, are also welded to the pipe. The pipe is bent to a large

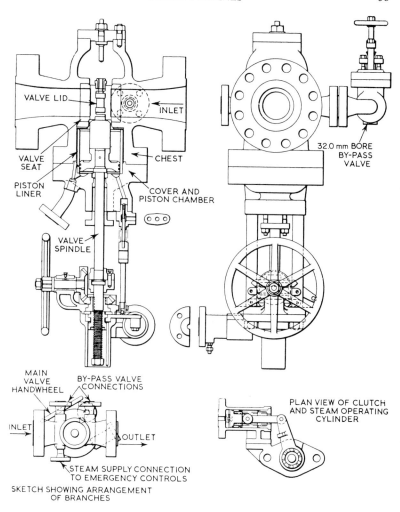

VALVE LID

INLET

VALVE SEAT

CHEST

PISTON LINER

COVER AND PISTON CHAMBER

VALVE SPINDLE

32.0 mm BORE BY-PASS VALVE

MAIN VALVE HANDWHEEL

BY-PASS VALVE CONNECTIONS

INLET

OUTLET

STEAM SUPPLY CONNECTION TO EMERGENCY CONTROLS

SKETCH SHOWING ARRANGEMENT OF BRANCHES

PLAN VIEW OF CLUTCH AND STEAM OPERATING CYLINDER

Figure 3.53 Details of the Cockburn parallel-slide, ahead turbine emergency and isolating valve

radius so that it can expand and contract without exerting force on the turbine which would distort the casing.

Interposed between the bulkhead stop valve and the manoeuvring valves is a steam-strainer (Figure 3.55), the purpose of which is to catch scale which might be carried over from the superheater elements of the boiler, and any loose object, such as a nut, which would damage the turbine. One form of

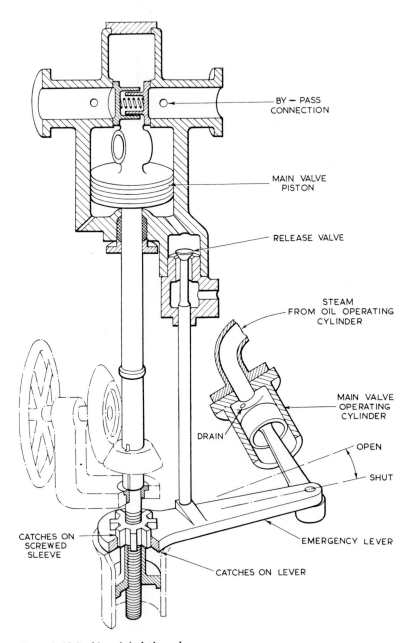

BY — PASS
CONNECTION

MAIN VALVE
PISTON

RELEASE VALVE

STEAM
FROM OIL OPERATING
CYLINDER

MAIN VALVE
OPERATING
CYLINDER

DRAIN

OPEN

SHUT

CATCHES ON
SCREWED
SLEEVE

EMERGENCY LEVER

CATCHES ON LEVER

Figure 3.54 Cockburn's isolating valve

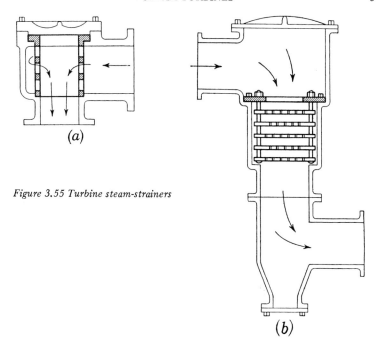

Figure 3.55 Turbine steam-strainers

steam-strainer consists of a cylindrical, cast-steel frame on which is secured a steel plate perforated with 5.0 mm holes (Figure 3.55a). Another arrangement consists of a number of flat steel, perforated plates secured together by bolts with distance pieces between the plates (Figure 3.55b).

In case of complete breakdown of either H.P. or L.P. turbine it is usual to provide steam- and exhaust-pipe connections to allow either H.P. or L.P. to run as a single-cylinder turbine, enabling the ship to proceed at reduced speed. Figure 3.56 shows the arrangement of emergency steam and exhaust.

Figure 3.57 shows a useful diagrammatic arrangement of a geared-turbine installation, illustrating most of the foregoing points.

EXAMPLES OF MODERN MARINE STEAM TURBINES

Figure 3.58 shows a cut-away view of a single cylinder turbine together with its condenser and reduction gear, and Figure 3.59 shows a sectional arrangement of the turbine. The tur-

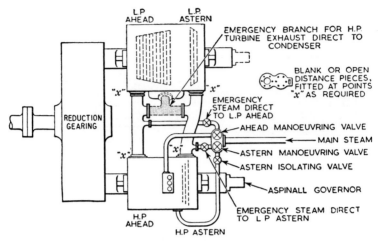

Figure 3.56 Emergency connections for complete breakdown of either H.P. or L.P. turbine

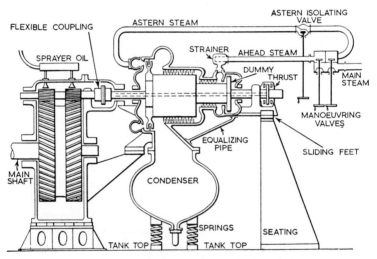

Figure 3.57 Diagrammatic arrangement of gear turbine installation

bine develops 13 000 kW at 86.7 rev/s with steam conditions 59.7 bar, 504.0°C and condenser pressure 0.05 bar. The propeller speed is 2.0 rev/s. This installation was designed and manufactured by the Industrial and Marine Steam Turbine Division of Messrs G.E.C. Turbine Generators Ltd, Manchester, by whose courtesy it is illustrated and described below.

The ahead turbine has fourteen single-row pressure stages and the astern turbine has one two-row Curtis stage followed by one single-row pressure stage. At the H.P. ahead end, the

Figure 3.58 Part cut-away view of 13 000 kW single-cylinder geared turbine and condenser

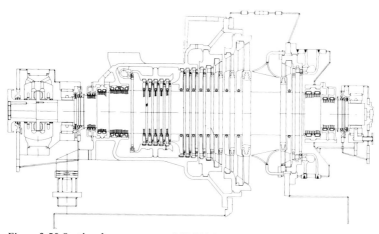

Figure 3.59 Sectional arrangement of 13 000 kW single-cylinder turbine

blading is of the impulse type with a moderate degree of reaction, the reaction gradually increasing towards the exhaust end, so that in the latter stages, the blading is in the reaction class. The blades subjected to the highest temperatures are of

molybdenum vanadium rustless steel and the remainder are
of stainless steel. With the exception of the last or last two
stages, all blades are shrouded to minimise leakage losses. The
last stage blades are fitted with stellite shields to minimise
erosion by the wet steam. The shields are attached to the
blades by brazing, or more recently, by electron beam weld-
ing. All blades are carefully designed to avoid any serious
vibration, and the long blades of the last stage are laced with
wire to provide safe vibration characteristics.

Both the ahead and astern first stage nozzles are of molybdenum vanadium steel, and are welded into annular segments
which are fitted into nozzle boxes of similar material. The
separately cast nozzle boxes are welded into the ahead and
astern cylinders before heat treatment.

The diaphragms, other than those at the exhaust end, are
of welded construction. Those for the higher temperatures
are made entirely of molybdenum vanadium steel, while the
others have low-carbon stainless steel nozzle division plates
and spacer bands with mild steel rims and centres. The
diaphragms towards the exhaust end are of cast construction
with low-carbon rustless steel nozzle division plates. Location
of the diaphragms and diaphragm carriers ensures alignment
co-axially with the cylinder, while providing ample radial
clearance for thermal expansion under all operating conditions.

The turbine rotor is a one-piece steel forging, the discs
being integral with the shaft. The turbine coupling and thrust
block are at the H.P. end which is located aft. Thermal expansion of the rotor is therefore in the forward direction,
which relieves the flexible coupling of any major expansion
effects. The major critical speed is well below the maximum
running speed, but above 50.0 per cent maximum speed. This
gives a well-proportioned rotor, having smooth running
characteristics and low gland losses.

Spring-backed shaft and diaphragm glands are used
throughout, as illustrated in Figure 3.60. The segmental gland
fins at the H.P. end are of 13.0 per cent chromium stainless
iron, but where the maximum working temperature does not
exceed 425.0°C they are machined from nickel leaded bronze.
This segmental design and material are now virtually standard
practice for marine turbines—they have been well-proven by
long experience. The gland segments are supported by light
leaf springs which maintain concentricity, but should contact
occur, they deflect and prevent damage to the shaft. On

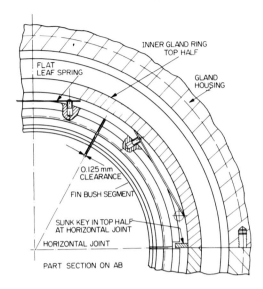

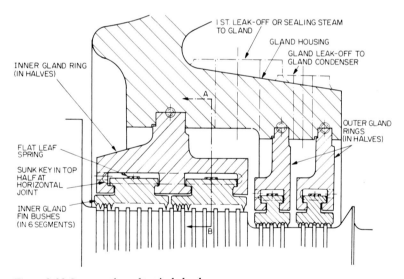

Figure 3.60 Construction of typical gland

starting up, all glands require to be steam-sealed, but with increasing load, the H.P. glands cease to require sealing, and will in fact leak steam back to the gland steam receiver, from which it is used to seal the astern cylinder gland.

The high pressure part of the turbine casing is of cast steel, and the exhaust chamber and astern casing are fabricated from boiler quality steel plate. The high pressure cylinder is designed to ensure ease and quality of casting, and to avoid any danger of thermal distortion in service, the diameter of the horizontal joint bolts is kept to a minimum, and the use of heavy flanges avoided, since these cause high thermal stresses and distortion during heating and cooling.

The supporting arrangements are designed to maintain internal alignment and so to ensure smooth running of the machinery unaffected by the hull movements which take place in service. Basically, the structure of the turbine—for an underslung condenser—is as shown in Figure 3.61. The ahead and astern cylinders are supported at their exhaust ends by the vertical joints, and at their steam ends at the horizontal joint by supports which are built on to the exhaust casing "legs". The two longitudinal beams, to which the ahead and astern vertical joints are rigidly secured form the main strength members, and as they are entirely surrounded by exhaust steam, they are not subjected to temperature variation, and therefore remain straight. The aft supporting feet of the beams are fixed in the fore-and-aft direction. Lateral alignment is maintained by keys on the vertical centre line at the forward end. This latter feature is illustrated very clearly in Figure 3.58.

Provision is made on the turbine casing for up to four bleeding points from which steam may be extracted for feed heating. Steam deflector hoods are fitted between the last ahead and last astern stages to minimise the windage loss of the idle running stages.

The turbine thrust bearing is of the Michell tilting-pad type, mounted in a spherical housing. The thrust collar is a separate shrunk-on item with hardened and ground faces. The collar to shaft shrink fit is designed to give a minimum interference of 0.025 mm at maximum speed to prevent any risk of fretting corrosion between the collar and shaft. Oil is introduced to the centre of the bearing, and flows outwards over the pads. The oil outlet is at the top of the bearing to ensure that the pads are always submerged in oil. The journal bearings have steel shells with white metal linings, and are mounted in adjustable housings, so that alignment can if necessary be adjusted in service.

The condenser is underslung and is placed axially i.e. with the tubes parallel to the turbine rotor. It has two water flows and the shell is integral with the exhaust casing of the turbine. The condenser is carried on spring feet which support its mass and control the vertical forces due to thermal expansion.

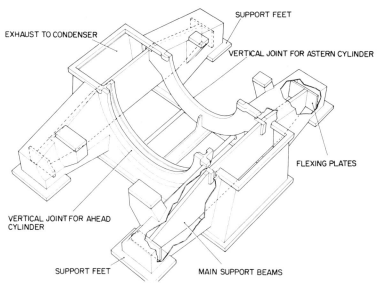

Figure 3.61 Supporting structure for single-cylinder turbines and for the L.P. turbine of cross-compound turbines

Figure 3.62 Two-cylinder cross-compound geared turbines with transverse under-slung condenser

The double-reduction gear is of the dual-tandem locked-train type generally as described in Chapter 4, except of course that there is only one primary pinion and only two intermediate shafts.

Figure 3.62 shows a partly cut-away view of a two-cylinder cross-compound turbine installation arranged with transverse underslung condenser, and Figure 3.63 the same type of turbines arranged with an "in-plane" condenser, i.e. condenser located at the same level as, but forward of, the turbines.

These turbines, designed and manufactured by the Industrial and Marine Steam Turbine Division of G.E.C. Turbine Generators Ltd, Manchester, are in the power range 28 000 to 35 000 kW with steam conditions 62.0 bar, 513.0°C and condenser pressure 0.1–0.05 bar. The range of double-reduction gears available enables a variation in propeller speed from 1.333 to 2.333 rev/s to be accommodated.

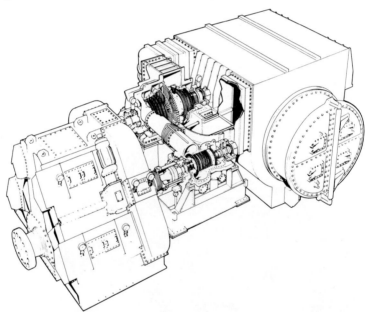

Figure 3.63 Two-cylinder cross-compound geared turbines with 'In-plane' condenser

Typical sectional arrangements of the H.P. and L.P. turbines are shown in Figures 3.64 and 3.65 respectively. The features of these turbines are generally similar to those already described for the single-cylinder turbine, with the additional points mentioned below which are relevant mainly to the different arrangements, and to developing technique.

The H.P. turbine has eight, and the L.P. ahead turbine seven single-row pressure stages. Compared with the single-cylinder turbine therefore, not only is there an extra stage, but the H.P. and L.P. turbines run at different speeds, which gives more flexibility in choosing values of u/C_0 commensurate with higher efficiency (see Chapter 10). The cross-compound arrangement is therefore more efficient than the single-cylinder arrangement.

Following on the concept of higher efficiency, the detail design of the stages includes some interesting features.

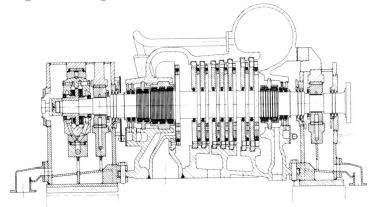

Figure 3.64 Sectional arrangement of H.P. turbine

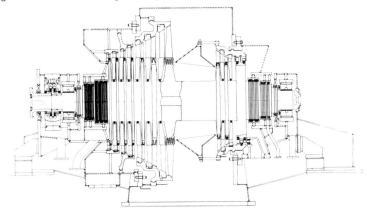

Figure 3.65 Sectional arrangement of L.P. turbine

Figure 3.66 Bull-nosed blades

Increased use has been made of "tear drop" or "bull-nosed" blades as illustrated in Figure 3.66. This blade section, because of its form at entry, is capable of accepting a wide range of steam angles (θ_1 in the velocity diagrams) without serious increase of the blade loss. This, of course, is ideal for marine turbines which have to operate at varying speeds. Also, the generous cross-sectional area renders the blade more robust, less prone to vibration, and makes possible the use of circular section blade tangs for fastening the shrouding. The shrouding material can then be jig-drilled, which is not only more economic than the punching which would otherwise be required, but with correct radiusing, it eliminates any risk of

Figure 3.67(a) Shrouding being fitted to astern element of a low pressure monobloc rotor (G.E.C.)

residual stresses, work-hardening, or micro-cracking in the shroud ring. Figure 3.67(a) shows an L.P. rotor of this type, and clearly illustrates the shrouding ring being fitted. All stages except the last, or last two in the L.P. turbine are shrouded to minimise leakage losses and so to contain the reaction. Figure 3.67(b) shows the blades and labyrinth gland rings.

In Chapter 10, we show how the application of some reaction to an impulse-type stage could materially increase the diagram efficiency, provided that the degree of reaction does not cause a large increase in thrust loss, and provided that the

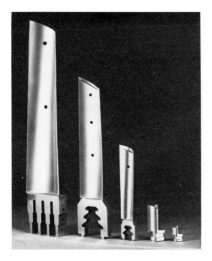

Figure 3.67(b) L.P. rotor block and labyrinth gland rings showing fin form and backing spring (G.E.C.)

reaction pressure drops can be contained within the nozzles and moving blades, i.e. any severe tip or root leakage can completely nullify any theoretical gain in efficiency.

In the first four ahead stages of the L.P. turbine, where the blade heights are still relatively small but the degree of reaction is significantly increasing, radial tip seals have been introduced in addition to the "end-tightened" shroud ring, as shown in Figure 3.68. The axial clearance between the sharp

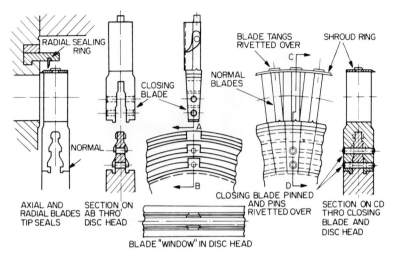

Figure 3.68 Axial and radial blade tip seals

edge of the shroud ring and the face of the diaphragm is made
sufficiently large as not to impose any operation limitations
(on rapid power changes or ahead and astern running), and
the radial clearance of the secondary seal is set to a practical
minimum making due allowance for centrifugal blade stretch.
The radial sealing strips are of annealed and softened chrome
iron, and are caulked into carriers that are virtually integral

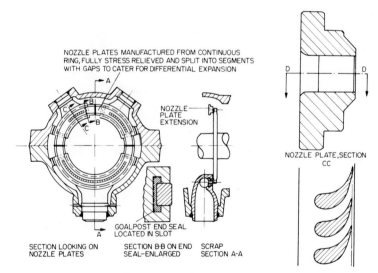

Figure 3.69 H.P. turbine first stage nozzle plate arrangement

with the diaphragm, thus minimising any differential expansion effects. It is likely that the use of radial tip seals will, in the future, be extended to H.P. turbine stages also.

The first stage nozzle box of the H.P. ahead turbine is illustrated in Figure 3.69. It is designed to limit parasitic leakage losses although three separate nozzle box castings are used to give flexibility and economy in operational power requirements, i.e. three nozzle groups. Although the three segments of nozzles facing the blades are fairly well isolated from one another, the T-section nozzle plate gives virtually 360° cover of the moving blades on the disc. The nozzle plate is made from one continuous ring which is split into three segments. The segments are entered circumferentially into the T-slots in the nozzle box castings, leaving circumferential gaps between the segments to accommodate differential expansion. Parasitic leakage in the circumferential direction between the T-section nozzle plate and the T-slot in the nozzle box casting is greatly reduced by copper end seals let into radial recesses in the T-slot, while the practically continuous nozzle plate minimises tip leakage over the blades—two of the major sources of loss in a stage having partial admission. The convergent–divergent astern nozzles are shown in Figure 3.70.

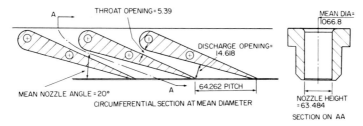

Figure 3.70 Convergent–divergent nozzles for astern Curtis stage

The last row of ahead blading is a most important factor in any turbine design. Indeed it has been said that in all turbine designs, the selection of proper staging begins at the exhaust end! When dealing with steam turbine theory in Chapter 10, we show how the large specific volume of the steam requires a large area through the nozzle and blade passages. A large area can be obtained only by a learge mean diameter and a large blade height, which means increased centrifugal stress, or by increasing the nozzle angle, which means reduced efficiency. Equally important is the need for absolute certainty that the vibration characteristics of the long last blades will not produce any destructive resonances, and that any vibration-excited stresses are sufficiently low as to prevent excessive fatigue damage to the blade material. Marine turbines have to be capable of running at various speeds, and hence with various steam forces on the blades and this renders the vibration aspect even more complicated. The blade root fixing too has a profound influence on the integrity of the last blades, and indeed of all blades.

The last L.P. stage of these turbines has a mean diameter of 1613 mm and a blade height of 470.0 mm, and when running at the maximum speed of 58.33 rev/s, the centrifugal load on each blade root is of the order of 270.0 kN. Not only must the blade root be capable of sustaining this load, but its behaviour under load must be such that the design prediction of the blade vibration characteristics will be achieved with the blade in its actual running condition. The last blades have multi-fork pinned roots which have excellent all-round mechanical and vibration-damping characteristics. These blade roots are shown in Figure 3.67.

An even more recent root fixing is shown in Figure 3.71, which promises further improvement, particularly for long last blades. The root is a curved, serrated fixing, approximately following the blade form. It makes use of the optimum amount of blade and disc material, and can be produced quite readily on blades and on solid rotors by milling techniques.

In Chapter 10, mention is made of the need—particularly in the long blades of the last or last few stages—to ensure that there is no radial flow of steam due to centrifugal force, and that there is unifom mass flow of steam through the blade passage at all sections between the root and the tip. The design of these long blades is not therefore based on the mean diameter, but on a series of diameters between root and tip, taking into account the velocity diagrams, the centrifugal force and the passage area. This results in the "twisted and tapered" type of blades which are clearly seen in the last stages in the illustrations. The design calculations are supported by extensive testing, using aerodynamic techniques.

It is the last stage blades which suffer most from erosion due to wet steam. The lower the exhaust pressure the greater is the amount of water in the steam (see Chapter 9), and the larger the mean diameter and blade height, the higher is the blade tip velocity as the water droplets strike the blades, and the more serious the erosion.

Figure 3.71 Curved serrated root for long L.P. turbines

It is of particular interest that in these turbines, centre line or near-centre line support is adopted. This feature on both the H.P. and the L.P. turbines is shown very clearly in Figure 3.63. This principle eliminates undesirable moments being imposed on the turbines, which could cause misalignment. Referring to Figure 3.63, the L.P. turbine exhausts to the condenser through twin trunks arranged to give complete access to the L.P. forward bearing, and allowing the bearing pedestal to be centre line supported in recesses machined into palm supports built out from the ahead and astern cylinders. The ship's seatings extend right up to the turbine cylinder palms, giving maximum support rigidity and freedom from moments and vibration.

Manholes are provided on the top wall of each trunk which allow practically "walk in" access to the L.P. cylinder exhaust and condenser, thus enabling thorough internal inspection to be made without lifting the top half of the L.P. cylinder or opening up the condenser shell access points.

The twin trunk entries to the condenser are adequately designed to withstand the very considerable forces imposed due to the sub-atmospheric condenser pressure, and to give efficient steam coverage of the condenser tube surface while sweeping the air and non-condensible gases towards the air pump suction take-off. Each trunk is constructed in one piece, and their strength enables the fore-and-aft anchor point of the L.P. turbine and condenser assembly to be located at the ship's seating, shared by the aft end of the condenser and the forward end of the L.P. forward bearing pedestal. In this way, the thermal expansion of the condenser and L.P. turbine are not additive, thus avoiding the problems associated with excessive axial movement at the flexible coupling.

Both the H.P. and L.P. turbines are self-contained and can be transported and installed as units. The H.P. turbine exhaust pipe is balanced by a tied bellows piece arrangement so that thrust loads from the cross-over exhaust pipe are entirely eliminated. Appropriate bleed belts are provided in both turbine cylinders, the L.P. cylinder being so arranged that bleed points can be selected from one or more than one of all the ahead stages after the first.

The turbine control valve assembly is illustrated in Figure 3.72. It consists of an integral steam chest and strainer mounted on substantial palm supports in such a manner as to resist forces and moments imposed by the steam piping. The steam inlet can be at either end of the strainer chamber (the latter is at the back of the chest in the illustration), the other end being access to the strainer. Steam flows outwards from the centre, through the strainer and into a common chest containing both the ahead and astern manoeuvring valves. The steam outlet from the ahead manoeuvring valve passes to the H.P. ahead turbine through three nozzle control points, two of which have individual hand-operated shut-off valves. With these three separate nozzle groups it is possible to select and to operate at any one of four discrete powers without throttling, or at any power from zero up to the maximum of the selected group or groups with minimum throttling. The maximum available powers are, typically as follows:

Figure 3.72 Control valve assembly

Group 1	20 136.5 kW
Groups 1+2	26 848.6 kW
Groups 1+3	29 831.8 kW
Groups 1+2+3	32 810.8 kW

The principles of this combined throttling and nozzle control are explained in Chapter 10.

Steam from the astern manoeuvring valve passes through an astern guardian valve before passing to the astern turbine.

The astern guardian valve has an automatic open/shut operation, opening being initiated by the first opening movement
of the astern manoeuvring valve gear, and completed before
steam is passing through the astern manoeuvring valve.

   The ahead manoeuvring valve is of the single-seated Venturi-
profile type with a pilot valve to reduce the out-of-balance
steam force on the valve at initial opening. The valve steam
path is designed to give a linear lift/flow characteristic. The
valve is opened hydraulically by oil at a pressure of 12.0 bar
supplied by an electric motor-driven positive displacement
pump; a standby pump is also provided. A trip piston provides
rapid closure of the valve when the trip cylinder is drained of
oil by the action of overspeed trip, high condenser pressure

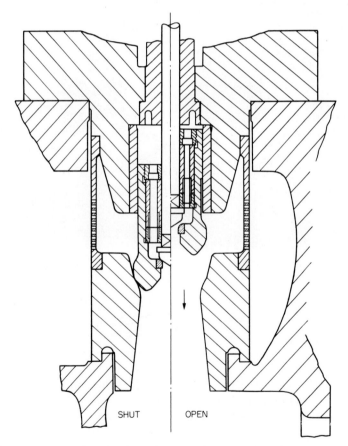

SHUT   OPEN

Figure 3.73 Typical section through obturated manoeuvring valve

trip, low lubricating oil pressure trip, etc. A speed-sensitive pilot valve operated by sensitive oil pressure partially closes the valve if the turbine speed rises above any desired value. This control can be preset to operate at any speed between about 75.0 to 100.0 per cent. The manoeuvring valve control gear has a cam-operated feedback to give an approximate linear relationship between the movement of the controller and the propeller speed.

The astern manoeuvring valve is similar to the ahead valve, but without the speed-sensitive element and without the trip valve mechanism.

The astern guardian valve also is a single-seated Venturi valve, but without linear lift/flow characteristic. Opening is

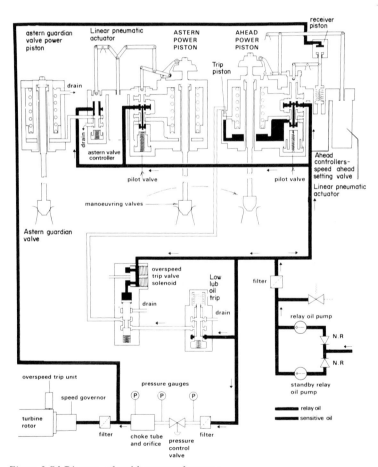

Figure 3.74 Diagram of turbine control system

initiated from the astern manoeuvring valve, and as the
guardian valve has no feedback, it opens fully once initiated.
Figure 3.73 shows a typical section through the manoeuvring
valve. The valves are operated by a pneumatic or electric
positional control from a remote control system, alternatively
by a local handwheel directly connected to the hydraulic
pilot valve sleeve. A normally-locked hand gear is also provided, acting directly on the valve spindles, for emergency use
in the event of loss of electricity supply or failure of both
pumps. Referring to the control system in Figure 3.74, the
operation is as follows:

Ahead valve gear

With the manoeuvring valves closed, relay oil pressure available, and all the protective devices in the safe to run condition, the trip piston is seated and the governor applies full
sensitive oil pressure to the receiver piston so that the pilot
valve is raised to its full lift position. In this condition the
manoeuvring valve remains closed until a control air signal is
applied to the linear pneumatic actuator. When the signal to
the ahead valve setting actuator increases above 1.22 bar the
actuator moves downwards and by means of levers pivoting
about an instantaneous fulcrum depresses the pilot valve
sleeve, admitting relay oil to the underside of the spring
loaded power piston. As the pressure under the power piston
builds up the piston lifts and raises the valve. As the valve
lifts a cam at the top of the spindle causes the linkage to lift
the sleeve to cancel the input signal and hold the valve at its
new lifted position. Further increase in the control air pressure increases the valve lift and as the valve lift increases the
feedback movement reduces so that the amount of valve lift
for a given change in control signal increases.

Should the low bearing oil pressure trip or the solenoid trip
valve (which is operated by overspeed, high condenser pressure
etc.) operate, then the oil to the trip piston is put to drain and
the pressure of the relay oil under the main power piston lifts
the trip piston and dumps the oil from under the main piston
to the top of the piston, allowing rapid valve closure.

When the turbine speed approaches the desired control
band the sensitive oil pressure starts to fall progressively with
speed increase until the spring load on the sensitive oil piston
overcomes the oil pressure on the piston. The piston then
moves upward to achieve a new balanced position as the

spring load is reduced, and this movement through a linkage depresses the pilot valve and so allows oil to drain from under the main power piston. The power piston moves down, reducing the valve opening, and the cam gear causes the pilot valve sleeve to move down until a new balanced position of the pilot valve and sleeve is attained.

The spring load on the sensitive oil piston, and hence the speed at which the turbine is controlled can be adjusted by operation of the speed setting linear actuator operated by a 1.22 to 2.05 bar air signal.

Astern valve gear

A single pneumatic linear actuator controls the opening of the astern manoeuvring and guardian valves. The ratio of lever movements and the overlap of the pilot valves is so arranged that initial movement of the pneumatic actuator allows oil to flow to the astern guardian valve, and since this valve has no feedback the valve opens to full lift. Further increase in the control air signal will cause the pilot valve to be depressed, admitting oil to the astern manoeuvring valve power piston. As the astern valve lifts, the cam gear at the top of the valve is arranged to lift the pilot valve to cancel the input signal. As with the ahead gear, the valve lift obtained for a given change in control signal increases as the valve lift increases, thereby giving accurate control at low powers.

Arrangement of turbines

Figures 3.75 and 3.76 shows several ways in which these types of turbines may be arranged.

The single-cylinder arrangement has the advantages of being smaller and less massive, lower initial cost, fewer rotating parts in both the turbine and the gearing suggesting increased reliability and reduced maintenance. Reduced width may be attractive for twin-screw or stern jobs. A possible disadvantage, at least in single-screw ships, is the need for emergency "get home" power in the unlikely event of major breakdown of the main turbine. This could be a small emergency turbine driving through the aft end of the primary pinion. The two-cylinder cross-compound arrangement however is more efficient, and with fuel economics as they are now, there can be no doubt that the efficiency of the turbine will have a much greater influence on the overall economics than in the past. Indeed this aspect may even in some cases

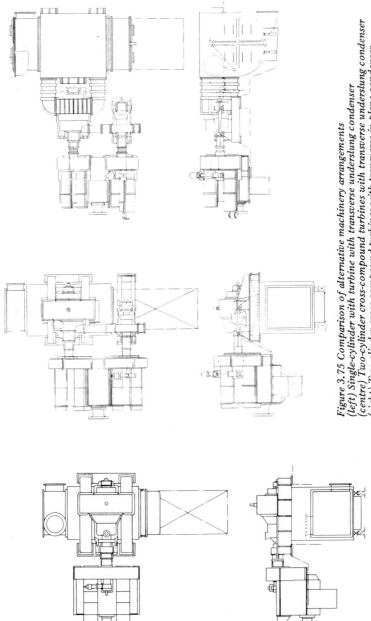

*Figure 3.75 Comparison of alternative machinery arrangements
(left) Single-cylinder with turbine with transverse underslung condenser
(centre) Two-cylinder cross-compound turbines with transverse underslung condenser
(right) Two-clinder cross-compound turbines with transverse in-plane condenser*

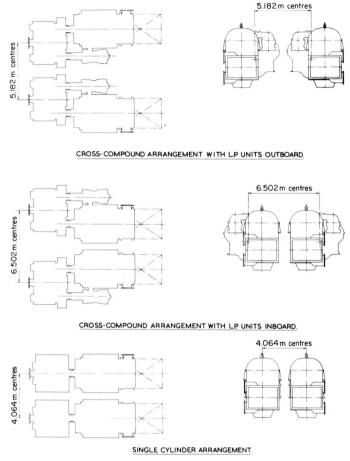

CROSS-COMPOUND ARRANGEMENT WITH LP UNITS OUTBOARD.

CROSS-COMPOUND ARRANGEMENT WITH LP UNITS INBOARD.

SINGLE CYLINDER ARRANGEMENT.

Figure 3.76 Comparison between cross-compound and single-cylinder turbine arrangements for twin-screw machinery of 14 920 kW/shaft at 2.0 rev/s

justify a three-cylinder cross-compound arrangement with or without reheat, and having either separate H.P., I.P. and L.P. turbines, or a combined H.P./I.P. turbine and an L.P. turbine.

Whether an axial or transverse underslung condenser, or an in-plane condenser is used depends on the ship's lines, the location of the engine room in the ship, and whether length, width or height is the more critical.

Tables 3.1 and 3.2 show the composition and physical properties of the major components of the H.P. and L.P. turbines.

Table 3.1 H.P. Turbine materials

Components				Chemical properties											Physical properties			
	C	Si	Mn	P	S	Cr	Ni	Mo	Va	Cu	Tensile kg/mm²	0.2% proof kg/mm²	Elongation %	Gauge	Red of area %	Izod impact test Nm	Hardness Brinell
Turbine casing	0.15 max.	0.45 max.	0.40 0.80	0.05 max.	0.05 max.	0.25 0.50	0.30 max.	0.5 0.7	0.22	0.20 max. 0.30	52 min.	31.5 min.	14 min.	L=5D	—	—	—
Nozzles and guide vanes stages 2–4: H.P.	0.08 0.13	0.30 max.	0.60 0.80	0.030 max.	0.030 max.	0.25 0.50	0.30 max.	0.50 0.70	0.22	0.20 max. 0.30	47 min.	31.5 min.	Transverse =15 min. Longitudinal 20 min.	L=5D	—	—	131 min.
Guide vanes stages 5–8	0.08 max.	0.50 max.	0.50 1.00	0.03 max.	0.03 max.	12.0 14.0	0.5 max.				44 min. 55 max.	—	20 min.	L=5D	—	—	123 163
Nozzles plates diaphragms 2–4	0.10 0.15	0.30 max.	0.40 0.60	0.040 max.	0.040 max.	0.25 0.50	0.30 max.	0.5 0.7	0.22	0.20 max. 0.30	47 min.	31.5 min.	15 trans 20 long min.	L=5D	—	—	131 min.

Diaphragms 5–8	0.20 max.	0.30 max.	1.50 max.	0.045 max.	0.050 max.	0.40 max.	0.40 max.	0.40 max.		39 / 47	20.5 (yield)	22 min.	L=5D		
Rotor	0.24 / 0.29	0.030 max.	0.70 / 0.90	0.030 max.	0.030 max.	0.9 / 1.2	0.65 / 0.85	0.65 / 0.85	0.30 Long / 0.35 Tang / Rad	71 / 71 / 71	55 / 55 / 55	16 / 14 / 14	L=5D		
Blades stage 1	0.07 / 0.15	0.60 max.	0.30 / 1.00	0.035 max.	0.035 max.	11.5 / 13.0	1.0 max.	0.4 / 0.8	0.10 Long / 0.25 Tang / Rad	79 min. / 94 max.	63 min. / 79 max.	15 / 15 / 15	L=5D	48 min.	227 / 270
Blades stages 2–8	0.18 / 0.25	0.50 max.	1.00 max.	0.045 max.	0.045 max.	12.0 / 14.0	0.50 max.	0.15 max.		71 min. / 86 max.	55 min.	18 min.	L=5D	34.2 min.	207 / 255
Labyrinth rings (highest temp. only)	0.08 max.	1.0 max.	1.0 max.	0.05 max.	0.05 max.	11.5 / 13.5	0.5 max.	0.15 max.	0.40 max.					20.5 min.	217 max.
Labyrinth rings	Sn = 1.5 – 2.0 / Pb = 4.5 – 5.0		Zn = 17.5 – 20.0			12.0 / 12.5			62.0 / 63.0	14.2 min.	10.0 min.	4			

Table 3.2 L.P. and astern turbine materials

Components	Chemical properties										Physical properties						
	C	Si	Mn	P	S	Cr	Ni	Mo	Va	Cu	Tensile kg/mm²	0.2% proof kg/mm²	Elongation %	Gauge	Red of area %	Izod impact test Nm	Hardness Brinell
L.P. turbine casing and astern turbine casing	0.22 max.	0.10 max.	0.65 1.20	0.050 max.	0.050 max.	0.25 max.	0.30 max.	0.10 max.		0.20 max.	41 50	23.3 min. (yield)	24 min.	L=200			
L.P. turbine diaphragms stages 1–4	0.20 max.	0.30 max.	1.5 max.	0.045 max.	0.050 max.	0.40 max.	0.4 max.	0.4 max.			39 47	20.5 min. (yield)	22 min.	L=5D			
Diaphragms stages 5–7 and last astern	3.40 3.60	1.70 2.00	0.50 0.70	0.10 0.12	0.30 0.50							22					
Nozzles and guide vanes	0.08 max.	0.50 1.00	0.50 max.	0.03 max.	0.03	12.0 14.0	0.5 max.				44 min. 55 max.	–	20 min.	L=5D			123 163
Rotor	0.25 0.35	0.30 max. 0.80	0.50 0.80	0.025 max.	0.025 max.	1.0 1.8	2.25 3.00	0.50 0.70	0.05 0.15	Long Tang Rad	78 min. 91 max.	Core 60 min. 63 min.	14 12 10	L=5D			
Blades	0.18 0.25	0.50 max.	1.00 max.	0.045 max.	0.045 max.	12.0 14.0	0.50 max.				71 min. 86 max.	55 min.	18 min.	L=5D	34.2 min.		207 255
Last stage ahead blade	0.08 0.15	0.60 max.	0.40 1.00	0.030 max.	0.030 max.	11.0 13.0	2.0 3.0	1.0 2.0	0.05 0.40		94 min. 110 max.	79 min.	12 min.	L=5D	48		271 321
Labyrinth rings	Sn = 1.5 – 2.0 Zn = 17.5 – 20.0 Pb = 4.5 – 5.0					12.0 12.5				62.0 63.0	14.2 min.	10.0 min.	4				

Feed heating and auxiliaries

On the grounds that simplicity of operation and maintenance is contributory to overall efficiency, these turbines have
only two L.P. surface feed heaters and one high-level direct-
contact deaerating heater—there are no H.P. heaters. Auxiliary
heat recoveries in the feed heating system are limited to gland
condenser, evaporator-distiller, boiler air preheater and
domestic steam-steam generator. The separate turbo-generator
can exhaust either to the main condenser or to an intermediate stage of the main turbines, the latter mode of operation giving a very worthwhile gain in efficiency. A separate
auxiliary condenser, working at atmospheric pressure, is
provided for use when the main engines are not operating,
and in the case of tankers, the cargo oil pump turbines would
also exhaust to the auxiliary condenser. In the case of ships
not requiring auxiliary steam in port, e.g. container ships
with electrically-driven auxiliaries, diesel generators could be
provided as an alternative, for port working.

APPROACH TO AUTOMATIC CONTROL

Extensive instrumented testing of these types of turbine has
shown that they are quite capable of accepting the temperature variations associated with normal operation and normal
manoeuvring without distress or adverse effect on the smooth-
ness of operation. The tests have also shown that from the
vibration aspect, no undue sensitivity exists which would
place any limitation on normal operation.

When considering automatic control therefore, a turbine
supervisory scheme would be devised which will continuously
monitor certain critical readings, and in the event of one or
more of these becoming abnormal, will bring up a visual and
audible "first alarm" in time for appropriate corrective action
still to be effective. In the event that this corrective action is
not taken, then the control would bring up a second alarm
which also trips the combined control and emergency valve
and stops the machinery. Even if an alarm is accepted by a
responsible engineer, visual indication of the fault would
remain until it is located and cleared. This is particularly
important for unmanned engine rooms.

Any turbine supervisory system must have at least these major alarm and trip facilities:

1. Turbine overspeed
2. Low lubricating oil pressure
3. High condenser pressure
4. High condensate level

In addition, a cross-compound turbine unit should monitor the following, and incorporate them into the turbine trip system:

1. H.P. turbine rotor eccentricity or rotor vibration
2. L.P. turbine rotor eccentricity or rotor vibration
3. H.P. turbine thrust wear
4. L.P. turbine thrust wear
5. H.P. turbine differential expansion
6. L.P. turbine differential expansion
7. Main thrust wear

Figure 3.77 shows a typical monitoring system for the latter seven items.

Automatic turbine control is itself a large and complicated subject, involving a thorough knowledge of highly specialised equipment including electronic, electrical, pneumatic and hydraulic devices, any extensive treatment of which is beyond the scope of a book of the present nature.

It is hoped however that these brief notes will show the principles as they apply to the turbines themselves, and will at least identify the starting point and the ultimate object of each item of protection.

The subject of automatic centralised control is dealt with in considerably more detail in *Marine Auxiliary Machinery*, a companion volume in this series.

Three-cylinder reheat turbines

Figures 3.78 and 3.79 show the turbines for a 22 380 kW installation having initial steam conditions 70.0 bar, with one intermediate reheat to 538.0°C. These illustrations and relevant information are from a paper by Mr. T. B. Hutchison,

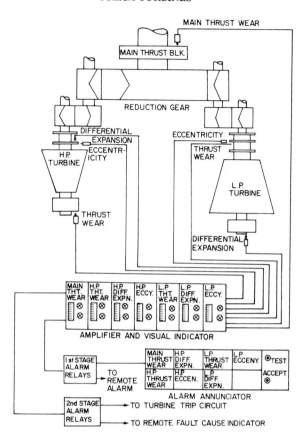

Figure 3.77 Typical monitoring system for turbine rotor protection. The diagram excludes the overspeed, high condenser pressure, relay oil, lubricating oil and other protective trips normally included in the complete turbine supervisory system

read to the Institute of Marine Engineers and reproduced herein by courtesy of the Institute.

The H.P. turbine (see Figure 3.78) has eight single-row impulse stages, running at 99.93 rev/s, and is of the double-casing design.

As this installation is designed for continuous full-power operation, nozzle control is not provided. The steam inlet and nozzle box are consequently of relatively simple and robust design, having approximately 120° of nozzle arc at the first stage in both the top and bottom halves. The remain-

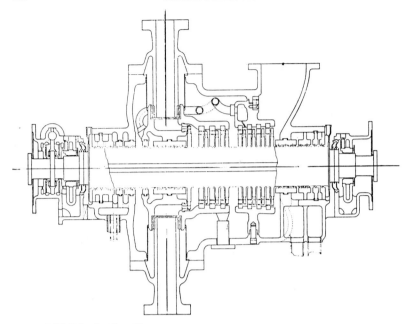

Figure 3.78 H.P. ahead turbine

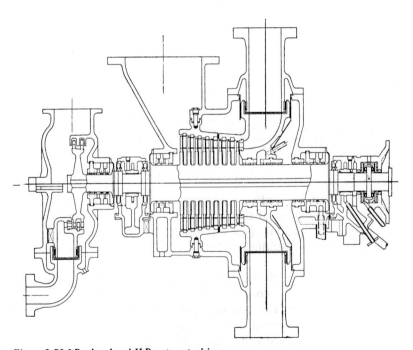

Figure 3.79 I.P. ahead and H.P. astern turbines

ing stages have full all-round admission. Note the inter-casing gland pocket leak-off to in front of the sixth stage, and the temperature shields round the steam inlet pipes between the outer and inner casings. These shields prevent loss of heat from the high-temperature steam in the inlet pipes to the lower-temperature steam in the outer casing.

The main feed pump is driven from the forward end of the H.P. turbine rotor.

The I.P. turbine (see Figure 3.79) has eight single-row impulse stages running at 83.93 rev/s. It is also of the double-casing design with full all-round admission to all stages. The H.P. astern turbine, consisting of one two-row Curtis stage housed in a separate casing, is overhung from the forward end of the I.P. turbine rotor. The combination of full admission, double casing and separate astern casing render the I.P. ahead turbine casing design simple, symmetrical and robust, which are important advantages, particularly as the I.P. ahead turbine receives reheated steam at $538.0°C$.

The L.P. turbine has six single-row impulse stages and four reaction stages and runs at 52.87 rev/s. The L.P. astern turbine, consisting of one two-row Curtis stages followed by one single-row impulse stage, is housed in the forward end of the L.P. turbine. The main electric generator is driven from the forward end of the L.P. turbine rotor through an epicyclic gear.

At full power of 22 380 kW the propeller speed is 1.334 rev/s and the power distribution between H.P., I.P. and L.P. turbines is 26.8, 29.8 and 43.4 per cent respectively. The astern turbines develop 12 090 kW.

The H.P. and I.P. turbines each drive through a single-tandem gear, and the L.P. turbine through a dual-tandem gear. The main wheel is located by the main thrust block and each primary train by integral thrusts. Each secondary pinion is driven by a quill shaft fitted with fine-tooth flexible couplings, to provide both torsional and axial articulation between the first and second reductions. This arrangement of turbines and gears facilitates full access to all parts (see Figure 3.80).

Figure 3.81(a), (b) and (c) shows the machinery arrangement for these turbines as applied to a large tanker. Note that the main and auxiliary boilers are arranged on a flat above the main turbines, but that the main boiler is located aft, and the auxiliary boiler to the port side, thus permitting full lifting access to the turbines.

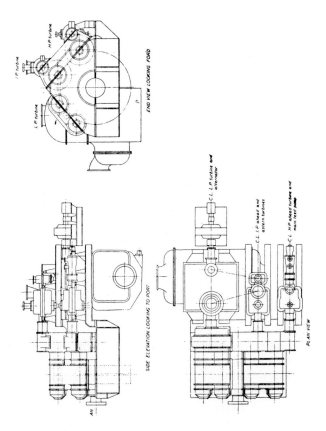

Figure 3.80 Outline arrangement of turbines, condenser and gearing

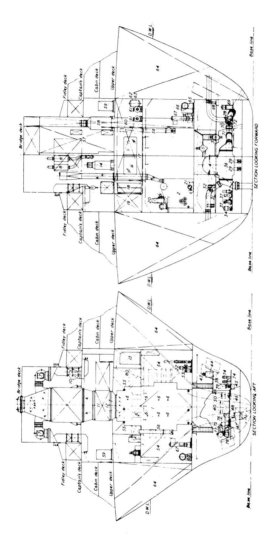

Figure 3.81 (a) Machinery arrangement—sectional views

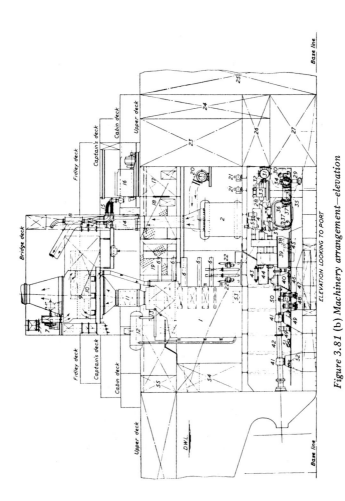

Figure 3.81 (b) Machinery arrangement—elevation

Key to Figures 3.81(a), (b) and (c)

1. Main boiler
2. Auxiliary boiler
3. H.P. turbine
4. L.P. turbine
5. I.P. turbine
6. Retractable soot blower
7. Main boiler F.D. blower
8. Diesel generator exhaust silencer
9. Air-heater
10. Steam/steam generator
11. Economiser
12. Main boiler steam drum
13. Lubricating-oil storage tank
14. Auxiliary de-aerator
15. Diesel generator lubricating-oil storage tank
16. 750-kW diesel generator
17. Machinery control room and switchboard room
18. Engineers' workshop
19. Electrical workshop
20. Auxiliary boiler F.D. blower
21. Main condenser vacuum pump
22. Fuel-oil unit
23. Fuel-oil settling tank
24. Pump-room entrance trunk
25. Ballast tank
26. Cargo pump turbine flat
27. Cargo pump room
28. Main boiler-feed pump
29. Main extraction pump
30. Auxiliary extraction pump
31. Auxiliary condenser

32. Auxiliary condenser air ejector
33. 750-kW engine-driven generator
34. Auxiliary condenser sea-water circulation pump
35. Auxiliary feed transfer pump
36. Main condenser
37. Auxiliary boiler feed pump
38. Lubricating oil centrifuge
39. Main reduction gearing
40. Main thrust block bearing
41. Shaft bearing
42. Main line shaft
43. Drain cooler
44. Steam/steam generator/feed tank
45. Lubricating-oil sludge tank
46. Dirty lubricating-oil tank
47. Lubricating-oil drain tank
48. Lubricating-oil pump
49. Sea-water service pump
50. Bilge pump
51. Diesel-oil transfer pump
52. Stern-tube lubricating-oil pump
53. Combined observation and filter tank
54. Fresh-water tank
55. Distilled-water storage tank
56. Main feed heater
57. Fire tower
58. Main de-aerator and storage tank
59. Lubricating-oil gravity tank
60. Elevator
61. Ship's service and control air compressors
62. Ship's service air reservoir

63. Control air reservoir
64. Bunker tank
65. L.P. heater and gland vapour condenser
66. Evaporating and distilling plant
67. Demineralising plant
68. L.P. heater drain pump
69. Fuel-oil transfer pump
70. Feed transfer pump
71. Main circulating pump
72. Bilge injection
73. Steam/steam generator feed pump
74. General service pump
75. Fire pump
77. Lubricating-oil coolers
78. Lubricating-oil filters
79. Centrifuge equipment
80. Auxiliary distilled-water storage tank
81. Air-conditioning machinery compartment
82. Auxiliary lubricating-oil centrifuge
83. Emergency diesel-driven air compressor
84. Starting-air reservoir
85. Diesel generator lubricating-oil sump tank
86. Diesel generator heat exchanger
87. Diesel-oil daily service tank
88. Auxiliary drain tank
89. Main drain tank
90. Lubricating-oil heater

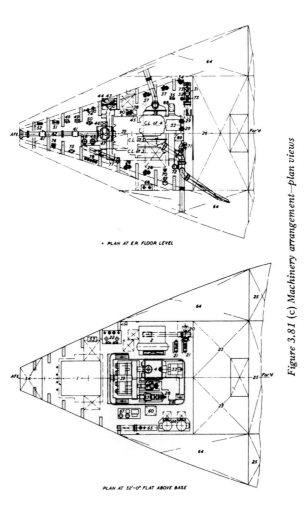

, PLAN AT E.R. FLOOR LEVEL

PLAN AT 32'-0" FLAT ABOVE BASE

Figure 3.81 (c) *Machinery arrangement–plan views*

TURBINE OPERATION, MAINTENANCE
AND OVERHAUL

In a book of this nature, it is not possible to lay down detailed procedures which would be applicable to the many different makes, types and ages of turbines which are at sea. The following notes attempt to describe certain general principles which apply in some degree to all turbines. *It is emphasised however, that for any particular installation, the engine builders' operating and maintenance instructions must always take precedence.*

Preparing the turbines for sea

Assuming that the turbines are initially cold, the general procedure is as follows:

1. Check that all drain valves and all pressure gauge isolating valves are open.
2. Check the main and standby gravity oil tank levels. Remove any water that may have settled at the tank bottoms, and top up the tanks with clean oil if necessary. Start the lubricating oil pump and check that oil is flowing at each bearing and at the gear sprayers. Check the oil pressure, and if necessary adjust by means of the relief valves. Assuming that the auxiliary circulating pump is already running, vent the water side of the lubricating oil cooler and establish a flow of circulating water through the cooler. (In very cold weather, the oil is viscous and circulation of water through the air cooler should not be started until the oil has heated up to about 50.0°C as indicated by the bearing oil thermometers).
3. Engage the turning gear and start turning the machinery.
4. Start the main circulating pump, vent the main condenser water boxes and establish circulating water flow through the condenser. Pass condensate into the condenser steam space until a level is showing in the condenser gauge glass. Start the condenser extraction pump drawing from the condenser bottom and recirculating back to the condenser. Start the condenser air pump.

5. Open up the gland steam on the auxiliary supply and adjust the control to give a pressure of approximately 1.1 bar in the gland steam reservoir, so as to establish and maintain a condenser pressure not less than 0.35 bar.

6. Ease the ahead and astern manoeuvring valves and re-close them lightly—this is to test if working freely.

7. Check the turbine protections, i.e. overspeed, low lubricating oil pressure, automatic start of standby pumps, etc., according to maker's instructions.

8. Open the bulkhead stop valve.

WARMING THROUGH

1. If the turbines are initially cold, continue turning the rotors, with sealing steam on the glands, for the period required by the maker's instructions (this may vary from one to four hours). During this period, lubricate the turbine sliding feet and longitudinal keys and check the movement at these points due to thermal expansion. Crack the main boiler stop valve (or open the small bypass round the valve) and warm through the main steam piping, using the drain on the upstream side of the turbine manoeuvring valves as a "bleed". At the end of this period, the turning gear should be stopped and disengaged.

2. Ensure that the main steam at the turbines has at least 50.0°C of superheat and that the turbine control gear is on "Manual"; slowly open the ahead manoeuvring valve sufficiently to just turn the rotors, then close the valve. Allow the rotors to come to rest, then slowly open the astern valve, again just sufficiently to break the turbine rotors from rest. Repeat this steam blasting cycle continuously for 15 minutes. The L.P. turbine casing temperature should not exceed 75.0°C.

Note that, with sealing steam on the glands, the turbines should not be left standing stationary for more than 3 minutes.

Note also that if the turbines are initially hot, i.e. if they are required within a limited period (possibly 8–12 hours) after shut-down, during which the rotors have been con-

tinuously turned, then it is likely that no warming through
period will be required.

STANDBY

After the warming through period, the turbines are ready to
be started on load. If the engines are not required immediately,
but remain on standby, then the steam blasting cycle should
be continued throughout the standby period. If the delay is
extended, then after a period of about one hour, steam blasting should be stopped (to prevent over-heating), the turning
gear engaged and the turbines turned until the normal standby is again rung.

UNDER WAY AT SEA

After full-away is received, the engines are gradually worked
up to full power. Starting drains are closed, the main circulating water and the air pump are adjusted to give the optimum
condenser pressure. Normally, the initial gland steam setting
will be adequate for any running condition, but regular
observation should be made, and immediate attention to the
gland steam sealing system should be the first step following
indication of rising condenser pressure.

As soon as the turbines are developing any appreciable
power, the condenser recirculating valve should be gradually
closed, and simultaneously the condensate isolating valve to
the feed heating system gradually opened, to maintain
constant water level in the condenser.

The oil tank level should be regularly checked as a pre-
caution against loss of oil through leaking joints. In the event
of a rise in level being observed, check that no leakage of
water into the oil system has occurred.

Regularly observe the bearing oil supply and the oil temperature leaving the bearings. If any journal or thrust bearing
shows excessive heat, the engines should be slowed down
immediately, and an investigation made.

The axial location of the rotors should be checked by the
movement indicator.

Auxiliary exhaust steam should not be discharged to the
main condenser unless the main turbines are on the turning
gear and the condenser pressure normal, or when under way,

running at not less than 60.0 per cent of full propeller speed with normal condenser pressure.

If the ship is a large modern job, the engines will ultimately be put on fully automatic control, with monitoring in the remote control room.

SHUTTING DOWN

As soon as the engines are stopped, the procedure is as described above for normal standby.

On receipt of "Finished with engines", engage the turning gear and start turning the machinery. Close the bulkhead stop valve and all drain trap byepasses. Open all drain valves and drain trap isolating valves. Close all pressure gauge isolating valves. Open the condenser recirculating valve and regulate as necessary.

Shut down the circulating pump, and when atmospheric pressure is established in the condenser, shut off the gland steam. Keep the air pump and the extraction pump working until the turbines are thoroughly drained.

Continue turning for at least 4 hours, and preferably 12 hours, then shut down the lubricating oil pump. Open up and clean the oil strainer. When the oil in the tank has completely settled, draw off a small sample from the bottom. If the sample shows deterioration, the oil supply should be renewed.

Every second day while shut down, start the lubricating oil pump and circulate clean oil through all the bearings and the gearing sprayers to prevent rusting and pitting while standing. While the oil is being circulated, turn the machinery through one and a half propeller revolutions in order to oil all the gear teeth and to make the rotors come to rest in a new position.

Unless the shut-down is to be of short duration, drain the condenser tubes and water boxes.

PROLONGED OPERATION AT LOW POWERS

No problems should occur at low ahead powers, but in the event of prolonged astern running in an emergency, distortion of the turbine casing could occur if the exhaust chamber temperature is allowed to exceed about 250.0°C. This condition will not be reached provided that the design limitation of the astern turbine is observed (see Chapter 10, page 549), e.g. if the astern turbine is specified to maintain 70.0 per cent of full ahead propeller speed for 30.0 minutes, then after this period, the propeller speed must be reduced probably to 40.0–50.0 per cent of full ahead speed. The condenser pressure must be maintained at not more than 0.07–0.1 bar.

BLACK-OUT

In the case of a ship having electrically driven auxiliaries, failure of the electric supply will cause all pumps to stop. The manoeuvring valve should be closed, (this will occur automatically if the engines are on automatic control). Check immediately that oil is being supplied from the gravity tank to the bearings and gear sprayers. Establish atmospheric pressure in the condenser by admitting air to the steam space, then shut off the gland sealing steam. When the rotors have come to rest, start to turn manually and continue until the electricity supply is restored.

FAULTS IN TURBINE ENGINES

The following notes attempt to list the symptoms and possibility of some faults which could occur.

1. *Excessive vibration*

This could be caused by:

(a) A bent rotor due to water carry-over from the boiler or the feed heating system, or by the engines being left standing with sealing steam on the glands, or by the gland steam being shut off while the condenser pressure is still sub-atmospheric thus drawing in relatively cold air over hot glands.

If either of these has occurred, then the propeller speed should be reduced to about 0.1 rev/s, and the rotors allowed to "soak" for at least one hour or until the eccentricity is back to normal. Every effort should be made to establish the cause of the bend, so as to prevent a recurrence of what could be a serious incident.

(b) Loss of balance, most probably due to mechanical damage to rotor(s).

(c) Damaged bearing, or bearing instability due to excessive wear, or inadequate oil pressure or quantity.

(d) Turbine casing distortion due to a too rapid build up of power having caused over-heating. In general, the rate of increase of steam temperature from the boiler,

and at any part of the turbines should not exceed
220.0°C per hour.

(e) Uneven or restricted expansion of turbine casing(s) due
to lack of maintenance and lubrication of sliding
pedestals and longitudinal keys. Also check that the
holding-down bolts at the sliding end are not too tight
—there should be slight clearance under the nuts.

(f) Failure of a flexible coupling membrane pack.

2. *Low oil pressure*
Possible causes are:

(a) Main oil filter choked.
(b) Leaking pipe joint(s).
(c) Jointing material partly blocking pipe bore after re-
making a joint.
(d) Oil pump suction partly blocked.
(e) Relief valve set pressure too low.
(f) Defect in oil pump or its driving unit.
(g) Damaged gear sprayer or choked sprayer strainer.
(h) Damaged or faulty pressure gauges on bearings and
sprayer manifolds.

3. *High bearing temperature*
Possible causes are:

(a) Low oil pressure.
(b) Bearing clearance insufficient.
(c) Bearing damage due to dirt in oil supply.
(d) Bearing joint in wrong position after examination or
replacement of bearing.

4. *High condenser pressure*
Possible causes are:

(a) Inadequate gland sealing steam. If pneumatic regulator,
check for dirt or moisture in the operating air supply.
(b) Abnormal air leak into condenser or other sub-atmospheric part(s) of system.
(c) Condenser flooding following extraction pump failure
or maloperation of condensate system valves.
(d) Inadequate quantity of circulating water due to circulating pump failure, or blocked C.W. suction or scoop,

or failure of internal condenser water box division plates, or blocked condenser tubes.

(e) Fouled or scaled condenser tubes.
(f) Faulty air pump.
(g) Damage to condenser steam side baffles.

5. *Impure condensate*
Possible causes are:

(a) Condenser tube failure.
(b) Condenser tube fixing failure.

LIFTING THE TOP HALF OF A TURBINE CASING

Compared with lifting the cover of a reciprocating engine cylinder, lifting the top half of a turbine casing presents difficulties only because it has to be *guided* to ensure that it does not foul the rotor at any point during the lift, otherwise damage to the blades, shroud rings, etc. could result. The blades are so finely finished and balanced that any pressure or knock from a heavy cover would bend them and probably necessitate re-blading. Included in the overhaul equipment therefore are four *guide pillars*, one to each corner, and their purpose is to prevent the cover swinging or rotating on to the blades while it is being lifted. The bottom ends of the guide pillars are secured into the bottom half of the casing, and pass through holes in the top half flange in which they are a sliding fit at the bottom. The pillars are sufficiently high to keep the top half in line until its horizontal joint face is well clear of the blades.

In most turbines, the first operation is to remove the cleading and the lagging in way of the horizontal joint, then to break the steam pipe joint(s), remove a length of the main steam piping and all other pipework attached to the top half. Wait until the turbine metal has cooled down, then slacken and remove the horizontal joint bolts, including those of the steam and exhaust end glands. In some casings, particularly those of large L.P. turbines, a few of the main horizontal joint bolts may be *internal*, in which case an engineer has to gain access through a door or manhole in the exhaust chamber to get at these bolts and remove them. Such a peculiarity may be well-known to the ship's engineers, or it may be called to attention by a warning notice plate on the turbine casing itself, or by a warning note in the overhauling and maintenance instructions. Either way, it is a reminder that force in lifting should be applied with great care.

After all the joint bolts have been removed, mount and lubricate the guide pillars, and ensure that the joint starting screws are clean, free and lubricated. Screw down the starting screws until the horizontal joint is parted uniformly by about 10.0 mm, and check that the top half diaphragms have separated at the tongue and groove joints from the bottom half. If this separation is found not to be complete, alternate lifting and lowering of the top half cover by the starting screws will force the diaphragm joints apart.

The cover lifting gear proper—provided when the ship is new—is now assembled in accordance with the maker's instructions. Usually there are brackets secured to the cover for the attachment of shackles, and chain blocks from overhead beams provide the means of lifting. Adjust the sling(s) of the lifting gear by a process of trial and error to transfer the mass load of the cover from the starting screws to the chain blocks (or crane) so that the cover is freely suspended without lateral displacement in any direction. During this process, the joint should be kept approximately 10.0 mm

Figure 3.82 H.P. turbine opened up, looking from forward end (Scott's Shipbuilding & Engineering Co. Ltd.)

open, and any "out-of-level" should not exceed approximately 3.0 mm measured at the joint gap. When in this condition, it is prudent to make records of the sling adjustment, by measurement at the respective shackles, to facilitate future lifts.

The cover is now lifted in small steps, the whole being closely observed to ensure that no binding occurs, and no fouling of the wheels and diaphragms, and that a level lift is maintained. Before lifting the cover clear of the guide pillars, ensure that there is no "side pull". When clear of the guide pillars, the cover may be run clear on the chain blocks (or crane), or it may be secured above the rotor on the cover *support columns*. The latter, four in number, are flanged at each end, with bolt holes for attachment to the horizontal joint flanges of the top half and bottom half casings.

Figure 3.82 shows an H.P. turbine opened up and illustrates the guide pillars and supporting columns in position.

Lifting the turbine rotor

The first essential is to disconnect from the rotor any attachment or component which cannot be lifted with it, e.g. the main bearing covers, the flexible coupling, the thrust bearing cover (removing the pads), the governor gear, etc. The details will vary with the different makes of turbine, and the maker's instructions should be adhered to rigidly.

The next essential is to ensure that the rotor, while being lifted, will not come in contact with the bottom half casing or diaphragms. To prevent fore-and-aft or athwartship movement, four *rotor guides* are fitted and secured to the bottom half casing horizontal joint flange. When in position, the guide faces are just clear of the shaft diameter thus preventing athwartship movement of the rotor, while the inner edges of the guides are shaped to fit into fillets in the shaft thus preventing fore-and-aft movement.

A wire-rope sling is used at either end, passing round the shaft, the upper end being attached to chain blocks (or crane). The rotor is lifted slowly and carefully, and when well clear of the bottom half casing, it may be suspended by passing steel bars through holes specially provided in the upper part of the rotor guides. Wood is placed on top of these bars and the rotor is lowered on to that. Alternatively, if space permits, the rotor may be run clear and landed on trestles, with the journals resting on V-blocks, and with soft material, such as sheet lead or copper between the journal and the V of the support. The journals should be covered, to prevent grit or dirt settling thereon, which could cause abrasion if the rotor is turned. The lifting of turbine casing cover and rotor is illustrated in Figure 3.83.

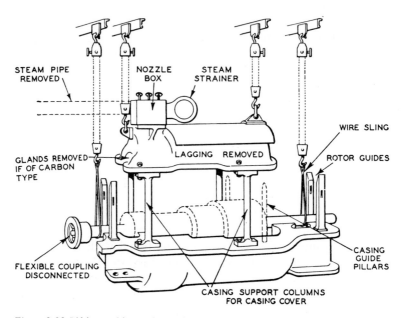

STEAM PIPE
REMOVED

NOZZLE
BOX

STEAM
STRAINER

WIRE SLING

GLANDS REMOVED
IF OF CARBON
TYPE

LAGGING REMOVED

ROTOR GUIDES

FLEXIBLE COUPLING
DISCONNECTED

CASING
GUIDE
PILLARS

CASING SUPPORT COLUMNS
FOR CASING COVER

Figure 3.83 Lifting turbine casing and cover

Internal inspection of rotor and casing

When the turbine has been opened up as described, inspection of the blading, etc., in the rotor and casing is carried out. The following are some of the faults to be found: loose blades, shrouding or lacing wire; fractured blades or blades missing; erosion or corrosion of blades and casing, particularly at the L.P. end; loose dummy strips or labyrinth gland fins; cracks in rotor, especially near the flexible coupling; nozzle passages and passages between blades choked by deposit; casing drain passages between diaphragms choked by deposit; loose discs or fractured discs; loose, or distorted, or damaged nozzle division plates; blades severely thinned and distorted by long usage.

The axial and radial clearances of the blading, glands, etc. should be examined, and where possible, checked dimensionsionally. It is important that all parts where measurements are being taken are clean, in order to avoid false readings. If a diaphragm (or diaphragms) has been removed from the casing to permit of more detailed inspection, then before the diaphragm is replaced, it should be given a thin polished coating of graphite.

Replacing the rotor and casing cover

This is carried out generally in the reverse order to lifting. The main horizontal joint of the casing is of some importance. A variation—amounting to 1.5 mm—in the thickness of an asbestos joint for a cylinder cover of a reciprocating engine would not be noticed in the running of the engine. Internal clearances in a turbine however are small—the radial blade tip clearance of a reaction turbine may be only 0.5 mm—therefore the joint is made almost face to face, and should be made with materials which will render the separation of the joint comparatively easy, even after an interval of say, one year, i.e. the material should not adhere to the joint surfaces too firmly.

A suitable jointing material is a mixture of three parts by weight of manganesite to one part of graphite made up to a thick cream consistency with boiled linseed oil, and applied sparingly to the joint surfaces. Alternatively, a mixture of red lead and copal varnish may be used. Some makers recommend that, in addition, a thin asbestos string should be laid on the joint face just inside the bolts.

For modern turbines, it is likely that most makers' instructions will call for *controlled tightening* of the horizontal joint bolts, by the use either of *torque spanners* or *bolt heaters*. Depending on the dimensions and the detail design of the joint, on the bolt and joint materials, and on the maximum working temperature, the cold bolt load is calculated by the designer, from which follows the bolt extension required when the bolts are tightened in the cold condition. This extension corresponds to a certain maximum tightening torque applied to the cold bolt, and a torque spanner is so designed that it will slip once this maximum torque is reached. Alternatively, the bolts are made with a central axial hole throughout the length, into which a powerful electric heater is inserted. As the bolt length increases, due to thermal expansion, up to a predetermined length, the nut is progressively screwed up, with little effort. When the heat is removed, the bolt cools down and contracts, so that when cold, it exerts the design cold load on the joint.

During overhaul, it is desirable to polish the screw threads of all bolts, particularly those subject to high temperature, by rubbing them with dry flake graphite. This prevents corrosion and reduces considerably the possibility of seizure.

Before replacing a rotor and casing cover, it is absolutely essential to check that without doubt, no tools, bolts, or other foreign bodies have been left inside the turbine.

Steam chests, strainers and manoeuvring valves

These should be opened up, in accordance with the maker's instructions, for examination, cleaning and, if necessary, adjustment. They should be replaced with the same main jointing material as described for the turbine casing horizontal joint.

Journal bearing

Remove the bearing housing cover and the top half bearing shell. Fit the appropriate *bearing bridge gauge* and check the gap against the previous bridge gauge reading. An increase of the gap dimension indicates sinking of the journal due to bearing wear. Bearing wear should be checked by comparing the actual bore against the original, and if the diametral clearance between the journal and the bearing exceeds 0.002 mm per 1.0 mm of diameter, the bearing should be remetalled, or a spare bearing fitted. Worn bearings should not be adjusted at the joint to reduce the bore.

Rotor easing gear is usually provided for each turbine to assist in turning out the bottom half bearing shells if necessary. Should any adjusting shims need to be replaced between the bearing housing and the bearing pedestal, care must be taken that the shims covering the oil inlet passage are drilled to permit entry of oil. Ensure also that any orifice plates in the oil passages are properly replaced.

Thrust bearings

The design axial "float" of the rotor, and the permissible maximum float will be given in the record of turbine clearances in the maker's instructions. Excessive float, caused by wear of the thrust pads, should be corrected by replacing the worn pads with a complete new set of pads of the correct

uniform thickness. With the thrust bearing and cover assembled, bedding marks should be taken on the thrust and surge
faces of the shaft collar to prove uniform distribution of load
on the thrust and surge pads. On final assembly of the thrust
bearing, ensure that all oil passages are clean and unobstructed.

General

Governor gear, lubricating oil pump and drive (if m.e. driven)
should be cleaned, and examined for mechanical damage,
worn joint pins, loose or missing split pins, etc.

Steam and exhaust, bled steam and drain lines should be
inspected with particular attention to:

(i) Open up all drain traps to check that the internals are
not damaged, and that the flow path is clear and unobstructed.

(ii) Check that all non-return valves operate freely, and
do not "pass" when in the closed position.

(iii) Inspect all relief valves and check that they are free
to operate. If it is necessary to dismantle a relief valve,
it *must be reset to the correct pressure* before refitting.

(iv) Where any turbine or pipe joints are broken during
overhaul, they should be re-made with the type and
thickness of jointing material specified by the makers.
This is important, since the different services, e.g.
steam, condensate, oil, etc. may require different
materials and thicknesses. Ready-cut joints for all
services are usually included in the spare gear, but if a
joint has to be made on board, it should be properly
cut with shears and the bolt holes cut with a punch of
the correct size. The practice of cutting a joint by
hammering against the flange should not be used. The
diameter of the central hole should be made about
6.0 mm greater than the pipe bore to avoid the possibility of encroachment on the latter.

Taking over a watch on a modern "turbine-water-tube boiler" vessel

Before entering the engine-room look at the funnel top to
ascertain the condition of the gases with regard to smoke and
also for *feathering* of the safety valves. Inspect the steering
gear. If it is of the electric-hydraulic type, see that the level
of oil in the sump is correct.

On entering the engine-room, if the feed system is fitted with a direct-contact heater, check the water level and pressure of the exhaust-steam inlet (about 1.7 bar). Down below, check all the turbine bearing temperatures ($50.0°C$) and note the flow of lubricating oil to and from the bearings.

The turbo-generator may be of the self-contained type, with separate condenser, extraction pump and air-ejector. Inspect the bearings as you have done on the main unit, steam pressure, gland pressure (1.1 bar) and condenser pressure.

Inspect the various pumps; main and auxiliary circulating pumps, main and auxiliary extraction or condensate pumps, lubricating-oil pumps and others in operation, special attention being given to the turbo-feed pumps, the governor spindle of which should be tested for freedom of action by the forked lever sometimes provided (see notes on breakdowns).

In the stokehold the boiler water-gauge should be blown through and the water level checked, uptake temperatures noted, fuel-oil temperatures and pressures checked (the pressures before and after the filters give a guide to the condition of these items). The size of the tips fitted to the spare oil-fuel burners, which have been cleaned by the previous watch, should be noted. If automatic-feed check valves are fitted with testing levers test them.

On the main turbine-control panel, H.P., I.P. and L.P. pressures and temperatures are noted, strict attention being given to the L.P. astern turbine temperatures. From these, a good indication of the condition of the astern manoeuvring and isolating valves, as regards steam tightness, may be obtained. Note the main condenser pressure and inlet and outlet circulating-water temperatures, the gland-steam and bled-steam gauge pressures, axial clearance, if possible, and the flow of oil to the main reduction gearing.

A good indication of the condition of the feed water can be had from the electric salinometer, and a reading must definitely be taken when taking over the watch and frequently during the watch. The maximum reading, as specified in the boiler maker's instructions must not be exceeded. Distilled water is usually kept in a reserve feed tank which is normally a double-bottom tank, but to avoid contamination with seawater it may be placed high up in the engine-room. It contains about 20 tonnes, and the level in the sight glasses or by test cocks, should be noted when coming on watch. By checking frequently, a check is kept on the amount of distilled water made by the evaporator or used during the watch. All these duties must be carried out when taking over a watch on a modern ship of this type and repeated frequently during the watch to ensure efficient running of the machinery.

Spare gear

The same remarks regarding the quantity and care of spares as have been made for reciprocating engines apply equally to those for the main engines of a turbine-driven vessel. An example of the spares carried for a turbine is as follows:

One set of bearing bushes for each size of rotor shaft; studs and nuts.

One set of bearing bushes for each size of pinion with studs and nuts.

One bearing bush for gear-wheel shaft with studs and nuts.

A number of bolts and nuts for the main turbine-casing joint.

A number of bolts and nuts for the gearcase joint.

One set gland segments and springs for each size fitted.

One main-gear pinion for each size, with claw piece or membrane pack for flexible coupling.

One set of pads for Michell-type thrust block on rotor spindle and some liners in halves for adjustment of same.

One set thrust pads for the main thrust block.

One escape-valve spring for each size fitted.

One set bolts and nuts for main-shaft coupling.

Several condenser tubes, ferrules and packing as for reciprocating engines.

A few spare thermometers.

An assortment of bolts and nuts for general use; iron bars of varying sizes and a few plates of iron sheet.

At least one complete set of joints for the engine room, and/or a quantity of jointing material of the correct types and thicknesses.

BREAKDOWN

The turbine is sturdy and most reliable when run in accordance with the maker's instructions; lubricating oil used of the best quality, kept clean and in good condition; pressures and temperatures to and from the bearings correct; properly warmed through before starting and drained thoroughly. The steam supply should be as pure as possible. This requires careful attention to feed and boiler water.

The following examples of trouble with turbine machinery will illustrate the sort of things to expect if great care is not taken.

Example 1

A turbine was kept running at slow speed for a lengthy period, when, without warning, there was heavy vibration and the whole engine shuddered. The manoeuvring valve was closed and the engine stopped. On examination of the main bearings it was found that they had run out and the rotor spindle had dropped on to the safety strips. This had caused the vibration, but had saved the turbine from further damage. The rotor was eased up with the special gear provided for such an eventuality and the damaged bearings removed. The spindle journals were examined and honed where marked by the bronze strips. The spare bearing shells were fitted, without lifting the turbine-casing cover, and the rotor lowered on to them. The turbine was ready to start within 12 hours of the stoppage. It was suspected that a quick drop in the sea temperature cooled the lubricating oil and increased its viscosity so much that the quantity passing through the bearings was insufficient to prevent overheating. It will be observed that, in this case, the bulkhead stop-valve emergency gear would not act because the pressure of oil was correct; only the temperature was low.

Example 2

In a double-reduction geared-turbine installation, while in port, the lubricating-oil cooler by-pass had been opened to allow of the cooler being cleaned out. The fact that the by-pass was open was later overlooked when the vessel left port, and in a short time a grinding noise came from the reduction gear-case. The engine was stopped, and it was found that the L.P. pinion had stripped some teeth and fractured others. The second reduction gear-wheel teeth were badly marked and grooved. The after L.P. pinion bearing had been overheated and the white metal had run out. The resulting misalignment of the pinion was probably the cause of the break-down of the teeth.

The damaged pinion was removed, the oil supply to its bearings shut off and the bearing ends blanked off. The H.P. emergency steam connections for exhausting directly to the condenser were fitted and the steam supply to the L.P. tur-bine blanked off so that the L.P. was out of commission. The superheated-steam temperature was reduced by opening the mixing valve, and the engine ran to the next port on the H.P. turbine only.

On reaching port, the second reduction wheel was removed and taken ashore to an engine works. The very badly damaged width of the teeth was turned off, leaving a reduced but workable width of sound teeth, which were honed as smooth as possible. The spare pinion was fitted, and the vessel com-pleted the voyage at slightly reduced power. The condenser pressure was not allowed to get below 0.14 bar. This was intended to relieve the load on the L.P. pinion, which was running with reduced tooth width.

Example 3

On examination of the magnetic strainer in the lubricating-oil system a number of metal chips and flakes were observed. The inspection doors of the gearcase were removed and a few pinion teeth were found to be fractured at the root and the ends of a few actually broken off. The fractured teeth were removed in way of the fractures, and the damaged teeth dressed up with a hone. The engine completed the voyage at reduced speed.

When fitting the new pinion, special care was observed to ensure that the alignment was correct, since it was suspected that misalignment had been the cause of the breakdown.

Example 4

While warming up a turbine, it was the usual practice to ease the ahead and astern manoeuvring valves and gland steam to give a steam pressure of 1.7 bar on the ahead H.P. and 1.35 bar on the astern. At the same time the vacuum breaker was eased to keep the condenser pressure about 0.88 bar, just enough to keep a steady flow of steam.

On one occasion, before leaving port, the turbine was warmed through in the usual way and the telegraph rang *stand-by.* The vacuum breaker was closed, the astern manoeuvring valve closed and the condenser pressure brought down to 0.07 bar. Due to some hitch on deck, the *stand-by* order remained for over half an hour, during which time the turbine was kept ready to move. When *slow ahead* was rung and steam was opened to the turbine, a screech came from the L.P. turbine casing. The turbine was stopped immediately. It was suspected that the rotor had warped during the long waiting period under low condenser pressure and that the blade tips had made contact with the inside of the casing. The condenser pressure was lowered again and the whole process of warming through was repeated for about an hour. When tried again everything appeared in order, and the turbine ran without further incident. On opening up at the home port there was evidence of contact at the blade tips but no real damage.

Example 5

A turbine installation, with a closed-feed system, was running normally at sea when the pressure governor spindle on the turbo-feed pump stuck. This reduced the output of feed water to the boilers, and the water level dropped. There were two boilers, and when the level in one got too low for safety the oil-fuel burners to that boiler were shut off and the feed check valves closed down. The other boiler now got all the feed water and, having to supply the turbine with steam alone, its pressure dropped.

When this was observed, the engine stop valve was *shut in* to reduce the speed of the turbine. Being in a hurry, the engineer omitted to adjust the gland steam, and in consequence, there was not sufficient to seal the L.P. turbine glands. Air was drawn in in sufficient quantity to cause a big drop increase in condenser pressure. This had the effect of reducing the speed of the turbo-generator, and the voltage on the switchboard dropped until the main automatic circuit-breaker tripped out. The electrically operated lubricating-oil and condensate pumps now stopped for want of power, and the whole plant of the engine-room came to a standstill.

This last example shows the necessity for careful watch-keeping, especially when the various items in the engine-room are interconnected.

Future developments

It seems likely that automatic control with its necessary accompaniment of data logging will be increasingly used in the future. Features of automatic control are dealt with in *Marine Auxiliary Machinery*, a companion volume in this series.

MEASUREMENT OF TURBINE POWER

In a turbine installation, it is not possible to estimate the power being developed by taking indicator diagrams from the cylinder as is done in reciprocating engines. The most usual method is by some form of *torsion meter* which measures the amount of twist of the propeller shaft. Various devices, both mechanical and electrical, have been employed to measure the angle of twist of the shaft while it is running.

The Hopkinson–Thring torsion meter is one example of the mechanical-optical type. Two discs are fixed to the shaft at a distance apart of about 1.5 m. One of the discs carries a cylindrical sheath which extends towards the other disc, and the angular movement of the end of the sheath and the disc is amplified by a lever and link gear connecting the two. The simplified diagram in Figure 3.84 shows the principle.

As the shaft twists under load, the angular movement of disc A relative to disc B is reproduced by the movement of disc C relative to disc B. This relative angular movement is magnified by the bell-crank lever, which through a suitable linkage mechanism alters the angular position of the mirror, thus altering the position of the reflected point of light on the scale. The distance moved by this point of light along the scale is proportional to the angle of twist of the shaft.

For a circular shaft, the torsion equation is $T/J = G\theta/L$, where

> T = applied, torque, Nm
> J = polar moment of inertia of the shaft, m^4
> G = modulus of rigidity of the shaft material, N/cm^2
>   (8.3×10^6 for steel)
> θ = angle of twist, radians
> L = twisting length, m.

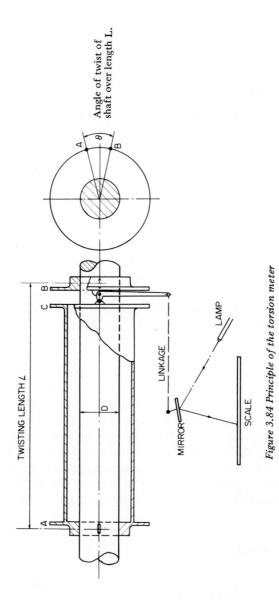

Angle of twist of
shaft over length L.

TWISTING LENGTH L

Figure 3.84 Principle of the torsion meter

The shafting usually is designed so that the angle of twist does not exceed $1.0°$ in a length of 6.0 m. The polar moment of inertia of a solid circular shaft, $J = \pi D^4/32$, and of a hollow circular shaft, $J = (\pi_1/32)(D^4 - d^4)$, where D and d are the external and internal diameters respectively.

Thus, if we have for example a solid circular steel shaft 254.0 mm dia. with the discs A and B 1.525 m apart, then

$$J = \frac{\pi \times 0.254^4}{32} = 0.00040865 \text{ m}^4$$

$L = 1.525$ m, and the maximum allowable angle of twist over the length L would be,

$$\theta = \frac{1.0 \times 1.525}{6.0} \times \frac{2\pi}{360} = 0.004436 \text{ radians}$$

From the torsion equation the maximum torque would be

$$T = \frac{JG\theta}{L} = \frac{0.00040865 \times 8.3 \times 10^6 \times 100^2 \times 0.004436}{1.525}$$

$$= 98\,660 \text{ Nm}$$

Now for any given shaft and torsion meter, JG/L is constant, and the torque T is directly proportional to the angle of twist θ. Hence if the torque of 98 660 Nm is made 100 on the torsion meter scale, then at any other scale reading,

$$\text{Torque} = \frac{\text{Scale reading}}{100} \times 98\,660 \text{ Nm}$$

and if the shaft speed is n rev/s

$$\text{Power transmitted} = \frac{\text{Scale reading}}{100} \times \frac{98\,660}{1000} \times 2\pi n$$

$$= 6.199 \times \text{Scale reading} \times n$$

The term 6.199 is called the torsion meter constant

i.e. if the speed at maximum torque 98 660 Nm is 1.667 rev/s, then

$$\text{Power} = \frac{98\,660 \times 1.667 \times 2\pi}{1000} = 1033.6 \text{ kW}$$

At this condition the torsion meter reading would be 100, hence

Power = 6.199 × 100 × 1.667 = 1033.6 kW as before

If at another power, the torsion meter scale reading was 65.0 at 1.334 rev/s, then the power = 6.199 × 65.0 × 1.334 = 537.5 kW.

Depending on the type of steel of which the shaft is made, the value of G can vary between 7.6×10^6 and 9.0×10^6 N/cm^2, hence in graduating a torsion meter scale, the shaft is tested for actual angle of twist under load by supporting it on trestles, and with one end fixed, the other end is made to deflect by applying a torsional load. For this purpose, a long steel bar is bolted to the free end flange, and weights are hung from the end of it to give a known torque. The torsion meter scale readings are then adjusted to represent the actual torque valves for that particular shaft.

4 Turbine reduction gears

All marine steam turbines are now invariably geared to the propeller shaft. The gearing is the means by which both the turbines and the propeller may run at their respective economical speeds—the turbines at high speed and the propeller at low speed. Turbine gears have to provide speed reduction ratios of the order of 30:1 up to 80:1, depending on the conditions, e.g. if a turbine runs at 50.0 rev/s and the required propeller speed is 1.667 rev/s, then the total speed reduction ratio required is 50.0/1.667 = 30:1. In order to limit the overall dimensions of the gearing in the thwartship plane, reduction ratios of this order require two stages of reduction, i.e. require *double-reduction* gearing.

Turbine gears invariably have *helical* teeth, i.e. the gear teeth are not parallel to the shaft axis as they are in ordinary *spur* gears, but each tooth is part of a helix on the periphery of the wheel, the majority of helical gears having a *helix angle* of 30° to the axis of the shaft. If one ordinary spur gear drives another, the forces between the teeth act entirely in the plane of the gears, i.e. there is no end thrust on either of the shafts. If a single helical gear drives another, the forces between the teeth act in a plane which is inclined to the plane of the gears, consequently there is a transverse component causing rotation, and an axial component causing end thrust. In order to balance the end thrust, turbine gears are almost invariably double-helical, i.e. there are two sets of teeth on each wheel, the helix of one set being of opposite hand to that of the other. The resultant end thrusts therefore cancel one another (see Figures 4.1 and 4.2).

This arrangement gives smooth running, the teeth sliding on to one another without impact, and several teeth being in mesh at any instant.

The smaller of two gears which mesh with one another is called the pinion, and the larger, the wheel.

The pinion is integral with the pinion shaft, being of forged

Figure 4.1 Main gearwheel
    Note the cast-iron wheel centre with steel rim shrunk on, and the double
helical teeth having opposite hand of helices

alloy steel. In the older turbines the main gear wheel was
generally of cast iron with a forged low-carbon steel rim about
100.0 m thick, shrunk on and pegged. In the latest designs,
both primary and secondary wheels are of fabricated steel
construction, the wheel centre being integral with the shaft,
the wheel side plates being of mild steel and the rim of alloy
steel. This type of construction is not so massive and is less
expensive than the cast iron wheel. Being thinner and less
massive, the wheels require some internal stiffening—usually
in the form of welded-in steel ribs or tubes—to reduce any
tendency to vibration, noise and fatigue.

Once a wheel of this type (see Figure 4.17) is welded up
and finished, it is in fact a sealed chamber, and care must be

Figure 4.2 Gear pinions
  This shows clearly the pinion clawpieces and part of the sleeve for the flexible coupling. The oil gutters on the claws should be noted

taken that no foreign matter, solid or liquid, is inadvertently left inside the fabrication, otherwise unbalance and severe vibration can occur when running at speed.

Experience with turbine reduction gears, and extensive testing over the past ten years has shown that tooth wear is influenced quite markedly by the nature and the extent of the *hardening* process which it is possible to apply to the teeth during manufacture. We will refer to this subject again later when dealing with specific examples of modern turbine gears.

Formerly the gearcase was of cast iron, but nowadays is invariably of fabricated steel. Here again, this means that being thinner and less massive, the modern gearcase would require additional ribbing to minimise vibration and noise. The earlier gearcases, almost invariably, were split at the horizontal centre line of the main (secondary) wheel, i.e. in the same manner as a turbine casing, but in modern gears, as described later in this section, this concept is now changing.

The gear teeth (which are dealt with rather more fully later in this section) are relatively small, the size depending on the size of the gear and on the power transmitted. The teeth are very carefully cut from the solid in a *hobbing* machine, housed in a room which is kept at constant temperature to ensure correctness and uniformity of the tooth form and pitch, which is essential for smooth and quiet operation. In the early gears, very slight variations in pitch were found to be the cause of noise, and to be a contributory factor to *flaking* of the teeth, in which the surface of the tooth comes off in flakes due to *slogger* between the teeth. Slogger is a hammer-like action which can be set up by variation of tooth pitch, or by torsional vibration, either from the propeller alone, or due to the natural torsional vibration characteristics of the whole system—turbines, gears, shafting, propeller. Early faults due to this cause were greatly reduced by the introduction of the *nodal* drive, this being designed so that the plane of contact of the gears, somewhere between the turbines and the propeller, was positioned at a *node*, i.e. a natural point of zero vibration. Flaking has also been attributed to an insufficient supply or an unsuitable quality of lubricating oil, and again to maladjustment or wear-down of the bearings putting the meshing wheels out of line with one another.

After cutting in the hobbing machine, the teeth go through an operation called *shaving*, which is rather the equivalent of *scraping* in that a very fine lamina is removed from the surface, giving the teeth a much finer finish. As distinct from the hobbing cutter, the shaving cutter is free to follow the contour of existing teeth. After shaving, the face of each tooth for about 12.0 mm from the end of the tooth is honed down, tapering from zero to about 1.0 mm. This prevents any excessive loads coming on the ends of the teeth which might cause fracture.

If the speed ratio of two meshing gears is to be say 10:1 and the pinion is to have 25 teeth, the number of teeth in the wheel is not made exactly 250, since if it is, the same tooth of the pinion wheels would engage with the same tooth of the wheel at every revolution of the wheel. If the number is made 251, then it will require 25 revolutions of the wheel before the same pair of teeth engage, thus ensuring that every tooth of the wheel engages in turn with every tooth of the pinion. This gives better running and more even wear.

Between a turbine rotor and its pinion shaft, some form of flexible coupling is fitted, of which the claw type has already been described. There is another type, with interlaced springs, called the Bibby coupling, and in more recent years, another type called the *membrane* flexible coupling has been increas-

ingly used. The membrane coupling is dealt with in more
detail later in this chapter.

The gears are lubricated from the main oil supply, the
lubricating points being the pinion and wheel bearings, the
flexible coupling if of the claw type, and each line of contact
between the pinion and wheel teeth. The oil is introduced
into the gear bearings in much the same manner as for the
turbine journal bearings, but in such a radial position as does
not coincide with the resultant ahead or astern bearing loads
(see Figure 4.21c). A claw-type flexible coupling is usually
lubricated by catching some of the oil leaving the adjacent
bearing (see Figure 3.25, Chapter 3).

The pinion and wheel teeth are lubricated by oil sprayers.
Oil at a pressure of 2.0–2.75 bar is projected through the
sprayers into the mesh of the teeth, the tips of the sprayers
being situated only 25.0–50.0 mm from the point at which
the teeth mesh. There may be three or more such sprayers on
each face of a double-helical arrangement, and on the astern
as well as on the ahead side. Figure 4.3 shows various forms
of gear oil sprayers, and Figure 4.4 shows the arrangement of
a single-reduction gear in which the position of the sprayers
can be seen.

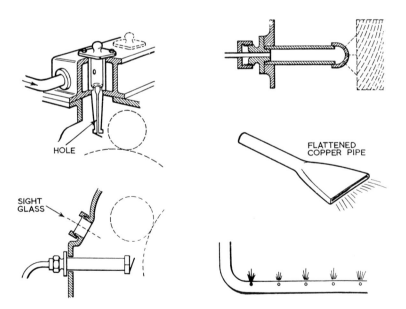

Figure 4.3 Gear oil sprayers

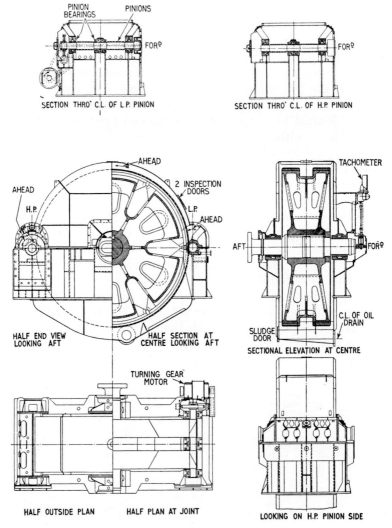

Figure 4.4 General arrangement of single-reduction gear

Ventilators are fitted at the top of the gearcase and, at sea in heavy weather, abnormal loading of the gear teeth heats the oil at the point of contact causing increased vapourisation of the oil which can be seen at the vent outlets.

The successful operation of a properly installed reduction gear is mainly a matter of attention to alignment and lubrication. Inspection should be made at regular intervals particularly when the gear is new, and records kept of the conditions observed.

While running, the flow of oil may be checked by a glance in the inspection windows if fitted. Alternatively each inlet pipe may be fitted with a "revolving flag" flow indicator, by which the condition of flow may be observed instantly. If the flow of oil to any one sprayer stops the inlet pipe becomes warmer than the others. The condition of the oil should be regularly observed.

When stopped, the condition of the teeth should be inspected. Correct tooth contact is indicated by uniform marking over the entire length of both the pinion and wheel teeth helices. Any abnormal marking on any part of the tooth faces may indicate incorrect alignment, which could ultimately cause pitting of the teeth and irregular bearing wear. All likely causes should be investigated and steps taken to correct them. The condition of the teeth as regards wear may be tested by taking a wax impression from both pinion and wheel, or by turning the gears while a lead wire is allowed to enter between the teeth. On removal of the wire, its thickness will show the clearance or "backlash" between the teeth. When examining this condition, the original form and clearance of the teeth must be borne in mind, and on no account should any attempt be made to alter the profile of the teeth. Should an inspection show that a tooth is fractured, the correct procedure is to remove as much of the tooth as contains the fracture—the whole tooth if in doubt.

Care should be taken when approaching a newly opened gear case with a naked light as there could be an accumulation of inflammable oil vapour.

If a reduction gear is to be out of use for an extended period of time, it may be necessary to protect the gears against internal condensation particularly if the atmosphere is humid.

Arrangement of gearing

The diagrams in Figure 4.5 show the various arrangements of double-reduction gearing, with the appropriate names.

Interleaved, split secondary means that the right-hand and left-hand helical teeth faces of the secondary reduction are placed sufficiently far apart in the fore-and-aft direction that the entire primary reduction can be accommodated between them.

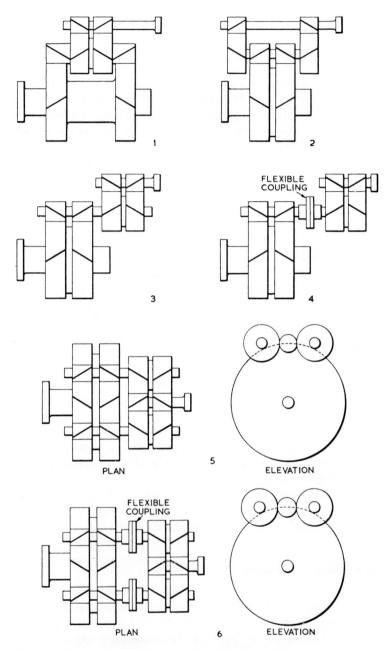

Figure 4.5 Various arrangements of double reduction gearing
1. Interleaved, split secondary 2. Interleaved, split primary 3. Tandem
4. Articulated tandem 5. Locked train dual tandem 6. Articulated locked train
(dual tandem)

Interleaved, split primary is the same in principle, but having the secondary reduction located between the right hand and left hand helical teeth faces of the primary reduction.

In either of the above two cases, the primary and secondary reductions are symmetrical about one thwartship plane.

Tandem means that the primary and secondary reductions are in two separate thwartship planes, the secondary reduction being usually, but not necessarily, aft of the primary reduction.

Articulated means that there is a flexible coupling, and also usually a quill shaft, between the primary and secondary reductions.

Single tandem means that *one* primary pinion gears with *one* primary wheel.

Dual tandem means that *one* primary pinion gears with *two* primary wheels.

Compared with the single tandem arrangement, dual tandem has the outstanding advantage that for each primary pinion there are two primary *gear contacts* instead of one, and two secondary gear contacts instead of one. For any given torque therefore, the individual tooth loads are reduced, and a greater proportion of the total number of teeth in the pinions and wheels is usefully employed. This offers the possibility of using a reduced tooth face width and a smaller tooth pitch, the latter allowing smaller diameter pinions and wheels to be used for any given reduction ratio.

This advantage however, can be obtained only if it is certain that the driving load is equally shared among all the gear contacts. Between every pinion and wheel there is always—however small it may be—some *backlash*, i.e. some difference between the thickness of a pinion tooth at the pitch line and the width of the space between two adjacent teeth on the mating wheel, and if one gear contact is in proper contact while the other is floating in the backlash, then the former will carry all the load and the latter will do nothing. Means must therefore be provided, so that when the gear has been set up with one gear contact in correct contact, the other members may be given slight relative rotation to ensure that all other gear contacts too are properly made, and then locked up so that they will remain so. It was this necessary feature which, in history, led to dual tandem gears being described by the rather unfortunate title of *locked train*. One means of achieving locked train is described in principle later in this chapter.

Otherwise, each of the gearing arrangements shown in Figure 4.5 has its own advantages and disadvantages as regards number of wheels and bearings, bearing centre distances, tooth loads, total mass, space occupied. A review of modern turbine gears appears to indicate that the dual tandem arrangement is most favoured, but that single tandem gears may show an advantage where extra height between the propeller shaft and the turbine shaft(s) is dictated by the preferred machinery arrangement.

The gear teeth

For the moment consider ordinary spur gears, i.e. gears in which the teeth are parallel to the wheel shaft.

The gear teeth are almost invariably of involute form, i.e. the working face of the tooth is part of an involute curve. An involute curve is the path described by the end of a string as it is unwound from a cylinder, the string always being kept taut—see Figure 4.6, which is self-explanatory. The cylinder is called the base circle, and the diameter d is the base circle diameter. It will be immediately obvious that, instantaneously, any tangent to the base circle is normal to the involute, e.g. the tangent $33'$ is instantaneously at right angles to the direction of motion of the involute.

Now imagine the base circle to be a wheel carrying a tooth of the involute form $01'2'3'4'$. Let this wheel rotate in the

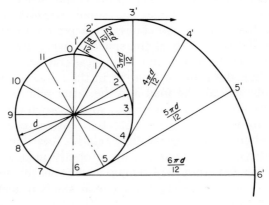

Figure 4.6 Involute curve

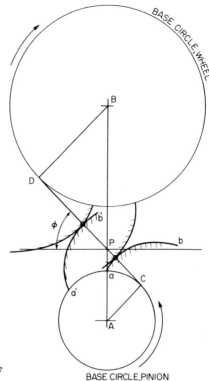

*Figure 4.7 Basic principle of involute
teeth in gear, pinion driving*

counter-clockwise direction, and gear with another generally
similar wheel, the distance between the wheel centres being
AB (Figure 4.7). The involute tooth ab will drive its counter-
part on the other wheel so as to cause the latter to rotate in
the clockwise direction, the involute faces of the two teeth
in contact rolling on one another such that the point of
contact always lies on the transverse common tangent CD to
the two base circles, and that the direction of the force
applied by the driving tooth to the driven tooth is always
along CD. At any instant, CD is normal to the tooth faces in
contact. The transverse common tangent to the two base
circles is called the line of action of the teeth. The point P at
which the line of action intersects the line of centres of the
two wheels is called the pitch point, and the angle ϕ which
the line of action makes with the perpendicular to the line of
centres at P is called the tooth pressure angle.

Let us redraw the diagram in Figure 4.8 exactly the same
as Figure 4.7, but for clarity, omit the involute curves. Refer-

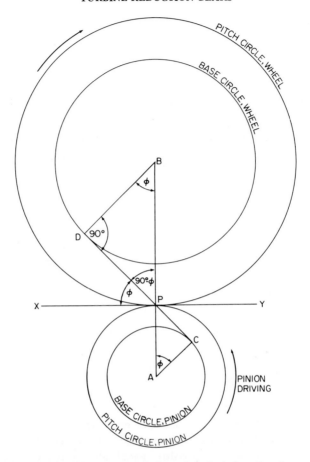

Figure 4.8 Relationships between base circles and pitch circles of involute gears

ring to Figure 4.8, the circle with centre A and radius AP is
called the pitch circle of the pinion, and the circle with
centre B and radius BP is called the pitch circle of the wheel.
The two pitch circles touch one another at the point point P,
and the perpendicular XPY to the line of centres at P is the
common tangent to the pitch circles.

Now a tangent to a circle is at right angles to a radius
drawn to the point of contact, hence in Figure 4.8, the angles
BDP and BPX are right angles, and since the sum of the
angles of a triangle is two right angles, it follows that the
angle DBP is equal to the tooth pressure angle ϕ. For the
same reasons, the angle PAC is also equal to ϕ.

By definition, $\cos \phi = BD/BP$ and $\cos \phi = AC/AP$, hence

$$BD = BP \cos \phi \quad \text{and} \quad AC = AP \cos \phi$$

BD and AC are the radii of the base circles; BP and AP are the radii of the pitch circles, hence follows the relationship

Base circle diameter = pitch circle diameter $\times \cos \phi$

$$\text{Conversely, pitch circle diameter} = \frac{\text{Base circle diameter}}{\cos \phi}$$

The circular pitch is the distance between two adjacent teeth of a wheel, measured round the circumference of the pitch circle. Any two wheels which gear together must have the same circular pitch, hence if the pitch circle diameters are d_1 and d_2, and the numbers of teeth are N_1 and N_2 respectively, then

$$\frac{\pi d_1}{N_1} = \frac{\pi d_2}{N_2} = \text{circular pitch,}$$

Hence $d_1/d_2 = N_1/N_2$, i.e. the pitch circle diameter of any wheel of given circular pitch is directly proportional to the number of teeth in the wheel.

If two wheels gear together, their pitch lines have a common linear velocity, hence if the wheels have speeds n_1 and n_2 rev/s, respectively, then

$$\pi d_1 n_1 = \pi d_2 n_2$$

$$\therefore \frac{n_1}{n_2} = \frac{d_2}{d_1} = \frac{N_2}{N_1}$$

i.e. the speeds of the two wheels are inversely proportional to the pitch circle diameters (or to the numbers of teeth.)

The addendum and the dedendum respectively, are the radial distances from the pitch circle to the tip and to the root of the pinion or wheel tooth, from which follows the tip circle and the root circle. The total tooth depth is the difference in radius between the tip and root circles, and the working depth is equal to the total depth minus the root clearance.

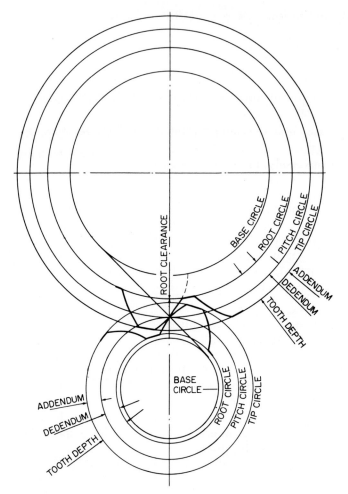

Figure 4.9 Root circles and tip circles of involute gears

Figure 4.9 has been purposely drawn exaggerated and out
of proportion in an attempt to illustrate these definitions
clearly. The actual magnitudes of the addendum and dedendum are chosen from consideration of tooth strength and
tooth action, and are quite independent of the fundamental
relationship between base circle, pitch circle and tooth
pressure angle.

In Figure 4.9, the root circles of both pinion and wheel are
greater in diameter than the respective base circles, hence the
entire working face of each tooth consists of an involute
curve. By definition, the involute curve cannot continue

below the base circle, hence if the root circle diameter is smaller than the base circle diameter, that part of the tooth face between the base circle and the root circle is not an involute curve, but is of some other form which, due to the gear cutting process, results in undercutting of the teeth, i.e. the thickness of the tooth diminishes below the base circle.

It will be noted from Figure 4.8 that the teeth will work with the same speed ratio if, within the limits of the tooth depth, the centre distance between the wheels is altered. This is equivalent to altering the pitch circle diameters without altering their ratio. The line of action will still pass through the appropriate pitch point, but the tooth pressure angle will be increased with increased centre distance, and vice versa. *This is an important property peculiar to involute gears.*

Note: Instead of being defined as circular pitch (C.P.), the pitch is sometimes defined as diametral pitch (D.P.), which is the number of teeth per unit of diameter. Alternatively the pitch may be defined as the module pitch (m) which is the reciprocal of the diametral pitch.

Hence if d is the pitch circle diameter and n the number of teeth, then in consistent units,

$$\text{C.P.} = \frac{\pi d}{n} \text{ and D.P.} = \frac{n}{d}, \text{ hence D.P.} = \frac{\pi}{\text{C.P.}},$$

$$\text{and } m = \frac{1}{\text{D.P.}} = \frac{\text{C.P.}}{\pi}$$

For our purpose, to avoid confusion we will use circular pitch throughout.

Forces acting between the gear teeth

The purpose of a reduction gear is to transmit a certain power which is developed by the turbines at high speed, to the propeller which absorbs that power at low speed. Consider the simple gear shown in Figure 4.10. Suppose the pinion, of pitch circle radius r_1, m, to be on the turbine shaft, and to run at a speed of n_1, rev/s.

The turbine develops at certain torque, which by definition, is the product of the force T, N, and the perpendicular distance r_1, m, between the line of action of T and the centre of the pinion, i.e.

Pinion torque = Tr_1, Nm

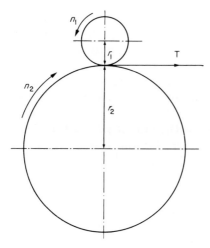

Figure 4.10 Simple gear

If the pinion makes one revolution, the force T acts through a distance $2\pi r_1$, hence the work done $= 2\pi T r_1$, Nm/rev. If the pinion runs at n_1 rev/s, then the work done $= 2\pi T r_1 n_1$, Nm/s, and since 1.0 Nm/s = 1.0 W, the power transmitted by the pinion $= (2\pi T r_1 n_1)/(1000)$, kW, i.e.

$$\text{Turbine power} = \frac{2\pi T r_1 n_1}{1000}, \text{ kW} \qquad (1)$$

Basically, the wheel must transmit the same power, and the force T is common to both the pinion and the wheel, hence

$$\text{Turbine power} = \frac{2\pi T r_2 n_2}{1000}, \text{ kW} \qquad (2)$$

$$\text{From 1, Pinion torque, } T r_1 = \frac{\text{turbine power} \times 1000}{2\pi n_1}, \text{ Nm}$$

$$\text{From 2, Wheel torque, } T r_2 = \frac{\text{turbine power} \times 1000}{2\pi n_2}, \text{ Nm}$$

$$\text{Equating 1 and 2 gives } \frac{2\pi T r_1 n_1}{1000} = \frac{2\pi T r_2 n_2}{1000}$$

$$\therefore T r_1 n_1 = T r_2 n_2$$

$$\therefore \frac{T r_1}{T r_2} = \frac{n_2}{n_1}$$

The torques are inversely proportional to the speeds, i.e. the pinion transmits the power with a low torque at high speed, and the wheel transmits the same power with a high torque at low speed. It is the torque that determines the shaft strength required, and it is for the above reason that in any reduction gear, the high speed shafts are always smaller in diameter than the low-speed shafts.

Knowing the turbine power and speed and the pitch diameters of the pinion and wheel, the force T in the line of the common tangent between the pinion and wheel may be found from the expressions given above.

Now, because of the necessary form of the gear teeth, the pinion cannot apply a force to the wheel along the line of the line of the common tangent, but it applies a force P along a line which is inclined at an angle ϕ to the common tangent. For the moment, consider ordinary *spur gears*, i.e. gears having the teeth parallel to the axes of the shafts.

Referring to Figure 4.11, the force P acts normal to (i.e. at right angles to) the surface of the teeth at the point of contact. The angle ϕ is of course the tooth pressure angle. For spur gears, the three forces P, T and S are all in the same plane, viz. the diametral plane. The actual force P applied by the pinion to the wheel may thus be considered to consist of two components, viz, a component T acting along the line of the

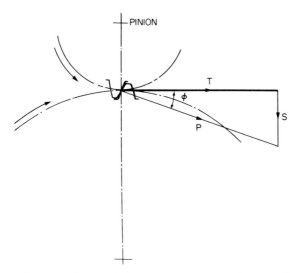

Figure 4.11 Forces applied to wheel tooth by pinion tooth (spur gears)

common tangent causing rotation of the wheel, and a component S at right angles to the common tangent tending to cause separation of the pinion and wheel along the line of their centres. From Figure 4.11, it will be seen that $P = T/\cos \phi$, hence we can consider the two forces T and S to be replaced by the single force P.

P is the resultant of T and S, and once P is determined, the forces T and S need be considered to exist only for the purposes of the present explanation.

In Figure 4.11, the forces shown are those applied to the wheel. Now action and reaction are equal and opposite, hence there are equal and opposite forces T', P' and S', say, applied to the pinion. The resulting state of affairs is shown in Figure 4.12(a) in which T, P and S are the forces applied to the wheel and T', P' and S' are the reaction forces applied to the pinion.

If the direction of rotation is changed, i.e. from ahead to astern, with the same torque, the forces on the pinion and on the wheel are reversed, as shown in Figure 4.12(b).

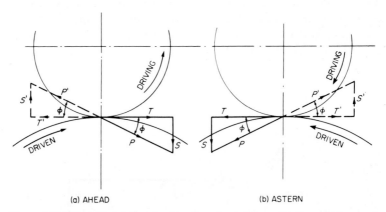

(a) AHEAD   (b) ASTERN

Figure 4.12 Effect of changing the direction of rotation on the forces between the teeth

Now, turbine reduction gears do not have straight spur teeth, but have helical teeth, i.e. each tooth is part of a *helix* on the pinion or wheel diameter (see Figure 4.13).

The angle α between the shaft centre line and the tangent to the helix at the mid-point of the wheel face is called the helix angle.

Now in a spur gear, the diametral plane, in which the forces T, P and S act, coincides with the plane normal to the

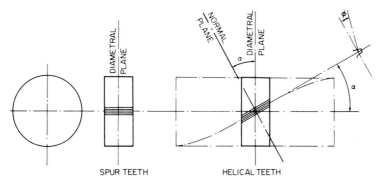

Figure 4.13 Spur teeth and helical teeth

tooth. In a helical gear, the normal plane, in which T, P and S act, is inclined to the diametral plane at an angle equal to the helix angle. This introduces an additional component force in the line of the shaft axis, i.e. it introduces end thrust. Turbine gears however are almost invariably made double-helical, i.e. each wheel is, in effect, two wheels mounted on the shaft, the helices of the two adjacent wheels being of opposite hand. With such an arrangement, the two end thrusts cancel one another, hence we need consider only the forces in the diametral plane.

The tooth pressure angle ϕ is in the normal plane, hence in a helical gear, the force P acts in the normal plane. If however, we attempt to observe the forces in the normal plane, the pitch circle of the wheel becomes an ellipse, and since by definition, the tangential force T, calculated from the power, speed and pitch circle diameter, must act in the diametral plane, and we must calculate all the forces as if they were in the diametral plane. To do this, we use quite a simple artifice, which consists of one operation only, viz, we first convert the tooth pressure angle ϕ in the normal plane into an equivalent pressure angle ϕ' in the diametral plane, and we can thence proceed as if all the forces P and S were acting in the diametral plane.

ϕ' is called the tooth pressure angle referred to the diametral plane or simply the tooth pressure angle in the diametral plane.

Referring to Figure 4.14, let α = helix angle of teeth in plane of common tangent, ϕ = tooth pressure angle in plane normal to tooth, ϕ' = tooth pressure angle in plane of wheel.

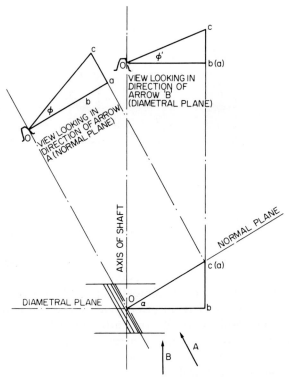

Figure 4.14 Tooth pressure angle referred to the diametral plane

From the plan, $ob = oa \cos \alpha$. From the view looking in direction of arrow 'A',

$$ac = oa \tan \phi$$

In the view looking in direction of arrow 'B',

$$\tan \phi' = \frac{ac}{ob} = \frac{oa \tan \phi}{oa \cos \alpha}$$

$$\therefore \tan \phi' = \frac{\tan \phi}{\cos \alpha}$$

Thus the tooth pressure angle in the diametral plane is ϕ' such that $\tan \phi' = \tan \phi / \cos \alpha$, where ϕ is the true pressure angle in the normal plane, and α is the helix angle. (Alternatively, we can write this relationship in the form $\phi' = \tan^{-1}$. $\tan \phi / \cos \alpha$, which has the same meaning.)

Since $\cos \alpha < 1.0$, $\tan \phi'$ is always greater than $\tan \phi$, and since ϕ increases as $\tan \phi$ increases, the pressure angle in the diametral plane is always greater than the pressure angle in the normal plane. Thus the force diagrams for a helical pinion and wheel will have the same appearance as shown in Figure 89, but the angle between T and P will be ϕ' instead of ϕ. For the same power, speeds and pitch circle diameters, the tangential force T is the same whether the gears are spur or helical.

If for example, the helix angle is $30°$ and the tooth pressure angle in the normal plane is $20°$, then

Tooth pressure angle in diametral plane =

$$= \tan^{-1} \frac{\tan 20°}{\cos 30°} = \tan^{-1} \frac{0.36397}{0.86603}$$

$$= \tan^{-1} 0.42027 = 22°48'$$

Gear bearing loads

Referring to Figure 4.12, the force P applied to the wheel has to be carried by the wheel shaft bearings, and the reaction force P' on the pinion has to be carried by the pinion shaft bearings. In addition, the wheel shaft bearings have to carry a vertically downward force G due to the mass of the wheel and its shaft, and the pinion bearings a vertically downward force G' due to the mass of the pinion shaft.

By drawing two triangles of forces for the pinion shaft therefore, we can find the magnitude and direction of the resultant reaction load R' which has to be carried by the pinion bearings for ahead and for astern running.

Depending on the arrangement of the turbines and gearing, there may be two or more pinions engaging with the same wheel. Each pinion is treated as described, to find the magnitude and direction of its bearing loads, due regard being had to its relative position around the wheel and to the direction of rotation.

The several forces applied by the pinions to the wheel, and the vertically downward force due to the mass of the wheel, are then applied in a polygon of forces at the wheel centre to determine the resultant ahead and astern loads on the wheel bearings.

The most satisfactory way of illustrating the procedure for determining gear bearing loads is to consider an actual numerical example. This we will do when considering an actual example of modern gearing.

Figure 4.15 (a) *Double-helical double-reduction articulated dual-tandem locked-train gear*

Figure 4.15 (b) *Double-helical double-reduction articulated locked-train gear*

Examples of modern turbine reduction gears

Figure 4.15(a) shows a modern double-helical double-reduction gear at an advanced stage of erection, and Figure 4.15(b) shows an outside view of the completed gear together with its turbines. This gear was designed and manufactured by Messrs G.E.C. Marine and Industrial Gears Ltd, Rugby, by whose courtesy it is illustrated and described below.

The gear is of the articulated, dual-tandem, locked-train type, transmitting 23 872 kW at a propeller speed of 1.3333 rev/s.

The technical particulars of the gear, relevant to our present purpose, are as follows.

Gear	H.P. primary pinion	H.P. primary wheel	L.P. primary pinion	L.P. primary wheel	H.P. sec. pinion	L.P. sec. pinion	Second-ary wheel
Power, kW	11936	5968	11936	5968	5968	5968	23972
Speed, rev/s	108.4	12.137	58.498	12.137	12.137	12.137	1.3333
Number of teeth	29	259	50	241	39	39	356
Circular pitch mm	23.34	23.34	23.34	23.34	36.858	36.858	36.858
Pitch circle dia, m	0.21264	1.899	0.3666	1.767	0.4575	0.4575	4.164
Helix angle	30°	30°	30°	30°	30°	30°	30°
Tooth pressure Angle in normal plane	20°	20°	20°	20°	20°	20°	20°
Face width	(2 × 209.55) + 76.2 gap				(2 × 460.375) + 101.6 gap		

Each turbine shaft is connected to its primary pinion shaft by a hollow spacer shaft or torque tube, the latter having at each end a flexible coupling of the membrane type, the principle of which is illustrated in Figure 4.16. The driving unit consists of a pack of thin steel plates clamped between two special washers at each bolt hole. The membrane pack is solidly bolted to the driving member at every second bolt, and to the driven member at each alternate bolt. There is thus no connection between the driving and driven members except through the membrane pack. The load is transmitted from the driving to the driven member by the membrane pack in tension between the bolt centres. The bolts are pre-tightened to a controlled torque to ensure that, in the plane

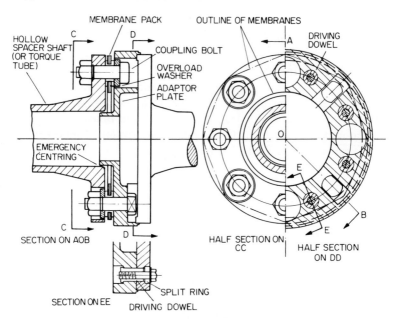

Figure 4.16 Membrane type flexible coupling

of the membrane pack, the driving load is transmitted by
friction in way of the membrane washers, thus ensuring that
no bending stresses are induced in the bolts. In this condition,
when cold, the torque tube and adaptor plate assembly is
slightly shorter than the distance between the turbine and
pinion coupling flanges when cold. When the setscrews (at
section EE) are tightened up therefore, the torque tube and
adaptor plate assembly as a whole is given a pre-stretch, so
that in the cold condition, the membranes are deflected
axially in the sense opposite to that in which they are deflected when the job is hot and the turbine shaft length is increased
by thermal expansion. The aim is to ensure that the membranes are not over-stressed by bending as a result of undue
deflection in one direction when hot.

The use of adaptor plates between the torque tube and the
turbine and pinion coupling flanges enables the torque tube,
membrane packs and adaptor plates to be assembled as a
unit, bolts torque-tightened, and the unit dynamically
balanced before fitting into place.

Since the driving and driven members are centred by the
membranes themselves, emergency centring is provided

between the hollow shaft and the adaptor plate to keep the coupling rotating reasonably concentrically while the shaft is brought to rest in the unlikely event of catastrophic failure of the membrane pack.

Couplings

Claw-type flexible couplings suffer from unpredictable friction forces between the teeth. Not only does this accelerate wear and necessitate adequate and continuous lubrication, but it can cause undesirable bending effects on the pinion shaft, and thus interfere with the tooth action. Membrane-type flexible couplings do not suffer from such friction forces, nor do they require any lubrication. Any relative axial movement between the shafts or any transverse misalignment is accommodated by flexing of the membranes. They have a high capacity for misalignment such as might be caused, for instance, by seating movement due to flexing of the ship's structure, and axial loading is readily controllable to safely accommodate turbine thermal expansion. It is for these reasons that membrane-type flexible couplings are being increasingly used.

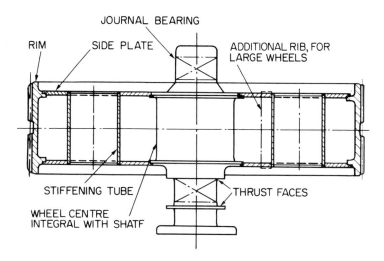

Figure 4.17 Construction of primary wheel

Gear wheels and pinions

The primary wheels are of fabricated construction as illustrated in Figure 4.17, the wheel centre being forged integral with the shaft. The wheel is stiffened by eight axial steel tubes welded to the side plates. This type of construction gives a strong and rigid wheel, which is not prone to any major structural vibration. As the fabricated wheel is a "sealed" cavity it is important that it should not contain any foreign matter, either solid or liquid, otherwise unbalance can result when running at speed.

Each primary wheel is connected to its secondary pinion by a quill shaft and flexible coupling arrangement which is illustrated in Figure 4.18.

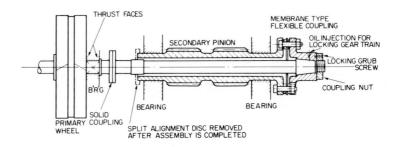

Figure 4.18 Intermediate quill shaft and flexible coupling

The forward end of the central shaft is solidly coupled to the intermediate wheel shaft, and the aft end is flexibly connected to the co-axial hollow shaft which is integral with the secondary pinion(s). The flexible coupling is of the membrane type, generally as already described. In the application shown in Figure 4.18, the driving member is carried on a conical seat on the central shaft. The cones have a taper of 1 in 16 on the diameter with an interference of 0.002 mm per 1.0 mm of diameter, which when the driving member is finally assembled on the shaft, is adequate to transmit the torque from the shaft to the driving member without the use of keys. If, during assembly, the driving member were to be directly pressed on to the shaft against this interference, the axial force required would be very large—in this particular case, it would be 5500 kN. Mention has already been made of the need to provide for some small relative rotation of the intermediate shaft during erection to ensure that all the gear contacts are properly made so that the load will be correctly shared among them. This relative rotation must actually take place between the shaft and the driving member of the flexible coupling, and with all the gear components in position. In Figure 4.18, the driving member of the flexible coupling is provided with a connection whereby very high-pressure oil can be injected, thus temporarily relieving the force fit between the cones and allowing the driving member to be pressed on or off the shaft by an axial force of about one tenth of the above "dry" axial force, i.e. a force which can be readily exerted by a portable hydraulic jack.

When assembling the gears, the driving member of the flexible coupling is initially mounted on the shaft with the cones in only very light contact with one another. This allows (*a*), the primary wheel to be rotated relatively to the primary and secondary pinions, thus to obtain correct gear contact between the primary pinion and primary wheel, and (*b*), the secondary pinion to be rotated relatively to the primary and secondary wheels, thus to obtain correct gear contact between the secondary pinion and secondary wheel. When all the gear contacts are properly made, an oil injection pump is operated to expand the conical bore of the driving member of the flexible coupling, and at the same time, the hydraulic jack is operated to force the driving member axially on to the shaft. When the driving member is in the correct axial position, the oil pressure is released, thus restoring the full interference fit between the coupling and shaft cones. The axial force exerted by the hydraulic jack is then released, the jack removed, and the coupling nut tightened and locked by the grub screw.

The split alignment disc is always fitted before the intermediate shaft is lifted from its bearings, but it must be removed after reassembly and alignment is completed.

The secondary wheel is of the same type of fabricated steel construction as the primary wheels, but being much larger, an additional rib is welded in between the side plates in way of each stiffening tube.

Up until about fifteen years ago, "through-hardened"

materials, viz. carbon steel wheel rims and nickel steel pinions were in almost universal use for marine turbine gears, and indeed are still quite widely used.

There are three factors which determine the suitability of a pinion/gear tooth material combination:

(i)   Surface strength, i.e. the ability of the material to resist pitting or flaking.
(ii) Tooth bending fatigue strength, i.e. the ability of the material to resist fracture at or about the root of the tooth due to cyclical application and removal of the tooth load.
(iii) Lubrication failure, i.e. the ability of the material to resist scuffing or scoring due to short-term lubrication failure.

Important advances in research, made in the early sixties, showed that from all these viewpoints, the best possible technique is to have both the pinion and wheel rim carburised, and subsequently ground to remove any distortion caused by the carburising process. This technique however, is very expensive and difficult to carry out, particularly on large diameter gears.

The gears illustrated in Figure 4.15, are designed on the "hard-on-soft" principle, which is a good compromise between the traditional through-hardened materials for both pinion and wheel and the ideal of carburised and ground pinion and wheel.

Briefly, the hard-on-soft principle means that after the gears are hobbed and shaved, the pinions only are surface-hardened by the nitriding process. The pinion shaft is heated up in an atmosphere of free nitrogen—the latter supplied by cracking of ammonia gas. The nitrogen combines with the alloying elements in the steel to give a very hard surface, with practically no distortion of the shaft or teeth. Subsequent grinding is therefore unnecessary, i.e. the relevant manufacturing operations on the pinion are hobbing, shaving, nitriding, and on the wheel, hobbing, shaving.

The hard-on-soft technique results, typically, in surface hardnesses of the order of 630–700 Brinell for the pinion teeth and 250–300 Brinell for the wheel teeth.

Nitriding of the pinion only means that the process is carried out only on the smaller item, which is quite con-

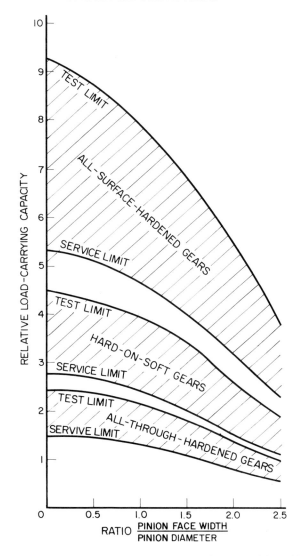

Figure 4.19 Relative load-carrying capacity with various material combinations

venient and economic, and is also logical on the grounds that
in service a pinion tooth comes round considerably more
often than a wheel tooth.

The curves in Figure 4.19 show the relative load-carrying
capacity of the three techniques. These indicate clearly the
advantage of the intermediate hard-on-soft principle compared with through-hardened gears.

As pointed out previously, when a reduction gear is in service, the shafts are subjected to twisting due to the torque, and to bending due to the tooth loads and bearing reactions. This combined bending and twisting, more particularly of the secondary pinion shaft, causes some distortion of the latter which tends to throw the load towards the outer ends of the teeth, and to counteract this effect, the helix angle is "corrected", and the shaving operation is adjusted so that rather more material is shaved off towards the outside of the teeth.

The disposition of the gears in the thwartship plane is shown in Figure 4.20, and from this and the table of technical particulars, the bearing loads may be illustrated as follows, using the methods previously described. For brevity, we will carry out the detailed calculations only for ahead running.

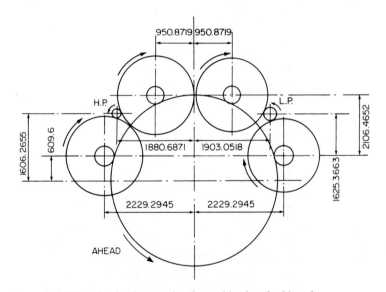

Figure 4.20 View of reduction gear in athwartship plane looking aft

H.P. TURBINE, Ahead full power, 11 936 kW at 108.4 rev/s

∴ H.P. turbine primary pinion shaft torque =

$$\frac{11\,936}{2\pi \times 108.4} = 17.526 \text{ kN m}$$

This is a dual-tandem locked-train gear, hence the primary pinion has two gear contacts, each contact dealing with one half of the torque, i.e.

$$\text{Torque} = \frac{17.526}{2} = 8.763 \text{ kNm}$$

The pitch circle diameter of the primary pinion is 0.21264 m, hence tangential force T between the primary pinion and the primary wheel is

$$T = \frac{8.763 \times 2}{0.21264} = 82.43 \text{ kN}$$

The tooth pressure angle ϕ in the normal plane is $20°$ and the tooth helix angle α is $30°$, hence tooth pressure angle in the diametral plane

$$\phi' = \tan^{-1} \frac{\tan \phi}{\cos \alpha} = \tan^{-1} \frac{0.36397}{0.86603} = \tan^{-1} 0.42027 =$$

$$= 22°48', \text{ and}$$

Tooth load along line of action in the diametral plane

$$P = \frac{T}{\cos \phi'} = \frac{82.43}{\cos 22° \, 48'} = \frac{82.43}{0.92186} = 89.42 \text{ kN}$$

The vertically downward force due to the mass of the primary pinion shaft, $G = 2.86$ kN, which we may assume concentrated at the centre line between faces.

The two forces P and the force G are set down as a polygon of forces (See Figure 4.21(a)), from which the resultant force R is obtained. From the diagram, $R = 66.8$ kN. The two bearings, and the two helical tooth faces of the pinion are symmetrical about the centre line between the faces, hence the resultant force R is shared equally between the two pinion faces, and between the two bearings. The primary pinion shaft may therefore be considered as a beam, simply supported at the bearing centres and carrying a concentrated load at the centre of each face, from which follows the maximum bending moment on the shaft. The combined effects of

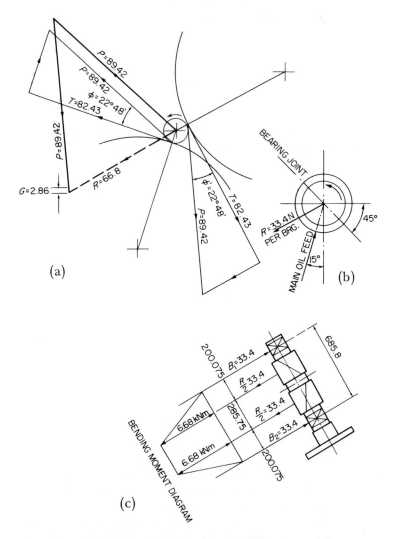

Figure 4.21 Tooth loads and bearing reactions for H.P. primary pinion

this bending and of twisting (due to the torque), together with the shaft diameters and the physical properties of the shaft material determine the strength and the stiffness of the shaft, and to what extent the helix angle has to be "corrected" and the shaving operation modified to compensate for the shaft deflection when under load.

Each bearing is 152.4 mm dia. and 101.6 mm long, hence the projected area of one bearing = (152.4 × 101.6)/(100) = 154.85 cm^2, and the bearing surface pressure = (33.4 × 1000)/ (154.85) = 215.72 N/cm^2, see Figure 4.21(b).

The H.P. primary pinion bearing shells are arranged as shown in Figure 4.21(c).

The forces acting on the intermediate shaft can be rather more complicated, since they act in two different planes. In the present case however, the intermediate shaft has four bearings, which has the effect of virtually separating almost completely the primary wheel bearing load from the second-ary pinion bearing load. The intermediate shaft is in fact a quill shaft (see Figure 4.18) hence it will be obvious that the mass of the central solid shaft is carried jointly by the aft bearing of the primary wheel and the aft bearing of the secondary pinion. For our purpose we will assume that the mass of the central shaft is shared equally by the four bear-ings—no significant error will result.

The tangential force 82.43 kN is common to the primary pinion and primary wheel, hence the tooth force P in the line of action is also the same viz, 89.42 kN but for the wheel, the sense of these forces is opposite to that for the pinion.

The pitch circle diameter of the primary wheel is 1.899 m, and that of the secondary pinion is 0.4575 m, hence the tan-gential force between the secondary pinion and the secondary wheel is

$$T = 82.43 \times \frac{1.899}{0.4575} = 342.2 \text{ kN, and}$$

$$\text{the tooth force in the line of action, } P = \frac{342.2}{0.92186} =$$

$$= 371.2 \text{ kN}$$

The downward forces due to the masses are, primary wheel 33.3 kN, secondary pinion 13.087 kN, central solid shaft 8.38 kN, hence using the assumption stated above, primary wheel G = 33.3 + 4.19 = 37.49 kN, secondary pinion G = 13.087 + 4.19 = 17.277 kN.

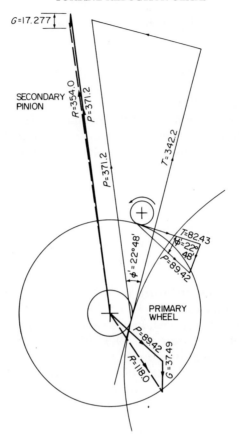

Figure 4.22 Tooth loads and bearing reactions for lower H.P. intermediate shaft

Figure 4.22 shows the triangles of forces for the primary wheel and secondary pinion of the lower intermediate shaft, from which the resultant forces are found, viz,

Primary wheel, R = 118.0 kN, Secondary pinion R = 354.0

The primary wheel and secondary pinion are each symmetrical about their own bearings, hence each 228.6 dia 127.0 long wheel bearing carries 59.0 kN, and the bearing pressure is

$$\frac{59.0 \times 1000 \times 100}{228.6 \times 127} = 203.0 \text{ N/cm}^2$$

Each 381.0 dia 254.0 long pinion bearing carries 177.0 kN, and the bearing pressure is

$$\frac{177.0 \times 1000 \times 100}{381.0 \times 254.0} = 182.0 \text{ N/cm}^2$$

The bending moments on the shaft are found by the means already described.

The upper H.P. intermediate shaft is treated in the same manner, but drawing the line of action in the appropriate direction. This results in the diagram shown in Figure 4.23.

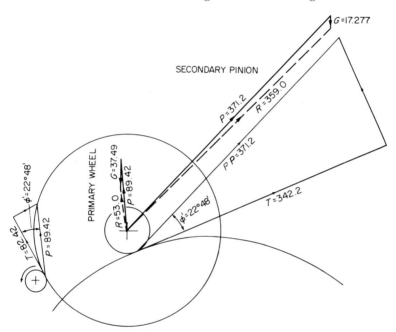

Figure 4.23 Tooth loads and bearing reactions for upper H.P. intermediate shaft

The L.P. primary pinion, primary wheels and secondary pinions also are treated in the same way using the appropriate values and lines of action between the teeth. This results in the following:

L.P. TURBINE   Ahead full power 11 936 kW at 58.493 rev/s.

∴ L.P. turbine primary pinion shaft torque

$$= \frac{11\,936}{2\pi \times 58.493} = 32.48 \text{ kNm}$$

i.e. Torque $= \dfrac{32.48}{2} = 16.24$ kNm/gear contact

Pitch circle diameter of primary pinion $= 0.3666$ m
Tangential force between primary pinion and primary wheel

$$T = \frac{16.24 \times 2}{0.3666} = 88.6 \text{ kN}$$

Tooth load along line of action in diametral plane

$$P = \frac{88.6}{0.92186} = 96.1 \text{ kN}$$

Primary pinion $G = 6.2$ kN

Pitch circle diameter of primary wheel $= 1.7671$ m

Pitch circle diameter of secondary pinion $= 0.4575$ m
Tangential force between secondary pinion and secondary wheel

$$T = 88.6 \times \frac{1.7671}{0.4575} = 342.2 \text{ kN}$$

$$P = \frac{342.2}{0.92186} = 371.2 \text{ kN}$$

Primary wheel $G = 37.49$ kN
Secondary pinion $G = 17.277$ kN

Figure 4.24 shows the force diagram for the L.P. primary pinion, and Figures 4.25 and 4.26 the force diagrams for the lower and the upper L.P. primary wheel and secondary pinion respectively. The bearing pressures and the bending moments on the intermediate shaft are found by the same general method as described for the H.P. primary pinion shaft.

The four secondary pinions each apply a force of 371.2 kN to the secondary wheel as shown in Figure 4.27. These four forces, and the vertically downward force $G = 333.5$ kN due to the mass of the secondary wheel and its shaft are set down in polygon of forces—also shown in Figure 4.27—from which the resultant load, $R = 1\,035$ kN, on the secondary wheel bearings is found.

A similar procedure is used for the astern bearing loads, using the appropriate torque, speed, tooth forces and lines of action.

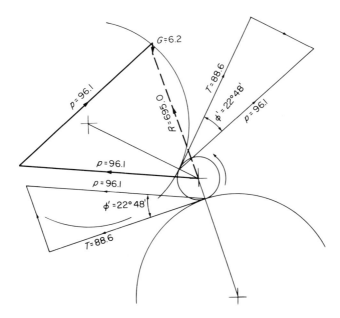

Figure 4.24 Tooth loads and bearing reactions for L.P. primary pinion

The bearing shells are of split cylindrical form, the two halves being dowelled to one another and to the bearing housing. The shells are of steel lined with white metal, and are provided with oil channels and reliefs positioned so that the oil will be carried round to the load point. The intermediate shaft flexible coupling does not give sufficiently positive axial location to prevent possible excessive movement of the primary wheel and consequently of the primary pinion, which could lead to possible damage to the turbine shaft flexible coupling. The intermediate shaft is therefore positively located in the axial direction by thrust faces provided at the forward and aft ends of the primary wheel aft bearing shell (see Figure 4.18).

As a result of continuing research into journal lubrication and bearing behaviour, modern gear bearings—and turbine

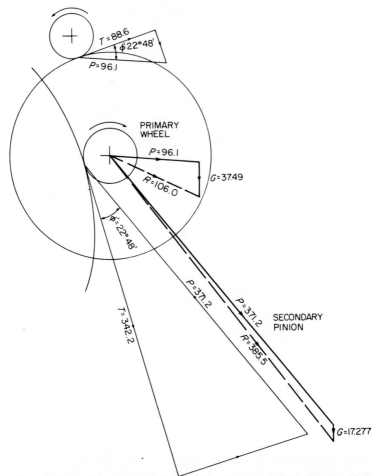

Figure 4.25 Tooth loads and bearing reactions for lower L.P. intermediate shaft

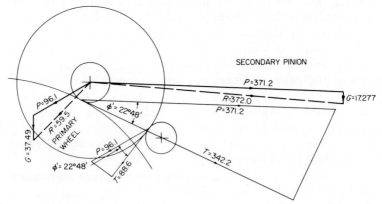

Figure 4.26 Tooth loads and bearing reactions for upper L.P. intermediate shaft

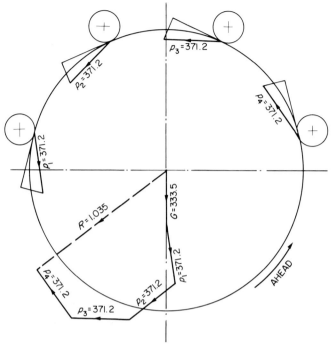

Figure 4.27 Ahead main gear bearing loads

bearings–have length to diameter ratio of 0.55–0.65 compared with 1.25–2.0 in the older designs.

All the bearing loads have to be carried by the gear case structure, and it is preferable that the structure should, so far as is possible and practicable, carry these loads within itself, i.e. so that the residual forces and moments at the gear case supports are kept to a minimum; also, there should be no undue deflection of the gear case structure in any plane. It is also preferable that no external forces from propeller thrust or ship's structure should be imposed on the gear case.

Some conception of the gear case ahead loading may be had by reference to Figure 4.28. Not only do the bearing loads all have different directions in the elevation, but they act nominally in two different thwartship planes, as shown in the plan view. The combined effect is quite complex, and may perhaps be best understood by imagining each bearing load to be replaced by a vertical component and a horizontal component, the combined effects of all the vertical components and of all the horizontal components being considered separately. In this way, the gear case can be considered in

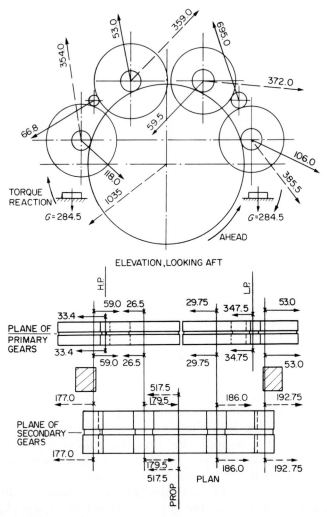

Figure 4.28 Forces acting on gear case structure

each separate plane for strength, stiffness and reaction at the supports.

Traditionally, the gear case was split, with a horizontal joint at the centre line of the secondary wheel, all the pinion and gear bearing housings being integral with the gear case structure. The gear case illustrated in Figure 4.15 departs somewhat from this concept in so far that the horizontal joint is located above the centre line of the secondary wheel (see Figure 4.29(a)). The bottom half of the gear case is a substantial fabrication, accommodating the bearings for the

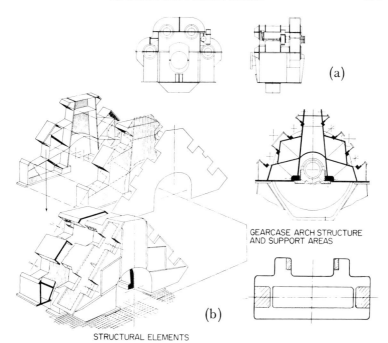

(a)

GEARCASE ARCH STRUCTURE
AND SUPPORT AREAS

(b)

STRUCTURAL ELEMENTS

Figure 4.29 Two piece and single piece gear cases

secondary wheel, and for both the lower intermediate shafts. The top half of the gear case—clearly seen in Figure 4.15(a)— is a fabricated structure carrying the bearings of both the upper intermediate shafts. The enclosure of the top half is completed by relatively light steel covers.

The mass of the gear case structure is 58 000 kg and of the complete reduction gear 116 000 kg. Table 4.1 shows the materials of the major components.

Table 4.1 **Materials of major components**

Component	C	Si	Mn	Ni	Cr	Mo	U.T.S. min kN/ cm^2
Primary and secondary pinions	0.2–0.3	0.1–0.35	0.4–0.65	0.4	2.9–3.5	0.4–0.7	93.0
Primary and secondary wheel rims	0.35–0.4	0.1–0.35	1.3–1.8			0.2–0.35	77.5
Intermediate and main wheel shafts	0.17–0.23	0.05–0.35	0.6–1.0				43.5
Flexible shafts	0.27–0.35	0.1–0.35	0.5–0.7	2.3–2.8	0.5–0.8	0.4–0.7	85.0

Figure 4.29(b) illustrates another more recent gear case also designed and manufactured by Messrs G.E.C. Marine and Industrial Gears Ltd, Rugby. It is for a 32 824 kW double-reduction gear, and certain novel principles have been used to the extent that the gear case design can be regarded as entirely new.

The gear case is primarily a fabricated steel structure of minimum size and maximum rigidity, designed primarily from the load-carrying aspect. It connects together all the interacting loads at the various bearings and support points, and achieves this purpose regardless of any potentially damaging external influences, e.g. movement of ship's structure. In this conception, the gears may be regarded as being grouped around the structure—rather than the gear case enclosing the gears—and the "oil tank" aspect is completed by simple light covers forming an enclosure.

The structure is basically of "arch" form, the two main members consisting of closed box sections formed from inherently open frames. Thus while the structure as a whole is very rigid, there exists some internal flexibility, i.e. in the planes in which the bearing loads act, which accommodate any slight deviations from correct tooth contact. The structure is supported under each "leg" of the arch on a plane which is close below the centre line of the secondary wheel, and it is through these local areas, where the support chocks are fitted, that the major parts of the dead load due to the mass and the live load due to the residual torque reaction are transmitted to the ship's structure. These relatively small-area supports, so positioned, minimise the effect on the gear case of any movement of the hull structure, which in these days of very large ships is known to be not uncommon. The two additional small support areas at the foward end are to assist in erection and lining-out—they are not functionally required by the gear case. With this type of gear case, it is necessary to erect completely in the manufacturer's works and install in the ship as a unit. Lifting points on the gear case are very simple and secure, the main near-vertical webs extending through the structure to form lifting eyes.

All the bearing housings are separate from, and are bolted to, the structure, the primary pinion and the intermediate shaft bearing housings being adjustable to permit correction of any misalignment occurring in service. The main wheel bearings are secured in such a manner that they virtually become integral parts of the gear case structure. Both vertical and horizontal bolting is used, the bolts being pre-tensioned by heat-tightening to a stress of 154.0 N/mm^2 for the vertical, and 308.0 N/mm^2 for the horizontal bolts, which represent factors of 10.0 and 4.5 respectively over the calculated static and dynamic forces occurring in service. In some cases, where required by the classification society, safety dowels and keys are fitted as additional protection.

Figure 4.30 New design of gear case during fabrication

An interesting view of the structure fabrication is shown in Figure 4.30, and complete reduction gears of this type in Figures 3.62 and 3.63 (Chapter 3).

This represents quite an advanced design of what we may call orthodox parallel-shaft gears, and the use of these techniques provides quite some scope for further development of orthodox gears into larger sizes, powers and reduction ratios should this prove necessary.

EPICYCLIC GEARS

It is often said that a turbine reduction gear costs as much to build, and occupies as much space as the turbines themselves. Whether or not this is true, there can be no doubt that the reduction gear is a large and costly item (see Chapter 3, Figures 3.1, 3.58 and 3.62).

In recent years, epicyclic gearing has been used for some marine turbines instead of the more orthodox single or double-reduction double-helical gears. In some cases, part of the reduction gear has been made epicyclic and part traditional. The main advantage of epicyclic gearing is that if it is judiciously designed, the reduction gear unit can be quite compact, resulting in a worthwhile saving in the space occupied. It is not possible to cover every aspect in a book of this nature, but it is hoped that the following notes will explain the principles involved, and illustrate the features of epicyclic gearing.

Simple gear

Consider the simple ordinary gear shown in Figure 4.31(a). Let each of the two wheels S and P have the same number of teeth. The gear case A is fixed. Hence if the wheel S makes one revolution in the clockwise direction, the wheel P will make one revolution in the counter-clockwise direction.

Let us now imagine the gearcase to be replaced by a link or arm A, which maintains the correct centre distance between

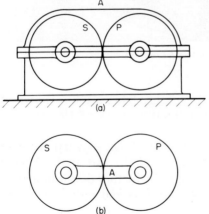

Figure 4.31 Simple gear

the wheels, i.e. the arm itself is fixed, but allows each wheel to rotate on its own axis (Figure 3.31(b)). If we nominate clockwise rotation as positive, and counter-clockwise rotation as negative, then in the example just considered, we can say that with A fixed, A makes zero revolutions, the wheel S makes one positive revolution and the wheel P makes one negative revolution, or we can write

$$\text{With } A \text{ fixed} \quad A = 0, \quad S = +1, \quad P = -1 \qquad (1)$$

Simple epicyclic gear

Now suppose that instead of fixing A, we fix S, and cause A to make one counter-clockwise revolution about the centre of S. The radius of the arm is equal to the pitch diameter, d say, of a wheel, hence as A makes one counter-clockwise revolution about the centre of S, the centre of P moves through a distance $2\pi d$. Since the free wheel P and the fixed wheel S remain in gear, the free wheel P will rotate on its own axis in the counter-clockwise direction, and a point on its pitch circle will move through a distance $2\pi d$ (just as if the wheel were rolled on a flat surface through a distance $2\pi d$.) Since the circumference of its pitch circle is πd, the free wheel P will make $2\pi d/\pi d = 2$ counter-clockwise revolutions about its own axis in the time that the arm makes one counter-clockwise revolution about the centre of S (see Figure 4.32).

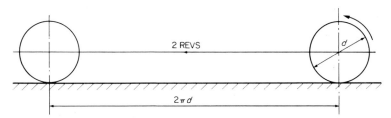

Figure 4.32 Equivalent revolutions of P

While this approach is reasonably easy to follow for the simple gear chosen, it becomes too difficult if we attempt to apply it to more complicated gears, hence we have to find a means of readily determining, with certainty, the speed ratios and directions of rotation for any gear.

Again consider the simple gear in Figure 3.31(b) for which we have determined the basis relationship (1):

With A fixed $A = 0$, $S = +1$, $P = -1$ (1)

Now again suppose that instead of fixing A, we fix S, i.e. we make $S = 0$. In order to make $S = 0$ in the relationship (1) we have to subtract +1, (i.e. we have to add −1). If however, we add −1 to S, we must, in order to retain the basis identities expressed by (1), also add −1 to A and to P, thus,

With A fixed $A = 0$ $S = +1$ $P = -1$ (1)
                      -1 -1 -1

With S fixed $A = -1$ $S = 0$ $P = -2$ (2)

Thus, if we fix the wheel S, and cause the arm A to make one counter-clockwise revolution about the centre of S, then the wheel P will make two counter-clockwise revolutions about its own axis. This result is exactly the same as that deduced above.

Figure 4.31(b), operating in this manner, is a simple epicyclic gear, i.e. a gear in which the arm A is not stationary, as it is in an ordinary gear, but itself revolves about the principle centre of rotation. The wheel whose axis is at the principle centre of rotation (wheel S in the example) is called the *sun* wheel, and the wheel whose centre revolves round the principle centre of rotation (wheel P in the example) is called the planet wheel. These names, based on analogy with the solar system, are in quite general use, as are the symbols S, P and A. An epicycle is a circle which rolls, without slipping on the circumference of another circle called the base circle, hence the general term epicyclic gears for gears which function in this manner. Formerly, epicyclic gears were sometimes called planetary gears, but this term is now used only for a particular form of epicyclic gear.

The simple epicyclic gear shown in Figure 4.31(b) and the derived relationship (2) illustrate rather clearly the quite simple artifice by which any epicyclic gear may be studied readily and with certainty. The artifice consists of *always* first imagining the arm to be fixed, i.e. as it is in an ordinary orthodox gear, thus enabling the basis speed ratios and

directions of rotation to be determined as in the relationship
(1) above. The procedure leading to any other relationship
such as (2) then follows quite readily provided the correct
signs are used throughout. Clockwise rotation is always +.
Counter-clockwise rotation is always −.

Simple practical epicyclic gear

The simple epicyclic gear shown in Figure 4.31(b) would be
of no use to us in practice. We can drive the arm, but there is
no output shaft.

Suppose that to the simple arrangement shown in Figure
4.31(b) we add a fourth member in the form of an internal-
teeth gear meshing with the planet wheel P. The internal-teeth
gear is called the annulus, or ring, which we will denote by R.
Referring to Figure 4.33, the centre of R coincides with the
principle centre of rotation (i.e. the centre of the sun), hence
the pitch diameter of R must be three times that of S or P.

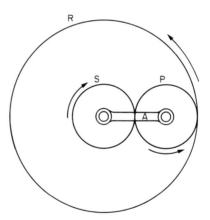

Figure 4.33 Simple practical epicyclic
gear

Adopting the procedure previously explained, first let the
arm A be fixed, and let S make one clockwise revolution. P
will make one counter-clockwise revolution, and R will make
one third of a counter-clockwise revolution.

We can therefore set down the basis relationship thus

$$\textit{With A fixed} \quad A = 0 \quad S = +1 \quad P = -1 \quad R = -\tfrac{1}{3} \tag{1}$$

Thus if we fix A, with the input shaft driving S, then R
will drive the coaxial output shaft at one third of the speed

of the input shaft, and in the opposite direction. The reduction gear ratio from S to R is -3.

This arrangement of epicyclic gear, when the arm is fixed, is called a star gear. The direction arrows in Figure 4.33 refer to this mode of operation.

Now let R be fixed instead of A, i.e add $+\frac{1}{3}$ to every term in (1)

With A fixed, $A = 0$ $S = +1$ $P = -1$ $R = -\frac{1}{3}$

              $+\frac{1}{3}$ $+\frac{1}{3}$ $+\frac{1}{3}$ $+\frac{1}{3}$

With R fixed, $A = +\frac{1}{3}$ $S = +\frac{4}{3}$ $P = -\frac{2}{3}$ $R = 0$

If we multiply throughout by $+3$, we can express the speed of A as unity without having altered the speed ratios and still keeping $R = 0$, viz.

With R fixed $A = +1$ $S = +4$ $P = -2$ $R = 0$

Thus if we fix R, with the input shaft driving S, then A will drive the coaxial output shaft at one quarter of the speed of the input shaft, and in the same direction. By fixing R instead of A, we have increased the gear ratio from -3 to $+4$ without having increased the overall dimensions. When the ring is fixed, the gear is called a planetary gear.

Now let S be fixed instead of A, i.e. add -1 to every term in (1)

With A fixed $A = 0$ $S = +1$ $P = -1$ $R = -\frac{1}{3}$

            -1 -1 -1 -1

         $A = -1$ $S = 0$ $P = -2$ $R = -\frac{4}{3}$

If we multiply throughout by $\frac{3}{4}$ we can express the speed of R as unity, viz.

With S fixed $A = -\frac{3}{4}$ $S = 0$ $P = -\frac{3}{2}$ $R = -1$

Thus, if we fix S, with the input shaft driving R, then A will drive the coaxial output shaft at three quarters of the speed of the input shaft, and in the same direction. When the sun is fixed, the gear is called a solar gear.

It is not necessary of course that the sun and planet wheels should have equal pitch circle diameters (equal numbers of teeth)—we can make these whatever we wish, to obtain the largest possible gear ratio within the given space, or, what is more important, to achieve the smallest possible space for a given gear ratio. Let us see what can be done within the overall dimensions of Figure 4.33.

In Figure 4.33, suppose S and P each to have 60 teeth, then it follows that R must have 60 × 3 = 180 teeth. In order to maintain the same overall diameter, let the ring in Figure 4.34 have 180 teeth, but let S have 30 teeth and P have 75 teeth. Note: $R = 2 (S/2 + P)$, i.e. $R = 2 (60/2 + 60) = 180$, or $R = 2 (30/2 + 75) = 180$.

Referring to Figure 4.34, first let A be fixed, and let S make one clockwise revolution, i.e.

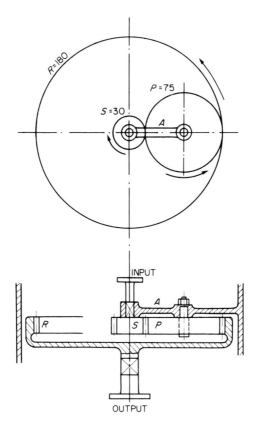

Figure 4.34 Epicyclic star gear

With A fixed

$$A = 0, \quad S = +1, \quad P = -\tfrac{30}{75} = -\tfrac{2}{5}, \quad R = \left(-\tfrac{2}{5}\right) \times \left(+\tfrac{75}{180}\right) = -\tfrac{1}{6}$$

$$(1)$$

Thus if we fix A with the input shaft driving S, then R will drive the output shaft at one sixth of the speed of the input shaft, and in the opposite direction. The gear is a star gear, and by altering S from 60 to 30 teeth, and P from 60 teeth to 75 teeth we have increased the gear ratio to -6 without having increased the overall dimensions.

Now let R be fixed instead of A, i.e add $+\tfrac{1}{6}$ to every term in (1) above. Refer to Figure 4.35.

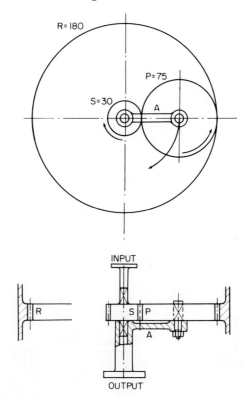

Figure 4.35 Epicyclic planetary gear

With A fixed, $\quad A = 0, \quad S = +1, \quad P = -\tfrac{2}{5}, \quad R = -\tfrac{1}{6}$
$\qquad\qquad\qquad\quad +\tfrac{1}{6} \qquad\quad +\tfrac{1}{6} \qquad +\tfrac{1}{6} \qquad\quad +\tfrac{1}{6}$

With R fixed, $\quad A = +\tfrac{1}{6} \quad S = +\tfrac{7}{6}, \quad P = -\tfrac{7}{30}, \quad R = 0,$

and multiplying throughout by +6 gives

With R fixed, $A = +1, \quad S = +7, \quad P = -\frac{7}{5}, \quad R = 0.$

Thus, if we fix R with the input shaft driving S, then A will drive the co-axial output shaft at one seventh of the speed of the input shaft, and in the same direction. The gear

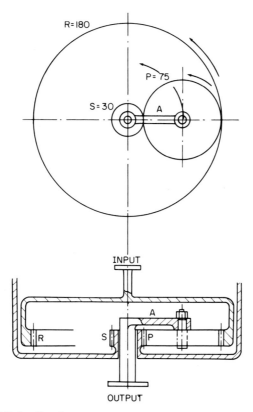

Figure 4.36 Epicyclic solar gear

is a planetary gear, and by using 30 and 75 teeth respectively in the sun and planet wheels, we have increased the gear ratio to +7 without having increased the overall dimensions.

Now let S be fixed instead of A, i.e. add -1 to every term in (1) above. Refer to Figure 4.36.

With A fixed, $\quad A = 0, \quad S = +1, \quad P = -\frac{2}{5}, \quad R = -\frac{1}{6}$
$$\qquad\qquad\qquad -1 \qquad\quad -1 \qquad\quad -1 \qquad\quad -1$$

With S fixed, $\quad A = -1, \quad S = 0, \quad P = -\frac{7}{5}, \quad R = -\frac{7}{6},$

and multiplying throughout by $\frac{6}{7}$ gives

With S fixed, $\quad A = -\frac{6}{7}, \quad S = 0, \quad P = -\frac{6}{5}, \quad R = -1$

Thus if we fix S, with the input shaft driving R, then A will drive the co-axial output shaft at six sevenths of the speed of the input shaft, and in the same direction. The gear is a solar gear, and by using 30 and 75 teeth respectively in the sun and planet wheels, we have a gear ratio of only +6/7 within the same overall dimensions as will give a gear ratio of --6 if arranged star, or +7 if arranged planetary.

From the foregoing example, it will be evident that there are many ways in which the simple epicyclic gear may be varied to give different speed ratios within the chosen overall dimensions. We may vary the numbers of teeth in the sun and planet wheels; we may fix either the arm (star gear), or the ring (planetary gear), or the sun (solar gear). The fixed member, whichever it may be, is called the *torque reaction member,* e.g. if the arm is fixed, it has to carry the reactions to the forces acting between the wheel teeth. The simple epicyclic gear, described in principle in the foregoing notes, forms the unit on which modern marine epicyclic gears are based, using either the star, planetary or solar modes, or some combination of these to suit the conditions.

The simple epicyclic gear illustrated in Figures 4.34, 4.35 and 4.36 may be regarded as a single-reduction gear. If arranged star as in Figure 4.34, it gives a reduction ratio of --6; if arranged planetary as in Figure 4.35, it gives a reduction ratio of +7. If two such gears be used, with the output shaft of the first connected to the input shaft of the second, then the arrangement is a double-reduction gear. For example, consider the primary reduction to be the star gear illustrated in Figure 4.34 having a reduction ratio of --6, and the secondary reduction to be the planetary gear illustrated in Figure 4.35, having a reduction ratio of +7.

The two gears together, illustrated in Figure 4.37, form a double-reduction epicyclic gear of the star/planetary mode, having a total reduction ratio of $(-6) \times (+7) = -42$.

In this example, we have assumed that the sun, planet and ring of the secondary reduction have the same numbers of teeth as the sun, planet and ring of the primary reduction; we

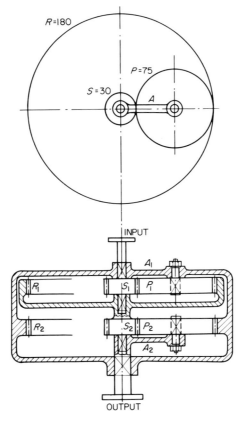

Figure 4.37 Double-reduction epicyclic gear (star/planetary mode)

have assumed the primary reduction to be a star gear $(A_1$ fixed) and the secondary reduction to be a planetary gear $(R_2$ fixed). In practice of course the numbers of teeth in the primary and secondary reductions may be varied, and the fixed members may be changed to suit the particular conditions.

We could also use three such gears in series thus making a triple-reduction epicyclic gear, again choosing the fixed members and the numbers of teeth to suit the particular conditions.

This arrangement, in principle, is in quite general use for modern turbine epicyclic reduction gears.

Note that in going from single to double or triple reduction, the overall *length* of the gear is increased.

The foregoing notes and diagrams attempt to deal only

with principles. Of the mechanical details of construction, one point in particular is necessary of special mention. In each example so far, we have considered the arm actually as a single arm carrying one planet wheel. In principle of course this is perfectly correct, but in practice, would be quite un-acceptable, particularly in a planetary or solar gear where the arm itself rotates. If we use a single rotating arm carrying a single planet wheel, the planet wheel generates a centrifugal force which is transmitted to the arm via the planet wheel bearings. The arm itself also generates a centrifugal force, hence the combined centrifugal force of the arm and planet wheel is imposed on the main bearings at the principal centre of rotation as an unbalanced revolving force. A double-reduction gear could have two such arms revolving in differ-ent planes, thus also imposing an unbalanced revolving couple on the gear case.

So far as the gear case itself is concerned, the centrifugal forces can be balanced by the use of multiple planet wheels, i.e. two, three, four, five, six, or more planet wheels are used, each in principle having its own arm, all the arms being rigidly fixed together to form a frame, or spider, or planet carrier.

This principle, illustrated in Figure 4.38, not only balances the centrifugal forces, but balances the forces acting between the wheel teeth so that the only load imposed on the main bearings is the vertically downward force due to the mass of the gears and shafts. Further, the total driving load is carried by a greater number of gear contacts, hence a greater propor-tion of the total number of teeth are in mesh, and therefore for a given torque, the individual tooth loads are reduced.

While the use of multiple planet wheels relieves the main bearings of any unbalanced centrifugal force, the centrifugal force of each planet wheel within the planet carrier remains unbalanced, and has to be carried by the planet wheel bear-ings. Now the centrifugal force varies directly as the square of the rotational speed, hence if a rotating planet carrier is used on the primary reduction of a turbine gear, the high speed will result in large centrifugal loads on the planet wheel bearings.

A rotating arm, or each arm of a multiple planet carrier, must not only be strong enough to withstand the centrifugal force, but it must be stiff enough to do so without significant stretch in the radial direction, otherwise the meshing of the planet wheel teeth with the sun wheel teeth and the ring teeth will be incorrect.

It is for these reasons that the primary reduction of a turbine gear is almost invariably made a star gear, i.e. fixed planet carrier. The planet carrier itself is almost invarably of the type shown in Figure 4.38(c), whether it is fixed or rotating.

The use of multiple planet wheels in no way affects the calculation of the speed ratios which is always carried out as if there was one planet wheel only.

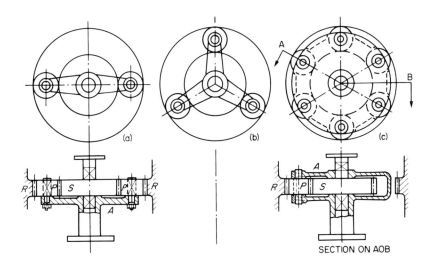

Figure 4.38 Multiple planet wheels
(a) Two planet wheels
(b) Three planet wheels
(c) Six planet wheels

It should however be particularly noted that where equally spaced multiple planet wheels are to be used, it is an essential condition for correct assembly that $(S + R)/n$ is an integer (i.e. a whole number), where S and R are the numbers of teeth in the sun and ring respectively, and n is the number of planets. This feature is referred to again later in this chapter.

DOUBLE-REDUCTION EPICYCLIC GEAR

Figure 4.39 shows a longitudinal section through a double-reduction epicyclic gear transmitting 3800 kW from a turbine shaft speed of 142.5 rev/s to an output shaft speed of 12.5 rev/s.

This gear was designed and manufactured by Messrs W.H. Allen, Sons & Co. Ltd.

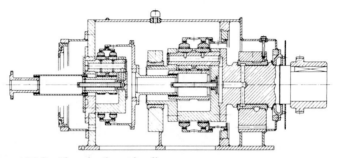

Figure 4.39 Double-reduction epicyclic gear

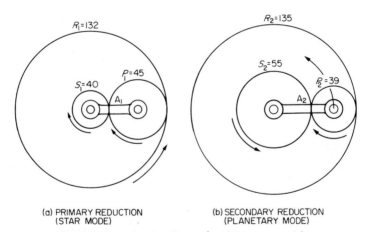

(a) PRIMARY REDUCTION
(STAR MODE)

(b) SECONDARY REDUCTION
(PLANETARY MODE)

Figure 4.40 Double-reduction epicyclic gear (star/planetary mode)

The primary reduction is a star gear having 40 teeth in the sun wheel, 45 teeth in each of the four planet wheels, and 132 teeth in the ring. The primary planet carrier (arm) is fixed to the gear case, and the primary ring drives the sun wheel of the secondary reduction.

The secondary reduction is a planetary gear having 55 teeth in the sun wheel, 39 teeth in each of the four planet wheels, and 135 teeth in the ring. The secondary ring is fixed to the gear case, and the secondary planet carrier (arm) drives the output shaft.

Applying the methods already explained, and referring to Figure 4.40(a) and (b), the reduction ratio may be demonstrated as follows:

Primary reduction Star gear with A_1 fixed, S_1 driving,
R_1 driven.

$$A_1 = 0 \quad S_1 = +1 \quad P_1 = -\frac{40}{45} \quad R_1 = -\frac{40}{132}$$

Primary speed reduction ratio, $\dfrac{\text{input}}{\text{output}} = \dfrac{S_1}{R_1}$

$$= (+1) \times \left(-\frac{132}{40}\right) = -\frac{66}{20} = -3.3$$

The $-$ sign means that the primary output R_1 rotates in the opposite direction to the primary input S_1.

Secondary reduction Planetary gear with R_2 fixed, S_2 driving,
A_2 driven

First, let A_2 be fixed

$$A_2 = 0, \quad S_2 = +1, \quad P_2 = -\frac{55}{39}, \quad R_2 = -\frac{55}{135},$$

Now let R_2 be fixed,

$$+\frac{55}{135} \qquad +\frac{55}{135} \qquad +\frac{55}{135} \qquad +\frac{55}{135}$$

$$A_2 = +\frac{55}{135}, \quad S_2 = +\frac{190}{135}, \quad P_2 = -\frac{5280}{5265}, \quad R_2 = 0$$

Secondary speed reduction ratio, $\dfrac{\text{input}}{\text{output}} = \dfrac{S_2}{A_2}$

$$= \left(+\frac{190}{135}\right) \times \left(+\frac{135}{55}\right) = +\frac{38}{11} = +3.4545$$

The $+$ sign means that the secondary output A_2 rotates in the same direction as the secondary input S_2.

∴ *Double reduction overall speed ratio* =

$$(-3.3) \times (+3.4545) = -11.4$$

Hence, for the turbine speed of 142.5 rev/s, the output shaft speed is $142.5/11.4 = 12.5$ rev/s, and the output shaft rotates in the opposite direction to the turbine shaft.

It will be noted that in these gears, the number of teeth in the ring is not equal to the number of teeth in the sun plus twice the number of teeth in the planet, as was the case in our earlier explanations which for simplicity, assumed one planet wheel only.

If we consider say the primary reduction of the present gear, $S = 40$ and $P = 45$, and there was only one planet, we should expect the ring to have $40 + (45 \times 2) = 130$ teeth. If however we used $R = 130$ with 4 planet wheels, then

$$\frac{S + R}{n} = \frac{40 + 130}{4} = \frac{170}{4} = 42.5,$$

which is not an integer, hence as stated previously, the planet wheels would not be equally pitched when the gear is assembled.

The number of teeth in the ring is therefore increased to 132, giving

$$\frac{S + R}{n} = \frac{40 + 132}{4} = \frac{172}{4} = 43.0$$

This is an integer, hence the gear will assemble with equally spaced planets. However if the same planet wheel is used, gearing basically with the ring at Q in Figure 4.41(b), then the centre distance y between the sun and planet will be slightly greater than the "standard centres" y in Figure 4.41(a). We have already seen that, with involute gears, the centre distance may be slightly increased, without affecting the ratio, but slightly increasing the pressure angle. The gear therefore works with standard centres and standard pressure angle at planet/ring but with slightly increased centres and slightly increased pressure angle at sun/planet. To utilise as much as possible of the tooth depth at this point, the addendum dedendum proportions of the sun wheel teeth are modified, as shown in Figure 4.42.

These artifices give a greater choice of numbers of teeth using standard pitch cutting tools, while ensuring correct assembly and minimum size of gear.

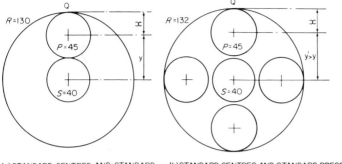

(a) STANDARD CENTRES AND STANDARD
PRESSURE ANGLE AT SUN / PLANET AND
AT PLANET/ RING

(b) STANDARD CENTRES AND STANDARD PRESSURE
ANGLE AT PLANET / RING; INCREASED CENTRES
AND INCREASED PRESSURE ANGLE AT SUN/PLANET

Figure 4.41 Practical requirements when using equally pitched multiple planet wheels

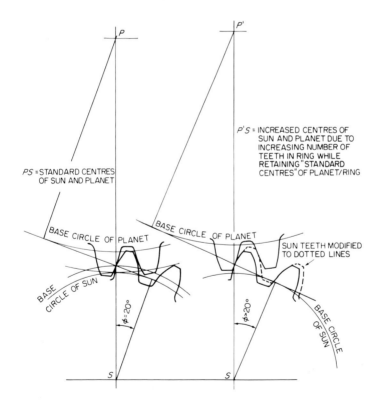

Figure 4.42 Standard centres and increased centres with involute gears

Referring to the longitudinal section in Figure 4.39, the following important points should be noted

1. The planet carrier (arm) of each reduction is in the form of a hollow cylinder. This type of construction has the advantages of ease and economy in manufacture, strength and stiffness, concentricity and potentially good balance. Practically all modern epicyclic gears have planet carriers of this type, which is very clearly illustrated in Figure 4.38(c). The primary planet carrier is rigidly fixed to the gear case. The secondary planet carrier is rigidly bolted to the output shaft, and has an outboard bearing located at the middle of the gear case. In the case of a rotating planet carrier, the centrifugal force generated by the planet wheels can impose large radial loads on the planet wheel bearings, particularly if the rotational speed is high. It is for this reason that the primary reduction is usually made a star gear, i.e. fixed planet carrier, and the lower speed secondary reduction can be made either a star, or a planetary, or a solar gear depending on the conditions and the desired direction of rotation.

2. Both the first and secondary rings and their supports are of relatively light construction. There is no input shaft bearing adjacent to either the primary or secondary sun wheel. This means that each sun wheel can "float" between its mesh contacts, i.e. between its tooth contacts with the four planet wheels. This feature, together with the flexibility of the ring and its support, enables the gear to accommodate any small manufacturing errors in the components, and thus to ensure that the load is shared evenly among the various gear contacts.

3. For assembly purposes, the right-hand and left-hand helices of each ring are made separately, and are connected together by a cylindrical sleeve through mating teeth which are helical to match the working teeth of the ring. The axial thrusts of the two separate ring helices are therefore transferred to, and balanced within, the single sleeve. The two helices of the ring are located axially by spring rings located in grooves formed in the sleeve teeth. This method permits of some flexibility between the two helices of the ring.

4. The primary ring and the secondary sun are coupled together to form one rotating unit. This rotating unit has no bearings—it is centred by the gear contacts between the primary ring and primary planet wheels at one end, and by the gear contacts between the secondary sun and secondary planet wheels at the other, and is located axially by the opposite-hand helices of the double helical teeth. This arrangement provides some further flexibility to ensure proper load sharing.

5. Lubricating oil for the gears is taken from the main turbine lubricating oil system. Oil at a pressure of 3.1 bar passes into an annular chamber in the aft main bearing shell, thence by radial holes and an axial hole in the output shaft to a cavity between the output shaft and the secondary planet carrier. From this cavity some of the oil passes radially outwards and into the open ends of the fixed hollow spindles on which the planet wheels rotate. The other ends of the hollow spindles being closed, oil passes through radial holes to the bearing surfaces on which the planet wheels run. From these bearing surfaces some oil passes outwards and escapes over the ends of the planet wheels, and some passes inwards to an annular chamber in the planet, and thence by radial holes in the planet (in the space between the R.H. and L.H. helices) to the teeth contacts between the planet and the sun, and between the planet and the ring. Also from the cavity between the output shaft and the secondary planet carrier, a central oil sprayer pipe projects into the hollow secondary sun wheel. Radial holes in the sprayer pipe spray oil on to the inside diameter of the sun wheel where it is retained by centrifugal force and passes through radial holes in the sun wheel to the actual tooth contact surfaces between the sun wheel and the planet wheels. The primary gear is lubricated in much the same manner, except that the oil is introduced into the hollow planet wheel shafts, oil for the sprayer pipe being transferred by means of radial holes in the aft end of the primary planet carrier.

Triple-reduction epicyclic gear

Figures 4.43 to 4.47 show a recent triple-reduction epicyclic gear, capable of transmitting 8550 kW from a turbine speed

Figure 4.43 8550 kW triple-reduction epicyclic gear

of 109.27 rev/s to a propeller speed of 1.867 rev/s. This gear, also designed and manufactured by Messrs W.H. Allen, Sons and Co, Ltd, is actually for a marine gas turbine installation, but the excellent photographs and diagrams illustrate very clearly the principles, details of construction and features which would be equally applicable to steam turbine gears.

The gear unit incorporates the integral main thrust block, also an auxiliary drive for a generator, lubricating oil pumps, etc.

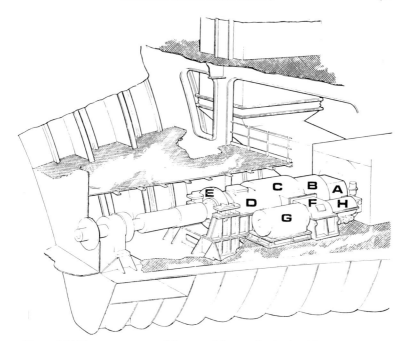

Figure 4.44 The arrangement of the propulsion gearing in the ship
A. First reduction star gear
B. Second reduction star gear
C. Third reduction planetary gear
D. Integral thrust block
E. Hydraulic caliper-type shaft brake and disc
F. Auxiliary drive gear
G. Alternator
H. Gear drive to lubricating oil-pumps, controllable-pitch propeller hydraulic
   system—pump and turning gear

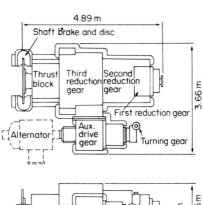

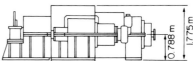

Figure 4.45 General arrangement
and approximate overall dimensions of the main propulsion
reduction gearing

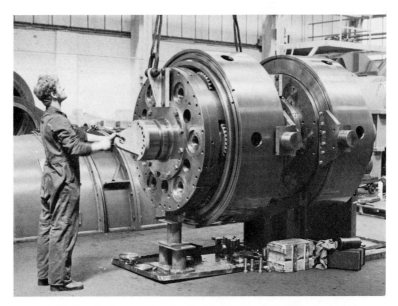

Figure 4.46 Two final gear trains after back-to-back testing in the manufacturer's works

The gear ratios of the main first, second and final reductions are respectively −4.51, −3.86 and 3.36, giving an overall reduction ratio of +58.53. Although this overall ratio is possible with double-reduction gears, triple-reduction was chosen since it enabled smaller diameter gears to be used in a "stern job" (i.e. a ship having machinery aft), and also gave an advantage in first cost.

The high turbine speed at the input to the gear required that the first reduction be a star gear, since the centrifugal forces would be too high to permit the use of a planetary gear. The planet carrier (arm), of hollow cylindrical construction, is bolted rigidly to the forward end of the gear case. The sun wheel is connected to the turbine shaft, and the ring, which is connected to the first reduction output shaft, rotates in the opposite direction to the input sun wheel.

The second reduction is also a star gear, which again reverses the direction of rotation, causing the second reduction output shaft to rotate in the same direction as the input turbine shaft to the first reduction.

The lower input speed to the third reduction enables a planetary gear to be used for the latter. The ring is fixed to the gear case, and the planet carrier drives the propeller shaft

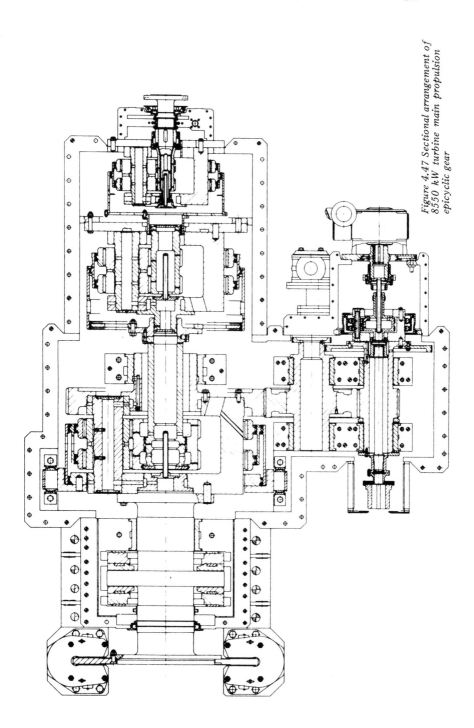

Figure 4.47 Sectional arrangement of 8550 kW turbine main propulsion epicyclic gear

in the same direction as the third reduction sun wheel, and therefore in the same direction as the turbine shaft.

The numbers of teeth in the three reductions are

Reduction	Sun	Planet	Ring
First	29	50	131
Second	28	39	108
Third	50	33	118

There are 4 planets each in the primary and secondary reductions, and 6 planets in the third reduction. The speed ratios may be demonstrated thus:

First reduction Star gear, A fixed, hence

$$A_1 = 0 \quad S_1 = +1 \quad P_1 = -\frac{29}{50} \quad R_1 = -\frac{29}{131}$$

$$\text{Speed ratio,} \quad \frac{\text{input}}{\text{output}} = \frac{S_1}{R_1} = -\frac{131}{29} = -4.51$$

Second reduction Star gear, A_2 fixed, hence

$$A_2 = 0 \quad S_2 = +1 \quad P_2 = -\frac{28}{39} \quad R_2 = -\frac{28}{108} = -\frac{7}{27}$$

$$\text{Speed ratio,} \quad \frac{\text{input}}{\text{output}} = \frac{S_2}{R_2} = -\frac{27}{7} = -3.86.$$

Third reduction Planetary gear, R_3 fixed, hence

$$A_3 \text{ fixed } A_3 = 0, \; S_3 = +1, \; P_3 = -\frac{50}{33} = -1.5151,$$
$$+0.4238 \quad +0.4238 \quad +0.4238$$

$$R_3 = -\frac{50}{118} = -0.4238$$
$$+0.4238$$

R_3 fixed $A_3 = +0.4238$, $S_3 = +1.4238$, $P_3 = -1.0913$,
$$R_3 = 0$$

$$\text{Speed ratio,} \quad \frac{\text{input}}{\text{output}} = \frac{S_3}{A_3} = \frac{+1.4238}{+0.4238} = +3.36$$

Overall speed ratio $= (-4.51) \times (-3.86) \times (+3.36) = +58.53$

With the exception of the auxiliary transfer wheels, all the gears have double-helical teeth with helix angle 30.0° and "standard" tooth pressure angle 22.5° in the normal plane. The running teeth of the external-teeth components of all three reductions are surface-hardened, while the rings of all three are of through-hardened alloy steel.

Referring to Figure 4.47, the first reduction input shaft is carried in two bearings and is connected to the first-reduction sun wheel by a gear coupling and quill shaft. In the second reduction, a single bearing on the planet carrier supports part of the weight of the second reduction output shaft. In the final reduction, the planet carrier is bolted rigidly to the final output shaft, and this assembly, which is supported in two bearings, carries the main transfer wheel for the auxiliary drive. A thrust collar, forged integral with the final output shaft, transmits the propeller thrust of 900.0 kN through a Michell thrust block, integral with the gear case, to the ship's structure.

During normal operation at sea, electric power for the ship's services is provided by a 500.0 kW shaft-driven alternating current generator. This is driven from the main transfer wheel through an idler wheel to a hollow pinion shaft which carries an overhung planetary epicyclic speed-increasing gear to give the generator a speed of 25.0 rev/s from a propeller speed of 1.867 rev/s.

An interesting feature is that the generator is so designed that it can be used as an emergency propulsion motor (using power provided by separately driven auxiliary generators) in the event of major breakdown of the main engines. To operate in this manner, it is necessary to change the generator rotor, and to change the ratio of the pinion-mounted auxiliary planetary gear to produce a propeller speed of 0.934 rev/s from a motor speed of 25.0 rev/s, with a "get home" power of 672.0 kW available. An interchangeable generator rotor and an interchangeable planetary gear of the required ratio for this purpose are carried on board as spare gear. The interchange is a quick and easy operation, requiring a minimum of dismantling. The auxiliary transfer gears have single-helical teeth, and the idler wheel and pinion are supported in adjustable bearings to permit correction of any deviation from correct tooth contact which may occur in service. Gears mounted at the forward ends of the idler and pinion respectively drive the main gear case lubricating oil pump and the hydraulic pump for the controllable-pitch propeller.

A motor-driven double-reduction worm gear unit manually clutched to the sun wheel of the generator gear provides means of turning the machinery at the rate of one propeller revolution in 6.67 minutes, for maintenance, inspection and testing purposes. Interlocks are provided to ensure that the main engines cannot be started with the turning gear engaged.

The shaft brake at the aft end is required only with gas turbine engines, to prevent rotation of the propeller during docking when the main engines are nominally stopped, but continue to develop some torque due to the necessity of keeping the gas generator on its minimum operating condition.

The gear case has its own self-contained lubricating oil system, functioning in much the same manner as already described for the smaller double-reduction gear. The main gear-driven lubricating oil pump draws oil from an oil tank built into the ship's double bottom, and is capable of supplying the full requirement of the gearing down to half speed. A motor-driven auxiliary oil pump, provided for starting, standby and tank filling, is arranged to start automatically if the oil pressure falls below a pre-set figure. A motor-driven, automatically self-cleaning, edge-type filter with magnetic filters is provided and is capable of filtering the oil down to 50.0 microns (0.051 mm). A differential pressure switch initiates cleaning of the filter, which can be carried out while the main machinery is running, and while maintaining the full supply of oil. High inlet oil temperature or low inlet oil pressure bring up alarms, and continuing fall of oil pressure after the alarm initiates shut-down of the main engines. The low oil pressure alarm and automatic starting of the standby oil pump can both be tested while the machinery is running.

Throughout manufacture and installation, these gears are subject to very rigorous inspection and testing, to ensure correct alignment and tooth action, to check noise and vibration levels, to demonstrate correct operation of auxiliary drives, standby equipment, interlocks and alarms, and to check oil flows, temperatures and pressures. The "get home" mode of operation is also tested.

For routine checks on board, *in situ* inspection of the gear teeth may be carried out by fibroscope or dental mirror through the inspection holes in the rings and planet carriers. These inspection holes are clearly seen in the illustrations.

Any one of the three main reduction gears may be removed for dismantling without disturbing the other two.

Similarly, any one of the auxiliary gear elements, except the main transfer wheel, may be removed individually.

Special equipment required to completely dismantle and re-erect the gears is carried on board. All this equipment is used during final assembly and dismantling in the works, to prove its complete suitability.

The total mass of the reduction gear is 45 000 kg.

Possible developments in parallel-shaft gears and epicyclic gears

We have seen that the orthodox parallel-shaft type of gearing is capable of further development, and that the epicyclic type of gearing offers possible advantages of reduced space occupied, and co-axial input and output shafts, but could have the possible disadvantage of increased number of rotating parts, so located that inspection and maintenance may be rather more difficult.

Depending on how ships and propellers develop, each type of gearing could develop accordingly, and there could be the possibility that combined gears—i.e. part parallel-shaft and part epicyclic, could in certain cases, be used to advantage.

It is possible, by using ahead and astern clutches—probably of the hydraulic coupling type for parallel-shaft gears or of the friction brake type for epicyclic gears—to adapt either type of gear for reversal of the direction of rotation of the propeller, thus permitting the use of uni-directional turbines. With steam turbines however, the provision of the usual astern turbine(s) is so simple by comparison with the complication of a reversing gear—whatever its type—that reversal by the gearing has not so far been seriously considered.

Although the initial interest in contra-rotating propellers does not for the moment appear to have been maintained, there remains the possibility that they could be used for large powers where the propeller diameter is limited, or the use of the more normal twin-screw arrangement is not favoured.

The following notes and illustrations briefly review some of these possibilities.

Combined parallel-shaft gears and epicyclic gears

Figure 4.48 shows in principle a double-reduction gear in which the primary reduction is an epicyclic planetary gear

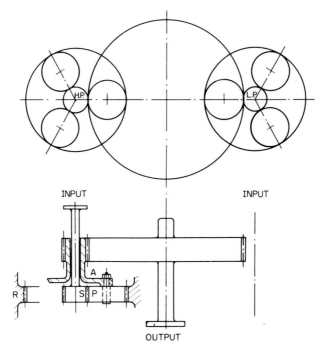

Figure 4.48 Double-reduction gear with planetary epicyclic primary reduction and parallel-shaft secondary reduction

and the secondary reduction is a parallel-shaft gear. Figure 4.49 shows an alternative arrangement in which the primary reduction is a parallel-shaft gear and the secondary reduction is an epicyclic planetary gear. In Figure 4.49, note that in the secondary reduction, the sun wheel is split into two sections with equal flexibilities in their concentric shafts, and the two sections of the secondary reduction ring are flexibly mounted. This ensures correct load-sharing among all the secondary reduction gear contacts.

Mechanical reversal of the propeller shaft

When dealing with astern turbines, we show that for a crash reversal from full ahead to full astern, the astern turbine itself acts as the "slipping device" which accommodates the opposing ahead and astern torques while destroying the ahead kinetic energy of the ship (see Chapter 10).

Basically, the object of mechanical reversal is to enable the propeller shaft to be reversed from full ahead to full astern smoothly, without causing any disturbance at all to the main

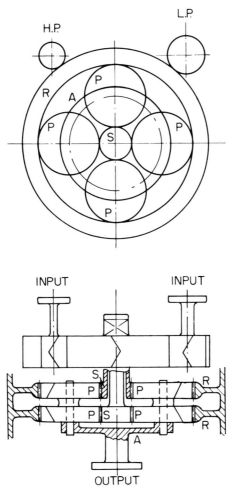

Figure 4.49 Double-reduction gear with parallel-shaft primary reduction and planetary epicyclic secondary reduction

turbines, which continue to run at full speed and full power and in the same direction.

The propeller must first be slowed down from full speed ahead until it is stationary, and then be accelerated to full speed astern. During this time, the propeller law will apply, viz. that the power absorbed by the propeller is directly proportional to the cube of the propeller speed. For example, if at one instant while slowing down, the propeller speed is 0.9 of its full speed, the propeller will absorb only $(0.9)^3 = 0.729$ of full power. The main turbines however continue to develop full power at full speed, hence $1.0 - 0.729 = 0.271$ of full power must be dissipated by some device which will allow the necessary slip between the turbine speed and the propeller speed. This is illustrated in principle by Figure 4.50, from which it will be noted that at the instant the propeller comes to rest, the entire turbine power is momentarily dissipated at the slipping device.

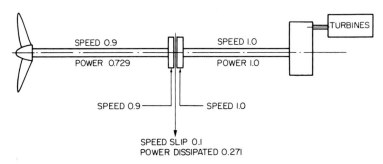

Figure 4.50 Principle of varying the propeller speed while maintaining constant engine speed and power

The slipping device could be either a friction clutch in which slipping is controlled by varying the axial force pressing the two clutch members together, or a hydraulic coupling in which slipping is controlled by filling and emptying (see Chapter 7, page 310).

To apply this principle to mechanical reversal, two slipping devices are required—one for ahead running and one for astern. Such a system might be as shown by the simplified diagram in Figure 4.51, which is drawn for an ordinary parallel-shaft double-reduction gear.

The primary pinion on the turbine shaft drives the ahead primary wheel directly, and the astern primary wheel through an idler wheel. A slipping clutch is interposed between each primary wheel and secondary pinion. When running ahead, the ahead clutch is fully engaged (zero split and zero power dissipation), and the astern clutch is fully disengaged (200.0 per cent slip and zero power dissipation).

Reversal is initiated by simultaneously relaxing the ahead clutch and engaging the astern clutch. The propeller begins to slow down thus absorbing less ahead power, the difference between the constant turbine power and the propeller power being dissipated by slipping of both the ahead and astern clutches. At the instant the propeller comes to rest, it is

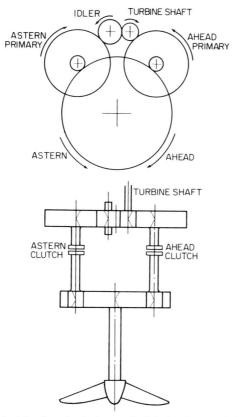

Figure 4.51 Principle of mechanical reversal of shaft using parallel-shaft gears

absorbing no power, and the whole of the turbine power is momentarily dissipated by slipping of the ahead and astern clutches, each of which at this point may be regarded as "half-engaged". As the astern clutch continues to engage and the ahead clutch to disengage, the propeller accelerates in the astern direction, absorbing progressively more power through the astern clutch and dissipating progressively less power at both clutches, until when the astern clutch is fully engaged it is transmitting full astern power to the propeller with zero slip, while the ahead clutch is fully disengaged and is dissipating zero power with 200.0 per cent slip.

This process is illustrated in Figure 4.52 which assumes equal power dissipation by the two clutches. It is not necessary of course that this should be so—the relative amounts of power dissipated and the rate of clutch engagement and

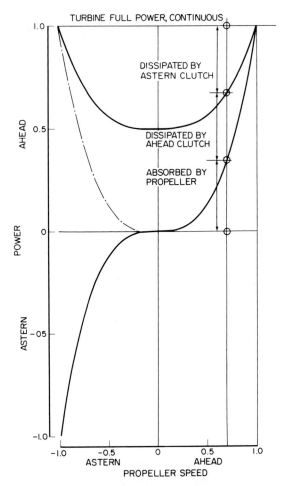

Figure 4.52 Power transmission and dissipation during mechanical reversal

relaxation are controlled by an acceptable speed of reversal on the one hand and an acceptable rate of energy dissipation on the other. Whether the slipping devices are friction clutches or hydraulic couplings, the energy destroyed is ultimately dissipated as heat.

Reversing epicyclic gears

Consider the simple epicyclic gear in Figure 4.53. The gear may be arranged in one of the three different ways shown.

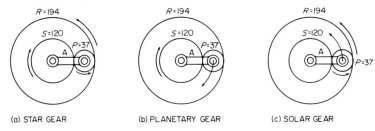

(a) STAR GEAR   (b) PLANETARY GEAR   (c) SOLAR GEAR

Figure 4.53 Principle of a reversing epicyclc gear

(a) *Star gear*, i.e. A fixed, in which case,

$$A = 0, \quad S = +1, \quad P = -\frac{120}{37}, \quad R = -\frac{60}{97},$$

$$\therefore \text{Speed ratio } \frac{\text{input}}{\text{output}} = \frac{S}{R} = -\frac{97}{60} = \underline{-1.6167}$$

(b) *Planetary gear*, i.e. R fixed, in which case

$$\begin{array}{cccc} +\frac{60}{97} & +\frac{60}{97} & +\frac{60}{97} & +\frac{60}{97} \\ A = +\frac{60}{97}, & S = +\frac{157}{97}, & P = -\frac{3140}{1163}, & R = 0 \end{array}$$

$$\therefore \text{speed ratio } \frac{\text{input}}{\text{output}} = \frac{S}{A} = +\frac{157}{60} = \underline{+2.6167}$$

(c) *Solar gear*, i.e. S fixed, in which case

$$\begin{array}{cccc} -1 & -1 & -1 & -1 \\ A = -1, & S = 0, & P = -\frac{157}{37}, & R = -\frac{157}{97} \end{array}$$

$$\therefore \text{Speed ratio } \frac{\text{input}}{\text{output}} = \frac{R}{A} = +\frac{157}{97} = \underline{+1.6186}$$

Thus, if a ready means could be found to change the gear from the star arrangement to the solar arrangement, the direction of rotation of the output shaft relative to the input shaft could be reversed, while maintaining nearly the same input/output speed ratio. This would require that

(i) When working star, the arm is fixed, input shaft on sun, output shaft on ring

(ii) When working solar, the sun is fixed, input shaft on ring, output shaft on arm.

This is practically impossible to achieve on a single gear because of the obvious mechanical complications. To overcome this, two similar gears in series are used, interconnected in such a manner that, for instance, *either*

(i) The first gear is a star gear with a speed ratio of -1.6167, and the second gear is a planetary gear with a speed ratio of $+2.6167$, giving an overall total speed ratio of $(-1.6167) \times (+2.6167) = -4.2304$, *or*

(ii) The first gear is a planetary gear with a speed ratio of $+2.6167$ and the second gear is a solar gear with a speed ratio of $+1.6186$, giving an overall total speed ratio of $(+2.6167) \times (+1.6186) = +4.2354$.

Figure 4.54 shows the principles of construction of such a possible reversing double epicyclic gear.

The arm A_1 and the ring R_1 of the first gear are both made capable of rotating, and each is provided with a clasp brake (B_{A1}, B_{R1}) arranged so that one brake is "on" while the other is "off", that brake which is "on" determining whether the arm A_1 or the ring R_1 is the fixed member of the first gear.

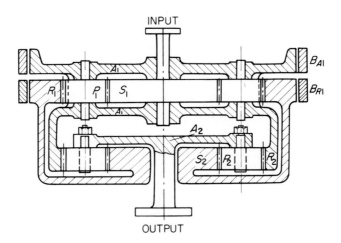

Figure 4.54 Principle of a reversing double epicyclic gear

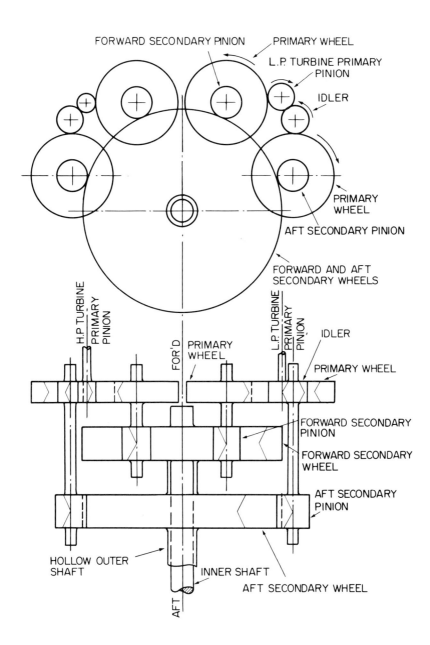

Figure 4.55 Double-reduction gear for contra-rotating propellers

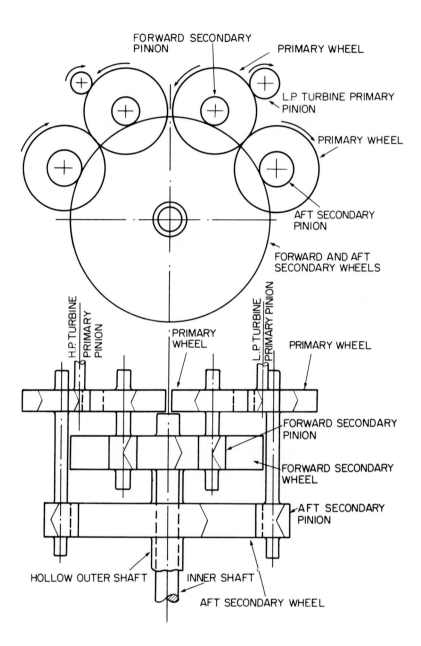

Figure 4.56 Double-reduction gear for contra-rotating propellers

The first arm A_1 is integral with the second ring R_2, and the first ring R_1 is integral with the second sun S_2.

If the brake B_{A1} is applied, A_1 is fixed, hence the first gear acts as a star gear with R_1 rotating in the opposite direction to the input S_1. Since R_2 also is fixed, the second gear acts as a planetary gear with A_2 rotating in the same direction as R_1. The output shaft therefore rotates in the opposite direction to the input shaft.

If the brake B_{A1} is now released and the brake B_{R1} applied, the first ring R_1 is fixed, and the first gear acts as a planetary gear with A_1 rotating in the same direction as the input S_1. Since S_2 also is fixed, the second gear acts as a solar gear, with A_2 rotating in the same direction as R_2. The output shaft therefore rotates in the same direction as the input shaft. The energy dissipation takes place at the brakes.

Figure 4.54—one of the many ways in which two epicyclic gears may be interconnected to permit mechanical reversal— is a compact arrangement having advantages in the manner in which the gears operate during reversal, but the speed ratios obtainable are inherently somewhat restricted.

Double reduction gears for contra-rotating propellers

In Figure 4.55 there are two secondary wheels, side by side, the shaft of the forward wheel passing co-axially through the hollow shaft of the aft wheel. Each primary pinion drives two primary wheels, one directly, and one through an idler wheel. The forward and aft secondary pinions and therefore the forward and aft secondary wheels rotate in opposite directions. The forward propeller is attached to the outer hollow shaft, and the aft propeller to the inner shaft.

In the case shown in Figure 4.56, opposite directions of rotation are obtained by meshing the two primary wheels, i.e. without the need for an idler wheel.

5 Balancing and critical speed of turbine rotors

The balancing of turbine rotors is carried out by the same principles as already explained for reciprocating engines.

A turbine rotor can suffer only from revolving forces—there are no reciprocating forces, and in this respect the turbine presents an easier problem. The consequences of unbalanced revolving forces can be much more serious in turbines, however, especially as the calculation of the unbalanced revolving masses is not so easy as it is in reciprocating engines. Indeed, it is impossible, since any such out-of-balance masses are the results of errors and inaccuracy in machining the discs and in fitting the blades and shroud rings.

Balancing grooves are turned in the outer faces of the end discs, and balance weights screwed or *caulked* into the grooves.

Static and dynamic balance

It is worthwhile noting at this stage the difference between static and dynamic balance. Suppose a rotor to be placed on knife edges. Then, if one part of the circumference of say the largest wheel is heavy compared with the rest, the rotor will turn on the knife edges until the heavy part comes to rest at the bottom centre.

Figure 5.1 shows this state of affairs in which the out-of-balance mass is imagined to be a mass attached to the disc. The moment tending to turn the rotor is WR.

It is obvious that the turning tendency can be cancelled by fitting opposite the unbalanced mass another mass at such a radius as will give an equal and opposite moment, e.g. W_B, R_B.

So far as this effect is concerned, the balance mass may be placed on any wheel. The only requirement is the correct moment. The rotor is then said to be in static balance, e.g., it will remain in equilibrium on the knife edges with no tendency to revolve.

Suppose that the balance mass W_B were attached to the first wheel at radius R_B as shown. The rotor would be in static balance. If, however, the rotor is run at speed, the two masses will each generate a centrifugal force F, say, acting radially outwards at a distance L from one another.

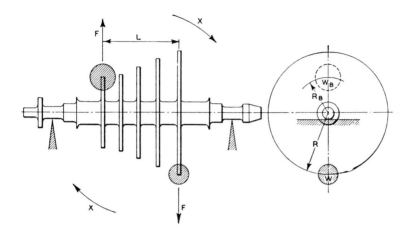

Figure 5.1 Static and dynamic balacing of turbine rotors

There is thus created a moment or *couple* tending to tilt the rotor in the manner shown by the arrow X, i.e., although the rotor is in static balance it is not in dynamic balance.

In the present case dynamic balance could be obtained by shifting the balance mass on to the last wheel, thus destroying the couple while still maintaining static balance. Turbine rotors may have anything up to eighteen or even twenty stages, and the determination of the out-of-balance masses, their angular and axial positions by the usual means is an impossibility. Dynamic balancing is largely a matter of trial and error, and calls for considerable experience and judgment on the part of those doing the balancing. Small rotors may be run up to speed on a hanging cradle, and the size and position of the balance masses adjusted until full speed is obtained without vibration. Within recent years, balancing machines have been developed. These machines indicate the requirements for dynamic balance quickly and accurately.

THE AVERY ELECTRODYNAMIC BALANCING
MACHINE

The modern trend in the design of dynamic machinery is for higher speeds of rotation. Any unbalance that is present will produce a centrifugal force which will increase as the square of the rotational speed.

In the past, mechanical balancing machines have been sufficiently sensitive to meet the demands of the day. The higher sensitivity now required, however, could not be obtained on mechanical machines due to the inertia of moving parts; this, and the friction inherent in a mechanical machine, tend to reduce the sensitivity of indication. Electrical balancing machines have been developed to meet this need for higher sensitivity and at the same time to reduce the skill needed.

As already described, in order to give dynamic balance two lateral planes of correction are necessary.

In Figure 5.2 the transverse movement of the supporting cradle, which is free to move laterally although controlled in extent by the deflection of vertical leaf springs, operates a moving-coil pick-up which generates alternating current with a frequency equal to the frequency of the vibrations. This current is fed to one coil of a dynamometer-type wattmeter.

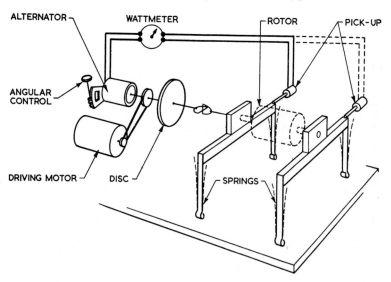

Figure 5.2 The Avery electrodynamic balancing machine made under licence from Carl Schenck Maschiren-fabrik, Darmstadt, Germany (W & T Avery Ltd.)

The other coil of the wattmeter is fed from one phase or other of a two-phase alternator driven by the machine at the same frequency as the current generated by the pick-up. The wattmeter then gives a reading which is proportional to the unbalance of the rotor.

The angular position of the alternator stator is not fixed, but can be adjusted through a small angle in either direction while the machine is running, i.e., it is possible to alter the phase difference between the current of the alternator and the current of the pick-up until they are 90 degrees out of phase, when the wattmeter will give a zero reading.

In the first instance therefore under the action of un-balanced forces the wattmeter gives a reading, and by altering the angular position of the alternator stator the wattmeter reading is made zero. The amount of movement to achieve this is recorded on a graduated disc, and from its final position the correct spot is indicated where metal must be added or removed from the rotor in order to obtain balance.

Loss of balance

If a turbine stage loses a blade or blades or a piece of shrouding, the dynamic balance is upset and will be evident by serious vibration. In such cases balance could be temporarily restored by removing an equal amount from the opposite side of the wheel, but in practice the whole row is removed because of lack of support in the remaining blades. Nevertheless, the very first opportunity should be taken to re-blade the wheel and restore the proper balance.

SHAFTING

The torque required to break a solid round shaft is $\pi/16D^3q$, where D is the diameter in inches and q is the ultimate shearing stress of the material; for a hollow shaft it is $\pi/16(D^4 - d^4/D)q$, where d is the internal diameter. It can be shown that, within limits, a hollow shaft is not as heavy as a solid shaft of the same strength. The hollow shaft also has the advantage that it is possible to inspect the interior metal for flaws before being put into service. This is of particular value in the forgings for turbine rotors.

Power (kW) in terms of torque is $2\pi TN/1000$, where T is the constant torque in Nm and N is the revolutions per second. Therefore, for a given shaft power it should be possible to fnd the torque at a given speed and from that the diameter of the shaft required. But no engine gives a constant torque, however near a turbine-driven shaft may approach that ideal state.

Variation of torque may be due to variation of pressure on the piston of a reciprocating engine (see Chapter 2). The propeller at the other end of the main shaft produces impulses depending on the number of blades and the variation in wake speed in the vicinity of the revolving blades.

Due to the property of elasticity in the metal, torsional vibrations are set up which often double the stress in the shaft and cause excessive pressure in the main drive gear teeth (see Chapter 4).

When power impulses coincide with the natural frequency of vibration of the whole system, synchronism is produced. The speed at which this occurs is called a *critical* speed. There are several critical speeds for one shaft; the first may be at 0.5 rev/s and the next at 5.0 rev/s. It is good practice to run through the critical range as quickly as possible when increasing speed during manoeuvring. Severe damage has been done to turbines which have unwittingly been run for long periods at critical speeds.

The Department of Trade and Lloyds have fixed formulae for shaft diameters, and for the foregoing reasons the diameter found by their formulae is much greater than that which would be required for a constant torque. In fact, the *factor of safety* will be found to be in the region of ten to twelve. Even then, shafts do break in service due to unexpected stresses.

Shafts transmitting the same power may for various reasons have different diameters. The turbine spindle at its high speed may be 75.0 mm diameter, while the *tunnel* or intermediate shaft is 254 mm diameter; the thrust shaft diameter may then be 267.0 mm, and that of the *tail end* shaft, to which the propeller is attached, may be 275 mm. The reason for this variation in diameter is, first, that the thrust shaft has a collar which takes the ahead and astern thrust loads as well as those imposed by longitudinal vibration from the propeller, producing complex stresses; secondly, the tail-end shaft, due to its position and the over-hanging mass of the propeller, which can be 10 000 kg or over, is subjected to torsion, compression, shear and bending; while going astern the shaft is in tension.

The stresses due to bending and shear may be very high in heavy seas due to the suddenly applied load of propeller and shaft when the lignum vitae lining in the stern bush is worn, allowing a play of, say, 6.0 mm.

CRITICAL SPEED OF TURBINE ROTORS

It is never possible to build a loaded shaft to run truly concentrically. Even if the workmanship were perfect, once the rotor is placed in its bearings, the natural sag changes the axis from a straight line to a curve, and hence the rotor may be regarded, to some extent, as running eccentrically.

The critical speed of a rotor may be defined as that speed of rotation at which any small differences between the mass centre and the centre of rotation causes the rotor to deflect by a relatively large amount.

So far as turbine rotors are concerned, the differences between the mass centre and the centre of rotation are very small, and under these circumstances, the critical speed coincides very closely with the natural frequency of transverse vibration of the shaft. The natural frequency of transverse vibration depends on the shaft masses and their distribution and on the strength of the shaft treated as a beam for bending.

The nature of such vibrations is very complex, and the following simplified method is based on treating the rotor as a beam freely supported at the bearing centres, and carrying a number of concentrated loads (due to the mass of the shaft, discs, blades, shroud rings, etc.).

The critical speed is calculated from the expression $N_c = 16.8/\sqrt{\delta}$, where δ is the maximum static deflection of the rotor in mm, i.e., the greatest amount of natural sag of the rotor when resting on knife edges at the bearing centres.

First draw down the rotor to scale and divide its length into a number of arbitrary convenient sections. Calculate the total mass and hence load of each section and mark it on the drawing on the appropriate line of action, which is usually assumed to be the middle of each section.

On the right of the diagram the various loads are set down vertically to scale, and a pole point O chosen, from which lines are drawn to the vertical lines representing the loads.

The simple shaft shown in Figure 5.3 illustrates this. W_1, W_2, W_3, etc., represent the various loads due to the shaft

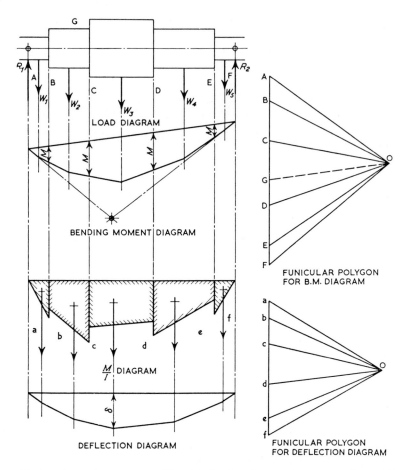

Figure 5.3 Bending moment, M/I and deflection diagrams for transversely loaded shafts

sections chosen, and the spaces between the lines of action of these loads are lettered. Thus the load W_1 is force AB, W_2 is BC, etc. When these are laid down vertically to scale in the funicular polygon the total length of the line AF therefore represents the total downward load due to the mass of the shaft.

In the space A in the load diagram a line is drawn parallel to OA in the funicular polygon, in the space B a line parallel to OB and so on, giving the shaft bending-moment diagram, which is then closed by drawing a straight line joining the extremities of the diagram. Another line OG is drawn in the funicular polygon parallel to the closing line of the bending moment (M) diagram, thus dividing AF into two parts viz. AG and GF.

AG is the left-hand bearing reaction and GF the right-hand bearing reaction. If the bending moment lines in the extreme spaces A and F are produced they will meet at the centre of gravity of the shaft. A diagram of M/I is then drawn for the shaft. M is the moment of inertia for bending, which for a circular solid shaft is $\pi D^4/64$ and for a hollow circular shaft is $\pi/64(D^4 - d^4)$.

It must be remembered that at any point where the shaft diameter changes, I and therefore M/I, has two values.

The area of each section of the M/I diagram is then calculated in the proper units thus:

If M is in Nmm and I in mm^4, then

$$M/I = \frac{\text{Nmm}}{\text{mm}^4} = \frac{\text{N}}{\text{mm}^3}$$

and the area of the M/I sections is

$$\frac{M}{I} \times L = \frac{\text{Nmm}}{\text{mm}^4} \times \text{mm} = \frac{\text{N}}{\text{mm}^2}$$

Assuming the M/I area of each section to act through the centre of gravity of the area, another funicular polygon is drawn from which is obtained the deflection diagram of the rotor. The maximum deflection δ is scaled off and the critical speed calculated from $N_c = 16.8\sqrt{\delta}$.

Scales of bending-moment diagram

Length scale 1 mm $= A$, mm   Load scale 1 mm $= B$, N
Polar distance $= P$, mm

then bending-moment scale is 1 mm $= (A \times B \times P)$ N mm

Scales of deflection diagram

Length scale 1 mm $= A$, mm M/I area scale 1 mm $=$
Polar distance $= Q$, mm C, N/mm^2

then deflection scale is

$$1 \text{ mm} = \frac{A \times C \times Q}{E}, \text{ mm}$$

where E is modulus of elasticity (206 920 N/mm² for steel).

Note: The M/I areas consist almost invariably of triangles and trapezia. The centre of gravity of a triangle is at the intersection of its medians.

The centre of gravity of a trapezium may be found by the following simple construction, illustrated in Figure 5.4.

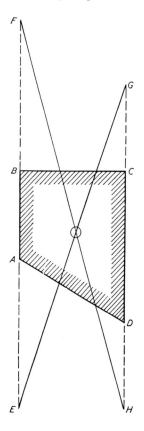

Figure 5.4 (left) Centre of gravity of a trapezium

Figure 5.5 (opposite) Critical speed calculation for a steam turbine rotor
Length scale 1.0 mm = 4.0 mm
Polar distance = 103.4 mm
E for steel = 206 920 n/mm²
Deflection scale

$$1.0 \ mm = \frac{0.1 \times 4.0 \times 103.4}{206 \ 920} = 0.0002 \ mm$$

$$
\begin{aligned}
Critical \ speed &= 16.8 \ \sqrt{(1/\delta \ max)} \\
&= 16.8 \ \sqrt{(1/0.0106)} \\
&= 16.8 \ \sqrt{(94.3)} \\
&= 16.8 \times 9.7 \\
&= 163.0 \ rev/s
\end{aligned}
$$

With the dividers, mark off AE and BF each equal to CD. Also mark off CG and DH each equal to AB. Then FH and GE intersect in the centre of gravity.

The area of a triangle is equal to one half of the base muliplied by the altitude, and the area of a trapezium is one half of the sum of the parallel sides multiplied by the perpendicular distance between them.

When finding these areas, of course, distances parallel to the axis of the shaft are expressed in units of length, viz. mm, and distances perpendicular to the axis of the shaft are expressed in units of M/I, viz., N/mm³.

Figure 5.5 shows these methods applied to a relatively simple impulse turbine rotor having one two-row Curtis and three single-row wheels. The notes and explanation should enable these methods to be used for any rotor.

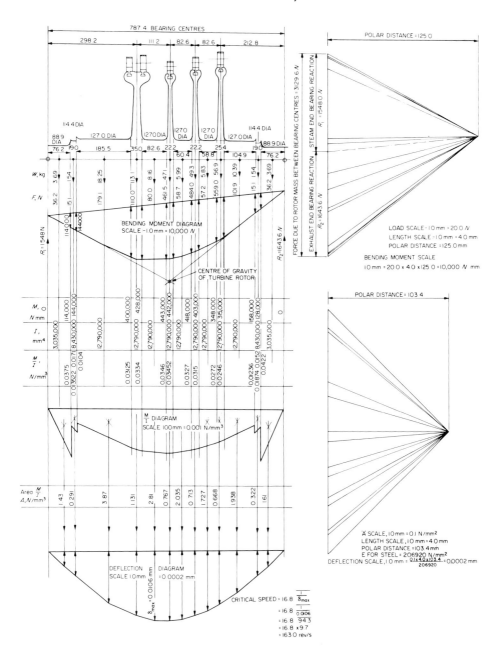

Turbines may be designed with *stiff* shafts or with *flexible* shafts.

In the former case the critical speed is well above the running speed, and in the latter case well below the running speed, the margin in either case being 30–90 per cent of the running speed.

Flexible shafts are of smaller diameters than stiff shafts, giving less weight, less shaft and diaphragm-gland leakage area. Care must be taken, however, with flexible shafts at starting and manoeuvring, so as to run through the critical speed as quickly as possible and thus allow the minimum possible time for the vibrations to build up a serious amplitude.

The critical speed calculated in the foregoing is called the major critical speed. Other minor critical speeds occur at multiples of the major, but these are usually of relatively little importance.

6 Condensers

A condenser is fitted to a reciprocating steam engine or steam turbine primarily to reduce the back pressure against which the engine works, thus allowing a greater amount of work to be done from a given quantity of steam and so giving a greater efficiency.

Steam-plants are almost invariably fitted with surface condensers in which the exhaust steam and cooling water are kept quite separate. When the steam condenses it forms practically pure water for boiler feed.

General construction

A modern surface condenser consists of a riveted or welded steel shell, through which pass a large number of brass, cupro-nickel or aluminium-bronze tubes. At each end of the shell is fitted a cast-iron water end, divided from the shell by a large brass tube plate. A circulating pump draws from the sea and

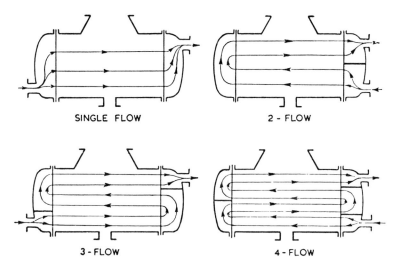

SINGLE FLOW   2 - FLOW

3 - FLOW   4 - FLOW

Figure 6.1 Condenser water flows

delivers through the condenser tubes and thence overboard. Depending on the number and arrangement of the divisions in the water-ends, the circulating water may be made to pass through the shell one, two, three or four times; hence the terms single-flow, two-flow, etc., condenser (Figure 6.1).

The tubes are fitted with screwed glands or ferrules where they pass through the tube plates or, at the water-inlet ends, they may be expanded and bell-mouthed to streamline the water flow at entry, thus reducing water-friction loss and pumping power (Figure 6.2). Alternatively, the tubes may be roller-expanded into the tube-plates at both ends, with the inlet ends bell-mouthed. In such cases means is incorporated in the condenser design to accommodate differential expansion between the steel shell and the non-ferrous tubes.

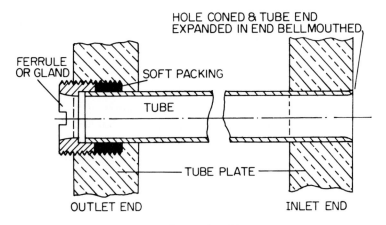

Figure 6.2 Condenser tubes, tube-plates and packing

Leakage and wear

The condenser of to-day, when fitted with tubes of copper-nickel alloy, gives little trouble due to leakage of tubes, but ordinary brass tubes have, in the past, been the cause of many stoppages at sea. Brass is a mixture of copper and zinc (70:30), and under the conditions of working, an electrolytic or galvanic action is set up between the particles of copper and zinc comprising the metal.

The action resembles that in a primary electric cell, with a rod of copper and a rod of zinc immersed in a weak solution of sulphuric acid. When the rods are joined externally, an electric current flows and the zinc rod is gradually eaten away. In much the same way, the zinc particles in the brass tube were eaten away (called de-zincification) until a hole was formed which allowed sea water to enter the steam space and mix with the pure condensate. As mentioned earlier, some of this action was due to water turbulence, and it was found that expanded tubes with bell-mouthed ends, giving a stream-line flow, were beneficial. Zinc plates, fitted to the tube plate or to the nuts of stays, helped to reduce the effects of galvanic action. Some firms used soft-iron plates attached to the end covers. Their effect was apparently to rust away, and in so doing to provide particles of iron oxide which coated the in-side of the tubes, thus protecting the brass surface.

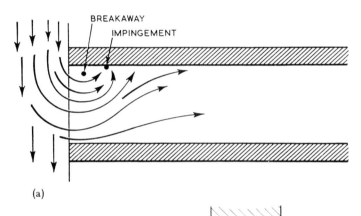

Figure 6.3 Inlet and impingement at tube inlet
(a) Breakaway and impingement at tube inlet
(b) Tube bell mouthed and plastic insert fitted at tube inlet

In addition to the above, condenser tubes wear through or fracture at the ends or at the division plate due to vibration caused by the high velocity of the exhaust steam. These are always possible sources of leakage.

Trouble is sometimes experienced with erosion of the first few inches at the inlet ends of the tubes. This was formerly attributed to excessive water velocity, but more recent investi-

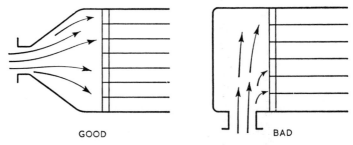

GOOD　　　　BAD

Figure 6.4 Water-box design for water flow

gations have shown that bad entry conditions are a more likely cause. In particular, pronounced water flow *across* the tube plate can cause breakaway of the flow at the inlet to the tube, and the resulting impingement erodes the tube (see Figure 6.3). This effect can be minimised by bell-mouthing the tubes at inlet (as shown in Figure 6.2) and by designing the water boxes to avoid pronounced cross flow (see Figure 6.4). Plastic inserts may be fitted also (see Figure 6.3).

Testing for leaky tubes

The method of testing for individual leaky tubes or stays is to blank off the condensate branch in the bottom of the condenser, fill the steam space with fresh water and remove the end covers to note the tube ends which are passing water.

If an independent air-pump is fitted, start the air-pump, creating a partial vacuum in the steam space which draws air in through the tubes which are leaking. These are found by testing the tube ends with a lighted candle, the flame being drawn in with the air.

A more recently adopted method of test makes use of fluorescent dye. Fluorescent dyes such as eosin and fluorescein have the property of changing the short waves of ultra-violet light, which are invisible, into long waves which can be seen. Many uses can be made of this property and one of these aboard ship is to detect leakage through condenser tubes.

Roughly, about 0.25 kg of the dyestuff is mixed with 20.0 tonnes of water, which mixture when introduced to the steam side of a condenser will flow out through any crack or hole in a tube. Without this aid small leaks are difficult to detect, since tubes and tube-plates are usually wet, but when introduced its presence is easily detected. This is done by directing the invisible rays from an ultra-violet lamp on to the

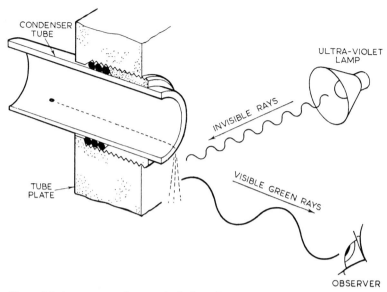

Figure 6.5 Apparatus used to test for leaky tubes

tube plate when, if there is any leakage, the water in the vicinity will appear greenish in colour. Figure 6.5 illustrates the method.

Alternatively, a sheet of thin plastic material is placed over the water side of each tube plate and the air pump started. The suction effect passes through the holed tube or tubes, drawing the plastic into the appropriate tube ends. Instead of the plastic sheets, a special foam has been sprayed over the water side of the tube plate to perform the same function.

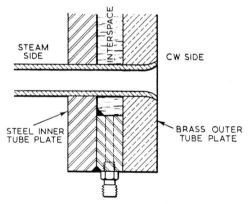

Figure 6.6 Condensate sealed double-tube plates

Very high-pressure boilers cannot tolerate impurities in the feed water, and in such cases double-tube plates have been used to positively eliminate leakage of sea-water past the tube fixings. The tubes pass through the inner steel tube plate and the outer brass tube plate as shown in Figure 6.6. The space between the two plates being sealed with pure condensate at a pressure higher than the maximum circulating-water pressure. The sealing pressure is usually obtained by a constant head tank. Any leakage past tube fixings is then always pure condensate from the interspace.

Instead of condensate sealing, the interspace is sometimes connected to a sub-atmospheric pressure, which quickly removes any circulating-water leakage.

Allowing for contraction and expansion

The ferruled tube ends are sealed with cotton-cord packing saturated with boiled oil, or by patent zinc metallic packing. The packing is inserted in a small stuffing-box and secured in place by the screwed ferrule.

Some means must be provided to allow for the relative expansion and contraction of the tubes and shell. In the method described the tube is free to expand and contract. When required, a projection on the inside of the ferrule prevents the tube from working out of the tube plate.

The tube plates, which are under compression from the combined action of pressure of the atmosphere and circulating water, are supported from the inside by stays, about 25.0 mm or more in diameter and set at about 450.0 mm pitch from one another. These stays are screwed at each end, pass through the tube plates and are fitted with nuts, washers and grommets inside and out.

In the latest condensers, the outside casing is given flexibility by the insertion of an expansion piece, allowing all the tubes to be expanded into the tube plates and so reducing the probability of leakage. In such cases, of course, the tube-plate stays cannot pass between the tube plates, since this would prevent the shell expansion piece from functioning correctly. The tube-plate stays then pass through the water box. The outer-stay nuts must be removed before removing the water-box cover. The weight of the water-box adjacent to the shell expansion piece is transmitted to the condenser-shell structure by cantilever brackets and not by the expansion piece. During manufacture, transport and installation the expansion piece is

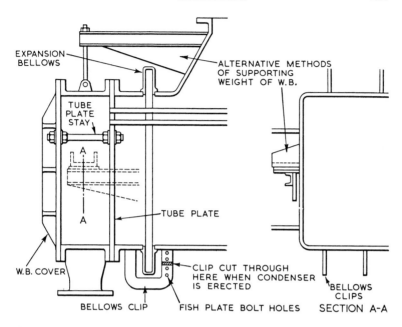

Figure 6.7 Features of condenser with tubes expanded both ends

rendered inoperative by welded-on clips. Once the condenser is finally erected in the ship and all pipe connections made, these clips are cut through. The clips may be bolted up again using fish plates if ever it should be necessary to take the water box off. These features are illustrated in Figure 6.7.

To prevent undue deflection at the centre of their length, it is usual to fit one or more support plates between the tube plates. These plates are drilled with clearing holes in line with the tube-plate holes, the tubes passing through the holes and being supported there. The support-plate positions and pitches are chosen to discourage transverse tube vibration.

Tube vibration can occur if the natural frequency of the tube coincides with the running speed of the turbines, and can be aggravated by "steam buffeting". The tube vibration characteristics depend on the pitching of the support plates, on the clearance between the tube and the support plate hole, on the tube diameter, thickness and material and is of course also influenced by the fact that when in operation, the tubes are full of sea water.

Tube vibration can result in the tubes hammering on one another, often to such an extent that flats are formed on the outer surfaces of the tube, ultimately wearing through the tube thickness. Vibration can also cause fatigue failure of the tubes at the support plates and behind the tube plates, and can cause slackening of the tube to tube plate fixing.

The modes of tube vibration are quite complex and usually nowadays form the subject of a computer investigation in the design stage. This invariably results in the adoption of unequal support plate pitches.

Shape and location of condenser

Condenser shells are not always made circular, but sometimes rectangular or nearly square and sometimes pear-shaped. These differences in no way affect the principles or calculations illustrated here, except in the cross-section of the condenser. On reciprocating engines, the condenser is carried on brackets on the back columns, but in turbines it is usually underslung, i.e. below the L.P. turbine, sometimes in the fore-and-aft, and sometimes in the athwartship direction. If underslung, the condenser is carried on spring feet to relieve the L.P. turbine exhaust flange of some of the very considerable downward force due to the mass of the condenser, and to control the upward forces due to thermal expansion.

Alternatively, the condenser may be solidly mounted, and a steel or special rubber bellows piece fitted between the turbine exhaust and the condenser. Such an arrangement

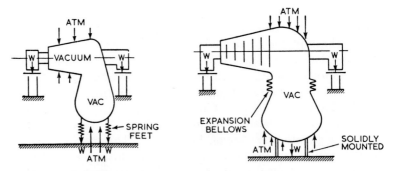

Figure 6.8 Condenser mounting and connection to turbine
(left) Only the weight of the L.P. turbine and condenser is imposed on the ship's structure. The atmospheric vacuum load is balanced within the turbine/condenser structure and is not transmitted to the ship's structure
(right) In addition to the weight of the L.P. turbine and condenser acting downwards, the atmospheric load on the L.P. exhaust chamber acts downwards on the engine seating, and the atmospheric load on the condenser acts upwards on the condenser seating

however introduces certain forces on the turbine condenser, and ships structure (see Figure 6.8).

While the majority of marine turbine condensers are under-slung, there were some installations made quite a number of years ago with wing condensers mounted separately from, and on roughly the same level as, the turbines (e.g. see Chapter 3, Figures 3.1 and 3.34). Within the last few years, several installations have been built which revert to this principle, but in a slightly different form. The modern version is called one-plane machinery. The turbines, gearing and con-denser are mounted at the same level, and the condenser is placed forward of the L.P. turbine, with some form of ex-haust trunk between.

LIMITATIONS DUE TO THE WORKING SUBSTANCE

The task of the condenser is indeed a sombre one—it has to reject to the atmosphere, in the form of low-grade heat, between 50 and 70 per cent of the high-grade fuel heat. It was probably an incomplete and subjective awareness of this fact which for many years caused the condenser to be regard-ed merely as a box of tubes—a convenient way of getting rid of the exhaust steam at low pressure and of providing more or less clean condensate for boiler feed water.

By providing a condenser operation at sub-atmospheric pressure, we increase very significantly the amount of work obtainable from each 1.0 kg of steam. Were there no conden-ser, this additional work, and the steam itself, would be thrown away. Were the condenser operated at atmospheric pressure, the steam/condensate would be recovered, but the additional work would be thrown away.

Thus, the dissipation to atmosphere of a large part of the fuel heat is not the fault of the condenser, or of the engines, but is an inherent feature of the steam/water working sub-stance itself. For example, steam at 60.0 bar, 500.0°C has specific enthalpy 3422.2 kJ/kg. If this steam were expanded to atmospheric pressure, 923.1 kJ/kg would become available for doing work, and 3422.2-923.1 = 2499.1 kJ/kg would be thrown out in the exhaust steam.

If instead, the steam were expanded to the lowest practic-able pressure, say 0.03 bar, 1381.2 kJ/kg would become available for doing work, and 3422.2-1381.2 = 2041.0 kJ/kg would be thrown out in the exhaust.

Thus by exhausting the heat engine at 0.03 bar instead of at atmospheric pressure, we increase the work obtainable from each 1.0 kg of steam by 49.6 per cent, and reduce the heat thrown out by 18.33 per cent. Even so, at the low exhaust pressure, 0.03 bar, the specific enthalpy of the steam is 2041.0 kJ/kg, of which the increment for evaporation (latent heat), 1940.0 kJ/kg, *must* be thrown away in the condensation process. This represents 56.7 per cent of the initial total enthalpy of steam at 60.0 bar, 500.0°C.

The large proportion of the fuel heat which must be rejected in the condenser results from an inherent physical property of the steam/water working substance itself, viz. that over a wide range of steam pressures and conditions, the increment for evaporation is a large proportion of the specific enthalpy.

Theoretical and practical condenser

As a matter of primary importance, it must be understood that, thermodynamically, the pressure at which the condenser will condense the exhaust steam is determined solely by the temperature of the heat sink, i.e. by the sea temperature. Thus if the sea temperature is say, 15.0°C, then theoretically the condenser should condense the exhaust steam at a pressure of 0.017 bar (i.e. that pressure whose saturation temperature is 15.0°C).

There are, however, certain practical matters which cause the condenser to differ considerably from the above theoretical conception.

Firstly, just as it is necessary to have a pressure difference to cause a fluid to flow from one vessel into another, so it is necessary to have a temperature difference between the exhaust steam and the circulating water to cause heat to flow from the steam to the water, i.e. the steam temperature must be higher than the water temperature at any point in the condenser.

Secondly, even after allowing some temperature difference for heat flow, the resulting condenser pressure might be lower than that which the engines can economically utilise. In this event, we would have to increase the temperature difference to raise the condenser pressure to that which can be economically justified.

Thirdly, the condenser works at sub-atmospheric pressure, as does a considerable part of the engines, steam and feed systems, etc. There is therefore always the tendency for atmospheric air to leak into the sub-atmospheric part of the system and ultimately to collect in the condenser. Air will not condense at ordinary temperatures, and if allowed to accumulate in the condenser, would cause the condenser pressure to rise, thus reducing the efficiency of the engine and creating other problems. Thus, we require to provide the condenser with an air pump, which must continuously remove any air (and other incondensible gas) which arrives in the condenser. The manner of air removal is of importance, as the presence of air in the condenser reduces the ability of the condenser to transmit heat from the steam to the water, and also causes under-cooling of the condensate. If the condensate is at saturation temperature, it cannot hold any air in solution, but undercooling, even by less than $1.0^{\circ}C$ renders it capable of absorbing and holding in solution, quite a significant quantity of air. This results in more difficult conditions for the feed water deaerator, or at worst, if there is no deaerator, release of air in the boiler drum, where saturation conditions exist. Oxygen in the boiler drum can cause corrosion.

Fourthly, the steam condenses at the saturation temperature corresponding to the condenser pressure, and for its complete condensation, it is necessary to remove only the increment of enthalpy for evaporation (latent heat). If any of the enthalpy of the saturated liquid (liquid heat) is removed, the temperature of the condensate falls below the saturation temperature corresponding to the condenser pressure (under-cooling), and this is a loss which has to be made good by the boiler or by the feed heating system. Also as stated, undercooled condensate can absorb air and hold it in solution.

Fifthly, the general design of the condensing plant can be based only on one set of conditions, i.e. sea temperature, circulating water quantity, main engine power, etc. By the nature of its function, a ship must be able to operate satisfactorily for extended periods in practically any part of the world, hence the conditions can vary drastically, even during any one voyage. This renders necessary some knowledge of the effects of these variations, so that judicious use may be made of any in-built means of meeting them.

Following the foregoing we may now examine the relevant points in more detail.

Temperature difference

We have seen how there must be a temperature difference between the steam and the circulating water at any point in the condenser.

The quantity of heat, kJ/s, which can be transmitted from steam to water is directly proportional to this temperature difference, e.g. if the temperature difference between steam and water is doubled, then twice the quantity of heat can be removed in the same time.

In passing through the condenser, the circulating water receives heat from the condensing steam, hence the water temperature rises from inlet to outlet. The steam temperature is constant and equal to the saturation temperature corresponding to the condenser pressure. At the water inlet end therefore, the temperature difference between steam and water is large, and the *rate* of water temperature rise is greater than at the water outlet end where the temperature difference is small. This may be illustrated diagrammatically as in Figure 6.9 which is drawn for a simple single-flow condenser.

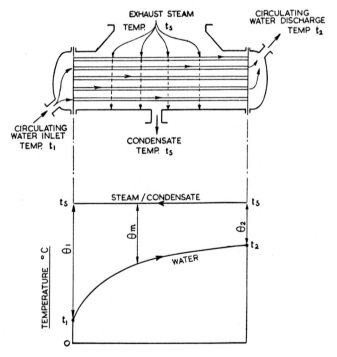

Figure 6.9 Temperature differences in a surface condenser

Since the temperature difference varies along the condenser, the heat flow from steam to water is controlled by the mean temperature difference between steam and water. It should be noted that because the *rate* of water temperature rise is not uniform, the mean temperature difference is not the arithmetic mean of θ_1 and θ_2, but is the logarithmic mean, viz.

$$\text{Mean temperature difference } \theta_m = \frac{\theta_1 - \theta_2}{\log_e \theta_1/\theta_2} \; ^\circ\text{C}$$

Change of sea temperature

Again referring to Figure 6.9, if the sea temperature t_1 rises, all other conditions remaining constant, the entire water temperature line $t_1 t_2$ will rise and tend to reduce θ_m. The same θ_m however is required to transmit the heat to condense the steam, hence the steam temperature line t_s will also rise, which means that the steam pressure will rise.

Hence, if the sea temperature rises, and no corrective action is taken, the condenser pressure will rise.

Circulating water quantity

For a given condenser heat load and t_1, the circulating water temperature rise r°C is determined by the circulating water quantity. Hence if, with any given heat load, the circulating water quantity is reduced, the water temperature rise will increase.

Again referring to Figure 6.9, an increase in r will tend to cause θ_m to diminish, but since the heat load is constant, the steam temperature line t_s will rise to restore the same θ_m which existed with the full water quantity. Hence if the c.w. quantity diminishes, and no corrective action is taken, the condenser pressure will rise.

Change of main engine power

If, with all other factors constant, the main engine power is reduced, the condenser heat load diminishes, hence the c.w. temperature rise diminishes and θ_m tends to increase. Because of the reduced heat load however, a smaller θ_m is required, and the steam temperature line t_s falls. Hence if the engine power is reduced, and no corrective action is taken, the condenser pressure will decrease.

Condenser surface

The condenser surface S is the total external surface area, m^2, of all the tubes between the inner faces of the tube plates. The quantity of heat, kJ/s, transmitted is directly proportional to the surface area which is transmitting the heat. Hence if say 10.0 per cent of the tubes become blocked with sand, weed, etc., all other conditions remaining as before, the quantity of heat transmitted would tend to diminish by the same percentage, but to enable the full quantity of heat to be transmitted, and so to maintain condensation, the mean temperature difference would increase accordingly, again leading to increased condenser pressure, if no corrective action is taken.

Thus if a proportion of the tubes become blocked and no corrective action is taken, the condenser pressure will rise.

The resistance to heat flow

The quantity of heat transmitted by unit surface in unit time with unit mean temperature difference varies inversely as the thermal resistance to heat flow, e.g. if the resistance is halved, the quantity of heat transmitted is doubled.

At first it might appear that the only resistance encountered by the heat flowing from the steam to the water is the metal of the tube wall. This however is far from the truth, since in actual fact the thermal resistance of the tube wall itself is usually quite small compared with the other resistances.

Firstly, water is passing along the inside of the tube, and depending on its mean temperature, the water has a certain viscosity, or *stickiness*, causing it to tend to adhere to, and form a water film on, the inside surface of the tube. At the same time, the water velocity along the tube is tending to tear any such film off the inside surface of the tube. Depending therefore on the mean water temperature and on the water velocity, there exists on the inside surface of the tube a stagnant water film of a certain thickness. The rate at which heat can be conducted through this water film depends on the film thickness and on the water temperature. The thermal resistance of the water film is also to some extent influenced by the tube diameter and by the water density. For our purpose, we may regard the thermal resistance of the water film on the inside of the tube as being controlled by the water velocity and the mean water temperature. The higher the velocity and mean temperature, the thinner is the water film and the lower the thermal resistance.

Secondly, steam is condensing to water on the outside surface of the tube, and again depending on the water temperature, the viscosity of the water tends to make it adhere to, and form a stagnant film on, the outside surface of the tube. At the same time, the exhaust steam sweeping over and around the tube tends to tear off this film. Depending therefore on the saturation temperature at which the steam is condensing, and on the rate of steam loading of the tube, there exists on the outside surface of the tube a stagnant water film of a certain thickness, and the rate at which heat can be conducted through this film depends on the film thickness and on the temperature. The higher the temperature and steam loading, the thinner is the water film and the lower the thermal resistance.

Thirdly after some time in service, the inside surface of the tube may become fouled by deposits from the circulating water. Of these, the most serious is scale, a hard deposit formed by calcium sulphate from the heated circulating water. The condenser tubes can also become fouled on the steam side by impurities in the steam. This is particularly so in the condensers of reciprocating engines where lubricating oil from the cylinder walls can be carried over by the exhaust steam and deposited on the tubes.

Fourthly, there is always present in the condenser a quantity—however small it may be—of air and incondensible gas. By far the worst offender in opposing heat transmission is the blanket of air and incondensible gas surrounding the tube on the steam side, since air is a very poor conductor of heat indeed.

The thermal resistance offered by the tube wall itself depends on the thermal conductivity of the metal, on the wall thickness, and on the ratio of the external to the internal diameter. If the thermal resistance of a brass tube wall 1.2 mm thick is taken as 1.0, the other thermal resistances are of the following order:

Water film 0.25 mm thick	100
Scale film 0.25 mm thick	100–200
Air film 0.25 mm thick	2000

The total resistance to heat transmission is the sum of the separate resistances outlined above. A reduction in one or more of the separate resistances reduces the total resistance.

The rate of heat transmission

Since the heat transmitted varies inversely as the total resistance, we may say that the heat transmitted varies directly as the reciprocal of the total resistance. The reciprocal of the total resistance is called the overall rate of heat transmission, denoted by K, in units kJ/m^{2}s °C, i.e. kW/m^2°C, since 1 kW = 1 kJ/s.

Fundamental equations for condenser

If we denote the heat rejection, kW, by H, the condenser surface m^2, by S and the mean temperature difference °C, by θ_m, then we may write

1 m^2 of surface with a mean temperature difference of 1°C
　　transmits K kW

S m^2 of surface with a mean temperature difference of 1°C
　　transmits KS kW

S m^2 of surface with a mean temperature difference of θ_m °C
　　transmits $KS\theta_m$ kW

　i.e. $H = KS\theta_m$　　　　　　　　　　　　　　　　　(1)

Also, if the circulating water quantity is Q m^3/s, and the circulating water temperature rise is r°C, and if the density of average sea water is taken as 1024 kg/m^3, and the specific heat as 3.935 kJ/kg°C, then from the relationship, heat absorbed = mass × specific heat × temperature rise, we may write

　　$H = 1024Q \times 3.935r$　　　　　　　from which

　　$H = 4030Qr$, kW　　　　　　　　　　　　　　　(2)

(1) and (2) are the fundamental equations for a condenser, and will be used later to illustrate both the basis design of the condenser and the effects of variation of the operating conditions.

Circulating water velocity through the tubes

As stated previously, the actual rate of heat transmission which it is possible to achieve depends in the first place largely on the circulating water velocity through the tubes. The higher the water velocity, the thinner is the water side film, the faster the heat is carried away, and hence the higher the rate of heat transmission.

With an increased value of K, examination of equation (1) will show that for a given value of θ_m, the surface S would be reduced, resulting in a smaller condenser for any given condenser pressure and heat load. The maximum tube velocity which it is possible to use is however limited by one or both of two factors, viz. the tube material, and the pumping power required to circulate the condenser.

TUBE MATERIAL

For any one tube material, there is a limiting velocity above which there is a danger of erosion. This risk can be aggravated if there is sand or other abrasive matter in the circulating water. There also exists the risk of partial blockage of a tube or tubes, resulting in high local velocity and erosion in way of the partial blockage. For these reasons, the maximum velocities generally in use with various tube materials are as follows:

Admiralty brass	1.5–1.8 m/s
Aluminium brass	1.8–2.4 m/s
90/10 copper nickel	3.0 m/s
70/30 copper nickel	3.6–4.0 m/s

Where aluminium brass tubes are used, the completed condenser has to be treated on the water side with ferrous sulphate in clean water, otherwise when working in estuarine waters the tubes can be attacked and holed by sulphides in the water. In addition, hollow plastic inserts may be fitted into the inlet ends of the tubes to prevent inlet-end erosion (see Figure 6.3).

Although 70/30 copper nickel should permit the use of the higher tube velocity shown above, there is in practice a reluctance to use tube water velocities much above 3.0 m/s even with this material, since in the event of partial blockage of a tube or tubes, the local water velocity past the partial blockage could well approach or exceed 5.5 m/s at which, for 70/30 copper nickel, adverse high velocity effects become significant.

TITANIUM TUBES

Within the last few years, the use of titanium tubes for condensers operating with sea water has become quite attractive. Formerly, by comparison with copper-based alloys, titanium was so expensive that its use for condenser tubes could not be economically justified. Recently however, much more has become known about those of its qualities which render it an excellent tube material for sea water applications, and it was tried experimentally, at first on a small scale, then on a large scale, and has now become established for land installations circulated by sea water. The larger potential market for titanium tubes, together with the astronomical rise over the years in the price of copper, has so narrowed the economic gap that it seems possible that, in marine installations also, titanium could become a serious competitor to the traditional copper-based alloys for condenser tubes.

The outstanding advantages of titanium for condenser tubes are:

1. It has a high strength/mass ratio. The density of titanium is about half that of 70/30 copper nickel, while the tensile strength is about the same. Hence for equal size, strength and number off, titanium tubes would have about one half the mass of 70/30 copper nickel tubes.
2. It has a very high resistance to corrosion, erosion, abrasion and all other forms of attack on both the steam and water sides, in a wide range of aggressive media, and at water velocities far in excess of the present accepted maxima for copper-based alloy tubes.
3. Its thermal conductivity is about 70.0 per cent of that of 70/30 copper nickel, hence for equal thermal performance, a titanium tube should have a wall thickness 0.7 of that of a 70/30 copper nickel tube of the same external diameter.

By its nature, a marine condenser circulating water system is essentially a low-head system; i.e. it is not likely to require a design circulating water pressure of more than about 15.0 m of sea water, which even including for the sub-atmospheric pressure in the steam side of the condenser, requires only quite a thin tube wall from the strength aspect, whatever the tube material.

With copper-based alloys however, strength is not the only criterion, but also wastage due to corrosion, erosion, etc., and experience has adopted a tube wall thickness of 1.2 mm for a 19.0 mm external diameter copper-based alloy tube.

With titanium tubes, the wastage criterion is eliminated, hence the tube wall thickness can be made considerably less, limited only by the need to ensure satisfactory vibration characteristics and sufficient stiffness to avoid distortion during handling. For a 19.0 mm external diameter titanium tube, present-day practice is to use a tube wall thickness of 0.72 mm. This is more than adequate for strength, reasonably stiff for handling, and with support plates pitched more closely, is adequate from the vibration aspect.

A 19.0 mm/0.72 mm titanium tube can be considered to be thermally equivalent to a 19.0 mm/1.2 mm 70/30 copper nickel tube, hence any given condenser with any given tube velocity would require approximately the same number and length of tubes whether titanium or 70/30 copper nickel.

The mass of the titanium tubes would however be considerably less:

$$\frac{18.28}{17.8} \times \frac{0.72}{1.2} \times \frac{1}{2} \times 100 = 30.8 \text{ per cent of the copper nickel tubes, i.e.}$$

We have used a smaller volume of a less dense material, and which is practically immune from any form of attack.

Further, since the danger of erosion is removed by using titanium tubes, the tube water velocity could be significantly increased, thus enabling one of the most fruitful means of improving the condenser performance to be exploited up to the economic limit of pumping power. For example, if the tube velocity could be raised from 3.0 m/s to 4.0 m/s, the rate of heat transmission would be increased by possibly 10.0–12.0 per cent, thus allowing a considerable reduction in surface to be made.

Pumping power

The pressure loss due to water friction in the condenser tubes varies directly as the square of the water velocity through the tubes. The condenser pressure loss is part of the pressure which has to be generated by the circulating pump, so that the power required to drive the circulating pump increases as the condenser tube velocity is increased, and there comes a point at which, in the overall economics, the benefit of the increased tube velocity is offset by the increased pumping power. To illustrate this, it might be possible, by running the circulating pump faster, to reduce the condenser pressure such that the steam consumption of the main engines is reduced by 1000 kg/h. This however, would be useless if the engine driving the circulating pump required an additional 1000 kg/h of steam to circulate the increased water quantity.

Arrangement of tubes

Condensers are no longer indiscriminately packed with tubes, but the tubes are carefully arranged with a view to achieving the following objects:

1. To attempt to ensure that each particle of steam encounters only the minimum amount of cold surface required for its complete condensation, and that the condensate so formed falls to the condenser bottom clear of any other tubes. This assists in the prevention of condensate under-cooling.
2. To bypass a certain proportion of steam round the tube nest, and cause it to pass through the "rain" of condensate falling from the tubes, so that any condensate which has been under-cooled will be reheated up to the steam temperature by condensing, by direct contact, some of the bypassed steam. Alternatively, a central untubed "steam lane" may be provided for this purpose. This process, sometimes called regeneration ensures that the condensate temperature is maintained practically at steam temperature.
3. To ensure that all tubes are continuously swept by steam, so to prevent the air blanket building up and reducing the rate of heat transmission.
4. To ensure that the steam can penetrate right down to the remote rows of tubes, and so to render effective the greatest possible amount of cooling surface.
5. To attempt to so streamline the steam flows through the condenser as will reduce the overall pressure drop to a minimum.
6. To ensure that steam cannot have direct access to the air pump suction, thus ensuring that the air cooling section is effective.

Figures 6.10 and 6.11 show methods of so arranging the tubes. Figure 6.11 also illustrates divided water ends, which permit one half of the condenser tubes to be cleaned on the water side while the other half is condensing the steam. Each half of the condenser has its own c.w. inlet and discharge

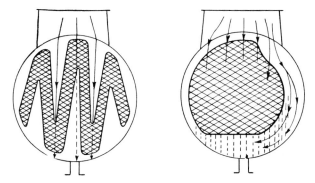

Figure 6.10 Surface condenser-tube arrangements
(left) ribbon arrangement
(right) side regenerative passage

pipes and its own air suction. The c.w. inlet and discharge
valves and the air suction valve of that half of the condenser
which is to be cleaned are closed, and the water boxes drained prior to opening up for cleaning. The cold tube surface
and the air suction of the half condenser remaining in service
attracts all the steam preferentially to that half. This means

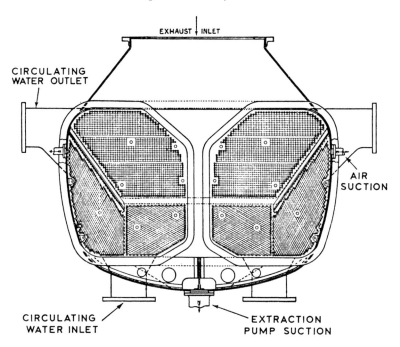

Figure 6.11 Regenerative condenser with centre regenerative passage

that only one half of the condenser surface is being used to condense all the steam, hence during condenser cleaning in this manner, either reduced power or increased condenser pressure must be accepted.

CONDENSER CALCULATIONS

Mention has already been made of the temperature differences between the steam and the water at inlet and outlet. In what follows, it is assumed that the steam saturation temperature is constant, and that the condensate leaves the condenser at the saturation temperature of the steam.

Detailed studies have shown that the economic temperature differences are in the following ranges

For reciprocating engines	$\theta_1 = 25.0°C$ to $50.0°C$
	$\theta_2 = 14.0°C$ to $20.0°C$
For turbine engines	$\theta_1 = 11.0°C$ to $28.0°C$
	$\theta_2 = 4.5°C$ to $9.0°C$

The economic values of θ_1 and θ_2 for reciprocating engines are higher than for turbine engines, since for the former, very low condenser pressures are not required.

Suppose a turbine job operates in a service where the average sea temperature is $17.0°C$, and the economic condenser pressure, as optimised for the entire installation, is 0.047534 bar. The saturation temperature corresponding to the condenser pressure is $32.0°C$, hence $\theta_1 = 32.0-17.0 = 15.0°C$.

Suppose $\theta_2 = 4.5°C$, then referring to Figure 6.12. The circulating water discharge temperature

$$t_2 = 32.0 - 4.5 = 27.5°C,$$

and the water temperature rise

$$r = t_2 - t_1 = 27.5 - 17.0 = 10.5°C$$

Suppose the steam quantity to be condensed amounts to 25 000 kg/hr and the specific enthalpy of the exhaust steam is 2325.0 kJ/kg.

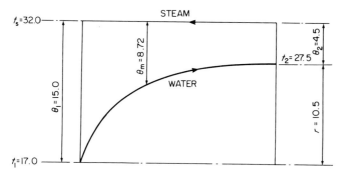

Figure 6.12 Temperatures and temperature differences in condenser

The enthalpy of the saturated liquid at 0.047534 bar is 134.0 kJ/kg. Hence heat to be removed from each 1.0 kg of steam = 2325.0 − 134.0 = 2191.0 kJ, from which,

$$\text{Condenser heat load } H = \frac{2191.0 \times 25\,000}{3600} = 15\,215 \text{ kW}$$

From fundamental equation (2), $H = 4030Qr$, the circulating water quantity,

$$Q = \frac{H}{4030r}$$

$$\therefore Q = \frac{15\,215}{4030 \times 10.5} = 0.3596 \text{ m}^3/\text{s}$$

$$\text{Mean temperature difference } \theta_m = \frac{\theta_1 - \theta_2}{\log_e \theta_1/\theta_2}$$

$$\therefore \theta_m = \frac{15.0 - 4.5}{\log_e 15.0/4.5}$$

$$\therefore \theta_m = \frac{10.5}{1.2039}$$

$$\therefore \theta_m = 8.72\,^\circ\text{C} \quad \text{(see Figure 6.12)}$$

In general, when tube water velocity, thermal resistances etc., are taken into account, the rate of heat transmission which can be achieved by normal condensers is between 2.2

and 4.5 kW/m^2°C. For present purposes, we will assume a tube velocity of 1.5 m/s, which could be expected to give an overall design rate of heat transmission, $K = 2.6$ kW/m^2°C.

Fundamental equation (1), $H = KS\theta_m$ from which

$$S = \frac{H}{K\theta_m}$$

$$\therefore S = \frac{15\,215}{2.6 \times 8.72}$$

$$\therefore S = 671.1 \text{ m}^2$$

From the equation of continuity $Q = Av$ for the water side of the tubes the required area of water flow through the tubes is

$$A = \frac{Q}{v} = \frac{0.3596}{1.5} = 0.23972 \text{ m}^2$$

Note that this is the total internal cross-sectional area of the tubes in one water flow.

Let the tubes be 19 mm external dia., 1.2 mm thick, then

Internal diameter of one tube =
$19.0 - (2 \times 1.2) = 16.6$ mm and
Internal area of one tube $= (\pi/4) \times 16.6^2 = 216.4$ mm^2
Hence, number of tubes per flow =

$$\frac{0.23972 \times 1000^2}{216.4} = 1108$$

Suppose there are two water flows, then the total number of tubes in the condenser is $1108 \times 2 = 2216$. Condenser tubes are generally arranged as shown in Figure 6.13. For 19.0 mm ext. dia. tubes, the pitch p would probably be 28.5 mm

Area of tubeplate section $= 2.5p \times 3.0p \times \sin 60.0°$
$$= \frac{2.5 \times 3.0 \times 0.866 \times 28.5^2}{1000^2}$$
$$= 0.005275 \text{ m}^2$$

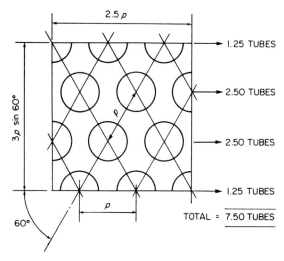

Figure 6.13 Typical condenser tube pitching

This area of tube plate accommodates 7.5 tubes, hence the gross tube density = 7.5/0.005275 = 1422 tubes/m² of tube plate area.

Now, not all of the tube plate is occupied by tubes—some untubed areas must be left in way of steam lanes, water box division bars, baffles, stays, etc. Suppose we assume a factor of 0.75 to allow for this, then

$$\text{Nett tube density} = 1422 \times 0.75 = 1066 \text{ tubes/m}^2$$

of tube plate area and to accommodate 2216 tubes would require tube plate area = 2216/1066 = 2.079 m².

If the condenser is of circular cross-section, this would give a condenser shell diameter of 1.63 m.

The cooling surface of the condenser is the total external surface area of all the tubes, hence if l is the length between the tube plates, m,

$$\text{External surface area of one tube} = \pi d l, \text{ m}^2.$$

There are 2216 tubes, 19.0 mm external diameter, and the total surface is 671.1 m², hence

$$\frac{2216 \times \pi \times 19.0 \times l}{1000} = 671.1$$

$$\therefore l = \frac{671.1 \times 1000}{2216 \times \pi \times 19.0} = 5.073 \text{ m}$$

The condenser dimensions are 1.63 m diameter, 5.073 m long between tube plates.

Variations possible in the original choice of condenser

Let us suppose that the above condenser cannot be accepted because it is too long. Excessive length causes problems of accommodation in the machinery arrangement; also if the condenser length is too large compared with the width (or length) of the L.P. turbine exhaust opening, problems of adequate steam access to the ends of the condenser arise.

Suppose we increase the number of water flows from two to three. Since the water quantity and tube velocity are not altered, the number of tubes per water flow is 1108 as before. There are however, now three water flows, hence total number of tubes = 1108 × 3 = 3324.

The required surface is 671.1 m^2 as before, hence

$$\text{Length between tube plates} = \frac{671.1 \times 1000}{3324 \times \pi \times 19.0} = 3.382 \text{ m}$$

The length is considerably reduced, but to accommodate 3324 tubes, we would require a tube plate area of 3324/1064 = 3.124 m^2, i.e. a condenser diameter of 2.0 m.

The total length, and therefore the total mass and cost of the *tubing* in this condenser, is the same as before, but we have increased the cross-section of the condenser. This means larger tube plates and water boxes, increased number of tube holes to be drilled in tube plates and support plates, increased number of tube expansions or packings. Since the increase in these is 50 per cent, and the reduction in length gives us only a minor saving on the simple shell plate, it is more than likely that this condenser would be rejected on the grounds of mass and first cost. The increased diameter (or depth) of the condenser could also adversely affect the head available over the condensate extraction pump suction. This is often an important factor.

Returning now to the original condenser, we have to consider what other variations are possible, in order to improve matters.

Inspection of the condenser equation $H = KS\theta_m$ will show that for a given heat load H, the required surface S can be reduced by increasing θ_m. To increase θ_m, we must increase either or both θ_1 or θ_2. Since in this case, the design sea temperature t_1 and the condenser pressure (corresponding to t_s) are fixed, we can increase θ_m only by increasing θ_2.

If we increase θ_2, we reduce the circulating water temperature rise r, and from the condenser equation $H = 4030Qr$, for a given heat load H we must increase the circulating water quantity Q. If we increase Q, but keep the tube water velocity as before, more water flow area will be required, and we will therefore have to increase the number of tubes, thus increasing the condenser cross-section. The reduction in surface which we get by increasing θ_m in this manner is a reduction in the *length* of the condenser.

Now, we have already seen that to reduce the length at the expense of increasing the number of tubes and the condenser cross-section has an adverse effect on the mass and cost of the condenser, therefore in trying to reduce the length, we should not increase—indeed we should try to reduce—the condenser cross-section.

In order to reduce the number of tubes and the condenser cross-section, we could leave θ_2 (and hence Q) unaltered, but make the condenser single-flow, i.e. instead of having two water flows doubling back on one another, we could "unfold" the two flows, making one. This however, would double the length between the tubeplates, which is already unacceptable. Alternatively, we could leave θ_2 unaltered, increase the water velocity through the tubes, and consider both the single and two-flow arrangements. Alternatively, we could increase both θ_2 and the tube velocity and again consider single and two-flow.

One possibility with modern turbine condensers is to use higher tube velocities in a single flow. This gives a condenser of relatively small cross-section, but at the expense of increasing the pumping power required to circulate the condenser. The tubes are usually of 70/30 copper nickel, permitting a maximum tube velocity of 3.0 m/s.

To illustrate this, suppose that in our example, we reduce the total number of tubes to 2000 in a single flow, and increase the tube velocity to 2.5 m/s, then

$$\text{Water flow area} = \frac{2000 \times 216.4}{1000^2} = 0.4328 \text{ m}^2 \text{, hence}$$

C.W. quantity, $Q = 0.4328 \times 2.5 = 1.082$ m^3/s.

C.W. temperature rise, $r = \dfrac{15\,215}{4030 \times 1.082} = 3.49°C$

C.W. discharge temperature, $t_2 = 17.0 + 3.49 = 20.49°C$

Discharge temperature difference, $\theta_2 = 32.0 - 20.49 = 11.51°C$

Mean temperature difference, $\theta_m = \dfrac{15.0 - 11.51}{\log_e \dfrac{15.0}{11.51}} = \dfrac{3.49}{0.2646} = 13.19°C$

The increased water velocity would give a higher overall rate of heat transmission, say $K = 3.5$ kW/m^2°C, hence

Condenser surface, $S = \dfrac{15\,215}{3.5 \times 13.9} = 329.6$ m^2 and

Length between tube plates $= \dfrac{329.6 \times 1000}{2000 \times \pi \times 19.0} = 2.761$ m

Again assuming 1066 tubes per 1.0 m^2 of tube plate area,

Tube plate area $= \dfrac{2000}{1066} = 1.876$ m^2, giving

Tube plate diameter $= 1.55$ m

The condenser would be 1.55 m dia., 2.761 m long between tube plates.

By comparison with the original condenser, not only have we approximately halved the length, but have reduced the number of tubes and the gross area of the tube plates, support plates and water boxes by about 10 per cent, thus making a very significant reduction in the dimensions, mass and first cost of the condenser.

As is always true however, we do not get this advantage for nothing. We have increased the tube water velocity from 1.5 m/s to 2.5 m/s, hence we have increased the hydraulic friction loss through the tubes by a factor of $(2.5/1.5)^2 = 2.78$. However, the condenser is only 0.545 of the original length, and being single-flow, the water has to go through once only instead of twice, therefore we have reduced the tube friction loss by a factor of 0.545/2 = 0.273. The nett result is that we have reduced the *condenser* head loss by a factor of 2.78 × 0.273 = 0.76. The effect on the total c.w. *system* head loss depends on what proportion of the total system head loss is due to the condenser and what proportion to the c.w. piping with its bends, valves, fittings, etc., but for our purpose, we will assume that the total system head loss is reduced by a factor of 0.8. The c.w. quantity we have increased from 0.3596 m^3/s to 1.0825 m^3/s, i.e. by a factor of 3.01. The power required by the circulating pump is directly proportional to the quantity pumped and to the head against which it is pumped, hence we have increased the c.w. pumping power required by a factor of 0.8 × 3.01 = 2.408.

The smaller, less expensive condenser requires two and a half times the c.w. pumping power required by the larger more expensive condenser.

The reduction in the number of tubes and the increase in water velocity were purposely chosen of large magnitude with the intention of more clearly illustrating how the choice of the condenser design can be varied in the light of the overall economics of the installation. The results shown should not be regarded as hard and fast rules, or what would necessarily be used in practice. What is correct for one ship is not necessarily correct for another. For any one ship or class of ship, the condenser design can be based only on one set of conditions—usually the weighted average conditions for the sea routes and type of trade visualised. The term "weighted average" implies that the variation in the conditions is taken into account in making the initial choice of condenser.

EFFECTS OF VARYING CONDITIONS ON THE PERFORMANCE OF THE CONDENSER

Condenser tube fouling

Condenser tubes which were initially clean, gradually become fouled in service. On the water side, fouling may be due to scale formation, marine biological growth, accumulations of sand, weed, etc., or protracted operation in polluted dock or river water. On the steam side, it may be due to oil, or impurities in the steam. Any such fouling of course means that there is increased thermal resistance to heat flow from steam to water, with the result that the overall rate of heat transmission diminishes, and if no corrective action is taken, the condenser pressure gradually rises. Depending on the nature and the rate of fouling, and on the intervals at which condenser tube cleaning can be carried out, there exists the tendency to continuous deterioration of efficiency.

Until comparatively recently, little precise knowledge of marine condenser fouling was available, and it has become customary to build margins into the condensing plant to enable some corrective action to be taken to eliminate, or at least to moderate the loss of efficiency due to fouling. To this end, the calculated overall rate of heat transmission K, kW/m^2 $°$C based on the design tube velocity, steam and water temperatures and steam loading is reduced by a fouling factor before being applied to the condenser equation $H = KS\theta_m$. This fouling factor—which may be of the order of 0.85 to 0.95—means that we build into the condenser some extra surface over and above that required by the design calculations. At design conditions therefore, when the tubes are clean, the condenser pressure will be lower than design.

In addition, the circulating pump and system is arranged so that it can be made to give either more water or less water than the design quantity Q through the condenser.

If at design conditions, with clean tubes, the main engines can take advantage of the lower condenser pressure, the main engine steam consumption will be reduced. This, in turn, means less heat load on the condenser, the condenser pressure will diminish, and the main engine steam consumption will be further reduced until balance is reached between the main engine steam and the condenser pressure. This implies higher overall efficiency, but we must now ask the question: is the saving in main engine steam greater or less than we would get by reducing the speed of the circulating pump, to reduce the water quantity to that which will give the design condenser pressure? In practice, this question can be answered only by the effect on the fuel consumption.

As the condenser fouls up in service, the condenser pressure tends to rise, and if the tubes cannot be cleaned when the fouling margin has been used up, then the opposite state of affairs exists, i.e. more water than design will be required to maintain the design condenser pressure.

As a rule, proper condenser tube cleaning can be carried

out only during a major refit, although in certain cases there exists the possibility of carrying out partial cleaning in port, or even at sea (see Figure 6.11). Ordinary fouling may be removed by brushing or bulleting the tubes with wire brushes or bullets. Hard scale can not generally be removed satisfactorily by brushing or bulleting, but necessitates treating the condenser on the water side with a 5 per cent solution of hydrochloric acid, to which a chemical inhibitor has been added to ensure that while the acid will attack the scale, it will not seriously attack the tube metal. If such a treatment proves necessary, it is prudent to have it done by chemical cleaning specialists, or at least to seek advice first from such specialists.

Oil fouling on the steam side of the condenser may be removed by washing out with a hot solution of soda or one of the newer detergents.

Change of sea temperature

One of the commonest variations which can occur in a marine installation is variation of the sea temperature. Suppose a ship to be steaming steadily at full power and the sea temperature rises from t_1 to t_1'. Now the sea temperature does not appear directly in either of the two fundamental equations, hence none of the terms in these equations changes, r and θ_m remaining as before. The immediate effect therefore when t_1 rises to t_1' is for all the other temperatures to rise by the same amount (Figure 6.14).

The condenser pressure then increases from that corresponding to t_s to that corresponding to t_s'. The increase in

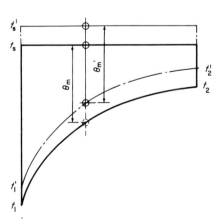

Figure 6.14 Effect of increased sea temperature on condenser temperatures and temperature differences

condenser pressure will cause the main engine steam consumption to increase which will increase the condenser heat load H. This will tend to cause the condenser pressure to rise further. At the same time however, the higher water and steam temperatures reduce the viscosity of the circulating water inside the tubes and of the condensate formed on the outside of the tubes, causing the water films on the inside and outside of the tubes to become thinner. The thermal resistance of these films will diminish, hence there will be some increase in the overall rate of heat transmission K. In the condenser equation $H = KS\theta_m$, the increase in H would probably be just about balanced by the increase in K, leaving θ_m unaltered. As a first approximation therefore, each 1°C change in sea temperature causes a change of 1°C in the saturation temperature corresponding to the condenser pressure.

With increased sea temperature, the rise in condenser pressure can be prevented, or reduced, by increasing the water quantity Q through the condenser. This reduces the c.w. temperature rise r, so increasing θ_m, and because of the increased tube velocity the rate of heat transmission K is also increased. The maximum sea temperature at which it is possible to run at full power with design condenser pressure is determined by what margin of power is built into the circulating pump, and whether the safe maximum water velocity through the tubes is likely to be exceeded.

With increased condenser pressure due to increased sea temperature, less work is available from each 1 kg of steam in the main engines. To maintain full power therefore, we can either

1. Accept the increased condenser pressure and put more steam through the main engines, or,
2. Increase the speed of the circulating pump to reduce the condenser pressure, thus requiring more steam for the circulating pump.

Depending on the margins built into the boilers, engines and condensing plant it may be necessary to use a combination of both.

Whatever method is used, some additional steam, and therefore some additional fuel will be required, and the object must be to keep this to a minimum.

If the sea temperature falls below design, the opposite state of affairs occurs. The condenser pressure diminishes, and the work per 1.0 kg of steam is increased, thus requiring less steam and less fuel. With falling sea temperature, this continues until the limiting condenser pressure is reached, i.e. the point at which the main engines cannot take advantage of any further reduction of condenser pressure. If the sea temperature continues to fall after this point is reached, a further saving in steam and fuel can be made by shutting in the circulating pump so that it is putting only sufficient water through the condenser to maintain the limiting condenser pressure. The c.w. quantity must not be reduced below that which corresponds to a tube velocity of 0.5–0.6 m/s, otherwise the change to laminar flow could drastically reduce the rate of heat transmission. With slow-moving water in the tubes, there is the risk of encouraging marine biological growth, but in the cold seas visualised in this instance, this is less likely.

In general, all the variations likely to be encountered, e.g. fouling, maximum and minimum tube velocities, capacity of circulating pump, etc., are taken into account in the original assessment and choice of the machinery, and it is likely that in any particular installation, there will exist a fair degree of flexibility of operation.

The sea-going engineer cannot be expected to know all the economic factors and design intentions of the machinery of which he is in charge, but the conscientious engineer will attempt continuously to satisfy two main criteria, viz.,

1. Is the main engine power being maintained?
2. Is the fuel consumption being maintained at the minimum which it can be for the prevailing conditions?

If the engine room is manually controlled, the engineer himself can establish the most economical way of meeting varying conditions, e.g. by experimenting with the circulating pump speed and noting the fuel consumption. If the engine room has automatic control, it is likely that the necessary corrective actions will be built into the control sequence.

Air in surface condensers

In the condenser proper, it is impossible actually to condense *all* the steam—there is always left behind at the air pump suction a certain quantity of vapour having roughly the same properties and behaving in the same manner as the exhaust steam. Compared with the quantity of exhaust steam entering at the top of the condenser, the vapour quantity at the air pump suction is very small.

Even in a well designed, well operated and well maintained steam plant, there is always a certain quantity of air present in the condenser, some of this being due to atmospheric air leakage into those parts of the system which are at sub-atmospheric pressure, and some entering with the exhaust steam due to there having been some air in solution in the feed water.

Hence there is always a mixture of steam and air in the condenser, and depending on the quantity and the proportion of air present, the effect on the performance of the condensing plant can be very significant.

The behaviour of a mixture of steam and air in a condenser is controlled by two laws:

1. Dalton's Law of Partial Pressures
Each constituent of a gas mixture exerts that pressure which it would exert if it alone occupied the containing vessel. The total pressure is the sum of the partial pressures.

2. The General Gas Law $PV = RT$
Although saturated or wet steam is not a perfect gas, its behaviour at low pressures is sufficiently close to enable the General Gas Law to be applied without appreciable practical error.

We may now examine the implications of these two laws.

Let P_A = partial air pressure, bar
P_S = partial steam pressure, bar
P = total pressure, bar

V_A = specific volume of air, dm^3/kg
V_S = specific volume of steam, dm^3/kg
$\overline{V}_A$ = total volume occupied by air, dm^3
$\overline{V}_S$ = total volume occupied by steam, dm^3

T_A = absolute air temperature, K
T_S = absolute steam temperature, K

R_A = gas constant for air (0.287 kJ/kg K)
R_S = gas constant for steam (0.462 kJ/kg K)

M_A = mass of air, kg
M_S = mass of steam, kg
M = mass of mixture, kg

Since it is only the steam which supplies the heat, the mixture temperature T is the temperature T_S corresponding to the partial steam pressure P_S, hence $T_A = T_S = T$.

The mass of the mixture is the sum of the masses of air and steam, thus $M = (M_A + M_S)$.

Now 1.0 bar dm^3 = 0.1 kJ, and to make the units consistent, we must write the General Gas Law in the form

$$0.1\, PV = RT$$

The units of which are $\dfrac{kJ}{bar\ dm^3} \cdot \dfrac{bar\ dm^3}{kg} = \dfrac{kJ}{kg\ K}\ K$

$$\therefore \frac{kJ}{kg} = \frac{kJ}{kg}$$

If we have M kg of gas occupying a total volume $\overline{V}$ dm^3, then

The specific volume, $V = \dfrac{\overline{V}}{M}$

and substituting this in the General Gas Law gives

$$\frac{0.1\, P\overline{V}}{M} = RT$$

$$\therefore\ 0.1\, P\overline{V} = MRT$$

For the air therefore, $0.1\, P_A\, \overline{V}_A = M_A\, R_A\, T_A$

$$\therefore\ \overline{V}_A = \frac{M_A\, R_A\, T_A}{0.1 P_A}$$

And for the steam, $0.1\, P_S\, \overline{V}_S = M_S\, R_S\, T_S$

$$\therefore\ \overline{V}_S = \frac{M_S\, R_S\, T_S}{0.1 P_S}$$

From the first statement of Dalton's Law, $\overline{V}_A = \overline{V}_S$ hence

$$\frac{M_A R_A T_A}{0.1 P_A} = \frac{M_S R_S T_S}{0.1 P_S}$$

Since $PV = RT$, we may put $R_A T_A = P_A V_A$ and $R_S T_S = P_S V_S$, hence

$$\frac{M_A P_A V_A}{0.1 P_A} = \frac{M_S P_S V_S}{0.1 P_S} \text{, from which}$$

$$M_A V_A = M_S V_S \tag{1}$$

$$\therefore \frac{M_S}{M_A} = \frac{V_A}{V_S}$$

Alternatively, from the General Gas Law, we have

$$0.1 P_A \overline{V}_A = M_A R_A T_A \quad \text{and} \quad 0.1 P_S V_S = M_S R_S T_S$$

Now $T_A = T_S$, hence,

$$0.1 P_A \overline{V}_A = M_A R_A \qquad \text{and} \quad 0.1 P_S V_S = M_S R_S$$

$$\therefore M_A = \frac{0.1 P_A \overline{V}_A}{R_A} \qquad \text{and} \quad M_S = \frac{0.1 P_S V_S}{R_S}$$

Again from the first statement of Dalton's Law, $\overline{V}_A = \overline{V}_S$, hence

$$M_A = \frac{0.1 P_A}{R_A} \qquad \text{and} \quad M_S = \frac{0.1 P_S}{R_S}$$

$$\therefore \frac{M_S}{M_A} = \frac{0.1 P_S}{R_S} \frac{R_A}{0.1 P_A}$$

$$\therefore \frac{M_S}{M_A} = \frac{R_A}{R_S} \frac{P_S}{P_A}$$

and putting $R_A = 0.287$ and $R_S = 0.462$ gives

$$\frac{M_S}{M_A} = \frac{0.287}{0.462} \frac{P_S}{P_A}$$

$$\therefore \frac{M_S}{M_A} = 0.622 \frac{P_S}{P_A} \tag{2}$$

From equation (1)

$$M_S = M_A \ \frac{V_A}{V_S}$$

The mass of mixture, $M = M_A + M_S$, and substituting the above values of M_S gives

$$M = M_A + M_A \ \frac{V_A}{V_S}$$

$$\therefore M = M_A \left(1 + \frac{V_A}{V_S}\right) \tag{3}$$

Alternatively, from equation (2), $M_S = 0.622 M_A \ P_S/P_A$.
   The mass of mixture $M = M_A + M_S$, and putting
$M_S = 0.622 \ M_A \ P_S/P_A$ gives

$$M = M_A + 0.622 M_A \ \frac{P_S}{P_A}$$

$$\therefore M = M_A \left(1 + 0.622 \ \frac{P_S}{P_A}\right) \tag{4}$$

Referring to equations (3) and (4), the term within the brackets is known as the mixture factor, and is that factor by which the mass of air must be multiplied to give the mass of the air/steam mixture with which the air pump has to deal, i.e.

$$\text{Mixture factor} = \left(1 + \frac{V_A}{V_S}\right), \text{ or}$$

$$\text{Mixture factor} = \left(1 + 0.622\right)\frac{P_S}{P_A}$$

From Dalton's law, each constituent of the mixture occupies the total volume of the containing vessel as if the other constituent did not exist, hence the total volume $\overline{V} = M_A V_A = M_S V_S$.
   (Note that it is *not* correct to add the total volume of the air to the total volume of the steam to obtain the total volume

of the mixture. The total volume of mixture = total volume of air = total volume of steam).

If the total volume $\bar{V}$ and the two specific volumes V_A and V_S are known, then the mass of air $M_A = \bar{V}/V_A$, and the mass of steam $M_S = \bar{V}/V_S$.

When dealing with condensing plant, the masses of air, steam and mixture are stated not in kg, but in kg/h. This makes no difference to the foregoing relationships, except of course that the total volume $\bar{V}$ becomes dm^3/h instead of dm^3.

Practical application to condenser

Let us consider further our single-flow condenser example, viz., 25 000 kg/h of steam with design condenser pressure 0.047534 bar, and sea temperature $17°C$, and suppose the "dry" air in-leakage allowed for is 10 kg/h.

Assume the condenser pressure to be uniform throughout the condenser, i.e. $P = 0.047534$ bar, and the corresponding saturation temperature $32.0°C$.

At the condenser inlet, $M_S = 25\,000$ and $M_A = 10.0$, hence the mass of mixture $M = M_S + M_A = 25\,000 + 10.0 = 25\,010$ kg/h, and from equation (4)

$$M = M_A \left(1 + 0.622 \frac{P_S}{P_A}\right)$$

$$\therefore \ 25\,010 = 10 \left(1 + 0.622 \frac{P_S}{P_A}\right)$$

$$\therefore \ 25\,010 = 10 + 6.22 \frac{P_S}{P_A}$$

$$\therefore \ \frac{P_S}{P_A} = \frac{25\,010 - 10}{6.22}$$

$$\therefore \ \frac{P_S}{P_A} = \frac{25\,000}{6.22}$$

$$\therefore \ \frac{P_S}{P_A} = 4019, \text{ from which}$$

$$P_S = 4019 P_A \qquad\qquad (5)$$

Now, from Dalton's law, we know that $P = P_S + P_A$, i.e.

$\qquad 0.047534 = P_S + P_A$, from which

$\qquad P_A = 0.047534 - P_S$ $\qquad\qquad\qquad\qquad\qquad$ (6)

Suustituting the value of P_S from equation (5) gives

$\qquad\quad P_A = 0.047534 - 4019\,P_A$

$\qquad \therefore\ P_A + 4019\,P_A = 0.047534$

$\qquad \therefore\ P_A = \dfrac{0.047534}{4020}$

$\qquad \therefore\ P_A = 0.000011822$ bar, and

$\qquad\quad P_S = 0.047534 - 0.000011822$

$\qquad \therefore\ P_S = 0.047522178$ bar

Hence at the condenser steam inlet, the partial pressure of the air is so small compared with the partial pressure of the steam that the mixture may be regarded as pure steam having a temperature of $32°C$, i.e. the saturation temperature corresponding to the condenser pressure 0.047534 bar.

As the mixture passes down the condenser, the mass of air M_A remains, but due to condensation, the mass of steam M_S is greatly reduced. Before arriving at the air suction take-off, the mixture passes through the condenser air cooling section (i.e. over that section of cold tubes under the baffle), in which the air is cooled to some temperature below the saturation temperature corresponding to the condenser pressure, accompanied by some further condensation of vapour. Suppose the temperature at the air pump suction is $4°C$ below the condenser temperature, i.e.

Air pump suction temperature $t = 32.0 - 4 = 28°C$

Again, at this point, $t_S = t$, hence $t_S = 28°C$ and from the steam tables, the partial steam pressure (corresponding to $t_S = 28.0°C$) is $P_S = 0.037782$ bar, and the specific volume of the steam, $V_S = 36\,728$ dm^3/kg.

The condenser pressure $P = 0.047534$ bar, and from Dalton's law

$$P_A = P - P_S$$

$$\therefore P_A = 0.047534 - 0.037782$$

$$\therefore P_A = 0.009752 \text{ bar}$$

The air temperature at this point, $t_A = 28°C$, hence

$$T_A = 28.0 + 273.15$$

$$\therefore T_A = 301.15 \text{ K}$$

From the General Gas Law $0.1 P_A V_A = R_A T_A$

$$\therefore V_A = \frac{R_A T_A}{0.1 P_A}$$

$$\therefore V_A = \frac{0.287 \times 301.15}{0.1 \times 0.009752}$$

$$\therefore V_A = 88\,632 \text{ dm}^3/\text{kg}$$

From equation (3), mass of mixture $M = M_A (1 + V_A/V_S)$

$$\therefore M = 10.0 \left(1 + \frac{88\,632}{36\,728}\right)$$

$$\therefore M = 10.0\,(1 + 2.413)$$

$$\therefore M = 10.0 \times 3.413$$

$$\therefore M = 34.13 \text{ kg/h}$$

Total volume of mixture to be dealt with by the air pump

$$\overline{V} = \overline{V}_A = \overline{V}_S$$

$$\therefore \overline{V} = M_A V_A \quad \text{or} \quad \overline{V} = M_S V_S$$

$$\therefore \overline{V} = \frac{10.0 \times 88\,632}{10^3} \quad \text{or} \quad \frac{24.13 \times 36\,728}{10^3}$$

$$= 886.32 \text{ m}^3/\text{h}$$

and the air pump would be designed accordingly.
(Note: The dry air allowance M_A expressed as a percentage of the steam entering the condenser is $10.0/25\,000 \times 100 = 0.04$ per cent. This will have a slightly adverse effect on the

overall rate of heat transmission, but will have been allowed for when the design rate was chosen.)

The dry air allowance—in this case 10.0 kg/h—on which the plant is designed, is usually quite a liberal allowance. For a well designed, well operated and well maintained system, the actual dry air leakage expected in service would be one third to one half of the design allowance, thus leaving a reasonable margin to accommodate the development of small additional air leaks without causing the performance of the condensing plant to deteriorate.

Effects of abnormal air leakage

If air in-leakage is allowed to increase abnormally, the performance of the condensing plant will deteriorate, the condenser pressure will rise and the overall efficiency of the engines will be reduced.

The deterioration in the performance of the condensing plant is due to two causes:

1. The additional air in the condenser tends to increase air-blanketing of the tubes, i.e. the air film surrounding a tube becomes thicker. Since air is one of the worst heat conductors, even a very slight increase in the thickness of the air film significantly increases the resistance to heat flow from steam to water, hence the overall rate of heat transmission K diminishes. Now the condenser heat load $= KS\theta_m$, and the condenser surface S is constant, hence the heat load can be maintained only if θ_m increases. If the c.w. temperature t_1 and the c.w. tempera-

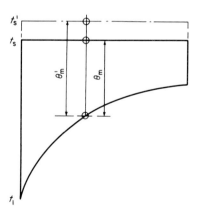

Figure 6.15 Increase of condenser pressure due to air

ture rise r remain unaltered, the condenser itself will increase θ_m (see Figure 6.15) by raising the steam temperature line from t_s to t'_s, i.e. the condenser pressure will increase. As the condenser pressure increases, less work is available from each 1.0 kg of steam and the main engines will require more steam if full power is to be maintained. This in turn increases the condenser heat load, which will require a further increase in θ_m, and a further increase in the condenser pressure, and so on until the balancing point between main engine steam and condenser pressure is reached. This is the pressure the condenser would maintain *provided* that the air pump is capable of removing the abnormally large air quantity.

2. The air pump, designed for 10.0 kg/h of dry air in our example, has a volumetric capacity of 886.32 m^3/h of air/vapour mixture. Any increase of dry air above 10.0 kg/h causes an increase in the total volume of air/vapour mixture, above the volumetric capacity of the air pump, and the air pump is therefore incapable of removing the increased volume of mixture. This causes air to accumulate in the condenser, causing the condenser pressure to rise to the point which will reduce the total volume of the mixture to 886.32 m^3/h, at which conditions will stabilise. This increase in condenser pressure can be very serious from the efficiency aspect.

These two causes of deterioration in performance are to some extent interdependent, i.e. rising condenser pressure due to air blanketing of the tubes makes matters easier for the air pump, but the condenser pressure will rise until the air pump aspect is satisfied, no matter what the condenser itself can do. The mechanism of all the changes which take place is quite complex, but the results may be illustrated in our example by making some credible assumptions.

Suppose, in the example, that a serious air leak develops such that the dry air quantity is twice the design allowance, i.e. $M_A = 20.0$ kg/h. This is about 0.08 per cent of the steam to condenser, which might reduce the overall rate of heat transmission K by a factor of 0.85, i.e. $K = 0.85 \times 3.5 = 2.975$ kW/m^2 °C.

The condenser surface area is as before 329.6 m^2.

The condenser heat load might increase by 1.0 per cent, i.e. $H = 1.01 \times 15\ 215 = 15367$ kW.

Hence the condenser would require

$$\theta_m = \frac{15\,367}{2.975 \times 329.6} = 15.67°C$$

Assuming that the circulating water temperature t_1 and quantity Q do not change, then the c.w. temperature rise

$$r = \frac{15\,367}{4030 \times 1.082} = 3.52°C$$

∴ C.W. discharge temperature, $t_2 = 17.0 + 3.52 = 20.52°C$

$$\theta_2 = \frac{r}{e^{r/\theta m} - 1}\text{, and}\quad \frac{r}{\theta_m} = \frac{3.52}{15.67} = 0.2246$$

$$∴ \theta_2 = \frac{3.52}{2.7183^{0.2246} - 1} = \frac{3.52}{0.2522} = 13.96°C$$

Saturation temperature $t_S = t_2 + \theta_2 = 20.52 + 13.96 = 34.48°C$, which corresponds to a condenser pressure of 0.0546 bar.

This is the pressure which the *condenser* would maintain *provided* that the air pump can remove 20.0 kg/h of dry air.

Now consider the air pump.

If we assume that the temperature at the condenser air take-off is still 4°C below the condenser steam temperature, then

Air pump suction temperature, $t = 34.48 - 4 = 30.48°C$

Again, at this point, $t_S = t$, hence $t_S = 30.48°C$, and from the steam tables, the partial steam pressure $P_S = 0.043613$ bar and the specific volume $V_S = 32\,096$ dm^3/kg.

The condenser pressure $P = 0.0546$ bar, and from Dalton's law, $P_A = P - P_S$,

$$∴ P_A = 0.0546 - 0.043613 = 0.010987 \text{ bar}$$

The air temperature at this point, $t_A = t = 30.48°C$, hence

$$T_A = 30.48 + 273.15 = 303.63 \text{ K}$$

From the General Gas Law,

$$V_A = \frac{R_A T_A}{0.1 P_A}$$

$$\therefore\ V_A = \frac{0.287 \times 303.63}{0.1 \times 0.010987} = 79\,310\ \text{dm}^3/\text{kg}$$

From equation (3), mass of mixture, $M = M_A\ (1 + V_A/V_S)$

$$\therefore\ M = 20.0\ \left(1 + \frac{79\,310}{32\,096}\right)$$

$$\therefore\ M = 20.0 \times 3.471$$

$$\therefore\ M = 69.42\ \text{kg/h}$$

Total volume of mixture to be dealt with by air pump

$$\overline{V} = M_A\ V_A$$

$$\therefore\ \overline{V} = \frac{20.0 \times 79\,310}{10^3}$$

$$\therefore\ \overline{V} = 1586.2\ \text{m}^3/\text{h}$$

The air pump is grossly overloaded, since it is capable of a volumetric capacity of only 886.32 m³/h. Consequently that part of the dry air with which the air pump cannot deal will remain behind in the condenser, air blanketing of the tubes will increase, the rate of heat transmission will diminish, and the condenser pressure will rise. This process will continue until the condenser pressure has risen so far as to bring the total volume of the air/vapour mixture within the volumetric capacity of the air pump, when conditions will stabilise, with the air pump again removing 20.0 kg/h of dry air, but at a much higher condenser pressure.

If for each of a series of rising condenser pressures, we repeat the calculation, we can plot graphs of total weight and total volume of mixture on a base of condenser pressure. For the present case, this is shown in Figure 6.16 from which it will be seen that the condenser pressure must rise to 0.112 bar to bring the total volume of mixture associated with 20.0 kg/h of dry air within the volumetric capacity of the air pump.

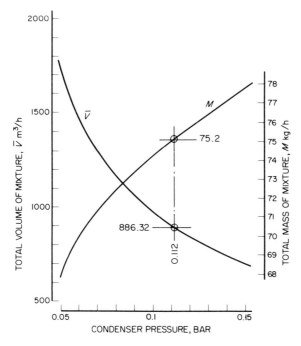

Figure 6.16 Overloading of air pump due to abnormally high air leakage

Note that in this condition, the total mass of mixture is 75.2 kg/h compared with 34.143 kg/h for the design air leakage of 10.0 kg/h, i.e. the total mass has more than doubled. However because of the increased condenser pressure, the pressure ratio over which the mixture has to be compressed by the air pump is reduced from 1.01325/0.047534 = 21.315 to 1.01325/0.112 = 9.047, i.e. the pressure ratio is now considerably reduced. Even so, the air pump is likely to be overloaded from the power aspect, i.e. although an increase of condenser pressure to 0.112 bar satisfies the volumetric aspect, it may not satisfy the power aspect.

The calculations given above are intended to be illustrative only, and are probably over-simplified. Nevertheless they do show how serious an abnormally large air leakage can be; from the efficiency aspect, an increase in condenser pressure from 0.047534 bar to 0.112 bar would be intolerable. Indeed, an increase of even one quarter of this would not be acceptable, particularly for turbines, which are usually very sensitive to changes of back pressure.

With some types of air pump, it is possible to obtain increased volumetric capacity and power by increasing the air pump speed. With the steam jet ejector type of air pump, the volumetric capacity cannot be increased above design unless by bringing in the standby ejector, if a standby is provided. Increasing the pressure of the driving steam to the air ejector jets above design gives little or no increase in capacity.

Whatever the type and number of air pumps, continued operation of the main engines and condenser with abnormally large air in-leakage is most undesirable.

Air cooling in the condenser

Suppose in the last example, with the design dry air allowance (10.0 kg/h), that in the condenser, we had cooled the air vapour mixture to only $1°C$ below the condenser temperature instead of to $4°C$ below, then

$$\text{Air pump suction temperature, } t_S = t_A = 32.0 - 1 = 31.0°C$$

Corresponding partial steam pressure p_S = 0.044911 bar, and

$$\text{Steam specific volume } V_S = 31\ 199 \text{ dm}^3/\text{kg}$$

Partial air pressure P_A = 0.047534 − 0.044911 = 0.002623 bar

$$\text{Air temperature } T_A = 31.0 + 273.15 = 304.15 \text{ K}$$

$$\text{Air specific volume } V_A = \frac{0.287 \times 304.15}{0.1 \times 0.002623}$$

$$= 332\ 800 \text{ dm}^3/\text{kg}$$

$$\text{Mixture factor} = 1 + \frac{332\ 800}{31\ 199} = 11.695$$

Mass of mixture M = 10.0 × 11.695 = 116.95 kg/h

Mass of air M_A = 10.0 kg/h

Mass of steam M_S = 106.95 kg/h

$$\text{Total volume of mixture } \bar{V} = \frac{10.0 \times 332\ 800}{1000} = 3328 \text{ m}^3/\text{h}$$

This means that if the mixture is cooled to only $1°C$ below the condenser steam temperature instead of to $4°C$

below, then the required volumetric capacity of the air pump is 3328 m³/h instead of 886.32 m³/h, i.e. nearly four times as much.

If we repeat the above calculation for a number of different air pump suction temperatures, we obtain the curve shown in Figure 6.17, from which it will be evident that cooling the mixture in the condenser before extraction results in quite a dramatic reduction in the required volumetric capacity of the air pump. The curve also shows why a difference of around 4°C is always aimed at in the original design of the conden-ser air cooling section.

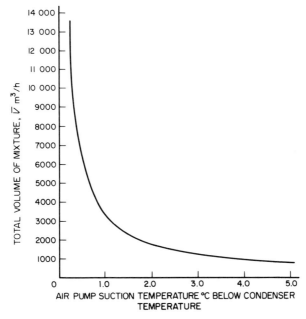

Figure 6.17 Effect of air pump suction temperature on the required volumetric capacity of the air pump. Based on dry air leakage 10.0 kg/h and condenser pressure 0.047534 bar

Suppose now that the air pump has been installed with a volumetric capacity of 886.32 m³/h on the basis that the condenser would cool the mixture to 4°C below the con-denser temperature, but that in fact, the condenser is capable of cooling the mixture to only 1°C below the condenser temperature.

The previous calculation shows that in this condition, the total volume of mixture is 3328 m³/h. With its installed

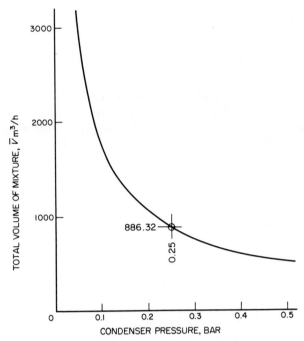

Figure 6.18 Effect of insufficient air cooling on condenser pressure based on dry air leakage 10.0 kg/h. Air pump section temperature 1°C below condenser temperature. Installed air pump capacity 886.32 m³/h

capacity of 886.32 m³/h, the air pump is grossly overloaded, and the condenser pressure will rise until the total volume of mixture is reduced from 3328 m³/h to 886.32 m³/h.

If the previous type of calculation is repeated for a series of progressively increasing condenser pressures, the curve shown in Figure 6.18 is obtained. This indicates that the condenser pressure would rise to 0.25 bar.

Once the condenser is built, tubed and installed, there is little or nothing that can be done to improve its air cooling. In the present instance, the only means of improving matters is to reduce the air leakage below 10.0 kg/h, e.g. if the air leakage could be reduced from 10.0 kg/h to

$$10.0 \times \frac{886.32}{3328} = 2.66 \text{ kg/h}$$

then the air pump could just cope, with condenser pressure 0.047534 bar and air pump suction temperature 1°C below condenser steam temperature.

In practice, the air pump capacity is made sufficiently generous to give a reasonable margin on the normal dry air leakage to be expected with a well maintained system, and the condenser is carefully designed with the object of making it capable of cooling the air vapour mixture to approximately 4°C below the condenser temperature. The practical achievement of 4°C is not always easy, and calls for a good deal of judgement in the original detail design of the condenser. Air is a very poor conductor and absorber of heat—it parts

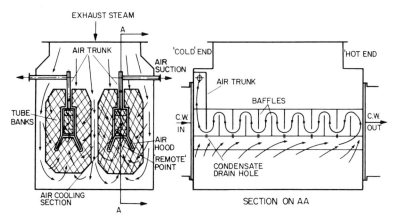

Figure 6.19 Air cooling and air extraction towards the cold end of a single-flow condenser

with its heat reluctantly, and hence would ideally require an efficient cooler with a relatively large surface. In a condenser, unfortunately, space is always limited, the air velocities are low, and the mean temperature difference between the air and the circulating water is limited to approximately that between the steam and the circulating water. Briefly, the best results are to be expected when, within the condenser proper, the air is swept by the steam towards a "remote point", and the mixture of air and steam, collected at the remote point, is made to pass over a section of the condenser tubes which is baffled off from the condenser proper, so that no fresh steam can pass directly to the air pump suction. In the air cooling section, some of the vapour is condensed out, thus raising the partial air pressure and so reducing the air volume. At the same time, the air is being cooled and its volume thereby further reduced. Ideally, to obtain the best air cooling, the air pump suction should be located at the "cold" end of the

condenser, and the mixture in the air cooling section made to
flow from the hot to the cold end, preferably with baffling to
give turbulence and thus to improve heat transfer. Some
modern condensers are arranged in this way, one typical case
being shown in principle in Figure 6.19.

To summarise, suppose that in practice, our condenser
example has a normal air leakage of 6.0 kg/h, and the condenser cools the mixture to $3°C$ below condenser temperature.

With design condenser pressure, air pump suction temperature = $32.0 - 3 = 29°C$. Corresponding partial steam pressure P_S = 0.04004 bar; steam specific volume V_S = 34 769
dm^3/kg. Partial air pressure P_A = $0.047534 - 0.04004$ =
0.007494 bar

$$\text{Air temperature } T_A = 29 + 273.15 = 302.15 \text{ K}$$

$\therefore$ Air specific volume V_A

$$= \frac{0.287 \times 302.15}{0.1 \times 0.007494} = 115\,710 \text{ dm}^3/\text{kg}$$

Total volume of mixture $\overline{V}$ =

$$M_A V_A = \frac{6.0 \times 115\,710}{1000} = 694.26 \text{ m}^3/\text{h}$$

This is well within the air pump capability of 886.32 m^3/h.

From the foregoing, it will be evident that reducing the air
leakage into the system is beneficial from every aspect.

Separate extraction of air and condensate from the condenser

For best efficiency, the condensate should be at condenser
temperature. For moderate air pump size, the air vapour mixture should be $4°C$ below condenser temperature.

In turbine condensers therefore—which work at low pressures—the air and condensate are extracted separately, with
the object of keeping the condensate as hot as possible and
the air take-off as cool as possible. Engine condensers work at
higher condenser pressures, hence the specific volumes are
lower, and separate extraction is not so important. Even so,
it seems likely that the combined extraction of air and condensate from engine condensers is a legacy from the old days
of the overtubed condensers, in which there was a considerable pressure drop down the condenser, and in which the

bottom rows of tubes acted merely as "condensate coolers", thus resulting in appreciable under-cooling of the condensate, and of the air.

Where an exhaust turbine is used with an engine, separate extraction of air and condensate is required.

Increase of condenser pressure

This may be due to one or more of the following causes:

1. Increased sea temperature
2. Failed or inadequate c.w. supply
3. Excessive air in-leakage (First check should be the turbine gland sealing system)
4. Fouled tubes
5. Failed or damaged air pump
6. Insufficient air cooling

Item 6 is not an operational variation as such. It is included as a possibility, since in one case, a serious increase of condenser pressure was ultimately traced to a baffle in the steam space having broken and been carried away, thus allowing direct access of steam to the air pump suction, and creating the situation illustrated by Figure 6.18.

7 Special engines and turbines

As steam expands in an engine or turbine, work is done at the expense of the heat content of the steam. Thus the pressure falls and the steam becomes progressively wetter. This leads to a considerable *wetness loss* in the L.P. stages, causing a drop in efficiency. Even when the steam is highly superheated initially, there comes a point in the expansion when the saturation point is reached and wetness occurs thereafter. In addition to the bad effect on efficiency, in the L.P. stages water causes endless trouble with leakage and wear in the valves and glands of reciprocating engines and with erosion and wasting of the blades in turbines.

As is shown later, steam passes through turbine stages with high velocity, and the water droplets—however small— strike the leading edges of the blades with considerable violence. The blades thus become torn and serrated, which may be dangerous, in addition to the bad effect on efficiency. Some manufacturers fit water-catchers in the L.P. turbines and special erosion-resisting shields on the leading edges of the blades.

REHEATER ENGINES

Another method of minimizing wetness in engines and turbines is by reheating the steam at one or more intermediate points during its expansion. There are two main systems, boiler reheater (Figure 7.1) and steam reheater (Figure 7.2).

In the first system superheated steam is first expanded in the H.P. cylinder and is then removed from the engine or turbine and passed through a reheater (similar to a superheater) in the boiler furnace. The steam is then passed to the I.P. or L.P. cylinder and expanded to the condenser pressure, this cylinder thus having the benefit of initially superheated steam with reduced wetness losses.

296

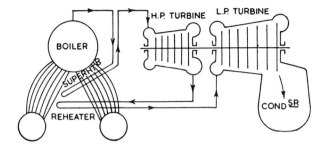

Figure 7.1 Boiler reheater as applied to two-cylinder turbines with one intermediate reheat

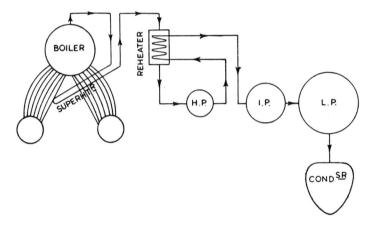

Figure 7.2 Steam reheater as applied to triple-expansion engine with one reheat

In the second system steam is generated in the boiler and leaves the superheater with a temperature much in excess of that with which it enters the H.P. cylinder of the engine or turbine. The steam temperature is then reduced by passing it through a reheater, the heat being used to reheat the H.P. exhaust steam on its way to the I.P. or L.P. cylinder. In both cases it is, of course, necessary that the steam be reheated at a point between the cylinders. This system is adopted on the North Eastern Marine Engineering Co.'s reheater triple and on the White compound engine and exhaust turbine.

Either of these systems may be adapted to give two inter-mediate reheats. Although the White engine is so fitted, one reheat is usually the limit. The two reheats give higher effic-iency than one reheat, but at the expense of more complicated and expensive machinery. These features, and the choice of the reheat pressure and temperature, and the probable effect of these on the efficiency are discussed in Chapters 9 and 12.

The North-Eastern reheater engine

Economy is effected in a reciprocating engine when the steam remains dry throughout the expansion from H.P. to L.P. exhaust. The presence of water assists the conduction of heat away from the cylinders, and is undesirable for that reason and also from the point of view of economy in the

Figure 7.3 Front of the "Sussex Trader's" main engine, showing Stephenson link-motion and high-pressure-cylinder valve gear (The North Eastern Marine Engineering Co. Ltd.)

Figure 7.4 The North-Eastern reheater engine (The North Eastern Marine Engineering Co. Ltd.)

amount of make-up water required for the boilers due to leakage. When steam remains dry, very little loss takes place at the glands. The total make-up required with this type of engine is given as about 2040 kg/1000 kW per day. The North-Eastern reheater engine is illustrated in Figures 7.3 and 7.4, and the general arrangement is shown diagrammatically in Figure 7.5.

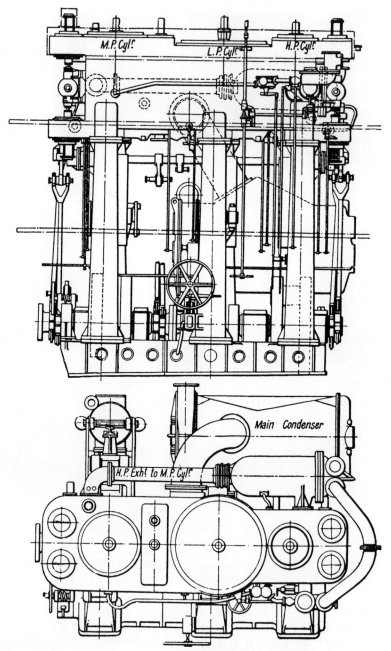

Figure 7.5 General arrangement of the North-Eastern reheater engine

Efficiency is increased by using steam at the highest possible temperature at the H.P. end. Not only does the engine

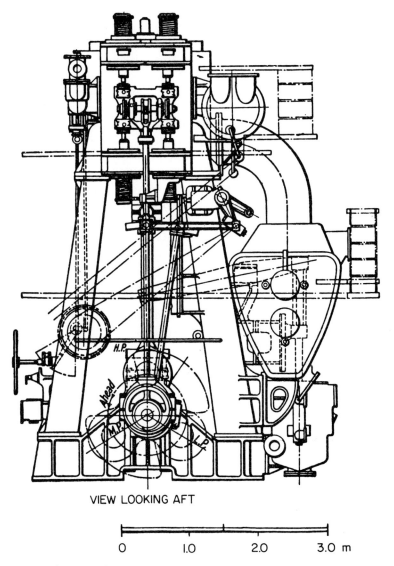

VIEW LOOKING AFT

```
|————————————|————————————|————————————|
0           1.0          2.0          3.0 m
```

Figure 7.5 (continued) North-Eastern reheater engine, view looking aft

gain in efficiency but also, since the heat in the superheated steam has been taken from the funnel gases, the efficiency of the whole installation is increased.

In one installation superheated steam leaves the boilers at 16.2 bar and at 400°C. Now, this temperature is too high to permit of efficient lubrication of the H.P. piston-rings and liner. The admission temperature of steam to the H.P. is therefore reduced by passing the high-temperature steam through tubes, on the outside of which is the lower-temperature steam on its way from the H.P. exhaust to the M.P. inlet. In this way the temperature of the steam being admitted to the H.P. cylinder is reduced to 315°C, and the heat given up by that steam is received by the H.P. exhaust steam on its way to the M.P. The admission temperature of the steam to the M.P., which would normally be 218°C, is thus raised to 300°C (at 5.85 bar). At the pressure of 5.85 bar the saturation temperature is 158°C, so that the steam now has 126°C of superheat.

This is sufficient to keep the steam drier during subsequent expansion. The fitting employed by which heat leaves the H.P. steam and is picked up by the M.P. steam is called the reheater or heat-exchanger. It consists of an outer casing with inlet and outlet branches. A tube plate on one end carries about one hundred looped tubes, which are expanded in place. The tube plate is held in place between the flange of the outer casing and the flange of an end cover which has a division plate and branches for inlet and outlet of the H.P. steam. Baffles are fitted within the tube nest to direct the H.P. exhaust so that it passes over the tubes four times. The reheater is illustrated in Figures 7.6 and 7.7.

Lubricating oil is supplied to points in the cylinder-liners and piston-rod glands by mechanical lubricators which can be adjusted to give the best results as regards wear of the parts and low oil consumption. Most of this oil is supplied at the

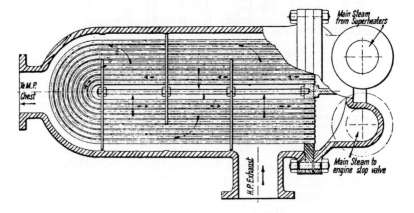

Figure 7.6 The North-Eastern reheater—sectional view

Figure 7.7 The North-Eastern reheater (The North Eastern Marine
Engineering Co. Ltd.)

H.P. end, because some of the oil finds its way into the other
cylinders, being carried there by the steam. The distribution
is as follows:

H.P. cylinder (three points)	35% of total oil
M.P. cylinder (three points)	32% of total oil
L.P. cylinder (five points)	20% of total oil
H.P. piston rod	7% of total oil
M.P. piston rod	3% of total oil
L.P. piston rod	3% of total oil

Stephenson valve gear is used to operate the H.P. and M.P.
poppet valves, there being four valves per cylinder, two steam
and two exhaust, operated by cams on an oscillating camshaft.
The valves are returned to their seats by external springs, and
are so designed that they rotate very slowly while opening
and shutting. This helps to keep the valves in good condition.
The valves and valve gear are illustrated in Figure 7.8.

The recorded fuel-oil consumption for engines of 3000–
3750 kW is 0.465–0.48 kg/kWh and 0.486–0.517 kg/kWh for
all purposes. For coal the consumption is 0.6–0.67 kg/kWh.

STEAM JACKETING

Many years ago, when a reciprocating steam-engine unit used
more than 0.9 kg coal/kWh using saturated steam, there was

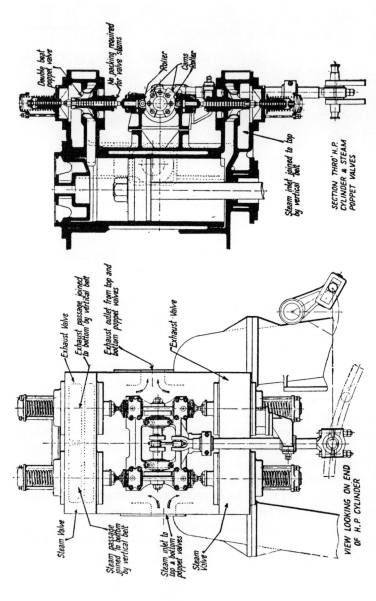

Double beat poppet valve

No packing required for valve stems

Roller

Cams

Roller

Steam inlet joined to top by vertical belt

SECTION THRO' H.P. CYLINDER & STEAM POPPET VALVES

Exhaust Valve

Exhaust passage joined to bottom by vertical belt

Exhaust outlet from top and bottom poppet valves

Exhaust valve

Steam Valve

Steam passage joined to bottom by vertical belt

Steam inlet to top & bottom poppet valves

Steam Valve

VIEW LOOKING ON END OF H.P CYLINDER

Figure 7.8 Arrangement of the poppet valves, cam gear and parts of the high-pressure cylinder of the North-Eastern reheater engine

an attempt to increase the efficiency by reducing the condensation in the cylinders. The method was called *steam-jacketing*,
and consisted of admitting boiler steam to a space provided
outside the cylinder-liners.

A water-gauge glass was fitted to each jacket, and the drain
from the jacket was adjusted to allow the condensate to drain
away to a feed tank at just sufficient speed to ensure water
showing in the glass. Many engines seemed to benefit by
jacketing so far as fuel consumption was concerned, while
others showed a definite loss.

So far as conditions in the cylinder were concerned there
was bound to be an improvement, the cylinder walls being
always heated to nearly the inlet-steam temperature, and
thereby giving heat to the steam as it expanded and dropped
in temperature. Condensation was thus prevented, and an
expansion curve obtained somewhere between the adiabatic
and hyperbolic, i.e., higher than that obtained without jacketing, due to re-evaporation of the particles of water formed.
But condensation was going on in the jackets. While that was
a loss which seemed to vary, the condensate was retrieved,
whereas when condensation took place in the cylinders, the
condensate often leaked past the gland packing and was lost.
This necessitated the introduction of cold fresh-water feed
into the system.

Theoretically there can be no gain from steam jacketing,
but the conditions in engines using saturated steam were, in
cases, so far removed from the theoretical that jacketing had,
in fact, a beneficial effect. There would, of course, be no
question of using jacketing in an engine using superheated
steam.

UNIFLOW ENGINES

One advantage of having steam expansion divided into a number of stages is that *heat drop* per stage is reduced. This has
the effect of reducing *initial condensation* caused by steam at
high temperature coming in contact with cylinder walls which
have been in contact with low-temperature exhaust steam.

Considering the ordinary design of engine, if steam was to
be expanded in one cylinder, the cut-off would require to be
at about one-twentieth of the stroke and the temperature
would drop from say $260°C$ to $50°C$, giving a relatively

cool liner for the incoming steam to contact. Since the engine
is double acting, the ends of the cylinder are alternately used
for steam and exhaust, resulting in condensation.

Stage expansion is never extended beyond four stages,
since any attempt to reduce the temperature-drop by the
addition of another cylinder would introduce more friction,
which would negative any theoretical gain.

Initial condensation losses may be very much reduced by
the use of a Uniflow engine, in which all the expansion takes
place in one cylinder, but which is arranged so that all the
steam is always flowing in one direction, from the steam inlet
at one end to the exhaust, through ports, at the middle of the
cylinder (Figure 7.9).

The Stephen engine uses the uniflow principle in the two
L.P. cylinders of the three-cylinder compound engine.

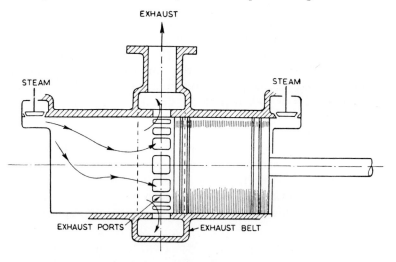

Figure 7.9 Diagram of the Uniflow engine cylinder

The Stephen marine steam engine

The engine is a three-cylinder compound, specially designed
to obtain the maximum economy possible in a reciprocating
steam engine using high superheat and a suitably low condenser pressure, but without the added complication and expense
of an exhaust turbine.

The main features are given overleaf, the information having
been supplied by the makers. The general appearance of the
engine is shown in Figure 7.10.

Figure 7.10 The Stephen three-cylinder compound marine steam engine

COMPOUND EXPANSION. The losses due to heat exchange with the walls of the cylinder are almost entirely absent when using superheated steam, which is a bad conductor of heat. Moreover, with independent steam and exhaust valves, both valves and steam ports remain at a constant temperature. As there is only one intermediate steam receiver, the heat losses from this source are reduced. Owing to the unidirectional flow of the steam in the L.P. cylinders, there is little loss from heat exchange in these cylinders.

INDEPENDENT VALVES. These allow of a small clearance volume in the cylinder, easy access for overhaul and small power required for operation. All valves are interchangeable. The best settings for inlet and cut-off can be arranged without any bad effect on the point of compression, as in ordinary valves combining both functions.

ANDREWS AND CAMERON VALVE. This comprises one slide valve having four openings for steam admission and exhaust.

VALVE-SPINDLE GLANDS. The valve spindles are of case-hardened steel, ground and lapped, and work in long, cast-iron bushes with oil-grooves and forced lubrication, thus eliminating the friction always present in a packed gland. With this arrangement there is no possibility of oil leaking into the steam space.

UNIFLOW L.P. CYLINDERS. The free exhaust through ports in the cylinder walls reduces the back pressure to within 0.035 bar of the condenser pressure. From tests made on the engine of the S.S. *Annan* the reduction in steam consumption due to the uniflow L.P. cylinders is about 9 per cent on a corresponding cylinder, or 3 per cent overall.

HYDRAULIC VALVE GEAR. An independent pump delivers oil at a high pressure to a rotary distributor driven off the engine crankshaft. In this distributor are situated a number of ports which allow the oil pressure to be distributed to small pistons on the ends of the various valve spindles. The valves are opened and closed by hydraulic pressure.

Variation in the point of cut-off and correction for the lag in the system are obtained by sloping the ports in the casing of the distributor at an angle to the axis. Reversal is obtained by means of a second series of ports. To alter the cut-off, or reverse, it is only necessary to move the rotating plug axially in the casing. The distributor is driven through gearing from the crankshaft, and the oil pressure is used as a transmitter of power, consequently, the timing of the engine once set, cannot be disturbed. The discharge from the oil-operating distributor is led to the engine forced-lubrication system.

This hydraulic valve gear has the following advantages over the Stephenson link motion: early cut-off, quick valve opening and closing, compression and release are independent of the point of cut-off, large variation in cut-off, speed regulation by varying the cut-off, shorter engine because valves are on front of the engine, cut-off equal top and bottom, fewer moving parts, pressure lubrication throughout. The distributor can be seen in Figure 7.10.

FORCED LUBRICATION. The engine is totally enclosed with forced lubrication throughout, on the same system as that employed in the best diesel-engine practice, the oil being discharged to the main bearings, and thence through holes drilled in the crankshaft to the crankpins, and from there up the connecting-rods to the crossheads and guide-shoes.

FABRICATED STEEL FRAME. The steel engine frame, while of a somewhat unorthodox type, is a very rigid structure, designed to transmit all loads with a minimum of material. The main stresses between the cylinders and the crankshaft are carried by heavy H-section beams, which are tied together in pairs by cast-steel main-bearing supports and cast-iron guide faces. The cylinders are rigidly held at their centre, leaving top and bottom free to expand. The crankpin is welded, and all holding-down bolts readily accessible while engine runs.

The whole design results in a shorter, more rigid and compact engine, with ample room to get at the running parts for inspection and maintenance. The saving in weight and length of the engine compared to the standard type of triple-expansion engine is approximately 20 per cent.

RECIPROCATING ENGINE-TURBINE COMBINATION

The lowest pressure to which a reciprocating steam engine can exhaust for best efficiency is between 0.135 and 0.1 bar. Reducing condenser pressure further merely cools the condensate without appreciably increasing the power. The L.P. cylinder cannot be made large enough to expand steam down to 0.07 or 0.035 bar vacuum because of the great increase in volume at low pressures. The increase in size would introduce condensation losses which would exceed any gain in power. The mass of the engine would be increased.

In large vessels, Parsons early made use of the turbine for completing expansion down to 0.035 bar or less by using three screws, the two outers being driven by reciprocating engines, and the centre one by his reaction turbine.

For smaller installations, while it is quite a simple matter to introduce a turbine after the L.P. cylinder, the problem of applying the turbine power to the shaft calls for ingenuity.

There are three well-known ways of doing this:

1. Connecting the turbine by gearing to the intermediate shafting.

2. Using the turbine to drive a steam compressor and thereby introducing steam at a higher pressure to an intermediate cylinder.
3. Connecting the turbine to an electric generator which
   then delivers its current to an armature on the intermediate shafting.

Bauer–Wach installation

In the Bauer–Wach arrangement by Barclay, Curle, Ltd, of
Glasgow, a reaction turbine receives the steam exhausted
from the L.P. cylinder and transmits its torque to the main
shaft through double-reduction gearing, with a ratio of 30:1
in the speed of the turbine and main shaft respectively. The
turbine is designed to run in one direction only, and because
of this, the arrangement becomes more complicated. Between
the turbine and main shaft some sort of clutch must be provided which can be easily disengaged, and at the same time
the exhaust from the L.P. cylinder must be diverted from the
turbine and passed straight to the condenser. It must be made
impossible to reverse the reciprocating engine while the turbine is still in gear.

The turbine runs at about 50 rev/s, and the pinion connected to its spindle engages with a first reduction wheel
which is secured to and surmounts one impeller of a hydraulic
coupling. The second reduction pinion is secured to the other
half (i.e., an impeller of similar shape) of this coupling and
engages with the second reduction wheel, which is secured to
the main shaft on a special sleeve. Single helical gears are
employed throughout. Suitable thrust collars and pads are
provided at the first and second reductions to take the
resultant end thrust.

Above the turbine there is a change-over valve which connects the passages to and from the turbine so that when it is
open, the exhaust steam by-passes the turbine and goes
straight to the condenser. When in this position, the fluid
coupling must be empty, and in order to perform the two
operations at almost the same time the hydraulic coupling or
servo-motor, which provides the power for changing the valve,
is operated from the same oil-line which supplies the oil for
filling the fluid coupling. Oil pressure is kept up by one of
two reciprocating pumps provided, the other being in reserve.
Circulation of the oil is necessary at sea, with the turbine in
gear, to keep the turbine bearings lubricated, to pass the oil

through a cooler, to keep the coupling full and to hold the change-over valve in position. Should the oil pressure drop, due to the pump stopping or other reason, the change-over valve will immediately disconnect the turbine. An overspeed governor is fitted on the end of the turbine-rotor spindle. It is a simple type, consisting of a spring-loaded bolt which flies out due to centrifugal force when the speed is excessive. It then engages with a lever which opens a valve connected to the underside of the change-over valve servo-motor, releasing the pressure and allowing the piston or the butterfly valve, whichever type is fitted, to swing over. Figures 7.11 and 7.12 illustrate the operation of the system.

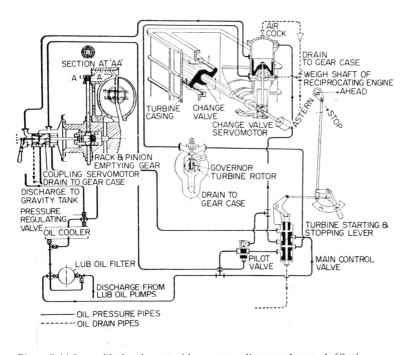

Figure 7.11 Bauer–Wach exhaust turbine system—diagram of controls (Out)

COUPLING. The coupling is of the Vulcan type, and there must always be a *slip* (i.e., a difference in speed between driving and driven member). It is in the order of 2 per cent. Examination of the principle will show why this is so. Supposing the driver, i.e., the turbine, to be started up with the coupling full, oil in the coupling will begin to move outwards due to

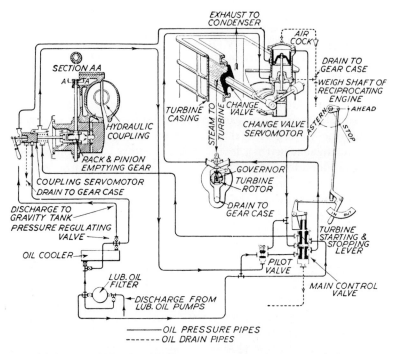

Figure 7.12 Bauer–Wach exhaust turbine system—diagram of controls (In)

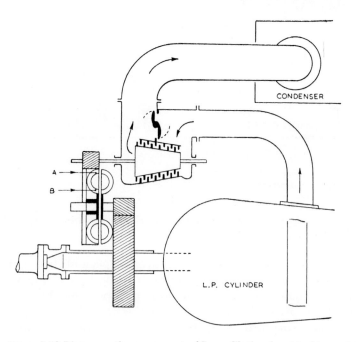

Figure 7.13 Diagrammatic arrangement of Bauer–Wach exhaust turbine system

centrifugal force, and the pressure at A in Figure 7.13 will be greater than at B. Looking now at the driven member, which is about 3.0 mm clear of the other, if the pressure of oil at A is greater than at B, oil will begin to flow inwards towards the centre because there is, as yet, no centrifugal force on the driven side, i.e., oil is thrown from one wheel to the other so long as there is a difference in speed. If the speeds became equal the pressure due to centrifugal force would be equal and flow would stop.

The oil being thrown from one wheel to the other, while there is a difference in speed between the two, impinges on the radial vanes and imparts a torque to the driven member.

USE AND MAINTENANCE. Steam reaches the turbine rotor while the main reciprocating engine is being warmed through so that it also becomes heated. When warming through, steam is admitted to the labyrinth glands of the turbine as in normal turbine practice. The condensate is removed by allowing it to drain to the air-pump suction.

Only the reciprocator is used while entering or leaving port, the turbine being engaged at *Full Away*, after the condenser pressure has been brought down to below 0.07 bar, by moving the hand-control lever at the starting platform.

With the machinery running, the oil supply to all bearings should be checked regularly by means of the test valves on the bearing covers. The bearing temperatures should also be observed, anything under 60°C being quite normal. Above that temperature care should be exercised, but no alarm need be felt so long as 80°C is not exceeded. The temperature of the oil leaving the cooler should not be allowed to drop below 32°C. This means that cooling water should not be allowed to pass through the cooler so long as the oil entering the cooler is below 35–38°C. Further, the minimum quanity of cooling water necessary to give the required temperature should be used, the quantity being regulated from the water-outlet valve.

EFFECT OF PUTTING TURBINE IN GEAR. The effect on the reciprocating engine produced by putting the turbine in gear is shown very well on the indicator diagrams.

The back pressure imposed at the L.P. end by the introduction of the turbine reduces the total power of the reciprocator, and the effect is to raise the back pressure on the M.P.

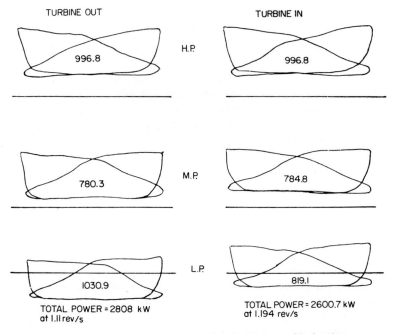

Figure 7.14 Indicator diagrams from engine fitted with Bauer–Wach exhaust turbine

and H.P. cylinders, reducing their power as well as that of the L.P.

The diagrams in Figure 7.14 show that the total indicated power with the turbine out of gear is 2808 kW when running at 1.11 rev/s, while it is reduced to 2600.7 at 1.194 rev/s with the turbine in gear.

Using the common assumption that power is proportional to (speed)^3 the equivalent power to give 1.194 rev/s will be

$$\left(\frac{1.194}{1.11}\right)^3 \times 2808 = 3493.7 \text{ kW}$$

Therefore the power being developed by the turbine is

$$3493.7 - 2600.7 = 893.0 \text{ kW}$$

This is only approximate, but owing to the variation in torque on the shaft it is not possible to use a torsionmeter to find the total power.

Götaverken arrangement

This method of using the L.P. energy of the steam consists of an exhaust turbine, of the impulse type, with two rows of moving blades, coupled directly to a rotary compressor which takes the exhaust steam from the H.P. valve-chest and compresses it to about 1.03 bar above the normal pressure of the M.P. casing (Figure 7.15).

In taking steam from the H.P. valve casing, the exhaust pressure of the H.P. cylinder is reduced by about 0.7 bar, being on the suction side of the compressor. This makes a total increase of 1.73 bar in the M.P. casing above the H.P. exhaust pressure while the compressor is in operation. The M.P. steam temperature (or dryness fraction) is also increased as a result of the compression.

The turbine is not connected in any way to the crankshaft of the reciprocator, and no alteration is required for astern running. The whole unit is comparatively small and attached to the back of the main engine at cylinder level.

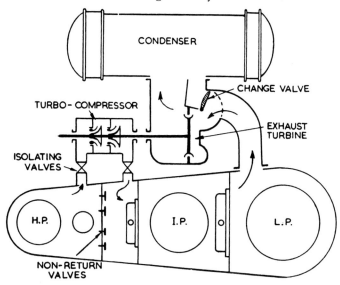

Figure 7.15 Diagrammatic arrangement of Götaverken exhaust steam-turbine system

The compressor may be put out of action by simply moving a lever controlling a change-over valve which deflects the exhaust from the L.P. cylinder directly to the condenser. When this is done, the H.P. exhaust steam now passes to the

M.P. valve casing in the usual way except that it must pass through several lightly loaded non-return valves. These valves, while the engine is running and with the turbine in operation, prevent the return of steam from M.P. to H.P.

While only the reciprocating engine is in use the condenser pressure is set at about 0.1 bar. When the turbine is to be used, the condenser pressure is reduced to under 0.035 bar by admitting steam to a vacuum augmentor or by increasing the speed of the air-pump.

The effect of the introduction of the turbo-compressor is shown on the indicator cards in Figure 7.16. The shaded portions show the increase of power in H.P. and M.P. cylinders, and the loss of power in the L.P. cylinder due to the higher back pressure in that cylinder.

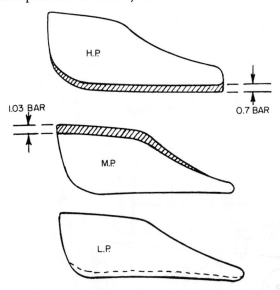

Figure 7.16 Effect of turbo-compressor on indicator diagrams

The White combined steam engine

This arrangement consists of a reciprocating engine running at the comparatively high speed of 4.66 to 5.0 rev/s, the exhaust of which is passed through a reaction turbine before reaching the condenser. They are coupled to the intermediate propeller shafting through reduction gearing, the reciprocating engine on one side driving through single reduction and the turbine on the other side of the main wheel through

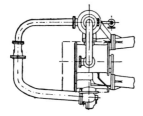

Figure 7.17 (left) White's combination engine-connections

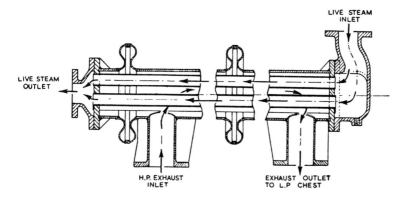

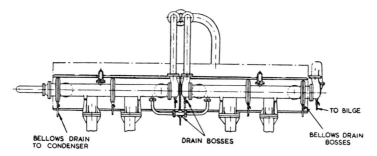

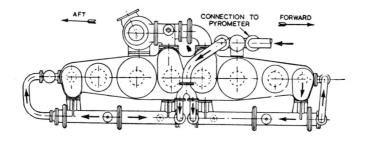

Figure 7.18 White's combination engine showing steam reheaters

double reduction. There is no hydraulic coupling. Further efficiency is gained by reheating the exhaust steam on its way from the H.P. cylinder to the L.P. and also the reciprocating-engine exhaust from the L.P. on its way to the turbine. Figures 7.17 and 7.18 show the steam reheaters for the H.P. exhaust steam.

The reciprocating engine is a four-cylinder compound with balanced cranks set at angles relative to one another to give correct balance to the engine. The balanced crankshaft is shown in Figure 7.19.

The valve gear may be the usual Stephenson type, operating piston or slide valves, or the White patent valve gear, of a type resembling the Marshall or Hackworth, employing poppet valves.

Figure 7.19 Crankshaft of the White engine

A change-over valve, operated from the weigh shaft, directs the engine exhaust to the turbine while running ahead, and to the condenser while running astern (Figure 7.20). A separate valve, also operated from the weigh shaft, admits H.P. steam to the astern turbine when the reciprocating engine is going astern.

Steam reheaters are used for both reheats, the H.P. exhaust steam being reheated by H.P., high-temperature steam on its way from the boilers to the H.P. cylinders and the L.P. exhaust steam by the H.P., high-temperature steam on its way from the boilers to the auxiliary steam range. The auxiliary exhaust steam is utilized in a surface feed heater to heat the feed water on its way to the boilers.

Normally, in a triple-expansion engine, even when using

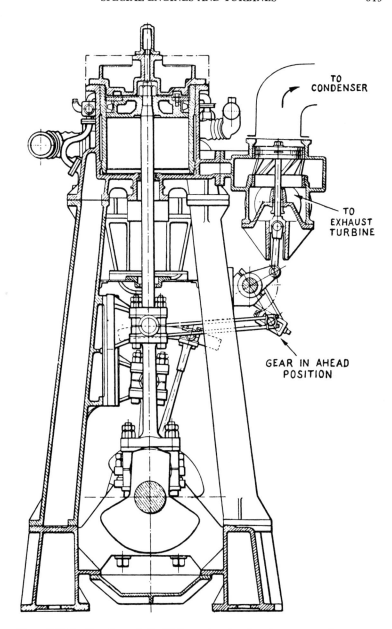

TO
CONDENSER

TO
EXHAUST
TURBINE

GEAR IN AHEAD
POSITION

Figure 7.20 Section through the White engine showing change-over valve

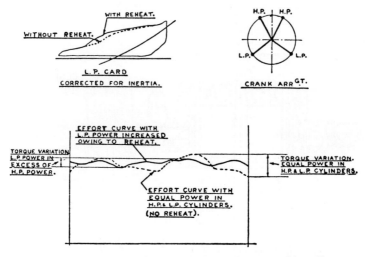

Figure 7.21 *The White engine-improvement from reheat on turbine-effort diagrams*

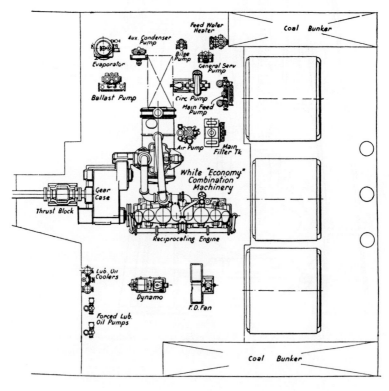

Figure 7.22 *The White engine installed in a typical engine room*

superheated steam, wetness occurs in the I.P. and L.P. cylinders and the overall diagram factor is of the order of 0.68.

Both cylinders of the White engine receive superheated steam, reducing wetness losses, and the overall diagram factor is about 0.79.

The exhaust turbine renders the resultant torque on the shaft much more uniform than on a comparable engine without exhaust turbine (Figure 7.21).

A plan of the engine-room of a White-engined ship is shown in Figure 7.22. Overall thermal efficiencies of the order of 23–24 per cent for all purposes, at the shaft, have been recorded compared with 16–19 per cent with orthodox engine installations.

DOUBLE COMPOUND ENGINES

The Christiansen and Meyer double compound engine

These engines with piston valves and rotating shaft valve-gear are of the enclosed type with forced lubrication and are based on the Woolf principle with direct expansion from H.P. to L.P. cylinder without receiver, and on the fact that it is not necessary to use triple expansion with superheated steam at about 16.0 bar pressure. This is because the exchange of heat between the steam and the cylinder walls with superheated steam is much lower than with saturated steam.

The design is characterised by the use of a semi-uniflow L.P. cylinder and one piston valve only for each cylinder pair, i.e., two valves for the whole four-cylinder engine.

Figure 7.23 is a sectional diagram showing the construction of a modern enclosed engine with forced lubrication.

Figure 7.24 is a sectional drawing showing the H.P. and L.P. cylinders and piston valve with the pistons at mid stroke, the H.P. one moving downwards and the L.P. one moving upwards, these being connected to cranks at 180°.

The steam enters the H.P. cylinder from the piston valve chamber and after cut-off, expands to the end of the stroke. On the return stroke this steam exhausts and expands direct into the L.P. cylinder (see lower part of Figure 7.24).

At the end of the L.P. stroke the steam leaves the cylinder by its circumferential ports and passes to the condenser or to an exhaust turbine if fitted. To keep down the degree of compression, exhaust is continued on the return stroke via the

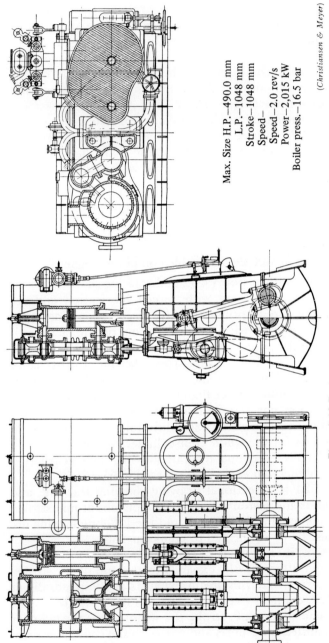

Max. Size H.P.–490.0 mm
L.P.–1048 mm
Stroke–1048 mm
Speed–
Speed–2.0 rev/s
Power–2,015 kW
Boiler press.–16.5 bar

(Christiansen & Meyer)

Figure 7.23 Enclosed engine with forced lubrication

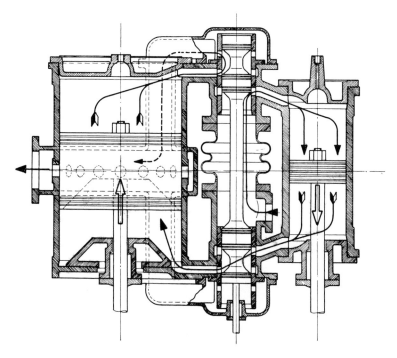

Figure 7.24 The H.P. and L.P. cylinders and piston valve with the pistons at mid-stroke

end port after the central ports are closed by the passage of the L.P. piston. The direct and quick passage of the steam through the engine without receiver, the small area of the surfaces in contact and the well-known advantages of the Uniflow principle with large area of L.P. exhaust ports, are responsible for the favourable steam consumption of 5.77–6.38 kg/kWh with superheated steam, depending on the size of the engine.

Typical indicator diagrams are shown in Figure 7.25.

The crankcase and bedplate are made in welded construction, as is usual with modern engines. Figure 7.26 shows the bedplate.

The front wall of the enclosed crankcase has large doors opposite the four cranks, and an oblong door on the rear wall enables the valve shaft system to be inspected and if necessary be removed completely.

The cover plate of the crankcase carries the columns for the two cylinder blocks and the wiper glands of the piston

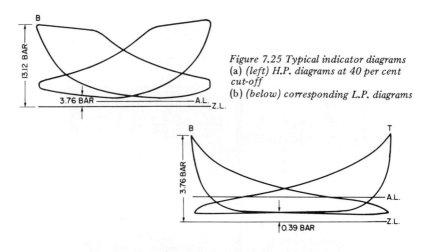

Figure 7.25 Typical indicator diagrams
(a) (left) H.P. diagrams at 40 per cent cut-off
(b) (below) corresponding L.P. diagrams

Figure 7.26 Double compound engine bedplate

and valve rods. The arrangement of these columns gives good accessibility to the piston-rod stuffing boxes.

The thrust block can be placed on a special bedplate bolted to the engine bedplate. In the smaller engines the thrust block is combined with the engines, the thrust collar being on the end portion of the crankshaft.

The crankshaft (Figure 7.27) is forged from ingot steel and is semi-built, i.e., crank webs and pins in one piece, the webs being shrunk on the corresponding shaft pieces. The diameters of the crank-pins and shaft pieces are equal. There are five main bearings of equal length. The crankshaft has four bore-holes (each from a main bearing to a crank pin) for the forced lubrication.

Figure 7.27 The crankshaft

To allow for the difference in temperature and vertical expansion of the H.P. and L.P. cylinder and piston valve chambers, a corrugated expansion piece is inserted in the latter item.

The cylinders do not have liners. The central L.P. exhaust ports are machined and made slightly oblique to correspond to the direction of the steam flow.

The cylinders are insulated with asbestos mats, which are filled with glass wool. The insulation is surrounded by galvanised or planished steel sheets.

By means of gear wheels, a rotating valve shaft in the upper part of the crankcase is driven from the crankshaft. This rotating shaft has two adjustable eccentrics by which the two piston slide valves are operated. These two slide valves along with the exhaust ports in the L.P. cylinder control all the steam events for the four cylinders. Figure 7.28 shows the control gear system, with driving wheel, regulating arrangement, and eccentrics. The two main parts are an external sleeve and an internal hollow shaft rotating together and having crank-pins at both ends driving the eccentrics.

The bore of the external sleeve has cut keyways like the rifling of a gun, and between internal and external shafts, a sleeve is arranged axially movable with keys in the keyways. By this motion the internal shaft may be twisted relative to the external one and thus by the crank-pins, the eccentrics altering their angle and degree of eccentricity. Because the sleeve parts are not in continuous relative movement they are subject to very little wear.

The offset arrangement of the valve gear, the absence of

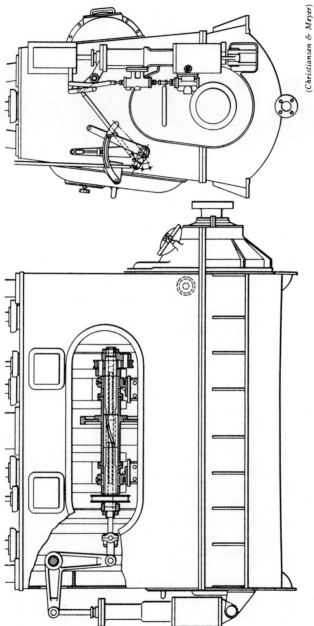

(Christiansen & Meyer)

Figure 7.28 Valve control gear

eccentrics from the crankshaft and the compact cylinder arrangement result in a very short engine.

Owing to the cranks being at $90°$ to one another no impulse valve is necessary, and the engine starts up immediately the reversing gear is moved to the ahead or astern position.

The use of superheated steam necessitates careful cylinder lubrication. This is effected by means of a multiple sight feed mechanical lubricator with regulation on each plunger. This delivers the oil through small tubes to the inlet steam pipe (to mix with the steam), to the H.P. cylinder walls, and to the H.P. stuffing boxes.

Manoeuvring of the engines is accomplished by only two controls—the lever which actuates the valve gear, and the

Figure 7.29 Geared 'Hamburg' engine unit with exhaust turbine

lever or handwheel of the main stop valve. The valve gear is hand operated in the smaller engines, and power assisted in the larger ones.

The Christiansen and Meyer geared "Hamburg" engines

It is claimed that this engine of enclosed type and with two piston slide valves only can operate at much higher speeds than would normally be acceptable for direct coupled engines, and to take advantage of this feature a special arrangement was evolved in the direct "Hamburg" engine (Figure 7.29) by using the Rembold system in combination with a Bauer–Wach exhaust turbine. The two cylinder pairs are arranged transverse to the ship, the pistons being connected to twin parallel crankshafts each with two cranks at 90° (Figure 7.30), and the valve gear is situated between the crankshafts.

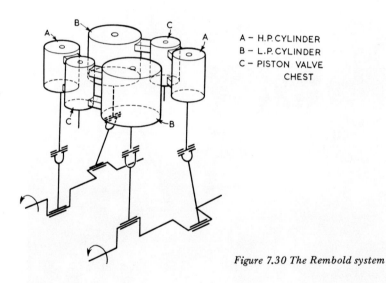

A – H.P.CYLINDER
B – L.P.CYLINDER
C – PISTON VALVE
         CHEST

Figure 7.30 The Rembold system

The Bauer–Wach Turbine is normally situated on top of the reduction gear, which combines the output of the two crankshafts of the engine with that of the turbine, and incorporates the thrust block also (Figure 7.31). This combination gives full advantage of the reduction in size and mass possible for a given H.P. output, especially for slow-running propellers.

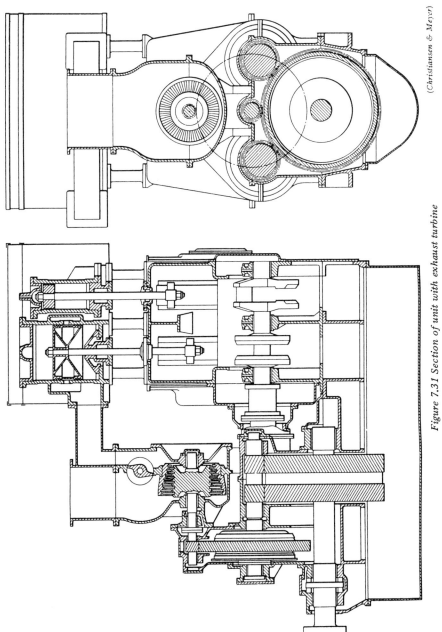

(Christiansen & Meyer)

Figure 7.31 Section of unit with exhaust turbine

8 Entropy and its uses: energy diagrams involving entropy

An energy diagram facilitates the study of thermodynamical operations and eliminates much tedious calculation and use of fairly advanced mathematics. All the information necessary to construct any form of energy diagram is contained in the Steam Tables.

Absolute zero of temperature

The *absolute zero of temperature* is that temperature at which the volume of a perfect gas theoretically becomes zero.

At ordinary temperatures, any perfect gas expands or contracts by 1/273.15 of its volume for each 1°C of temperature change, provided the pressure is kept constant. This statement is called *Charles' Law*.

Thus if we have 273.15 dm^3 of gas at 0°C,

then we have 272.15 dm^3 of gas at -1.0°C
and we have 271.15 dm^3 of gas at -2.0°C
and we have   0 dm^3 of gas at -273.15°C

-273.15°C is called the absolute zero of temperature on the Celsius (Centigrade) scale, and in thermodynamics it is called zero on the Kelvin scale.

From Figure 8.1 it will be noted that the magnitude of 1.0 K is the same as the magnitude of 1.0°C, and since 0.0 K is equivalent to -273.15°C, then the thermodynamic temperature, T kelvins, is equal to the Celsius temperature t°C + 273.15.

In what follows in the present chapter we shall use the Kelvin scale throughout unless stated otherwise.

In the Students' Steam Tables all temperatures are tabulated both as ordinary temperature θ/K, expressed in degrees Celsius (°C), and as thermodynamic temperature T, expressed in kelvins (K).

The measure of the quality, or grade of availability of heat is its temperature level, and one of the simplest and most instructive and useful energy diagrams is *a graph whose vertical axis is absolute temperature, and on which areas are enthalpies (heat quantities).*

Let the vertical scale start at 0.0 K and go up to say 900.0 K, thus including a large part of the range of temperatures in the Steam Tables. Consider, in stages, the formation of steam at say 7.0 bar, 280.0°C.

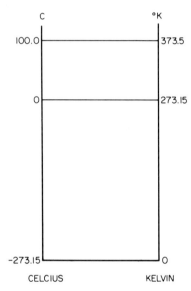

Figure 8.1 Celsius and Kelvin temperature scales

Referring to Figure 8.2, at point A we have 1.0 kg of water at 273.15 K which in the steam tables is reckoned to have zero enthalpy. Thus at A there is *no diagram area*. Let the water now receive liquid heat until it reaches the saturation temperature $T_s = 438.15$ K corresponding to the pressure of 7.0 bar. The specific enthalpy of the saturated liquid is then 697.1 kJ/kg. This state is represented by the point B, on a horizontal line where $T = 438.15$ K, and at such a horizontal distance OC that the area OABC is 697.1 kJ/kg. The *state point* has moved from A to B, and if at this stage we assume

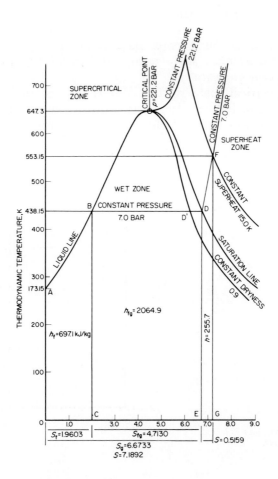

Figure 8.2 Construction of the temperature entropy diagram

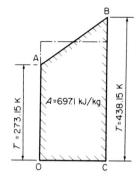

Figure 8.3 Approximate value of OC

AB to be a straight line, then the horizontal distance OC may be calculated as follows:

Referring to Figure 8.3

$$\text{Average } T = \frac{273.15 + 438.15}{2} = \frac{711.3}{2} = 355.65 \text{ K}$$

$$\text{Hence OC} = \frac{697.1}{355.65} = 1.9603 \text{ kJ/kg K}$$

This may be drawn to any convenient scale.

Let the water now receive the increment of enthalpy for evaporation, to cause complete evaporation at the constant saturation temperature 438.15 K. The state point moves from B along a horizontal line to D, such that the area CBDE is equal to the increment of enthalpy for evaporation h_{fg} = 2064.9 kJ/kg.

The horizontal distance CE = 2064.9/438.15 = 4.713 kJ/kg K, which is drawn down to the chosen horizontal scale. The saturated vapour has specific enthalpy h_D = area OABC + area CBDE = 697.1 + 2064.9 = 2762.0 kJ/kg.

Let the steam now receive the increment of enthalpy to superheat it to 280.0°C (553.15 K) at constant pressure 7.0 bar. From Table 3

Specific enthalpy of superheated steam h = 3017.7 kJ/kg
Specific enthalpy of saturated vapour h_g = 2762.0 kJ/kg
Increment of enthalpy for superheating $h - h_g$ =   255.7 kJ/kg

During superheating the temperature rises to 280.0 + 273.15 = 553.15 K.

The state point moves from D to F, such that the vertical height of F above the origin is 553.15 K, and the area EDFG

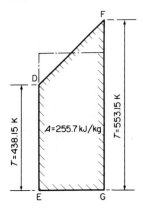

Figure 8.4 Approximate value of EG

is 255.7 kJ/kg. Again assuming DF to be a straight line, and referring to Figure 8.4.

$$\text{Average temperature} = \frac{438.15 + 553.15}{2} = \frac{991.3}{2} = 495.65 \text{ K}$$

$$\therefore \text{Horizontal distance EG} = \frac{255.7}{495.65} = 0.5159 \text{ kJ/kg K}$$

The area OABDFG represents the specific enthalpy of steam at 7.0 bar, 553.15 K (280°C), and F is the state point of steam at these conditions. Specific enthalpy $h_F = 3017.7$ kJ/kg.

Horizontal distances on the diagram are called *entropy*, which in the SI steam tables is denoted by s. The unit of entropy is kJ/kg K. For instance,

OC is the specific entropy of the saturated liquid,

$$s_p = 1.9603 \text{ kJ/kg K}$$

CE is the increment of entropy for evaporation,

$$s_{fg} = 4.713 \text{ kJ/kg K}$$

EG is the increment of entropy for superheat,

$$s - s_g = 0.5159 \text{ kJ/kg K}$$

OE is the specific entropy of the saturated vapour

$$s_g = s_f + s_{fg}$$
$$\therefore s_g = 1.9603 + 4.713$$
$$\therefore s_g = 6.6733 \text{ kJ/kg K}$$

OG is the specific entropy of the superheated steam

$$s = 6.6733 + 0.5159$$
$$\therefore s = 7.1892 \text{ kJ/kg K}$$

BDF is called a *line of constant pressure* or an *isobar*.

If instead of being superheated to 553.15 K, the steam had been 0.9 dry, the final state point would be D' such that

Increment of enthalpy for evaporation

$$= 0.9 \times 2064.9 = 1858.41 \text{ kJ/kg}$$

Increment of entropy for evaporation

$$= 0.9 \times 4.7134 = 4.2421 \text{ kJ/kg K}$$

Specific enthalpy of wet vapour

$$h = 697.1 + 1858.41 = 2555.51 \text{ kJ/kg}$$

Specific entropy of wet vapour

$$s = 1.9603 + 4.2421 = 6.2024 \text{ kJ/kg K}$$

The point D' lies on a *line of constant dryness* 0.9.

If the foregoing procedure is carried out for various other pressures, any number of lines of constant pressure and lines of constant dryness may be drawn on the diagram.

It will be observed that the specific entropies tabulated in the steam tables for steam at 7.0 bar, 553.15 K differ somewhat from those which we have calculated above:

Entropy	Calculated	Tabulated	Difference
s_f	1.9603	1.9918	0.0315
s_{fg}	4.713	4.7134	—
s	7.1892	7.2112	0.022

The differences are due to our having, in order to facilitate this conception of entropy, assumed AB and DF to be straight lines, whereas they are in fact curves. In subsequent calculations, the proper Steam Table entropies are used.

Referring again to Figure 8.2, it should be noted that all points such as D lie on a continuous curve called the *satura-*

tion line, and all points such as B on another continuous curve called the *liquid line*. These two curves merge together at the *critical pressure* 221.2 bar, where the increments of enthalpy and of entropy for evaporation are zero, and where the specific volume of the steam is equal to the specific volume of the water. The temperature at this point is 647.3 K, but it is not correct to refer to this as the saturation temperature since there is no constant temperature evaporation. It is referred to as the critical temperature.

That part of the diagram below the curve formed by the liquid line and the saturation line is called the wet zone. That part of the diagram above the saturation line and to the right of the line of constant pressure 221.2 bar is called the superheat zone. That part of the diagram above the liquid line and to the left of the line of constant pressure 221.2 bar is called the supercritical zone.

Note that at the point F, the steam temperature exceeds the saturation temperature by $553.15 - 438.15 = 115.0$ K. The steam has a superheat of 115.0 K, and all points such as F lie on a line of constant superheat. Lines of constant superheat for various other superheats could be drawn by the same methods.

We could also plot lines of constant specific volume, but for the present, these we will not consider so as to avoid too much complication.

A complete temperature–entropy diagram, as illustrated in Figure 8.5, having lines of constant pressure, dryness, superheat and specific volume could be drawn. Since however, the use to which we propose to put the temperature–entropy diagram in the next chapter is to illustrate the thermodynamical steam cycles, it is necessary only to sketch a skeleton temperature–entropy diagram on which appear only the lines and state points applying to the particular cycle being studied at any one time.

Relation between temperature, reception of heat and change of entropy

We have seen that on a temperature–entropy (Ts) diagram, areas represent heat quantities (enthalpies). Hence in Figure 8.6, the shaded area $h_2 - h_1 = T(s_2 - s_1)$ from which

$$s_2 - s_1 = \frac{h_2 - h_1}{T}$$

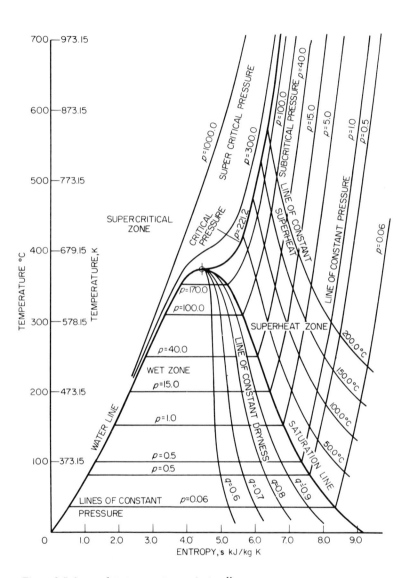

Figure 8.5 A complete temperature entropy diagram

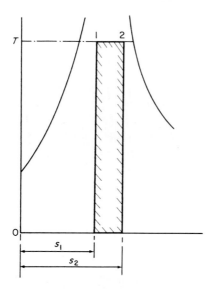

Figure 8.6 Heat quantities on Ts diagram

Thus, if a substance receives heat,

$$\text{The change of entropy} = \frac{\text{heat received}}{\text{average temperature of heat reception}}$$

and the unit of entropy is therefore kJ/kg K. (In practice, it has become conventional to omit the units, i.e. when writing down an entropy, it is written only as a number).

The above is also valid for rejection of heat.

Entropy has been variously defined, e.g. entropy is that characteristic, or state, or function of a substance which increases or diminishes accordingly as the substance receives or rejects heat; or again, entropy is a measure of the unavailability of a system's thermal energy for conversion into mechanical work.

Such definitions are somewhat pedantic and are not at all easy to understand, with the result that the conception of entropy has to some extent been shrouded in mystery, imaginary or otherwise. As engineers, we need not concern ourselves with these features, but by remembering that *entropy is the horizontal axis of a graph whose vertical axis is absolute temperature and on which areas are heat quantities*, quite extensive use may be made of entropy to simplify and illustrate various operations and to investigate the efficiencies of the theoretical steam cycles.

Adiabatic operations

If the pressure, volume and temperature of a fixed mass of steam change in such a manner that no heat is added to or taken away from the steam *externally* during the change then the change is called an *adiabatic change*.

Suppose 1.0 kg of steam to expand adiabatically from a high pressure to a low pressure. The volume increases, and thus external mechanical work is done. Since by definition, no heat is received by the steam during expansion, all of the external work done must be done at the expense of the original enthalpy of the steam. The loss of enthalpy of the steam is therefore equal to the external work done during expansion. Suppose now that the same quantity of external work is done on the steam to compress it adiabatically. As no heat enters or leaves the steam during compression, all the compression work goes back into the steam, and the enthalpy, pressure, volume and temperature return to their original values before expansion.

An adiabatic operation is therefore thermodynamically reversible, i.e. it can be carried out naturally in the reverse direction with no more external assistance than in the original direction.

Further, by definition,

$$\text{Change of entropy} = \frac{\text{heat received or rejected}}{\text{average temperature}}$$

During an adiabatic operation, no heat is received from any external source and no heat is rejected to any external sink, hence the change of entropy is zero. Thus *an adiabatic operation is carried out at constant entropy*, and is therefore represented on the temperature-entropy diagram by a perpendicular straight line. Such an operation is sometimes also called an isentropic operation.

Isothermal operations

If the pressure and volume of a fixed mass of steam change in such a manner that the temperature is constant, the change is called an isothermal change.

Suppose 1.0 kg of steam to expand isothermally from a high pressure to a low pressure. The volume increases and external mechanical work is done. Since the steam temperature remains constant, the external work cannot be done at the expense of the original enthalpy of the steam (otherwise the steam temperature would fall). Hence as the external work is being done, heat from an external source must enter the steam at a rate sufficient to keep the steam temperature constant. Hence the heat received from the external source is equal to the external work done plus any increase in enthalpy of the steam.

If now, the same quantity of external work is done on the steam to compress it isothermally, the steam must reject heat continuously to an external sink, otherwise the steam temperature would rise.

An isothermal operation is thermodynamically reversible, and is represented on the temperature–entropy diagram as a horizontal straight line.

Illustration of adiabatic and isothermal operations on Ts diagram

Let steam at 15.0 bar, dry saturated expand to 2.0 bar (1) adiabatically (2) isothermally.

$$\text{Initially, } p = 15.0, \; T = 471.43, \; h_g = 2789.9, \; s_g = 6.4406,$$
$$v_g = 131.67$$

(1) ADIABATIC EXPANSION

The initial state point is shown by D in Figure 8.7. The specific enthalpy of the saturated vapour, $h_D = 2789.9$, is represented by the area OABCDEF.

By definition, adiabatic expansion is carried out at constant entropy, so that the state point moves vertically downwards from D to a point E on the line of constant pressure 2:0 bar. The total entropy at E = 6.4406.

Reference to the Steam Tables will show that for dry saturated steam at 2.0 bar, $s_f = 1.5301$ and $s_{fg} = 5.5967$. Hence the increment of entropy from B to E is $6.4406 - 1.5301 = 4.9105$, and the dryness fraction at E is

$$q_E = \frac{4.9105}{5.5967} = 0.8773$$

The specific enthalpy at E

$$h_E = h_f + q_E \cdot h_{fg}, \text{ where } h_f \text{ and } h_{fg}$$

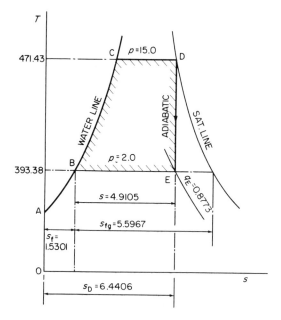

Figure 8.7 Adiabatic expansion

are read from the Steam Tables for a pressure of 2.0 bar, thus

$$h_E = 504.7 + (0.8773 \times 2201.6)$$
$$\therefore h_E = 504.7 + 1931.4$$
$$\therefore h_E = 2436.1 \text{ kJ/kg}$$

The loss of enthalpy of the steam $(h_D - h_E)$ is equal to the external work done, i.e.

$$h_D - h_E = 2789.9 - 2436.1$$
$$h_D - h_E = \underline{353.8 \text{ kJ/kg}}$$

This is of course represented by the area BCDE.

[Note that where a symbol has a suffix in capital letters, it refers to a state point on the diagram, e.g. h_E means the specific enthalpy of the wet vapour at the state point E. Where a symbol has a suffix in *small* letters it refers to the value read from the Steam Tables, e.g. at point B, $s_f = 1.5301$ means the specific entropy of saturated water at a pressure of 2.0 bar as read from the Steam Tables.

The specific entropy at D, viz. s_D = 6.4406, is of course the same as the specific entropy s_g of saturated steam at 15.0 bar as read from the Steam Tables.]

The specific volume v_E at the end of adiabatic expansion is $v_E = v_f (1 - q_E) + q_E v_g$, where v_f and v_g are read from the steam tables for a pressure of 2.0 bar:

$$v_E = (1.0608 \times 0.1227) + (0.8773 \times 885.4)$$
$$\therefore \ v_E = 0.1302 + 776.75$$
$$\therefore \ v_E = 776.88 \ \text{dm}^3/\text{kg}$$

If we choose several intermediate pressures on the adiabatic line DE, and calculate the specific volume at each pressure point on DE by the method given above, we obtain the following

Adiabatic expansion line DE

p, bar	15.0	12.0	10.0	5.0	2.0
v, dm^3/kg	131.67	160.25	186.17	346.16	776.88
$\log p$	1.1761	1.0792	1.0	0.699	0.301
$\log v$	2.1177	2.2048	2.2699	2.5393	2.8903

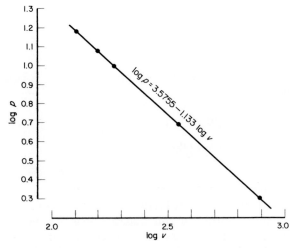

Figure 8.8 Relation between log p and log v during adiabatic expansion in the wet zone

Referring to Figure 8.8, if we plot $\log p$ on a base of $\log v$, the points lie on a straight line. The equation of a straight line graph is of the form $y = ax + b$, which in this case may be written,

$$\log p = n\log v + c$$

If we put any two corresponding values of $\log p$ and $\log v$ into this (say the first and the last) we get

$$1.1761 = 2.1177n + c \tag{1}$$
$$0.3010 = 2.8903n + c \tag{2}$$

and subtracting (2) from (1),

$$0.8751 = -0.7726n$$
$$\therefore n = -\frac{0.8751}{0.7726}$$
$$\therefore n = -1.133$$

The minus sign implies that the gradient of the graph is negative, i.e. it slopes downwards when going from left to right.

If we substitute this value of n in (1), we get

$$1.1761 = (-1.133 \times 2.1177) + c$$
$$\therefore 1.1761 = -2.3994 + c$$
$$\therefore c = 1.1761 + 2.3994$$
$$\therefore c = 3.5755$$

The equation of the graph is therefore $\log p = -1.133 \log v + 3.5755$, from which $\log p + 1.133 \log v = 3.5755$. By the laws of logarithms, this means that $pv^{1.133} =$ antilog 3.5755.

Hence during adiabatic expansion in the west zone, the relation between the pressure and the specific volume of the steam is given by

$$pv^{1.133} = \text{constant}$$

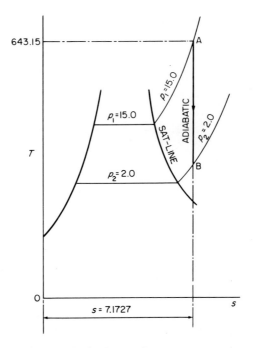

Figure 8.9 Adiabatic expansion in the superheat zone

If we consider an adiabatic expansion lying entirely in the superheat zone we find the form of the relationship is the same, but the value of the index of v is different. To show this, we need consider only two points. Referring to Figure 8.9 let steam at 15.0 bar, 643.15 K expand adiabatically to 2.0 bar, i.e. from A to B.

Initial specific entropy = final specific entropy

$$s_A = s_B = 7.1727$$

Reference to the steam tables will show that steam at 2.0 bar having a specific entropy of 7.1727 is still superheated, therefore the adiabatic expansion line AB lies wholly in the superheat zone.

From the Steam Tables

Specific volume at A = 193.13 dm^3/kg

Specific volume at B = 907.2 dm^3/kg

Hence, since $p_A v_A^n = p_B v_B^n$

$$\log p_A + n \log v_A = \log p_B + n \log v_B$$

$$\therefore 1.17609 + 2.28586n = 0.30103 + 2.95771n$$

$$\therefore 2.95771n - 2.28586n = 1.17609 - 0.30103$$

$$\therefore 0.67185n = 0.87506$$

$$\therefore n = \frac{0.87506}{0.67185}$$

$$\therefore n = 1.3$$

Hence during adiabatic expansion in the superheat zone, the relation between the pressure and the specific volume of the steam is given by

$$pv^{1.3} = \text{constant}$$

Although in actual fact, the exact value of n varies slightly for different locations on the Ts diagram, we are at present merely calling attention to the relationship $pv^n = \text{constant}$ for adiabatic expansion, and in general. *If expansion is wholly in the wet zone,*

$$pv^{1.133} = \text{constant, i.e. } p_1 v_1^{1.133} = p_2 v_2^{1.133}$$

If expansion is wholly in the superheat zone,

$$pv^{1.3} = \text{constant, i.e. } p_1 v_1^{1.3} = p_2 v_2^{1.3}$$

In cases where an adiabatic crosses the saturation line, from the superheat zone to the wet zone, or vice versa, where the pv characteristics are concerned it may be necessary to consider it in two separate parts.

Note that in the steam tables, the unit of specific volume is dm^3. This means $(\text{decimetres})^3 = (0.1 \text{ metre})^3 = 0.001 \text{ m}^3$. It does *not* mean $0.1 \ (m^3)$.

(2) ISOTHERMAL EXPANSION
In Figure 8.10, the initial state point D is as before, and the specific enthalpy of the saturated vapour $h_D = 2789.9$ is again represented by the area OABCDF.

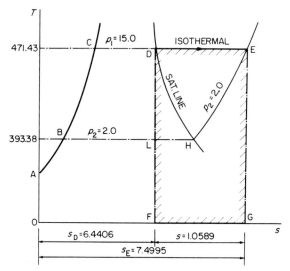

Figure 8.10 Isothermal expansion

By definition, isothermal expansion is carried out at constant temperature, so that the state point moves horizontally from D to a point E on the line of constant pressure 2.0 bar. The point E is in the *superheat zone*, hence from the Steam Tables (Table 4) we must find the specific enthalpy, specific entropy and specific volume at E, i.e. at 2.0 bar, 471.43 K.

The steam temperature 471.43 K lies between the tabulated values 463.15 K and 473.15 K, hence it is necessary to *interpolate* between the tabulated values.

For this interpolation, we assume that h, s and v are each linear functions of T. For a pressure of 2.0 bar, from the Steam Tables

At $T = 473.15$ K	$h = 2870.5$	$s = 7.5072$	$v = 1080.4$
At $T = 463.15$ K	$h = 2850.3$	$s = 7.4639$	$v = 1056.5$

Difference

10.0 K	20.2	0.0433	23.9
∴ 1.0 K	2.02	0.0043	2.39
∴ 8.28 K	16.74	0.0356	19.8
∴ 471.43 K	$h_E = 2867.04$	$s_E = 7.4995$	$v_E = 1076.3$

The differences for 8.28 K are *added* to the table values for 463.15 K since h, s and v all increase as T increases.

The change of entropy from D to E = 7.4995 − 6.4406 = 1.0589, and

Heat received from D to E = change of entropy × average temperature
$$= 1.0589 \times 471.43$$
$$= 499.2 \text{ kJ/kg}$$

Specific enthalpy at E = area OABHEG = 2867.04 kJ/kg
Specific enthalpy at D = area OABCDF = 2789.9 kJ/kg
Increase in enthalpy of steam from D to E = 77.14 kJ/kg

Of 499.2 kJ/kg of heat received from the external source, only 77.14 kJ/kg appears in the steam as an increase of enthalpy, hence

External work done from D to E =

$$499.2 - 77.14 = 422.06 \text{ kJ/kg}$$

The specific volume after isothermal expansion is of course that interpolated from the steam tables, viz v_E = 1076.3 dm^3/kg.

Note. Although the isothermal expansion from D to E is in tion (the reverse of evaporation) are isothermal operations since they are carried out at constant temperature.

Note Although the isothermal expansion from D to E is in the superheat zone, the amount of superheat (0.0 K to 78.05 K) is relatively so small that the steam is practically still a vapour, i.e. a gas near its condensing point. As such, the steam does not strictly obey the gas laws, the latter which apply to a perfect gas, i.e. a gas whose pressure and temperature are far removed from its condensing point.

In the case of a perfect gas expanding isothermally, *all* of the heat received goes to do external work, and *none* to increase the internal energy (enthalpy) of the gas.

In the case of steam, as the superheat increases, the behaviour of the steam approaches more nearly to that of a perfect gas, and if an isothermal expansion is carried out entirely at high superheat, then the gas laws would apply exactly as for a perfect gas.

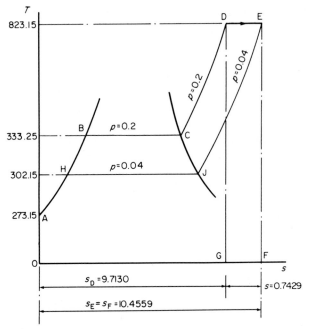

Figure 8.11 Isothermal expansion of highly superheated steam

To illustrate this, let us consider steam expanding iso-thermally from 0.2 bar, 550.0°C to 0.04 bar, i.e. from D to E in Figure 8.11.

$$\text{Initial temperature} = 550 + 273.15 = 823.15 \text{ K}$$
$$\text{Initial sat. temp} \quad = 60.1 + 273.15 = 333.25 \text{ K}$$
$$\therefore \text{Initial superheat} \qquad\qquad\qquad = 489.9 \text{ K}$$
$$\text{Final sat. temp} \quad = 29.0 + 273.15 = 302.15 \text{ K}$$
$$\text{Final superheat} \qquad\qquad\qquad = 521.0 \text{ K}$$
$$\text{The superheat is } \textit{high throughout} \quad \doteq 500.0 \text{ K}$$

From the Steam Tables (Table 4)

$$h_D = 3596.4 \text{ kJ/kg}, \; s_D = 9.713, \; v_D = 18\,992 \text{ dm}^3/\text{kg}$$
$$\text{and} \; h_E = 3596.5 \text{ kJ/kg}, \; s_E = 10.4559, \; v_E = 94\,971 \text{ dm}^3/\text{kg}$$

$$\text{Change of entropy, D to E} = 10.4559 - 9.7130 = 0.7429$$
$$\text{Heat received, D to E} = 823.15 \times 0.7429 = 611.52 \text{ kJ/kg}$$

Specific enthalpy at E = 3596.5 kJ/kg (area OAHJEF)

Specific enthalpy at D = 3596.4 kJ/kg (area OABCDG)

Increase in enthalpy of steam from D to E = 0.1 kJ/kg

Of 611.52 kJ/kg of heat received from the external source, only 0.1 kJ/kg appears in the steam as an increase of enthalpy, hence

External work done = 611.52 − 0.1 = 611.42 kJ/kg

These differences are negligible, hence heat received = external work done, as for a perfect gas. Note that $p_D v_D = 0.2 \times 18\,992 = 3798.4$ bar dm^3, and $p_E v_E = 0.04 \times 94\,971 = 3798.4$ bar dm^3, hence during isothermal expansion from D to E in Figure 8.11, the steam obeys the law $pv = $ constant, as for isothermal expansion of a perfect gas whereas from D to E in Figure 8.10 the connection is $pv^{0.96} = $ constant.

Within the wet field, an isothermal is either evaporation or condensation.

Reception and rejection of heat

Referring to Figure 8.2, 1.0 kg of water receives heat from A to B causing the water temperature to rise from 273.15 K to 438.15 K. Therefore the temperature of the heat source must be at least 438.15 K, since heat will not, of its own accord, flow from a cold to a hot body, (just as compressed air, for instance, will not of its own accord, pass upward from a low-pressure receiver to a high-pressure receiver). Hence at all points on AB, except B, heat will flow from the hot source into water which is colder than the heat source, but cannot of its own accord flow backwards from the colder water into the hot source. This operation is therefore *thermodynamically irreversible*, and from the foregoing reasoning we may state a rule:

If any process necessitates the transfer of heat from a source to a substance, the process is reversible *only if the temperature of the source is equal to the temperature of the substance.*

Conversely, if a substance rejects heat to a sink, the process is reversible only if the temperature of the substance is equal to the temperature of the sink.

This qualification is known as *equality of temperature* and is a necessary requirement for reversibility of a heat transfer operation. Theoretically, evaporation and condensation are both reversible, since they are both carried out at constant temperature.

Following consideration of the last three operations, viz. adiabatic operations, isothermal operations, reception and rejection of heat, the laws of thermodynamics may be stated. These are two in number.

1. Heat and work are mutually convertible, 1.0 kJ of heat being equivalent to 1.0 kNm of work.
2. Heat will not, of its own accord pass upward from a cold to a hot body.

Bearing in mind these two laws, and what we have said concerning equality of temperature and reversibility, we may in the next chapter proceed to examine the theoretical process of the conversion of heat into work, using steam as the working substance. For this purpose, the temperature-entropy diagram is used, as it makes all the processes and arguments very easy to follow.

It is worthwhile repeating that it is not necessary to work on a complete *Ts* diagram, but only to make a little hand sketch, marking on the appropriate values in each case. This is fully explained in Chapter 9.

Enthalpy-entropy diagram (Mollier diagram)

Another energy diagram involving entropy is the enthalpy-entropy diagram, which as its name implies is essentially a graph in which the specific enthalpy of steam is plotted on a base of entropy. The enthalpy-entropy diagram is often referred to as the Mollier diagram, on account of its having been first developed by Dr. Mollier, a German engineer of Dresden, whose work on the properties of steam corresponds with that of Professor Callendar in Great Britain.

Referring to Figure 8.12, if the specific enthalpy of the saturated liquid (h_f from the Steam Tables), is plotted on a base of specific entropy of the saturated liquid (s_f from the Steam Tables), a curve OCBAE is obtained.

If the specific enthalpy of the saturated vapour (h_g from the Steam Tables) is plotted on a base of specific entropy of the saturated vapour (s_g from the Steam Tables) on the same diagram, a curve EDHFG is obtained, merging into the curve OCBAE at E.

OCBAE is called the liquid line and EDHFGA the saturation line.

Consider steam at a pressure of 7.0 bar. Then from the Steam Tables,

Specific enthalpy of the saturated liquid h_f = 697.1 kJ/kg
Specific entropy of the saturated liquid s_f = 1.9918

These are the coordinates of the point B, where the line of constant pressure 7.0 bar leaves the liquid line.

Also from the Steam Tables for the same pressure, 7.0 bar,

Specific enthalpy of the saturated vapour h_g = 2762.0 kJ/kg
Specific entropy of the saturated vapour s_g = 6.7052

These are the coordinates of the point F, at which the line of constant pressure 7.0 bar crosses the saturation line.

Suppose the steam at pressure 7.0 bar to be 0.9 dry, then

Specific enthalpy of the wet vapour =
    697.1 + (0.9 × 2064.9) = 2555.5 kJ/kg
Specific entropy of the wet vapour =
    1.9918 + (0.9 × 4.7134) = 6.2339

These are the coordinates of a point F'. If the above calculation be repeated for a dryness fraction of 0.8 another point F'' can be obtained on the line of constant pressure 7.0 bar. Since the increment of enthalpy for evaporation and the increment of entropy for evaporation are each linear functions of the dryness fraction, the line of constant pressure 7.0 bar is a straight line in the wet zone.

Now consider steam at a pressure of 7.0 bar but superheated to a temperature of 300°C. From the Steam Tables

Specific enthalpy of the superheated steam = 3059.8 kJ/kg
Specific entropy of the superheated steam = 7.2997

These are the coordinates of a point J on the line of constant pressure 7.0 bar. By considering a steam temperature of 200°C in the same way, another point J' can be obtained on the line of constant pressure 7.0 bar, and so on.

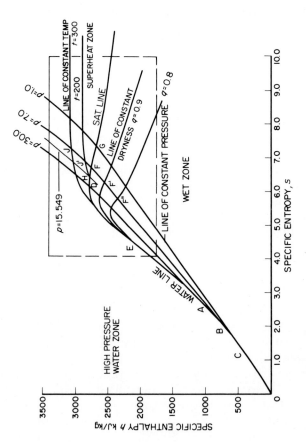

Figure 8.12 Enthalpy–entropy diagram for saturated and superheated steam

By repeating these methods for other pressures (e.g. 30.0 bar and 1.0 bar in Figure 8.12) any number of lines of constant pressure may be drawn. By joining all points such as F' on these lines of constant pressure, a line of constant dryness 0.9 may be drawn. By joining all points such as J on the lines of constant pressure, a line of constant temperature 300°C may be drawn. By joining all points such as J' a line of constant temperature 200°C may be drawn.

The saturation temperature corresponding to a pressure of 7.0 bar is 165°C, hence if the steam temperature is 300°C it has a superheat of 300 − 165 = 135°C. Hence the point J lies on a line of constant superheat 135°C and the point J' on a line of constant superheat 35°C.

Lines of constant specific volume may also be drawn, but as the additional complication might be confusing to the relatively inexperienced student, these lines are not included in the present explanation.

Note that areas on a Mollier diagram have no significance, and that the practical (Celsius) scale of temperature is used, i.e. °C.

Note also that each line of constant temperature meets the saturation line at the intersection of the saturation line and a line of constant pressure whose saturation temperature is equal to that constant temperature; e.g. in Figure 8.12 the line of constant temperature 200°C meets the saturation line at the point where the line of constant pressure 15.549 bar crosses the saturation line. In other words 200°C is the saturation temperature corresponding to a pressure of 15.549 bar.

The enthalpy-entropy diagram is used in the practical investigation of steam engines and steam turbines, and provided the scale is not too small, state points can be plotted and enthalpy quantities read, reasonably accurately, direct from the diagram.

As will be shown in succeeding chapters, we are interested mainly in that part of the Mollier diagram enclosed in the rectangular frame (Figure 8.12), and the various diagrams sold consist of this part plotted to a large scale.

For our purpose a very convenient average-scale diagram is available. This is titled *Enthalpy Entropy Chart for Steam– SI Units* (Juza) published by Messrs Edward Arnold (Publishers) Ltd, London.

9 Steam engine and turbine cycles and efficiencies

When dealing with the thermodynamical aspects of steam cycles, we are not concerned with the shortcomings of the boiler, or of the engine, or of any of the other units in the system.

We are concerned only with the recurring sequence of physical changes through which the steam passes, and with what heat we must supply to the steam, and what work we can get back from the steam. Whether our practical engine can in fact carry all this out perfectly is of no consequence to the theoretical cycle. It is also of no consequence to the cycle whether we use a reciprocating piston engine or a turbine engine, whether a water-tube boiler or a Scotch boiler, etc.

Once we fix the cycle steam conditions and the physical nature of the cycle operations, then there exists a definite maximum efficiency which can be attained, irrespective of the type of engine, etc.

Suppose, for example, the efficiency of a certain theoretical cycle is 35 per cent. No practical engine is capable of attaining that efficiency but will attain something less than 35 per cent, and the fraction of the theoretical cycle efficiency which is attained in practice depends on the type of engine and boiler, and the extent of their losses. Thus, we have:

(a) *The cycle efficiency* which depends only on the steam pressures and condition and on the nature of the cycle operations.
(b) *The actual efficiency* which is a fraction of the cycle efficiency, depending on how good, or how bad, the practical engine is made.

This chapter is concerned only with the cycle efficiency, i.e., the maximum efficiency which can be attained with any given steam conditions and any given cycle operations, independent of the type of engine or of its losses.

Carnot's principle

In 1824 the French physicist Nicholas Joseph Sadi-Carnot laid down the fundamental requirements of a heat-engine cycle of maximum efficiency in a short statement called Carnot's Principle.

> *No heat engine can be more efficient than one which is completely reversible within itself when working between the same temperature limits.*

This statement is quite general—it does not say that we must use a steam engine, or a steam turbine, or a oil engine, or a gas turbine; it merely states that if we wish to aim at maximum efficiency, then there are only two qualifications: (i) Reversibility;* (ii) Temperature limits.

Bearing in mind the two laws of thermodynamics and the qualifications for reversibility, let us examine the implications of Carnot's Principle.

In all heat-engine cycles it is necessary to add heat to the working substance at some point in the cycle. To be reversible, such heat reception must be at constant temperature (see page 349). Similarly, it is necessary to take heat from the working substance at some point in the cycle, and this heat rejection is reversible only if it takes place at constant temperature. Thus, to comply with Carnot's Principle, all heat received must be received at constant temperature, and all heat rejected must be rejected at constant temperature.

Carnot's Principle also states *when working between the same temperature limits*. This means that for maximum efficiency the upper temperature limit should be as high as possible and the lower temperature limit as low as possible. Now, at any point in the cycle other than the upper and lower temperature limits, the temperature is not constant,

---

Note that reversibility does not mean *Ahead* and *Astern*, but thermodynamical reversibility as referred to in Chapter 8.

but variable, and if heat is taken in and rejected at any temperature other than the upper- and lower-temperature limits respectively, then that heat is not being exploited over the maximum temperature range. We may therefore amplify a previous statement thus: *All heat received must be received at constant high temperature and all heat rejected must be rejected at constant low temperature, these two temperatures being the limits between which the cycle works.*

The working substance must be brought up from the lower to the upper temperature limit by some process other than by receiving heat from the source of heat. The means proposed by Carnot for so doing is a reversible adiabatic compression.

The cycle proposed by Carnot for initially saturated steam consists of four operations:

1. Reception of heat at constant high temperature T_1 (evaporation).
2. Adiabatic expansion, external work being done at the expense of the total heat of the steam, the temperature falling from T_1 to T_2.
3. Rejection of heat at constant low temperature T_2 (partial condensation).
4. Adiabatic compression, work being done on the steam to return the temperature from the lower limit T_2 to the upper limit T_1.

Consider 1.0 kg of steam applied to this cycle, and refer to Figure 9.1(a) and (b) which show the pv diagram and the Ts diagram respectively.

Let the initial steam conditions be 14.0 bar, dry saturated, and the final pressure be 0.07 bar.

AB is evaporation at constant temperature 468.19 K and constant pressure 14.0 bar, the entropy increasing from 2.2836 to 6.4651 and heat to the extent of area $EABF$ being received

$$\text{Area } EABF = AE \times EF$$

$$\therefore \text{Heat received} = T_1 \left(s_2 - s_1 \right)$$

The steam then expands adiabatically from B to C, during which the temperature falls from 468.19 K to 312.18 K at constant entropy, and during which external work is done at the expense of the enthalpy of the steam.

The steam is then partially condensed from C to D at constant temperature 312.18 K and constant pressure 0.07 bar, the entropy diminishing from 6.4651 to 2.2836, and heat to the extent of area $EDCF$ being rejected.

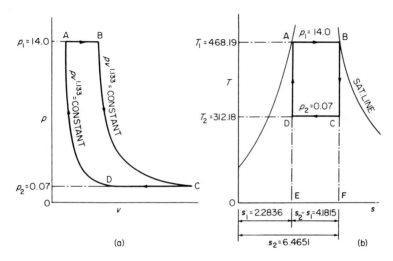

Figure 9.1 Carnot cycle for initially saturated steam between the limits 14.0 bar and 0.07 bar
(a) The pv diagram
(b) The Ts diagram

The steam is then adiabatically compressed from D to A, during which the pressure rises from 0.07 to 14.0 bar and the temperature from 312.18 to 468.19 K.

Now the heat rejected = area $EDCF$
$$= ED \times EF = T_2 \left(s_2 - s_1\right)$$

This means that the Carnot engine receives heat to the extent of $T_1 \left(s_2 - s_1\right)$, converts some of this heat to work, and rejects the remainder, $T_2 \left(s_2 - s_1\right)$. Thus the heat converted to work is

Heat received -- heat rejected = area $ABCD$
$$= \left(T_1 - T_2\right) \left(s_2 - s_1\right)$$

The cycle efficiency is as usual given by heat converted to work/heat received

$$\therefore \text{Cycle efficiency} = \frac{(T_1 - T_2)(s_2 - s_1)}{T_1(s_2 - s_1)}$$

$$\therefore \text{Cycle efficiency} = \frac{T_1 - T_2}{T_1}$$

This is the Carnot efficiency, or the maximum efficiency of *any* heat engine cycle working between temperature limits 468.19 K and 312.18 K. As all four cycle operations are already reversible the cycle efficiency can be increased only by raising T_1 and/or lowering T_2.

Applying the appropriate values,

$$\text{Cycle efficiency} = \frac{468.19 - 312.18}{468.19} = \frac{156.01}{468.19}$$

$$= 0.3332 \ (\text{or } 33.32 \text{ per cent})$$

The heat received, or cycle heat = 468.19 × 4.1815

$$= 1957.8 \text{ kJ/kg}$$

Work done, or cycle work = (468.19 − 312.18) 4.1815

$$= 156.01 \times 4.1815$$

$$= 652.4 \text{ kJ/kg}$$

The heat rejected = 312.18 × 4.1815 = 1305.4 kJ/kg.

While the Carnot cycle must remain the ideal to be aimed at, it is quite impracticable to design and build an engine to work on this cycle. The practical complications are numerous, and so far, insurmountable. For instance, all the operations are supposed to take place within the actual working cylinder, which must therefore be a perfect heat insulator, a perfect heat conductor, an engine cylinder and a compressor cylinder at will. It must also act as a condenser and as a boiler at will, and in these capacities, must be capable of transmitting heat without any temperature difference between the heat source and the steam, or between the steam and the heat sink. Nevertheless Carnot's principle is quite immutable— it must remain and guide us in our quest for high efficiency, using practicable cycles and practicable plant.

The Rankine cycle

As a result of the growth of the steam engine and of a realisa-
tion of the practical difficulties in making a workable Carnot
engine, a modified cycle was proposed practically simultaneously by Rankine in Great Britain and by Clausius in Germany. This modified cycle, called the Rankine Cycle, assumes
all the operations to be carried out in the necessary separate
units, boiler, engine, condenser, feed pump etc., and is the
ideal practical cycle for steam engines and steam turbines.

Consider 1.0 kg of steam applied to the cycle and refer to
Figure 9.2. The cycle operations are as follows:

1. The steam is completely condensed at constant temperature from D to A.
2. At A, the feed pump delivers the water into the boiler,
   and the water then receives heat from A to B causing the
   water temperature to rise from 312.18 K to 468.19 K.
   During this operation there is a slight decrease in the
   volume of the water due to the compression of the pump
   and a slight increase in the volume of the water due to
   heating. These are of importance for the higher pressures, but will be ignored at present, for simplicity.
3. The steam then receives further heat in the boiler at

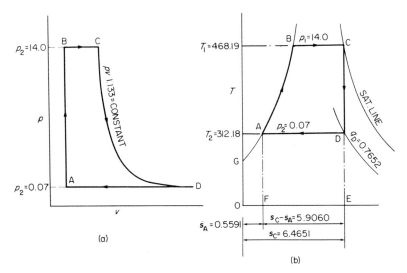

*Figure 9.2 Rankine cycle for initially saturated steam between the limits 14.0 bar
and 0.07 bar*
(a) The pv diagram
(b) The Ts diagram

constant temperature from B to C causing complete evaporation.

4. The steam then expands adiabatically in the engine from C to D, during which external work is done at the expense of the enthalpy, the steam temperature falling to the lower limit.

It will be noted that the second operation (which replaces Carnot's reversible adiabatic compression) is a reception of heat at varying temperatures which is irreversible. According to Carnot's principle therefore, the efficiency of the Rankine cycle will be less than that of the Carnot cycle between the same temperature limits.

Referring to Figure 9.2(b) water entering the boiler at A has enthalpy represented by area $OGAF$, i.e. the enthalpy of saturated water at a pressure of 0.07 bar, which from the steam tables is $h_f = 163.4$ kJ/kg. The dry saturated steam leaving the boiler at C has enthalpy represented by area $OGABCDE$, i.e. the enthalpy of saturated vapour at a pressure of 14.0 bar, which from the steam tables is $h_g = 2787.8$ kJ/kg. The nett heat received in the boiler, or the cycle heat is therefore $2787.8 - 163.4 = 2624.4$ kJ/kg, and is of course represented by area $FABCDE$.

At the end of adiabatic expansion, the enthalpy of the steam is represented by the area $OGADE$, and the state point D lies in the wet zone. During adiabatic expansion from C to D, the entropy remains constant, i.e. $s_C = s_D = 6.4651$.

From the steam tables, the entropy of the saturated liquid at a pressure of 0.07 bar is $s_A = 0.5591$, hence the increment of entropy from D to A is $6.4651 - 0.5591 = 5.9060$. From the steam tables, the increment of entropy for evaporation of dry saturated steam at a pressure of 0.07 bar is 7.7176, hence the dryness fraction at D is

$$q_D = \frac{5.9060}{7.7176} = 0.7652, \text{ and the enthalpy of the steam at } D \text{ is}$$

$$h_D = 163.4 + (0.7652 \times 2409.2) = 2007.0 \text{ kJ/kg}$$

The cycle work is the area $OGABCDE$ less the area $OGADE$, which is equal to area $ABCD$, or simply,

$$\text{Cycle work} = h_C - h_D = 2787.8 - 2007.0 = 780.8 \text{ kJ/kg}$$

$$\text{Cycle efficiency} = \frac{\text{cycle work}}{\text{cycle heat}} = \frac{780.8}{2624.4} = 0.2975$$

(or 29.75 per cent)

Thus the substitution of the irreversible reception of heat at varying temperature for the reversible adiabatic compression has lowered the cycle efficiency from 0.3332 to 0.2975, i.e. a reduction of 10.7 per cent on the Carnot efficiency. This is the price which has to be paid for contravening Carnot's principle in order to obtain practicability.

Note that the Rankine cycle work is greater than the Carnot cycle work between the same temperature limits, but is produced less efficiently.

Note also that the steam is expanded adiabatically over the entire pressure drop from p_1 to p_2. When this is so, the Rankine cycle is said to have complete expansion.

When dealing with the Rankine cycle, or any of its variations, we should, strictly speaking, deduct the theoretical feed pump work from the cycle work, since the cycle could not operate without the expenditure of this feed pump work. The theoretical feed pump work is given by $v_{f2} (p_1 - p_2)$ where v_{f2} is the specific volume of the saturated liquid, dm^3/kg, at the lower cycle pressure limit p_2 bar, and p_1 bar is the upper cycle pressure limit. In the present case, theoretical feed pump work = 1.0074 (14.0 − 0.07) = 14.0331 bar dm^3/kg and since 1.0 bar dm^3 = 0.1 kJ,

Theoretical feed pump work = 14.0331 × 0.1 = 1.4 kJ/kg

To render certain aspects of this chapter more readily understood, however, we will at this stage ignore the feed pump work, but we will bear in mind that when we use the terms cycle work and cycle efficiency it is the *gross cycle work* and *gross cycle efficiency* which are implied. (Note: all the other auxiliaries are required for practical reasons, to enable the practical engine to work. The feed pump work is required for thermodynamical reasons, to enable the cycle to work, hence the reason why only the feed pump work is mentioned at this point.) Appropriate corrections for all auxiliary power are illustrated in Chapter 12, in which we deal with the more practical aspects of the Rankine cycle and its variations.

The constant volume cycle

This is the cycle on which a non-expansive engine would work, e.g. an engine taking steam throughout the length of the stroke and exhausting throughout the length of the return stroke. While such a cycle has nothing to recommend it thermodynamically, it is of interest to examine it from two viewpoints:

1. To emphasise the inefficiency of a cycle working without expansion of the steam.
2. To demonstrate how a line of constant specific volume is drawn on the *Ts* diagram.

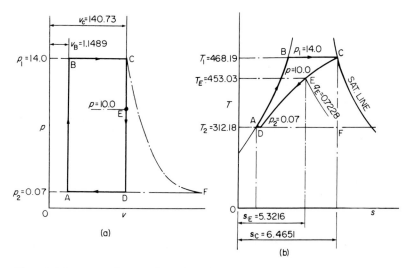

Figure 9.3 Constant volume cycle for initially saturated steam between the limits
14.0 bar and 0.07 bar
(a) The pv diagram
(b) The Ts diagram

Referring to Figure 9.3, the operations *AB* and *BC* are the same as for the Rankine cycle between the same limits. *CD* is expansion at constant volume and *DA* is complete condensation. The cycle heat is the same as in Figure 9.2; viz.

$$\text{Cycle heat} = h_C - h_A = 2787.8 - 163.4 = 2624.4 \text{ kJ/kg}$$

The simplest way of obtaining the cycle work in this instance is from the *pv* diagram.

The pressures are in bar, and 1.0 bar = 10^5 N/m^2.

The specific volumes are in dm^3/kg = $(0.1 \text{ m})^3$/kg

$$= 0.001 \text{ m}^3/\text{kg} = \frac{\text{m}^3}{\text{kg}} \times \frac{1}{10^3}$$

Hence areas on the pv diagram are bar dm^3

$$= \frac{10^5}{10^3} \frac{\text{N}}{\text{m}^2} \frac{\text{m}^3}{\text{kg}} = \frac{\text{Nm}}{\text{kg}} \times 10^2$$

i.e. areas on the pv diagram are *work* quantities and since

$$1 \text{ Nm} = 1 \text{ J, then Nm/kg} = \text{J/kg} = \frac{\text{kJ}}{\text{kg}} \frac{1}{1000}$$

Hence areas on the pv diagram are

$$\frac{\text{kJ}}{\text{kg}} \times \frac{10^2}{10^3} = \frac{\text{kJ}}{\text{kg}} \times 0.1$$

Now v_1 is the specific volume of the saturated water

$$= 1.1489 \text{ dm}^3/\text{kg}$$

v_2 is the specific volume of the saturated steam

$$= 140.73 \text{ dm}^3/\text{kg}$$

And if we neglect the change in volume from A to B, which has only a small effect,

Area of pv diagram $= (p_1 - p_2)(v_2 - v_1)$

$$= [(14.0 - 0.07) - (140.73 - 1.1489)]$$
$$\times 0.1, \text{ kJ/kg}$$

$$= 13.93 \times 139.5811 \times 0.1, \text{ kJ/kg}$$

$$= 194.43 \text{ kJ/kg, that is}$$

Cycle work $= 194.43$ kJ/kg

Cycle efficiency $= \dfrac{194.43}{2624.4} = 0.0741$ (or 7.41 per cent)

If this is compared with the efficiency 0.2975 (or 29.75 per cent) of the Rankine cycle, the inefficiency of using the steam non-expansively at once becomes most obvious. Only the change in volume during evaporation is being utilised to do work (see Chapter 1), and none of the inherent capability of the steam to expand. The area CDF on the energy diagrams is not utilised.

The construction of the line of constant volume CD is of some importance. The specific volume of the steam remains constant at 140.73 dm^3/kg from C to D. Consider a line of constant pressure 10.0 bar, and find the dryness fraction at E. From the steam tables for a pressure of 10.0 bar,

$$v_f = 1.1274 \text{ dm}^3/\text{kg}; \quad v_g = 194.3 \text{ dm}^3/\text{kg}$$

But the specific volume at $E = v_E = 140.73 \text{ dm}^3/\text{kg}$

$$\therefore v_E = q_E v_g + (1 - q_E) v_f$$
$$\therefore 140.73 = 194.3 q_E + 1.1274 - 1.1274 q_E$$
$$\therefore 193.1726 q_E = 139.6026$$
$$\therefore q_E = \frac{139.6026}{193.1726}$$
$$\therefore q_E = 0.7228$$

Hence the entropy

$$s_E = s_f + q_E \, s_{fg} \text{ (s_f and s_{fg} from the tables for or} \atop \text{10.0 bar)}$$
$$\therefore s_E = 2.1382 + (0.7228 \times 4.4447)$$
$$\therefore s_E = 2.1382 + 3.2124$$
$$\therefore s_E = 5.3506$$

The saturation temperature corresponding to a pressure of 10.0 bar is 453.03 K, i.e.

$$T_E = 453.03$$

T_E and s_E are the coordinates of a point E on the constant volume line, and by choosing a series of pressures between

14.0 bar and 0.07 bar and carrying out a similar calculation for each pressure, the curve of constant volume CD may be drawn.

The Rankine cycle with incomplete expansion

In this chapter we have already defined *complete expansion* as adiabatic expansion over the entire cycle pressure drop, and we established the dryness fraction at D as $q_D = 0.7652$. Hence the specific volume at D is given by

$$v_D = q_D v_g + (1 - q_D) v_f$$
$$\therefore v_D = (0.7652 \times 20\,530.4) + (0.2348 \times 1.0074)$$
$$\therefore v_D = 15\,709.9 + 0.2365$$
$$\therefore v_D = 15\,710.14 \text{ dm}^3/\text{kg}$$

For convenience, we may repeat the pv and Ts diagrams in Figure 9.4.

If now instead of expanding adiabatically from C to D, adiabatic expansion is stopped at X where the pressure is, say, 1.0 bar, and the remainder of the pressure drop is carried out at constant volume from X to E, it is obvious that the cycle work will be reduced by the shaded area XED and the cycle efficiency will be reduced accordingly.

Let us first find the dryness fraction at X.

$$s_X = s_C = 6.4651$$
$$\therefore 6.4651 = s_f + q_X\, s_{fg} \text{ (s_f and s_{fg} from the steam}$$
$$\text{tables for } p = 1.0 \text{ bar)}$$
$$\therefore 6.4651 = 1.3027 + 6.0571 q_X$$
$$\therefore q_X = \frac{6.4651 - 1.3027}{6.0571}$$
$$\therefore q_X = \frac{5.1624}{6.0571}$$
$$\therefore q_X = 0.8522 \text{, and the specific volume at } X \text{ is}$$

$$v_X = q_X v_g + (1 - q) v_f \text{ (v_g and v_f from the steam tables for}$$
$$p = 1.0 \text{ bar)}$$
$$\therefore v_X = (0.8522 \times 1693.7) + (0.1478 \times 1.0434)$$

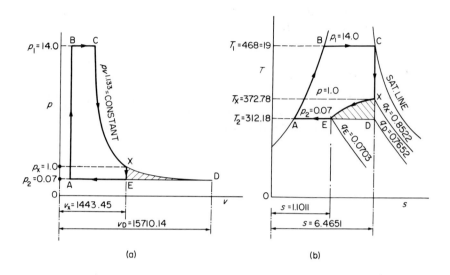

*Figure 9.4 The Rankine cycle for initially saturated steam between the limits
14.0 bar and 0.07 bar with incomplete expansion
(a) The pv diagram
(b) The Ts diagram*

$$\therefore\ v_X = 1443.3 + 0.1542$$

$$\therefore\ v_X = 1443.4542 \text{ dm}^3/\text{kg}$$

Since the specific volume is constant from X to E, then
$v_E = 1443.45$ dm^3/kg.

The dryness fraction at E is q_E and is found from

$$1443.45 = 20530.4q_E + 1.0074\ (1 - q_E)$$

$$\therefore\ 1443.45 = 20530.4q_E + 1.0074 - 1.0074q_E$$

$$\therefore\ 20529.393q_E = 1442.443$$

$$\therefore\ q_E = \frac{1442.443}{20529.393}$$

$$\therefore\ q_E = 0.0703$$

The entropy at E is $s_E = 0.5591 + (0.0703 \times 7.7176)$

$$\therefore \ s_E = 0.5591 + 0.5420$$

$$\therefore \ s_E = 1.1011$$

If, as an approximation, we treat area XED as a triangle, then loss of cycle work due to incomplete expansion = area XED

$$= \frac{6.4651 - 1.1011}{2} \ (372.78 - 312.18)$$

$$= \frac{5.3640 \times 60.6}{2}$$

$$= 162.54 \ \text{kJ/kg}$$

Hence the cycle work = $780.8 - 162.54 = 618.26$ kJ/kg approx. and the

$$\text{Cycle efficiency} = \frac{618.26}{2624.4} = 0.2356 \ \text{approx.}$$

Thus by sacrificing work to the extent of the shaded area EXD and accepting the resulting lower cycle efficiency, we reduce the final specific volume of the steam from 15710.14 dm³/kg to 1443.45 dm³/kg.

This means that if we design a reciprocating engine to work on the above Rankine cycle with incomplete expansion, the volume of the L.P. cylinder need be only 1443.45 compared with 15710.14 for complete expansion, i.e. less than one-tenth of the size. For this reason reciprocating engines invariably have incomplete expansion in the L.P. cylinder. The pressure at X is called the terminal pressure.*

Although steam engines invariably have incomplete expansion, it is customary to refer the actual performance of an engine or an engine cylinder to the Rankine cycle having complete expansion, i.e. the engine is debited with the thermodynamical loss due to incomplete expansion. For example, the cycle efficiency of the engine in Figure 9.4 would not be taken as 0.2356, but as 0.2975 as for the engine in Figure 9.2.

*The H.P. and I.P. cylinders of steam engines are also likely to have incomplete expansion, but for a different reason (see Chapter 2).

Turbines operate with steam which is moving at high velocity, and it is therefore not only the steam specific volume which determines the flow area, but also the steam velocity (see Chapter 10). The combined effect of these factors invariably enables steam turbine cycles to be designed with complete expansion.

Average temperature of cycle heat reception

In the Rankine cycle shown in Figure 9.2, the cycle heat is received in two parts, one at varying temperature from A to B, and one at constant temperature from B to C, the total cycle heat being the area $FABCDE$.

By definition,

Heat received = average temperature of heat reception × change of entropy

Hence the average temperature of heat reception T, for the whole cycle is

$$T = \frac{\text{cycle heat}}{s_C - s_A}, \text{ from which}$$

$$T = \frac{2624.4}{5.9060} = 444.4 \text{ K}$$

corresponding to a pressure of 8.16 bar.

Referring to Figure 9.5, this means that the Rankine cycle heat (area $FABCDE$) which is received at varying temperature from A to C is equal to a Carnot cycle heat (area $FAXYDE$) having heat reception at constant temperature from X to Y.

The two cycles have the same efficiency, viz.

$$\text{Carnot cycle efficiency} = \frac{T - T_2}{T}$$

$$= \frac{444.4 - 312.18}{444.4}$$

$$= \frac{132.22}{444.4}$$

$$= 0.2975$$

The heat rejected, area *FADE* is the same for the two cycles, hence the cycle work *ABCD* is also equal to the cycle work *AXYD*.

Thus for any given lower cycle temperature limit, the efficiency of any Rankine cycle is equal to the efficiency of a Carnot cycle whose upper temperature limit is equal to the average temperature of heat reception of the Rankine cycle.

This is a most important relationship.

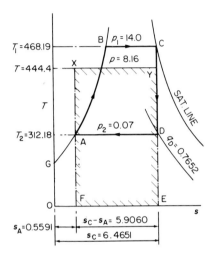

Figure 9.5 Carnot cycle having the same efficiency as a Rankine cycle for initially saturated steam between the limits 14.0 bar and 0.07 bar

We may now use it to examine how the simple Rankine cycle shown in Figure 9.2 may be modified to give higher efficiency, and so lead to a clear appreciation of the advanced cycles of the present day. In all cases we will assume complete expansion.

For purposes of efficiency comparison, any Rankine cycle can be regarded as being replaced by its equivalent Carnot cycle as explained above and as illustrated in Figure 9.5.

To increase the efficiency of any Rankine cycle, we must increase the efficiency of its equivalent Carnot cycle, and the only means by which we can do so are these:

1. By lowering the lower temperature limit of the Carnot cycle, which means lowering the exhaust pressure of the Rankine cycle.
2. By raising the upper temperature limit of the Carnot cycle which means raising the *average* temperature of heat reception of the Rankine cycle. There are several ways of achieving this.
3. By some combination of 1 and 2.

LOWERING THE EXHAUST PRESSURE

Suppose we lower the exhaust pressure to 0.034 bar. Referring to Figure 9.6 and using the same methods as before, then from the steam tables h_C = 2787.8 kJ/kg, h_A = 109.8 kJ/kg.

$$\text{Cycle heat} = h_C - h_A = 2787.8 - 109.8 = 2678.0 \text{ kJ/kg}$$

Dryness fraction at D

$$q_D = \frac{6.4651 - 0.3838}{8.5336 - 0.3838} = \frac{6.0813}{8.1498} = 0.7463$$

Enthalpy at D

$$= 109.8 + (0.7463 \times 2439.7) = 109.8 + 1820.6$$
$$= 1930.4 \text{ kJ/kg}$$

$$\text{Cycle work} = h_C - h_D = 2787.8 - 1930.4 = 857.4 \text{ kJ/kg}$$

$$\text{Cycle efficiency} = \frac{857.4}{2678.0} = 0.32$$

$$\text{Average temperature of heat reception } T = \frac{\text{cycle heat}}{s_C - s_A}$$

$$\therefore T = \frac{2678.0}{6.0813} = 440.33 \text{ K}$$

$$\text{(Check, cycle efficiency} = \frac{T - T_2}{T} = \frac{440.33 - 299.35}{440.33}$$

$$= \frac{140.98}{440.33}$$

$$= 0.32 \text{ as before)}$$

Specific volume at exhaust

$$v_D = (0.7463 \times 40576.4) + (0.2537 \times 1.0032)$$

$$\therefore v_D = 30280.0 + 0.2545$$

$$\therefore v_D = 30280.26 \text{ dm}^3/\text{kg}$$

By reducing the exhaust pressure from 0.07 bar to 0.034 bar, the line AD has been lowered, the point A thus moving down the water line to the left, with these effects on the cycle:

1. The cycle heat is increased from 2624.4 kJ/kg to 2678.0 kJ/kg which is an increase of 2.0422 per cent.
2. The cycle work is increased from 780.8 kJ/kg to 857.4 kJ/kg, which is an increase of 9.8115 per cent.
3. The percentage increase in cycle work is greater than the percentage increase in cycle heat, hence the cycle efficiency is increased, viz. from 0.2975 to 0.32, which is an increase of 7.56 per cent.
4. The dryness fraction at exhaust is reduced from 0.7652 to 0.7463.
5. The specific volume at exhaust is increased from 15710.14 dm^3/kg to 30280.26 dm^3/kg.

   Or if we consider what we may call the "equivalent Carnot cycle" shown in ghost lines in Figure 9.6.

1. The additional cycle heat is received at low temperature which reduces the average temperature of cycle heat reception from 444.4 K to 440.33 K, that is a reduction of 4.07 K in the upper temperature limit.
2. The lower cycle temperature limit is reduced from 312.18 K to 299.35 K, that is a reduction of 12.83 K.
3. Since the reduction in T_2 is greater than the reduction in T, the cycle efficiency $T - T_2/T$ is increased.

In common with all other benefits we do not obtain this increase in cycle efficiency free--some sort of price has to be paid for it.

Thus to create the lower exhaust pressure, a larger and more expensive condenser must be provided, which will probably require more circulating water, and more space and more power for the condenser auxiliaries. The sea temperatures also have a marked effect on the exhaust pressure.

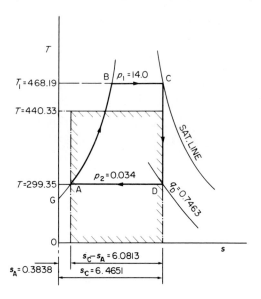

Figure 9.6 Rankine cycle for initially saturated steam between the limits 14.0 bar and 0.034 bar

Because of the lower final dryness fraction associated with the lower exhaust pressure, there will be correspondingly more water in the steam as it approaches the exhaust end, causing increased wetness losses, and possible erosion to last-stage turbine blades.

Because of its higher efficiency, the cycle exhausting at 0.034 bar will take only 0.2975/0.32 of the mass flow of steam required by the cycle exhausting at 0.07 bar, but the specific volume at exhaust is increased in the proportion 30280.26/15710.14.

The total volume of steam in dm^3/h exhausted by the cycle exhausting at 0.034 bar will therefore be

$$\frac{0.2975}{0.32} \times \frac{30280.26}{15710.14} = 1.793$$

times that of the cycle exhausting at 0.07 bar. This means that the steam flow areas through exhaust-end nozzles and blades, and other exhaust passages must be increased accordingly.

The exhaust pressures chosen for the last two examples, viz. 0.07 bar and 0.034 bar, represent the extremes of the range, which in the light of the factors outlined above, might be regarded as economic for large modern turbine steamers. The author's survey of modern marine steam turbine cycles indicates that to date, 0.05 bar is by far the most common design exhaust pressure, implying that this is the best compromise among the various conflicting features mentioned above. The features which influence the choice of steam and exhaust conditions are further discussed in Chapter 12. Meantime we will recalculate the simple Rankine cycle as before, but using the agreed lower limit of 0.05 bar.

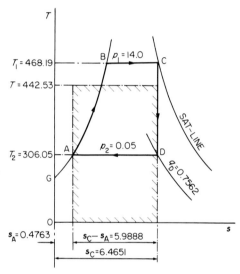

Figure 9.7 Rankine cycle for initially saturated steam between the limits 14.0 bar and 0.05 bar

Referring to Figure 9.7 and calculating as before

Cycle heat = 2787.8 − 137.8 = 2650.0 kJ/kg

Dryness fraction at D

$$q_D = \frac{6.4651 - 0.4763}{8.3960 - 0.4763} = \frac{5.9888}{7.9197} = 0.7562$$

Enthalpy at D

$$h_D = 137.8 + (0.7562 \times 2423.8)$$
$$\therefore \ h_D = 137.8 + 1832.9$$
$$\therefore \ h_D = 1970.7 \ \text{kJ/kg}$$

Cycle work $= 2787.8 - 1970.7 = 817.1$ kJ/kg

Cycle efficiency $= \dfrac{817.1}{2650.0} = 0.3083$

Specific volume at D

$$v_D = (0.7562 \times 28194.5) + (0.2438 \times 1.0052)$$

$$\therefore \; v_D = 21320.0 + 0.2451$$

$$\therefore \; v_D = 21320.2451 \text{ dm}^3/\text{kg}$$

Average temperature of cycle heat reception

$$= \dfrac{2650.0}{5.9888} = 442.53 \text{ K}$$

We may now use this cycle as a basis to examine how the cycle efficiency may be increased by modifying the upper limits, so leading to the advanced cycles of the present day.

Since we have fixed the lower temperature limit, then the Rankine cycle efficiency will be increased if we can raise the upper temperature limit of the equivalent Carnot cycle, i.e. if we can raise the *average* temperature of heat reception of the Rankine cycle.

INCREASING THE INITIAL PRESSURE

It will be immediately obvious that one of the most fruitful ways of increasing the average temperature of heat reception is to raise the initial pressure. At the present time, the maximum steam pressure which would be used in marine practice is of the order of 100.0 bar.

Suppose we raise the initial pressure to 100.0 bar, keeping the exhaust pressure at 0.05 bar. Referring to Figure 9.8 and calculating as before,

Cycle heat $= 2727.7 - 137.8 = 2589.9$ kJ/kg

Dryness fraction at D

$$q_D = \dfrac{5.6198 - 0.4763}{8.3960 - 0.4763} = \dfrac{5.1435}{7.9197} = 0.6495$$

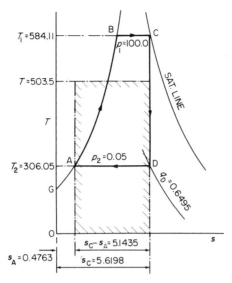

Figure 9.8 Rankine cycle for initially saturated steam between the limits 100.0 bar and 0.05 bar

Enthalpy at D

$$h_D = 137.8 + (0.6495 \times 2423.8)$$
$$\therefore \ h_D = 137.8 + 1574.1$$
$$\therefore \ h_D = 1711.9 \text{ kJ/kg}$$
$$\therefore \ \text{Cycle work} = 2727.7 - 1711.9 = 1015.8 \text{ kJ/kg}$$
$$\therefore \ \text{Cycle efficiency} = \frac{1015.8}{2589.9} = 0.3923$$

Specific volume at D

$$v_D = (0.6495 \times 28194.5) + (0.3505 \times 1.0052)$$
$$\therefore \ v_D = 18309.0 + 0.3523$$
$$\therefore \ v_D = 18309.35 \text{ dm}^3/\text{kg}$$

Average temperature of heat reception

$$T = \frac{2589.9}{5.1435} = 503.5 \text{ K}$$

Raising the initial pressure from 14.0 bar to 100.0 bar has increased the cycle efficiency from 0.3083 to 0.3923. This dramatic increase—27.25 per cent—is a consequence of having raised the average temperature of heat reception from 442.53 K to 503.5 K, thus complying with Carnot's principle as regards temperature limits. Consider however, the dryness fraction at D—it is now only 0.6495 compared with 0.7562 for the 14.0 bar cycle. The expansion line CD of the 100.0 bar cycle therefore proceeds further into the wet zone, and we must now consider further modification of the cycle, which while retaining the benefit of the increased pressure, will reduce the wetness of the steam during expansion, thus reducing wetness losses and possible blade erosion.

INCREASING THE INITIAL TEMPERATURE—THE SUPERHEAT CYCLE
Another method of raising the average temperature of heat reception is to apply superheat to the steam. In practice, superheating is done at constant pressure i.e. at the initial pressure, and the present-day maximum steam temperature which would be used in marine practice is of the order of 520°C, i.e. 793.15 K.

Suppose we retain the initial pressure of 100.0 bar and the final exhaust pressure of 0.05 bar, but superheat the steam to an initial temperature of 793.15 K. Referring to Figure 9.9 and calculating as before,

The specific enthalpy of the superheated steam at C, from the Steam Tables,

$$h_C = 3425.1 \text{ kJ/kg}$$

Cycle heat $= 3425.1 - 137.8 = 3287.3$ kJ/kg

Dryness fraction at D

$$q_D = \frac{6.6640 - 0.4763}{8.3960 - 0.4763} = \frac{6.1877}{7.9197} = 0.7814$$

Enthalpy at D

$$h_D = 137.8 + (0.7814 \times 2423.8)$$

$$\therefore h_D = 137.8 + 1893.9$$

$$\therefore h_D = 2031.7 \text{ kJ/kg}$$

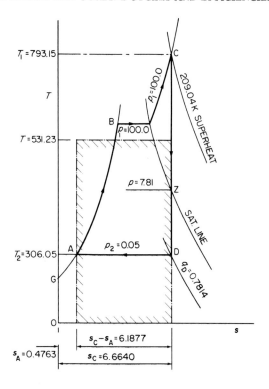

Figure 9.9 Rankine cycle for initially superheated steam between the limits 100.0 bar, 793.15 K and 0.05 bar

Cycle work = 3425.3 − 2031.7 = 1393.6 kJ/kg

Cycle efficiency = $\dfrac{1393.6}{3287.3}$ = 0.4239

Specific volume at D

$$v_D = (0.7814 \times 28194.5) + (0.2186 \times 1.0052)$$
$$\therefore \ v_D = 22028.0 + 0.2197$$
$$\therefore \ v_D = 22028.22 \ dm^3/kg$$

Average temperature of heat reception

$$T = \dfrac{328.3}{6.1877} = 531.23 \ K$$

Thus compared with the saturated steam cycle illustrated in Figure 9.8, initial superheating at constant pressure to 793.15 K has raised the average temperature of heat reception from 503.5 K to 531.23 K, resulting in an increase of cycle efficiency from 0.3923 to 0.4239, that is, an improvement of 8.06 per cent.

It is important at this stage, to examine in some detail the Rankine cycle illustrated in Figure 9.9 in relation to Carnot's principle. For this purpose, let us regard the initial and final pressures as the fixed basis of comparison.

A Carnot cycle between these limits would be as illustrated in Figure 9.10(a). All four of the cycle operations are reversible, the average temperature of heat reception is constant, and equal to the upper cycle temperature limit, and the cycle efficiency is the maximum which can be attained when working between the limits $T_1 = 584.11$ K and $T_2 = 306.05$ K.

The Rankine cycle in Figure 9.9 has two irreversible operations, viz. reception of sensible heat at varying temperature in the boiler and reception of superheat at varying temperature in the superheater. This cycle therefore contravenes Carnot's principle on two counts. Let us consider, however, the separate and combined effects of these two irreversible operations. Figure 9.10(b) shows that the effect of replacing only the adiabatic compression by an irreversible reception of sensible heat in the boiler is to reduce the average temperature of heat reception from 584.11 K to 503.5 K. Thus, not only is this operation irreversible, but it also lowers the average temperature of cycle heat reception. Both of these effects are contrary to Carnot's principle and the cycle efficiency is reduced from 0.476 to 0.3923 in consequence.

If we now add superheating at constant pressure as in Figure 9.10(c), while it is true that this is yet another irreversible operation, its effect is to raise the equivalent upper cycle temperature limit from 503.5 K to 531.23 K, because the additional heat is received at high temperature. The irreversibility of superheating is contrary to, but the raising of the equivalent upper cycle temperature limit is in accordance with, Carnot's principle. In this case the effect of the latter is greater than that of the former, and in consequence, the cycle efficiency is improved from 0.3923 to 0.4239.

The application of superheating at constant pressure in (c) may be regarded as a practical means of improving (b) to bring the latter nearer to (a). It could be argued that because

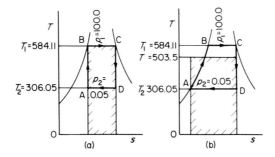

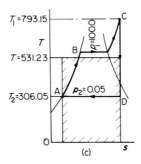

Figure 9.10 Effect of introducing irreversible operations into a basic Carnot cycle working between pressure limits 100.0 bar and 0.05 bar
(a) Carnot cycle: cycle efficiency = 0.476
(b) Rankine cycle without superheat: cycle efficiency = 0.3923
(c) Rankine cycle with superheat: cycle efficiency = 0.4239

we have raised the initial steam temperature from 584.11 K to 793.15 K, we have raised the upper cycle temperature limit, and that we should therefore compare (c) not to a Carnot cycle having an initial pressure of 100.0 bar, but to a Carnot cycle having an upper cycle temperature limit of 793.15 K. Such an argument is logical, but we have already decided that 100.0 bar is the highest initial pressure at present acceptable in marine practice, hence our object is to establish the best that can be done, in a practicable manner, with that initial pressure.

The question might also be asked, why not apply superheat to the Carnot cycle? Suppose we were desirous of applying superheat to the Carnot cycle having an initial pressure of 100.0 bar. Obviously, we could not superheat at constant pressure because this is irreversible and a Carnot cycle must have all its operations reversible. It must therefore receive all of its cycle heat at constant high temperature, i.e. at the upper cycle temperature limit. Thus for the given pressure limit, the superheating would have to be done at constant temperature 584.11 K, i.e. by an isothermal expansion of the steam from E to C in Figure 9.11.

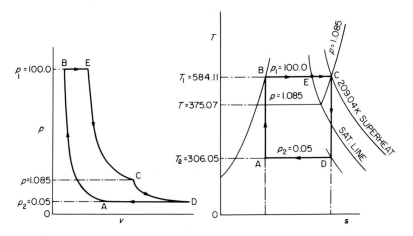

Figure 9.11 Carnot cycle for superheated steam between the limits 100.0 bar, 209.4 K superheat, and 0.05 bar
(a) The pv diagram
(b) The Ts diagram

We allow the same superheat range i.e. $793.15 - 584.11 = 209.04$ K as in the Rankine cycle illustrated in Figure 9.9. This fixes the point C at which isothermal expansion ends and adiabatic expansion begins.

Since we have not altered the temperature limits and have retained reversible operations throughout, the efficiency of this cycle is exactly the same as that of the Carnot cycle for initially saturated steam as shown in Figure 9.10(a). Such a Carnot cycle for superheated steam is of academic interest only.

Reverting to the Rankine cycle, we may say that that illustrated in Figure 9.9 represents the limits of the present-day "straight" Rankine cycle for marine installations. (The purists claim that it is not correct to refer to this type of cycle as a straight Rankine cycle, since, they say, the superheating operation is not in accordance with Rankine's original conception.) There remain however, two areas which may still be exploited to further improve the cycle efficiency.

1. Additional heat may be applied to the cycle at high temperature even if the additional heat reception is irreversible. This modification is known as reheating.
2. The reception of sensible heat at varying temperature in the boiler may be modified so as to reduce the "degree" of its irreversibility. This modification is known as *feed heating*.

We may now consider, in some detail, the thermodynamical aspects of each of these modifications.

Reheating–the reheat cycle

Comparing Figure 9.9 with 9.8, the application of superheat has improved the final dryness fraction from 0.6495 to 0.7814. Even so, we have ultimately to design and operate a practical engine or turbine, and a final dryness fraction of 0.7814 is much too low from the practical viewpoints of wetness losses and exhaust-end blade erosion. A considerable part, ZD, of the expansion line still lies in the wet zone, and we may now consider what can be done to reduce ZD to a minimum such that the dryness fraction q_D is not less than about 0.88.

For any given initial and final steam pressures this can be achieved by

(i) Increasing the initial steam temperature. Since we have, for our example, chosen the present day maximum steam temperature, we cannot increase this further.
(ii) Withdrawing the steam from the engines, or turbines, at some intermediate point in its expansion and re-superheating it at constant pressure before it passes through the remaining engine or turbine stages.

The resuperheating process is called *reheating*.

There are two methods of reheating, both of which are used in marine practice

(i) *The boiler reheater.* The steam to be reheated is passed through a series of tubes extending across the hotter parts of the boiler furnace, in exactly the same manner as the initial superheater.

(ii) *The steam reheater.* The steam is initially superheated to a temperature considerably higher than required at the engine or turbine stop valve, and is reduced to the latter temperature by giving up some of its heat to the steam to be reheated. The heat exchanger—usually of the shell and tube type—in which this heat transfer takes place is called a steam reheater.

Dealing firstly with the boiler reheater, and considering the application of one intermediate reheat to the cycle having conditions as in the last example, i.e. 100.0 bar, 793.15 K to 0.05 bar, two questions immediately present themselves:

1. To what temperature will we reheat the steam?
2. At what pressure will we reheat the steam?

The first question is quite readily answered; we have already noted the beneficial effect of heat reception at the highest possible temperature level, and we have fixed the maximum acceptable steam temperature at present as 793.15 K (i.e. 520°C). Therefore so far as the reheat temperature is concerned, the best that can be done is to make it the same as the initial steam temperature, i.e. 793.15 K.

The answer to the second question is considerably more involved. Referring to Figure 9.9, we could argue that the steam should be first expanded down to the point Z (at which it becomes dry saturated) before reheating. The pressure at Z is 7.81 bar (i.e. the pressure of dry saturated steam having total entropy 6.6640). For convenience in reading the Steam Tables, and in minimising the need for interpolation, let us make the reheat pressure = 8.0 bar.

Figure 9.12 shows the reheat cycle with these conditions. Compared with the non-reheat cycle of Figure 9.9, the cycle heat is increased by the area $JDEF = h_E - h_D$.

From the Steam Tables reading directly $h_E = 3523.7$ kJ/kg. Now $p_D = 8.0$ bar and $s_D = 6.6640$, hence from the Steam Tables and interpolating,

383

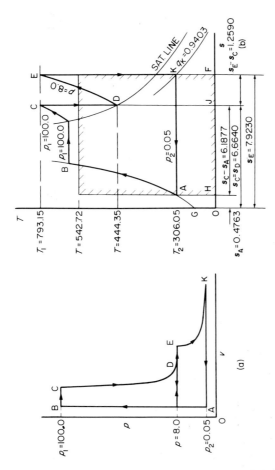

Figure 9.12 Reheat cycle between the limits 100.0 bar, 793.15 K, and 0.05 bar with one reheat at 8.0 bar to 793.15 K

s	T	h
6.7122	453.15	2791.10
6.6596	443.55	2767.50
0.0526	9.60	23.60
0.0044	0.80	1.98

At D 6.6640   444.35   2769.48

$\therefore$ Additional cycle heat

$$= 3523.7 - 2769.48 = 754.22 \text{ kJ/kg}$$

$\therefore$ Total cycle heat = 3287.3 + 754.22 = 4041.52 kJ/kg

Average temperature of cycle heat reception

$$T = \frac{4041.52}{7.923 - 0.4763} = \frac{4041.52}{7.4467} = 542.72 \text{ K}$$

$\therefore$ Cycle efficiency =

$$\frac{542.72 - 306.05}{542.72} = \frac{236.67}{542.72} = 0.4361$$

Dryness fraction at exhaust,

$$q_K = \frac{7.9230 - 0.4763}{8.3960 - 0.4763} = \frac{7.4467}{7.9197} = 0.9403$$

Thus the application of the reheat has raised the cycle efficiency from 0.4239 to 0.4361—an increase of 2.878 per cent. This is because we have raised the average temperature of cycle heat reception, i.e. we have raised the upper temperature limit of the equivalent Carnot cycle.

The final dryness fraction also has been increased, from 0.7814 to 0.9403.

Suppose we raise the reheat pressure to 17.0 bar, keeping all other conditions as before. Then, referring to Figure 9.13,

Additional cycle heat = $h_E - h_D$ = 3514.4 − 2928.05
$$= 586.35 \text{ kJ/kg}$$

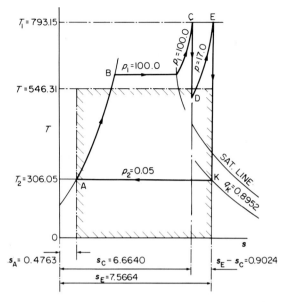

Figure 9.13 Reheat cycle between the limits 100.0 bar, 793.15 K, and 0.05 bar with one reheat at 17.0 bar to 793.15 K

Total cycle heat = 3287.3 + 586.35   = 3873.65 kJ/kg

$$\text{Average temperature of heat reception} = \frac{3873.65}{7.5664 - 0.4763}$$

$$= \frac{3873.65}{7.0901} = 546.31 \text{ K}$$

Cycle efficiency =

$$\frac{546.31 - 306.05}{546.31} = \frac{240.26}{546.31} = 0.4398$$

Dryness fraction at exhaust

$$q_K = \frac{7.5664 - 0.4763}{8.3960 - 0.4763} = \frac{7.0901}{7.9197} = 0.8952$$

Compared with the non-reheat cycle, the improvement in cycle efficiency is 3.751 per cent.

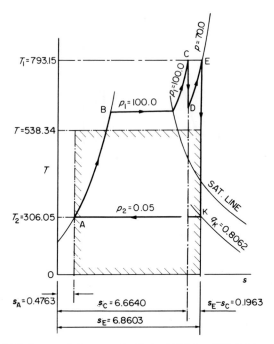

Figure 9.14 Reheat cycle between the limits 100.0 bar, 793.15 K and 0.05 bar with one reheat at 70.0 bar to 793.15 K

Suppose we further raise the reheat pressure to 70.0 bar, again keeping all other conditions as before. Referring to Figure 9.14,

$$\text{Additional cycle heat} = h_E - h_D$$

$$= 3458.3 - 3308.84$$

$$= 149.46 \text{ kJ/kg}$$

$$\text{Total cycle heat} = 3287.3 + 149.46$$

$$= 3436.76 \text{ kJ/kg}$$

Average temperature of cycle heat reception

$$= \frac{3436.76}{6.8603 - 0.4763}$$

$$= \frac{3436.76}{6.3840}$$

$$= 538.34 \text{ K}$$

$$\text{Cycle efficiency} = \frac{538.34 - 306.05}{538.34}$$

$$= \frac{232.29}{538.34}$$

$$= 0.4315$$

Dryness fraction at exhaust

$$q_K = \frac{6.8603 - 0.4763}{8.3960 - 0.4763} = \frac{6.3840}{7.9197} = 0.8062$$

The average temperature of cycle heat reception is lower than that of the cycle having the reheat at 17.0 bar. The improvement over the non-reheat cycle is 1.793 per cent compared with 3.751 per cent for the cycle with 17.0 bar reheat pressure.

Thus, as the reheat pressure is progressively raised, the cycle efficiency increases up to a certain point, and thereafter diminishes.

For any given initial pressure, initial temperature and exhaust pressure, there is therefore an optimum reheat pressure for which the cycle efficiency is a maximum.

Let us examine the reasons why this is so.

Reheating at constant pressure is an irreversible operation. The ultimate effect of the reheat on the overall cycle efficiency is determined by two factors, i.e.

(i) The quantity of additional cycle heat received.
(ii) The average temperature at which the additional cycle heat is received.

It will immediately be obvious that the improvement over the non-reheat cycle efficiency will be a maximum when *simultaneously* the combined effect of these two factors is a maximum.

Reference to the cycle calculations already carried out for three different reheat pressures will show that as the reheat pressure is increased, the quantity of additional cycle heat diminishes, while the average temperature at which the additional cycle heat is received increases. This is conveniently illustrated by the diagrams in Figure 9.15, noting that for any particular reheat pressure, the average temperature T' of additional heat reception is equal to the additional heat

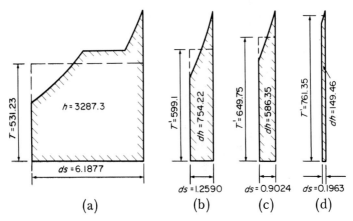

Figure 9.15 Additional cycle heat and average temperature of its reception for three different reheat pressures (a) Non-reheat (b) p = 8.0 (c) p = 17.0 (d) = 70.0

quantity dh divided by the change of entropy ds during the reheat. The cycle heat for the non-reheat cycle is shown by Figure 9.15(a).

If we add (b) to (a) we have added 754.22 kJ/kg to the cycle at an average temperature of 599.1 K, i.e. a large quantity of heat at a low average temperature.

If we add (c) to (a) we have added 586.35 kJ/kg to the cycle at an average temperature of 649.75 K, i.e. a smaller quantity of heat at a higher average temperature.

If we add (d) to (a) we have added only 149.46 kJ/kg to the cycle at an average temperature of 761.35 K, i.e. a small quantity of heat at a high average temperature.

The relative effect of the three different reheat pressures on the overall cycle efficiency may readily be seen by redrawing Figure 9.15 in such a manner as to add in turn to the non-reheat cycle (a), the additional cycle heats (b), (c) and (d) using the equivalent rectangles. Such a composite diagram is shown in Figure 9.16, and demonstrates clearly how, as the reheat pressure is raised, the combined effects of the increasing average temperature of the reheat and the diminishing additional heat received cause the average temperature of overall cycle heat reception—and therefore the overall cycle efficiency—to increase up to a maximum and thereafter to diminish.

It is interesting to speculate on the theoretical extremes of this conclusion. If, on the one hand we continue to raise the reheat pressure above 70.0 bar, the tall narrow rectangle on

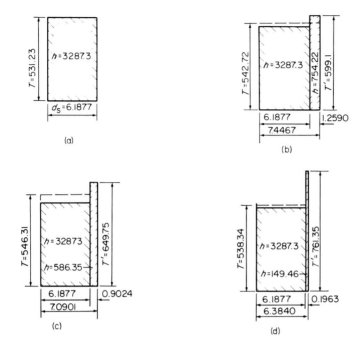

Figure 9.16 Effect of varying the reheat pressure on the average temperature of the overall cycle heat reception

(a) Non-reheat, $T = \dfrac{3287.3}{6.1877} = 531.23$

(b) $p = 8.0$, $T = \dfrac{3287.3 + 754.22}{7.4467} = 542.72$

(c) $p = 17.0$, $T = \dfrac{3287.3 + 586.35}{7.0901} = 546.31$

(d) $p = 70.0$, $T = \dfrac{3287.3 + 149.46}{6.3840} = 538.34$

the right-hand side of Figure 9.16(d) would become taller and narrower, until in the limit, when the reheat pressure is equal to the initial pressure, it would become a vertical straight line enclosing no area. The reheat would then be non-existent, and the cycle efficiency would revert to that of the non-reheat cycle, Figure 9.16(a).

If on the other hand, we continue to lower the reheat pressure below 8.0 bar, the rectangle on the right-hand side of Figure 9.16(b) would become lower and wider until a point is reached when it is the same height as the left-hand rectangle. The reheat would then not raise the average temperature of overall cycle heat reception above 531.23 K and the cycle efficiency would revert to that of the non-reheat cycle. For the given initial and final steam conditions this point is reached when the reheat pressure is about 2.415 bar. If we continue to lower the reheat pressure below 2.415 bar, the height of the right-hand rectangle in Figure 9.16 becomes less than that of the left-hand rectangle, the average temperature of overall cycle heat reception becomes less than 531.32 K, and the cycle efficiency becomes less than that of the non-reheat cycle.

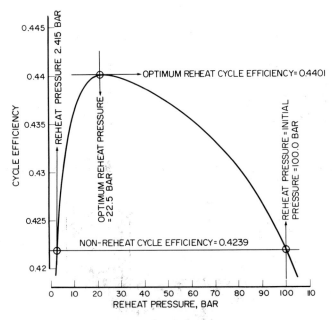

Figure 9.17 Theoretical optimum reheat pressure for reheat cycle between the limits 100.0 bar, 793.15 K and 0.05 bar with one reheat to 793.15 K

If, for the given initial steam conditions and exhaust pressure, viz., 100.0 bar, 793.15 K and 0.05 bar, we carry out a series of calculations similar to those illustrated by Figures 9.12 to 9.14, we can plot a graph of cycle efficiency on a base of reheat pressure as shown in Figure 9.17, from which we may obtain the optimum reheat pressure and the optimum cycle efficiency. Note that compared to the non-reheat cycle, the improvement due to reheating at the optimum reheat pressure is

$$\frac{0.4401 - 0.4239}{0.4239} \times 100 = 3.822 \text{ per cent}$$

For reference, we may set down the *Ts* diagram and calculations for the optimum reheat cycle with initial steam conditions 100.0 bar, 793.15 K, exhaust pressure 0.05 bar,

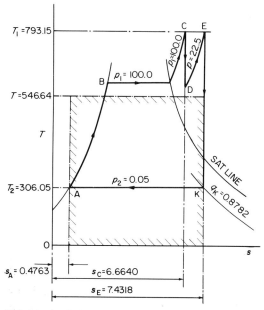

Figure 9.18 Reheat cycle between the limits 100.0 bar, 793.15 K and 0.05 bar with one reheat at 22.5 bar to 793.15 K (optimum single reheat cycle for these steam conditions)

with one reheat at 22.5 bar to 793.15 K. This is representative of the maximum steam conditions which would normally be used in marine practice at the present time. Referring to Figure 9.18 and calculating as before,

Additional cycle heat = 3508.7 − 2994.22

= 514.48 kJ/kg

∴ Total cycle heat = 3287.3 + 514.48

= 3801.78 kJ/kg

Average temperature of cycle heat reception

$$T = \frac{3801.78}{7.4318 - 0.4763} = \frac{3801.78}{6.9555} = 546.64 \text{ K}$$

$$\text{Cycle efficiency} = \frac{546.64 - 306.05}{546.64}$$

$$= \frac{240.59}{546.64}$$

$$= 0.4401$$

Dryness fraction at exhaust

$$q_K = \frac{7.4318 - 0.4763}{8.3960 - 0.4763} = \frac{6.9555}{7.9197} = 0.8782$$

The student should select other initial steam conditions and exhaust pressures, and calculate similar curves for these. these.

Suggested conditions are 63.0 bar, 753.15 K to 0.05 bar
46.0 bar, 723.15 K to 0.068 bar

An ordinary slide rule may give some "scatter" among the points in the vicinity of the optimum where the differences are small, but even so, the form of the curve is quite unmistakable and, in general, shows that the optimum reheat pressure always lies between 0.22 and 0.26 of the initial pressure.

The double reheat cycle

Although used only rarely even in modern land practice, the average temperature of cycle heat reception—and therefore the cycle efficiency—can be further increased by the application of a second reheat.

Taking as a basis the optimum single reheat cycle illustrated in Figure 9.18, the optimum second reheat pressure is obtained by the methods already explained, the object being to obtain the greatest increase of average temperature of heat reception above 546.64 K. The optimum second reheat

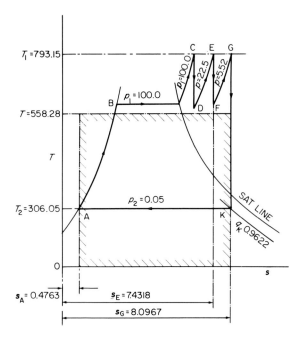

Figure 9.19 Optimum double reheat cycle between the limits 100.0 bar, 793.15 K and 0.05 bar

pressure is 5.52 bar, resulting in the cycle illustrated in Figure 9.19

$$\text{Additional cycle heat} = h_G - h_F$$
$$= 3526.28 - 3073.72$$
$$= 452.56 \text{ kJ/kg}$$

$$\text{Total cycle heat} = 3801.78 + 452.56$$
$$= 4254.34 \text{ kJ/kg}$$

Average temperature of cycle heat reception

$$T = \frac{4254.34}{8.0967 - 0.4763}$$

$$\therefore T = \frac{4254.34}{7.6204} = 558.28 \text{ K}$$

$$\text{Cycle efficency} = \frac{558.28 - 306.05}{558.28}$$

$$= \frac{252.23}{558.28}$$

$$= 0.4518$$

Dryness fraction at exhaust

$$q_K = \frac{8.0967 - 0.4763}{8.3960 - 0.4763} = \frac{7.6204}{7.9197} = 0.9622$$

Optimum reheat pressures

It is interesting to superpose on the curve shown in Figure 9.17, another curve showing the effect of the second reheat. This is shown in Figure 9.20. The two dotted curves on Figure 9.20 show that if any first reheat pressure other than the optimum is used, then the second optimum reheat pressure changes, but the resulting double reheat cycle efficiency is always lower than if the first reheat is done at the optimum pressure. In other words, 22.5 bar remains an optimum reheat pressure whether or not a second reheat is used at all.

It is interesting to note that just as the first optimum reheat pressure is about one quarter of the initial pressure, so the optimum second reheat pressure is about one quarter of the first optimum reheat pressure.

Since the last three cycles represent the most advanced cycles likely to be used in marine practice to date, we may summarise their main features in tabular form, thus

Cycle	Non-reheat	Single reheat	Double reheat	
Initial steam pressure, bar	100.0	100.0	100.0	
Initial steam temperature °C	520.0	520.0	520.0	
Reheat pressure, bar	—	22.5	22.5	5.52
Reheat temperature, °C	—	520.0	520.0	520.0
Exhaust pressure, bar	0.05	0.05	0.05	
Cycle efficiency	0.4239	0.4401	0.4518	
Improvement, per cent	0	3.822	6.582	

Note that in the above table, the temperatures are given in the practical Celsius units, i.e. $(°C = K - 273.15)$. The Kelvin

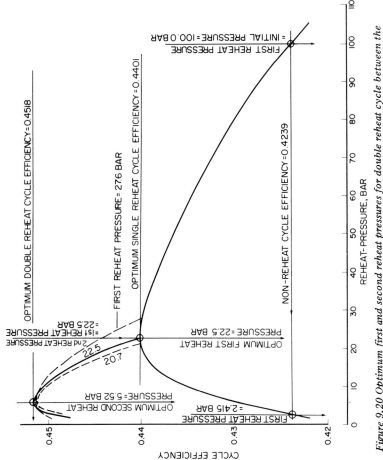

Figure 9.20 Optimum first and second reheat pressures for double reheat cycle between the limits 100.0 bar, 793.15 K, and 0.05 bar, reheating to 793.15 K

units are always used for thermodynamical theory, and the Celsius units for practical cycle calculations, with which we shall deal in later chapters.

The steam reheater

Dealing now with the steam reheater, the most usual application of this method of reheating is in cases where the initial steam temperature at the engine or turbine is, or must be, limited. Thus a reciprocating engine would be limited to about $343°C$ on account of cylinder lubrication difficulties with higher temperatures. There could be cases of turbines

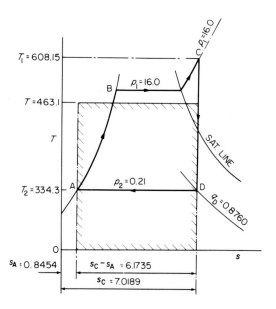

Figure 9.21 Rankine cycle for initially superheated steam between the limits 16.0 bar, 608.15 K and 0.21 bar

where the expense of providing high temperature materials in the H.P. and I.P. turbines is not justified. There are now many land installations having a particular type of nuclear-fuelled boiler which produces steam at quite limited temperatures.

Let us consider the case of the engine described on page 298. The initial steam conditions are 16.0 bar, $335°C$ (608.15 K) and the final exhaust pressure 0.21 bar.

The basic Rankine cycle, i.e. without reheat, is therefore as shown in Figure 9.21, from which,

$$\text{Cycle heat} = h_C - h_A$$
$$= 3113.9 - 255.9$$
$$= 2858.0 \text{ kJ/kg}$$

Dryness fraction at D

$$q_D = \frac{7.0189 - 0.8454}{7.8925 - 0.8454} = \frac{6.1735}{7.0471} = 0.876$$

Enthalpy at D

$$h_D = 255.9 + (0.876 \times 2355.8)$$
$$\therefore \ h_D = 255.9 + 2063.7$$
$$\therefore \ h_D = 2319.6 \text{ kJ/kg}$$

$$\text{Cycle work} = h_C - h_D$$
$$= 3113.9 - 2319.6$$
$$= 794.3 \text{ kJ/kg}$$

Average temperature of cycle heat reception

$$T = \frac{2858.0}{7.0189 - 0.8454} = \frac{2858.0}{6.1735} = 463.0 \text{ K}$$

$$\text{Cycle efficiency} = \frac{463.0 - 334.3}{463.0} = \frac{128.7}{463.0} = 0.278$$

If the steam temperature at the boiler is now raised to 410.0°C (683.15 K), and on its way to the engine, the steam is passed through a reheater in which its temperature is reduced from 683.15 K to 608.15 K by giving up heat to the H.P. exhaust steam at 5.86 bar, the temperature of the H.P. exhaust steam will be raised (Figure 9.22).

An additional quantity of cycle heat represented by area $KCC'G$ is received at constant pressure in the superheater

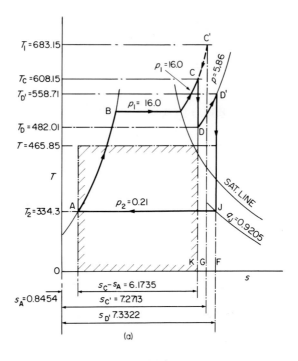

(a)

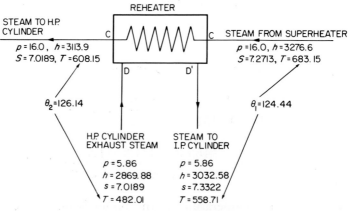

NOTE THAT $h_{C'} - h_C$ $h_{D'} - h_D$ = 162.7 kJ/kg

Figure 9.22 Reheat cycle for initially superheated steam between the limits 16.0 bar, 683.15 K and 0.21 bar with one steam reheat at 5.86 bar to 558.71 K

from C to C'. This additional quantity of heat is transferred to the H.P. exhaust steam at constant pressure in the reheater from D to D'.

$$\text{Thus area } KCC'G = \text{area } KDD'F = h_{C'} - h_C$$
$$= 3276.6 - 3113.9$$

i.e. additional cycle heat = 162.7 kJ/kg

The H.P. cylinder exhausts at 5.86 bar, so that the pressure at D is 5.86 bar and the specific entropy at D is 7.0189.

Inspection of the Steam Tables shows that this specific entropy is greater than the specific entropy of dry saturated steam at 5.86 bar, hence we conclude that the steam at D is superheated, and we must now find its specific enthalpy and its temperature by interpolating the Steam Table values, vide,

6.0 bar:	s	h	T	5.8 bar:	s	h	T
	7.0567	2893.5	493.15		7.0294	2872.7	483.15
	7.0121	2871.7	483.15		6.9836	2850.8	473.15
tab. diff.	0.0446	21.8	10.0		0.0458	21.9	10.0
diff. reqd.	0.0068	3.32	1.53		0.0353	16.88	7.71
	7.0189	2875.02	484.68		7.0189	2867.68	480.86

Bar	h_D	T_D
6.0	2875.02	484.68
5.8	2867.68	480.86
0.2	7.34	3.82
0.06	2.20	1.15
5.86	2869.88	482.01

Specific enthalpy of steam at D'

$$h_{D'} = h_D + \text{additional cycle heat}$$
$$\therefore h_{D'} = 2869.88 + 162.7$$
$$\therefore h_{D'} = 3032.58 \text{ kJ/kg}$$

We must now interpolate the Steam Table values to get s_D and $T_{D'}$

6.0 bar:	h	s	T	5.8 bar:	h	s	T
	3041.5	7.3374	563.15		3042.0	7.3537	563.15
	3020.6	7.3000	553.15		3021.1	7.3164	553.15
tab. diff.	20.9	0.0374	10.0		20.9	0.0373	10.0
reqd. diff.	11.98	0.0214	5.73		11.48	0.0205	5.49
	3032.58	7.3214	558.88		3032.58	7.3369	558.64

Bar	$s_{D'}$	$T_{D'}$
6.0	7.3214	558.88
5.8	7.3369	558.64
0.2	0.0155	0.24
0.06	0.0047	0.07
5.86	7.3322	558.71

Total cycle heat = 2858.0 + 162.7 = 3020.7 kJ/kg

Average temperature of cycle heat reception

$$= \frac{3020.7}{7.3322 - 0.8454}$$

$$= \frac{3020.7}{6.4868}$$

$$= 465.7 \text{ K}$$

Cycle efficiency $= \dfrac{465.7 - 334.3}{465.7} = \dfrac{131.4}{465.7} = 0.2822$

Dryness fraction at exhaust

$$q_J = \frac{7.3322 - 0.8454}{7.8925 - 0.8454} = \frac{6.4868}{7.0471} = 0.9205$$

Thus in this particular case, the application of the steam reheat has raised the cycle efficiency from 0.278 to 0.2822— an increase of only 1.51 per cent. To understand why this increase is relatively small, let us examine the reheating operation itself.

The additional cycle heat, 162.7 kJ/kg, is received in the

superheater from C to C' at an average temperature of

$$\frac{162.7}{7.2713 - 7.0189}$$

$$= \frac{162.7}{0.2524}$$

$$= 644.6 \text{ K}$$

The additional heat however is not received by the cycle at this high temperature, but is received from D to D' at an average temperature of

$$\frac{162.7}{7.3322 - 7.0189} = \frac{162.7}{0.3133} = 519.3 \text{ K}$$

The temperature of the additional heat has been degraded from 644.6 K to 519.3 K before being applied to the cycle.

This temperature degradation which is irreversible, and is a total thermodynamical loss, is necessary for two practical reasons, i.e.

1. The H.P. exhaust pressure is necessarily lower than the initial pressure.
2. A temperature difference must be maintained across the reheater so that heat will flow from the heating steam to the steam being reheated.

The reheater temperature difference, illustrated in Figure 9.22(b) is θ_1 = 124.44 K at the 'hot end' and θ_2 = 126.14 K at the 'cold end', these being so chosen to give reasonable reheater dimensions. (For any given heat load, kJ/s, the total surface area of the reheater tubes varies inversely as the mean temperature difference between the heating steam and the steam being reheated.)

So far as the cycle efficiency is concerned, the cycle with the steam reheater is exactly the same as a cycle with a boiler reheater reheating the H.P. exhaust steam at constant pressure 5.86 bar from D to D'. However, in the case of the steam reheater, no matter what the reheat pressure is, the additional cycle heat due to the reheat is fixed, and is equal to area

KCC'G in Figure 9.22 (a). If the reheat pressure is raised above 5.86 bar then,

1. The temperature of the additional cycle heat is degraded by a lesser amount, hence the cycle efficiency will increase and will continue to increase with increasing reheat pressure.
2. The temperature difference across the reheater will diminish, hence a larger reheater will be required.
3. The adiabatic enthalpy drop for the H.P. cylinder will diminish, and that for the I.P. cylinder will increase, hence the H.P. power will increase and the I.P. power diminish.

   If the reheat pressure is lowered, 1, 2 and 3 will change in the opposite manner.

There is therefore no optimum reheat pressure such as there is in the case of a boiler reheater in which the additional cycle heat *varies* with the reheat pressure. The reheat pressure is chosen to give the best compromise among the three effects stated above. For high cycle efficiency, the reheat pressure should be high, but if it is too high, a prohibitively large reheater is required, and the H.P. power will be relatively low.

We may restate these conclusions. The steam reheater degrades the average temperature of the additional cycle heat before the latter is applied to the cycle. The reheat pressure is fixed by considerations other than the conception of an optimum reheat pressure. The improvement in *cycle* efficiency is relatively small.

Although in this chapter, we are supposed to be dealing exclusively with thermodynamical theory, it has, in the present example been necessary to introduce practical features such as the reheater temperature difference. This has been necessary to show that the introduction of the steam reheater —the object of which is practical—does not render the cycle efficiency any worse than that of the comparable cycle without the steam reheater.

In the case of turbines with a steam reheater, the general principles and the cycle calculations do not differ from those of the foregoing example for which a reheater engine was used.

The regenerative cycle

The complete regenerative cycle, described by Stirling in 1829, eliminates the irreversible reception of sensible heat in the boiler and replaces it by a process of regenerative feed heating, which, in the ideal case, could be regarded as reversible, and therefore a cycle efficiency could be attained equal to the Carnot efficiency between the same temperature limits.

Some conception of the requirements of such a cycle can be had by reference to the diagram in Figure 9.23.

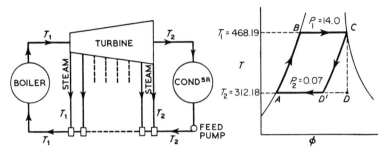

Figure 9.23 Regenerative ϕ cycle

The turbine is supposed to have an infinite number of stages, and from each turbine stage, steam is extracted to heat the feed water in a very small direct-contact feed heater.

Thus feed water entering the first of the feed heaters encounters steam at a temperature only marginally above the water temperature, and the water temperature is raised by this very small amount. The feed water then passes on to the second of the heaters, where again it encounters steam at a temperature infinitesimally higher than its own temperature and is thereby raised to that temperature. If this process is carried on right up to the steam end of the turbine, and if the number of feed-heating stages is sufficiently large, then the infinitesimal temperature difference between the steam and water at each feed-heating stage, while sufficient to cause heat flow from steam to water, is so small as not to differ from equality of temperature between steam (source) and feed water (substance)! If such a feed-heating process can be imagined, then the feed water is heated reversibly by regeneration right up to the upper cycle temperature limit T_1 and only latent heat is received at constant temperature in the boiler.

Thus, the irreversible reception of sensible heat in the boiler is replaced by a reversible operation, and the Carnot efficiency attained in consequence. This cycle in no way contravenes Carnot's principle, which makes reference only to reversibility and temperature limits.

On the *Ts* diagram the single adiabatic *CD* is replaced by the curve CD^1, which is in fact a series of infinitesimally small adiabatics moving progressively to the left. The simplified sketch is shown in Figure 9.24.

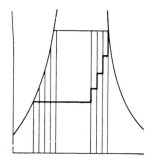

Figure 9.24 Regenerative cycle

Such a complete regenerative cycle is utterly impossible in practice. We cannot make an infinite number of feed-heating stages. Nor can we make heat flow from steam into water without a finite temperature difference between the two.

The regenerative cycle is nevertheless the basis of the modern partial-regenerative cycle, with up to nine stages of feed heating by steam extracted from the engine or turbine, as described in Chapter 11 (see also Figure 9.25).

Further work done on the partial-regenerative cycle in Chapter 11 will be illustrated by an enthalpy entropy diagram, as the calculation of such a cycle on a *Ts* diagram can become very tedious.

The three shaded areas on the right-hand side of the diagram in Figure 9.25 must be transferred to the left-hand side, and on a *Ts* diagram this can involve a great deal of repetitive calculation.

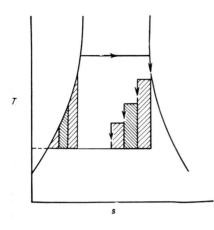

T

s

Figure 9.25 Partial regenerative cycle (three stage)

Conclusions

The following must be clearly understood:

Once one of the above cycles is chosen, and its steam conditions fixed, then the above efficiency is the *maximum* thermal efficiency which can be attained. This is dependent only on the thermodynamical characteristics of the changes which take place in the steam.

Having decided on the cycle and found its efficiency, we now have to design and build an engine which, if operated correctly, will approach as closely as possible to its cycle efficiency.

No engine will ever attain the cycle efficiency because of practical losses, and the ratio of the actual engine efficiency to the cycle efficiency is called the *efficiency ratio* of the engine.

There are therefore two requirements.

1. To choose a cycle which will give the greatest cycle efficiency commensurate with economical considerations such as first cost, reliability, etc.
2. To design and operate an engine which will approach closely to the cycle efficiency.

The first of these is theoretical, the second practical, and the relation of these two requirements forms the subject of Chapter 12.

10   Steam turbine theory

While it is not intended that this chapter be regarded as a treatise on turbine design, it is hoped that a moderate excursion into turbine design theory will enable the student to recognise the various features of turbines, why these features are adopted and how they are applied in practice, e.g. how the requisite form and dimensions of nozzles are determined and how these nozzles are accommodated; how the blades are arranged to do work in an efficient manner; why we have multistage turbines, etc.

Very often in practice we hear comments—for example, "turbine A is more efficient than turbine B because it has an extra stage" or "although turbines A and B have the same number of stages, A is better because it is more judiciously staged", or again "turbine A has a two-row Curtis stage followed by seven single-row pressure stages". Such comments can be very bewildering unless we have some knowledge of what they imply.

FUNDAMENTAL TYPES OF TURBINES

Up until comparatively recently, it had remained customary to broadly classify turbines into two types (a) impulse turbines and (b) reaction turbines. When viewed in relation to the features of practical turbines however, particularly in modern practice, such a broad classification becomes somewhat loose, and indeed could even cause confusion and lack of understanding.

Let us first examine the implications of the terms impulse and reaction by considering a simple turbine having one revolving wheel. Steam at high pressure and having high enthalpy enters the turbine, and leaves the turbine at low pressure and with low enthalpy. There is thus a pressure drop and a corresponding enthalpy drop in passing through the turbine.

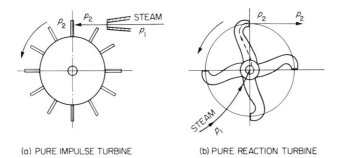

(a) PURE IMPULSE TURBINE   (b) PURE REACTION TURBINE

Figure 10.1 Impulse and reaction turbines

If we arrange the simple turbine so that the entire pressure drop—and hence enthalpy drop—takes place in fixed nozzles separate from the wheel, and direct the high-velocity steam jets on to blades mounted on the periphery of the wheel, then the turbine is a pure impulse turbine. Such an arrangement is shown in Figure 10.1(a). There is no pressure drop through the moving blades of a pure impulse turbine; the blades merely cause a change of steam velocity, this change of velocity thereby exerting a driving force on the blades. The kinetic energy is generated entirely in a fixed element which is quite separate from the moving element.

If we arrange the simple turbine as shown in Figue 10.1(b), there is no separate fixed element, the entire pressure drop— and hence enthalpy drop -taking place in the moving element itself, the turbine is a pure reaction turbine. The kinetic energy is generated entirely in the moving element itself.

For practical reasons, turbines are not arranged in either of the two ways shown in Figure 10.1 but in the manner shown in Figure 10.2, which shows a circumferential section at the

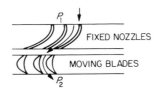

Figure 10.2 Practical simple turbine

mean diameter. While it is quite possible to make such a turbine a pure impulse turbine, it will be obvious that it cannot
be made a pure reaction turbine, since some part of the
pressure drop, and hence part of the enthalpy drop, must
always take place in the fixed nozzles. The percentage of the
total enthalpy drop which takes place in the moving blades is
called the degree of reaction. The maximum degree of reaction
which is used in practice is about 50 per cent.

Thus a turbine can be a pure impulse turbine, i.e. having
zero reaction, or it can be an impulse-type turbine having a
degree of reaction which can be from 1.0 per cent to 50 per
cent depending on the conditions. A turbine having 50 per
cent reaction has, traditionally, been called a reaction turbine,
and whenever the term is used, it must be clearly understood
that it means 50 per cent reaction.

Whether a single-wheel turbine be a pure impulse turbine
or a so-called reaction turbine, it consists of a fixed element—
the nozzles—and a moving element—the blades, as shown in
Figure 10.2.

We will first examine the fixed element—the nozzles—since
the general theory is the same whether the turbine is impulse
or reaction.

STEAM TURBINE NOZZLES

Referring to Figure 10.3, consider the open end of a circular
pipe of cross-sectional area A, mm^2, discharging fluid with
velocity C, m/s, and imagine the fluid to retain the same
cross-sectional area after leaving the pipe. Then in 1.0 s there
will be discharged a cylinder of fluid whose cross-sectional
area is A, mm^2, and whose length is C, m.

Hence the volume discharged in 1.0 s is area × velocity, or

$$\text{Volume discharged} = \frac{10\,AC}{100^2} \ \text{dm}^3$$

[Note the units; A is mm^2, C is m, 10 is dm/m and 100^2 is
mm^2/dm^2, hence

$$\text{Volume is } \frac{\text{dm}}{\text{m}} \times \text{mm}^2 \times \text{m} \times \frac{\text{dm}^2}{\text{mm}^2} = \text{dm}^3 \,]$$

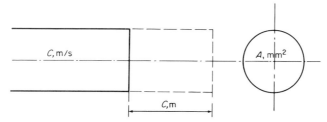

Figure 10.3 Steady flow of a fluid in a pipe or passage

If the specific volume of the fluid is v dm^3/kg then the weight of fluid discharged = volume discharged/specific volume, i.e.

$$M = \frac{10\,AC}{100^2 v} \text{ kg/s}$$

$$\therefore M = \frac{AC}{1000v} \text{ kg/s}$$

$$\therefore 1000Mv = AC$$

This is called the equation of continuity which in words means mass flow × specific volume = area × velocity.

Note the units used; M is in kg/s, v is in dm^3/kg, C is in m/s and A is in mm^2.

The equation of continuity, operated in these units, is used repeatedly in studying steam turbine theory. Usually three out of the four factors are known, or can be established from the conditions, and the equation of continuity is used to find the fourth.

Expansion of steam in turbine nozzles

This process may be regarded as a Rankine cycle in which the steam does work upon itself. The cycle work (or the adiabatic heat drop as we will now call it) is not utilised to do mechanical work on a piston as it is in a reciprocating engine, but to increase the kinetic energy of the steam passing through the nozzles, so that the steam jets leave the nozzles with high velocity.

Steam at any given pressure and condition (i.e. superheat or dryness fraction) has a certain heat energy content, stated in kilojoules per kilogramme (kJ/kg), and therefore called the specific enthalpy. A nozzle is a passage specially designed to convert part of the heat energy of the steam to kinetic energy. By the principle of the conservation of energy, the specific enthalpy of the steam leaving the nozzle is less than the specific enthalpy of the steam entering the nozzle by the amount of kinetic energy generated. Bearing in mind the first law of thermodynamics, viz. that heat and work are mutually convertible, it follows that kinetic energy can be expressed either in heat units or in work units provided that we use the correct relationship between units.

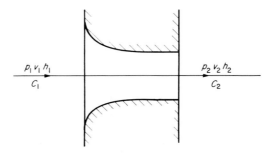

Figure 10.4 Expansion of steam in turbine nozzles

The kinetic energy E, newton metres (Nm) of a body of mass M kilogrammes (kg) moving with velocity C metres per second (m/s) is given by $E = \frac{1}{2} M C^2$.

We will consider unit mass i.e. 1 kg, of steam, hence

$$E = \frac{C^2}{2}, \text{ Nm/kg and since 1 Nm = 1 joule (J) then}$$

$$E = \frac{C^2}{2}, \text{J/kg from which}$$

$$E = \frac{C^2}{2000}, \text{kJ/kg}, \quad \text{or } E = \left(\frac{C}{44.725}\right)^2 \text{kJ/kg}$$

Referring to Figure 10.4, steam enters the nozzle at high pressure p_1 with velocity C_1 and leaves at low pressure p_2 with velocity C_2.

The initial enthalpy h_1 is greater than the final enthalpy h_2. The final velocity C_2 is greater than the initial velocity C_1, thus the increase of kinetic energy through the nozzle is

$$\left(\frac{C_2{}^2}{2000} - \frac{C_1{}^2}{2000}\right) \text{ kJ/kg}$$

This increase of kinetic energy is obtained at the expense of the enthalpy of the steam, hence we may write

$$h_1 - h_2 = \frac{C_2{}^2}{2000} - \frac{C_1{}^2}{2000}$$

Ideally the nozzle should expand the steam adiabatically, then the enthalpy drop $h_1 - h_2$ is the adiabatic enthalpy drop denoted by dh_s, thus

$$dh_s = \frac{C_2{}^2}{2000} - \frac{C_1{}^2}{2000}, \text{ from which}$$

$$\frac{C_2{}^2}{2000} = dh_s + \frac{C_1{}^2}{2000}$$

$$\therefore \; C_2{}^2 = 2000\left(dh_s + \frac{C_1{}^2}{2000}\right)$$

$$\therefore \; C_2 = \sqrt{\left[2000\left(dh_s + \frac{C_1{}^2}{2000}\right)\right]}$$

$$\therefore \; C_2 = \sqrt{(2000)}\sqrt{\left(dh_s + \frac{C_1{}^2}{2000}\right)} \qquad \text{Now}\sqrt{2000} = 44.725$$

$$\therefore \; C_2 = 44.725\sqrt{\left[dh_s + \left(\frac{C_1}{44.725}\right)^2\right]} \text{ m/s}$$

Thus, if for any nozzle, the initial steam velocity C_1 is known, and if the adiabatic enthalpy drop is found from the Mollier Diagram, then the theoretical nozzle discharge velocity can be found from the above expression. If the initial velocity C_1 is zero, the expression becomes $C = 44.725\sqrt{(dh_s)}$ m/s.

Further, the final condition of the steam leaving the nozzle can be read from the Mollier Diagram, and hence the final specific volume, v dm^3/kg. Note that the adiabatic enthalpy drop is the same as the Rankine cycle work between the given limits.

Knowing the mass flow of steam M kg/s, the cross-sectional area A mm^2 of the nozzle may be calculated from the equation of continuity as described at the beginning of this chapter.

At this point we may consolidate the foregoing by a worked example.

Example. The nozzles of a steam turbine stage have to expand 5.94 kg/s of steam from 24.0 bar, 370.0°C to 14.0 bar. Assuming the expansion to be adiabatic and the initial steam velocity to be zero, find the steam velocity at the nozzle discharge in m/s and the total nozzle discharge area in mm^2.

The initial state point of the steam is found on the Mollier Diagram at the intersection of the line of constant pressure 24.0 bar and the line of constant temperature 370.0°C. This is the point X in Figure 10.5.

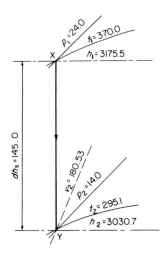

Figure 10.5 Adiabatic expansion of steam in a nozzle

Since for the present we are assuming adiabatic expansion, a perpendicular straight line drawn from X to meet the line of constant pressure 14.0 bar will give the state point Y at the nozzle discharge.

Examination of the diagram will show that the adiabatic enthalpy drop $dh_s = 145.0$ kJ/kg and that the steam temperature at the nozzle discharge is 295.1°C. The nozzle discharge velocity

$$C = 44.725 \sqrt{145.0} = 538.61 \text{ m/s}$$

The specific volume at the nozzle discharge is found by interpolating the steam tables for a temperature of 295.1°C at a pressure of 14.0 bar. Alternatively, the specific volume may be read directly from the chart if lines of constant specific volume are included thereon. Specific volume at $Y = v_2 = 180.53$ dm³/kg.

The nozzle discharge area $A = 1000Mv/C$

$$\therefore A = \frac{1000 \times 5.94 \times 180.53}{538.61}$$

$$\therefore A = 1991 \text{ mm}^2$$

Note: On at least this one occasion, the student should himself, by the methods explained in Chapter 9, check and satisfy himself that the above adiabatic enthalpy drop is equal to the cycle work of a Rankine cycle between the given limits. There may be some slight discrepancy, particularly if reading a small-scale Mollier Diagram and using an ordinary slide rule, but for our purpose this is not of any significance.

Suppose now that instead of expanding the steam to a final pressure of 14.0 bar, we had expanded it to a final pressure of 2.0 bar. Referring to Figure 10.6 the adiabatic enthalpy drop would be $dh_s = 544.0$ kJ/kg and the nozzle discharge velocity $C = 44.725\sqrt{544.0} = 1043.1$ m/s.

The adiabatic expansion line now crosses the saturation line, hence the steam at the nozzle discharge is wet, the dry-

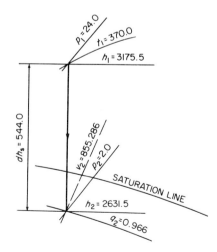

Figure 10.6 Adiabatic expansion of steam in a nozzle

ness fraction being 0.966. The specific volume at the nozzle discharge is given by $v = q.v_g + v_f (1 - q)$, v_g and v_f being read from the Steam Tables for saturated steam at 2.0 bar, i.e.

$$v = (0.996 \times 885.4) + (0.034 \times 1.0608)$$

$$\therefore \; v = 855.25 + 0.0361$$

$$\therefore \; v = 855.2861 \; dm^3/kg$$

The nozzle discharge area

$$A = \frac{5.94}{1043.1} \times \frac{855.286}{1000} \times 1\,000\,000 = 4870.4 \; mm^2$$

Thus although the nozzle discharge velocity has increased from 538.61 m/s to 1043.1 m/s, i.e. about twice, the specific volume at discharge has increased from 180.53 dm^3/kg to 855.286 dm^3/kg, i.e. about 4.7 times, thus resulting in a larger discharge area being required for the lower final pressure.

The relative rates of increase of velocity and specific volume over any particular pressure range, as explained in the following section, are of primary importance in the study of nozzles.

Adiabatic expansion of steam in nozzles—the critical pressure ratio

Consider a nozzle expanding 1.0 kg/s of steam from 7.0 bar, dry saturated, to a fairly low pressure, say 1.0 bar. Let the initial velocity be zero, and the expansion be adiabatic. Refer to Figure 10.7.

As steam passes through the nozzle, the pressure falls progressively from p_1 to p_2. Consider a series of cross-sections (1), (2), (3) etc. at which the pressures are 7.0, 6.0, 5.0, etc. bar respectively, and for each section calculate the velocity, the specific volume and the nozzle area required to pass 1.0 kg/s (i.e. $M = 1.0$). The methods illustrated in the previous example are used.

At section 1, the steam velocity is zero and $A = v/0$, hence, theoretically, the nozzle entrance area is infinity (i.e. infinitely large).

At section 2, the pressure has fallen to 6.0 bar, and from Figure 10.7(b), this results in an adiabatic enthalpy drop $dh_s = 31.5$ kJ/kg, and a dryness fraction of 0.9891, hence

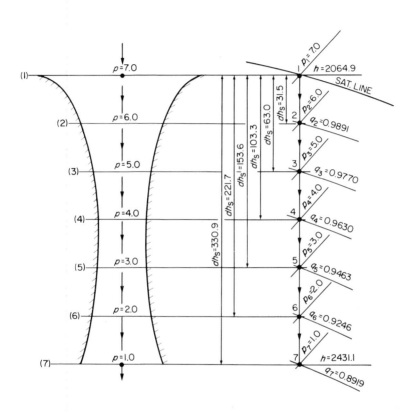

Figure 10.7 Progressive adiabatic expansion of steam in a nozzle

Steam velocity = 44.725 $\sqrt{31.5}$ = 251.0 m/s, and

Specific volume

= (0.9891 × 315.46) + (0.0109 × 1.1009) = 312.02 dm³/kg

From which, nozzle area

$$A = \frac{1000v}{C} = \frac{1000 \times 312.02}{251.0} = 1243.2 \text{ mm}^2$$

At section 3 the pressure has fallen to 5.0 bar, and from the Mollier Diagram, dh_s = 63.0 kJ/kg, and q = 0.977, hence

V = 44.725 $\sqrt{63.0}$ = 355.0 m/s, and

v = (0.977 × 374.66) + (0.0230 × 1.0928)
   = 366.03 dm³/kg

and nozzle discharge area

$$A = \frac{1000v}{C} = \frac{1000 \times 366.03}{355.0} = 1031.2 \text{ mm}^2$$

If this procedure is repeated for the remaining sections, the following table may be drawn up

p Bar	dh_s kJ/kg	C m/s	v dm³/kg	A mm²
7.0	0	0	272.68	∞
6.0	31.5	251.0	312.02	1243.2
5.0	63.0	355.0	366.03	1031.2
4.0	103.3	454.0	445.18	980.2
3.0	153.6	554.0	573.08	1034.4
2.0	221.7	666.5	818.67	1228.3
1.0	330.9	815.5	1510.613	1852.4

From this table, the steam velocity, specific volume and nozzle area are plotted on a base of pressure as shown in Figure 10.8.

Inspection of Figure 10.8, will show the following. As the steam begins to expand at first, the steam velocity begins to increase very rapidly and the specific volume to increase very slowly. The required cross-sectional area of the nozzle therefore diminishes and keeps on diminishing until a point X is

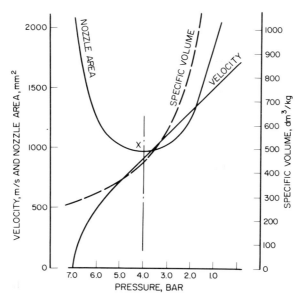

Figure 10.8 Adiabatic expansion characteristics for steam between 7.0 bar dry sat. and 1.0 bar

reached, at which the specific volume begins to increase more rapidly than the velocity. Beyond this point X the nozzle area begins to increase again.

The point X occurs at a pressure of 4.0 bar, which is $4.0/7.0 = 0.57$ of the initial pressure, and with reference to the initial pressure, is called the *critical pressure* (Note: this definition of critical pressure refers only to expansion in a nozzle from given initial steam conditions—it must not be confused with *the critical pressure* viz., 221.2 bar, as defined in Chapter 8).

This critical pressure ratio, $p_2/p_1 = 0.57$, remains constant for any initial pressure provided that the steam is initially dry saturated or wet. If the steam is initially superheated, the critical pressure ratio $p_2/p_1 = 0.5455$.

Thus if we wish our nozzle to expand initially dry saturated or wet steam to any final pressure greater than 0.57 of the initial pressure, the pressure ratio is said to be under critical, and the nozzle must converge, i.e. its cross sectional area must diminish continuously from the entrance to the exit— see the curve of nozzle area in Figure 10.8. Such a nozzle is a convergent nozzle.

If we wish our nozzle to expand initially dry saturated or

wet steam to any final pressure less than 0.57 of the initial pressure, then the pressure ratio is said to be over critical, and the nozzle must first converge and then diverge—see the curve of nozzle area in Figure 10.8. Such a nozzle is a *convergent-divergent nozzle*.

The minimum cross-section (i.e. at *X* in Figure 10.8) is called the nozzle throat, and if the steam is initially dry saturated or wet, the pressure at the throat of a convergent-divergent nozzle is always 0.57 of the initial pressure. If the steam is initially superheated, the pressure at the throat of a convergent-divergent nozzle is always 0.5455 of the initial pressure.

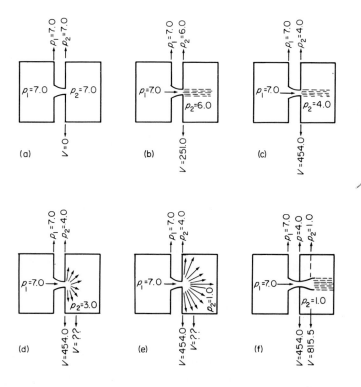

Figure 10.9 Expansion of steam in a nozzle of throat area 980.2 mm²
with constant upstream pressure 7.0 bar, dry saturated, and with
varying downstream pressure
(a) No expansion; steam flow zero
(b) Expansion under critical; steam flow 0.7884 kg/s
(c) Expansion critical; steam flow 1.0 kg/s
(d) Expansion over critical; steam flow 1.0 kg/s
(e) Expansion over critical; steam flow 1.0 kg/s
(f) Expansion over critical; steam flow 1.0 kg/s

It is interesting to note that in the throat of a convergent–divergent nozzle, the steam attains sonic velocity i.e. the velocity of sound in steam at the throat conditions.

It is important for the student to appreciate other features of critical expansion. Whether a nozzle be convergent or convergent–divergent, the pressure at the minimum cross-section (called the throat) can never be less than $0.57p_1$ if the steam is initially dry saturated or wet, or less than $0.5455p_1$ if the steam is initially superheated. Suppose that in the case illustrated by Figure 10.8, we had omitted the divergent part of the nozzle (i.e. that part to the right of X) and attempted to make the convergent part (i.e. that part to the left of X) expand to pressures below 4.0 bar. Consider two closed vessels each containing steam at 7.0 bar, dry saturated, and let these two vessels be connected by the convergent nozzle. Since there is no pressure difference between the two vessels, there will be no steam flow through the nozzle (Figure 10.9(a)).

Now let the pressure in the right hand vessel be lowered to 6.0 bar (Figure 10.9(b)). The table on page 416 shows us that this will result in adiabatic enthalpy drop of 31.5 kJ/kg, a nozzle discharge velocity of 251.0 m/s and a specific volume of 312.02 dm³/kg at the nozzle discharge. Since the nozzle discharge area is 980.2 mm², the steam flow through the nozzle, from $1000Mv = AC$ will be

$$M = \frac{AC}{1000v} = \frac{980.2 \times 251.0}{1000 \times 312.02} = 0.7884 \text{ kg/s}$$

Let the pressure in the right-hand vessel be further lowered to 5.0 bar. The steam flow through the nozzle will be

$$M = \frac{980.2 \times 355.0}{1000 \times 366.03} = 0.9505 \text{ kg/s}$$

Lowering the back pressure (i.e. downstream pressure) has increased the steam mass flow through the nozzle.

As the back pressure is further progressively lowered, the steam flow through the nozzle will continue to increase, but at a diminishing rate of increase, until when the downstream pressure is 4.0 bar, it becomes 1.0 kg/s. At this point the pressure at the nozzle discharge is equal to the pressure in the downstream (i.e. right hand) vessel; see Figure 10.9(c).

The enthalpy drops, velocities, specific volumes and steam flows up to this point are shown in the table below.

p_2 bar	dh_s, kJ/kg	C, m/s	v dm^3/kg	M, kg/s
7.0	0	0	272.68	0
6.0	31.5	251.0	312.02	0.7884
5.0	63.0	355.0	366.03	0.9505
4.0	103.3	454.0	445.18	1.0

Suppose now that the pressure in the right hand vessel is lowered to 3.0 bar. The table on page 416 shows us that to pass 1.0 kg/s with a pressure of 3.0 bar *at the nozzle discharge* then the nozzle discharge area would have to be 1034.4 mm^2. The nozzle discharge area, however, is only 980.2 mm^2, hence the steam cannot expand from 4.0 bar to 3.0 bar *within the convergent nozzle*. There is not enough nozzle discharge area to pass 1.0 kg/s of steam at the velocity and specific volume associated with the down-stream pressure of 3.0 bar. The pressure at the nozzle discharge will remain at 4.0 bar, and immediately beyond the nozzle discharge the steam will simply "explode" from 4.0 bar at the nozzle discharge down to 3.0 bar in the downstream vessel; see Figure 10.9(d)).

When the pressure at the nozzle discharge is 4.0 bar, the pressure ratio is critical, and the nozzle is said to be "choked".

By lowering the back pressure (in the downstream vessel) we cannot lower the pressure at the nozzle discharge below 4.0 bar, nor can we make the nozzle pass more than 1.0 kg/s of steam.

If the final downstream pressure is further lowered to 1.0 bar as in Figure 10.9(e), the pressure at the nozzle throat will still remain at 4.0 bar, and the steam quantity passed at 1.0 kg/s. The "explosion" or uncontrolled expansion beyond the nozzle throat will merely become more violent because of the greater free pressure drop from the nozzle throat to the downstream vessel. This free or uncontrolled expansion does not generate the properly directed steam velocity appropriate to the adiabatic enthalpy drop between 4.0 bar and 1.0 bar, and indeed it may destroy some of the properly directed velocity already generated during the controlled expansion up to the nozzle throat.

From Figure 10.9(f) it will be seen that the addition of the divergent part to the nozzle does not in any way affect the throat pressure or the maximum steam flow through the nozzle. All it does is to make the steam expand from the nozzle throat pressure to the final downstream pressure *in a controlled manner*, thus generating the full final steam velocity corresponding to the adiabatic enthalpy drop from 7.0 bar to 1.0 bar, and to direct the steam jet at this velocity in the desired manner.

Note that in Figure 10.9(f), if the back pressure is raised above 1.0 bar, the steam will not "fill" all of the divergent part of the nozzle, and in the limit, if the back pressure reaches or exceeds 4.0 bar, the steam will behave exactly as in Figure 10.9(b) and (c) i.e. as if the divergent part did not exist at all.

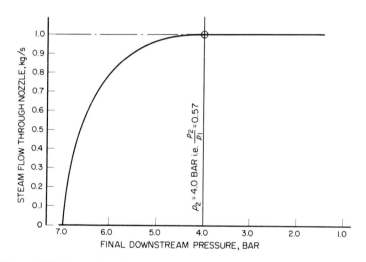

*Figure 10.10 Steam flow through a nozzle of throat area 980.2 mm²
with constant upstream pressure 7.0 bar dry saturated and with
varying downstream pressure*

Figure 10.10 shows the change in the steam mass flow through the nozzle as the back pressure is reduced. Note that the steam flow reaches a maximum when $p_2/p_1 = 0.57$. This is so whether the nozzle be convergent or convergent-divergent.

Note: In the foregoing, the number of intermediate pressures between 7.0 bar and 1.0 bar has been limited, for clarity of explanation. The student should choose additional intermediate pressures, say 6.5, 5.5, 4.5 etc. bar, and himself

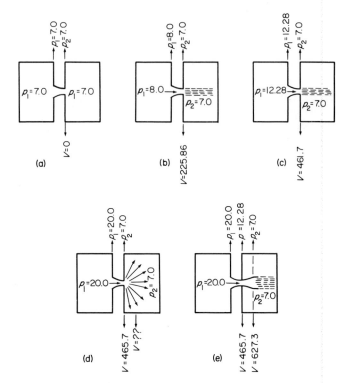

*Figure 10.11 Expansion of steam in a nozzle of throat area
980.2 mm with constant downstream pressure 7.0 bar with
varying upstream pressure*
(a) no expansion; steam flow zero
(b) Expansion under critical; steam flow = 0.8198 kg/s
(c) Expansion critical; steam flow = 1.7306 kg/s
(d) Expansion over critical; steam flow = 2.7614 kg/s
(e) Expansion over critical; steam flow = 2.7614 kg/s

calculate additional points for plotting the curves in Figures
10.8 and 10.10.

Suppose we now revert to the convergent nozzle of throat
area 980.2 mm^2 and consider the effects of varying the initial
pressure. Figure 10.11(a) shows the same starting conditions
as before, namely equal pressures, 7.0 bar, in the two vessels,
and hence zero steam flow through the nozzle. Now keeping
the pressure in the right-hand vessel constant at 7.0 bar, let
the pressure in the left-hand vessel be increased to 8.0 bar.
The pressure ratio p_2/p_1 = 7.0/8.0 = 0.875 which is greater
than 0.57, and hence the expansion is *under critical* and the
steam can expand from the initial to the final pressure within
the convergent nozzle.

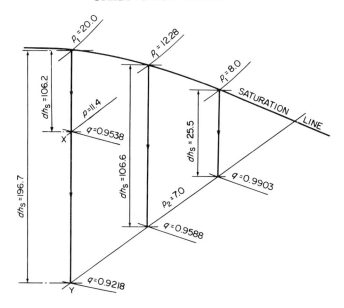

Figure 10.12 Adiabatic expansion of initially saturated steam from various initial pressures to a final pressure of 7.0 bar

The Mollier Diagram (see Figure 10.12) shows that the adiabatic enthalpy drop dh_s = 25.5 kJ/kg and the final dryness fraction q = 0.9903. The steam velocity at the nozzle throat is therefore C = 44.725 $\sqrt{25.5}$ = 225.86 m/s, and the steam specific volume at the nozzle throat is v = (0.9903 × 2064.9) +(0.0097 × 1.1082) = 270.03 dm³/kg.

The nozzle throat area A = 980.2 mm², hence the steam flow through the nozzle is

$$M = \frac{AC}{1000v} = \frac{980.2 \times 225.86}{1000 \times 270.03} = 0.8198 \text{ kg/s}$$

The conditions are as shown in Figure 10.11(b).

Let the initial pressure now be raised to 12.28 bar. The pressure ratio p_2/p_1 = 7.0/12.28 = 0.57 which is *critical*, and the steam can only just expand from the initial to the final pressure within the convergent nozzle. By the same methods as before, and using the Mollier Diagram as in Figure 10.10, the steam flow through the nozzle is

$$M = \frac{980.2 \times 461.7}{1000 \times 261.51} = 1.7306 \text{ kg/s}$$

The conditions are as shown in Figure 10.11(c).

Let the initial pressure now be raised to 20.0 bar. The pressure ratio p_2/p_1 = 7.0/20.0 = 0.35, which is over critical, and the steam cannot expand from the initial to the final pressure within the convergent nozzle. The pressure at the nozzle throat is 0.57 × 20.0 = 11.4 bar, and the steam "explodes" in an uncontrolled manner from 11.4 bar at the nozzle throat down to 7.0 bar in the right-hand vessel. Examination of the Mollier Diagram in Figure 10.12 shows that the adiabatic enthalpy drop to the throat pressure (point X) is 106.2 kJ/kg and that the dryness fraction at the throat is 0.9538. Hence steam velocity at throat V = 44.725 $\sqrt{106.2}$ = 461.7 m/s, and specific volume at throat v = (0.9538 × 171.43) + (0.0462 × 1.1353) = 163.58 dm^3/kg. The steam flow through the nozzle

$$M = \frac{980.2 \times 461.7}{1000 \times 163.58} = 2.7614 \text{ kg/s}$$

The conditions are as shown in Figure 10.11(d).

If we now add a divergent part to the nozzle, the divergent part does *not* alter the throat pressure or the steam flow through the nozzle; it merely controls the expansion from 11.4 bar down to 7.0 bar, thus constraining it to follow the adiabatic line from X to Y in Figure 10.12, and generating a steam velocity at the nozzle discharge C = 44.725 $\sqrt{196.7}$ = 627.3 m/s.

Since in these circumstances, the final specific volume is v = (0.9218 × 272.68) + (0.0782 × 1.1082) = 251.43 dm^3/kg, the discharge area of the divergent part of the nozzle would be

$$A = \frac{1000Mv}{C} = \frac{1000 \times 2.7614 \times 251.43}{627.3} = 1106.8 \text{ mm}^2$$

The conditions are as shown in Figure 10.11(e).

Keeping the nozzle throat area constant at 980.2 mm^2 and the back pressure constant at 1.0 bar, let us now consider various initial pressures from 1.0 bar to 36.0 bar, thus including in the range pressure ratios which are under critical and pressure ratios which are over critical. These are shown in the table on page 426, three of the pressures having been examined in detail above, the others calculated by the same method.

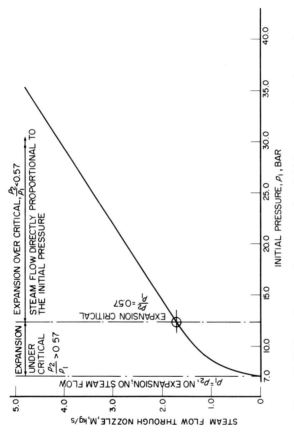

Figure 10.13 Flow of saturated steam at various initial pressures through a nozzle of throat area 980.2 mm² to a constant final pressure of 7.0 bar

p_1 bar	7.0	8.0	9.0	10.0	12.28	15.0	20.0	26.0	36.0
dh_s, kJ/kg	0	25.5	47.7	67.6	106.6	107.3	106.2	109.0	105.1
q_2	1.0	0.9903	0.9819	0.9742	0.9588	0.9570	0.9538	0.9501	0.9442
v_2, dm^3/kg	272.68	270.03	271.31	269.19	261.51	215.93	163.58	126.78	91.829
C, m/s	0	225.86	309.0	367.5	461.7	463.24	460.84	467.05	458.48
M, kg/s	0	0.8198	1.1164	1.3380	1.7306	2.1027	2.7614	3.6110	4.8940

If from the above table, we plot the steam flow M, kg/s, on a base of initial pressure p_1 bar, we obtain the interesting curve shown in Figure 10.13. Note that when the expansion is over-critical the graph is a straight line, hence the steam flow through the nozzle is directly proportional to the initial pressure. To be quite correct, when the expansion is *over-critical*, the steam flow is in fact directly proportional to $\sqrt{(p_1/v_1)}$, and the steam flow can be calculated from the expression $M = 0.00652A \sqrt{(p_1/v_1)}$ for initially saturated or wet steam, or $M = 0.00666A \sqrt{(p_1/v_1)}$ for initially superheated steam where

M = steam mass flow, kg/s

A = total nozzle *throat* area, mm^2

p_1 = initial pressure, bar

v_1 = initial specific volume, dm^3/kg

The properties and characteristics of steam are such that $\sqrt{(p_1/v_1)}$ is practically proportional to p_1, as illustrated by the graphs in Figure 10.14. Hence when the expansion is over critical, the steam flow through the nozzle is directly proportional to the initial pressure.

We may summarise these important features as follows:

1. The quantity of steam discharged by any nozzle expanding to a final pressure higher than about 0.56 of the initial pressure is controlled by the initial pressure, by the final pressure and by the throat area.
2. The quantity of steam discharged by any nozzle expanding to a final pressure lower than about 0.56 of the initial pressure is controlled by the initial pressure and

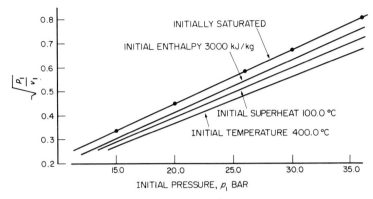

Figure 10.14 Linear relation between p_1 and $\sqrt{(p_1/v_1)}$ for initially saturated steam and for initially superheated steam

by the throat area, and is directly proportional to both. The pressure at the throat is *always* $0.57p_1$ if the steam is initially saturated or wet, or $0.5455p_1$ if the steam is initially superheated.

Losses in nozzles–the nozzle efficiency and the coefficient of discharge

As stated at the beginning of this chapter, the process of expansion of steam in an ideal nozzle is in fact the adiabatic expansion operation of a Rankine cycle. The steam should expand adiabatically, i.e. at constant entropy, from the initial state point to the final pressure. It will be obvious from the Mollier Diagram that such expansion gives the greatest possible enthalpy drop between any given initial steam conditions and any given final pressure.

No practical working nozzle, however, is perfect. Due to minute imperfections and unavoidable minute manufacturing defects on the nozzle surfaces, fluid friction, shock and eddying occur. These effects destroy some of the velocity, and thus some of the kinetic energy is reconverted to heat which goes back into the steam.

The *efficiency ratio* of the nozzle is that fraction of the adiabatic enthalpy drop which is actually converted into kinetic energy. Referring to the Mollier Diagram in Figure 10.15 the nozzle efficiency ratio $= dh/dh_s$.

The difference $dh_s - dh$ is called the *nozzle loss* and causes reheat of the steam from A to N.

In addition to reducing the steam velocity, the fractional

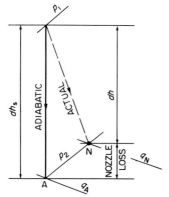

Figure 10.15 *Nozzle loss and nozzle efficiency*

nozzle efficiency ratio (commonly called nozzle efficiency in practice) is to render the dryness fraction or the superheat, and hence the specific volume at N, greater than at A. Hence, on two counts, the fractional nozzle efficiency means that the discharge area of the nozzle must be *greater* than it would be if there were no losses.

When dealing with convergent nozzles, the losses must of course take place in the converging passage, and since the throat area and discharge area are one and the same, the nozzle efficiency correction is applied to that area.

When dealing with convergent–divergent nozzles, it is usual to assume that all the losses take place in the divergent part after the throat, i.e. *the nozzle efficiency correction is applied only to the discharge area.* Depending on the design and manufacture, the practical value of nozzle efficiency lies between about 0.85 and 0.94.

The throat area of a convergent-divergent nozzle is calculated as if the expansion up to the throat were adiabatic, and the actual throat area is made slightly larger than that calculated. This correction, called the nozzle coefficient of discharge, is applied to allow for the well known fact that no fluid jet ever completely fills the throat, due probably to inertia in changing from convergent to divergent flow (see Figure 10.16).

The coefficient of discharge applies only to the throat area of a convergent-divergent nozzle. Depending on the design, the practical value of the coefficient of discharge lies between 0.95 and 0.98.

Again referring to Figure 10.15 the theoretical nozzle discharge velocity = $44.725 \sqrt{dh_s}$, m/s, and the actual nozzle discharge velocity = $44.725 \sqrt{dh}$, m/s. The theoretical nozzle

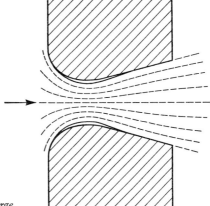

Figure 10.16 Coefficient of discharge

discharge velocity is denoted by C_0 and the actual nozzle discharge velocity by C_1.

We may summarise the foregoing by a worked example. This example we will make in two parts—one to cover a convergent-divergent nozzle working with initially superheated steam, and one to cover a convergent nozzle working with initially wet steam. In each case, let the steam flow be 5.124 kg/s.

1. Initial steam conditions 18.0 bar, 260°C, final pressure 3.0 bar. Nozzle efficiency 0.9; nozzle coefficient of discharge 0.95.
2. Initial steam conditions 2.8 bar 0.97 dry, final pressure 1.9 bar. Nozzle efficiency 0.85.

In each case, assume the initial steam velocity to be zero.

1. Pressure ratio p_2/p_1 = 3.0/18.0 = 0.167. The steam is initially superheated, hence since the pressure ratio is less than 0.5455, the expansion is over critical, and convergent-divergent nozzles are required. Pressure at nozzle throat = 0.5455 × 18.0 = 9.8 bar.

Set down the initial state point A on the Mollier Diagram and draw a perpendicular straight line from A to meet the final pressure line at B. Mark the point C at which AB crosses the throat pressure line. Since, as previously stated, we assume the expansion to be adiabatic up to the throat, C is the state point of the steam

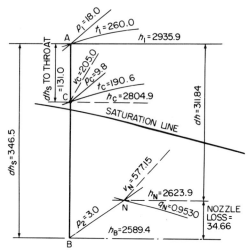

Figure 10.17 Expansion of steam in turbine nozzles from 18.0 bar 260.0° C to 3.0 bar

shows that the adiabatic enthalpy drop up to the throat is 131.0 kJ/kg and the steam velocity at the throat is therefore $C_c = 44.725 \sqrt{131.0} = 511.94$ m/s.

If the Mollier chart has lines of specific volume, the specific volume at the throat, v_c, can be read directly. If the Mollier chart does not have lines of specific volume, but has lines of constant temperature, the steam temperature at C can be read directly and the specific volume at C obtained by interpolating the Steam Tables. By either of these methods $v_c = 205.0$ dm^3/kg.

Theoretical total throat area

$$A_c = \frac{1000 M v_c}{C} = \frac{1000 \times 5.124 \times 205.0}{511.94} = 2051.9 \text{ mm}^2$$

This has to be increased so as to include the coefficient of discharge. Hence,

$$Actual \ total \ nozzle \ throat \ area = \frac{2051.9}{0.95} = \underline{2159.8 \text{ mm}^2}$$

Inspection of the Mollier Diagram shows that the overall nozzle adiabatic enthalpy drop is 346.5 kJ/kg. Since the nozzle efficiency is 0.9, then only 0.9 of the adiabatic heat drop is converted to kinetic energy, i.e. actual nozzle enthalpy drop $dh = 0.9 \times 346.5 = 311.84$ kJ/kg, and the actual nozzle discharge velocity $C_N = 44.725 \sqrt{311.84} = 789.8$ m/s.

The nozzle loss $= dh_s - dh = 346.5 - 311.84$
$$= 34.66 \text{ kJ/kg}$$

The point N may now be found on the line of constant pressure 3.0 bar, from which the dryness fraction at N, $q_N = 0.935$.

Specific volume at N,
$$v_N = (0.953 \times 605.53) + (0.047 \times 1.074)$$
$$= 577.15 \text{ dm}^3/\text{kg}$$

Hence *total nozzle discharge area,*
$$A_N = \frac{1000 \times 5.124 \times 577.15}{789.8} = 3744.5 \text{ mm}^2$$

2. Pressure ratio $p_2/p_1 = 1.9/2.8 = 0.68$. The steam is initially wet, hence since the pressure ratio is greater than 0.57, the expansion is under critical and convergent nozzles are required.

Inspection of the Mollier diagram (Figure 10.18) shows that the adiabatic enthalpy drop is $dh_s = 66.6$ kJ/kg. The nozzle efficiency is 0.85, hence actual enthalpy drop

$$dh = 0.85 \times 66.6 = 56.6 \text{ kJ/kg}$$

$\therefore$ Steam velocity at nozzle discharge
$$C = 44.725 \sqrt{56.61} = 336.5 \text{ m/s}$$

Dryness fraction at nozzle discharge $= 0.9527$

$\therefore$ Specific volume at nozzle discharge
$$v_N = (0.9527 \times 928.95) + (0.0473 \times 1.0594)$$
$$\therefore v_N = 885.0 + 0.05$$

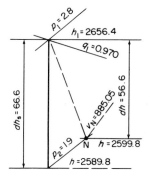

Figure 10.18 Expansion of steam in turbine nozzle from 2.8 bar 0.970 dry to 1.9 bar

$$\therefore v_N = 885.05 \ dm^3/kg$$

$$\therefore Nozzle\ discharge\ area = \frac{1000 \times 5.124 \times 885.05}{336.5}$$

$$= \underline{13476.0\ mm^2}$$

For any one turbine stage, the total nozzle area required can be found by the above methods, and it is now necessary to see how the staging and the stage pressure drops are determined, and how the resulting total nozzle areas can best be accommodated within the turbine. Before proceeding to do so however, we require to consider at some length the turbine as a whole so as to appreciate certain fundamental features of the different ways in which a turbine can be arranged.

Pure impulse turbines

The simplest form of turbine is one having a single row of fixed nozzles followed by a single wheel having a single row of blades as illustrated in Figure 10.19. The whole of the steam pressure drop takes place in the nozzles; there is no pressure drop through the blades, the latter causing only change of velocity of the steam. Such a turbine is called a *pure impulse* turbine, or more generally an impulse turbine. It will probably be immediately obvious that for maximum efficiency, the nozzle angle α should be as small as possible, since in this condition, the thrust of the steam jet on the blades has a greater component in the direction of blade motion, i.e. the steam jet is travelling more nearly in the same direction as the blades.

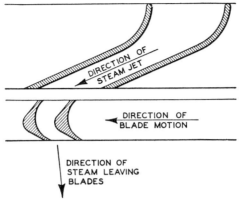

Figure 10.19 Circumferential section through the nozzles and blades of a simple-impulse turbine stage

The action of steam issuing from the nozzles and passing through the blades of such a turbine may now be considered. This is best done by vector velocity diagrams.

A velocity may be represented by a *vector*, i.e. a straight line on paper, the length of the line being proportional to the magnitude of the velocity, and the direction of the line—with reference to some fixed point—being the same as the direction of the velocity. For example, a jet of steam is discharged from a turbine nozzle at C_1 m/s in a direction inclined at an angle α to the plane of the wheel. Now the direction is relative to some fixed point on the turbine casing, and in consequence, C_1 is called the *absolute entrance velocity*.

If the mean diameter D_m, m, of the blade ring and the revolutions per second, R, are known, then the mean blade velocity u, m/s, may be calculated from $u = \pi D_m R$.

These velocities may be shown in vector form as in Figure 10.20. The steam jet may be regarded as moving away from the point X at C_1 m/s and in a direction inclined at an angle α to the plane of the wheel. At the same time, the blades are moving away from the point X at u m/s in the direction of blade motion, i.e. in the plane of the wheel. In the diagram, u and C_1 are drawn to scale, each pointing away from X at the appropriate angle.

The closing line w_1 of the entrance vector triangle gives us the magnitude and direction of the steam jet relative to the blade at entrance to the latter. Thus the steam jet strikes the blade at an angle θ_1 to the plane of the wheel. θ_1 is called the steam entrance angle and theoretically the blade entrance angle β_1 should be equal to θ_1, if the steam jet is to enter the blades without shock and consequent loss. In practice, the blade entrance angle β_1 is made a few degrees greater than θ_1 to preclude the possibility of the steam striking the back of the blade, particularly when running at reduced powers with the turbines throttled down, in which condition the changes in u and C_1 can cause the steam entrance angle θ_1 to vary up or down by a few degrees.

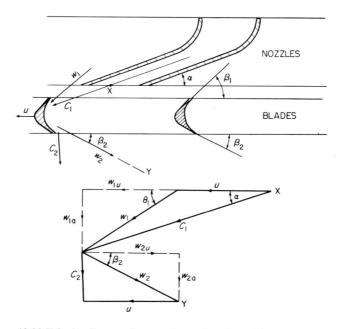

Figure 10.20 Velocity diagrams for a single-row impulse turbine stage

The function of a pure impulse blade is solely to deflect the steam jet, i.e. to change its direction. There is no change of pressure through a pure impulse blade. If the blade surfaces were perfectly formed and perfectly smooth, therefore, relative to the blade, the steam would leave with the same velocity with which it entered, i.e. w_2 would be equal to w_1. In practice, minute imperfections in form and minute roughness on the blade surfaces cause some shock and fluid friction, which result in some loss of velocity, the lost velocity being reconverted to heat which goes back into the steam. w_2 is therefore somewhat less than w_1, the difference

$$\left(\frac{w_1}{44.725}\right)^2 - \left(\frac{w_2}{44.725}\right)^2 \text{ kJ/kg}$$

being called the *blade loss*, and the ratio w_2/w_1 the *blade velocity coefficient*. If the blades become eroded or fouled by impurities in the steam, the blade loss is increased.

Referring again to Figure 10.20, therefore, relative to the blades, the steam jet leaves the blades and approaches the fixed point Y with a velocity w_2 and in a direction determined by the blade discharge angle β_2. At the same time, the blades are moving away from Y with velocity u in the plane of the wheel. w_2 and u may therefore be set down to scale on the velocity diagram, and the discharge triangle completed by drawing in C_2, the absolute velocity of the steam leaving the blades.

The steam leaving the blades with absolute velocity C_2, m/s, carries with it kinetic energy to the extent of $(C_2/44.725)^2$ kJ/kg. If the turbine consists of this one stage only, this kinetic energy is a complete loss and is called the leaving loss.

Interpreting velocity diagrams

Relative to the blades, the steam enters at w_1 m/s (Figure 10.20) and leaves at w_2 m/s. In passing through the blades therefore the change of velocity is basically $w_1 - w_2$ m/s. However, these velocities are vector quantities (i.e. directed quantities), and in assessing the change of velocity, we must consider direction as well as magnitude. One way to appreciate this is to consider, separately, the composition of w_1 and w_2.

w_1 can be replaced by a tangential component w_{1u} in the direction of blade motion, and an axial component w_{1a} at right angles to the direction of blade motion.

w_2 can be replaced by a tangential component w_{2u} in the direction of blade motion, and an axial component w_{2a} at right angles to the direction of blade motion.

The two tangential components have opposite sense (i.e. their arrowheads point opposite ways), hence w_{1u} and w_{2u} are of opposite sense. The component change of velocity in the direction of motion is $w_{1u} - (- w_{2u}) = w_{1u} + w_{2u}$ m/s.

The two axial components have the same sense, hence they are of the same sign, and the component change of velocity at right angles to the direction of motion is $w_{1a} - w_{2a}$ m/s.

Perhaps the most convenient method of drawing the velocity diagrams is to superpose the two triangles on a common base of blade velocity u, as shown in Figure 10.21. This method is in fact an artifice which automatically gives us the sum $(w_{1u} + w_{2u})$ and the difference $(w_{1a} - w_{2a})$.

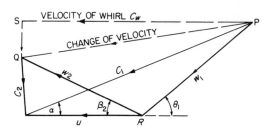

Figure 10.21 Convenient method of drawing velocity diagrams

In passing through the blades, the change of velocity of the steam is represented by the vector PQ. This change has a component PS in the direction of blade motion causing rotation of the wheel, and a component SQ at right angles to the direction of motion causing axial thrust. Note that in an impulse stage as described, the axial component SQ, and hence the end thrust, are small. In practice, the tangential component PS is called the velocity of whirl and may be denoted by C_w. Comparison of Figures 10.20 and 10.21 will show that $C_w = w_{1u} + w_{2u}$, and that the axial component $SQ = w_{1a} - w_{2a}$.

Now C_w m/s is the change of velocity in the direction of motion and if the mass flow of steam through the stage is M kg/s, then the product $M C_w$ has units

$$\frac{\text{kg}}{\text{s}} \times \frac{\text{m}}{\text{s}} = \text{kg} \ \frac{\text{m}}{\text{s}^2}$$

m/s² is the rate of change of velocity i.e. the acceleration, and $M C_w$ is therefore (mass × acceleration), which is of course the force on the blades in newtons (N).

If the rotor makes one revolution, this force acts through a distance πD_m metres, hence the work done on the blades is given by $(M C_w \times \pi D_m)$, Nm/rev. (D_m is the stage mean diameter, m).

If the rotor makes R rev/s, then work done on blades = $(M\,C_w \times \pi D_m \times R)$, Nm/s. Now the term $\pi D_m R$ is the mean velocity u, m/s, hence

Blade work = $uC_w M$, Nm/s, and since 1.0 Nm = 1.0 J,

Blade work = $uC_w M$, J/s, and we may therefore write

$$\text{Blade work} = \frac{uC_w M}{1000M} = \frac{uC_w}{1000} \text{ kJ/kg}$$

This is the work output from the combined nozzles and blades.

Steam leaves the stage with absolute velocity C_2, m/s, thus carrying with it kinetic energy, $C_2^2/2000$, kJ/kg. The purpose of the stage is to do work, hence so far as this particular stage is concerned, the kinetic energy of the steam leaving the stage is a complete loss. It is called the leaving loss.

The work input to the stage is the theoretical kinetic energy of the steam jets, i.e. $C_0^2/2000$, kJ/kg (C_0 is the steam velocity which would be generated by the full stage adiabatic enthalpy drop dh_s —see Figure 10.35.

Hence the combined efficiency of the nozzles and blades

$$= \frac{\text{work output}}{\text{work input}} = \frac{uC_w}{1000} \div \frac{C_0^2}{2000} = \frac{uC_w}{1000}\,\frac{2000}{C_0^2} = \frac{2uC_w}{C_0^2}$$

This efficiency takes into account the nozzle loss, the blade loss and the leaving loss, all of which affect the velocity diagrams. It is therefore called the *diagram efficiency*.

$$\text{Diagram efficiency} = \frac{2uC_w}{C_0^2}$$

Note: If our turbine stage is followed by another stage, and if the nozzle inlet angle of the next stage is suitably designed (see Figure 10.41), to reduce shock losses, it is possible to carry over part of C_2 as velocity to the next stage, in which case the heat equivalent of that fraction of C_2 which is carried over as velocity is added to the adiabatic enthalpy drop of the next stage, but is *not* shown on the Mollier Diagram. The remainder of C_2 which is not carried over as velocity, but is destroyed and reconverted to heat appears on the Mollier Diagram as a loss causing reheat of the steam in the first of the two stages. The Mollier Diagram is drawn for enthalpy; i.e. any one state point shows the enthalpy, kJ/kg, irrespective of whether the steam is at rest or is moving at high velocity. The state point moves only if velocity is created at the expense of enthalpy, or if enthalpy is created at the expense of velocity.

Thus if it is possible to carry over a fraction k of the first stage leaving velocity C_2 as velocity to the next stage,

$$\text{Energy carried over as velocity} = k \, \frac{C_2{}^2}{2000} \text{, kJ/kg, and}$$

Energy reconverted to heat in first stage

$$= (1 - k) \, \frac{C^2}{2000} \text{, kJ/kg}$$

In detailed calculations, it is convenient to express the kinetic energy of steam moving at C m/s as $(C/44.725)^2$, kJ/kg, rather than $C^2/2000$, kJ/kg.

These two expressions are exactly the same, but $(C/44.725)^2$ involves smaller numbers and facilitates location of the decimal point.

It should be noted that although for any given mass flow of steam, the axial thrust for any one stage is determined by the velocity diagrams, the total axial thrust work is determined not only by the sum of the stage thrusts, but also by the type, size, condition and lubrication of the rotor thrust block. The thrust block work is therefore an external mechanical loss in the same way as is the rotor journal bearing loss, flexible coupling loss, gear loss, etc. External losses do not appear on the Mollier Diagram, since they do not cause reheat of the steam.

Relation between the mean blade velocity and the steam velocity

The ratio of the mean blade velocity u to the steam velocity C_1 is one of the most important factors in steam turbine theory. We may best approach this by first imagining a simple turbine having steam velocity C_1 in the plane of the wheel and considering the three extreme cases. For this purpose, the blade loss may be neglected.

1 Blade Velocity Zero

i.e. $\dfrac{u}{C_1} = 0$

The steam jet enters the blade with velocity C_1 in the plane of the wheel, is deflected through $360°$ by the blade, and leaves the blade at C_1 m/s in the plane of the wheel, but in the opposite sense (see Figure 10.22(a)). The velocity diagram then consists of two equal straight lines PQ and QP which coincide with one another but have their arrowheads pointing opposite ways (see Figure 10.22(b)).

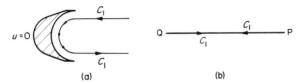

Figure 10.22 Blade velocity zero, i.e. $u/C_1 = 0$

The change of velocity is $C_1 - (-C_1) = 2C_1$ m/s, which with a steam mass flow of M, kg/s, results in a force on the blades of $2M/C$. Since however, $u = 0$, the blade remains stationary and no work is done. The efficiency of such an arrangement is therefore zero.

2 Blade Velocity Equal to Steam Velocity

i.e. $\dfrac{u}{C_1} = 1.0$

In this case u and C_1 are each represented by a straight line PQ with both arrowheads pointing away from P. The relative velocity entering the blade is $C_1 - u = 0$, hence there is no change of velocity through the blade, no work is done on the blades and the efficiency is zero. Refer to Figure 10.23(a) and (b).

Note: In 1 there is force on the blade but no blade *motion*; in 2 there is blade motion but no *force* on the blade, and since work done = force × distance moved, both arrangements give no work and zero efficiency.

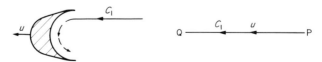

Figure 10.23 Blade velocity equal to steam velocity, i.e. $u/C_1 = 1.0$

3 BLADE VELOCITY GREATER THAN STEAM VELOCITY

i.e. $\dfrac{u}{C_1} > 1.0$

If such a condition can be visualised, it implies that the blades are driving the steam round—clearly, for a turbine, this would be impossible and absurd.

Thus, from cases 1, 2 and 3 our first conclusion is that the value of u/C_1 must lie between 0 and 1.0.

Let us now examine the general case in which u/C_1 lies between 0 and 1.0, i.e. $u/C_1 < 1.0 > 0$.

In this case, referring to Figure 10.24, the steam jet may be regarded as moving away from the fixed point X at C_1 m/s in the direction of blade motion at the same time as the blade is moving away from X at u m/s in the direction of blade motion.

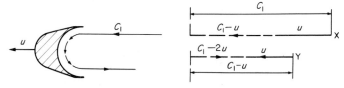

Figure 10.24 Blade velocity/steam velocity $> 0 < 1.0$

Relative to the blade therefore, the steam enters the blade at $(C_1 - u)$ m/s, is deflected through $360°$, and relative to the blade leaves the blade at $(C_1 - u)$ m/s towards a fixed point Y. At the same time however, the blade is moving away from Y at u m/s hence the absolute velocity of the steam leaving the blade (i.e. relative to Y) is $(C_1 - 2u)$ m/s. The overall change of velocity = initial velocity − final velocity

$$= C_1 - [- (C_1 - 2u)]$$
$$= C_1 - [- C_1 + 2u]$$
$$= C_1 + C_1 - 2u$$
$$= 2C_1 - 2u$$
$$= 2(C_1 - u) \text{ m/s}$$

The work done on the blades

$$= \frac{u \times 2(C_1 - u)}{1000} = \frac{2u(C_1 - u)}{1000} \text{ kJ/kg}$$

The work available is as before, equal to the kinetic energy of the steam jet travelling at C_1 m/s

$$= \frac{C_1{}^2}{2000} \text{ kJ/kg, and}$$

$$\text{Efficiency} = \frac{\text{blade work}}{\text{k.e. of jet}} = \frac{2u\,(C_1 - u)}{1000}\frac{2000}{C_1{}^2} = \frac{4u\,(C_1 - u)}{C_1{}^2}$$

Suppose we now choose several values of u/C_1 between 0 and 1.0, and keeping C_1 constant at 1.0 unit, calculate the blade efficiency η for each. This may be conveniently done in tabular form as follows.

					$C_1 = 1.0$						
u/C_1	0	0.1	0.2	0.3	0.4 0.5 0.6	0.7	0.8 0.9	1.0
u	0	0.1	0.2	0.3	0.4 0.5 0.6	0.7	0.8 0.9	1.0
$4u$	0	0.4	0.8	1.2	1.6 2.0 2.4	2.8	3.2 3.6	4.0
$C_1 - u$	1.0	0.9	0.8	0.7	0.6 0.5 0.4	0.3	0.2 0.1	0
$4u(C_1 - u)$	0	0.36	0.64	0.84	0.96 1.0 0.96	0.84	0.64 0.36	0
$\eta = 4u(C_1 - u)/\ C_1{}^2$	0	0.36	0.64	0.84	0.96 1.0 0.96	0.84	0.64 0.36	0

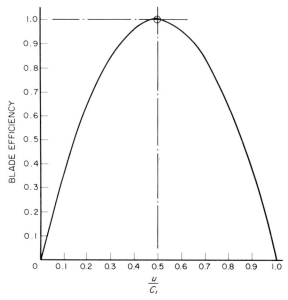

Figure 10.25 Blade efficiency for varying values of u/C_1 when $\alpha = 0$

If we plot the blade efficiency η on a base of u/C_1 we obtain the curve illustrated in Figure 10.25, which shows that maximum efficiency is obtained when the mean blade velocity u m/s is one half of the steam velocity C_1 m/s at the nozzle discharge, and that for the notional turbine with the steam jet in the plane of the wheel (i.e. nozzle angle $\alpha = 0$), if u/C_1 is made $\frac{1}{2}$ then the fundamental blade efficiency is 1.0, (i.e. 100 per cent).

The vast majority of practical steam turbines, however, do not have the steam jets in the plane of the wheel, but inclined at an angle α, the nozzle angle (see Figure 10.26).

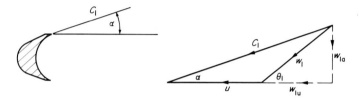

Figure 10.26 Effect of the nozzle angle

The result is that the steam does not enter the blade in the direction of motion with velocity $(C_1 - u)$ m/s, but enters at an angle θ_1 with velocity w_1 m/s. Although w_1 is greater than $(C_1 - u)$, only the tangential component w_{1u}, which is smaller than $(C_1 - u)$, develops a force on the blade in the direction of motion. Similarly, the tangential component w_{2u} at the blade discharge is less than $(C_1 - u)$, hence for the same mass flow of steam, the work done and the efficiency are less than for zero nozzle angle. It therefore follows, as has been stated previously, that the smaller the nozzle angle, the higher is the efficiency.

Further, if the nozzle angle is α, the optimum value of u/C_1 is no longer $1/2$, but $1/2\cos\alpha$, and the fundamental optimum blade efficiency is no longer 1.0, but $\cos^2\alpha$.

In practice of course, the blade discharge angle and the blade velocity coefficient further modify the optimum value of u/C_1. Also, in what follows, we require to base our arguments, not on the steam velocity C_1 at the nozzle discharge, but on the theoretical steam velocity C_0 corresponding to the full adiabatic enthalpy drop for the stage, hence actually we will be dealing with u/C_0, so also including the nozzle loss.

However, in general the nozzle angles are small, and the values of $\cos\alpha$ are large, i.e. if $\alpha = 14°$, $\cos\alpha = 0.9703$ and if

$\alpha = 20°$, $\cos\alpha = 0.9397$. Thus practical values of u/C_0 can be expected to be of the order of 0.45 to 0.48. In the next section however we will, for convenience, assume that we can take the best value of u/C_0 for a single-row wheel as 0.5, i.e. ignoring the effects of the nozzle angle, the nozzle and blade losses, and the blade discharge angle.

COMPOUNDING PURE IMPULSE TURBINES

A turbine steamer might have initial steam conditions 26.0 bar, 420°C, and may exhaust to the condenser at 0.07 bar. Setting these conditions down on the Mollier Diagram shows that the total adiabatic enthalpy drop over this range of expansion is 1097.3 kJ/kg. Were this used in a single impulse stage, the steam velocity generated would be $C_0 = 44.725$ $\sqrt{1097.3} = 1475.0$ m/s. For optimum efficiency, the mean blade velocity would be half of this, i.e. $u = 1475/2 = 737.5$ m/s.

If the turbine speed were 50 rev/s, then the mean diameter of the wheel would be $D_m = 737.5/(\pi \times 50) = 46.9$ m. Such a wheel would be quite impracticable on account of sheer size, centrifugal stress, etc. We could of course reduce the mean diameter of the wheel by increasing the speed, e.g. suppose an acceptable mean diameter to be 1.0 m, then the speed would be $(737.5 \times 60)/(\pi \times 1.0) = 234.67$ rev/s.

Such a turbine speed would be inadmissible in marine practice on account of excessive centrifugal stress, high journal speed, large reduction gear ratio to give relatively low propeller speed required.

To combine high efficiency with reasonable turbine speed and dimensions, the turbine must be *compounded*.

Pressure compounding

In this system, the turbine consists of a number of simple impulse stages, each consisting of one row of nozzles followed by one row of blades on a wheel, the wheels being on one common shaft. The total pressure drop, and hence the total enthalpy drop, is divided up over the stages so that each stage deals with only a fraction of the total enthalpy drop. The steam velocity, and therefore the blade velocity at each stage, is much reduced and hence the stage mean diameters and/or the turbine speed may be reduced accordingly.

For instance, suppose the total enthalpy drop in the previous example to be equally shared by four single-row pressure stages.

$$\text{Each stage enthalpy drop} = \frac{1097.3}{4} = 274.3 \text{ kJ/kg}$$

$$\text{Each stage steam velocity } C_0 = 44.725\sqrt{274.3} = 737.5 \text{ m/s}$$

$$\text{With } \frac{u}{C_0} = \tfrac{1}{2} \text{, mean blade velocity } u = \frac{737.5}{2} = 368.75 \text{ m/s}$$

$$\text{For 50 rev/s, stage mean diameter } D_m = \frac{368.75}{\pi \times 50}$$
$$= 23.45 \text{ m}$$

By using four single-row pressure stages instead of one for the same speed, viz. 50 rev/s, we have halved the stage mean diameter. This mean diameter is still much too large, but the object of the calculation at present is to show how the mean diameters may be reduced by increasing the number of pressure stages. As the number of stages is increased, so the length of the turbine is increased. If we imagine the turbine rotor to be a beam simply supported at its bearing centres, it will be immediately obvious that if we increase the number of stages we have to increase the bearing centres, both of which increase the natural "sag" of the rotor, with consequent adverse effect on the critical speed of the rotor (see Chapter 5). To correct this, we could increase the diameter of the rotor shaft to make it stiffer, but if we do so, we increase the leakage area through the diaphragm glands, with consequent increased leakage loss from stage to stage and reduced efficiency.

Our example assumes that the same mean diameter would be acceptable for all four stages. Actually, the stage mean diameters usually increase progressively towards the exhaust end to obtain the increasing flow area necessary to pass the larger volumes of steam associated with the lower pressures. To obtain sufficient steam flow area it is necessary to progressively increase not only the mean diameters but also the nozzle heights (and hence the blade heights) towards the exhaust end. The blade heights can be increased only up to that limit imposed by centrifugal stress, usually about one-quarter of the stage mean diameter. If when approaching this limit, more steam flow area is still required, it is necessary also to increase the nozzle angle and very probably the blade discharge angle, resulting in some loss of efficiency as explained previously. The necessity of having to increase the mean diameters towards the exhaust end means that these stages have increased mean blade velocities, and hence for the same u/C_0, higher steam velocities. The larger diameter stages can therefore deal with higher stage enthalpy drops, and it is possible that one, or two, fewer stages will be required than would have been had all the stages been of the same mean diameter. These features will be illustrated by examples later in this chapter.

Velocity compounding

In this method of compounding, the entire pressure drop, and hence the entire enthalpy drop takes in one row of nozzles, but the total change of velocity is divided up over two or over three rows of blades on the wheel. A row of fixed blades is fitted between each pair of rows of moving blades to redirect the steam jets.

If there are two rows of moving blades, maximum efficiency is obtained when the mean blade velocity is about one quarter of the steam velocity; if there are three rows of moving blades maximum efficiency is obtained when the

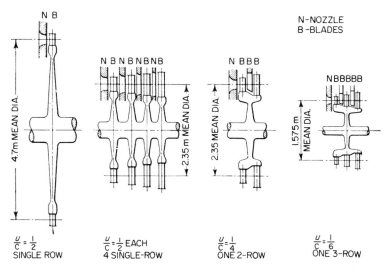

Figure 10.27 Equivalent impulse turbines

Single row	*4 single-row*	*One 2-row*	*One 3-row*
$u/C_0 = \frac{1}{2}$	$u/C_0 = \frac{1}{2}$ *each*	$u/C_0 = \frac{1}{4}$	$u/C_0 = \frac{1}{6}$

mean blade velocity is about one sixth of the steam velocity.

For example, were the total enthalpy drop of 1097.3 kJ/kg (as quoted in the previous example) dealt with by one two-row wheel, the steam velocity would be 1475.0 m/s, as for the simple single-row turbine, but the mean blade velocity would be one quarter of 1475.0, i.e. 368.75 m/s, which at speed 50 rev/s would give a mean diameter of 23.45 m. If one 3-row were used the mean blade velocity would be one sixth of 1475.0, i.e. 245.833 m/s, which at speed 50 rev/s would give a mean diameter of 15.62 m.

Each of the four arrangements described above and illustrated in Figure 10.27(a) expands steam over the same total range, has the same total enthalpy drop, the same speed, and the same theoretical efficiency. Actually in practice, any of the compound arrangements is less efficient than the comparable simple single-row turbine, due to the multiplication of the *parasite* losses, e.g. disc friction, windage, diaphragm gland leakage, nozzle and blade losses etc., in the compound arrangements. Also, as previously mentioned the actual practical values of the optimum u/C_0 are not exactly $\frac{1}{2}$, $\frac{1}{4}$ and $\frac{1}{6}$.

Figure 10.27(a) shows that theoretically, four single-row pressure stages can be replaced by one two-row velocity-compounded pressure stage of the same mean diameter and speed. In practice, because of the deviation of the optimum u/C_0 from $\frac{1}{2}$ and $\frac{1}{4}$, and of the possibility of varying the mean diameters, one two-row stage can be equivalent to four, three, or even two single-row stages.

Of the three compound arrangements shown in Figure 10.27(a), in practice four single-row pressure stages usually have higher efficiency than either the two-row or three-row nominally equivalent velocity stages.

Pressure-velocity compounding

Figure 10.27 shows that one two-row wheel is theoretically equivalent to four single-row wheels of the same mean diameter and running at the same speed. Very often, the first two, three or four single-row stages of a pressure-compounded impulse turbine are replaced by one 2-row stage; this reduces the turbine length. Also, since the two-row stage expands steam over the same total pressure drop as the number of single-row stages which it replaces, the steam pressure and temperature on the steam end shaft gland are significantly reduced.

Such an arrangement is obviously a combination of pressure compounding and velocity compounding, and in consequence, is known as *pressure-velocity compounding*. It is illustrated in Figure 10.28. The single-row stages have comparatively small pressure drops and thus have convergent nozzles. The 2-row stage has a large pressure drop and almost invariably requires convergent–divergent nozzles. This feature has already been dealt with earlier in this chapter.

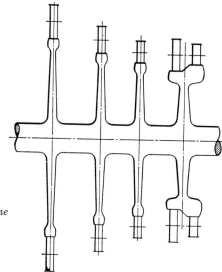

Figure 10.28 Pressure-velocity compounded impulse turbine, one two-row and three single-row wheels

Impulse turbine compounding in practice

The initial steam conditions chosen for our last example, viz., 26.0 bar, 420.0°C are quite low by modern standards. Even so, the total enthalpy drop is large enough to result in excessively large mean diameters with any form of compounding to the extent illustrated for example if we were to use four single-row stages at 50 rev/s, the mean diameter would be 23.45 m, which is unacceptably large.

For such a marine turbine, reasonable and acceptable mean diameters might be 0.5 m at the high pressure end to 1.0 m at the exhaust end. If at the moment, we assume the average mean diameter to be 0.7 m, then the average mean blade velocity would be $u = \pi \times 0.7 \times 50 = 109.5$ m/s, and if $u/C_0 = 1/2$, the average stage steam velocity $C_0 = 109.5 \times 2 = 219.0$ m/s, and the average stage adiabatic enthalpy drop $dh_s = (219.0/44.725)^2 = 24.0$ kJ/kg.

Since the total adiabatic enthalpy drop is 1097.3 kJ/kg, then 46 single-row pressure stages would be required. The turbine, however would now be much too long. We must now extend the principles of compounding to give us a turbine, or turbines, which will be the best compromise among all the conflicting requirements.

Firstly, we can divide up our turbine into two or three separate turbines. If the latter, this gives us the conception of H.P., I.P. and L.P. turbines, and immediately results in a proportionate reduction in individual turbine length. Since all three turbines drive a common propeller shaft through a single or a double reduction gear, it is possible to adopt three different speeds for the three turbines by adopting different numbers of teeth in the pinions of a single reduction gear, or in the primary pinions and primary wheels of a double reduction gear.

One of the major limiting factors on turbine speed is centrifugal stress in the blades, blade roots and discs. The centrifugal force generated by a body of mass M kg revolving at u m/s and at a radius r m around a point is given by

$$\text{C.F.} = \frac{Mu^2}{r} \text{ newtons}$$

Let us consider a turbine blade whose mass is M, kg. Its velocity is the mean blade velocity u m/s and its radius about the shaft centre is $D_m/2$ m. If the speed is R rev/s, its centrifugal force is

$$\text{C.F.} = Mu^2 \; \frac{2}{D_m} \quad \text{and since } u = \pi D_m R, \text{ then}$$

$$\text{C.F.} = \frac{M\pi^2 D_m{}^2 R^2}{D_m}$$

$$\text{C.F.} = \pi^2 \times M D_m R^2 \text{ newtons}$$

The centrifugal force therefore varies directly as the mass of the blade, directly as the mean diameter of the stage, and directly as the square of the speed.

Now in the H.P. turbine, the blades are small hence their mass is small, and the stage mean diameters are small. For any given centrifugal force therefore, the speed can be made higher than for the L.P. turbine where the mean diameters are large and the blades long and of greater mass.

The centrifugal stress however is determined not only by the centrifugal force, but by the cross-sectional area of the blade or blade root sustaining that force. The first-stage H.P. turbine blades might be 12.0 mm high on 0.5 m mean diameter; the last-stage L.P. turbine blades might be 250 mm high on 0.9 m mean diameter.

Thus from the mass and mean diameter aspects alone, the centrifugal force on the last-stage L.P. turbine blades, for the same rev/min would be about

$$\frac{250.0}{12.0} \times \frac{0.9}{0.46} = 41$$

times that on the first H.P. blades.

Now, the last-stage L.P. blade root areas could not be made 41 times that of the first-stage H.P. blade root areas, hence the L.P. turbine running speed must be reduced to that which will give acceptable stresses in the particular blade material, while retaining reasonable blade root areas.

In our example, let us assume that a speed of 50 rev/s is satisfactory for the L.P. turbine, but let us increase the I.P. turbine speed to 75 rev/s, and the H.P. turbine speed to 108.33 rev/s, all of which can be conveniently accommodated by the reduction gear as explained above.

If the I.P. turbine average mean diameter is made 0.7 m, and the L.P. turbine 0.9 m then the average mean blade velocities would be

H.P. turbine $u = \pi \times 0.5 \times 108.33 = 170.0$ m/s

I.P. turbine $u = \pi \times 0.7 \times 75 \quad = 164.5$ m/s

L.P. turbine $u = \pi \times 0.9 \times 50 \quad = 141.5$ m/s

If we make $u/C_0 = \frac{1}{2}$ throughout, then for each stage, the steam velocity would be

H.P. turbine $C_0 = 170.0 \times 2 = 340.0$ m/s

I.P. turbine $C_0 = 164.5 \times 2 = 329.0$ m/s

L.P. turbine $C_0 = 141.5 \times 2 = 283.0$ m/s

and the individual heat drops

$$\text{H.P. turbine } dh_s = \left(\frac{340.0}{44.725}\right)^2 = 57.6 \text{ kJ/kg}$$

$$\text{I.P. turbine } dh_s = \left(\frac{329.0}{44.725}\right)^2 = 54.2 \text{ kJ/kg}$$

$$\text{L.P. turbine } dh_s = \left(\frac{283.0}{44.725}\right)^2 = 40.0 \text{ kJ/kg}$$

If we divide the total adiabatic enthalpy drop of 1097.3 kJ/kg equally among the three turbines, each turbine will deal with 1097.3/3 = 365.8 kJ/kg and the number of stages would be

H.P. turbine $\dfrac{365.8}{57.6}$ = 6.3, say 7 stages, average mean dia. 0.5 m, speed 108.33 rev/s

I.P. turbine $\dfrac{365.8}{54.2}$ = 6.7, say 7 stages, average mean dia. 0.7 m, speed 75 rev/s

L.P. turbine $\dfrac{365.8}{40}$ = 9.2, say 9 stages, average mean dia. 0.9 m, speed 50 rev/s

Thus by pressure-compounding, and by judicious selection of mean diameters and speeds, we have replaced the unacceptably large-diameter single-stage, or the unacceptably long 46-stage pressure-compounded single turbine by three short compact turbines, of high efficiency, running at acceptable speeds and which may be conveniently arranged around a double reduction gear.

In the foregoing calculations we have imagined the H.P., I.P. and L.P. turbines to have constant mean diameters 0.5 m, 0.7 m and 0.9 m respectively. As the steam expands through each turbine, the pressure falls and the specific volume increases progressively. In the H.P. turbine the rate of increase of the specific volume is small, and it is likely that the constant mean diameter of 0.5 m can be used for all the H.P. turbine stages. Somewhere, probably in the I.P. turbine, the rate of increase of the specific volume begins to rise and subsequent mean diameters have to be increased to give the

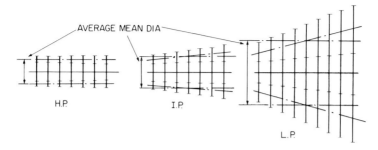

Figure 10.29 Turbine staging about an "average" mean diameter

larger nozzle and blade annulus areas required. Figure 10.29 attempts to give some conception of "average" mean diameter of a turbine such as we have used up to this point.

The actual stage mean diameters are chosen quite arbitrarily relative to the average mean diameter, and the stage enthalpy drops modified to suit the actual stage mean diameters.

Further variations may sometimes, with advantage, be made by using a 2-row pressure stage instead of some of the single-row stages at the H.P. end.

Equivalent turbines—Parsons' K

In studying the subject of turbine staging, it is useful to know what the effect on the staging will be if one dimension is changed; e.g. in a turbine having a given total enthalpy drop we may wish to increase the number of stages. What must we do to the original stages to maintain the same overall efficiency?

Now, the steam velocity $C_0 = 44.725 \sqrt{(dh_s)}$, hence for any one stage C_0 varies as $\sqrt{(dh_s)}$.

The mean blade velocity $u = \pi D_m R$, therefore u varies as $D_m R$

Hence $\dfrac{u}{C_0}$ varies as $\dfrac{D_m R}{\sqrt{(dh_s)}}$,

i.e. $\dfrac{u}{C_0} \propto \dfrac{D_m R}{\sqrt{(dh_s)}}$ or

$\dfrac{u}{C_0} \sqrt{(dh_s)} \propto D_m R$, and hence for any one stage having a constant value of $\dfrac{u}{C_0}$, $\sqrt{dh_s} \propto D_m R$

$\therefore dh_s \propto D_m{}^2 R^2$

If the turbine has n stages and a total adiabatic enthalpy drop of Dh_s, then Dh_s varies as $D_m{}^2 R^2 n$.

Thus for a turbine or a section of a turbine having a given overall adiabatic enthalpy drop and if the stages have a constant value of u/C_0, then the quantity $D_m{}^2 R^2 n$ must be constant. This constant is called the turbine coefficient, often referred to as Parsons' K.

For example, the H.P. turbine in our previous example has 7 stages, average mean diameter 0.5 m, speed 108.33 rev/s.

Parsons' K = $0.5^2 \times 108.33^2 \times 7 = 20533$

If for example we wish to increase the number of stages to eight, while retaining the same speed and the same overall efficiency, we must alter the average mean diameter to keep the same value of Parsons' K as before, i.e. $D_m{}^2 \times 108.33^2 \times 8 = 20533$.

from which $D_m = \sqrt{\left(\dfrac{20533}{108.33^2 \times 8}\right)} = 0.467$ m

i.e. we reduce the average mean diameter from 0.5 m to 0.467 m.

Alternatively, suppose we wished to retain seven stages, but to reduce the speed to 100 rev/s. We must adjust the average mean diameter to again retain the original value of Parsons' K:

$D_m{}^2 \times 100^2 \times 7 = 74\,000\,000$

$\therefore D_m = \sqrt{\left(\dfrac{20533}{100^2 \times 7}\right)} = 0.535$ m

i.e. we increase the average mean diameter from 0.5 m to 0.535 m.

If we consider the implications of Parsons' K to a single-row pressure stage having a stage adiabatic enthalpy drop dh_s kJ/kg and a constant speed R rev/s, then we may write

$dh_s \propto D_m{}^2 R^2 n$, but R is constant and $n = 1$, hence

$dh_s \propto D_m{}^2$

or in words, the *stage adiabatic enthalpy drop varies as the square of the stage mean diameter*. Applying this to say the I.P. turbine of our last example, we decided on 7 stages with an average mean diameter of 0.7 m. Let us make the middle stage 0.7 m mean diameter and arbitrarily choose the other stage mean diameters in steps of 0.05 m, thus again referring to Figure 10.27,

Stage	1	2	3	4	5	6	7	
D_m, m	0.55	0.6	0.65	0.7	0.75	0.8	0.85	
$D_m{}^2$	0.303	0.36	0.424	0.49	0.563	0.64	0.723	$\Sigma D_m{}^2 = 3.503$
dh_s, kJ/kg	31.6	37.6	44.3	51.2	58.7	66.8	75.6	$\Sigma dh_s = 365.8$

The overall adiabatic enthalpy drop for the I.P. turbine we decided to make 365.8 kJ/kg. If we divide this by $\Sigma D_m{}^2$ and multiply in turn by each stage $D_m{}^2$, we have divided up the total adiabatic enthalpy drop among the stages in proportion to the squares of their mean diameters; e.g.

$$\text{For Stage 1, } dh_s = \frac{365.8}{3.503} \times 0.303 = 31.6 \text{ kJ/kg}$$

$$\text{For Stage 2, } dh_s = \frac{365.8}{3.503} \times 0.36 = 37.6 \text{ kJ/kg}$$

A similar procedure would be used to decide the stage mean diameters for the L.P. turbine, but bearing in mind that towards the exhaust end where the specific volume increases rapidly, the mean diameters may have to be increased rather more to obtain sufficient nozzle and blade annulus areas. The nozzle angles also may have to be increased, hence requiring lower values of u/C_0.

STEAM FLOW AREA

Earlier in this chapter we have seen how the work (kJ/kg) obtainable from the steam may be calculated. The work done (kJ/s) from which follows the power (kW) developed, is therefore dependent on the mass flow of steam (kg/s) passing through the stages. We have also, knowing the stage adiabatic enthalpy drop (kJ/kg) and the mass flow (kg/s) seen how the total nozzle area for a stage is obtained.

In the present section we shall consider how for one stage of an impulse turbine, the total nozzle area, and the appropriate area through the blade passages is accommodated.

Impulse turbine nozzles, convergent type

Normally, single-row pressure stages are arranged so that the nozzle pressure ratio is under critical, thus requiring convergent nozzles.

We have already shown that the steam velocity C_1 m/s, at the nozzle discharge is given by $C_1 = 44.725 \sqrt{(dh_n)}$, where dh_n is the actual nozzle enthalpy drop (kJ/kg). Using this velocity, and the specific volume v_n (dm^3/kg) at the nozzle discharge, the total nozzle discharge area required to pass a mass flow M, kg/s, is found from the equation of continuity $1000 \, Mv_n = AC_1$.

Convergent nozzles may be either cast-in nozzles, or built-up annular nozzles, the former normally used for intermediate and low pressure stages and the latter for the higher pressure stages. These two types are illustrated in Figures 10.30 and 10.31 respectively. Within recent years, new and revolutionary machining techniques have enabled the required nozzle forms to be accurately produced from the solid.

Whatever type is used, the circumferential section xx remains essentially as shown in Figures 10.30 and 10.31.

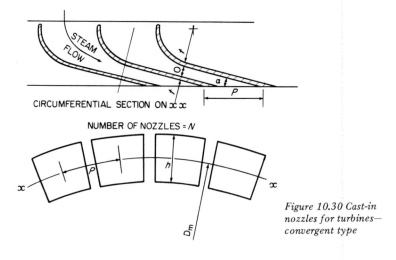

Figure 10.30 Cast-in nozzles for turbines— convergent type

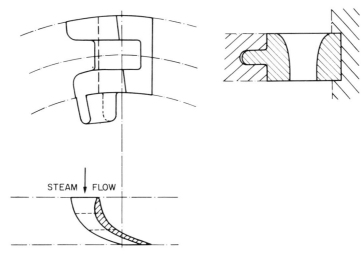

Figure 10.31 Built-up annular nozzles for turbines—convergent type

The discharge area of any one nozzle is the product of the nozzle opening O and the nozzle height h. Hence if there are N nozzles, the total nozzle discharge area is NOh.

Also, if P is the nozzle pitch, α the nozzle angle, and t the thickness of the nozzle division plate, then by simple trigonometry

$$\sin\alpha = \frac{O + t}{P}, \text{ from which } O = P\sin\alpha - t$$

It has already been shown that for high efficiency, the nozzle angle α should be small. If α is small, then $\sin\alpha$ is small, and the nozzle opening O is small, so that for any given total nozzle discharge area, the nozzle height h will be greater than it would have been had the nozzle angle been greater. Thus, the smaller the nozzle angle the greater is the nozzle height.

Now to avoid spillage losses, the blade height must always be slightly greater than the nozzle height, consequently, as the nozzle height increases, the blade height also increases, the maximum blade height which can be tolerated being determined by the maximum centrifugal stress which can be permitted in the blade material. Towards the L.P. end of a turbine, the specific volume of the steam is increasing rapidly, and it is usually necessary to increase the nozzle angle of such stages, thus increasing the nozzle opening, and so permitting the larger steam flow area to be obtained without exceeding the limiting blade height.

For high efficiency, the nozzle angle should be small. For large steam flow area, the nozzle angle may have to be increased.

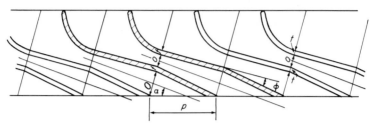

Figure 10.32 Turbine nozzles—convergent-divergent type
Throat opening = o
Discharge opening = 0
Nozzle angle for velocity diagrams = α + φ/2

Figure 10.32 shows one type of convergent–divergent nozzle. Note that the trailing end of the nozzle division plate is, of necessity, inclined at an angle ϕ to the centre line of the nozzle passage. Consequently, for the velocity diagrams, the nozzle angle is taken as $\alpha + (\phi/2)$ (instead of α, as it would be for the nozzles shown in Figures 10.30 and 10.31).

Impulse turbine blades

The blade discharge area may be approached as follows.

Referring to Figure 10.33, suppose the blades to be replaced by dimensionless wires marking only the blade positions x and y say, then the total flow area through the blade annulus is $\pi D_m h$. If the annulus is now bladed, the width of the channel available for steam flow at discharge between any two blades is reduced from P to O. (P is the blade pitch and O the blade opening). Hence the total flow area through the blades at discharge is now $\pi D_m h \, O/P$. Also, for the usual blade form, by simple trigonometry

$$\sin\beta_2 = \frac{O + t}{P}$$

$$\therefore \frac{O}{P} = P \sin \beta_2 - \frac{t}{P}$$

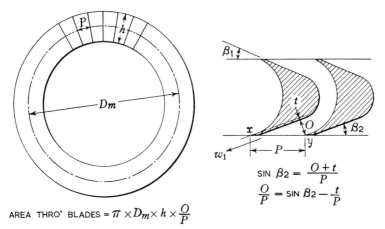

$$\text{AREA THRO' BLADES} = \pi \times D_m \times h \times \frac{O}{P}$$

Figure 10.33 Impulse turbine blade

Steam leaving the blades has a velocity w_2 m/s, and a specific volume v_b depending on its pressure and condition. If the mass flow is M kg/s, then the total blade discharge area A mm² is again calculable from $1000Mv_b = Aw_2$, and the blade height h mm from

$$A = \frac{\pi D_m\, h}{1000}\,\frac{O}{P}, \text{ where } D_m \text{ is the stage mean diameter, m.}$$

It will again be noted that the smaller the blade discharge angle β_2, the smaller is $\sin\beta_2$ and hence the smaller the blade O/P. Hence for any given blade discharge area, a small blade discharge angle gives a large blade height. Towards the exhaust end where the specific volume of the steam is increasing rapidly, larger blade discharge areas (i.e. in the channels between the blades) are required and the blade angles have to be increased, so that the blade heights do not become excessive and create difficulty with centrifugal stress.

It will be clearly noticed on a turbine rotor that the channels between the blades at the L.P. end are much wider than those at the H.P. end, giving the well known appearance of flattening out of those blade sections towards the L.P. end. This feature is quite clearly seen in Figures 3.62 and 3.63.

Partial admission and nozzle grouping

It very often happens that the first or first few stages of impulse H.P. turbines have partial admission; i.e. the entire circumference of the nozzle pitch circle is not occupied by nozzles; only part is occupied by nozzles, the remainder being solid. See Figure 3.29.

Partial admission is adopted for either or both of the following reasons:

1. At the H.P. end, the specific volume of the steam is small and if the whole circumference were occupied by nozzles the resulting nozzle and blade heights may be so small as to create difficulties in manufacture. The solution is therefore to use fewer nozzles, so that greater height is required to give the necessary steam flow area.
2. Certain ships may have to operate for long periods at reduced power or indeed at overload. If the first stage nozzles are divided into a number of groups, each group being controlled by a valve downstream of the manoeuvring valve, the turbine power may be regulated by opening up or closing down nozzle groups, thus reducing to a minimum the need for throttling the steam at the manoeuvring valve. Under these conditions the steam expands usefully over a greater pressure range in the turbines so improving the efficiency.

Overload bypass

Steam turbines are often required to be designed to give overload, i.e. to be capable of developing power in excess of the normal full power. We have already seen, earlier in this chapter, that the power developed by a steam turbine depends on the quantity of steam, kg/s, which is capable of being passed through the nozzle and blade passages. This in turn, depends on the nozzle area and the specific volume of the steam. Referring to Figure 10.34, if the bypass valve is opened and the main steam valve is closed, then H.P. steam, having a small specific volume, is admitted to the fourth stage in which the nozzle area is considerably greater than in the first stage. It is therefore possible to pass considerably more steam through the fourth and succeeding stages than it is at normal full power with the bypass closed, and hence the turbine may be made to develop more power. Under these conditions, the stages preceding the byepass belt run idle—they do not develop any power. The stages before the bypass belt are sometimes called "cruising stages".

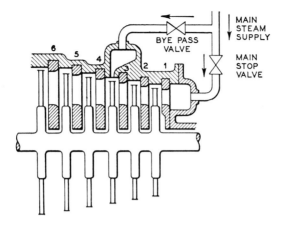

Figure 10.34 Overload bypass

Nowadays, when on overload, almost invariably the by-pass valve and the main steam valve are both open. This still gives a considerable increase in steam quantity through the stages after the bypass, but the stages before the bypass develop some power, and the distribution of the stage pressures, etc., is quite different.

The principles, and the effects on efficiency of power variation by throttling, by nozzle control, and by overload byepass are dealt with in some more detail towards the end of this chapter.

We may now proceed to work through, in detail, a numerical example of an impulse stage.

CALCULATIONS FOR A SINGLE-ROW PURE IMPULSE TURBINE STAGE

The following typical example is intended to make clear the several points discussed earlier in this chapter, and to lead up to important variations.

A single-row pure impulse stage has a mean diameter of 0.762 m and runs at 50 rev/s. The nozzles expand steam from 5.80 bar 180°C to 4.80 bar. The nozzle efficiency is 0.94 and the quantity of steam passing through the stage is 4.762 kg/s. At present, the stage will be treated in isolation, i.e. unaffected by previous or succeeding stages.

Nozzle dimensions

The initial state point for the stage is found on the Mollier Diagram at the intersection of the line of constant pressure 5.80 bar and the line of constant temperature 180°C. A perpendicular from this point to the line of constant pressure 4.80 bar gives the stage adiabatic enthalpy drop $dh_s = 37.2$ kJ/kg (see Figure 10.35).

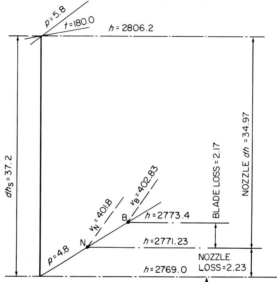

Figure 10.35 *Mollier diagram for nozzle and blades of pure impulse turbine stage having* $u/C_0 = 0.4392$
N = state point of steam at nozzle discharge
B = state point of steam at blade discharge

The nozzle efficiency is 0.94 hence the actual nozzle enthalpy drop

$$dh_N = 0.94 \times 37.2 = 34.97 \text{ kJ/kg}$$

Nozzle loss $= 37.2 - 34.97 = 2.23$ kJ/kg

Actual nozzle discharge velocity

$$C_1 = 44.725\sqrt{34.97} = 264.47 \text{ m/s}$$

Setting down the actual nozzle enthalpy drop on the Mollier Diagram gives the actual state point N at the nozzle discharge and shows that the steam at this point is still in the superheat zone and has a specific volume of 401.8 dm^3/kg.

The total nozzle discharge area

$$= \frac{1000Mv}{C_1}$$

$$= \frac{1000 \times 4.762 \times 401.8}{264.47}$$

$$= 7234.0 \text{ mm}^2$$

Suppose the circumferential pitch of the nozzles to be 44.5 mm,

Then the number of nozzles

$$= \frac{\pi D_m}{P} = \frac{\pi \times 0.762 \times 1000}{44.5}$$

$$= 53.8$$

Say 54 nozzles, hence exact nozzle pitch

$$P = \frac{\pi \times 0.762 \times 1000}{54} = 44.3 \text{ mm}$$

If the nozzle division plate thickness at discharge is made 1.5 mm and the nozzle angle 14°, then from the trigonometrical tables (or the slide rule) sin 14° = 0.2419, and the nozzle opening,

$$O = P \sin \alpha - t = (44.3 \times 0.2419) - 1.5 = 10.7 - 1.5$$
$$= 9.2 \text{ mm}$$

The nozzle height $h = \dfrac{\text{total nozzle discharge area}}{\text{number of nozzles} \times \text{opening}}$

$$= \frac{7234}{54 \times 9.2}$$

$$= 14.56 \text{ mm (see Figure 10.30)}$$

Note that as the nozzle pressure ratio $p_1/p_2 = 4.8/5.8 = 0.828 > 0.5455$, and the steam is superheated throughout, the nozzles are convergent.

Stage velocity diagrams

The velocity diagrams for the stage may now be drawn (Figure 10.36)

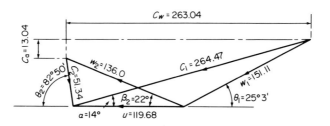

Figure 10.36 Velocity diagrams for single-row pure impulse turbine stage. Velocities are in metres per second

Mean blade velocity

$$u = \pi D_m R = \pi \times 0.762 \times 50 = 119.68 \text{ m/s}$$

The mean blade velocity u is laid down to scale and C_1 drawn in at an angle of $14°$ to u. The entrance triangle is completed by drawing in w_1, the steam velocity relative to the blades at entrance. w_1 may now be scaled from the diagram and the steam angle θ_1 measured by a protractor. Alternatively w_1 and θ_1 may be calculated as follows, with reference to Figure 10.37, which is simply the entrance triangle segregated from the complete diagram, for clarity.

$$w_{1a} = C_1 \sin\alpha = 264.47 \times 0.2419 = 63.98 \text{ m/s}$$

$$\begin{aligned} w_{1u} &= C_1 \cos\alpha - u = (264.47 \times 0.9703) - 119.68 \\ &= 256.63 - 119.68 = 136.95 \text{ m/s} \end{aligned}$$

$$\begin{aligned} \theta_1 &= \tan^{-1} \frac{w_{1a}}{w_{1u}} = \tan^{-1} \frac{63.98}{136.95} = \tan^{-1} 0.4672 \\ &= 25°3' \end{aligned}$$

$$w_1 = \frac{w_{1a}}{\sin\theta_1} = \frac{63.98}{0.4234} = 151.11 \text{ m/s}$$

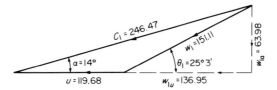

Figure 10.37 Calculation of relative velocity and steam angle at inlet for single-row pure impulse turbine stage

The blade inlet angle β_1 would be made rather greater than the steam angle θ_1 — possibly $28°$, thus giving approximately $3°$ of "cover".

Suppose that in passing over the blade surfaces, the relative velocity is reduced by 10 per cent due to fluid friction, etc., i.e. the blade velocity coefficient $\psi = 0.9$. The relative velocity leaving the blades is

$$w_2 = \psi \, w_1 = 0.9 \times 151.11 = 136.0 \text{ m/s}$$

$$\text{and the blade loss} = \left(\frac{w_1}{44.725}\right)^2 - \left(\frac{w_2}{44.725}\right)^2$$

$$= \left(\frac{151.11}{44.725}\right)^2 - \left(\frac{136.0}{44.725}\right)^2$$

$$= 11.415 - 9.245$$

$$= 2.17 \text{ kJ/kg}$$

Assuming the blade discharge angle β_2 to be $22°$, the relative velocity w_2 may be laid down at an angle of $22°$ to u (Figure 10.38) and the exit triangle completed by drawing in the absolute velocity C_2 of the steam leaving the blades.

The velocity of whirl C_w, the absolute velocity C_2 of the steam leaving the blades and the absolute discharge angle θ_2

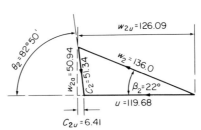

Figure 10.38 Calculation of absolute discharge velocity and angle for single-row pure impulse turbine stage

may be scaled from the diagram (Figure 10.36). Alternatively these may be calculated as follows, with reference to Figure 10.38 which is simply the exit triangle segregated from the complete diagram, for clarity.

$$w_{2u} = w_2 \cos\beta_2 = 136.0 \times 0.9272 = 126.09 \text{ m/s}$$

$$C_{2u} = w_{2u} - u = 126.09 - 119.68 = 6.41 \text{ m/s}$$

$$w_{2a} = w_2 \sin\beta_2 = 136.0 \times 0.3746 = 50.94 \text{ m/s}$$

$$\theta_2 = \tan^{-1} \frac{w_{2a}}{C_{2u}} = \tan^{-1} \frac{50.94}{6.41} = \tan^{-1} 7.949$$
$$= 82°50'$$

$$C_2 = \sqrt{(w_{2a}^2 + C_{2u}^2)} = \sqrt{(50.94^2 + 6.41^2)} = 51.34 \text{ m/s}$$

$$\text{equivalent to } \left(\frac{51.34}{44.725}\right)^2 = 1.32 \text{ kJ/kg}$$

The velocity of whirl

$$C_w = w_{1u} + w_{2u} = 136.95 + 126.09 = 263.04 \text{ m/s}$$

$$\text{The blade work} = \frac{u\, C_w}{1000} = \frac{119.68 \times 263.04}{1000} = 31.48 \text{ kJ/kg}$$

The axial component of the change of velocity

$$C_a = w_{1a} - w_{2a} = 63.98 - 50.94 = 13.04 \text{ m/s}$$

$$\text{The axial thrust} = M\, C_a = 4.762 \times 13.04 = 62.1 \text{ N}$$

The blade work and the axial thrust so calculated, are of course only for the stage under consideration. The axial thrust is ultimately carried on the turbine rotor thrust block, and the friction work done at the thrust block is of course done at the expense of the blade work. The axial thrust is therefore not an internal loss but is an external mechanical loss.

BLADE HEIGHT

Due to the blade loss, the enthalpy of the steam leaving the blades is 2.17 kJ/kg greater than the enthalpy of the steam leaving the nozzles at the same pressure; i.e. in Figure 10.35, the steam leaves the blades at the point B where the specific volume is 402.83 dm^3/kg. The steam velocity relative to the blade at exit is $w_2 = 136.0$ m/s, hence the blade discharge area

$$A = \frac{1000Mv}{w_2} = \frac{1000 \times 4.762 \times 402.83}{136.0} = 14\,106 \text{ mm}^2$$

Suppose the mean blade pitch to be 10.2 mm and the thickness of the discharge edge to be 0.5 mm, then

$$\text{Blade } \frac{O}{P} = \sin \beta_2 - \frac{t}{P}$$

$$= 0.3746 - \frac{0.5}{10.2}$$

$$= 0.3746 - 0.0490$$

$$= 0.3256$$

Clear blade height at discharge

$$h_B = \frac{\text{total blade discharge area}}{\pi D_m \ O/P}$$

$$\therefore \ h_B = \frac{14\,106}{\pi \times 0.762 \times 0.3256 \times 1000} = 18.1 \text{ mm}$$

Blade lap = blade height – nozzle height = 18.10 – 14.56 = 3.54 mm, which is equivalent to

$$\frac{3.54}{14.56} \times 100 = 24.3 \text{ per cent of the nozzle height.}$$

There must always be some blade lap to ensure that steam does not bypass the blades at the tip, or strike the solid blade roots, as this would cause a loss. On the other hand, the blade lap must not be too great, or the steam will, to an excessive extent, spread radially in the blade channels to "fill" the blade discharge area, thus also creating a loss. 25 to 30 per cent lap is considered to be about the maximum acceptable for blade heights of this order. The percentage lap of course diminishes as the blade heights increase.

The nozzle and blade heights calculated above are, as previously stated, based on full all-round admission. If for example, all the nozzles were to be located in the top half of the diaphragm, then the above nozzle and blade heights would be doubled.

LEAVING LOSS

The steam leaves the blades with absolute velocity C_2 m/s, carrying with it kinetic energy

$$= \left(\frac{C_2}{44.725}\right)^2 = \left(\frac{51.34}{44.725}\right)^2 = 1.32 \text{ kJ/kg}$$

This quantity of kinetic energy is a complete loss so far as this particular stage is concerned.

DIAGRAM EFFICIENCY

The adiabatic enthalpy drop for the stage is 37.2 kJ/kg hence the theoretical nozzle discharge velocity $C_0 = 44.725\sqrt{37.2} = 272.5$ m/s. The diagram efficiency

$$= \frac{2u\,C_w}{C_0{}^2} = \frac{2 \times 119.68 \times 263.04}{272.5 \times 272.5} = 0.847$$

(Note also that diagram efficiency =

$$\frac{\text{stage adiabatic enthalpy drop} - \text{nozzle loss} - \text{blade loss} - \text{leaving loss}}{\text{stage adiabatic enthalpy drop}}$$

$$= \frac{37.2 - 2.23 - 2.17 - 1.32}{37.2} = \frac{31.48}{37.2} = 0.847, \text{ as before)}$$

$$\text{Note that the stage } \frac{u}{C_0} = \frac{119.68}{272.5} = 0.4392$$

OTHER STAGE LOSSES

The diagram efficiency is only the first criterion of efficiency. In addition to the diagram losses, there are other losses which do not affect the velocity diagrams, but which must be taken into account before the Mollier Diagram for the stage can be completed.

The nozzle loss, blade loss and leaving loss we have already established in the stage calculations. The other losses are quite complex in nature and any detailed investigation of these is beyond the present scope. The majority of these losses are not susceptible of precise calculation or even of direct measurement, hence they must be established largely by inference, and their overall effect judged by the comparative performance of actual turbines. Nevertheless, it is hoped that the notes in this section will illustrate the effect of the various stage losses on the working and the efficiency of the turbines.

Referring to the pure impulse stage for which we have already carried out some calculations, the stage losses are as follows:

1. *Nozzle loss*:
   2.23 kJ/kg, as already determined
2. *Blade loss*:
   2.17 kJ/kg, as already determined
3. *Leakage loss*:
   This is caused by steam leaking through the diaphragm gland instead of passing through the nozzles. Depending on the gland diameter, the gland clearance and the number of gland fins, a small quantity of steam leaks through the diaphragm gland, and in doing so, is throttled from A to B in Figure 10.39, while the remainder of the steam expands through the nozzles from A to N. In the wheel case, the small quantity of steam with enthalpy B mixes with the large quantity of steam having enthalpy N, resulting in a mixed enthalpy C. The perpendicular distance between N and C is the leakage loss. In the present instance, let us allow a leakage loss of 0.8 kJ/kg.

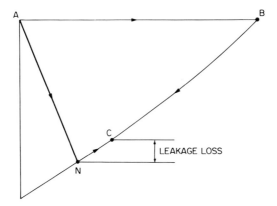

Figure 10.39 Leakage loss

4. *Spillage loss*:

This is due to steam from the nozzle discharge spilling over the shroud ring, and/or passing through balance holes in the disc. This means that a small quantity of high-velocity steam from the nozzles is baffled through the spill paths, and ultimately has its velocity reduced to approximately C_2 without having done any work. The kinetic energy therefore goes back into the steam as heat.

The spillage loss depends on the blade lap, on the axial clearance between the shroud ring and the face of the diaphragm and on the number and size of the balance holes in the disc. In the present instance, let us allow a spillage loss of 0.3 kJ/kg.

5. *Disc friction and windage loss*:

This is due to the fast-moving surfaces of the disc "rubbing" on the steam in the wheel case, to the centrifugal pumping action of the disc on the steam, and to the "fanning" action of those of the blades which are not covered by nozzles. This loss should also include a share of the energy required to drive the astern turbine idle in the ahead direction. The magnitude of this loss depends on the stage diameter and speed, on the density of the steam in the wheel case and on the admission ratio. In the present instance, let us allow a total of 0.27 kJ/kg for the disc friction and windage loss.

6. *Wetness loss*:

If the steam is wet, the water particles themselves do not have sufficient energy to enable them to acquire anything like the same velocity as the steam, and the water has therefore to be accelerated at the expense of the steam. Water particles striking the blades can oppose the blade motion. Matters are further complicated by flashing of the water as the pressure falls. A rule laid down many years ago appears to give satisfactory results, and is still in general use, viz. a wetness correction factor equal to the dryness fraction at the blade discharge is applied. In the present instance, the steam remains in the superheat zone throughout, hence there is no wetness loss.

7. *Leaving loss*:

1.32 kJ/kg as already determined.

In drawing a turbine condition curve, it is customary to assume that for any one stage, the energy available (adiabatic enthalpy drop) is either converted to work, or appears as lower-grade heat in the steam. This assumption is perfectly justifiable, except for the leaving loss, which is a little more troublesome. Referring to Figure 10.40(a), which regards the stage in isolation, the nozzle loss and blade loss are stepped up in that order, from the lower end of the adiabatic line so that the correct specific volume points N and B for the nozzles and blades may be found. Thereafter, the remaining losses may be stepped up in any order. (In Figure 10.40(a) the leaving loss has been shown last, for the purpose of the present explanation).

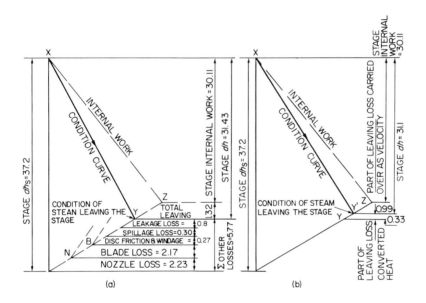

Figure 10.40 Mollier diagram for a single-row pure impulse turbine stage, showing losses
(a) Leaving velocity as a total loss
(b) 75.0 per cent of leaving velocity carried over

Since we are regarding the stage in isolation, the leaving loss is a velocity, which strictly speaking, cannot be shown on the Mollier Diagram, since any state point on the latter is enthalpy, irrespective of whether the steam is at rest or is moving with high velocity. On the other hand, if we try to show the stage useful internal work on the Mollier Diagram, we must show the heat equivalent of the leaving loss. Hence, in Figure 10.40(a), XY is the true condition curve since Y shows the condition of the steam leaving the stage. The line XZ does not in fact exist at all, but is merely a "ghost" line, whose sole purpose is to show the useful internal work done by the stage.

Now, the ratio dh/dh_s is as usual, the efficiency ratio of the stage as a Rankine Cycle, and in practice is always called the *stage efficiency*.

Hence, by putting stage efficiency = dh/dh_s we are in fact crediting the stage with giving us not only the useful internal work (kJ/kg) but the heat equivalent (kJ/kg) of the leaving velocity as well.

If there is only this one stage, the heat equivalent of the leaving loss cannot be used, hence

$$\text{nett internal work} = dh - \text{leaving loss, and the}$$

$$\text{True internal efficiency ratio} = \frac{dh - \text{leaving loss}}{dh_s}$$

$$= \frac{dh}{dh_s} - \frac{\text{leaving loss}}{dh_s}$$

$$= \text{Stage efficiency} - \frac{\text{leaving loss}}{dh_s}$$

If however the stage is followed by another stage, the internal work and the condition line XY do not change, but if the succeeding stage can use all of the leaving loss, then we are quite justified in crediting the first stage with its leaving loss. The stage efficiency, dh/dh_s, is then the true efficiency.

Generally in practice not all of the leaving velocity can be carried over as velocity to the next stage. There are always some shock losses which result in reconversion of part of the leaving velocity to heat in the steam. Figure 10.41 shows how the nozzle inlet angle of the next stage is arranged to minimise the shock loss. In the present instance let us assume that 75.0 per cent of the leaving velocity is carried over as velocity to the next stage, and 25.0 per cent is reconverted to heat, i.e.

Carry over = 0.75 × 1.32   = 0.99 kJ/kg

Leaving loss not carried over = 0.25 × 1.32 = 0.33 kJ/kg

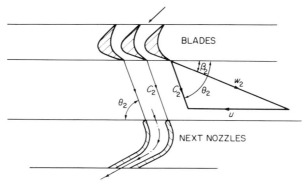

Figure 10.41 Nozzle design to receive steam at C_2 and θ_2 from previous stage with minimum shock loss

The latter figure is stepped up on the Mollier Diagram, giving us the final state point Y' of the steam leaving the stage and the true condition line XY' in Figure 10.40(b).

$$\text{The stage efficiency} = \frac{dh}{dh_s} = \frac{31.1}{37.2} = 0.836$$

The stage internal work $= dh -$ carry-over $= 31.1 - 0.99$
$$= 30.11 \text{ kJ/kg}$$

[Note that the ratio $\dfrac{\text{stage internal work}}{\text{stage } dh} = \dfrac{dh - \text{carry-over}}{dh}$

$$= 1 - \frac{\text{carry-over}}{dh}$$

The term $1 - \dfrac{\text{carry-over}}{dh}$ is called the *carry-over factor*,

which in this case is $1 - \dfrac{0.99}{31.1} = 1 - 0.03183 = 0.96817$, i.e.

Stage internal work $=$ stage $dh \times$ carry-over factor
$$= \text{stage } dh_s \times \text{ stage efficiency} \times$$
$$\text{carry-over factor}$$
$$= 37.2 \times 0.836 \times 0.96817$$
$$= 30.11 \text{ kJ/kg}$$

[Note also that if the dryness fraction at the blade discharge had been, say, 0.98, we would have to apply a wetness correction factor of 0.98 to the above. For this reason, the stage efficiency described above is sometimes called the *dry* stage efficiency].

The steam leaving the stage passes on to the nozzles of the next stage, the calculations for which are carried out in a similar manner. Where there is carry-over velocity entering any stage, it is converted to its equivalent enthalpy drop and added to the stage adiabatic enthalpy drop, C_0 and all the stage calculations are based on this increased value, but the Mollier Diagram is still drawn for the initial and final *enthalpy* conditions, as explained.

The foregoing section attempts to illustrate an arbitrarily chosen pure impulse stage, the dimensions of which are shown in Figure 10.42. Apart from the need to introduce the conception of carry-over, the stage is treated in isolation. We may now consider in some detail what modifications it is possible to make to the stage design to improve the efficiency and what price we have to pay for any such improvement.

The diagram efficiency is the first criterion, and the next section deals with this aspect.

Effect of varying the value of u/C_0 in a pure impulse stage

We have already seen that a pure impulse stage theoretically attains maximum efficiency when $u/C_0 = \frac{1}{2}\cos\alpha$, which in the last example would give,

$$\text{best } \frac{u}{C_0} = \tfrac{1}{2}\cos 14° = \frac{0.9703}{2} = 0.4851$$

whereas we actually used stage $u/C_0 = 0.4392$, i.e. less than the theoretically ideal value.

Let us now therefore retain the same steam flow, mean diameter and speed, same nozzle angle and nozzle efficiency, same blade discharge angle and blade velocity coefficient and the same initial steam conditions, but let u/C_0 be increased to the theoretically ideal value of 0.4851.

The mean blade velocity is as before $u = 119.68$ m/s, hence theoretical nozzle discharge velocity

$$C_0 = \frac{119.68}{0.4851} = 246.68 \text{ m/s}$$

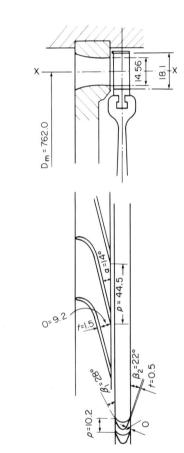

Figure 10.42 Dimensions of single-row pure impulse turbine Circumferential section at XX

From which the stage adiabatic enthalpy drop

$$dh_s = \left(\frac{246.68}{44.725}\right)^2 = 30.42 \text{ kJ/kg}$$

Actual nozzle enthalpy drop

$$dh_N = 0.94 \times 30.42 = 28.59 \text{ kJ/kg}$$

Actual nozzle discharge velocity

$$C_1 = 44.725 \sqrt{28.59} = 239.12 \text{ m/s}$$

Nozzle loss $= 30.42 - 28.59 = 1.83 \text{ kJ/kg}$

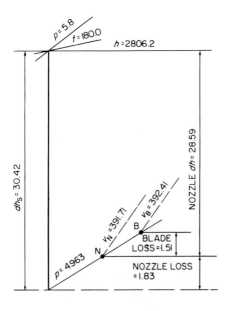

Figure 10.43 Mollier diagram for nozzles and blades of pure impulse turbine stage having $u/C_0 = \frac{1}{2} \cos \alpha$

To accommodate the reduced stage adiabatic enthalpy drop, the final stage pressure has to be increased from 4.8 bar to 4.963 bar (see Figure 10.43). The specific volume at the nozzle discharge is $v_N = 391.71 \text{ dm}^3/\text{kg}$, hence

Total nozzle discharge area

$$A_N = \frac{1000 \times 4.762 \times 391.71}{239.14} = 7800.2 \text{ mm}^2$$

Assuming the same number, pitch, etc. of nozzles,

$$\text{Nozzle discharge height} = \frac{7800.2}{54 \times 9.2} = 15.702 \text{ mm}$$

The velocity diagrams may now be drawn and the relevant calculations carried out (see Figure 10.44).

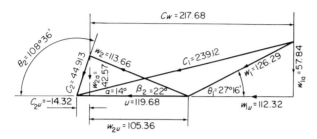

Figure 10.44 Velocity diagrams for single-row pure impulse turbine stage having $u/C_0 = \frac{1}{2}\cos\alpha$

$$w_{1a} = C_1 \sin\alpha = 239.12 \times 0.2419 = 57.84 \text{ m/s}$$

$$w_{1u} = C_1 \cos\alpha - u = (239.12 \times 0.9703) - 119.68$$

$$= 232.0 - 119.68$$

$$= 112.32 \text{ m/s}$$

$$\theta_1 = \tan^{-1}\frac{w_{1a}}{w_{1u}} = \tan^{-1}\frac{57.84}{112.32} = \tan^{-1} 0.515 = 27°16'$$

$$w_1 = \frac{w_{1a}}{\sin\theta_1} = \frac{57.84}{0.4580} = 126.29 \text{ m/s}$$

$$w_2 = \psi\, w_1 = 0.9 \times 126.29 = 113.66 \text{ m/s}$$

Blade loss

$$w_1 - w_2 = \left(\frac{126.29}{44.725}\right)^2 - \left(\frac{113.66}{44.725}\right)^2 = 7.98 - 6.47$$

$$= 1.51 \text{ kJ/kg}$$

Specific volume at blade discharge $v_B = 392.41 \text{ dm}^3/\text{kg}$

Total blade discharge area

$$A_B = \frac{1000 \times 4.762 \times 392.41}{113.66} = 16\,442 \text{ mm}^2$$

Blade discharge height

$$= \frac{16\,442}{\pi \times 0.762 \times 0.3256 \times 1000} = 21.09 \text{ mm}$$

Blade lap $= 21.09 - 15.702 = 5.388$ mm $= 34.2$ per cent

$w_{2a} = w_2 \sin\beta_2 = 113.66 \times 0.3746 = 42.57$ m/s

$w_{2u} = w_2 \cos\beta_2 = 113.66 \times 0.9272 = 105.36$ m/s

$C_{2u} = w_{2u} - u = 105.36 - 119.68 = -14.32$ m/s

$C_2 = \sqrt{w_{2a}^2 + C_{2u}^2} = \sqrt{42.57^2 + (-14.32)^2} = 44.913$ m/s

$$180° - \theta_2 = \sin^{-1}\frac{w_{2a}}{C_2} = \sin^{-1}\frac{42.57}{44.913} = \sin^{-1}0.9478$$
$$= 71°24'$$

$\therefore \theta_2 = 108°36'$

$$\text{Leaving loss} = \left(\frac{C_2}{44.725}\right)^2 = \left(\frac{44.913}{44.725}\right)^2 = 1.01 \text{ kJ/kg}$$

Axial thrust $= (w_{1a} - w_{2a})\, M = 4.762\,(57.84 - 42.57)$
$$= 4.762 \times 15.27 = 72.51 \text{ N}$$

Velocity of whirl

$$C_w = w_{1u} + w_{2u} = 112.32 + 105.36 = 217.68 \text{ m/s}$$

Diagram efficiency

$$\frac{2u\,C_w}{C_0^2} = \frac{2 \times 119.68 \times 217.68}{246.68 \times 246.68} = 0.8563$$

$$\text{Blade work} = \frac{u\,C_w}{1000} = \frac{119.68 \times 217.68}{1000} = 26.05 \text{ kJ/kg}$$

The blade work is reduced but the diagram efficiency is increased.

If we choose various values of u/C_0 and carry out the above stage calculations for each, we may plot the diagram efficiency η_D, the stage adiabatic enthalpy drop dh_s, and the absolute discharge velocity C_2 on a base of u/C_0. These curves are shown in Figure 10.45, from which the following important conclusions may be drawn.

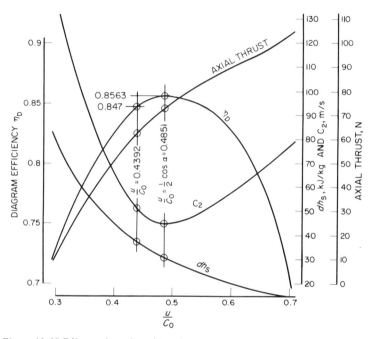

Figure 10.45 Effects of varying u/C_0 of a pure impulse turbine stage

(i) For a single-row pure impulse stage working under the given conditions, $u/C_0 = 0.4851$ represents the best that can be done so far as the diagram efficiency of the stage is concerned, giving a diagram efficiency of 0.8563.

    0.4851 is the *optimum* u/C_0, i.e. that u/C_0 which gives maximum diagram efficiency under a given set of conditions.

    In what follows later, we shall be referring back to these optimum values of u/C_0 and diagram efficiency.

(ii) Originally, the stage dealt with an adiabatic enthalpy drop of 37.2 kJ/kg and had $u/C_0 = 0.4392$ which gave a diagram efficiency of 0.847. By increasing u/C_0 to

0.4851, the diagram efficiency is increased to 0.8563, but the stage will deal with an adiabatic enthalpy drop of only 30.42 kJ/kg.

The stage uses less heat and does less work but does it more efficiently.

The implications of these conclusions may now be examined.

Suppose we have a turbine consisting of eight of the original stages. For convenience let us assume that each of the eight stages behaves in the same way as our original stage, i.e. each stage deals with an adiabatic enthalpy drop of 37.2 kJ/kg and has a diagram efficiency of 0.847.

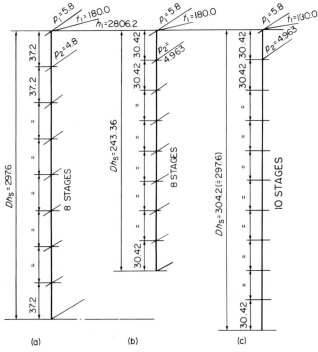

Figure 10.46 Effect of varying u/C_0 on the staging of single-row pressure-compounded pure impulse turbines
(a) $u/C_0 = 0.4392$
Blade work = 297.6 × 0.847 = 252.05 kJ/kg
(b) $u/C_0 = 0.4851$
Blade work = 243.36 × 0.8563 = 208.37 kJ/kg
(c) $u/C_0 = 0.4851$
Blade work = 297.6 × 0.8563 = 254.81 kJ/kg

If we retain the same number of stages, the same stage dimensions and speed, and only alter each u/C_0 to 0.485, then the result is shown in Figure 10.46(b). The stages each operate more efficiently, but each deals with only 30.42 kJ/kg, hence the eight stages together cannot utilise the full overall adiabatic enthalpy drop and therefore cannot produce the required blade work of 252.05 kJ/kg.

If however we add two more stages, as shown in Figure 10.46(c), the ten stages together can utilise the full overall adiabatic heat drop and can produce 1.1 per cent *more* blade work per 1.0 kg of steam than the original turbine (a). Turbine (c) will require 1.1 per cent less steam, and therefore 1.1 per cent less fuel than (a), but at the expense of requiring ten stages instead of eight.

(*Note*: To maintain the given initial steam conditions and final pressure, we should of course have to make each stage $dh_s = 297.6/10 = 29.76$ kJ/kg. Figure 10.45 shows that this would not cause the diagram efficiency to differ sensibly from the optimum value).

From the efficiency viewpoint, the original turbine is said to be *under-staged*.

We could, instead of adding two more stages, increase the mean diameters, i.e. eight stages, each having $u/C_0 = 0.4851$, and each dealing with an adiabatic enthalpy drop of 37.2 kJ/kg.

Hence $C_0 = 44.725 \sqrt{37.2} = 272.5$ m/s, and

$$u = 272.5 \times 0.4851 = 132 \text{ m/s and}$$

$$\text{Average mean diameter} = 0.762 \times \frac{132}{119.68} = 0.8405 \text{ m}$$

Alternatively we could retain eight stages having the original mean diameter 0.762 mm, and increase the speed to $50 \times 132/119.68 = 55.33$ rev/s.

Instead of either of the above we could use any combination of extra stage(s), mean diameter and speed.

Note that under-staging is usually dictated by the need—for first-cost or other reasons—to minimise the turbine diameter, length and speed, at the expense of operating efficiency.

Although it is possible to imagine a turbine which is *over-staged*, it is not likely to be encountered in practice. Such a turbine would have greater dimensions and/or speed, and lower efficiency, and would therefore lose on both first cost and running cost. Figure 10.47 shows the comparative velocity diagrams for the three conditions.

Note that in Figures 10.44, 10.45 and 10.47(b), when u/C_0 is ideal, C_2, and hence the stage *leaving loss* is a minimum. Note also from Figure 10.45 that the value of u/C_0 for maximum efficiency of a pure impulse stage does not differ sensibly from $\frac{1}{2}\cos\alpha$.

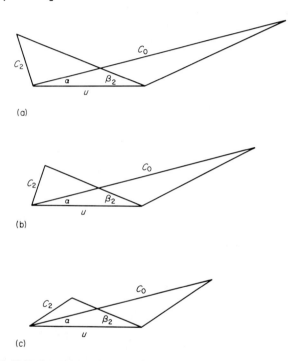

Figure 10.47 Understaging and overstaging of single-row, pressure-compounded pure impulse turbines
(a) Understaged $u/C_0 < \frac{1}{2}\cos\alpha$
(b) Optimum $u/C_0 = \frac{1}{2}\cos\alpha$
(c) Overstaged $u/C_0 > \frac{1}{2}\cos\alpha$

REACTION TURBINES

It is worthwhile to repeat that in this section, the meaning of the term *reaction turbine* is the traditionally accepted meaning, viz., a turbine having 50 per cent impulse and 50 per cent reaction.

A reaction stage can be approached by the same general methods as an impulse stage, but there are some important differences which must be understood.

Earlier in this chapter, we saw that, for maximum efficiency, a single-row impulse stage should have the mean blade velocity about one half of the steam velocity corresponding to the stage adiabatic enthalpy drop, or to be more correct $u/C_0 = \frac{1}{2}\cos\alpha$, where α is the nozzle angle. Theoretically, for maximum efficiency, a reaction stage should have $u/c_0 = \cos\alpha$, and since α is generally quite a small angle, $\cos\alpha$ is relatively large, hence the steam velocity is more nearly equal to the mean blade velocity. The underlying reason for this important difference may perhaps best be appreciated firstly by reference to Figure 10.48 which shows an imaginary pure reaction turbine with the steam jets in the plane of the wheel, i.e. $\alpha = 0$.

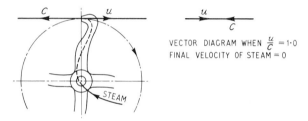

Figure 10.48 *Maximum efficiency of a pure reaction stage*

Maximum efficiency is achieved when *all* the kinetic energy of the steam jets is utilised in driving the rotor, i.e. when the final velocity of the steam is zero. This can be so only when the blade velocity is equal to the steam velocity, i.e. when $u/C_0 = 1.0$.

The vectors u and C_0 are then two equal coincident straight lines and the efficiency is 1.0 (i.e. 100 per cent).

Practical reaction turbine arrangement is such that α cannot be zero, nor can the running blades have 100 per cent reaction. The nozzle angle α may be anywhere between $14°$ and $35°$, and the running blades have 50 per cent reaction; i.e. one half of the stage adiabatic enthalpy drop takes place in the running blades. The effect of these is to make the theoretical optimum value of $u/c_0 = \cos\alpha$, where c_0 is the theoretical steam velocity generated by *one half* of the stage adiabatic enthalpy drop.

To emphasise an important point
An impulse stage has optimum

$$\frac{u}{C_0} = \tfrac{1}{2}\cos\alpha, \text{ where } C_0 = 44.725\ \sqrt{(dh_s)}$$

A reaction stage has optimum

$$\frac{u}{c_0} = \cos\alpha, \text{ where } c_0 = 44.725\ \sqrt{\left(\frac{dh_s}{2}\right)}$$

Staging of reaction turbines

A traditional reaction stage consists of one row of fixed blades and one row of moving blades of identical blade section, and having equal blade discharge angles. Basically, one half of the stage adiabatic enthalpy drop is converted to kinetic energy in the fixed blades (which correspond to the nozzles of an impulse turbine stage), and one half in the moving blades (which therefore also function as moving nozzles, giving something of the effect shown in Figure 10.48).

Let us examine the implications of the differences between an impulse stage and a reaction stage. Assume the two stages to be of equal mean diameter and to run at the same speed, i.e. the two stages have equal mean blade velocity u.

For the impulse stage

$$u/C_0 \doteqdot \tfrac{1}{2}, \text{ i.e. } C_0 \doteqdot 2u, \text{ and } C_0 = 44.725\ \sqrt{(dh_s)}, \text{ hence}$$

$$44.725\ \sqrt{(dh_s)} \doteqdot 2u, \text{ from which } dh_s \doteqdot 4\left(\frac{u}{44.725}\right)^2$$

For the reaction stage

$$\frac{u}{c_0} \doteqdot 1 \text{ i.e. } c_0 \doteqdot u, \text{ and } c_0 = 44.725\ \sqrt{\left(\frac{dh_s}{2}\right)}, \text{ hence}$$

$$44.725\ \sqrt{\left(\frac{dh_s}{2}\right)} \doteqdot u, \text{ from which } dh_s \doteqdot 2\left(\frac{u}{44.725}\right)^2$$

Thus for a given mean blade velocity (i.e. given mean diameter and speed), the stage adiabatic enthalpy drop with which the reaction stage can deal is *one half* of that with which an impulse stage can deal. This means that for any given initial steam conditions, exhaust pressure, mean diameter and speed, *a reaction turbine would have twice the number of stages of an impulse turbine.*

In practice of course, it does not follow that we need always compare impulse and reaction turbines on the basis of the same mean blade velocity; we could use greater mean diameters or higher running speeds. The principle remains however, that in going from impulse to reaction, we must increase *something*, whether it be the number of stages, or the mean diameters, or the running speed, or indeed all three of these. In general, a reaction turbine for given initial steam conditions has significantly more stages than an impulse turbine for the same conditions.

Reaction blading

The front and back profiles of the usual reaction blade section are composed of a series of blended curves of different radii, the passages between blades being curved and converging. The stage adiabatic enthalpy drops in a reaction turbine are relatively small, and since the fixed blades (nozzles) and the moving blades each deal with one half of the stage adiabatic enthalpy drop, the pressure drop across either a fixed or a moving blade row is small, critical expansion is never reached, hence only *convergent* passages are required.

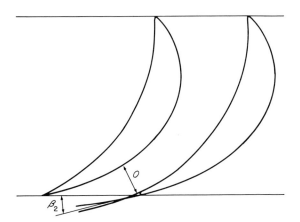

Figure 10.49 Discharge angle of reaction type blades

Referring to Figure 10.49, the front and back surface curves extend right up to the tail of the blade section, hence the discharge angle is not so clearly defined as it is in say the impulse nozzles and blades illustrated in Figure 10.42. Since expansion is continuous through both the fixed and moving blades, the steam "fills" the channels between blades, and it is therefore customary to take the blade discharge angle as the mean between the tangents to the two curves at the theoretical tail point.

Also because of the continuous blended curves forming the front and back surfaces, the calculation of the blade O/P is much more involved than it is for the usual type of impulse nozzles and blades.

Steam flow area

The fixed blades of a reaction stage function in exactly the same way as the nozzles of an impulse stage, and the total discharge area is found by exactly the same methods, except that the steam velocity and specific volume are based on *one half* of the stage adiabatic enthalpy drop.

The total discharge area through the moving blades also is found by the same method as for impulse blades except that the area is based on the relative velocity w_2 and the specific volume *after expansion* in the moving blades.

The relation $A = \pi D_m\, h\, O/P$ also is valid for both the fixed and moving blades of a reaction stage, but if the blades are radial-clearance blades (i.e. do not have a shroud ring), the blade height h calculated from this expression has to be corrected to take into account that part of the steam flow which passes through the radial clearance.

As for impulse turbines, it is generally necessary to increase the blade discharge angles towards the exhaust end—where the specific volume of the steam is increasing more rapidly— to obtain sufficient area without having to use excessive blade heights.

Because of the continuous nature of the expansion, partial admission cannot be used in a reaction stage. Since the steam velocities c_1 and w_2 leaving the fixed and moving blades respectively are approximately equal, and since there is a relatively small increase in specific volume at the moving blade compared with the fixed blade, it follows that the total area through the moving blades must always be approximately equal to, or only slightly greater than the total area through the fixed blades. The fixed and moving blades have identical blade sections and equal discharge angles, hence the height of the moving blades must be approximately equal to the height of the fixed blades. Now there is a pressure drop through the moving blades, and this pressure drop must take place through *all* the moving blades of the stage. If the fixed blades were made for say 50 per cent partial admission, the pressure drop through the fixed blades would be confined within 50 per cent of the circumference of the blade annulus, but the pressure drop through the moving blades cannot confine itself to 50 per cent of the moving blade annulus — it will take place all round the moving blades. To give approximately equal fixed and moving blade areas, this would imply that the moving blade height would be only one half of the fixed blade height—an absurd and impossible condition. For these reasons, reaction turbines always have full all-round admission, and power variation by nozzle control is therefore not possible.

Velocity diagrams for a reaction stage

The velocity diagrams for a reaction stage have the appearance shown in Figure 10.50(b).

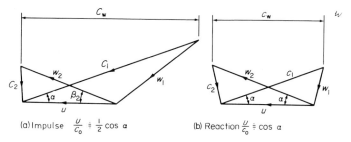

(a) Impulse $\frac{U}{C_0} \doteq \frac{1}{2} \cos a$ (b) Reaction $\frac{U}{C_0} \doteq \cos a$

Figure 10.50 Relative work done in impulse and reaction stages having equal mean blade velocity and equal nozzle and blade angles
(a) Impulse $u/C_0 \doteq \frac{1}{2} \cos \alpha$
(b) Reaction $u/c_0 \doteq \cos \alpha$

If the blade velocity and the blade angles are assumed to be the same as for the single-row pure impulse stage in Figure 10.50(a), then the steam velocity c_0 for the reaction stage, and hence the velocity of whirl c_w are only about one-half of those for the impulse stage. The work done on the blades is proportional to c_w, hence two reaction stages are required to deal with the same enthalpy drop dealt with by one single-row impulse stage.

Another interesting feature of the velocity diagrams for a reaction stage is the relative proportion of blade work done by the impulse force and by the reaction force. Referring to Figure 10.51, if there were no reaction, the relative velocity

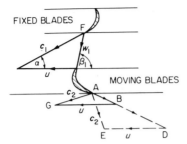

*Figure 10.51 Velocities in a reaction
turbine stage*

leaving the moving blade would be $AB(= \psi w_1)$ and the exit
triangle would be ABG. The expansion through the moving
blades, however, increases the relative velocity of the steam
leaving the moving blades to

$$AD = \psi w_1 + 44.725 \sqrt{\left(\frac{k\ dh_s}{2}\right)}$$

giving an exit triangle ADE.

Figure 10.52 shows these diagrams superposed on a
common u. The total change of velocity through the stage
is $F(A)$. This total is made up of the impulse component FA
and the reaction component $A(A)$. The velocity of whirl
c_w is the sum of the components of these two in the direction

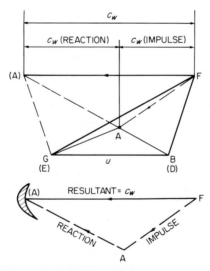

*Figure 10.52 Proportions of blade work due
to impulse and reaction in a reaction turbine
stage*

of motion. The components of FA and $A(A)$ at right angles to the direction of motion cancel one another since they are equal and of opposite sign. In this type of reaction stage therefore, there is no *impulse thrust*.

Since however in any stage having any degree of reaction, there is a pressure drop across each row of moving blades, there is an axial thrust equal to the product of the pressure drop and the blade annulus area. The sum of the axial thrusts across each moving row is called the *reaction thrust* and acts towards the exhaust end. The reaction thrust can be quite considerable, often requiring a dummy cylinder to balance it (see 490).

Steam leaves the moving blades with absolute velocity c_2 (denoted by $A(E)$ in Figure 10.52) carrying with it kinetic energy $(c_2/44.725)^2$ kJ/kg.

This kinetic energy is lost so far as this particular stage is concerned. The leading edges of the next stage fixed blades however are arranged as nearly as practicable to receive the steam at the absolute discharge angle, and it is therefore possible to *carry over* quite a large part of c_2 as *velocity* to the next stage. The remaining part of c_2, which is not carried over as velocity, is destroyed by shock between the fixed moving blades, and is reconverted to heat which goes back into the steam.

Reaction turbine blading arrangements

There are several ways in which a reaction turbine may be arranged. Basically, each reaction stage (or reaction *pair*) should have its own dimensions based on much the same principles as an impulse stage, with the mean diameters, blade heights and blade discharge angles continually increasing towards the exhaust end to accommodate the larger volume of steam as the pressure diminishes. Reaction turbines are often designed in this manner, the turbine casing, and possibly also the rotor, being coned accordingly. The turbine then has the appearance of the ahead turbine illustrated in Figure 3.38, page 77. Another method is to design the turbine with several *expansions*, each expansion consisting of a number of reaction pairs of constant mean diameter and constant blade height. The reaction turbines shown in Figures 3.35, 3.36 and 3.37 in Chapter 3 are arranged in this manner. While not theoretically correct, this system was adopted for convenience and economy of manufacture.

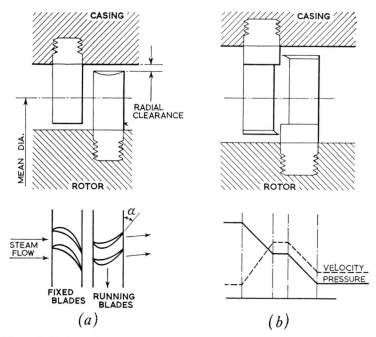

Figure 10.53 A reaction stage
(a) with radial clearance blading
(b) with end-tightened blading

Figure 10.53(a) illustrates one stage of the ordinary type of reaction blading. There is no shroud ring, and for practical reasons, a radial clearance of about 0.5 mm is necessary between the tips of the moving blades and the casing bore and between the tips of the fixed blades and the rotor diameter. The tips of both fixed and moving blades are thinned to minimise contact and subsequent damage in the event of a rub. This type of reaction blading is called *radial-clearance* blading, and the radial clearance is responsible for one of the most significant losses in reaction turbines viz., *blade-tip leakage*. A proportion of the steam passes through the clearance space at the tips of the fixed blades, adversely affecting expansion and direction of steam through the latter. A proportion of steam passes through the clearance space at the tips of the moving blades without doing work on the latter. Blade tip leakage is most serious at the H.P. end, where the blade heights and blade discharge angles are small, and the clearance area is therefore a larger proportion of the steam flow area through the blade channels. Also the pressure drop across any row of blades is likely to be greater at the H.P. than at the L.P. end.

To reduce this large blade-tip leakage loss, the H.P. section—and possibly all or part of the I.P. section—of the turbine may be fitted with *end-tightened* blading as illustrated in Figure 10.53(b). The blade tips are fitted with a shroud ring having a sharp edge running about 0.07–0.13 mm clear of the adjacent blade root. The leakage area is thus considerably reduced, so materially reducing the tip leakage loss compared with radial-clearance blading. An adjusting gear is provided to enable the rotor to be moved axially, to increase the blade-tip axial clearance to about 1.5 mm for manoeuvring, when sudden temperature variation and rotor vibration might otherwise cause a rub between fixed and moving elements. In the event of such a rub, the sharp edge of the shroud ring ensures minimum contact between fixed and moving elements, thus minimising damage.

Another method of minimising blade tip leakage is to replace a number of the first H.P. stages by a 2-row impulse stage. This arrangement, shown in Figure 10.54, also has the advantage of considerably shortening the H.P. turbine. Further, because of the continuous nature of the steam expansion, a reaction turbine must have full all-round admission of steam from the first stage onward. The adoption of a two-row impulse first stage permits nozzle grouping to be used in the first stage. The rotor for such an impulse-reaction turbine is illustrated in Figure 10.54.

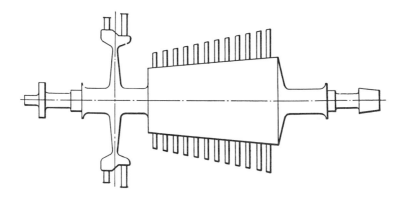

Figure 10.54 Impulse reaction rotor

Axial thrust in reaction turbines

Since, in a reaction turbine, there is a pressure drop across each row of moving blades, there is a considerable *reaction thrust* acting in the axial direction towards the exhaust end. This thrust is often too heavy to be carried by a normal rotor thrust block, and a *dummy cylinder-and-piston* is fitted to balance the reaction thrust. The dummy piston (see Figure 10.55), is a wheel mounted on the rotor at the H.P. end, and connected by an equalising pipe to a turbine stage whose pressure when acting over the annular area of the dummy piston is suitable to balance the reaction thrust. The dummy cylinder and the dummy piston are provided with labyrinth packing, as shown in Figure 10.55 to minimise steam leakage between the turbine cylinder and the dummy cylinder. The steam leaking through the dummy cylinder is of course carried away by the equalising pipe (see Figure 3.57).

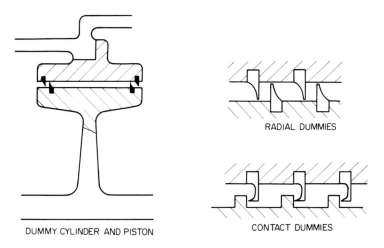

RADIAL DUMMIES

DUMMY CYLINDER AND PISTON

CONTACT DUMMIES

Figure 10.55 Dummy cylinder and piston, and labyrinth packing

H.P. turbines are usually fitted with *contact dummies*, and L.P. and astern turbines with *radial dummies*, for the same reason as end-tightened blading is used on H.P., and radial-clearance blading on L.P. turbines.

Another method of balancing the reaction thrust, used particularly in L.P. turbines is to make the turbine *double-flow*, i.e. the steam flows simultaneously in two opposite directions as shown in Figure 10.56.

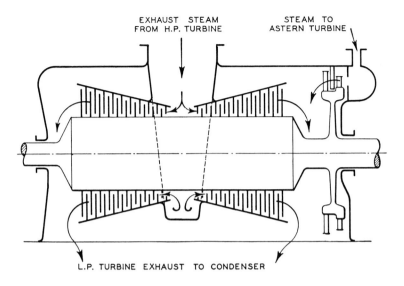

EXHAUST STEAM
FROM H.P. TURBINE

STEAM TO
ASTERN TURBINE

L.P. TURBINE EXHAUST TO CONDENSER

Figure 10.56 Double-flow L.P. turbine

This arrangement also has the advantage that only half the total steam quantity passes through each flow. The stages—and more particularly the last few stages—can therefore have smaller mean diameters, shorter blades and smaller blade angles, thus compensating for increased L.P. turbine length, and maintaining efficiency.

Calculations for a reaction turbine stage

To enable us ultimately to directly compare impulse and reaction stages, let us begin with the same conditions as were used for our original impulse stage; viz. $p_1 = 5.8$ bar, $t_1 = 180.0°C$, $p_2 = 4.8$ bar, $u = 119.68$ m/s. Normally the fixed and moving blades of a reaction stage are identical in section, and again to be comparable, let us assume that the blade discharge angle—which we will denote by α—is $14°$ (as for the impulse stage nozzle angle) and that the blade $O/P = \sin \alpha = 0.2419$.

We have already seen that for the same mean blade velocity, we require two reaction stages to replace one impulse stage. The adiabatic enthalpy drop from 5.8 bar, $180.0°C$ to 4.8 bar is 37.2 kJ/kg, hence each of the two reaction stages has $dh_s = 37.2/2 = 18.6$ kJ/kg. The theoretical steam velocity is based on one half of this, i.e. $c_0 = 44.725\sqrt{9.3} = 136.4$ m/s, hence

$$\frac{u}{c_0} = \frac{119.68}{136.4} = 0.8774$$

For our purpose, we need consider only the first of the two reaction stages, as the behaviour of the second is, in this case, very nearly the same. Setting down the initial steam conditions and adiabatic enthalpy drops on the Mollier

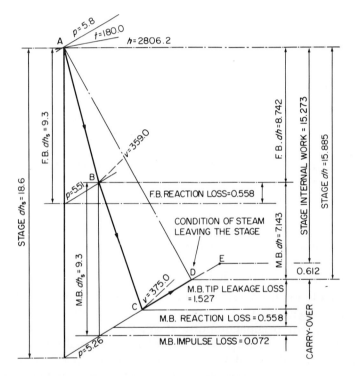

Figure 10.57 Mollier diagram for a reaction turbine stage

Diagram (Figure 10.57) gives the pressure at the fixed blade discharge = 5.51 bar, and at the moving blade discharge = 5.26 bar.

If we assume that the efficiency of expansion in the blades (comparable to nozzle efficiency) is 0.94, then fixed blade actual enthalpy drop

$$= 9.3 \times 0.94 = 8.742 \text{ kJ/kg},$$

and fixed blade expansion loss (nozzle loss)

$$= 9.3 - 8.742 = 0.558 \text{ kJ/kg}$$

Stepping this up on the Mollier Diagram gives the stage point B at the fixed blade discharge, for which the specific volume of the steam = $359.0 \text{ dm}^3/\text{kg}$.

The actual steam velocity c_1 at the fixed blade discharge is

$$c_1 = 44.725 \sqrt{(8.742)} = 132.2 \text{ m/s}$$

If we assume the same mass flow of steam as before, viz. 4.762 kg/s, then total discharge area through the fixed blades = $1000Mv/c_1$

$$= \frac{1000 \times 4.762 \times 359.0}{132.2} = 12932 \text{ mm}^2$$

$$\text{Fixed blade height} = \frac{A}{\pi D_m \ O/P} = \frac{12932}{\pi \times 762 \times 0.2419}$$

$$= 22.34 \text{ mm}$$

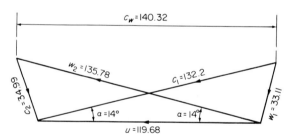

Figure 10.58 Velocity diagrams for a reaction turbine stage

The stage velocity diagrams, Figure 10.58, may be built up as the calculations proceed, vide,

$$w_{1u} = c_1 \cos \alpha - u = (132.2 \times 0.9703) - 119.68 = 8.59 \text{ m/s}$$

$$w_{1a} = c_1 \sin \alpha = 132.2 \times 0.2419 = 31.98 \text{ m/s}$$

$$w_1 = \sqrt{(w_{1u}^2 + w_{1a}^2)} = \sqrt{(8.59^2 + 31.98^2)} = 33.11 \text{ m/s}$$

or in heat units,

$$w_1 = \left(\frac{33.11}{44.725}\right)^2 = 0.548 \text{ kJ/kg}$$

If there were no expansion in the moving blades, then $w_2{}^1 =$ ψw_1 (as for impulse blades). Suppose $\psi = 0.87$, then $w_2{}^1 =$ $0.87 \times 0.548 = 0.476$ kJ/kg, and moving blades impulse loss $= 0.548 - 0.476 = 0.072$ kJ/kg.

There is also however an adiabatic enthalpy drop of 9.3 kJ/kg through the moving blades, and again assuming that the efficiency of expansion is 0.94, gives actual enthalpy drop through moving blades $= 0.94 \times 9.3 = 8.742$ kJ/kg, and moving blades reaction loss $= 9.3 - 8.742 = 0.558$ kJ/kg.

Hence absolute velocity leaving moving blades,

$$w_2 = 0.476 + 8.742 = 9.218 \text{ kJ/kg}$$

$$\therefore w_1 = 44.725 \sqrt{(9.218)} = 135.78 \text{ m/s}$$

Stepping up the moving blade impulse loss and expansion loss on the Mollier Diagram gives the state point D at which the steam leaves the moving blades. The specific volume at D is 375.0 dm³/kg, hence the total discharge area required through the moving blades is

$$A = \frac{1000 \times 4.762 \times 375.0}{135.78} = 13\,152 \text{ mm}^2, \text{ and}$$

$$\text{Moving blade height} = \frac{13\,152}{\pi \times 762.0 \times 0.2419} = 22.71 \text{ mm}$$

From the velocity diagrams, Figure 10.58,

$$w_{2u} = w_2 \cos \alpha = 135.78 \times 0.9703 = 131.73 \text{ m/s}$$

$$w_{2a} = w_2 \sin \alpha = 135.78 \times 0.2419 = 32.845 \text{ m/s}$$

$$c_{2u} = w_{2u} - u = 131.73 - 119.68 = 12.05 \text{ m/s}$$

$$c_2 = \sqrt{(w_{2a}{}^2 + c_{2u}{}^2)} = \sqrt{(32.845^2 + 12.05^2)}$$
$$= 34.99 \text{ m/s},$$

or in heat units,

$$c_2 = \left(\frac{34.99}{44.725}\right)^2 = 0.612 \text{ kJ/kg}$$

Let us assume that all of this is carried-over as velocity to the next stage, i.e. in Figure 10.57, the point E appears on the Mollier Diagram only as a "ghost" point to remind us that in addition to the work output internally at the shaft, the stage gives us 0.612 kJ/kg of kinetic energy in the leaving steam which is available for doing work in the next stage.

$$\text{Velocity of whirl } c_w = w_{1u} + w_{2u} = 8.59 + 131.73$$
$$= 140.32 \text{ m/s}$$

$$\text{Blade work} = \frac{u \; c_w}{1000} = \frac{119.68 \times 140.32}{1000} = 16.792 \text{ kJ/kg}$$

The efficiency of the blading

$$= \frac{\text{blade work}}{\text{stage adiabatic enthalpy drop}}$$

$$= \frac{16.792}{18.6} = 0.9027$$

We can call this the *diagram efficiency*, and obtain it from the usual expression $2uC_w/C_0^2$, where C_0 is based on the *full* stage adiabatic enthalpy drop, vide, $C_0 = 44.725\sqrt{18.6} = 192.88$ m/s

$$\text{Diagram efficiency} = \frac{2 \times 119.68 \times 140.32}{192.88^2} = 0.9027$$

By so doing, we can directly compare impulse and reaction stages by the diagram efficiency as a first criterion.

In addition to the diagram losses, however, we must consider the other losses, since the latter also affect significantly the overall efficiency. The major losses in this category, for a reaction turbine, are

1. Blade tip leakage loss.
2. Axial thrust loss.

Since these two losses are of some importance in what follows, let us examine their effects with reference to the reaction stage under consideration.

BLADE TIP LEAKAGE LOSS
Whether radial-clearance blading or end-tightened blading is used, there must always be some *tip clearance*. This means

that the total flow area = area through the blades + clearance area. The calculated blade heights must therefore be reduced in the proportion that the clearance area bears to the total calculated area. In the present case, we may assume a radial clearance of 0.5 mm, and since both the fixed and moving blade heights have to be corrected for tip leakage, the clearance area may be based on the mean diameter (see Figure 10.53), thus

$$\text{Average clearance area} = \pi \times 762.0 \times 0.5 = 1196.9 \text{ mm}^2$$

$$\text{Average total area} = \frac{12\,932 + 13\,152}{2} = 13\,042 \text{ mm}^2$$

$$\therefore \frac{\text{Average clearance area}}{\text{Average total area}} = \frac{1196.9}{13\,042} = 0.09176, \text{ hence}$$

Corrected fixed blade height

$$= 22.34\,(1 - 0.09176) = 22.34 \times 0.90824 = 20.29 \text{ mm}$$

Corrected moving blade height

$$= 22.71 \times 0.90824 = 20.63 \text{ mm}$$

The steam leaking through the clearance spaces does no work, and this results in a *tip leakage loss*. If we assume the leakage steam to move axially, to expand and to behave generally in the same way as the working steam, then the steam quantities through the blades and through the clearance space are in proportion to the respective areas of flow, i.e. if radial clearance = x,

$$\frac{\text{Leakage steam}}{\text{Working steam}} = \frac{\pi D_m\, x}{\pi D_m\, h\ O/P} = \frac{x}{h\ O/P}$$

that is, the leakage steam is proportional to the clearance x, and the working steam to the moving blade height h and to the blade O/P. Hence the efficiency correction factor for tip leakage

$$= \frac{\text{working steam}}{\text{working steam} + \text{leakage steam}}$$

$$= \frac{h \, O/P}{(h \, O/P) + x} = \frac{1}{1 + \dfrac{x}{h \, O/P}} \text{, which in this case gives}$$

$$\text{Tip leakage factor} = \frac{1}{1 + \dfrac{0.5}{20.63 \times 0.2419}} = \frac{1}{1.10021}$$

$$= 0.909$$

All the *work* is done in the moving blades. If there were no tip leakage loss, the moving blades would do work = diagram blade work = 16.792 kJ/kg because of tip leakage, the moving blades do only 0.909 of this, i.e. 0.909 × 16.792 = 15.265 kJ/kg. The blade tip leakage loss is therefore 16.792 − 15.265 = 1.527 kJ/kg. This also is stepped up on the Mollier Diagram as shown in Figure 10.57. (Note also,

$$\text{Nett blade work} = \text{stage } dh_s \times \text{diagram efficiency} \times \text{tip leakage factor}$$

$$= 18.3 \times 0.9207 \times 0.909$$

$$= 15.3 \text{ kJ/kg})$$

$$\text{The } \textit{stage efficiency} = \frac{dh}{dh_s} = \frac{15.885}{18.6} = 0.8541$$

(Compare with 0.836 for the original pure impulse stage).

AXIAL THRUST LOSS
From the velocity diagrams, Figure 10.58,

$$C_a = w_{1a} - w_{2a} = 31.98 - 32.845 = -0.865 \text{ m/s, hence}$$

$$\text{Impulse thrust} = -0.865 \times 4.762 = -4.12 \text{ N}$$

Because of the pressure drop across the moving blades however, there is a *reaction thrust* equal to the product of the pressure drop across the moving blades and the moving blade annulus area, thus

$$\text{Pressure drop across moving blades} = 5.51 - 5.26$$
$$= 0.25 \text{ bar}$$

$$\text{Moving blade annulus area} = \pi \times 0.762 \times \frac{20.5}{1000}$$

$$= 0.04908 \text{ m}^2$$

$\therefore$ Reaction thrust $= 0.25 \times 10^5 \times 0.04908 = 1226.9$ N

$\therefore$ *Resultant axial thrust* $= 1226.9 - 4.12 = 1222.78$ N, towards exhaust end.

This is the axial thrust for the stage under consideration. The total axial thrust is the sum of the thrusts of all the stages and the total axial thrust *loss* also depends on the speed, size, condition and lubrication of the rotor thrust. Since we cannot deal with all these we will use the resultant axial thrust as indicative of the thrust loss.

This rather extreme example illustrates the serious blade tip leakage loss due to using radial-clearance blading where the blade heights are small. A loss of this magnitude would not be contemplated, and even with end-tightened blades of this height, the tip leakage loss could be significant. In modern marine steam turbines, the use of radial-clearance blades is confined to the last, or the last two reaction-type L.P. stages, where the blade heights are large compared with the radial clearance (see Figure 10.53, page 488).

The axial thrust loss of a reaction turbine is considerably greater than that for an impulse turbine. If the axial thrust is balanced by a dummy, an efficiency correction for dummy leakage is still required. If the axial thrust is balanced by going to a double-flow turbine, the turbine is longer and more expansive, and tip leakage and other parasitic losses are multiplied by two.

Depending on the design, a reaction stage may or may not suffer from disc friction and windage losses, diaphragm gland leakage losses, wetness loss, etc. In the present instance there is no wetness loss as the stage(s) works wholly in the superheat zone. These losses are considered further in a later part of this chapter.

Effect of varying the value of u/c_0 in a reaction stage

For our example of the calculations for a reaction stage, we chose to work with $u/c_0 = 0.8774$.

If we carry out a series of similar stage calculations using a different u/c_0 for each one of the series, we can plot the curve shown in Figure 10.59.

The implications of this curve, with regard to over and under-staging are generally similar to those described earlier in this chapter for pure impulse turbines, except that since the velocity diagrams for a reaction stage are always symmetrical or nearly symmetrical, the impulse thrust is zero, or at most, very small. For any given blade velocity however, diminishing values of u/c_0 mean larger stage enthalpy drops, hence increased reaction thrust.

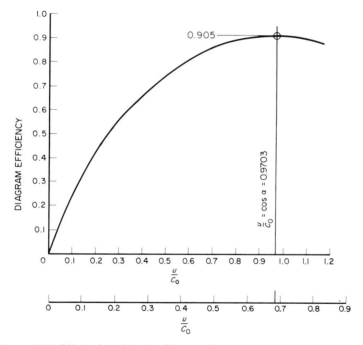

Figure 10.59 Effect of varying u/c_0 for a reaction stage

To enable us to directly compare pure impulse stages and reaction stages on diagram efficiency as the first criterion, we must use u/C_0 for both types, c_0 being the theoretical steam velocity generated by the *full* stage adiabatic enthalpy drop,

i.e., $\dfrac{u}{C_0} = \dfrac{u/c_0}{\sqrt{2}}$

REACTION STAGE

$\dfrac{u}{c_0}$	0.5	0.6	0.7	0.8	0.9	0.9703	1.1
$\dfrac{u}{C_0}$	0.354	0.425	0.495	0.566	0.635	0.686	0.776
η_D	0.743	0.818	0.86	0.89	0.903	0.905	0.898

If we plot the diagram efficiency η_D on a base of u/C_0, we obtain the curve marked "50 per cent reaction" in Figure 10.60. If we superpose on this the curve of diagram efficiency for an impulse stage (taken from Figure 10.45) we can compare directly the diagram efficiencies of the two extreme types of stage.

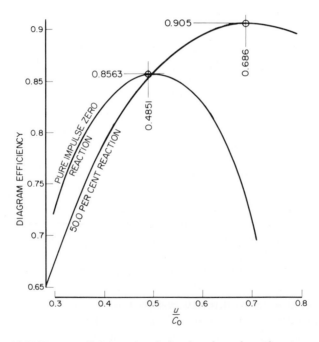

Figure 10.60 Diagram efficiency of equivalent impulse and reaction stages

We may now summarise some of the results of our calculations for the optimum impulse and reaction stages up to this point

Type of stage	Impulse	Reaction
Adiabatic enthalpy drop, kJ/kg, total	30.42	30.42
u/C_0	0.4851	0.686
Degree of reaction per cent	0	50
Diagram efficiency	0.8563	0.905
Number of stages	One	Two
Axial thrust, N, total	72.51	2393.72

Owing to the fact that the reaction process and the reaction blade forms are in practice somewhat more efficient, the optimum reaction stage shows an improvement of 5.68 per cent in diagram efficiency over the comparable pure impulse stage. To obtain this improvement however, we have to provide two stages instead of one, requiring a longer and more expensive turbine, and in addition we have to accommodate a very much greater axial thrust which, if balanced by a dummy cylinder causes a leakage loss, or if carried on a thrust bearing causes an increased external work loss; there is also a significant tip leakage loss. All these losses have to be set against the improvement in diagram efficiency.

Nevertheless, Figure 10.60 shows clearly that there exists an area between $u/C_0 = 0.4851$ with zero reaction and $u/C_0 = 0.686$ with 50 per cent reaction in which a worthwhile improvement in efficiency might be obtained, while retaining a more moderate end thrust and requiring something less than two stages instead of one.

To explore this area, we should choose several values of u/C_0, and for each, apply various degrees of reaction, e.g. 5, 10, 15 etc. per cent, hence obtaining the diagram efficiency, adiabatic enthalpy drop and axial thrust. We will carry out only one such calculation in detail, viz. $u/C_0 = 0.4851$ with 10 per cent reaction. For moderate degrees of reaction, the nozzles and blades are of the same form and construction as already described for the pure impulse stage, and the detailed calculations will show the necessary differences.

Calculations for an impulse type stage with slight reaction

As suggested, let us consider the optimum impulse stage already dealt with, viz. 0.762 m mean diameter, 50.0 rev/s, initial steam conditions 5.8 bar, 180°C, nozzle angle 14°, $u/C_0 = 0.4851$, nozzle efficiency = 0.94.

The mean blade velocity is as before, viz. $u = 119.68$ m/s, and since $u/C_0 = 0.4851$

$$C_0 = \frac{119.68}{0.4851} = 246.68 \text{ m/s, as before}$$

Now C_0 is the theoretical steam velocity based on the full adiabatic enthalpy drop hence $dh_s = (246.68/44.725)^2 = 30.42$ kJ/kg as before, and the final stage pressure = 4.963 bar as before.

In this case however, the nozzles deal with only 90.0 per cent of the stage adiabatic enthalpy drop i.e. nozzle $dh_s = 0.9 \times 30.42 = 27.38$ kJ/kg which fixes the pressure at the nozzle discharge 5.05 bar (see Figure 10.61).

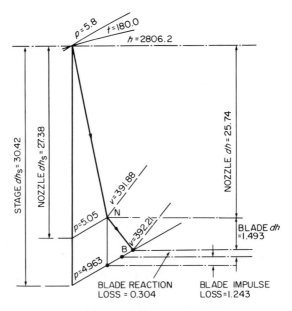

Figure 10.61 Mollier diagram for impulse stage with 10.0 per cent reaction steam leaves the nozzles at N. Steam leaves the blades at B

The actual nozzle enthalpy drop = $0.94 \times 27.38 = 25.74$ kJ/kg, and the actual nozzle discharge velocity $C_1 = 44.725 \sqrt{25.74} = 226.96$ m/s.

The nozzle loss = $27.38 - 25.74 = 1.64$ kJ/kg, hence the steam leaves the nozzles at the state point N in Figure 10.58 where the specific volume $v_N = 391.88$ dm^3/kg.

$$\text{Total nozzle discharge area} = \frac{1000 \times 4.762 \times 391.88}{226.96}$$

$$= 8222.5 \text{ mm}^2$$

Let the number, pitch and plate thickness of nozzles be as before, hence

$$\text{Nozzle discharge height} = \frac{8222.5}{54 \times 9.2} = 16.551 \text{ mm}$$

The stage velocity diagrams are drawn and the relevant calculations made generally by the same methods as before, except that allowance must be made for the steam expansion in the blades.

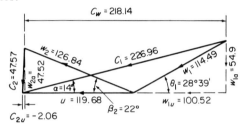

Figure 10.62 Velocity diagrams for impulse stage with 10.0 per cent reaction

Thus referring to Figure 10.62.

$$w_{1a} = C_1 \sin\alpha = 226.96 \times 0.2419 = 54.9 \text{ m/s}$$

$$w_{1u} = C_1 \cos\alpha - u = (226.96 \times 0.9703) - 119.68$$

$$= 100.52 \text{ m/s}$$

$$\theta_1 = \tan^{-1} \frac{w_{1a}}{w_{1u}} = \tan^{-1} \frac{54.9}{100.52} = \tan^{-1} 0.5461 = 28°39'$$

The blade entrance angle would be made $31°$ or $32°$.

Assuming the same blade velocity coefficient $\psi = 0.9$ gives

$$\psi w_1 = 0.9 \times 114.49 = 103.04 \text{ m/s}$$

and expressing this in heat units gives

$$\psi w_1 = \left(\frac{103.04}{44.725}\right)^2 = 5.309 \text{ kJ/kg}$$

To obtain w_2, we must now add to ψw_1, the actual re-action enthalpy drop through the blades. From Figure 10.58, the adiabatic enthalpy drop through the blades $\doteqdot 30.42 - 27.38 = 3.04$ kJ/kg, and if we assume that the efficiency of expansion is 0.9 then the actual reaction enthalpy drop through the blades is $0.9 \times 3.04 = 2.736$ kJ/kg.

Hence $w_2 = \psi w_1 +$ actual reaction enthalpy drop

$$\therefore w_2 = 5.309 + 2.736 = 8.045 \text{ kJ/kg},$$

and converting this back to velocity units gives

$$w_2 = 44.725 \sqrt{8.045} = 126.84 \text{ m/s}$$

The blade impulse loss is

$$\left(\frac{w_1}{44.725}\right)^2 - \left(\frac{\psi w_1}{44.725}\right)^2 = 6.552 - 5.309 = 1.243 \text{ kJ/kg}$$

The blade reaction loss is

$$3.04 - 2.736 = 0.304 \text{ kJ/kg, hence}$$

Total blade loss $= 1.243 + 0.304 = 1.547$ kJ/kg. In Figure 10.61, this gives the state point B at the blade discharge, where the specific volume is 392.21 dm^3/kg; hence

$$\text{Total blade discharge area } A_B = \frac{1000 \times 4.762 \times 392.21}{126.84}$$

$$= 14723.0 \text{ mm}^2$$

and assuming the same blade O/P viz. 0.3256

$$\text{Blade discharge height} = \frac{14723.0}{\pi \times 0.762 \times 0.3256 \times 1000}$$

$$= 18.89 \text{ mm}$$

Blade lap $= 18.89 - 16.551 = 2.339$ mm $= 14.2$ per cent of nozzle height. Referring again to Figure 10.62, $w_{2u} = w_2 \cos \beta_2 = 126.84 \times 0.9272 = 117.62$ m/s.

$$w_{2a} = w_2 \sin \beta_2 = 126.84 \times 0.3746 = 47.52 \text{ m/s}$$

$$C_{2u} = w_{2u} - u = 117.62 - 119.68 = -2.06$$

$$C_2 = \sqrt{(w_{2a}^2 + C_{2u}^2)} = \sqrt{(47.52^2 + (-2.06)^2)}$$

$$= 47.57 \text{ m/s}$$

Steam discharge angle

$$\theta_2 = \sin^{-1} \frac{w_{2a}}{C_2} = \sin^{-1} \frac{47.52}{47.57} = \sin^{-1} 0.9988 = 92°48'$$

Velocity of whirl

$$C_w = w_{1u} + w_{2u} = 100.52 + 117.62 = 218.14 \text{ m/s}$$

$$\text{Blade work} = \frac{u \, C_w}{1000} = \frac{119.68 \times 218.14}{1000} = 26.11 \text{ kJ/kg}$$

$$\text{Leaving loss} = \left(\frac{C_2}{44.725}\right)^2 = \left(\frac{47.57}{44.725}\right)^2 = 1.131 \text{ kJ/kg}$$

$$\text{Diagram efficiency} = \frac{2 \times 119.68 \times 218.14}{246.68 \times 246.68} = 0.858$$

$$C_a = w_{1a} - w_{2a} = 54.9 - 47.52 = 7.38 \text{ m/s}$$

$$\text{Impulse thrust} = 4.762 \times 7.38 = 35.14 \text{ N}$$

Pressure drop across the blades = 5.05 − 4.963 = 0.087 bar

$$\text{Reaction thrust} = \pi \times 0.762 \times \frac{18.89}{1000} \times 0.087 \times 10^5$$

$$= 393.34 \text{ N}$$

Total axial thrust = 35.14 + 393.34 = 428.48 N

Hence by applying 10 per cent reaction to the impulse-type stage, we increase the diagram efficiency from 0.8563 to 0.858, and increase the axial thrust from 72.51 N to 428.48 N. Since we have retained the same u and u/C_0, the stage adiabatic enthalpy drop is still 30.42 kJ/kg, hence only one stage is necessary.

In the foregoing example, the degree of reaction, viz. 10.0 per cent was chosen quite arbitrarily. If we now choose varying degrees of reaction, from zero to, say, 20.0 per cent, and, with constant u/C_0 = 0.4851, carry out calculations similar to the above for each we may plot the diagram efficiency and the axial thrust on a base of per cent reaction as shown in Figure 10.63. This shows that for the stage under consideration maximum diagram efficiency viz. 0.8593 is attained when the stage has about 5.0 per cent reaction. This is an improvement of 0.35% over the pure impulse stage, and is obtained in a single stage with an increase in axial thrust from 72.5 N to 250.0 N. The latter is quite moderate when compared with the equivalent two reaction stages having a total axial thrust of 1196.86 N.

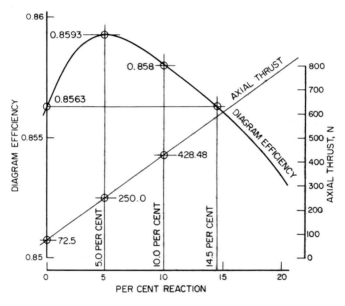

Figure 10.63 Optimum degree of reaction for an impulse-type turbine stage having $u/C_0 = 0.4851$

Note that any degree of reaction greater than 14.5 per cent will give a diagram efficiency lower than that of the pure impulse stage, accompanied by a useless increase of axial thrust.

If we now choose various values of u/C_0 above and below 0.4851 and apply various degrees of reaction to each, we obtain the instructive curves shown in Figure 10.64, from which we may conclude:

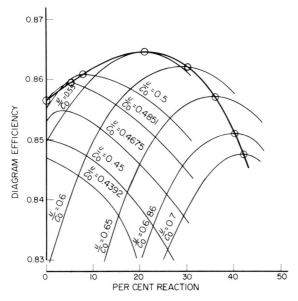

Figure 10.64 Effect of applying reaction to an impulse-type stage having u = 119.68 m/s, α = 14°, β₂ = 22°

1. That if u/C_0 is significantly less than $\frac{1}{2}\cos\alpha$, (0.4851), then the application of any reaction will actually worsen the diagram efficiency.
2. That if u/C_0 is equal to $\frac{1}{2}\cos\alpha$, then the application of any degree of reaction between zero and 14.5 per cent will improve the diagram efficiency, the maximum improvement being obtained when the degree of reaction is about 5.0 per cent.
3. That if u/C_0 is made progressively greater than $\frac{1}{2}\cos\alpha$, then the application of increased reaction will give increasing diagram efficiency up to an optimum point for each value of u/C_0; thereafter the diagram efficiency again diminishes.
4. The heavy-line curve, drawn through the optimum points shows that for the particular stage with which we are dealing, the best diagram efficiency, 0.8645, is obtained when the stage has $u/C_0 = 0.55$ and 21 per cent reaction.

This means that $C_0 = \dfrac{119.68}{0.55} = 217.57$ m/s

and the stage adiabatic enthalpy drop

$$dh_s = \left(\frac{217.57}{44.725}\right)^2 = 23.67 \text{ kJ/kg}$$

Now the pure impulse stage dealt with an adiabatic enthalpy drop of 30.42 kJ/kg. Hence if we use $u/C_0 = 0.55$ with 21.0 per cent reaction, we would require $30.42/23.67 = 1.285$ stages to replace one pure impulse stage. Also, with $u/C_0 = 0.55$ and 21.0 per cent reaction, the total axial thrust, approximately, would be (impulse thrust + reaction thrust) $\times$ 1.285 = (9.65 + 564.0) $\times$ 1.285 = 737.2 N.

In practice of course, we cannot replace one stage by 1.285 stages; the entire turbine has to be restaged so that the total number of stages is 1.285 times the original number, e.g. if the original turbine had 7 pure impulse stages each with $u/C_0 = 0.4851$, we would require $7 \times 1.285 = 9$ stages, each with $u/C_0 = 0.55$ and 21.0 per cent reaction.

The curves in Figure 10.64 refer only to that one stage with which we have dealt in detail, i.e. to the steam conditions, nozzle and blade angles, nozzle efficiency and blade velocity coefficient used in the example. Thus each of the 9 stages postulated in the previous paragraph would not necessarily have optimum $u/C_0 = 0.55$ and optimum reaction 21.0 per cent, and the overall arrangement would have to be adjusted in the light of each stage having been considered in the same detail as our example.

When applying increasing reaction to impulse-type stages, there comes a point—probably between 10.0 and 15.0 per cent reaction—when the spillage factor associated with pure impulse stages must be replaced by the tip leakage factor associated with reaction stages.

We may again summarise the relevant results of our stage calculations up to this point,

Type of stage	Pure impulse	Impulse type with reaction	Reaction
Adiabatic enthalpy drop kJ/kg	30.42	30.42	30.42
u/C_0	0.4851	0.55	0.686
Degree of reaction %	0	21.0	50.0
Diagram efficiency	0.8563	0.8645	0.905
Number of stages	One	1.285	2
Total axial thrust, N	72.5	737.2	2393.72

Whether or not the full optimum u/C_0 and degree of re-action are used depends on the increased thrust and tip leak-age losses compared with the improvement in diagram efficiency.

When u/C_0 = 0.686, the impulse stage and the reaction stage should be nominally equal, i.e. same u/C_0, same degree of reaction, same number of stages (two) and same diagram efficiency. Examination of the curve u/C_0 = 0.686 for the impulse-type stages however, will show that it reaches a maximum diagram efficiency of 0.851 with 40 per cent reaction compared with a diagram efficiency of 0.905 with 50 per cent reaction for the reaction-type stages. This is because we have based the impulse-type stages on the impulse type of blading throughout, thus including a constant blade velocity coefficient of 0.9, a loss from which the reaction type of blade does not suffer. Thus ideally, in this particular case, if the axial thrust and the blade tip leakage losses show that a degree of reaction greater than 20.0 per cent is justi-fied, then we should use reaction-type blades.

The application of a judicious degree of reaction to an impulse type stage improves the stage efficiency by reducing certain losses in the blade passages (virtually increasing the blade velocity coefficient). The degree of reaction applied to a single-row pressure stage can vary from 2.0 to 25.0 per cent depending on the conditions. Two-row velocity-compounded pressure stages, in certain conditions, show improvements with total reaction of up to 30.0 per cent suitably distributed among the moving and fixed blades. Reaction however is effective only if the pressure drops across the moving and fixed blades can be contained. Tip and root leakage, if significant, will negate any theoretical increase in efficiency. The end-tightened type of blading is quite effective in so doing, provided that the axial clearance between the shroud ring and the diaphragm face can be kept to a minimum of 0.3 mm to 1.0 mm. This is not always possible, and certain other steps may have to be taken to minimise tip leakage (see Figure 3.68).

A problem sometimes arises in applying reaction to long impulse-type blades, due to centrifugal force throwing the steam outwards, so causing an increase of pressure at the blade tips and a reduction of pressure at the blade roots. This reduction of pressure, if too large, could cause *negative reaction*, a most undesirable feature. Figure 10.65 illustrates this feature which can generally be avoided by design.

Towards the L.P. end of a turbine, where the blades are

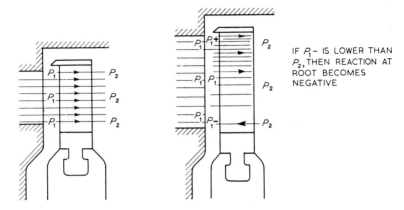

Figure 10.65 Negative reaction at blade root

long, the opening between any two adjacent blades is much greater at the blade tip than at the root. This feature, combined with the centrifugal force, necessitates a departure from the conception of the stage calculations carried out on the mean diameter, and leads to the "twisted and tapered" type of blade, which is virtually an impulse blade at the root and a reaction blade at the tip, and aims at achieving uniform mass flow throughout the length of the blade, and zero steam flow in the radial direction. This type of blade is clearly shown in Figure 3.62.

Fundamental efficiency of a turbine stage

Any turbine stage attains maximum fundamental efficiency only if simultaneously,

1. The nozzle loss is zero
2. The blade loss is zero
3. The change of velocity C_w is entirely in the direction of blade motion, i.e. the axial component of the change of velocity is zero.

The velocity diagrams for an impulse stage would be as shown in Figure 10.66, and to satisfy (3) above, it is obvious that the blade discharge angle β_2 must equal the steam entrance angle θ_1, and that $C_w = 2u$.

Hence maximum fundamental efficiency $= \dfrac{2u\,C_w}{C_0{}^2}$

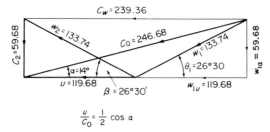

$$\frac{u}{C_0} = \frac{1}{2}\cos a$$

Figure 10.66 Velocity diagrams for fundamental efficiency in a single-row impulse stage

but $C_w = 2u$

$$\therefore \eta_m = \frac{4u^2}{C_0{}^2}, \text{ also } \frac{u}{C_0} = \frac{\cos\alpha}{2}, \therefore \frac{u^2}{C_0{}^2} = \frac{\cos^2\alpha}{4}$$

$$\therefore \eta_m = \frac{4\cos^2\alpha}{4}$$

$$\therefore \eta_m = \cos^2\alpha, \text{ which in this case is}$$

$$\eta_m = \cos^2 14° = 0.9703^2 = 0.9414$$

The only loss is the leaving loss $= \left(\dfrac{59.68}{44.725}\right)^2 = 1.78 \text{ kJ/Kg}$

So that we may also write

$$\eta_m = \frac{\text{stage adiabatic enthalpy drop} - \text{leaving loss}}{\text{stage adiabatic enthalpy drop}}$$

$$\eta_m = \frac{30.42 - 1.78}{30.42} = \frac{28.64}{30.42} = 0.9414$$

which again is the same as

$$\eta_m = \frac{2u\,C_w}{C_0{}^2} = \frac{2 \times 119.68 \times 239.36}{246.68^2} = 0.9414$$

The velocity diagrams for fundamental efficiency in a reaction stage would be as shown in Figure 10.67, from which it is obvious that $c_w = u$.

Now in a reaction stage, the steam velocity c_0 is generated by *one half* of the stage adiabatic enthalpy drop dh_s

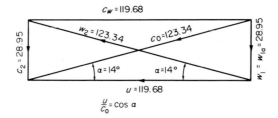

Figure 10.67 Velocity diagrams for fundamental efficiency in a reaction stage $u/c_0 = \cos \alpha$

$$\text{Thus } c_0 = 44.725 \sqrt{\left(\frac{dh_s}{2}\right)}$$

The steam velocity which would be generated by the *full* stage adiabatic enthalpy drop is

$$C_0 = 44.725\sqrt{(dh_s)}, \text{ hence } \frac{C_0}{c_0} = \frac{44.725\sqrt{(dh_s)}}{44.725\sqrt{\left(\dfrac{dh_s}{2}\right)}}$$

$$= \sqrt{2}, \text{ i.e. } C_0 = \sqrt{(2)}\,c_0$$

The diagram efficiency

$$= \frac{2u\,c_w}{C_0{}^2} = \frac{2u\,u}{(\sqrt{(2)}c_0)^2} = \frac{2u^2}{2c_0{}^2} = \left(\frac{u}{c_0}\right)^2$$

and putting $\dfrac{u}{c_0} = \cos\alpha$,

maximum fundamental efficiency $= \cos^2\alpha$,

which is exactly the same as for the impulse stage, but two reaction stages are required compared with one impulse stage.

In practice of course, we cannot have zero nozzle loss and zero blade loss. Also, because of its influence on the blade height, the blade discharge angle cannot always be such as to give zero axial impulse thrust. Thus, in practice, the basic efficiency of a stage is the diagram efficiency which includes the nozzle loss, the blade loss and the leaving loss. The theoretical work done on the blades is then given by

Stage adiabatic enthalpy drop × diagram efficiency

Because of the other stage losses, the net work done on the blades is less than the theoretical work, and the net work done *internally* at the shaft is less than the net blade work. Of the total work done internally at the shaft, some is dissipated by several external losses, and the remainder is delivered to the propeller. The various external losses are considered later in this chapter.

Two-row velocity-compounded impulse-type stages

The calculations are generally similar to those for a single-row impulse stage, except that the velocity diagrams have two sets of entrance and exit triangles instead of one, and that four specific volume points have to be found on the Mollier Diagram in the correct order instead of two (see Figure 10.68).

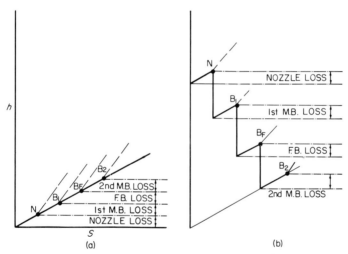

Figure 10.68 Specific volume points on the Mollier diagram for a two-row velocity-compounded impulse-type turbine
(left) Pure impulse stage
(right) Impulse-type stage with reaction

Theoretically, a two-row velocity-compounded stage has optimum $u/C_0 = \frac{1}{4}\cos\alpha$, but in practice, the best compromise value is generally less than this—of the order of 0.22 or even 0.2. Thus the stage adiabatic enthalpy drop—and hence pressure drop—is about 4.0 to 5.0 times that of a single-row stage having the same mean blade velocity. This usually necessitates convergent–divergent nozzles as explained earlier in this chapter.

Because of the multiplication of stage losses, the stage efficiency of a 2-row stage is significantly lower than that of the equivalent four single-row stages. Consequently in modern practice, its use is confined to

(a) The first stage of the H.P. turbine in cases where it is necessary to reduce the length of the turbine, and/or to reduce the pressure on the H.P. steam end gland. These necessities may be dictated by space, first cost or operational considerations.

(b) Astern turbines, where one or two two-row stages (sometimes followed by one or two single-row stages) are mounted generally on the L.P. ahead turbine rotor, but having the nozzles and blades of opposite hand to the ahead turbine stages. Although this arrangement results in some loss of both ahead and astern efficiency due to windage loss in driving the idle stages, it is compact and relatively simple. The windage loss can be reduced by fitting hoods over the last stage ahead and astern blades (Figure 3.59, page 99) or by interposing a diaphragm between the ahead and astern turbines (Figure 3.24, page 66), or by putting the astern turbine in a separate casing (Figure 3.79, page 126). In general, from the efficiency aspect, windage loss is more serious at the high pressure end where the steam is more dense, i.e. smaller specific volume. At the low-pressure end, the effect on efficiency is not so serious, but a problem may arise due to overheating of the long last-stage blades of the ahead turbine when they are being driven astern, and are merely churning comparatively dead steam.

Calculations for a two-row velocity-compounded impulse-stage having symmetrical (or equiangular) blades

For convenience in manufacture, some blade rows are fitted with symmetrical—or equiangular—blades. This means that the blade discharge angle is made equal to the blade entrance angle. As stated previously, the blade entrance angle theoretically, should be equal to the steam entrance angle, the latter being fixed solely by the nozzle angle and the value of u/C_1. In this section, to avoid confusion, we shall assume that this is so, i.e. we shall ignore "cover", and make

Blade discharge angle β_2 = blade entrance angle β_1
= steam entrance angle θ_1

This arrangement does not necessarily give the best diagram efficiency, and for this reason it is usually confined to astern turbines which normally operate for only a small fraction of steaming time.

For example, the nozzles of a two-row velocity-compounded impulse stage discharge steam at 668 m/s, at an angle of 18° to the plane of the wheel. The mean blade velocity is 133 m/s, and the blade velocity coefficient for the first row moving blades, the fixed blades and the second row moving blades is 0.9 for each.

For convenience, we may consider the velocity diagrams in two parts, viz. (1) the nozzles and first row moving blades, and (2) the fixed blades and second row moving blades. Note that it is the actual steam velocity C_1 at the nozzle discharge which is given.

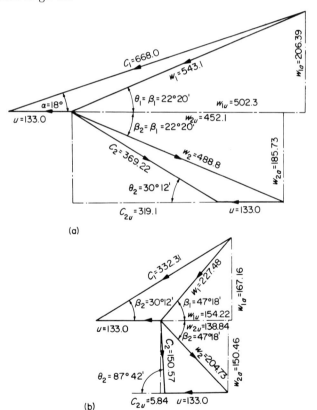

Figure 10.69 *Velocity diagrams for two-row velocity-compounded impulse stage with symmetrical blading and without "cover"*
(a) Nozzles and first row moving blades
(b) Fixed blades and second row moving blades

1. NOZZLES AND FIRST ROW MOVING BLADES (Refer to Figure 10.69)
The mean blade velocity u and the steam velocity C_1 are set
down to scale, the angle α between u and C_1 being $18°$—the
nozzle angle. The entrance triangle is then completed, from
which the steam velocity w_1 relative to the blade at entrance
and the steam entrance angle θ_1 may be scaled, or calculated
by the usual methods, viz.,

$$w_{1a} = C_1 \sin\alpha = 668.0 \times 0.309 = 206.39 \text{ m/s}$$

$$w_{1u} = C_1 \cos\alpha - u = (668.0 \times 0.9511) - 133$$
$$= 635.3 - 133.0 = 502.3 \text{ m/s}$$

$$\theta_1 = \tan^{-1}\frac{w_{1a}}{w_{1u}} = \tan^{-1}\frac{206.39}{502.3} = \tan^{-1}0.4109 = 22°20'$$

$$w_1 = \frac{w_{1a}}{\sin\theta_1} = \frac{206.39}{0.380} = 543.1 \text{ m/s}$$

Since the blade velocity coefficient $\psi = 0.9$,

$$w_2 = \psi w_1 = 0.9 \times 543.1 = 488.8 \text{ m/s}$$

The blade discharge angle $\beta_2 =$ steam entrance angle θ_1
$$= 22°20'$$

w_2 is set down to scale at an angle β_2 to w, and the discharge triangle is completed, from which the absolute discharge
velocity C_2 and the absolute discharge angle θ_2 from the first
row moving blades may be scaled, or calculated by the usual
methods viz.

$$w_{2a} = w_2 \sin\beta_2 = 488.8 \times 0.380 = 185.73 \text{ m/s}$$

$$w_{2u} = w_2 \cos\beta_2 = 488.8 \times 0.925 = 452.1 \text{ m/s}$$

$$C_{2u} = w_{2u} - u = 452.1 - 133.0 = 319.1 \text{ m/s}$$

$$\theta_2 = \tan^{-1}\frac{w_{2a}}{C_{2u}} = \tan^{-1}\frac{185.73}{319.1} = \tan^{-1}0.5820$$
$$= 30°12'$$

$$C_2 = \frac{w_{2a}}{\sin\theta_2} = \frac{185.73}{0.5030} = 369.22 \text{ m/s}$$

The fixed blade entrance angle $\beta_1 = \theta_2 = 30°12'$, and the
steam enters the fixed blades at 369.22 m/s.

2. FIXED BLADES AND SECOND ROW MOVING BLADES (Refer to Figure 10.69)

Since the fixed blade velocity coefficient $\psi = 0.9$, the absolute velocity leaving the fixed blades is $C_1 = 0.9 \times 369.22 = 332.31$ m/s. The fixed blade discharge angle $\beta_2 = 30°12'$, i.e. equal to the fixed blade entrance angle β_1.

The entrance triangle may be drawn to scale, from which the velocity w_1 of the steam relative to the second row moving blades and the steam entrance angle θ_1 may be scaled, or calculated by the usual methods, viz.,

$$w_{1a} = C_1 \sin\beta_2 = 332.31 \times 0.5030 = 167.16 \text{ m/s}$$

$$w_{1u} = C_1 \cos\beta_2 - u = (332.31 \times 0.8643) - 133.0$$
$$= 287.22 - 133.0 = 154.22 \text{ m/s}$$

$$\theta_1 = \tan^{-1}\frac{w_{1a}}{w_{1u}} = \tan^{-1}\frac{167.16}{154.22} = \tan^{-1}1.084 = 47°18'$$

$$w_1 = \frac{w_{1a}}{\sin\theta_1} = \frac{167.16}{0.7349} = 227.48 \text{ m/s}$$

Second row moving blade entrance angle $\beta_1 = \theta_1 = 47°18'$

Since the blade velocity coefficient $\psi = 0.9$, the steam velocity w_2 relative to the blade at exit is $w_2 = 0.9 \times 227.48 = 204.73$ m/s.

The blade discharge angle $\beta_2 =$ blade entrance angle β_1
$= 47°18'$

The exit triangle may now be completed, and the absolute discharge velocity C_2 and the absolute discharge angle θ_2 scaled or calculated by the usual methods, viz.,

$$w_{2a} = w_2 \sin\beta_2 = 204.73 \times 0.7349 = 150.46 \text{ m/s}$$

$$w_{2u} = w_2 \cos\beta_2 = 204.73 \times 0.6782 = 138.84 \text{ m/s}$$

$$C_{2u} = w_{2u} - u = 138.84 - 133.0 = 5.84 \text{ m/s}$$

$$C_2 = \sqrt{(w_{2a}^2 + C_{2u}^2)} = \sqrt{(150.46^2 + 5.84^2)}$$
$$= \sqrt{(22636.0 + 34.105)}$$
$$= \sqrt{(22670.105)} = 150.57 \text{ m/s}$$

$$\theta_2 = \sin^{-1}\frac{w_{2a}}{C_2} = \sin^{-1}\frac{150.46}{150.57} = \sin^{-1}0.9992$$
$$= 87°42'$$

Thus, the blade angles are

First row moving blades $\beta_1 = \beta_2 = 22°20'$

Fixed blades $\beta_1 = \beta_2 = 30°12'$

Second row moving blades $\beta_1 = \beta_2 = 47°18'$

The velocity of whirl

$$C_w = \Sigma w_u = (502.3 + 452.1) + (154.22 + 138.84)$$
$$\therefore\ C_w = 954.4 + 293.06$$
$$\therefore\ C_w = 1247.46 \text{ m/s}$$

The blade work

$$= \frac{u\,C_w}{1000} = \frac{133.0 \times 1247.46}{1000} = 165.89 \text{ kJ/kg}$$

Note that the proportion of the total work done on the first row moving blades is $954.4/1247.46 \times 100 = 76.51$ per cent and on the second row moving blades is $293.06/1247.46 \times 100 = 23.49$ per cent.

$$\text{The blade efficiency} = \frac{2\,u\,C_w}{C_1{}^2} = \frac{2 \times 133.0 \times 1247.46}{668.0 \times 668.0}$$
$$= 0.7436$$

Note: Since the mathematics involved in velocity diagrams are relatively simple and straightforward, the student is recommended always to first draw the velocity diagrams to scale, then to calculate the required values, then to check the calculated values by scaling from the diagram. In cases such as the present, it will become immediately obvious from initially drawing the velocity diagrams to scale, that the absolute discharge angle θ_2 from the second row moving blades is in the neighbourhood of $90°$. When this is so, it is better to calculate C_2 from

$$C_2 = \sqrt{(w_{2a}^2 + C_{2u}^2)}, \text{ from which } \theta_2 = \sin^{-1}\frac{w_{2a}}{C_2},$$

rather than to calculate θ_2 from

$$\theta_2 = \tan^{-1} w_{2a}/C_{2u}, \text{ from which } C_2 = w_{2a}/\sin\theta_2$$

When θ_2 is in the neighbourhood of $90°$, then C_{2u} is small compared with w_{2a} and $\tan^{-1} w_{2a}/C_{2u}$ is large. If $\tan^{-1} w_{2a}/C_{2u}$ exceeds about 2.0, then the evaluation of θ_2 from the ordinary trigonometrical tables can be insufficiently accurate.

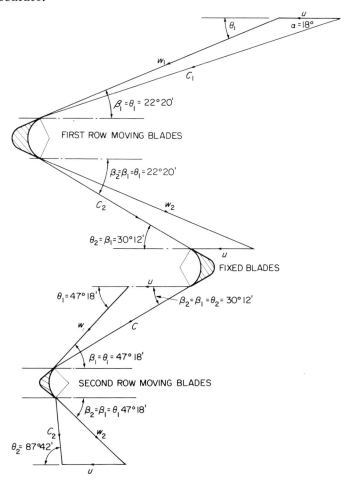

Figure 10.70 Expanded velocity diagrams for two-row velocity compunded stage

Figure 10.70 shows another conception of the same velocity diagrams for this two row velocity-compounded stage.

Note: In this example we are not given the nozzle efficiency, but C_1 is given as 668 m/s, hence the stage nozzle $dh = (668/44.725)^2 = 223.1$ kJ/kg.

Assuming a nozzle efficiency of 0.94 gives stage $dh_s = 223.1/0.94 = 237.35$ kJ/kg, hence $C_0 = 44.725 \sqrt{(237.35)} = 689.1$ m/s, hence

$$\text{Stage } \frac{u}{C_0} = \frac{133.0}{689.1} = 0.193$$

Compare with theoretical optimum value of $\frac{1}{4}\cos\alpha$

$$= \frac{0.95106}{4} = 0.2376$$

$$\text{The diagram efficiency} = \frac{2u\,C_w}{C_0{}^2} = \frac{2 \times 133.0 \times 1247.46}{689.1 \times 689.1}$$

$$= 0.6988$$

TYPE NAMES OF TURBINES

Having examined the various turbine types, it may be prudent at this stage to recollect that towards the end of the nineteenth century, several names became famous because of their association with the development of certain types of turbines. Such was the impact of these names on the subject, that even today, as we move through the last quarter of the twentieth century, they are still commonly used to identify a type of turbine.

PARSONS. A reaction turbine in which steam expansion takes place in the channels between both the fixed and moving blades. One row of fixed blades and one row of moving blades constitutes a stage. The stage adiabatic enthalpy drop is usually divided up more or less equally between the fixed and the moving blade rows; i.e. the stages have 50 per cent reaction. The early Parsons marine steam turbines—before the advent of accurate and reliable single and double reduction gears—had the turbine rotors directly coupled to the propeller shafts. The turbines were therefore slow-running, and reflection on Parsons' K will show that the turbines had to be of large diameter and/or to have many stages if any reasonable efficiency was to be achieved. Following the development of satisfactory reduction gears, the turbine diameters were drastically reduced, and assumed the proportions illustrated by Figures 3.35, 3.36, 3.37, and 3.38 in Chapter 3.

DE LAVAL. A high-speed (330 rev/s or more) pure impulse turbine having one set of nozzles and a single wheel having one row of blades, such as in Figure 10.27(a). Although this arrangement offers the highest efficiency of all impulse turbines, its inherent high efficiency cannot be exploited for main turbines, since for the large adiabatic enthalpy drops required to give high thermodynamical cycle efficiency its mean diameter and speed would be prohibitive (see page 443)

RATEAU. An impulse turbine employing a number of stages, each stage having one row of nozzles followed by one row of blades, otherwise referred to as pressure-compounded, and illustrated in Figure 10.27(b).

CURTIS. An impulse turbine having one row of nozzles and a single wheel having two or three rows of moving blades, otherwise referred to as velocity-compounded, and illustrated in Figure 10.27(c) and (d).

These notes on names will explain what is meant when a turbine is described as, for example, "a two-row Curtis stage followed by three Rateau stages"; alternatively this type might be described as "a two-row Curtis followed by three singles". The latter two descriptions have the same meaning, viz. a pressure-velocity compounded turbine as in Figure 10.28.

MULTISTAGE TURBINES

Condition curve

So far, apart from the leaving loss and carry-over aspect, we have dealt with one stage in isolation. Main turbines however consist of a considerable number of stages in series, and we now have to consider how our knowledge of the behaviour of individual stages can be used to illustrate the features, the efficiency and the behaviour of the multistage turbine as a whole.

If, on the Mollier Diagram we set down the conditions shown in Figure 10.40(b) as the first stage, we obtain the points X, Y' and Z in Figure 10.71. Taking Y' as the initial state point and adding the carry-over from the first stage to dh_{s2}, the second stage calculations are carried out in the same manner as for the first, and its state points added to the Mollier Diagram. This process is continued for each succeeding stage throughout the turbine.

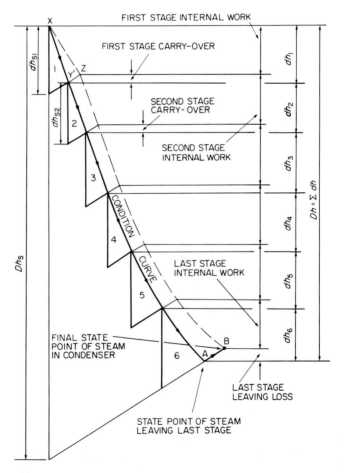

Figure 10.71 Condition curve, enthalpy drops and work done in multistage turbines. Total internal work = Σ stage internal work = (Dh − leaving loss)

Part of the kinetic energy (carry-over) developed in the first stage is carried over from stage to stage and is ultimately thrown out by the last stage. The *whole* of the leaving velocity of the last stage is destroyed in the condenser and the kinetic energy reconverted to heat which is ultimately lost in the circulating water.

Referring to Figure 10.71, steam leaves the last stage with enthalpy A and velocity C_2 m/s. In the condenser C_2 is converted to $(C_2/44.725)$ kJ/kg, causing the enthalpy of the steam to increase to B, thus enabling B to be shown on the Mollier Diagram as the final state point of the condition curve. The enthalpy at B is sometimes called the *stagnation enthalpy*; i.e. the final enthalpy of the steam when it has been brought to rest. The perpendicular distance between A and B, i.e. the enthalpy equivalent of the last stage C_2 is the overall *turbine leaving loss* since it is the only point at which kinetic energy is completely lost by velocity being converted to heat.

Note that since Σ internal work $= (Dh - \text{leaving loss})$, we may also write

$$\Sigma \text{ internal work} = Dh \left(1 - \frac{\text{leaving loss}}{Dh}\right)$$

The term $\left(1 - \dfrac{\text{leaving loss}}{Dh}\right)$ is called the *leaving loss factor*

i.e. that factor by which we must multiply the internal enthalpy drop to obtain the total useful internal work:

$$\text{Total internal work} = Dh \times \text{leaving loss factor},$$

or alternatively

$$\text{Total internal work} = Dh_s \times \text{internal efficiency ratio} \times \text{leaving loss factor}$$

The reheat factor

Reference to the printed Mollier Chart will show that the lines of constant pressure diverge upward and to the right, this effect being more pronounced in the superheat zone. Thus in Figure 10.72 CD is greater than AB. This means that

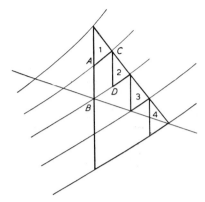

Figure 10.72 Reheat factor

due to the fractional efficiency ratio of the first stage, the second stage receives steam at C instead of at A, with the result that it has the increased adiabatic enthalpy drop CD instead of AB.

The effect of this is that the sum of the individual stage adiabatic enthalpy drops of a multistage turbine is greater than the overall adiabatic enthalpy drop. Referring to Figure 10.71, $\Sigma dh_s > Dh_s$, and the ratio $\Sigma dh_s/Dh_s$ is called the *reheat factor*. Σdh_s is called the *cumulative enthalpy drop*.

The actual value of the reheat factor depends on the initial steam conditions, on the range of expansion and on the turbine design. For example, a turbine expanding steam from 100.0 bar, 510.0°C to 0.05 bar with an internal efficiency ratio of 0.8 has a reheat factor of about 1.1.

Thus any particular stage benefits to some extent from the inefficiency of the preceding stages. The overall result of course, is still a loss compared with adiabatic expansion throughout, since no matter the value of the reheat factor, $Dh < Dh_s$ always.

Because of the reheat factor therefore, the available energy to be divided up amongst the stages of a multistage turbine is greater than the overall adiabatic enthalpy drop shown on the Mollier Diagram, and the reheat factor must be assessed by the turbine designer and taken into account in the staging. Earlier in this chapter, when dealing with staging, we divided up the overall adiabatic enthalpy drop in proportion to $D_m{}^2$, but it is in fact the cumulative enthalpy drop which is so divided up. To do so however, requires some pre-knowledge of the stage efficiency ratios and the expansion line.

Stage efficiency

Again referring to Figure 10.71, the ratio dh_1/dh_{s1} = stage efficiency of first stage, dh_2/dh_{s2} = stage efficiency of second stage, and so on. Thus each stage is debited with that part of its leaving velocity which is destroyed and reconverted to heat. Now, *all* of the last stage leaving velocity is lost in this way, but it is not correct to debit the last stage alone with this loss, since it is not the fault of the last stage itself that its leaving velocity cannot be utilised. We therefore debit the *whole* turbine with the last stage leaving loss, thus total internal enthalpy drop $Dh = \Sigma dh$, and total internal work = Dh — leaving loss. It is always the *true condition curve* from which the correct specific volume points for the nozzle and blade areas are found. Steam extracted for feed heating ultimately comes to rest in the heater, hence theoretically the enthalpies of extracted steam should be found from the stagnation enthalpy curve (*XZB* in Figure 10.71). Since the differences are relatively small, we will in what follows, assume that the true condition curve applies to both the turbine steam and the extracted steam, but will correct the total internal work for the leaving loss.

INTERNAL EFFICIENCY RATIO

The ratio Dh/Dh_s is the *internal efficiency ratio* of the turbine. Hence we may write

Total internal work at shaft = $(Dh_s \times$ internal efficiency ratio$)$ — leaving loss

OVERALL EFFICIENCY RATIO

Of the total internal work done at the shaft, some is absorbed by the external losses, such as thrust and journal bearing friction, gear losses, oil pump power, gland losses, etc. These external losses do not cause reheat of the working steam, and they cannot therefore be shown on the Mollier Diagram. Typically, the external and mechanical losses might amount to 5.0 per cent of turbine internal work, i.e. the *external loss factor* is 0.95. The work done at the propeller shaft in kJ/kg is therefore given by

$[(Dh_s \times$ internal efficiency ratio$)$ — leaving loss$]$ × external loss factor

The ratio $\dfrac{\text{work done at propeller shaft}}{Dh_s}$ is the *overall*

efficiency ratio of the turbine.

Steam consumption

Knowing the initial steam conditions, the final pressure and the expected *internal* efficiency ratio, an estimated condition curve can be laid down on the Mollier Diagram, but before we can proceed with the individual stage calculations, we must know the steam flow (in kg/s) through the stages.

If the turbine were perfect, i.e. with no losses at all it would do Dh_s, kJ/kg, of work and the specific steam consumption would be $3600/Dh_s$, kJ/kWh.

Because of all the losses, however, the nett work at the propeller shaft is not Dh_s, but (Dh_s × overall efficiency ratio), kJ/kg. Hence the specific steam consumption

$$= \frac{3600}{Dh_s \times \text{overall efficiency ratio}}, \text{ kg/kWh}$$

[Note the units, $3600 = (s/h)$, $Dh_s = (kJ/kg)$, overall efficiency ratio (dimensionless). Hence, specific steam consumption

$$= \frac{s}{h} \div \frac{kJ}{kg} = \frac{s}{h} \frac{kg}{kJ}, \text{ and since } 1.0 \text{ kJ/s} = 1.0 \text{ kW}$$

$$\text{Specific steam consumption} = \left[\frac{kg}{kWh}\right]$$

Steam consumption, kg/h = specific steam consumption kg/kWh × turbine power, kW

$$\text{Steam flow through stages, kg/s} = \frac{\text{steam consumption kg/h}}{3600}$$

Alternatively, from the above, we may write

$$\text{Steam flow through stages} = \frac{\text{turbine power at propeller shaft}}{Dh_s \times \text{overall efficiency ratio}}$$

The turbine power is in kW and Dh_s in kJ/kg. The turbine power must include any power required by main-engine driven auxiliaries.

This steam flow is then used in the stage calculations as previously illustrated, the calculated expansion line built up stage by stage on the Mollier Diagram, and the turbine internal efficiency ratio ultimately found. If this differs significantly from that originally assumed, the steam flow and the condition curve are modified and the calculations repeated until agreement is reached. If steam for feed heating is to be extracted from some of the turbine stages, then the steam flows through the various sections of the turbines must be modified accordingly (see Chapters 11 and 12).

These processes can be quite complex, involving as they do, many interdependent factors and much repetitive work, and nowadays are tending more to be carried out by computer methods. A computer, however, can do the repetitive work and satisfy all the interdependent factors, only if it is "programmed" to do so by someone who has done the fundamental work outlined, albeit comparatively briefly, in this and other chapters.

Modern steam turbine development is such that it is no longer strictly correct to classify turbines as impulse *or* reaction, implying that either all or half respectively of the stage adiabatic enthalpy drop takes place in the nozzles. So-called reaction turbines have always had approximately 50 per cent reaction, and nowadays most so-called impulse stages have some reaction. To be correct a stage is defined by its u/C_0 and its degree of reaction. Even so, the terms impulse and reaction tend to remain, but where used, they should be understood to mean the class of blade used; i.e. whether an impulse type such as that shown in Figure 10.42 or a reaction type such as shown in Figure 10.49. Reference to Figure 10.64 will show that for the given conditions, the change-over point is $u/c_0 = 0.55$ and 21 per cent reaction i.e. below these values we should use impulse-type blades, and above we should use reaction-type blades.

General application of Parsons' K to any type of turbine

Earlier in this chapter, we used Parsons' K to illustrate equivalent pressure-compounded impulse turbines having single-row stages. Since we have now dealt with several other types of turbine, it is of interest to apply the principle of Parsons' K so as to enable us approximately to compare any one type of turbine with any other. Neglecting losses, let us examine pure impulse stages and reaction stages:

1. Single-row impulse-type stages having $u/C_0 = \frac{1}{2}$
2. Two-row impulse-type stages having $u/C_0 = \frac{1}{4}$
3. Three-row impulse-type stages having $u/C_0 = \frac{1}{6}$
4. Reaction-type stages having $u/c_0 = 1$.

For an impulse stage, $C_0 = 44.725 \sqrt{(dh_s)}$, hence $C_0 \propto \sqrt{dh_s}$

also $u = \pi D_m R$, hence $u \propto D_m R$

$$\therefore \frac{u}{C_0} \propto \frac{D_m R}{\sqrt{(dh_s)}}, \text{ from which } dh_s \propto \frac{D_m{}^2 R^2}{\left(\dfrac{u}{C_0}\right)^2}$$

If the turbine has n stages having a total adiabatic enthalpy drop Dh_s, then $Dh_s = n\, dh_s$, hence

$$Dh_s \propto \frac{D_m{}^2 R^2 n}{\left(\dfrac{u}{C_0}\right)^2} \tag{1}$$

For a reaction stage, $c_0 = 44.725 \sqrt{\left(\dfrac{dh_s}{2}\right)}$, hence

$$c_0 \propto \sqrt{\left(\dfrac{dh_s}{2}\right)}$$

also $u = \pi D_m R$, hence $u \propto D_m R$

$$\therefore \frac{u}{c_0} \propto \frac{D_m R}{\sqrt{\left(\dfrac{dh_s}{2}\right)}}, \text{ from which } dh_s \propto \frac{2 D_m{}^2 R^2}{\dfrac{u}{c_0}}$$

If the turbine has n stages having a total adiabatic enthalpy drop Dh_s, then

$$Dh_s \propto \frac{2 D_m{}^2 R^2 n}{\left(\dfrac{u}{c_0}\right)^2} \tag{2}$$

Substituting the appropriate values of u/C_0 and u/c_0^2 in (1) and (2) gives

Reaction, $$Dh_s \propto \frac{2D_m{}^2 R^2 n}{(1.0)^2} \quad \therefore Dh_s \propto 2D_m{}^2 R^2 n$$

Impulse, single row, $$Dh_s \propto \frac{D_m{}^2 R^2 n}{(\frac{1}{2})^2} \quad \therefore Dh_s \propto 4D_m{}^2 R^2 n$$

Impulse, two-row, $$Dh_s \propto \frac{D_m{}^2 R^2 n}{(\frac{1}{4})^2} \quad \therefore Dh_s \propto 16D_m{}^2 R^2 n$$

Impulse, three-row, $$Dh_s \propto \frac{D_m{}_2 R^2 n}{(\frac{1}{6})^2} \quad \therefore Dh_s \propto 36D_m{}^2 R^2 n$$

And if we divide throughout by the common factor of 2, we may write

Reaction, $Dh_s \propto D_m{}^2 R^2 n$, i.e. Parsons' $K = D_m{}^2 R^2 n$

Impulse, single-row, $Dh_s \propto 2D_m{}^2 R^2 n$, i.e. Parsons' $K = 2D_m{}^2 R^2 n$

Impulse, two-row, $Dh_s \propto 8D_m{}^2 R^2 n$, i.e. Parsons' $K = 8D_m{}^2 R^2 n$

Impulse, three-row, $Dh_s \propto 18D_m{}^2 R^2 n$, i.e. Parsons' $K = 18D_m{}^2 R^2 n$

If we are dealing only with *one type* of turbine, we need consider only $D_m{}^2 R^2 n$, as we did previously for the pressure-compounded impulse turbine with single-row stages.

If we are dealing with *two or more* types, we must use the appropriate values of Parsons' K given above.

All four of the above turbines utilise the same total adiabatic enthalpy drop and theoretically have the same efficiency.

For instance, with any given mean diameter and speed, two reaction stages can be replaced by one single-row impulse stage, one two-row impulse stage can be replaced by 8/2 = 4 single-row impulse stages, eighteen reaction stages can be replaced by one three-row impulse stage, one three-row impulse stage can be replaced by one two-row plus five single-row impulse stages, and so on.

These comparisons are of course "first estimates" only; they are affected ultimately by the actual values of u/C_0 and u/c_0, by the relative parasitic stage losses, by possible variations of D_m and R, and by the overall reheat factor (see page 523).

Performance of marine steam turbines at reduced power and at overload

Marine steam turbines are designed to give their maximum efficiency at that service power at which the ship will operate for the greatest part of its sea time. This power is called design full power, or more simply *full power*.

Depending however, on the service conditions and on the type of trade in which the ship is to be involved, there may be significant periods of time when it is required to operate at reduced power, or indeed at power greater than normal full power (overload). It is of some importance that we examine the means of so doing, and the behaviour of the main turbines in these conditions.

From what we have learned of steam turbine theory, it will be appreciated that the power developed by the turbines is, fundamentally, the product of the adiabatic enthalpy drop in kJ/kg of steam, and the steam quantity, kg/h, passing through the turbines. Thus, to reduce the power, we must reduce either the adiabatic enthalpy drop, or the steam quantity, or both.

In practice it has, up to the present, been customary to maintain the full boiler pressure and temperature at reduced power. Further, the characteristics of the condenser are such that power variations do not markedly change the final exhaust pressure. This means that for reduced power there is available approximately the full power adiabatic enthalpy drop. To reduce the turbine power we must therefore either reduce the adiabatic enthalpy drop *and* the steam quantity by *throttling* at the manoeuvring valve, or, keeping the adiabatic enthalpy drop constant, we must reduce the steam quantity by reducing the nozzle area available for steam flow; i.e. by *nozzle control*, shutting off one or more nozzle groups (see Figure 3.29, page 71). We can also adopt a combination of throttling and nozzle control. Since the boiler pressure and temperature are constant, and the condenser pressure changes within quite narrow limits, we cannot increase the adiabatic heat drop, hence to obtain power greater than full power, we must increase the steam quantity through the turbines either by providing a group of overload nozzles or by providing an overload byepass.

THROTTLING
Partial closing in of the turbine manoeuvring valve causes pressure drop of the steam during which no external work is

531

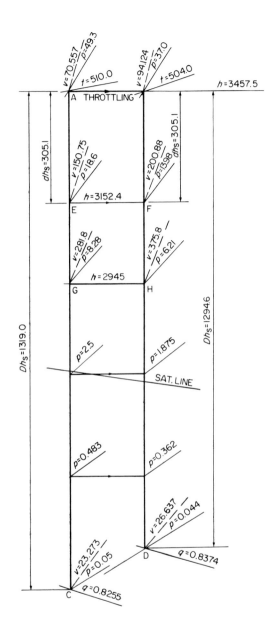

Figure 10.73 Full power and reduced power adiabatic expansion lines for throttling turbines

done, and as the restricted area past the partially closed valve is designed in such a manner that no appreciable additional steam velocity is generated, then no heat energy is taken from the steam. Such a process is called a *throttling* process. If we assume that there are no external heat losses, then the throttling process can be regarded as an expansion at constant enthalpy, and can be represented by a horizontal straight line on the Mollier Diagram.

Figure 10.73 shows the simplified full power adiabatic expansion line AC for 14 920 kW steam turbines taking steam at 49.3 bar, 510.0°C and exhausting at 0.05 bar. If we neglect the relatively small pressure drop through the fully-open manoeuvring valve when it is passing the full power steam quantity, then at A the steam pressure is 49.3 bar and the steam specific volume is 70.557 dm^3/kg.

Suppose we now partially close the manoeuvring valve such that the steam is throttled to a pressure of 37.0 bar after the valve. The state point moves along the horizontal throttling line from A to B, where the pressure is 37.0 bar and the specific volume 94.124 dm^3/kg. The ratio of the pressure p_B/p_A = 37.0/49.3 = 0.75, and the ratio of the specific volumes v_A/v_B = 70.557/94.124 = 0.75. Thus for the initial throttling operation, the pressure varies inversely as the specific volume. The other stage state points behave in the same manner, i.e. E moves to F, and G moves to H and so on, such that from E to F, p_F/p_E = 13.98/18.6 = 0.751, and v_E/v_F = 150.75/200.88 = 0.7504

$$\text{from } G \text{ to } H, \quad \frac{p_H}{p_G} = \frac{6.21}{8.28} = 0.75 \text{ and } \frac{v_G}{v_H} = \frac{281.8}{375.8} = 0.7499$$

Thus for any throttling line between the two adiabatic lines, the pressure varies inversely as the specific volume, and the ratio

$$\frac{\text{Throttled pressure}}{\text{Unthrottled pressure}} = \frac{\text{Unthrottled specific volume}}{\text{Throttled specific volume}}$$

remains remarkably constant.

With the exception of the last few stages (which are influenced to a greater extent by the condenser), all the stage pressures tend to change along horizontal straight lines such as *EF* or *GH*. This means that, with the exception of the last few stages, the stage adiabatic enthalpy drops at reduced power are practically the same as at full power, and therefore the steam velocities in the nozzle throats do not change. Since the total nozzle throat areas remain constant, the quantity of steam which can be passed through the nozzles is therefore inversely proportional to the specific volume of the steam. We have seen that for throttling, the specific volumes are almost exactly inversely proportional to the pressures. Hence the steam quantity is directly proportional to the pressure. This conclusion gives us an important and useful rule for turbines which are controlled by throttling, viz., *so long as the nozzle areas remain unaltered, the stage pressures of a multistage turbine are directly proportional to the steam quantity passing through the stages.* This may perhaps be further explained by considering that since the steam quantity M, kg/s, varies inversely as the specific volume v, dm^3/kg, then the value of Mv remains constant. Now the two expressions which determine the steam quantity through any stage are $v = 1000Mv/A$ and $v = 44.725 \sqrt{(dh_s)}$, hence we may write

$$44.725 \sqrt{(dh_s)} = \frac{1000Mv}{A} \text{, from which}$$

$$dh_s = \sqrt{\left(\frac{1000Mv}{44.725A}\right)}$$

The nozzle area A is constant, and the term Mv remains constant, hence for a throttled turbine, the stage adiabatic enthalpy drops also remain constant.

The behaviour of the stages towards the exhaust end differs from the above. Because of the reduced steam quantity, the condenser pressure at reduced power is somewhat lower than at full power, in this instance say 0.044 bar. Because of the condenser pressure, the point C cannot move horizontally as the higher stage state points do, but is constrained to move to D. In doing so, the steam specific volume increases from 23 273 to 26 637 dm^3/kg. However at reduced power, the last stage nozzles, operating at D, have to pass only 0.75 of the steam quantity which they have to pass when operating at C. Since the nozzle area does not change, the last stage nozzle steam velocity will be only $0.75 \times 26\,637/23\,273 = 0.8583$ of the velocity at full power.

The last stage adiabatic enthalpy drop at reduced power will therefore be

$$\left(\frac{0.8583C_0}{44.725}\right)^2 = 0.7367 \quad \left(\frac{C_0}{44.725}\right)^2 = 0.7367$$

of the last stage adiabatic enthalpy drop at full power. This reduction in adiabatic enthalpy drop means that the last stage will run 'lighter', developing a smaller fraction of the total turbine power. This enthalpy drop establishes the last stage pressure; the second last stage, etc., behave in a similar manner, the stage adiabatic enthalpy drops progressively increasing backwards up the turbine, until at possibly the third last or fourth last stage, the perpendicular distance between C and D due to the condenser is dissipated, and the behaviour of the higher stages is that due to throttling alone as is described above. For the sake of clarity, Figure 10.73 illustrates this feature as if it affected only the last stage.

Throttling at the manoeuvring valve has reduced the overall adiabatic enthalpy drop from 1319.0 to 1294.6 kJ/kg, and has reduced the steam throughput to 0.75 of the full power steam throughout. If the overall internal efficiency ratio of the turbines remained constant, the reduced power to be expected would be $0.75 \times 1294.6/1319.0 = 0.736$, or 73.6 per cent of full power.

However, one of the characteristics of an ordinary marine propeller is that it can absorb a certain power only at a certain speed. The "propeller law" states that the power absorbed is approximately directly proportional to the cube of the propeller speed, thus the propeller speed is proportional to the cube root of the power. This means that for geared turbines at reduced power, the turbine speed and hence the mean blade velocity u, m/s, will fall in direct proportion to the propeller speed, i.e. in direct proportion to the cube root of the power. Since the majority of the stage adiabatic enthalpy drops, and therefore the nozzle steam velocities C_0, m/s, do not change significantly, the value of u/C_0 throughout these stages will be reduced well below the optimum value, and the diagram efficiencies will diminish accordingly. This is illustrated by Figure 10.74 which shows in full lines the velocity diagram for the pure impulse stage dealt with earlier in this chapter (see Figure 10.44) and superposed on it in dotted

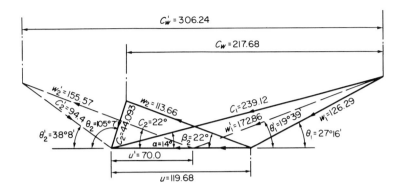

$C_w' = 306.24$

$C_w = 217.68$

$W_2' = 155.57$

$C_2' = 94.48$

$\theta_2' = 38°8'$

$\theta_2 = 105°7'$

$C_2' = 44.093$

$W_2 = 113.66$

$C_2 = 22°$

$a = 14°$

$\beta = 22°$

$C_1 = 239.12$

$W_1' = 172.86$

$\theta_1 = 19°39'$

$W_1 = 126.29$

$\theta_1 = 27°16'$

$u' = 70.0$

$u = 119.68$

Figure 10.74 Effect of reduction of mean blade velocity of a pure impulse stage when running throttled at reduced power. Full power conditions shown in full lines $u/C_0 = 119.68/246.68 = 0.4851$. Reduced power conditions shown in broken lines $u/C_0 = 70.0/246.68 = 0.2838$

lines, the velocity diagram for the same stage when running throttled at reduced power such that the mean blade velocity is reduced to 70.0 m/s.

Note that the blade work at reduced power

$$= \frac{u' \, C_w'}{1000} = \frac{70.0 \times 306.24}{1000} = 21.437 \text{ kJ/kg}$$

compared with 26.05 kJ/kg at full power.

$$\text{The diagram efficiency} = \frac{2u' \, C_w'}{C_0^2} = \frac{2 \times 70.0 \times 306.24}{246.68^2}$$

$$= 0.7046$$

compared with 0.8563 at full power.

The velocity of whirl C_w is increased, but this is more than offset by the reduced blade velocity. The leaving loss C_2 is more than doubled. These effects are fundamental, and so affect the diagram efficiency. The relations of steam angles to blade angles and nozzle entrance angles are no longer ideal, thus increasing shock losses, and in particular, reducing the fraction of C_2 which it is possible to carry over as velocity to the next stage.

On the other hand, more stages work in the superheat zone

so that wetness losses throughout the turbines will be reduced. The reduced rev/s and reduced steam density (increased specific volume) reduce the disc friction and windage losses. The reduced pressure drops across the stages reduce the diaphragm gland leakage losses.

For our purpose, we will assume that the sum of the parasitic losses (friction, shock, carry-over fraction, disc friction, windage, leakage) remains constant, and consider only the diagram efficiency correction which then virtually becomes a correction factor on the stage efficiency. Figure 10.75 shows typical correction factors for varying u/c_0 for three different types of turbine stage. This diagram assumes, for example that a single-row impulse stage at full power has an optimum $u/C_0 = 0.455$. This of course is not necessarily true for all single-row impulse stages, but Figure 10.75, as a

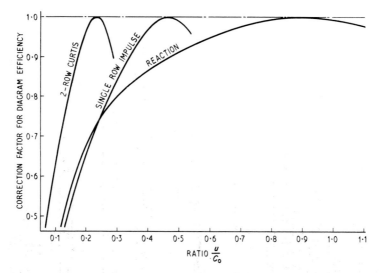

Figure 10. 75 Typical efficiency correction factors for turbine stage with varying value of u/C_0

general diagram, is quite adequate for our purposes. The reduced power u/C_0 of any stage is estimated and the correction factor read from Figure 10.75. The reduced power stage efficiency is then obtained by multiplying the full power stage efficiency by the correction factor, e.g. referring to Figure 10.74, the reduced power $u/C_0 = 0.2838$, and from Figure 10.75 the efficiency correction factor for a single-row impulse stage is 0.82. The reduced power diagram efficiency = 0.8563 × 0.82 = 0.702, which checks quite well with that calculated for Figure 10.74. By assuming constant parasitic losses, the correction factor can be applied also to the stage efficiency.

From the foregoing, it will be evident that the turbine internal efficiency ratio diminishes at reduced power, and that in the example shown in Figure 10.73, 75.0 per cent steam will not give 73.6 per cent power (as might be thought from consideration of the adiabatic enthalpy drops), but some power rather less than 73.6 per cent of full power.

Referring now to Figure 10.76(a), AC and AB are the adiabatic and actual expansion lines respectively at full power. Consider the case when the turbines are running throttled such that only 75.0 per cent of the full power steam quantity is passing. The first stage nozzle box pressure is reduced by throttling to 49.3 × 0.75 = 37.0 bar. All the other stage pressures (with the exception of the last two) are also reduced to 0.75 of the full power pressures. The reduced power adiabatic line is DE.

The first stage is a two-row Curtis stage having full power $u/C_0 = 0.23$ and full power stage efficiency 202.3/305.1 = 0.663. At the reduced power the first stage adiabatic enthalpy drop does not differ sensibly from that at full power, hence the steam velocity C_0 does not change. Assuming that 75.0 per cent steam will give about 72.0 per cent power, the propeller speed, and hence the mean blade velocity u will be reduced to $\sqrt[3]{0.72} = 0.895$ of its full power value. Thus, for the first stage, u/C_0 will be reduced to 0.895 × 0.23 = 0.206, and from Figure 10.75, the correction factor for a two-row Curtis stage is 0.978. Hence, the stage efficiency at reduced power = 0.663 × 0.978 = 0.6484, and the first stage internal enthalpy drop $dh' = 305.1 × 0.6484 = 197.83$ kJ/kg.

By treating the succeeding stages in the same way—but using the appropriate correction factors for single-row stages, the actual reduced power expansion line DF is built up, which gives an internal enthalpy drop $Dh' = 1079.3$ kJ/kg compared with 1128.8 kJ/kg at full power. Thus the actual reduced power will be 0.75 × (1079.3/1128.8) × 100.0 = 71.72 per cent of full power, i.e. 0.7172 × 14920 = 10 700 kW. (Note: this result checks closely enough with our original estimate of 72.0 per cent).

The overall internal efficiency ratio at reduced power = 1079.3/1284.6 = 0.8402 compared with 1128.8/1319.0 = 0.8558 at full power.

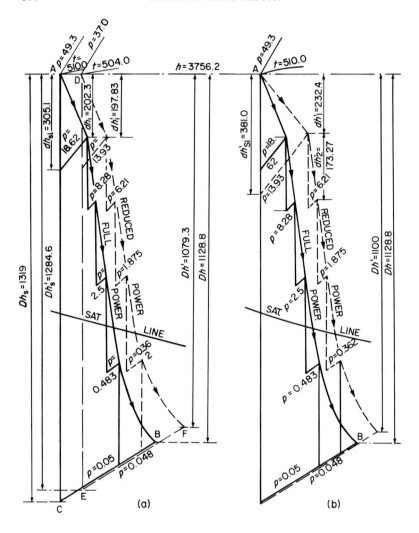

Figure 10.76 Mollier diagram for turbines at full power and at reduced power
(a) Power reduced by throttling
(b) Power reduced by nozzle control

If we allow an external loss factor of 0.95, the specific steam consumption of the turbines at full power = 3600/1128.8 × 0.95 = 3.357 kg/kWh, and the full power steam consumption = 3.357 × 14 920 = 50 080 kg/h. Thus 100.0 per cent steam (50 080 kg/h) gives 100.0 per cent power

(14 920 kW) and 75.0 per cent steam (37 560 kg/h) gives
71.72 per cent power (10 700 kW).

If the steam consumption, kg/h, of a *throttling* turbine is
plotted on a base of power, kW, the resulting points lie on a
straight line. This statement is known as *Willans' Law* and
the straight-line graph as the *Willans' Line*. The two points we
have established may therefore be plotted at *A* and *B*, and
Willans' line drawn through them as shown in Figure 10.77(b),
from which the steam consumption at any power may be
found, or calculated by simple algebra. The Willans' line
intersects the vertical axis at the point *C*, where the power
is zero and the steam consumption 6500 kg/h. This is known
as the *light load* steam consumption, and is virtually that
steam quantity required to supply *all* the turbine losses.

Marine geared turbines of course, cannot run at zero
power, since because of the propeller law, zero power would
require zero speed. (Constant-speed turbines, such as would be

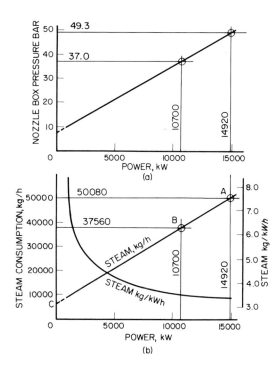

Figure 10.77 Characteristics of turbine power control by throttling only
(a) First stage nozzle box pressure
(b) Willans line and specific steam consumption

used for a turbo-electric installation, run under control of a speed governor. Such turbines can run at full speed but delivering no power at the generator terminals). In the present case of geared turbines, C is a theoretical point, and the steam consumption at this point is usually between 6.0 and 10.0 per cent of the full power steam consumption.

If for the various powers we divide the steam consumption in kg/h by the power in kW, we obtain a curve of specific steam consumption, kg/kWh, and this curve may conveniently be plotted on the same diagram as the Willans' line, as shown in Figure 10.77(b).

We already know that the steam quantity passing through a stage is directly proportional to the pressure in front of the nozzles. From Willans' Law, the steam quantity is directly proportional to the power, therefore the stage pressures (except the last three) are also directly proportional to the power. This is shown in Figure 10.77(a) which is drawn for the pressure in front of the first stage nozzles. A graph of this type is the *reference* for throttle control, e.g. if we wish to reduce power from 100.0 per cent to 72.0 per cent, we must close in the manoeuvring valve until the first stage nozzle box pressure is reduced from 49.3 bar to 37.0 bar. Sometimes the pressure in front of the second stage is used for this purpose— this makes no difference in principle—only the pressure corresponding to any particular power will be lower.

From Figure 10.77(b) it will be evident that the lowest specific steam consumption is at full power. This is the most economical power at which to operate throttling turbines, i.e. the power at which we get the greatest amount of work from 1.0 kg of steam. However, full power implies full ship speed, and if there is a protracted period during which only 0.895 of the full ship speed is justified, then the turbines may be throttled in to the requisite 72.0 per cent power, so reducing the steam consumption to 75.0 per cent of full power steam, which, allowing for some fall off in boiler efficiency, would reduce the fuel consumption to possibly 77.0 per cent of full power fuel consumption.

Note that with throttle control, the power is *infinitely variable* throughout the power range, i.e. the manoeuvring valve can be adjusted to give *any* power variation, large or small.

Strictly speaking, we should in each case have corrected

Dh by the leaving loss factor, but as the relative effect is small, it has been omitted for clarity.

NOZZLE CONTROL

In this system of varying the power, the full steam pressure and temperature are maintained in front of the first stage nozzles, and the *steam quantity* passing through the turbines is varied by varying only the nozzle throat areas.

Theoretically and ideally, this would mean varying the nozzle throat areas of *all* the turbine stages in the same proportion as the power variation required, e.g. for half power, the total throat areas of all the stages would be reduced roughly by half, and the overall expansion line would not differ much from the full power expansion line. Such an arrangement however, would be much too complicated and expensive in practice, and in consequence, only the first stage nozzle area is made variable, and even then, only in several distinct steps (several *discrete powers*).

Consider the turbines in the last example, but with the first stage nozzles divided into four groups, each group having the same total nozzle throat area, and each of three of the groups having its own shut-off valve, all steam first passing through the manoeuvring valve. At full power, the manoeuvring valve and all three nozzle control valves would be fully open, and the full power expansion line *AB* in Figure 10.76(b) would be exactly the same as the full power expansion line *AB* for the throttling turbines in Figure 10.76(a).

To reduce the power, let one nozzle control valve be fully closed. The first stage nozzle area is reduced to 75.0 per cent of the full power area, hence only 75.0 per cent of the full power steam now passes through the turbines. The nozzle areas of the remaining stages however, are unaltered, hence the pressures in front of all the stages *except the first* fall to 0.75 of the full power pressures. Thus the adiabatic enthalpy drop across the first stage is increased, but the adiabatic enthalpy drops across the remaining stages do not differ sensibly from the full power adiabatic enthalpy drops.

Reference to Figure 10.76(b) will show that the first stage adiabatic enthalpy drop at reduced power is 381.0 kJ/kg compared with 305.1 kJ/kg at full power, i.e. 1.249 times. Thus at reduced power, the first stage C_0 increases by $\sqrt{1.249} = 1.1176$. Again assuming that 75.0 per cent steam will give about 72.0 per cent power, the propeller speed, and hence all the mean blade velocities will fall to $\sqrt[3]{0.72} = 0.895$ of the full power velocities, and

$$\text{First stage } \frac{u}{C_0} = 0.23 \times \frac{0.895}{1.1176} = 0.1842$$

From Figure 10.75,

Efficiency correction factor = 0.92, hence
First stage efficiency = 0.663 × 0.92 = 0.61, and
First stage internal enthalpy drop = 381.0 × 0.61
$$= 232.4 \text{ kJ/kg}$$

This is plotted on the Mollier Diagram, Figure 10.76(b), and the succeeding stages treated similarly, e.g. for the second stage which is a single-row impulse, the adiabatic enthalpy drop, and hence C_0, do not change

$$\therefore \text{ Reduced power } \frac{u}{C_0} = 0.455 \times 0.895 = 0.4072$$

Corrector factor from Figure 10.75 = 0.98
$\therefore$ Stage efficiency = 0.8 × 0.98 = 0.784
Stage internal enthalpy drop = 221.0 × 0.784
$$= 173.27 \text{ kJ/kg}$$

The expansion line, shown dotted in Figure 10.76(b), gives an overall internal enthalpy drop of 1100 kJ/kg compared with 1128.8 kJ/kg at full power. With 75.0 per cent steam therefore, the reduced power is 0.75 × 1100/1128.8 = 0.7308, or 73.08 per cent of full power = 0.7308 × 14920 = 10 904 kW. The reduced power internal efficiency ratio = 1100/1319 = 0.834.

Thus for the same steam quantity, nozzle control gives us more power than throttling, i.e. power reduction by nozzle control is *more efficient than by throttling*. The underlying reasons for this are:

1. The throttled adiabatic heat drop is always the lesser
2. The reduced power internal efficiency ratio of the nozzle controlled turbines is only very slightly worse than that of the throttled turbines. Figure 10.78 will make this clear.

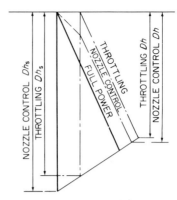

Figure 10.78 Comparison of enthalpy drops for throttling and nozzle control
Throttling Dh$_s$ < nozzle control Dh$_s$
Throttling Dh/Dh$_s$ $\doteq$ nozzle control Dh/Dh$_s$
Throttling Dh < nozzle control Dh

If two nozzle control valves are closed, the above type of calculation is carried out using 50.0 per cent steam, and so on.

COMBINED THROTTLING AND NOZZLE CONTROL

Again consider the turbines in the last example, running at full power with all three nozzle control valves open, i.e. all four nozzle groups open. If the manoeuvring valve is progressively closed in, all four nozzle groups still being open, the power will be reduced solely by throttling, and the steam consumption and nozzle box pressure characteristics will be the same as in Figure 10.77, i.e. *AB* in Figure 10.79.

If, when the power is so reduced to 72.0/73.0 per cent of full power, and one nozzle control valve is then closed fully, a *reduced quantity* of steam is passed through the turbines, and hence to maintain the reduced power we must open up the manoeuvring valve to restore full nozzle box pressure so that the *enthalpy drop is increased* to compensate for the reduced steam quantity. In this condition, the operating point would be *C* in Figure 10.79. Thus for this particular power, we can operate either at *B* or at *C*—obviously *C* is the more economical operating point since it requires less steam, and therefore less fuel than *B*. At *C* we have not reduced the heat drop by throttling.

If with three nozzle groups remaining open, we again progressively close in the manoeuvring valve, the power is further reduced below 72.0/73.0 per cent by throttling and the operating point moves from *C* to *D* in Figure 10.79. At *D*, we may fully close a second nozzle control valve, and again open up the manoeuvring valve, when the operating point

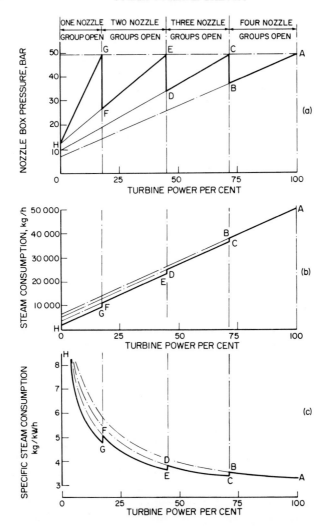

Figure 10.79 Characteristics of turbine power variation by combined throttling and power control
(a) Nozzle box pressure
(b) Steam consumption
(c) Specific steam consumption

would move from *D* to *E*. Further power reduction by throttling can then be obtained from *E* to *F*, when the third nozzle group could be shut off causing the operating point to move from *F* to *G*. Very low powers would then be obtained by throttling between *G* and *H* with only one nozzle group open.

There are virtually four separate Willans' lines (see Figure 10.79(b)), depending on whether one, two, three or four nozzle groups are open, and opening or closing of a nozzle control valve changes the operation from one Willans' line to another. The points G, E, C and A show the maximum powers respectively which can be obtained with one, two, three or four nozzle groups in operation. For clarity, the reduced power lines have been drawn somewhat out of proportion.

Our choice of four nozzle groups, of equal total throat area, was made quite arbitrarily to demonstrate a principle. In practice, the nozzle control points are chosen to give that combination of service powers which will best suit the anticipated variation of operating conditions. In some cases, the nozzle groups are arranged so that one of them gives a power greater than full power, hence the term *overload nozzles*.

BYPASS OVERLOAD

Another method of obtaining powers higher than the most economical nominal full power is to use an overload bypass. Steam at the initial conditions, byepasses the first or first few stages of the H.P. turbine in such a manner that more than full power steam may be passed through the suceeding stages.

Again consider the turbines in the previous examples, with only throttle control up to full power. For overload, let 15.0 per cent additional steam byepass the first (Curtis) stage; hence 15.0 per cent more steam will pass through the stages after the byepass. Basically, this means that all the stage pressures will increase by 15.0 per cent. The first stage pressure = $18.6 \times 1.15 = 21.4$ bar, and since this is still less than 0.5455 times the first stage nozzle box pressure, expansion through the first stage nozzles remains critical, and the quantity of steam passing through the first stage will be unaltered. The additional 15.0 per cent of steam is throttled through the byepass valve from 49.3 bar, 510.0°C to 21.4 bar, and then mixes with the steam leaving the first stage, the mixture then passing on through the second and succeeding stages.

The behaviour of the stages preceding the bypass belt is complex, and a full treatment of this is beyond present scope. For our purpose, we may assume that the first-stage internal efficiency ratio when the bypass is open is very low—possibly of the order of 0.4. If this is so, then referring to Figure 10.80

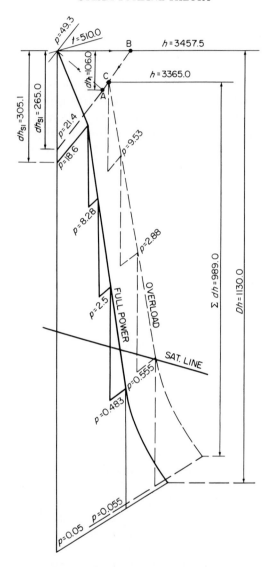

Figure 10.80 Mollier diagram for full power and for overload on bypass

the first stage internal enthalpy drop on overload = 265.0 ×
0.4 = 106.0 kJ/kg, hence the enthalpy of the steam leaving
the first stage = 3457.5 − 106.0 = 3351.5 kJ/kg, i.e. the point
A. Hence 1.0 kg of steam at A having enthalpy 3351.5 kJ/kg
mixes with 0.15 kg of steam which has been throttled through

the bypass valve to B, having enthalpy 3457.5 kJ/kg. The enthalpy of the mixed steam at C passing to the second stage is therefore

$$\frac{(1.0 \times 3351.5) + (0.15 \times 3457.5)}{1.0 + 0.15} = \frac{3351.5 + 518.6}{1.15}$$

$$= \frac{3870.1}{1.15} = 3365.0 \text{ kJ/kg}$$

The overload expansion line for the stages following the bypass is then built up as explained previously, and the overall internal heat drop 989.0 kJ/kg for these stages so obtained. For every 1.0 kg of steam passing through the first stage and doing 106.0 kJ of work, 1.15 kg passes through the remaining stages doing 989.0 kJ of work. Thus the increased power is found from

$$\frac{(1.0 \times 106.0) + (1.15 \times 989.0)}{1.0 \times 1130.0} = \frac{106.0 + 1137.4}{1130.0}$$

$$= \frac{1243.4}{1130.0} = 1.1 \text{ or } 110.0$$

per cent of full power or $1.1 \times 14920 = 16\,412$ kW.

The steam consumption is $1.15 \times 50\,080 = 57\,592$ kg/h and the specific steam consumption $= 57\,592/16\,412 = 3.5096$ kg/kWh. This is higher than the full power specific steam consumption since increased power by overload byepass involves a throttling loss, a poor performance of the stage(s) preceding the bypass, and a u/C_0 efficiency correction on all other stages.

The provision of a bypass for overload has little or no effect on efficiency when the turbines are running at normal full power. If we omit the bypass, and obtain overload by throttling, then the turbines would run throttled at full power, and there would be a considerable throttling loss at this, the power which should be the most economical. If we omit the bypass and provide an additional group of overload nozzles, then there is an adverse efficiency effect at full power, since the blades facing the closed nozzles do no work, other than churning the steam in the wheel case, which is *negative* work.

All-reaction turbines must have full all-round admission of steam because of the pressure drop through the moving blades, hence nozzle control cannot be used. Reduced power is obtained by throttling and overload by bypass. A two-row Curtis impulse first stage is sometimes used in reaction turbines, thus permitting the use of nozzle control. Most modern marine steam turbines have impulse-type stages at the H.P. end and reaction-type stages at the L.P. end. Power variation is almost invariably obtained by combined throttling and nozzle control.

The provision of overload facilities on turbines implies that the boilers are capable of producing the additional steam, and that the turbines are capable of withstanding the increased pressures and forces.

The turbines used in this section have been considerably simplified with the object of simplifying the principles of power variation. In practice, the turbines would have many more stages than is shown in the various hs diagrams, and if they are feed heating turbines, the steam quantities through the different sections would vary. The principles which this section attempts to explain are, however, in no way altered by the simplifications which have been adopted for clarity.

Reversal and astern running

If a ship is steaming full ahead, then before it can be made to move astern at all, the entire kinetic energy of the ship in the forward direction must be destroyed. If in the first place, ahead steam is merely shut off, the forward way of the ship, and the tendency of the propeller to turn in the ahead direction will continue until the ship's kinetic energy is exhausted by the hull resistance. The period of time required for this, prior to the application of astern torque, would be much too long to give safe and satisfactory manoeuvring characteristics, and to reduce it, the main engines and/or the transmission system and propeller are used as a "brake" on the ship.

Thus, if astern torque is applied while the ship is still moving ahead, there must be some "slipping device" in the engines, or in the transmission, or in the propeller, which will accommodate the ahead torque applied by the ship while it is slowing down, and the astern torque applied by the engines, and which by this slipping, will simultaneously dissipate the entire forward kinetic energy of the ship.

When all the forward kinetic energy has been dissipated, the ahead torque becomes zero, slipping ceases, and the astern torque then accelerates the ship in the astern direction.

Depending on the type of engine, transmission and propeller, there are several alternative ways in which the above requirements can be met. With steam turbine-driven ships, by far the most usual way is by the provision of an astern turbine (or turbines). A possible alternative is to use a variable pitch propeller. Other alternatives are discussed in Chapter 4, dealing with reduction gears.

Astern turbines

The astern turbine is mounted on the same shaft as one, or more, of the ahead turbines, but has nozzles and blades of the opposite hand.

Based on satisfactory manoeuvrability of the ship, the most usual requirements for the astern turbine(s) are:

1. That it will give 80.0 per cent of the full power ahead torque at 50.0 per cent of the full ahead propeller speed with 100.0 per cent full ahead steam flow.
2. That it can maintain 70.0 per cent of full ahead propeller speed for at least 30.0 minutes without distress in any part of the plant.

To understand these requirements properly, we have to consider the turbine characteristic with full steam in relation to the propeller law.

Earlier in this chapter, when dealing with the velocity diagrams for a turbine stage, we saw that the *force* on the blades = $M\,C_w$, N, where M is the steam flow, kg/s, and C_w is the velocity of whirl, m/s.

Now, the radius of the blade ring is $D_m/2$, hence the *torque* on the blades = force × radius = $M\,C_w\,D_m/2$, Nm, thus for any given mean diameter D_m and any given steam flow M, the *blading torque* is directly proportional to C_w.

If for our present purpose, we assume that due to internal and external losses, only 0.9 of the blading torque is available at the shaft, then the shaft torque is proportional to $0.9C_w$. For example, at full power with full steam, the turbine stage illustrated in Figure 10.44 of this chapter gives $C_w = 217.68$ m/s, hence the shaft torque is proportional to $0.9 \times 217.68 = 195.92$. This figure we may regard as 100.0 per cent torque.

Now, Figure 10.74 of this chapter shows that if the mean blade velocity u is reduced from 119.68 m/s (i.e. 100.0 per cent propeller speed) to 70.0 m/s (58.5 per cent propeller speed), then C_w is increased from 217.68 m/s (100.0 per cent) to 306.24 m/s (140.7 per cent). Hence *if full power steam flow is maintained*, the shaft torque is increased from

$$\begin{array}{lll}
(0.9 \times 217.68) & \text{to} & (0.9 \times 306.24) \\
= 195.92 & \text{to} & 275.62, \text{ i.e. from} \\
100.0 \text{ per cent} & \text{to} & 140.07 \text{ per cent}
\end{array}$$

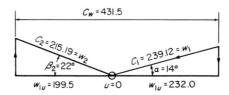

Figure 10.81 Effect of zero blade velocity on C_w

If the propeller speed is reduced to zero (i.e. $u = 0$), then from Figure 10.81, $C_w = 431.5$ m/s, and with constant full power steam flow M kg/s, shaft torque $\propto 0.9 \times 431.5 = 388.85$, which is

$$\frac{388.35}{195.92} \times 100.0 = 198.2 \text{ per cent of full ahead torque}$$

This means that at zero propeller speed and with full steam flow, a single-row stage with full power $u/C_0 = 0.4851$ develops 1.982 times the full power shaft torque. This is called the *standstill* torque, i.e. the torque developed by the turbines when full steam is applied against a stationary propeller. This particular stage has a *standstill torque ratio* of 1.982. By repeating the above procedure for this stage at varying propeller speeds, we can plot the curve shown in Figure 10.82, which for our purpose is near enough a straight line.

If, using the above methods, we calculate the standstill torque ratio for a series of stages having various values of full

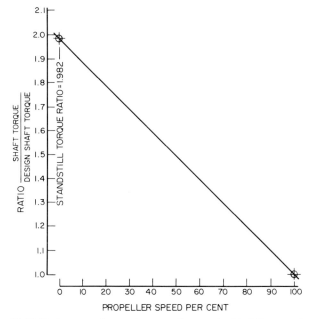

Figure 10.82 Shaft torque for varying propeller speed with full steam flow for a single-row impulse stage having full power $u/C_0 = 0.4851$

power u/C_0, we can plot the curve shown in Figure 10.83, from which it will be seen that for a given full power u/C_0, there exists a certain definite standstill torque ratio. This is equally true for two-row velocity-compounded stages provided that we use the appropriate value of the full power u/C_0 as shown in Figure 10.83. For any given full power u/C_0, the curve of standstill torque ratio on a base of per cent propeller speed, i.e. the *turbine torque characteristic*, may be assumed to be a straight line.

If we assume the approximate propeller law that the power absorbed varies directly as the cube of the propeller speed, then we may write that power $\propto$ speed^3. Also for the propeller, power = torque × speed × 2π, hence power $\propto$ (torque × speed) and therefore we may write that

$$\text{Torque} \times \text{speed} \propto \text{speed}^3$$

$$\therefore \text{Torque} \propto \text{speed}^2$$

Thus for the propeller, power $\propto$ speed^3, and torque $\propto$ speed^2, which enables us to draw the propeller power and torque curves shown in Figure 10.84.

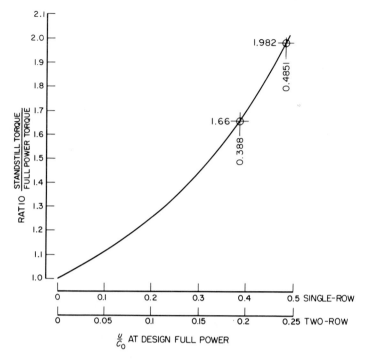

Figure 10.83 Standstill torque ratio for various values of design u/C_0

The astern turbine is specified to develop 80.0 per cent of full ahead torque at 50.0 per cent of full ahead propeller speed, therefore the astern turbine torque characteristic must pass through point A (Figure 10.84), and the slope of this characteristic will determine the design full astern power DB', the design full astern torque DB, and the standstill torque ratio OC/DB of the astern turbine. This torque ratio enables the design astern u/C_0 to be found from Figure 10.83.

For example, suppose the design astern power is made 52.0 per cent of full ahead power (point B' in Figure 10.84), then the standstill torque $OC = 106.6$ per cent, and the design astern torque $DB = 64.0$ per cent of the ahead full power and torque respectively. Thus the standstill torque ratio for the astern turbine $= 106.6/64.0 = 1.66$, which from Figure 10.83 requires the astern turbine to be designed with $u/C_0 = 0.194$ for two-row stages and 0.388 for single-row stages.

To summarise, this means that the astern turbine(s) would be designed to give 52.0 per cent of full ahead power at 80.0

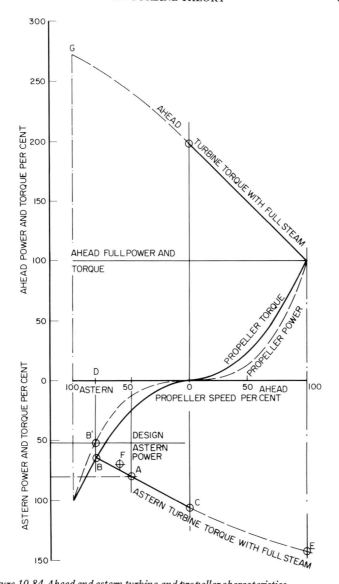

Figure 10.84 Ahead and astern turbine and propeller characteristics

per cent of full ahead propeller speed with full ahead steam flow, and with $u/C_0 = 0.194$ for two-row stages and 0.388 for single-row stages.

Referring to Figure 10.84, the following points should be noted:

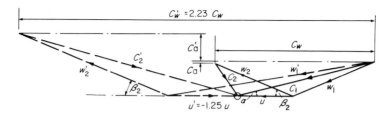

Figure 10.85 Typical velocity diagrams for astern turbine
Full line = normal full astern condition
Broken line = approximate condition at instant of initiating crash reversal

1. If at the instant of initiating reversal, it is assumed that
   full ahead steam is shut and full astern steam is opened
   simultaneously, then at this instant the propeller is running ahead at 100.0 per cent speed and the astern
   turbine mean blade velocity u is $1/0.8 = 1.25$ *times
   normal astern value but is in the ahead direction.*

   This is illustrated in Figure 10.85 in which the full
   lines show typical velocity diagrams for the astern
   turbine when running at full astern power and speed,
   and the dotted lines at the instant when full ahead
   steam is shut off and full astern steam is applied. In the
   latter condition, the instantaneous value C_w' is 2.23
   times the normal full astern value C_w, i.e. the instantaneous torque applied by the astern turbine is 2.23 times
   the normal full astern torque, which, from Figure 10.84,
   is $2.23 \times 64.0 = 143.0$ per cent of full ahead torque.

   This means that at the instant of initiating a "crash"
   reversal from full ahead to full astern, the propeller
   is turning at 100.0 per cent ahead speed and exerting
   100.0 per cent ahead torque on the astern turbine, while
   the astern turbine is exerting 143.0 per cent of ahead
   torque (point E in Figure 10.84). The excess of astern
   turbine torque over ahead propeller torque rapidly slows
   down the propeller, until it comes to rest momentarily
   at C in Figure 10.84, at which point the astern turbine is
   exerting its standstill torque. During this period, the
   astern turbine itself acts as the "slipping" device, i.e.
   although it has full astern steam, the propeller is still
   driving it in the ahead direction, and the propeller power
   (i.e. the forward kinetic energy of the ship) is being
   destroyed by doing negative work (on the steam) in the

astern turbine. The greatly increased values of C_2' (leaving loss $> C_0$) and C_a' (axial thrust) in Figure 10.85 compared with C_2 and C_a are indicative of this energy dissipation. C_2' appears as heat in the steam leaving the astern turbine and is ultimately dissipated in the condenser, while C_a' is ultimately dissipated as heat at the turbine thrust block.

After the propeller comes to rest at C in Figure 10.84, it is accelerated in the astern direction by the excess of the astern turbine torque over the propeller torque until at B the propeller speed is 80.0 per cent of the full ahead speed, when the astern turbine is developing full astern power and full astern torque, having in the process passed through the specified point A. At B in Figure 10.84 the astern turbine torque and the propeller torque are in balance, hence the propeller speed remains constant at 80.0 per cent of the full ahead speed.

2. The increase of enthalpy of the steam due to the destruction of energy must not overheat either the astern or the ahead turbine to an undesirable extent, otherwise trouble could result from rotor or casing distortion, relaxation of blade fixings, etc. The materials and the detail design of the turbines must be such as to eliminate any such possibilities. The turbines must be designed to safely withstand the maximum instantaneous reversal torques.

3. Full ahead steam applied to the ahead turbine(s) produces 100.0 per cent power. The same steam quantity applied to the astern turbine produces only 52.0 per cent power. The astern turbine is much smaller and simpler than the ahead turbine(s) but at the expense of being much less efficient. Normally, however, the astern turbine is used much less frequently and for much shorter periods, hence efficiency is of less importance than the saving in space, mass and first cost.

3. The astern turbine shown in Figure 10.84, designed for 80.0 per cent of full ahead torque at 50.0 per cent full ahead propeller speed, would also meet 70.0 per cent full ahead torque at 60.0 per cent full ahead propeller speed (point F in Figure 10.84) had the latter been specified.

5. In a "crash" reversal from full astern to full ahead, although less energy has to be destroyed, it has to be destroyed in a shorter period of time since the opposing

torque of the ahead turbine(s) is relatively much greater. The transition from full astern to full ahead is faster than from full ahead to full astern and the turbine design must safely accommodate the greater *rate* of energy dissipation.

Controllable-pitch propeller

The propeller blades can be rotated about the vertical axes through their roots by hydraulic/mechanical means (see *Marine Auxiliary Machinery* of the Marine Engineering Series published by Butterworths) over the entire range from full ahead pitch to full astern pitch. The turbines are *unidirectional* (i.e. there is no astern turbine), and on reversal, the dissipation of the ahead kinetic energy of the ship takes place at the propeller itself by "churning", the resultant large forces due to the opposing torques being carried by the propeller blades and the pitch-changing mechanism inside the propeller boss.

11 Regenerative feed heating

The majority of modern steam jobs, whether fitted with reciprocating or turbine engines or with both, are designed for heating of the boiler feed water by steam extracted from the engines or turbines at some intermediate point or points in its expansion.

Many engineers find some difficulty in understanding clearly why economies can be made by this means, since by any such extraction of steam, the engines or turbines are *robbed* of a certain amount of work, thus causing the steam-consumption rate in lb/h.p. hour to increase.

It must, however, be remembered that thermal economy in a steam power-plant depends not only on how much work is *got out* of the steam, but also on how much fuel heat had to be *put into* the steam to produce it.

Thus, economy will result if for any given weight of steam/hour:

(a) The work obtained from the steam can be increased.
(b) The fuel heat put into the steam can be reduced.

Extraction feed heating causes the work obtained from the steam to diminish, but provided the system is correctly designed and operated, the fuel-heat input is reduced to such an extent that it more than compensates for the reduced work, hence the net result is a thermal gain, i.e., more heat goes back to the boiler in the feed water than the equivalent work-heat lost by the engine.

This chapter—dealing with theory and practice of feed heating—attempts to approach the subject in two ways. Firstly, without having recourse to thermodynamical theory, a straight triple-expansion engine is considered:

1. without feed heating;
2. with a single stage of feed heating utilizing some of the I.P. exhaust steam;
3. with a single stage of feed heating utilizing some of the H.P. exhaust steam;
4. with two stages of feed heating utilizing some of the H.P. and I.P. exhaust steam;

and the effect of these different feed-heating arrangements on the overall efficiency demonstrated in a practical manner.

Secondly, the theoretical aspects of feed heating are examined and the association of such thermodynamical theory with practical feed heating is shown.

1. STRAIGHT TRIPLE EXPANSION ENGINE WITHOUT FEED HEATING

Figure 11.1 shows a typical example of such an engine as is used in marine practice.

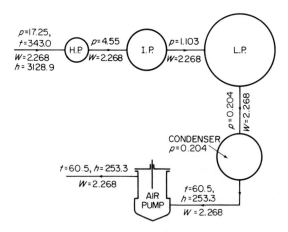

Figure 11.1 Straight triple-expansion engine without feed heating

The steam pressures p are in bar, the temperatures t in °C. The steam quantity W, kg/s, is the same throughout the engine, and any pressure and temperature drops between cylinders are ignored. The H.P. cylinder develops an indicated power of 517.0 kW, the I.P. cylinder 442.0 kW and the L.P. cylinder 373.0 kW, giving a total engine power of 1332.0 kW.

Now, by definition 1 W = 1 J/s, hence 1 kW = 1 kJ/s, hence the work *output* of the engine, stated in heat units is 1332.0 kJ/s.

To produce this output, the engine requires 2.268 kg/s of steam, at 17.25 bar, 343.0°C, which from the Steam Tables, has a specific enthalpy of 3128.9 kJ/kg reckoned above 0°C. The feed temperature however, is not 0°C but is 60.5°C. Hence the feed water entering the boiler already has enthalpy 253.3 kJ/kg, and the nett heat received in the boiler is therefore $3128 - 253.3 = 2875.6$ kJ/kg.

Thus the net heat *input* to the engine is $2.268 \times 2875.6 = 6521.87$ kJ/s and the indicated thermal efficiency

$$= \frac{\text{output}}{\text{input}} = \frac{1332.0}{6521.87} = 0.2043, \text{ or } 20.43\%$$

Note that the steam consumption rate is

$$\frac{2.268}{1332.0} \times 3600 = 6.13 \text{ kg/kWh,}$$

and since each 1 kg of steam requires a nett heat input of 2875.6 kJ, the heat consumption rate of the engine is $6.13 \times 2875.6 = 17627.43$ kJ/kWh.

(*Note*: The latter figure is sometimes called the *water* heat consumption rate, since it includes only the engine and condenser. The *fuel* heat consumption rate is that of the whole plant, including the boiler).

It is assumed in the foregoing calculation that the exhaust steam is condensed and the condensate is returned as feed water at the saturation temperature corresponding to the condenser pressure, i.e. there is no under cooling of the condensate.

2. TRIPLE EXPANSION ENGINE WITH A SINGLE STAGE OF FEED HEATING UTILISING SOME OF THE I.P. EXHAUST STEAM

Let the total quantity of steam supplied to the engine be the same as before, viz. 2.268 kg/s. Assume the same receiver pressures and same condenser pressure, and let the heater drain be returned to the condenser (see Figure 11.2).

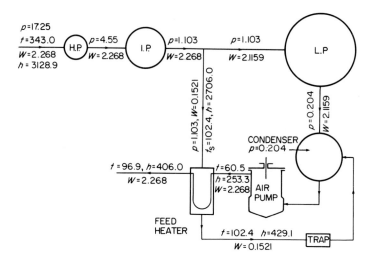

Figure 11.2 Triple-expansion engine with a single stage of feed heating utilising I.P. exhaust steam

The H.P. and I.P. cylinders will function exactly as before, since no alteration has been made to the initial or back pressures or to the steam quantity through the cylinders. The H.P. cylinder will develop indicated power 517 kW, and the I.P. cylinder 442 kW as before. The H.P. and I.P. cylinders together develop 959 kW, and since 1 kW = 1 kJ/s, these two cylinders together extract 959 kJ/s from the steam and convert this to work. A total of 2.268 kg/s of steam passes through these cylinders, hence heat extracted from the steam is 959.0/2.268 = 422.9 kJ/kg.

The specific enthalpy of the steam entering the H.P. cylinder is 3128.9 kJ/kg, hence the specific enthalpy of the steam leaving the I.P. cylinder at 1.103 bar is 3128.9 − 422.9 = 2706.0 kJ/kg. From the Steam Tables, steam at 1.103 bar has liquid enthalpy 429.1 kJ/kg, hence the increment for evaporation (latent heat) of the steam in the L.P. receiver is 2706.0 − 429.1 = 2276.9 kJ/kg. This is the quantity of heat given up by each 1 kg of steam in the feed heater, again assuming that the steam condenses in the heater and that the drain leaves at the saturation temperature.

Steam extracted from the I.P. exhaust at 1.103 bar has a saturation temperature of 102.4°C. A surface heater for this application would normally be designed to heat the feed water to within about 5.5°C of the saturation temperature of the heating steam, i.e. the feed temperature leaving the heater would be $102.4 - 5.5 = 96.9°C$. Thus 2.268 kg/s of water have to be heated from 60.5°C to 96.9°C. Water at 96.9°C has liquid enthalpy 406.0 kJ/kg hence

$$\text{Steam required} = \frac{2.268\,(406.0 - 253.3)}{2276.9} = 0.1521 \text{ kg/s},$$

to be extracted for the heater. The steam passing through the L.P. cylinder will be reduced to $2.268 - 0.1521 = 2.1159$ kg/s, causing the L.P. power to be reduced to

$$373.0 \times \frac{2.1159}{2.268} = 348.0 \text{ kW}$$

The total engine power will be $517 + 442 + 348 = 1307$ kW. The feed temperature is, however increased to 96.9°C which has liquid enthalpy 406.0 kJ/kg; hence the net heat received in the boiler is now $3128.9 - 406.0 = 2722.9$ kJ/kg. The net heat input is $2722.9 \times 2.268 = 6175.0$ kJ/s, and the indicated thermal efficiency $1307.0/6175.0 = 0.2117$ or 21.17%, compared with 20.43% for the non-feed heating engine.

Note that the *steam* consumption rate is *increased* to $2.268/1307.0 \times 3600 = 6.247$ kg/kWh but that the *heat* consumption rate is *reduced* to $2722.9 \times 6.247 = 17004.0$ kJ/kWh.

This represents a saving in fuel of $17627.43 - 17004.0/17627.43 \times 100 = 3.536$ per cent compared with the non-feed heating engine.

3. TRIPLE- EXPANSION ENGINE WITH A SINGLE STAGE OF FEED HEATING UTILISING SOME OF THE H.P. EXHAUST STEAM

Suppose that we had supplied the heater with steam extracted from the H.P. exhaust instead of the I.P. exhaust. (Refer to Figure 11.3).

The H.P. cylinder passes 2.268 kg/s of steam and develops 517.0 kW as before, hence the heat extracted from the steam in that cylinder is $517.0/2.268 = 228.0$ kJ/kg and the specific enthalpy of the steam at the H.P. exhaust is $3128.9 - 228.0 = 2900.9$ kJ/kg. From the Steam Tables, the liquid enthalpy of steam at 4.55 bar is 625.0 kJ/kg, hence the heat available for feed heating is $2900.0 - 625.0 = 2275.9$ kJ/kg. The

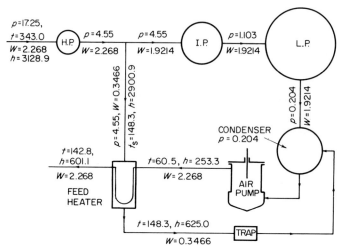

Figure 11.3 Triple expansion engine with a single stage of feed heating utilising H.P. exhaust steam

saturation temperature is 148.3°C hence the heater has to raise 2.268 kg/s of water from 60.5°C to 142.8°C requiring an extracted steam quantity of

$$\frac{2.268 \,(601.1 - 253.3)}{2275.9} = 0.3466 \text{ kg/s}$$

The steam through the I.P. and L.P. cylinders is 2.268 − 0.3466 = 1.9214 kg/s and the powers developed by these cylinders are

$$\text{I.P.} \ = 442.0 \times \frac{1.9214}{2.268} = 374.5 \text{ kW}$$

$$\text{L.P.} = 373.0 \times \frac{1.9214}{2.268} = 316.0 \text{ kW}$$

The total engine power is 517.0 + 374.5 + 316.0 = 1207.5 kW

The liquid enthalpy of feed water at 142.8°C is 601.1 kJ/kg hence the nett heat received in the boiler is 3128.9 − 601.1 = 2527.8 kJ/kg, and the indicated thermal efficiency is

$$\frac{1207.5}{2527.8 \times 2.268} = 0.2106, \text{ or } 21.06 \text{ per cent}$$

compared with 20.43 per cent for the non-feed heating engine, and with 21.17 per cent for the engine with I.P. exhaust heater.

Thus the improvement over the non-feed heating engine when the heater takes steam from the H.P. exhaust is actually less than that when the heater takes steam from the I.P. exhaust. Although we have further reduced the nett heat required in the boilers, we require a larger quantity of steam for the feed heater hence both the I.P. and L.P. cylinders are "robbed" of a greater amount of work. The reduced net heat is tending to be cancelled by the increased steam consumption rate. Our first conclusion therefore is that with the given steam conditions and with a single stage of feed heating, there is a definite feed temperature which gives maximum improvement in efficiency.

4. TRIPLE EXPANSION ENGINE WITH TWO STAGES OF FEED HEATING UTILISING SOME OF THE H.P. EXHAUST STEAM AND SOME OF THE I.P. EXHAUST STEAM

Let us now consider the effect of heating the feed to $142.8°C$ in two stages, i.e. two heaters, one using H.P. exhaust steam and one using I.P. exhaust steam. For simplicity at this stage, let the two heater drains be returned independently to the condenser. The temperatures, enthalpies, etc., would be as shown in Figure 11.4.

The H.P. cylinder passes 2.268 kg/s of steam and develops 517.0 kW as before, hence the specific enthalpy of the H.P. exhaust steam is 2900.9 kJ/kg as in Case 2.

$$\text{Steam to H.P. exhaust heater} = \frac{2.268\,(601.1 - 406.0)}{2900.9 - 625.0}$$

$$= \frac{2.268 \times 195.1}{2275.9} = 0.19442 \text{ kg/s}$$

$$\text{Steam through I.P. cylinder} = 2.268 - 0.19442$$
$$= 2.07358 \text{ kg/s}$$

$$\text{I.P. power} = 442.0 \times \frac{2.07358}{2.268} = 404.1 \text{ kW}$$

$$\text{Heat extracted from steam in I.P. cylinder} = \frac{404.1}{2.07358}$$

$$= 194.9 \text{ kJ/kg}$$

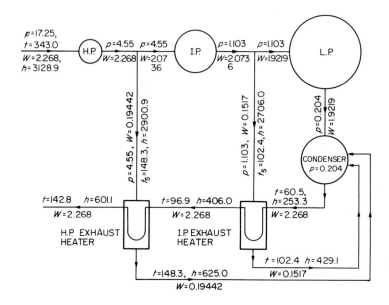

Figure 11.4 Triple-expansion engine with two stages of feed heating utilising I.P. exhaust steam and H.P. exhaust steam

∴ Specific enthalpy of I.P. exhaust steam
= 2900.9 − 194.9 = 2706.0 kJ/kg

$$\text{Steam to I.P. exhaust heater} = \frac{2.268\,(406.0 - 253.3)}{2706.0 - 429.1}$$

$$= \frac{2.268 \times 152.3}{2276.9}$$

$$= 0.15172 \text{ kg/s}$$

Steam through L.P. cylinder = 2.07358 − 0.15172
= 1.92188 kg/s

$$\text{L.P. power} = 373 \times \frac{1.92186}{2.268} = 316.1 \text{ kW}$$

Total engine power = 517 + 404.1 + 316.1 = 1237.2 kW

The net heat received in the boiler = 3128.9 − 601.1

$$= 2527.8 \text{ kJ/kg}$$

Hence indicated thermal efficiency $= \dfrac{1237.2}{2527.8 \times 2.268}$

$$= 0.2158 \text{ or } 21.58\%$$

compared with 20.43% for the non-feed heating engine.

We may summarise these results as follows

Case	Indicated thermal efficiency	Difference (per cent)
Non-feed heating	0.2043	0
Single stage of feed heating, I.P. exhaust	0.2117	+3.622
Single stage of feed heating, H.P. exhaust	0.2106	+3.084
Two stages of feed heating, I.P. and H.P. exhaust	0.2158	+5.629

For the same feed temperature, the two-stage system shows a considerable improvement over either of the two single-stage systems.

The reason for this is because in the two-stage system, some of the steam for feed heating is extracted further *down* the engine, i.e. nearer the L.P. end, and has thus done a greater amount of work before it is extracted.

Feed temperature, number of feed heating stages and efficiency

Consideration of the last three examples will clearly illustrate the two conflicting features:

1. The higher the feed temperature, the less the net heat required in the boilers from the fuel, and therefore the higher the efficiency.

2. The higher the feed temperature, the higher the last stage extraction pressure. Steam extracted at a high pressure has done only a small amount of work in the engine, and consequently large quantities of steam extracted at high pressures lead to *less gain* in efficiency, and indeed, in the limit, to worsening the efficiency compared with the non-feed heating engine.

Good feed heating design and operation aims at making a compromise between these features to obtain the highest possible increase in efficiency commensurate with simplicity, reliability and first cost.

The foregoing examples attempt to explain, as simply as possible at this stage, the broad principles of feed heating, and to achieve this object we have over-simplified certain factors. The next section attempts to describe, in practical terms, what modifications are made to our over-simplified system to further increase the efficiency, to ensure reliability, and to meet certain other requirements, thus leading to understanding of the apparently complicated feed heating systems now in general use at sea.

DEVELOPMENT OF THE FEED HEATING SYSTEM

Disposition of the heater drains

Figure 11.4 shows both the I.P. and H.P. exhaust heater drains returned directly and independently to the condenser. The drain water leaving the H.P. exhaust heater has liquid enthalpy 625.0 kJ/kg, and in the condenser this is reduced to 253.3 kJ/kg. Each 1.0 kg of drain water therefore loses $625.0 - 253.3 = 371.7$ kJ in the condenser, this 371.7 kJ/kg being transferred to the circulating water and lost in the overboard discharge. This loss therefore amounts to $371.3 \times 0.19442 = 72.19$ kJ/s. If instead of passing to the condenser, the H.P. exhaust heater drain could be returned to the feed pipe after the H.P. exhaust heater, the 72.19 kJ/s would be retained in the system and would cause a feed water enthalpy rise of $72.19/2.268 = 31.83$ kJ/kg. The enthalpy of the feed water entering the boiler would be increased to 601.1+

31.83 = 632.93 kJ/kg, the net heat received in the boiler would be reduced to 3128.9 − 632.93 = 2495.97 kJ/kg and the overall thermal efficiency increased to

$$\frac{1237.2}{2495.97 \times 2.268} = 0.21826$$

or 21.826 per cent. This is an improvement of

$$\frac{21.826 - 20.43}{20.43} \times 100 = 6.83\%$$

over the non-feed heating engine, and an improvement of

$$\frac{21.826 - 21.58}{21.58} \times 100 = 1.14 \text{ per cent}$$

over the two-stage system with both drains discharged to the condenser.

Similarly, by returning the I.P. exhaust heater drain into the feed pipe between the heaters, a further improvement could be made.

Provided the feed temperature leaving any heater is less than the temperature of the drain water leaving that heater, this is the most efficient method of disposing of the heater drains, as it returns the drain heat to the system at the highest possible temperature level. A drain pump however, would be required for each heater, which causes complication and expense. In practice, the H.P. heater drain is often *cascaded* into the I.P. exhaust heater shell in which it is cooled down from 148.3°C to 102.4°C, the liquid enthalpy difference 625.0 − 429.1 = 195.9 kJ/kg being transferred to the feed water passing through that heater, thus requiring less I.P. exhaust steam.

The combined drain from the I.P. exhaust heater may be pumped forward into the feed pipe as previously explained, or it may be passed through a drain cooler before being discharged to the feed tank or to the condenser. Neither of the latter methods is as efficient as individual pumping forward, since the drain heat is degraded (i.e. has its temperature reduced) before being applied to the feed water. Normally the number of drain pumps in any system is limited to not more than one, some systems having no drain pump at all.

Referring to Figure 11.4 if the H.P. exhaust heater drain is cascaded to the I.P. exhaust heater, it is cooled down from 148.3°C to 102.4°C in that heater, the liquid enthalpy difference 625.0 − 429.1 = 195.9 kJ/kg being transferred to the feed water. Thus, the cascaded drain enthalpy difference will cause a feed water enthalpy rise of

$$\frac{0.19442 \times 195.9}{2.268} = 16.79 \text{ kJ/kg}$$

hence the steam to the I.P. exhaust heater will be reduced to

$$0.15172 \times \frac{152.7 - 16.79}{152.7} = 0.1350 \text{ kg/s}$$

thus the steam through the L.P. cylinder will be increased to 2.0736 − 0.1350 = 1.9386 kg/s, and the L.P. power increased to

$$373 \times \frac{1.9386}{2.268} = 318.85 \text{ kW}$$

The total engine power will be increased to 517 + 404.1 + 318.85 = 1239.95 kW, and assuming the I.P. heater drain discharged to the condenser, the overall thermal efficiency

$$= \frac{1239.95}{2527.8 \times 2.268} = 0.2163 \text{ or } 21.63\%$$

This is an improvement of

$$\frac{21.63 - 20.43}{20.43} \times 100 = 5.87\%$$

over the non-feed heating engine.

A further improvement of course could be made by pumping forward the I.P. exhaust heater drain, or by passing it
through a drain cooler before discharging it to the condenser.

FLASHING OF HEATER DRAINS

It will be evident that in cascading the H.P. exhaust heater
drain to the I.P. exhaust heater, some device is necessary to
break down the pressure from 4.55 bar to 1.103 bar so as to
prevent steam and water blowing straight through from heater
to heater. A water level gauge may be fitted to the H.P.
exhaust heater and the level kept correct by manual manipu-
lation of a drain valve on the heater bottom. In modern feed
heating systems an automatic drain valve is used, operated
either electrically or pneumatically, operation of the valve
being initiated by the heater water level such that rising level
opens up the valve and falling level closes it in. Alternatively,
an orifice plate may be fitted in the drain pipe between the
heaters, the orifice being sized to pass the full power drain
quantity with the appropriate pressure difference. Although
such an arrangement works fairly well over the entire power
range, drainage is not necessarily correct at reduced powers
and under certain emergency conditions. Another method is
to use a drain trap. One such trap is shown in Figure 11.5. As

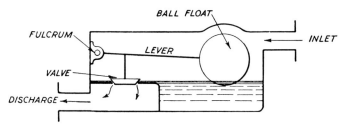

Figure 11.5 Ball-float trap for draining feed heater

the water level in the trap rises the ball float rises and opens
up the valve. The steam pressure difference blows some of the
water out, the level falls and the ball float closes in the valve
when such a trap is operating correctly, the discharge should
be practically continuous, the valve merely floating between
closed and slightly open.

Whichever method of drain control is used, one important
feature of drain cascading is *flashing* of the drain water resulting from the pressure reduction. If in Figure 11.4 we had
cascaded the H.P. exhaust heater drain to the I.P. exhaust

heater, saturated water at 148.3 °C and having liquid enthalpy
625.0 kJ/kg passes through the restriction of the drain orifice
or trap and comes under the influence of the I.P. exhaust
heater pressure where it can no longer exist as water at
148.3 °C, but must immediately reduce its temperature to
102.4 °C (the saturation temperature corresponding to 1.103
bar) and its liquid enthalpy to 429.1 kJ/kg. The liquid enthalpy difference $625.0 - 429.1 = 195.9$ kJ/kg is flashed off
as saturated steam at 1.103 bar. The enthalpy of evaporation
at this pressure is 2250.6 kJ/kg. Hence for every 1.0 kg of
drain water the pressure reduction will cause $195.9/2250.6 =$
0.08705 kg to flash into saturated steam. This process is
illustrated in Figure 11.6.

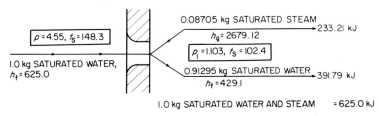

Figure 11.6 Steam flashing due to pressure reduction on saturated water

Although the mass of saturated steam flashed off is small,
its specific volume (1545.4 dm^3/kg), compared with that of
the associated water (1.0456 dm^3/kg) is large. Consequently,
steam flashing can be quite violent, and the resulting mixture
of water and steam can cause physical damage, by erosion
and impingement, to orifice plates, drain pipes and feed heater
tubes, particularly if the flashing takes place in a confined
space. In modern practice therefore, a cascaded drain is not
passed directly from heater to heater but is first passed into
an intermediate vessel called a *flash chamber* or flash box in
which the flash steam and residual drain water are separated,
and the flash steam only is introduced into the heater. The
drain orifice or drain valve should be situated as closely as
possible to the flash box so that flashing will take place into
the flash box and not into the drain pipe. The drain pipe upstream of the orifice should be generously sized to ensure low
drain water velocity thus preventing pre-flashing due to loss
of pressure by hydraulic friction in the pipe. These features
are illustrated in Figure 11.7 and it should be noted that
thermally, there is no difference between (a) and (b).

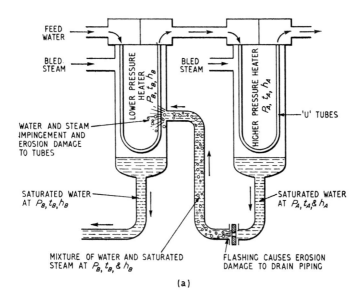

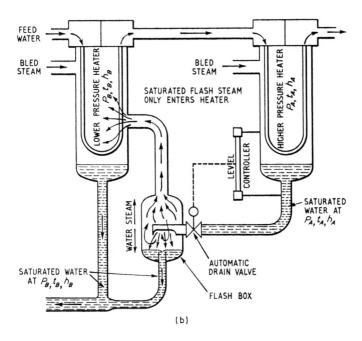

Figure 11.7 Feed heater drain cascading stage
(a) with simple orifices in drain pipe
(b) with flash box and automatic drain control valve

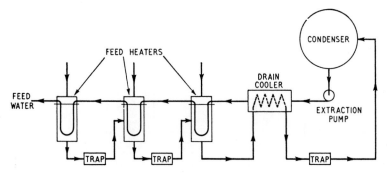

Figure 11.8 Heater drain cascading system with water drain cooler

In most feed-heating systems the combined drain from the lowest pressure heater is passed through a *drain cooler* before going to the condenser. A drain cooler is a tubular heat exchanger similar to a feed heater, and may be either a *water water* cooler or a *flash* cooler. A system with a water water drain cooler is shown in Figure 11.8 and with a flash drain cooler in Figure 11.9.

Alternatively, the combined drain may be *pumped forward* by a small independent pump called a drain pump (see Figure 11.10). This is an efficient method, as all the liquid heat of the combined drain is retained in the system and none is lost in the condenser.

However, the drain pump is an item of running plant requiring maintenance and, of course, power to drive it.

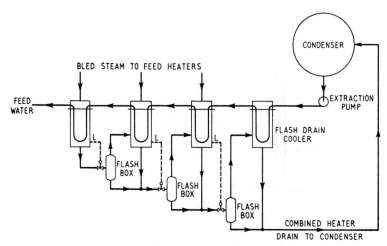

Figure 11.9 Heater drain cascading system with flash drain cooler

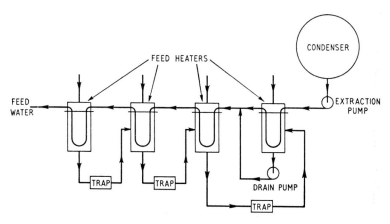

Figure 11.10 Heater drain cascading system with drain pump

Utilization of evaporator vapour, auxiliary exhaust steam, gland steam leakage, etc.

Most steam jobs have an evaporator, i.e., a L.P. boiler evaporating sea-water for make-up feed. The heat is supplied not by a fire but by a steam-coil submerged in the sea-water in the shell.

The vapour and steam-coil drain may be passed into a feed heater instead of using steam bled from the engine or turbine.

Evaporating is usually done at the lowest pressure possible for two reasons:

(a) If the evaporation temperature is not too high, the calcium sulphate in the sea-water will not form hard scale on the coils.

(b) If the evaporator is supplied with steam bled from the main engines or turbines, then the lower the steam pressure, the more economical is the operation as already shown. Further, the latent heat of saturated steam is greater at low pressure than at high pressure, hence less is required.

Sometimes the evaporator vapour is passed into the L.P. cylinder of the engines or turbine and the sensible heat of the coil drain recovered in a drain cooler or by passing it into the feed tank.

Auxiliary exhaust steam is another fruitful field for economy by feed heating where one or more auxiliary engines are steam driven. All auxiliaries exhaust into a common main, this passing to a feed heater and being used instead of bled steam. Here again, a compromise has to be made since the use of auxiliary exhaust steam for feed heating implies that the auxiliaries may have to exhaust against a pressure higher than that of the main or auxiliary condenser, hence the auxiliary steam consumption may be increased in consequence. In turbine jobs, air ejector exhaust steam is condensed in a separate heater.

De-aeration of boiler feed water

Even in fully closed systems, not open to the atmosphere, there is always the possibility of the feed water being contaminated by dissolved oxygen. This is due to small quantities of air coming over with the steam, and to air leakage into sections of the steam and exhaust and feed systems which work at pressures less than atmospheric pressure. The amount of oxygen which water will hold in solution decreases with increased water temperature, and theoretically becomes zero when the water is at the saturation temperature corresponding to its pressure. Thus any oxygen which is in solution in the feed water will be released at any point or points in the system at which saturation conditions exist. Such conditions exist: (a) in the boiler drum, and (b) in the condenser.

Oxygen released in the boiler drum could accumulate and become a potential danger for boiler corrosion, hence means must be provided in the feed-heating system to remove as much dissolved oxygen as possible from the feed water. To achieve this, there are several requirements:

1. The feed water must be at the saturation temperature corresponding to its pressure.
2. The feed water must be broken up into droplets—the smaller these droplets, then the easier it is for the dissolved oxygen to be released.
3. The water droplets must be in contact with steam in such a manner and for sufficient time to enable the steam to "scrub" the ogygen and other incondensable gas from the water.
4. The oxygen and incondensable gas must be continuously removed.
5. The equipment used for de-aeration should operate at a pressure above atmospheric pressure at all times.

By the nature of its function, the condenser fulfils these requirements to some extent, and gives a reasonable degree of de-aeration. However, unless primarily designed for de-aeration in addition to its other functions, the condenser cannot give the low oxygen content necessary for modern high-pressure boilers. Towards the condenser bottom for example, the condensate falling from the tubes is likely to be in large masses rather than droplets; any undercooling of the condensate below the saturation temperature will render it capable of reabsorbing small quantities of oxygen, particularly if there should be any air concentrations in the condenser; air leakage into the extraction pump suction piping or into the extraction pump glands can also cause aeration.

To reduce the dissolved oxygen to the necessary low figure, a special direct-contact feed heater designed to meet all the above requirements is included in the feed-heating system. Steam is introduced into the heater shell and the feed water is sprayed into this steam, falling through a series of perforated trays in the opposite direction to the steam flow. Steam condenses in the incoming water spray, giving up its latent heat to the water and raising the temperature of the latter to saturation temperature. To reach the incoming water spray, the steam has to pass upwards through the curtains of falling water, removing the oxygen and driving it towards the vent, and thence to the condenser, where it is removed by the air pump. A de-aerator heater of this type—illustrated in Figure 11.11—will reduce the oxygen content of the feed water to not more than 0.005 cm^3/litre, whereas condenser de-aeration could not normally be expected to give less than 0.015–0.02 cm^3/litre. The condenser can therefore be regarded as the primary stage, and the d.c. heater the final stage of de-aeration.

H.P. and L.P. feed heaters

As is well known, water boils at $100.0°$C when at atmospheric pressure. If we reduce the pressure, the water will boil at a lower temperature. Conversely, if we have water at a high temperature, the pressure on the water must be sufficient to prevent the water turning into steam in the pipes, e.g., in Figure 11.4 the final feed temperature is $142.8°$C. Hence to prevent vaporization, the water at this point must be under a pressure of at least 3.9 bar. If the boiler feed pump follows this heater, the pressure will almost certainly

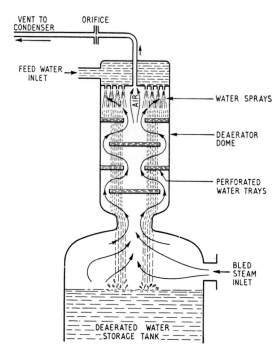

Figure 11.11 Principle of de-aerator heater

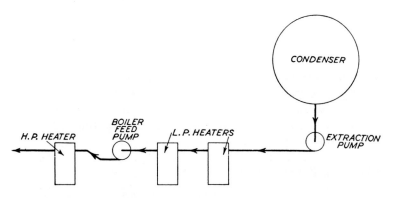

Figure 11.12 H.P. and L.P. feed heater

be less than this and the water will vaporize in the suction pipe—a most undesirable feature. On of three things must be done:

(a) The heater(s) must be placed on the delivery side of the boiler feed pump where the full feed pressure is available. The heater then becomes a *high-pressure* heater and should have cast- or forged-steel water-ends and copper or copper-nickel tubes capable of withstanding the boiler pressure (Figure 11.12).

(b) The condensate pump must be capable of generating sufficient pressure to give an ample margin at the heater discharge.

(c) The I.P. exhaust heater must be placed high up in the engine-room so that the static head imposed on the H.P. exhaust heater will be sufficient to prevent the water vaporizing at 142.8 °C. The minimum static head could be calculated as follows: Pressure corresponding to 142.8°C is 3.9 bar. 1 metre head is equivalent to 0.098 bar. Height required from I.P. exhaust heater.

$$\frac{3.9}{0.098} = 40.0 \text{ m}$$

If a further 5.0 m be allowed for margin we would require to place the I.P. exhaust heater about 45.0 m above the H.P. exhaust heater—clearly impossible. Thus the last heater would almost certainly have to be on the discharge side of the boiler-feed pump.

In practice, the feed-heating stages are chosen so that the direct-contact heater (called the de-aerator) can be accommodated high up in the engine-room casing. In large turbine jobs this may well be some 18–28 m above the tank top. The de-aerator heater is combined with a de-aerated water-storage tank containing about ten minutes' supply of feed water at full power. This stored de-aerated water acts as a "buffer" in the system, to accommodate any transient differences between condenser-extraction-pump output and boiler-feed-pump demand during power changes or manoeuvring, without having to spill excess water to, or receive make-up water from, atmospheric feed tanks in which the water could absorb oxygen. The de-aerator storage-tank level can vary over a reasonably wide range, and as this level reflects storage or excess of water in the system, it is used to initiate operation of the de-aerator control valves. High de-aerator level opens the spill valve to pass excess water to the reserve feed tanks, while low de-aerator water level opens the make-up valve to pass water into the system via the condenser. As the water in the reserve feed tanks is in contact with the atmosphere, it is likely to contain dissolved oxygen, and all such make-up water entering the main system is first passed into the condenser for primary de-aeration.

At reduced powers all the engine- or turbine-stage steam pressures fall, and at low powers could be sub-atmospheric. To prevent the de-aerator pressure falling below atmospheric pressure and therefore encouraging air leakage, an automatic valve is sometimes fitted which opens when the de-aerator pressure is slightly above atmospheric pressure and maintains this pressure down to the lowest powers. This automatic low-load valve takes steam from a source which is always above atmospheric pressure, e.g., the auxiliary steam range.

By combining the d.c. heater and the de-aerated water-storage tank, then the pressure on the water passing to the feed-pump suction is normally equal to the saturation pressure plus the static height of the de-aerator over the pump. The static height can therefore be regarded as the margin of pressure over the vaporization condition. The actual static height required depends on the design and the speed of the feed-pump suction stages, on the quantity of water in the de-aerator storage tank and on the size and configuration of the feed-pump suction piping. In this connection one important point is the effect of sudden power reduction, when the de-

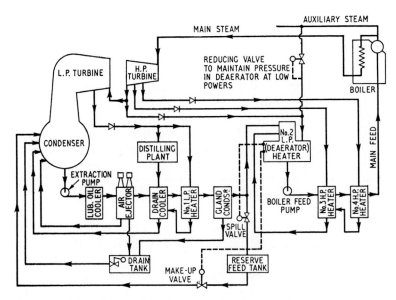

Figure 11.13 Simplified feed heating system for a large turbine steamer

aerator pressure could fall quite rapidly, thus reducing the margin of pressure on any hot water still in the suction piping with the risk of vaporization and consequent damage to the pump. While this problem did cause trouble in the earlier variable-pressure de-aerators, it is now much better understood, and de-aerators, feed pumps and piping are now designed to satisfactorily accommodate all conditions of operation.

These features are illustrated in Figure 11.13, which is a simplified diagram of a typical feed system for a large turbine steamer.

Closed feed controller

The quantity of water passing through a feed system may be reasonably constant, as when a ship is steaming at constant speed for long periods under favourable conditions, or it may be subject to sudden unpredictable variations, e.g., manoeuvring, rough weather, etc. Suppose a turbine job to be running in rough weather. The ship pitches and the propeller comes out of the water. The turbines tend to race, and the Aspinall governor closes the emergency valve, i.e., the turbine power is *reduced* to limit the propeller speed, and the demand for steam is also reduced. The feed regulator on the boilers will partially close and the condensate pump will temporarily deliver more water than is required by the boiler feed pump. Means have to be found to store this excess water, holding it in reserve until the opposite state of affairs occurs, viz., the feed pump demanding more water than is coming from the condenser. A method of dealing with these variations is to include a closed-feed controller in the system. This consists

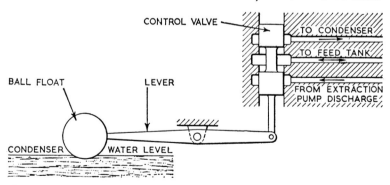

Figure 11.14 Principle of the closed-feed controller

essentially of a piston valve controlled by a ball float. The position of the latter is regulated by the water level in the condenser bottom (Figure 11.14).

So long as the condensate and feed quantities are balanced, the condenser-water level is constant and the control valve remains closed to all connections. Under these circumstances the extraction pump delivers condensate through the heaters direct to the feed-pump suction. A sudden demand for more water by the boiler feed pump causes the condenser water level to fall, and the control valve then allows water to pass from the feed tank to the condenser, thus equalizing the system during the time lag. If the condensate quantity is in excess of the feed-pump requirements, the condenser-water level rises, changing the control valve and allowing the excess water to pass from the extraction-pump discharge through the controller to the feed tank. This is shown in Figure 11.15. Note that the return pipe from the extraction-pump discharge through the feed controller to the condenser or feed tank is taken off *after* the air-ejector. This is to ensure the maximum quantity of water always passing through the air-ejector to condense the exhaust steam from the air-ejector jets.

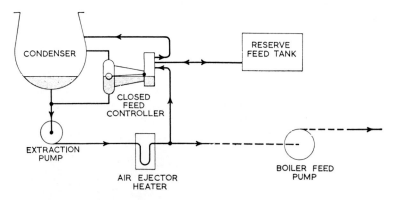

Figure 11.15 Simplified diagram of closed-feed system

Number of feed-heating stages

So far as reciprocating engines are concerned, the receiver pressures fix the saturation temperature of the steam and hence the feed temperature which it is possible to obtain at the various heaters. Turbines have a large number of stages, with comparatively small pressure drops across each. Hence there is a much wider choice of extraction points, and in general the feed system may be designed to give the best possible results. It is worth remembering that for the best results, the feed temperature rises across each feed heater should be about equal, i.e., it is quite wrong to have one heater heating feed from 40°C to 65°C, while the next is heating from 65°C to 120°C. The total rise, 80°C, should be divided up as equally as possible between the two heaters, and the extraction pressures chosen accordingly. The greatest possible use should be made of low-grade heat which would otherwise be wasted.

For practical reasons the number of stages rarely exceeds five in marine installations. Two of these heaters would be arranged to utilize evaporator vapour and auxiliary exhaust steam as alternative to bled steam.

The economy obtainable increases as the number of feed-heating stages is increased. If this statement is carried to the limit we would have the maximum possible economy when we have an infinite number of heaters each giving a small temperature rise, and raising the water temperature to the saturation temperature corresponding to the boiler pressure. Under such circumstances the boiler would supply only latent heat, all the liquid heat having been supplied in the feed system. Such a system is obviously impossible.

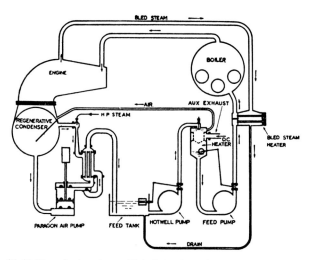

Figure 11.16 Open-feed system with independent air pump

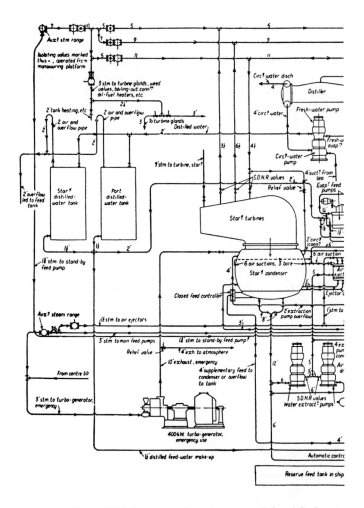

Figure 11.17 Diagrammatic arrangement of closed-feed system

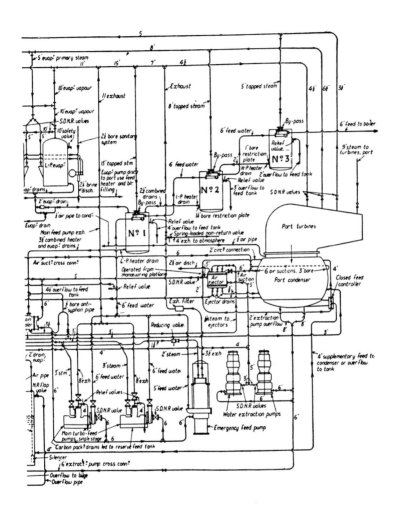

for twin-screw turbine installation with water tube boiler

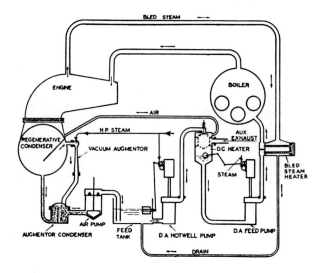

Figure 11.18 Feed system for reciprocating engines with engine-driven air pump

Typical feed systems

Sufficient has been said to enable the reader to study the illustrations in Figures 11.16 to 11.28. These have been prepared with the co-operation of Weir Pumps Ltd, Glasgow. Typical feed systems may be traced from the simplest open type to a modern closed-feed system for a twin-screw turbine installation with water-tube boilers.

While the subject of feed heating and feed systems has been introduced herein from the main-engine viewpoint, the reader is reminded that a close study of the all-important auxiliary

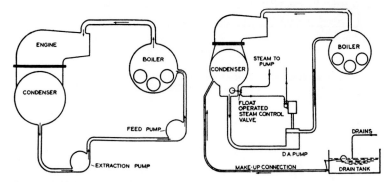

Figure 11.19 Fundamental circuit of modern closed-feed systems

Figure 11.20 Simple form of closed-feed system

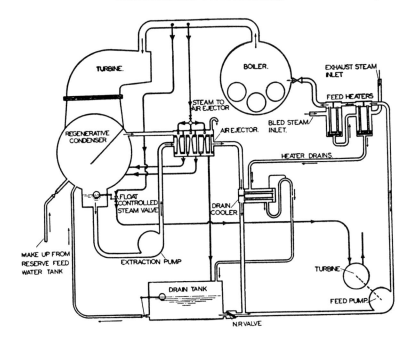

Figure 11.21 Closed-feed system for tank boilers

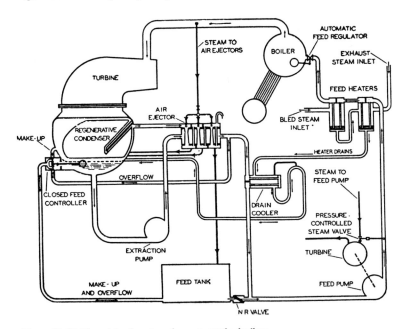

Figure 11.22 Closed-feed system for water-tube boilers

machinery will amply repay itself, and that reliable and efficient operation of any feed system is a close integration of boiler, engine and auxiliary technique.

Figures 11.16 and 11.18 show typical open-feed systems such as might be applied to reciprocating steam jobs with independent and main-engine-driven pumps respectively. Note the direct-contact feed heater to ensure satisfactory de-aeration of the feed water.

Development of the closed-feed system

Figures 11.19 to 11.22 show the development of the closed-feed system. The following points are worthy of note:

1. In a closed-feed system, feed water is not at any time open to the atmosphere, and all drains, make-up water, etc., pass through the condenser and are de-aerated therein before passing to the boilers. A separate d.c. heater and its associated hotwell pump are necessary only if the boiler pressure is high.
2. A Scotch boiler has a large water capacity as compared with a water-tube boiler, and the former could be run for some time without any appreciable fall in the water level.

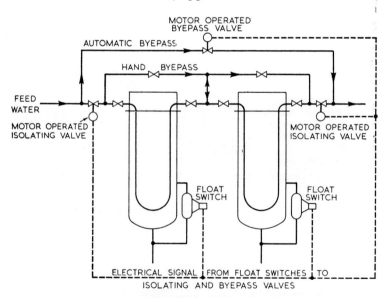

Figure 11.23 Automatic heater feed bypass. Rising water level in either heater shell causes float switch to signal by-pass valve to open and isolating valves to close. Faulty heater then isolated on hand by-pass and remaining heater reset

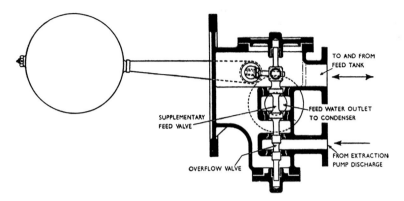

Figure 11.24 Closed-feed controller (Weir Pumps Ltd.)

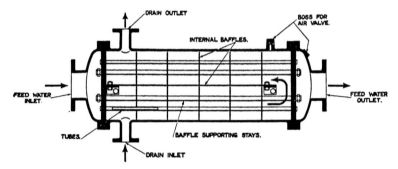

Figure 11.25 Drain cooler (Weir Pumps Ltd.)

No direct control of the water level is required, and the system shown in Figure 11.21 does not have a closed-feed controller or feed regulator. The water-tube boilers in Figure 11.22 have a small water capacity, and in consequence require a closed-feed controller and feed regulator to give close control of the water levels.

Figure 11.17 shows a modern closed-feed system for a twin-screw turbine job with water-tube boilers and three-stage feed heating. Note the following points:

1. All three feed heaters on discharge side of boiler-feed pumps.
2. Drain cooler in system with combined drain to condenser.
3. Utilization of evaporator vapour and auxiliary exhaust steam for feed-heating.

4. Cross-connections between port and starboard sets.
5. Heater drain cascading with restriction plates instead of traps or valves.
6. By-pass gear to enable a feed heater to be by-passed on the feed side in the event of heater flooding due to a burst tube. In the latest practice this by-pass is operated automatically, being initiated by high water level in the heater (see Figure 11.23).

Figure 11.26 Pair of primary and secondary 'Multiflow' feed water-heaters

Figure 11.24 shows a closed-feed controller. Note that the valve is balanced, requiring very little effort to move it. Figures 11.25 and 11.26 illustrate Weir's drain cooler and feed heaters respectively.

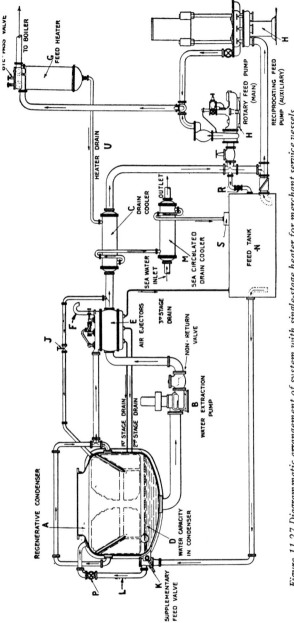

Figure 11.27 Diagrammatic arrangement of system with single-stage heater for merchant service vessels

A. Condenser.
B. Rotary water-extraction pump.
C. Drain cooler.
D. Water capacity in condenser.
E. Air ejector.
F. Air escape pipe.
G. Main feed heater.
H. Main (rotary) and auxiliary (reciprocating) feed pumps.
J. Hand-controlled recirculating valve and connection.
K. Supplementary feed valve.
L. Supplementary feed to condenser.
M. Sea water circulated drain cooler.
N. Reserve feed tank.
P. Isolating valve.
R. Hand-controlled overflow valve.
S. Filter for heater drain.
U. Heater drain.
(G. & J. Weir, Ltd.)

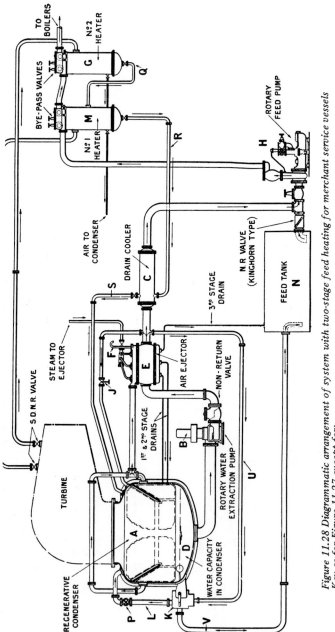

Figure 11.28 Diagrammatic arrangement of system with two-stage feed heating for merchant service vessels
Key as for Figure 11.27 except for:

G. High-pressure feed heater.
H. Rotary feed pump.
J. Hand-controlled recirculating connection.
K. Closed feed controller.

M. Low-pressure feed heater.
Q. High-pressure heater drain.
R. Low-pressure heater drain.
S. Drain cooler connection to condenser.

Starting up with the closed-feed system

Figures 11.27 and 11.28 show feed systems for merchant ships. In Figure 11.27 U is the extraction pump discharge to the feed tank through K, and V is the supplementary feed to the condenser through K and L and extraction pump discharge to the feed tank through K.

The following working instructions apply to these systems:

1. Start circulating pump.
2. Start condensate-extraction pump, having first ensured that its suction is *drowned* to the level of the closed-feed controller.
3. Open slightly the recirculating valve J.
4. Open air-ejector drain valves, and immediately water is circulating through the air-ejector, open steam valves to ejector. As condenser pressure falls water will be drawn into condenser through the closed-feed controller from the feed tank as necessary.
5. Open air-cocks on ejector, and thus release air. Close cocks.
6. Start main engines.
7. Close recirculating valve J.

If at any time, the condenser well is empty of water, proceed as follows:

1. Start up the air-ejector. The condenser pressure will begin to fall, and when water has been drawn into the condenser and flooded the water-extraction pump suction, then
2. Start up the water-extraction pump;
3. Open the recirculating valve J;
4. Open the air-cocks on the air-ejector and free the coolers of air; then close cocks.

The condenser pressure will then fall to normal, the water level in the condenser well will be maintained by the closed-feed controller K, and pressure will be shown in the extraction-pump discharge.

To shut down the system:

1. Shut the steam off the air-ejector;
2. Stop the water-extraction pump.

The air-ejector is designed to work at a certain steam pressure, and no advantage is to be gained by carrying a higher pressure. The pressure should not be allowed to fall unduly. See that the drain valves are always open when the ejector is in operation.

Don't neglect to test the closed-feed controller twice daily by means of the handle provided, as this valve must be quite free.

Don't start the water-extraction pump without ensuring an ample supply of water at the pump suction.

Don't forget to open air-cocks on water spaces of air-ejector and to close them when free of air.

Don't run the air-ejector with a steam pressure above the designed steam pressure.

Don't run air-ejector with drain valves shut.

Don't forget to open air-cocks on steam and water spaces of surface feed-water heater.

Don't forget to clean all strainers occasionally.

GENERAL THEORY OF FEED HEATING

So far, this chapter has attempted to explain the practical application to engines and turbines of feed heating by extracted steam. In Chapter 9 it was shown that the straight Rankine Cycle is inferior to the Carnot Cycle on account of the irreversible reception of sensible heat in the boiler while the feed-water temperature is being raised from the lower- to the upper-cycle temperature limit. It was also demonstrated that could this irreversible operation be replaced by a reversible reception of sensible heat, as in the Stirling Cycle, then the Carnot efficiency could be attained.

The purpose of the remainder of this chapter is to show the clear connection between practical feed heating and thermodynamical theory as outlined in Chapter 9.

The student should bear in mind Carnot's Principle and the following two essentials which have already been emphasized:

1. By adopting feed heating, the aim is to modify the first operation of the Rankine Cycle so as to make it *more nearly reversible*, thus increasing the *cycle efficiency* and so rendering the latter nearer to the Carnot Cycle efficiency.

2. Having done so, the engine must be designed, built and operated in such a manner as to enable it to approach as closely as possible to its cycle efficiency.

Consider first a straight Rankine Cycle between the limits 14.0 bar dry saturated and 0.07 bar. These steam conditions— and these only—fix the cycle efficiency as 0.2975, thus dh_s = 2787.8 − 2007.1 = 780.7 kJ/kg, and

$$\text{Cycle efficiency} = \frac{780.7}{2787.8 - 163.4} = 0.2975$$

Now let the actual working engine have an efficiency ratio of 0.75, i.e. it attains only 0.75 of the cycle efficiency. Its actual thermal efficiency would be 0.75 x 0.2975 = 0.2231.

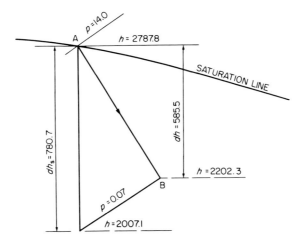

Figure 11.29 Mollier diagram for straight Rankine cycle

From the Mollier Diagram (shown in Figure 11.29) the adiabatic enthalpy drop dh_s = 780.7 kJ/kg. As the efficiency ratio is 0.75, and ignoring external losses, the actual heat drop dh = 0.75 x 780.7 = 585.5 kJ/kg. Let the expansion line AB be assumed meantime to be a straight line.

Irrespective of whether it be a reciprocating engine or a turbine engine, all it is required to assume at the moment is that steam for feed heating can be extracted at any point on

the expansion line AB. Obviously there are practical limitations to this assumption which will be discussed later. If a
turbine engine is used, then a simplified diagram of the cycle
would be as shown in Figure 11.30.

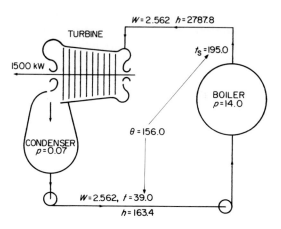

Figure 11.30 Simplfied diagram of straight Rankine cycle

Condensate leaves the condenser at 39°C (the saturation
temperature corresponding to the condenser pressure) and is
pumped into the boiler at this temperature. The boiler temperature is 195°C (the saturation temperature corresponding
to the boiler pressure). Thus when the feed water enters the
boiler, heat will flow from the hot boiler (195°C) to the
cold feed (39°C). By the second law of thermodynamics,
heat cannot, of its own accord, flow from the cold feed to
the hot boiler hence the reception of liquid enthalpy in the
boiler while the feed is being heated from 39°C to 195°C
is an irreversible operation, and a simple measure of the *degree
of irreversibility* of the operation is the temperature difference
between the hot boiler and the cold feed. In the present
instance, this temperature difference $\theta = 195 - 39 = 156$°C.

Each 1.0 kg of steam passing through the turbine does
585.5 kJ of work, and 1 kW = 1 kJ/s. Hence to develop 1 kW
of power, the turbine requires 1/585.5 = 0.001708 kg/s of
steam, i.e. the *specific steam consumption* is 0.001708 kg/kWs.
Suppose the turbine is required to develop 1500 kW, then th
the steam consumption = 0.001708 × 1500 = 2.562 kg/s. The

net heat received in the boiler is $2787.8 - 163.4 = 2624.4$ kJ/kg and the actual thermal efficiency of the cycle

$$= \frac{1500}{2624.4 \times 2.562} = 0.2231$$

(i.e. same as previously calculated from actual efficiency = cycle efficiency × efficiency ratio).

Single stage of feed heating

Suppose we apply a single stage of feed heating to raise the feed temperature to 90°C. To avoid complication at this stage, let us assume a direct-contact feed heater capable of heating the feed water up to the saturation temperature of the steam extracted from the turbine. Hence saturation temperature of extracted steam = 90°C, which corresponds to a pressure of 0.7011 bar, and the turbine must be "bled" at a stage where the pressure is 0.7011 bar. Reference to the Mollier Diagram in Figure 11.31 shows that steam at this pressure has specific enthalpy 2430.0 kJ/kg.

For the moment assume the same steam quantity, 2.562 kg/s, passing to the turbine and this quantity passes through all the turbine stages before the extraction point. Up to this point each 1 kg of steam does work $dh_1 = 357.8$ kJ/kg, hence the work done in this section of the turbine = 357.8×2.562 = 916.56 kJ/s.

W_B kg/s of steam is then extracted for feed heating and $(2.562 - W_B)$ kg/s of steam passes through the remaining turbine stages and thence to the condenser. A simple heat exchange equation enables the quantity of bled steam W_B kg/s to the heater to be calculated.

Total heat, kJ/s, entering heater = total heat, kJ/s, leaving heater

$$\therefore 163.4 \, (2.562 - W_B) + 2430 W_B = 2.562 \times 376.9$$

$$\therefore 418.57 - 163.4 W_B + 2430 W_B = 965.45$$

$$\therefore 2266.6 W_B = 546.88$$

$$\therefore W_B = 0.2413 \text{ kg/s}$$

The steam quantity passing through those turbine stages following the extraction point is therefore $2.562 - 0.2413 =$

2.3207 kg/s, and the work done in this section of the turbine is $227.7 \times 2.3207 = 528.38$ kJ/s. The total turbine work is $916.56 + 528.38 = 1444.94$ kJ/s, i.e. the power developed by the turbine is 1444.94 kW.

Since the feed temperature is now 90°C, the liquid enthalpy of the feed water is 376.9 kJ/kg, and the nett heat received in the boiler is $2787.8 - 376.9 = 2410.9$ kJ/kg, hence the actual thermal efficiency of the cycle is

$$\frac{1444.94}{2410.9 \times 2.562} = 0.2339$$

Comparing this with the straight Rankine cycle without feed heating shows an improvement of

$$\frac{0.2339 - 0.2231}{0.2331} \times 100 = 4.84 \text{ per cent}$$

Note that for 2.562 kg/s of steam, only 1444.94 kW is now obtained, hence the *steam* consumption rate is 2.562/1444.94 = 0.001773 kg/kWs, an increase of 3.805 per cent compared with the non feed heating cycle. The *heat* consumption rate however is reduced by 4.84 per cent.

Thus *less* power is developed but is developed more efficiently. Although the steam consumption rate is increased, the net heat input to the boiler has been reduced to a greater extent. Reference to the simplified diagram of the single stage feed heating system in Figure 11.31 shows the theoretical reasons for the improvement in thermal efficiency. The temperature difference between the boiler and the feed water entering the boiler has been reduced from 156.0°C to 105.0°C. The *degree of irreversibility* of the feed heating operation in the boiler has been reduced and this has been done by introducing another secondary feed heating operation whose degree of irreversibility is no worse than that of the boiler feed heating operation. The temperature difference between the hot steam in the feed heater and the cold feed water entering the feed heater is only 51°C compared with 105°C at the boiler. To put this another way, the feed heating cycle is more efficient than the straight Rankine cycle because each of its two feed heating operations (heater and boiler) are *less irreversible* than the single feed heating operation (boiler) of the straight Rankine Cycle.

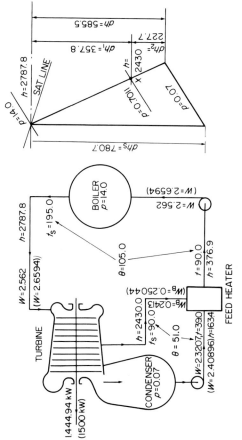

Figure 11.31 Simplified diagram of single-stage feed heating cycle

It will be appreciated that if it requires 1500 kW to propel the ship at contract speed, then obviously it could not attain contract speed if the power were only 1444.94 kW. Even the advantage of the reduced fuel consumption would not necessarily compensate the owners for a slow ship. It therefore becomes necessary to find some means of restoring the power to 1500 kW while still retaining the high-effiency feed heating cycle.

Bearing in mind that the steam consumption of the feed heating cycle is 2.562 kg/s, 1500 kW could be obtained by increasing the steam quantity to the turbine to roughly

$$2.562 \times \frac{1500}{1444.94} = 2.6595 \text{ kg/s}$$

However, in order to understand thoroughly the theoretical features of the more complicated feed heating cycles, it is better to approach the question of compensation for power by considering the work lost in the various sections of the turbine due to bleeding steam for feed heating. Referring to the Mollier Diagram in Figure 11.31, every 1 kg of steam bled at X *robs* the turbine of 227.7 kJ of work. How much extra steam must be passed into the turbine stop valve, which expanding through all the turbine stages (and thus doing 585.5 kJ/kg of work) will compensate for 227.7 kJ lost?

$$\text{Obviously } \frac{227.7}{585.5} = 0.3889 \text{ kg}$$

Thus for every 1 kg of steam extracted at X, an additional 0.3889 kg must be supplied at the turbine stop valve. This is called *compensating steam*, and 0.3889 is the *compensating factor* for this particular extraction point. The provision of compensating steam of course means that the steam quantity to the heater will also increase slightly. The modified steam and water quantities as calculated below are indicated in brackets in Figure 11.31.

Feed heater

$$163.4(2.562 + 0.3889W_B - W_B) + 2430W_B = 376.9\ (2.562 + 0.3889W_B)$$

$$\therefore 418.57 + 63.546W_B - 163.4W_B + 2430W_B = 965.45 + 146.56W_B$$

$$\therefore 2183.586W_B = 546.88$$

$$\therefore W_B = 0.25044 \text{ kg/s}$$

$$\text{Steam to turbine stop valve} = 2.562 + (0.25044 \times 0.3889)$$

$$= 2.562 + 0.0974$$

$$= 2.6594 \text{ kg/s}$$

Turbine power = $(2.6594 \times 357.8) + 227.7 (2.6594 - 0.25044)$

$\qquad\qquad\quad = 951.5 + 548.5$

$\qquad\qquad\quad = 1500$ kW

Thermal efficiency $= \dfrac{1500}{2410.9 \times 2.6594}$

$\qquad\qquad\qquad = 0.2339$ as before

Effect of increasing the feed temperature

Consider the significance of the compensating factor. If 1 kg of steam is bled from the turbine exhaust, no compensating steam is required since the full turbine power has been developed before the steam is extracted. If 1 kg is extracted at the turbine stop valve another 1 kg must be supplied at the stop valve to enable the turbine to develop the power. The compensating factor therefore varies from 1.0 at the high pressure end of the turbine to zero at the exhaust end. From the turbine power aspect therefore, the lower down the turbine the steam is bled the lower the compensating factor and the higher the efficiency. On the other hand the higher up the turbine the steam is bled, the higher is the feed temperature, the less heat is required from the boiler and the higher the efficiency. This is one of the apparently conflicting results of thermodynamical theory, and the following is intended to show how to apply Carnot's principle to obtain that compromise between the conflicting features which will give the maximum improvement over the non-feed heating cycle.

Retaining a single stage of feed heating recalculate the system for a feed temperature of $117°C$ and again for a feed temperature of $150°C$. In each case, the net heat required from the boiler will be less, but the compensating factor will be higher, hence more steam will be required. The methods of calculation are exactly as for the case of the $90°C$ feed temperature and the conditions, quantities etc. are shown in Figure 11.32, on which, for convenience, the $90°C$ feed temperature case has been repeated. The compensating factor is denoted by C, and the compensating steam quantity by W_C.

The results, tabulated below, show that as the feed temperature is increased with a single stage of feed heating, the thermal efficiency increases up to a certain feed temperature and thereafter again begins to diminish. There is therefore an optimum feed temperature, i.e. that at which maximum

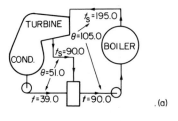

. (a)

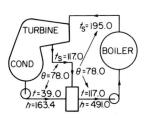
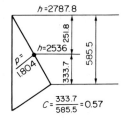

(b)

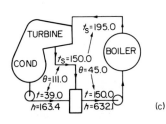
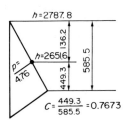

(c)

Figure 11.32 Effect of increasing the feed temperature with a single stage of feed heating
(a) Total turbine steam = 2.6594 kg/s. Thermal efficiency = 0.2339
Improvement over non feed heating cycle = 4.84 per cent
(b) Feed heater, 163.4 (2.562 + 0.57W_B − W_B) + 2536W_B = 491.0
(2.562 + 0.57W_B)
∴ W_B = 0.3839 kg/h W_C = 0.3839 × 0.57 = 0.2188 kg/s
Total turbine steam = 2.5620 + 0.2188 = 2.7808 kg/s
Turbine power = (2.7808 × 251.8) + (2.3969 × 333.7) = 700.2 + 799.8 = 1500 kW
Thermal efficiency = 1500/2.7808 × 2296.8 = 0.23484
Improvement over non-feed heating cycle = 5.262 per cent.
(c) Feed heater 163.4 (2.562 + 0.7673W_B − W_B) + 2651.6W_B = 632.1
(2.562 + 0.7673W_B)
∴ W_B = 0.5642 kg/s W_C = 0.5642 × 0.7673 = 0.4329 kg/s
Total turbine steam = 2.5620 + 0.4329 = 2.9949 kg/s
Turbine power = (2.9949 × 136.2) + (2.4307 × 449.3) = 407.9 + 1092.1 = 1500 kW
Thermal efficiency = 1500/2.9949 × 2155.7 = 0.2323
Improvement over non-feed heating cycle = 4.124 per cent.

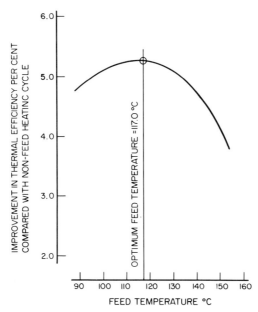

Figure 11.33 Improvement in thermal efficiency due to a single stage of feed heating

efficiency is achieved under the given conditions, this optimum feed temperature giving the best compromise between increased steam consumption and decreased net heat from boiler. See Figure 11.33 for a single stage of feed heating.

Cycle	Non-feed heating	Single stage	Single stage	Single stage
Feed temperature °C	39.0	90.0	117.0	150.0
Thermal efficiency,	0.2231	0.2339	0.23484	0.2323
Improvement, per cent	0	4.84	5.262	4.124

Consider the diagrams shown in Figure 11.32. In each of the three cases there are two feed heating operations, that is, the feed heater and the boiler. The temperature difference θ is a measure of the irreversibility of each operation.

For 90°C feed temperature, the boiler θ is 105°C, and the heater θ is 51°C. The boiler feed heating is therefore less efficient thermodynamically than the feed heater.

For 150°C feed temperature, the boiler θ is 45°C and the heater θ is 111°C. The feed heater has now become the less efficient of the two.

For 117°C feed temperature, the boiler and feed heater temperature differences are equal, and it is at this feed temperature that the maximum improvement in thermal efficiency is attained. Thus, the following rule may be stated:

For any given number of feed heating operations, the optimum feed temperature is attained when the degrees of irreversibility of all the feed heating operations are simultaneously a minimum.

To put this in more practical terms, optimum feed temperature is attained when the total feed temperature *range*, i.e. the difference between the boiler saturation temperature and the condenser saturation temperature, is equally divided amongst the feed heating operations. The single stage feed heating cycle has two feed heating operations, viz., one in the heater and one in the boiler. The feedheating range is 195 − 39 = 156°C, hence each operation should raise the feed temperature by 156/2 = 78°C. This fixes the saturation temperature of the steam for the heater at 39 + 78 = 117°C, which corresponds to an extraction pressure of 1.806 bar. Hence the choice of 117°C for example (b) in Figure 11.32. This is the best that can be done with the basic single stage of feed heating.

Effect of increasing the number of feed heating stages

Let us take the optimum feed temperature 117°C calculated for the single-stage feed heating cycle, but do the feed heating first in two, then in three stages. Let the feed water temperature rise 117 − 39 = 78°C be divided equally among the heaters.

Hence for the two-stage feed heating cycle, the first stage heater would heat the feed water from 39°C to 78°C, and the second stage heater from 78°C to 117°C. Since the second stage heater has to raise the feed water temperature to 117°C, it will require steam at the same condition as was required for the single stage, i.e. the bled steam for No. 2 heater will have a compensating factor of 0.57. The No. 2 heater however has to raise the feed temperature by only 39°C compared with 78°C for the single-stage heater, and the bled steam quantity for the No. 2 heater will thus be roughly only half that required for the single-stage heater. The No. 1 heater has the same feed water temperature rise as the No. 2 heater, hence it will require roughly the same bled steam quantity as No. 2 heater.

Thus instead of a single heater taking 0.3839 kg/s of steam at a compensating factor of 0.57, there are now two heaters each taking 0.3839/2 = 0.192 kg/s of steam, but only the 0.192 kg/s for No. 2 heater has to be compensated for by the high compensating factor (0.57), the 0.192 kg/s for the No. 1 heater being compensated for by a lower compensating factor (0.3064). Hence for the same power and same feed temperature, less compensating steam (and therefore less total turbine steam) is required for the two stage system and its thermal efficiency is thus higher than that of the single stage system.

By adopting three stages of feed heating only *one third* of the total bled steam has to be compensated by the factor 0.57, one third by the lower factor 0.3984 and one third by the still lower factor 0.2113. This results in a further reduction of steam consumption, rendering the three-stage system more efficient again than the two-stage system.

Figure 11.34 illustrates the conditions and approximate quantities for these alternatives and for convenience, the single-stage system has been included in this diagram. To enable the foregoing explanation to be kept simple, the diagrams in Figure 11.34(b) and (c) assume equal bled steam quantities to the heaters. Because of the different enthalpies of the bled steam to the heaters, and because of the different water quantities to the heaters, the bled steam quantities to the heaters are not exactly equal. The exact heat balances are shown in Figures 11.35 and 11.36.

In practical terms, the adoption of n stages of feed heating instead of one stage means that only $1/n$ of the total bled steam quantity has to be compensated for at the compensating factor of 0.57 (instead of all of the total bled steam quantity), and the remainder at smaller compensating factors depending on the number of stages.

Effect of increasing the number of feed heating stages and the feed temperature

Figures 11.32 and 11.33 show that with a single stage of feed heating, the highest efficiency is attained when the feed temperature is 117°C, i.e. with equal temperature differences at each feed heating operation.

(a) SINGLE STAGE

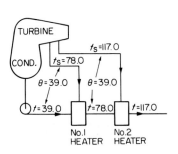

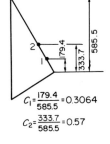

(b) TWO-STAGE

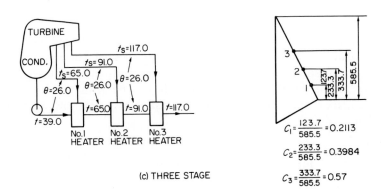

(c) THREE STAGE

Figure 11.34 Approximate effect of increasing the number of feed heating stages with constant final feed temperature

Key to Figure 11.34
(a) Single stage
$W_B = 0.3839$ kg/s
$W_C = 0.3839 \times 0.57 = 0.2188$ kg/s
$\therefore$ Total steam $= 2.562 + 0.2188$
$\qquad\qquad\quad = 2.7808$ kg/s

$C = 333.7/585.5 = 0.57$
(b) Two stage
$W_{B_1} \doteqdot W_{B_2} \doteqdot 0.3839/2 \doteqdot 0.192$
$W_{C_1} = 0.192$

(b) Two stage
$W_{B_1} \doteqdot W_{B_2} \doteqdot 0.3839/2 \doteqdot 0.192$
$W_{C_1} = 0.192 \times 0.3064 = 0.05884$ kg/s
$W_{C2} = 0.192 \times 0.57 \quad = 0.10945$ kg/s
$W_{C1} + W_{C2} \qquad\quad = 0.1683$ kg/s
$= 117.0$

$\therefore$ Total steam $= 2.562 + 0.1683 \qquad\qquad C_1 = 179.4/585.5 = 0.3064$
$\qquad\qquad\quad = 2.7303$ kg/s $\qquad\qquad\qquad C_2 = 333.7/585.5 = 0.57$

(c) Three stage
$W_{B_1} \doteqdot W_{B_2} \doteqdot W_{B_3} \doteqdot 0.3839/3 \doteqdot 0.12793$ kg/s
$W_{C_1} = 0.12793 \times 0.2113 = 0.02703$ kg/s
$W_{C2} = 0.12793 \times 0.3984 = 0.05097$ kg/s
$W_{C3} = 0.12793 \times 0.57 \quad = 0.07291$ kg/s
$W_{C1} + W_{C2} + W_{C3} \qquad = 0.15091$ kg/s
$\therefore$ Total steam $= 2.5620 + 0.1509 = 2.7129$ kg/s

$C_1 = 123.7/585.5 = 0.2113$
$C_2 = 233.3/585.5 = 0.3984$
$C_3 = 333.7/585.5 = 0.57$

Examination of Figures 11.35 and 11.36 will show that while the two-stage system is more efficient than the single stage, and the three-stage system is more efficient than the two-stage neither the two-stage nor the three-stage system has been fully exploited, since by retaining the same final feed temperature, 117°C, we have a boiler temperature difference of 78°C, compared with a heater temperature difference of 39°C for the two stage, and 26°C for the three-stage. To obtain maximum benefit, the temperature differences at all feed heating operations—including the boiler—should be equal.

The total feed temperature rise from the condenser to the boiler is, in all cases $195 - 39 = 156$°C. Hence for the two-stage system, temperature difference at each feed heating

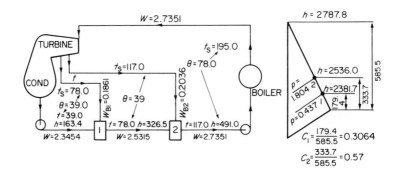

Figure 11.35 Exact heat balance for two-stage feed heating cycle with $117°C$ final feed temperature

No. 2 heater

Heat entering in feed + heat entering in bled steam = heat leaving in feed

$\therefore 326.5 (2.7351 - W_{B2}) + 2536.0W_{B2} = 2.7351 \times 491.0$

$\qquad \therefore W_{B2} = 0.2036 \ kg/s \qquad W_{C2} = 0.2036 \times 0.57 = 0.1161 \ kg/s$

No. 1 heater

$163.4 (2.7351 - 0.2036 - W_{B1}) + 2381.7W_{B1} = 326.5 (2.7351 - 0.2036)$

$\qquad \therefore W_{B1} = 0.1861 \ kg/s \qquad W_{C1} = 0.1861 \times 0.3064 = 0.057 \ kg/s$

Basis steam = 2.5620 kg/s

$W_{C2} \qquad = 0.1161$

$W_{C1} \qquad = 0.0570$

_____

Total steam = 2.7351

$W_{B2} \qquad = 0.2036$

_____

$\qquad \qquad 2.5315$

$W_{B1} \qquad = 0.1861$

_____

Steam to

condenser = 2.3454

Turbine power = $(2.7351 \times 251.8) + (2.5315 \times 154.3) + (2.3454 \times 179.4)$

$\qquad \qquad = 688.7 + 390.6 + 420.7$

$\qquad \qquad = 1500 \ kW$

Thermal efficiency $= \dfrac{1500}{2.7351 (2787.8 - 491.0)} = 0.23875$

Improvement over non-feed heating cycle $= \dfrac{0.23875 - 0.2231}{0.2231} \times 100.0 = 7.014$

$\qquad \qquad \qquad \qquad \qquad \qquad \qquad \qquad \qquad \qquad \qquad \qquad$ *per cent*

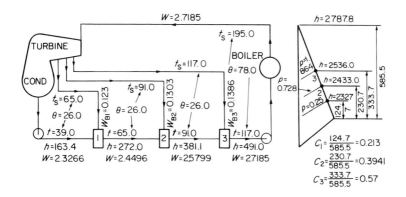

Figure 11.36 Exact heat balance for three-stage feed-heating cycle with 117°C final feed temperature

No. 3 heater

$381.1 (2.7185 - W_{B3}) + 2536.0W_{B3} = 491.0 \times 2.7185$

$\therefore W_{B3} = 0.1386 \ kg/s \qquad W_{C3} = 0.1386 \times 0.57 = 0.079 \ kg/s$

No. 2 heater

$272.0 (2.7185 - 0.1386 - W_{B_2}) + 2433.0W_{B_2} = 381.1 (2.7185 - 0.1386)$

$\therefore W_{B2} = 0.1303 \ kg/s \qquad W_{C2} = 0.1303 \times 0.3941 = 0.0513 \ kg/s$

No. 1 heater

$163.4 (2.7185 - 0.1386 - 0.1303 - W_{B1}) + 2327.0W_{B1} = 272.0$
$(2.7185 - 0.1386 - 0.1303)$

$\therefore W_{B1} = 0.123 \ kg/s \qquad W_{C1} = 0.123 \times 0.213 = 0.0262 \ kg/s$

Basis steam = 2.5620

$W_{C3} \quad = 0.0790$
$W_{C2} \quad = 0.0513$
$W_{C1} \quad = 0.0262$

Total steam = 2.7185
$W_{B3} \quad = 0.1386$

$\qquad \quad \ 2.5799$
$W_{B2} \quad = 0.1303$

$\qquad \quad \ 2.4496$
$W_{B1} \quad = 0.1230$

Steam to
condenser = 2.3266

Turbine power $= (2.7185 \times 251.8) + (2.5799 \times 103.0) + (2.4496 \times 106.0)$
$\qquad \qquad \quad + (2.3266 \times 124.7)$
$\qquad \qquad = 684.53 + 265.71 + 259.64 + 290.12$
$\qquad \qquad = 1500 \ kW$

Thermal efficiency $= \dfrac{1500}{2.7185 (2787.8 - 491.0)} = 0.2402$

Improvement over non-feed heating cycle $= \dfrac{0.2402 - 0.2231}{0.2231} \times 100.0 = 7.664$
$\qquad \qquad \qquad \qquad \qquad \qquad \qquad \qquad \qquad \qquad \qquad \qquad per \ cent$

operation = 156/3 = 52°C, and optimum feed temperature = 195 − 52 = 143°C.

The quantities and conditions for this condition are shown in Figure 11.37(a). This is the best that can be done with the basic two-stage feed heating system.

For the three-stage system, temperature difference at each feed heating operation = 156/4 = 39°C, and optimum feed temperature = 195 − 39 = 156°C. This results in the quantities and conditions shown in Figure 11.37(b) this is the best that can be done with the basic three-stage feed heating cycle.

By repeating these types of calculation for one, two and three stages of feed heating with various feed temperatures, a table may be compiled from which the curves in Figures 11.38 and 11.39 may be drawn. These will show that for a given boiler pressure and a given condenser pressure.

1. For any given feed temperature, the thermal efficiency increases as the number of feed heating stages is increased.
2. For any given number of feed heating stages there is an optimum feed temperature at which the improvement in thermal efficiency is a maximum.
3. The *rate* of improvement in thermal efficiency diminishes as the number of feed heating stages is increased, viz., at the optimum feed temperatures.

One stage is 5.262 per cent better than no feed heating. Two stage is 7.369 per cent better than no feed heating. Three stage is 8.248 per cent better than no feed heating.

If we plot the optimum improvement in thermal efficiency for various numbers of feed heating stages, we obtain the curve in Figure 11.39, which shows the continuous fall-off in the *rate* of improvement as the number of feed heating stages is increased. Obviously, for the chosen conditions, it would not be economic to have more than two or three stages, since the improvement by going to more stages is too small to justify the additional heaters, piping, valves, etc.

It will however be readily obvious that if the boiler pressure is increased, and/or the condenser pressure is reduced, the total range of feed heating is increased, and a higher feed temperature, and a greater number of feed heating stages will be justified. For example, suppose the boiler pressure were

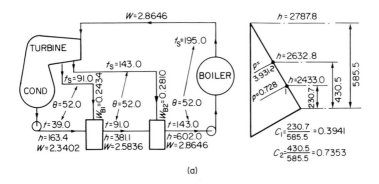

(a)

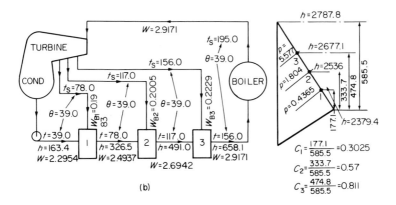

(b)

Figure 11.37 Optimum two-stage and three-stage feed heating cycles for constant turbine power = 1500 kW

(a) Two-stage feed heating cycle with optimum feed temperature

$W_{C2} = 0.281 \times 0.7353 = 0.2067 \ kg/s; \qquad W_{C1} = 0.2434 \times 0.3941 = 0.0959 \ kg/s$

Total steam = 2.562 + 0.2067 + 0.0959 = 2.8646 kg/s

$$\text{Thermal efficiency} = \frac{1500.0}{2.8646 \ (2787.8 - 602.0)} = 0.2395$$

(b) Three-stage feed heating cycle with optimum feed temperature

$W_{C3} = 0.2229 \times 0.811 = 0.1808 \ kg/s; \qquad W_{C2} = 0.2005 \times 0.57 = 0.1143 \ kg/s$

$W_{C1} = 0.1983 \times 0.3025 = 0.06 \ kg/s$

Total steam = 2.562 + 0.1808 + 0.1143 + 0.06 = 2.9171 kg/s

$$\text{Thermal efficiency} = \frac{1500}{2.9171 \ (2787.8 - 658.1)} = 0.2415$$

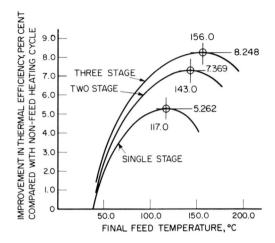

Figure 11.38 Optimum feed temperature for various numbers of feed heating stages with boiler pressure 14.0 bar, dry sat., and condenser pressure 0.07 bar

Boiler pressure 14.0 bar, condenser pressure 0.07 bar, power 1500 kW

Cycle	Final feed temperature °C	Net heat from boiler kJ/kg	Total steam kg/s	Thermal efficiency	Improvement (per cent)
Non feed heating	39.0	2624.4	2.562	0.2231	0
Single stage	90.0	2410.9	2.6594	0.2339	4.84
	117.0	2296.8	2.7808	0.23484	5.262
	150.0	2155.7	2.9949	0.2323	4.124
Two stage	90.0	2410.9	2.6382	0.2358	5.675
	117.0	2296.8	2.7351	0.23875	7.014
	143.0	2185.8	2.8646	0.23954	7.369
Three stage	90.0	2410.9	2.6315	0.2364	5.971
	117.0	2296.8	2.7185	0.2402	7.664
	156.0	2129.7	2.9171	0.2415	8.248

increased to 50.0 bar, and the condenser pressure reduced to 0.034 bar, the total range of feed heating, i.e. from condenser saturation temperature to boiler saturation temperature, is increased to $263.9 - 26.2 = 237.7°C$. For maximum improvement in thermal efficiency, we require equal temperature difference at each feed heating operation, hence we would have

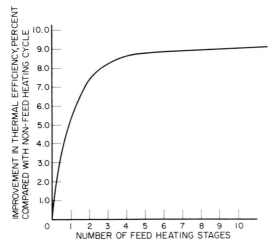

Figure 11.39 Optimum improvement for varying number of feed heating stages with boiler pressure 14.0 bar, dry sat., and condenser pressure 0.07 bar

Single stage, $\theta = \dfrac{237.7}{2} = 118.8°C$

optimum feed temp. = 263.9 − 118.8 = 145.1°C

Two stage, $\theta = \dfrac{237.7}{3} = 79.2°C,$

optimum feed temp. = 263.9 − 79.2 = 184.7°C

Three stage, $\theta = \dfrac{237.7}{4} = 59.4°C$

optimum feed temp. = 263.9 − 59.4 = 204.5°C

Four stage, $\theta = \dfrac{237.7}{5} = 47.5°C$

optimum feed temp. = 263.9 − 47.5 = 216.4°C

Five stage, $\theta = \dfrac{237.7}{6} = 39.6°C$

optimum feed temp. = 263.9 − 39.6 = 224.3°C

A series of calculations similar to those already shown enables us to draw the curves shown in Figures 11.40 and 11.41, from which it will be noted that for the higher boiler pressure and lower condenser pressure, probably four stages

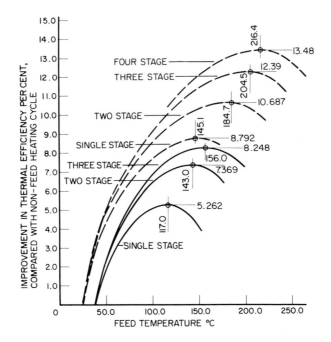

Figure 11.40 Optimum feed temperature for various numbers of feed heating stages with different boiler pressure and condenser pressure. Full lines = boiler pressure 14.0 bar, condenser pressure 0.07 bar. Broken lines = boiler pressure 50.0 bar, condenser pressure 0.034 bar

and a final feed temperature of 216.4°C would be justified.

In endeavouring to make the foregoing explanation of principles as clear as possible, we have over-simplified certain features, which in practice, would have a significant effect on the choice of the actual feed heating system, and on the resulting improvement in efficiency.

For instance, we have used direct-contact (d.c.) heaters throughout. A multiplicity of d.c. heaters would not however be used in practice as each one requires its own extraction pump. The main principles however are equally adaptable to surface type heaters, and the foregoing arguments may also be applied, albeit modified to some extent to allow for departures from our over-simplified system. Some of these departures are worthy of comment. Feed heating system calculations are rendered more complicated by the practice of heater drain *cascading*, i.e. passing the drain water—resulting from condensation of the bled steam—backwards from heater to heater to recover some of the liquid enthalpy at the

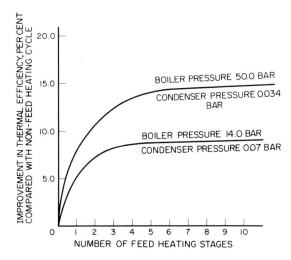

Figure 11.41 Effect of increasing the number of feed heating stages with different boiler pressures and condenser pressures and with optimum feed temperature maintained throughout

highest practicable temperature level. The term *cascading* means *falling downwards*, and is here used in the sense of temperature. The hottest drain, i.e. that from the highest pressure heater is passed into the next highest pressure, and the combined drain from the latter is then passed into the next again heater, and so on right down to the de-aerator or the condenser, a proportion of liquid enthalpy of the drain water being utilised to heat the feed water at each temperature level. Less bled steam is therefore required at each feed heating stage which receives a cascaded drain.

A further complication is that a surface heater cannot always heat the feed water up to the saturation temperature of the steam, but requires a *terminal temperature difference*, usually from 3 to 6°C. Such surface heaters are therefore slightly less efficient than direct contact heaters, since the terminal temperature difference is a further departure from equality of temperature (see Chapter 8).

We credited all the feed heating operations with equal efficiency, e.g. we assumed a feed temperature rise of 78°C in a heater, to be carried out equally as efficiently as a 78°C rise in the boiler. This is not necessarily true, nor does it follow that the boiler design will accommodate the same feed temperature rise as an ideal feed heating stage. There may be practical reasons why the boiler design will demand a lower or a higher feed temperature than that resulting from our simplified treatment. Only the boiler designer can say.

In any practical system it is not always possible to extract steam where ideally it is desired to do so. With reciprocating engines, steam may be extracted only from the receivers between cylinders, the receiver pressures being fixed by considerations other than feed heating (see Chapter 2). With turbines, steam may be extracted at any of the stage pressures, i.e. from between the nozzles of any two adjacent stages, but many more of these are available than with reciprocating engines and there is therefore a greater choice. Even so, the choice of turbine bleeding points may be restricted by the need to use existing patterns, or to simplify the turbine cylinder casting, etc.

Where auxiliary exhaust steam or evaporator vapour is available, it may be used in one of the feed heaters instead of bled steam. The efficiency will be increased, as less bled steam and therefore less compensating steam will be required, and this of course will be a further departure from our simplified conception of the feed heating system.

In modern practice it is usual also to recover the heat dissipated in the turbine lubricating oil coolers by circulating these coolers with condensate. Heat from turbine gland leak-offs, distilling plant drains etc. is also recovered in the feed heating system. All these auxiliary heat recoveries of course mean that a more complicated system is required—not always a welcome feature.

Types of feed heaters

We have already seen that feed heaters are of two main types.

1. DIRECT CONTACT HEATERS. The steam bled from the turbines is introduced into a vessel into which the feed water is sprayed. The steam condenses by direct contact with the water sprays, transferring its latent heat to the water, and thereby raising the water temperature right up to the saturation temperature corresponding to the steam pressure. The combined feed water and condensate is removed from the heater by a pump.

2. SURFACE HEATERS. The feed water passes through a nest of tubes contained in the heater shell. The bled steam is intro-

duced into the heater shell and condenses on the outer surfaces of the tubes, giving up its latent heat to the feed water passing through the tubes. The heaters are arranged in series on the feed side, feed-water flow through the tubes being maintained by the extraction pump, or by the feed pump, depending on whether the heaters are situated on the suction side (L.P. heaters) or the discharge side (H.P. heaters) of the feed pumps. Condensate from the steam side is progressively cascade drained from the higher- to the lower-pressure heaters.

These two main heater types are illustrated in Figure 11.42.

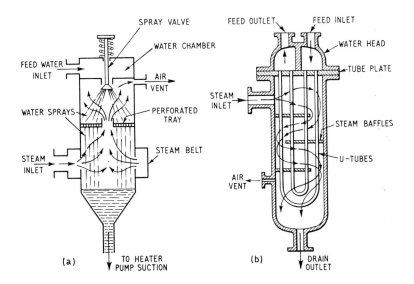

Figure 11.42 Types of feed heater
(a) direct contact heater
(b) surface heater

Surface feed heater with desuperheating section

To appreciate the fundamental difference in principle between these two types we must remember that when steam condenses it can only condense at the saturation temperature corresponding to the pressure, hence the surface on which the steam condenses must be at saturation temperature. In the case of the direct-contact heater the steam condenses on the water droplets in the sprays, hence the water temperature is brought up to the saturation temperature. In the case of the surface heater the condensing steam is not in contact with the outside surface of the tube, but is in contact with the outside surface of the condensate film on the outside of the tube. Therefore the outer surface of the condensate film is at saturation temperature. To drive the heat from the outer surface of the condensate film into the feed water inside the tubes requires a *temperature difference* to do so. The heat has to pass through the condensate film on the outside of the tube, through the tube wall itself and through the layer of water next to the inside of the tube wall. These three each form *resistances to heat flow*, the total resistance being the sum of the three. Because of this total resistance, a temperature drop is required to cause heat flow, just as a volt drop is required to cause a flow of electric current against a resistance.

Thus a surface heater of the type illustrated in Figure 11.42(b) will not be capable of raising the feed-water temperature up to the steam saturation temperature. There will always be a *terminal temperature difference*, which in practice will vary between 3 and 6°C. For given steam saturation temperature and inlet feed temperature the surface heater in Figure 11.42(b) will be somewhat less efficient than the direct-contact heater in Figure 11.42(a).

If either type of heater is supplied with superheated steam the latter cannot condense until its temperature has been reduced to the saturation temperature. Thus the outgoing feed temperature cannot be any higher than if the steam had been saturated or wet—the steam temperature has been *degraded* down to saturation temperature by introducing the superheated steam into a heater in which saturation temperature *must* exist. Because of the higher heat content, however, less superheated steam will be required for the same feed temperature rise than if the steam had been saturated or wet.

With the increasing use of high initial steam temperatures, and of reheat, the bled steam passing to certain feed heaters may have quite a high superheat. If instead of passing the superheated steam indiscriminately into the condensing heater it is first passed through a desuperheating heater in which the steam temperature is reduced to saturation temperature by feed water leaving the condensing heater, then the feed-water temperature may be raised apprecialy above that which would be obtained from the condensing heater only (see Figure 11.43).

In certain cases it is possible to arrange the desuperheating section within the shell of the condensing heater, and thus to

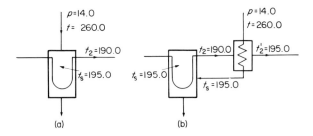

Figure 11.43 Effective utilisation of superheat in a surface feed heater
(a) condensing heater
(b) condensing and desuperheating heater

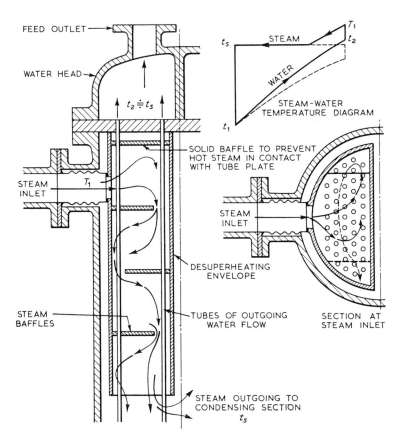

Figure 11.44 Desuperheating section in feed heater

obtain the advantage of stage desuperheating without having to provide a separate vessel.

Such an integral desuperheating section is illustrated in Figure 11.44, from which it will be seen that the outlet end of the tubes of the outlet flow are enclosed by the desuperheating envelope. Steam is admitted to the top end of the envelope and passes downwards—counterflow to the water passing up the tubes—until when it arrives at the lower open end of the envelope it has been desuperheated down to saturation temperature. With this arrangement the feed-water temperature may be raised right up to the saturation temperature of the steam, or even a degree C or so above it. It is thus possible to take advantage of zero terminal temperature difference where this is economically justified.

It should be noted that were we to imagine an infinite number of baffles, the steam temperature would approach the water temperature at each baffle, and such an ideal case could be regarded as reversible. In fact, the number of baffles is limited to that necessary to desuperheat the steam without causing an excessive pressure drop through the desuperheating section, as such a pressure drop causes an excessive loss in the condensing surface by depressing the saturation temperature.

Surface-feed heater with drain-cooling section

If we consider one stage of heater drain cascading such as that shown in Figure 11.45(a) it will immediately be evident that the sensible heat difference is degraded from $127.43\,^{\circ}\text{C}$ to $99.63\,^{\circ}\text{C}$ before being recovered in the lower pressure heater.

Referring to Figure 11.45(b), if we interpose another heat exchanger, called a drain cooler, between the two heaters it is possible to recover some of the sensible heat at a higher temperature level, resulting in a higher feed temperature entering the higher-pressure heater, and thus requiring less steam to that heater. The temperature difference between the heat source (the steam) and the substance receiving the heat (the feed water) has been reduced at each stage, hence the operation is more nearly reversible. This principle is, of course, true for any drain cascading stage, but it would not be economic to build a separate drain cooler for each heater.

In certain cases it has, however, been possible to arrange the drain-cooling section in the shell of the appropriate

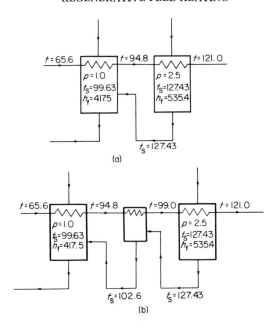

Figure 11.45 Principle of surface heater with drain cooling section
(a) Cascading without drain cooling
(b) Cascading with drain cooling

heater, thus obtaining the advantage of stage drain cooling
without the necessity of providing a separate vessel.

Figure 11.46(a) illustrates the principle of a horizontal
surface heater with drain-cooling section, and (b) the principle
of a vertical drum heater with desuperheating and drain-
cooling section.

Direct contact heaters in cascade

We have seen that a direct-contact heater is more efficient
than an equivalent condensing surface heater and that a direct-
contact heater provides de-aeration of the feed water, whereas
a surface heater does not. It is also generally true that a direct-
contact heater is simply a shell with sprays and trays, and is
therefore likely to be less expensive than a surface heater
with its relatively large number of tubes. However, any direct-
contact heater is a "break" in the condensate system, and
requires its own pump to transfer the feed water to the next
highest pressure.

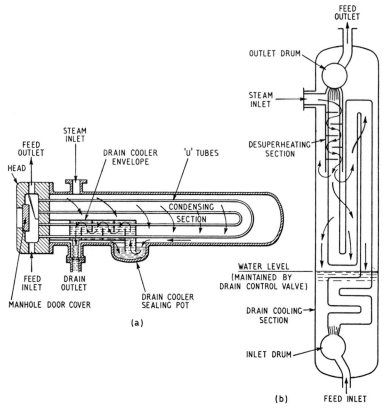

Figure 11.46 Surface heaters
(a) Horizontal surface heater with integral drain cooler
(b) All-steel welded drum heater with desuperheating and drain cooling sections

Reference to Figure 11.47 will illustrate this (for simplicity, air ejector heater, lubricating-oil cooler, drain cooler and gland condenser are omitted).

Figure 11.47(a) shows that only one pump—the condenser extraction pump—is required, and that this pump has to deal with a quantity of condensate equal to the turbine exhaust steam plus the combined drain from LP_1 and LP_2 heaters. It has to pump against the de-aerator pressure plus the static head of the de-aerator plus the friction head loss through the L.P. heaters and piping.

Figure 11.47(b) shows that three pumps are required. The condenser extraction pump has to pump a quantity of condensate equal to the turbine exhaust steam against the LP_2

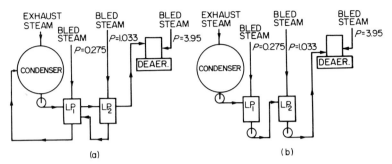

Figure 11.47 L.P. feed heating system comparison
(a) System with surface L.P. heaters
(b) System with direct-contact L.P. heaters

heater pressure. The LP_1 heater pump has to pump a quantity equal to the turbine exhaust steam plus the LP_1 heater bled steam from LP_1 heater pressure to LP_2 heater pressure. The LP_2 heater pump has to deal with a quantity of condensate equal to the turbine exhaust steam plus the total bled steam to the two L.P. heaters and has to pump from LP_2 heater pressure against the de-aerator pressure plus the de-aerator static head plus the friction head loss in the piping to the de-aerator.

By using a cascade arrangement all the advantages of D.C. heaters may be exploited, while reducing the number of pumps required.

The D.C. heater pump should have a net positive suction head of 6-8 m, which fixes the height of LP_2 heater. LP_1 heater is then situated at a height above LP_2 heater which will balance the steam pressure difference between the two heaters, in this case

$$1.033 - 0.275 = 0.758 \text{ bar} = \frac{0.758 \times 1.0197}{0.1} = 7.75 \text{ m}$$

giving a total cascade height of some 15 m, which is probably comparable with the de-aerator height. The LP_1 heater thus drains by gravity into the LP_2 heater, and one d.c. heater pump is eliminated. The total pumping power is less than for a surface heater system, since the main extraction pump does not have to handle the combined drain from the two L.P. heaters.

The cascade system of L.P. heaters has been applied to some large land turbine installations, but experience with it to date has not been good, the U-pipe seals in particular having shown a tendency to hydraulic instability on changing conditions. Pending a great deal more operating experience, the cascade system is not likely to be generally adopted, and certainly not at sea.

The cascade system can be applied only to L.P. heaters, since the pressure differences between H.P. heaters are so great that the necessary cascade height could not be accommodated in even the largest engine-room. In any case, it is possible that the H.P. heaters would have desuperheating and drain-cooling sections which would render surface heaters at least as efficient as direct contact heaters.

Pumps, de-aerators, etc., have been dealt with in this chapter with the intention only of indicating their effect on the cycle. These items are fully dealt with in detail as auxiliaries in *Marine Auxiliary Machinery*, a companion volume in the Marine Engineering series published by Newnes-Butterworths.

12 The Rankine cycle in practice

Having shown the construction of the enthalpy-entropy diagram in Chapter 8, we can now proceed to show how the Rankine cycle is indicated on this diagram.

Figure 12.1 shows the *hs* diagram for the straight Rankine cycle for initially saturated steam between the limits 14.0 bar and 0.07 bar, as has already been dealt with on the *Ts* diagram in Chapter 9, Figure 9.2.

The four operations shown in Figure 12.1 below are exactly the same as described for this cycle in Chapter 9 and illustrated by a *Ts* diagram in Figure 9.2.

The beauty of the *hs* diagram is that the cycle heat may be found merely by plotting the initial state point C, drawing a perpendicular from C to the lower pressure limit at D, and reading off the value CD on the enthalpy scale.

The dryness fraction at D may also be read directly from the diagram without any calculation whatsoever.

As previously explained, the cycle efficiency is given by

$$\eta = \frac{h_C - h_D}{h_C - h_A}$$

Since h_A can be readily obtained from the Steam Tables, we really need plot only the two points C and D to obtain the cycle work (or the *adiabatic enthalpy drop* as it is more generally called in practical work).

Thus, a Rankine cycle is indicated on the *hs* diagram by one perpendicular straight line—the one shown by CD on the diagram in Figure 12.1. This gives all the information required.

A complete Mollier chart is in fact a graphical steam table, on which a single state point gives all the information contained in the steam tables, and from which the changes resulting from a change of state point can be read directly from the chart, or at least, can be obtained with the minimum amount of calculation.

624

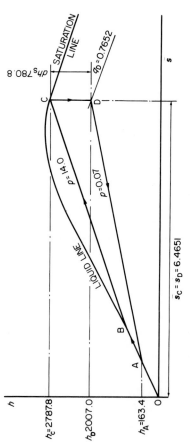

Figure 12.1 Complete hs diagram for Rankine Cycle between the limits 14.0 bar
dry saturated and 0.07 bar

AB = reception of the enthalpy of the liquid
BC = reception of the increment of enthalpy for evaporation
CD = adiabatic expansion
DA = complete condensation

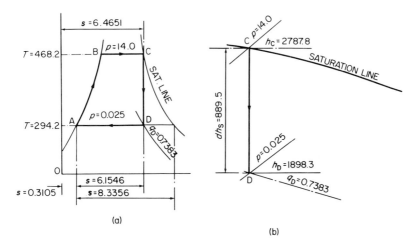

Figure 12.2 Ideal Rankine Cycle for initial conditions 14.0 bar dry saturated in which the lower cycle pressure limit is that corresponding to the temperature of the heat sink
(a) Ts diagram
(b) hs diagram

Again referring to Figure 12.1, the cycle work or adiabatic enthalpy drop is given by the difference in enthalpy of the steam at C and D. The adiabatic enthalpy drop is usually denoted by the symbol dh_s, meaning simply, the heat drop at constant entropy. Hence for the conditions chosen

$$dh_s = h_C - h_D = 2787.8 - 2007.0 = 780.8 \text{ kJ/kg}$$

The cycle heat or *heat received above exhaust* is given by

$$h_C - h_A = 2787.8 - 163.4 = 2624.4 \text{ kJ/kg}$$

and the cycle efficiency $= \dfrac{780.8}{2624.4} = 0.2975$ as before.

It will be remembered that when dealing with cycles on a Ts diagram, it was not necessary to work on a proper Ts chart, but merely to make a hand sketch and mark on it the various values obtained from the steam tables or by calculation.

When working on an hs diagram, as we are now, it is desirable to actually use a large-scale chart for reading off the values, and then to mark these values on an hs sketch made as the calculations proceed. The student is recommended to purchase a large-scale chart*.

In dealing with practical cycles, the first point which must be appreciated is that the operations are not ideal as they are in theory—there are always losses and practical limitations. For example, expansion is not adiabatic, isentropic and reversible, nor can heat be received or rejected reversibly since practically, the condition of equality of temperature cannot be realised. There is also always some pressure drop in steam pipes.

Confining our attention to the engine and condenser aspects, let us consider first a straight Rankine cycle having an upper limit of 14.0 bar, dry saturated, i.e. an upper temperature limit of 468.2 K.

In thermodynamic theory, the minimum lower cycle temperature limit is the temperature of the environment, i.e. of the earth, the sea, the atmosphere, since it is to that temperature that all heat rejected—and indeed all work done—is ultimately degraded. For a marine engine cycle we may regard the sea as the immediate heat sink, and thermodynamically therefore, the minimum lower cycle temperature limit is the sea temperature.

Suppose the sea temperature to be 21°C (294.2 K). This corresponds to a saturation pressure of 0.025 bar, and an ideal Rankine condenser would therefore give a minimum lower cycle pressure of 0.025 bar, resulting in the cycle illustrated in Figure 12.2(a) and (b).

To achieve the Rankine ideal of reversible condensation however, would mean that the sea water would have to pass through the condenser at constant temperature 21°C—clearly impossible in practice, since cold water cannot receive heat without its temperature rising, nor can heat flow from the exhaust steam to the circulating water unless there is a temperature difference between the steam and the water at all points in the condenser (see Chapter 6).

Suppose the temperature difference at the cold water end of the condenser to be 18°C. The steam now condenses at a constant temperature of 21 + 18 = 39°C (312.2 K), which is the saturation temperature corresponding to 0.07 bar. This results in the cycle illustrated in Chapter 9, Figure

*Enthalpy–Entropy Chart for Steam (S.I. units) (Jůza), published by Edward Arnold (Publishers) Ltd.

9.2, which if we superpose on the present Figure 12.2 appears as in Figure 12.3. Because of the necessary condenser temperature difference, the cycle work of the practical cycle is reduced by 889.5 − 780.8 = 108.7 kJ/kg compared with the ideal thermodynamical Rankine cycle. This loss is called the *loss of availability of energy due to irreversible heat transmission in the condenser*; it can be reduced by reducing the condenser temperature difference, but at the expense of requiring a larger condenser. Clearly, there is a limit to what can be done, on account of sheer size, mass and cost of the condenser.

Again, in thermodynamic theory, expansion of the steam in the engine or turbine is adiabatic, isentropic and reversible. In practice, various losses cause the expansion to depart from the adiabatic, isentropic mode, resulting in an increase of entropy during expansion, and causing some of the theoretical adiabatic enthalpy drop to be converted into *reheat* of the steam, this amount of energy ultimately going to increase the heat rejected. Obviously this expansion process is irreversible, and the actual efficiency will be lower than the theoretical cycle efficiency.

Suppose we actually design, build and operate a steam engine to work with steam at 14.0 bar dry saturated and to exhaust at 0.07 bar—the latter dictated by the condenser temperature difference as explained above. For the present, assume a simple single-cylinder engine, which on test, develops 1000 kW by the indicator (i.e. internal power) and consumes 10 940 kg/h of steam.

Note that the *steam consumption rate* or the *specific steam consumption* is 10 940/1000 = 10.94 kg/kWh.

Now 1.0 W = 1.0 J/s, hence 1.0 kW = 1.0 kJ/s = 3600 kJ/h, hence the work *output* of the engine, expressed in heat units = (1000 × 3600) kJ/h.

To obtain this output requires 10 940 kg/h of steam, hence the work obtained from each 1.0 kg of steam = 1000 × 3600/ 10 940 = 329.1 kJ.

This is called the *indicated enthalpy drop* (or the *internal enthalpy drop* in the case of a turbine) and is denoted by the symbol *dh*.

Thus our engine extracts 329.1 kJ of work from each 1.0 kg of steam. Had it behaved as a Rankine engine should, the expansion would have been adiabatic and isentropic, and it would have extracted 780.8 kJ of work from each 1.0 kg of

628

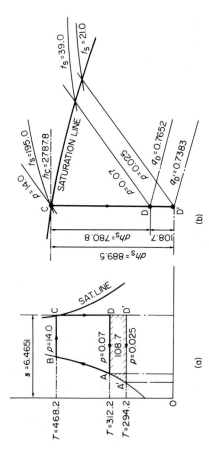

Figure 12.3 Loss of availability of energy due to irreversible heat transmission in the
condenser
(a) Ts diagram
(b) hs diagram

steam. The engine has attained only $329.1/780.8 = 0.4215$ or 42.15 per cent of what it is possible to attain.

This ratio is known as the *indicated efficiency ratio relative to the Rankine cycle*, or simply the *indicated efficiency ratio*. In the case of a turbine it would be called the internal efficiency ratio. (*Note*: the efficiency ratio is sometimes called the *isentropic efficiency*).

Thus, indicated efficiency ratio =
$$\frac{\text{Actual indicated enthalpy drop}}{\text{adiabatic enthalpy drop}} = \frac{dh}{dh_s}$$

Note that as the heat input to the actual engine is the same as the heat input to the Rankine engine, the indicated thermal efficiency of the actual engine is

$$\frac{1000 \times 3600}{10\,940\,(2787.8 - 163.4)} = 0.1254, \text{ or again}$$

Indicated thermal efficiency = Rankine cycle efficiency × efficiency ratio

$$= 0.2975 \times 0.4215 = 0.1254, \text{ or again}$$

Indicated efficiency ratio $= \dfrac{\text{indicated enthalpy drop}}{\text{adiabatic enthalpy drop}}$

$$= \frac{329.1}{780.8} = 0.4215$$

Referring now to Figure 12.4 in which for comparison, we show the *hs* diagram along with the *Ts* diagram, instead of expanding adiabatically from *C* to *D* as it would in a Rankine engine, the steam expands along some other line such that the actual indicated, or internal enthalphy drop $dh = 329.1$ kJ/kg.

In Figure 12.4(b) therefore, the final state point of the steam is a point *E* on the line of constant pressure 0.07 bar, where the enthalpy is $2878.8 - 329.1 = 2458.7$ kJ/kg, and plotting this point on the *hs* diagram shows that the dryness fraction at *E* is 0.953. The temperature of 451.7 kJ/kg of heat energy has been uselessly *degraded* from 468.2 K to 312.2 K—an irreversible process.

The effect of the irreversible expansion in the engine is to increase the heat rejected by 451.7 kJ/kg, not at the expense of the theoretical cycle work, but at the expense of the amount of theoretical cycle work *available to us*. Thus, on

630

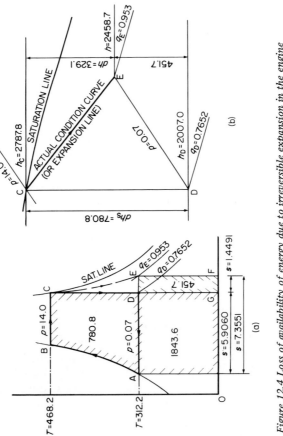

Figure 12.4 Loss of availability of energy due to irreversible expansion in the engine
(a) Ts diagram
(b) hs diagram

the Ts diagram, the cycle work is *not* the area $ABCE$, but is the area $ABCD$ as before. The cycle work available to us however is only area $ABCD$ − area $DEFG = 780.8 − 451.7 = 329.1$ kJ/kg.

The curve CE on the Ts diagram is a "ghost" line, indicating only the location of the point E on the line of constant pressure 0.07 bar, and hence the additional quantity of heat rejected.

The additional quantity of heat rejected, viz. 451.7 kJ/kg is called the *loss of availability of energy due to irreversible expansion in the engine*. The magnitude of this loss is controlled by many factors, including the initial steam conditions, the exhaust pressure, the type of cycle, the type of engine or turbine, the detail design of the engine or turbine stages, etc. These factors are discussed further in this and other appropriate chapters. In general we should aim at minimising this loss of availability (i.e. aim at the highest efficiency ratio), commensurate with reasonable dimensions, mass and cost of engines, and without any undue complication which could adversely affect safety, reliability, maintenance, staffing, etc.

Of the two losses of availability of energy with which we have dealt up to this point, it is of some importance to clearly understand in what manner each of these works against us. Irreversibility of heat transmission in the condenser forces us to accept a bottom cycle temperature limit which is higher than that thermodynamically possible. It therefore forces us to accept a *lower cycle efficiency*. Having accepted this cycle efficiency, the irreversibility of expansion in the engine forces us to accept the fact that we cannot obtain all of the cycle work associated with that cycle efficiency. It forces us to accept a *fractional efficiency ratio*. Figure 12.5 attempts to illustrate these two effects.

The Ts diagram is the ideal means of illustrating the theoretical thermodynamical cycles, as has been attempted in Chapter 9. Once the theoretical cycles are understood, and we come to examine actual working cycles and their relation to the theoretical cycles, as we are now about to do, the hs (Mollier) diagram is preferred. This is simple and convenient for our purpose and, if a reasonably large-scale diagram is used, it enables most of the relevant values to be read off directly with sufficient accuracy, thus reducing calculation to a minimum. We will use the Mollier diagram throughout the remainder of this chapter.

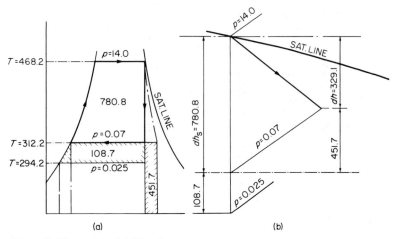

Figure 12.5 Loss of availability of energy
(a) Ts diagram
(b) hs diagram
108.7 kJ/kg due to irreversible heat transmission in the condenser
451.7 kJ/kg due to irreversible expansion in the engine

The calculation procedure adopted in producing Figure 12.4(b) may be used for each cylinder of a multiple-expansion engine. The indicated power of each cylinder is found from the indicator diagrams, and knowing the steam consumption, the condition points for each cylinder may be plotted on the Mollier diagram, and the complete expansion line for the whole engine thus built up. The same procedure may be used for turbines using condition points at H.P., I.P. and L.P. turbine exhaust, and at any intermediate stages from which steam is bled for feed heating. Each individual stage of a turbine is in fact treated in this way in the design stage. Appropriate examples of all of the foregoing are given in this and in other chapters.

Referring to Figure 12.4(b) the actual condition curve is usually shown as a straight line between C and E for any one engine cylinder, or any one turbine stage, or any one section of a turbine. While this is not necessarily correct theoretically, as will be obvious from the turbine stage calculations in Chapter 10, it is of importance only in the latter. At present we are concerned only with condition points *between* cylinders or sections or stages, and these we can identify correctly. We can therefore regard the complete expansion line as the locus of a series of correct condition points such as C and E in Figure 12.4(b).

Triple expansion engine

As a first example, consider a straight triple expansion engine receiving 8165 kg/h of steam at 14.0 bar, dry saturated and exhausting to the condenser at 0.2 bar. The indicated powers developed in each of the three cylinders are, H.P. 320.0 kW, I.P. 338.0 kW, L.P. 300.0 kW, and the I.P. and L.P. receiver pressures are 4.5 bar and 1.1 bar respectively. It is required to find the indicated efficiency ratio of each cylinder and the overall indicated efficiency ratio of the engine. The initial state point A (Figure 12.6) of the steam is found on the Mollier diagram at the intersection of the line of constant pressure 14.0 bar and the saturation line.

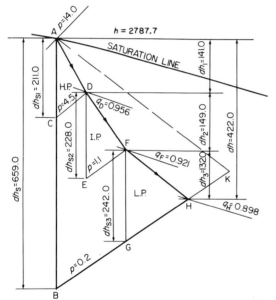

Figure 12.6 Mollier diagram for straight triple expansion with initially saturated steam

A perpendicular straight line is then drawn from A to meet the L.P. exhaust pressure line, 0.2 bar, in the point B. The length of the line AB, to the enthalpy scale of the diagram gives the overall adiabatic heat drop dh_s for the whole engine, viz.,

$$dh_s = 659.0 \text{ kJ/kg}$$

This would be the work done in a perfect Rankine engine working between these limits. No practical working engine is perfect however, and in order to assist our engine to approach more nearly to its Rankine ideal, we divide the total range of expansion into three separate stages, so reducing the temperature range at each stage and thus reducing the total condensation, wetness and reevaporation losses accordingly.

The engine is now considered as three separate Rankine cycles in series, these three together forming one large Rankine cycle. The point C is found at the intersection of the adiabatic line and the H.P. exhaust (I.P. receiver) pressure line 4.5 bar. The adiabatic heat drop dh_{s1} for the H.P. cylinder is given by the length of the line AC to the enthalpy scale of the diagram, viz. $dh_{s1} = 211.0$ kJ/kg.

Now the H.P. cylinder actually indicates 320.0 kW and takes 8165.0 kg/h of steam to do so, therefore the work actually done inside the H.P. cylinder (or its indicated enthalpy drop dh_1) is given by

$$dh_1 = \frac{320.0 \times 3600}{8165} = 141.0 \text{ kJ/kg}$$

The efficiency ratio of the H.P. cylinder =
$$\frac{dh_1}{dh_{s1}} = \frac{141.0}{211.0} = 0.668, \text{ that is,}$$

the H. P. cylinder attains 66.8 per cent of its Rankine efficiency.

If the actual indicated enthalpy drop is set down vertically from h_A, the actual state point D at H.P. exhaust is found on the line of constant pressure 4.5 bar. The dryness fraction at this point $q_D = 0.956$, and the temperature $t_D = 148.0°C$ (the saturation temperature corresponding to a pressure of 4.5 bar).

The above procedure is now repeated for the I.P. cylinder, taking D as the initial state point for this cylinder.

From the Mollier diagram,

$$dh_{s2} = 228.0 \text{ kJ/kg}$$

$$dh_2 = \frac{338.0 \times 3600}{8165} = 149.0 \text{ kJ/kg}$$

Efficiency ratio of I.P. cylinder = $\dfrac{149.0}{228.0} = 0.653$

Dryness fraction at I.P. exhaust, $q_F = 0.921$

The procedure is again repeated for the L.P. cylinder taking F as the initial state point for that cylinder.

From the Mollier diagram

$$dh_{s3} = 242.0 \text{ kJ/kg}$$

$$dh_3 = \frac{300.0 \times 3600}{8165} = 132.0 \text{ kJ/kg}$$

Efficiency ratio of L.P. cylinder $= \dfrac{132.0}{242.0} = 0.543$

Dryness fraction at L.P. exhaust, $q_H = 0.898$

We have thus, in turn, compared the performance of each cylinder with its Rankine cycle, so establishing the actual expansion line $ADFH$, each of the three sections AD, DF and FH being assumed to be a straight line.

Considering now the engine as a whole, we find that it expands the steam from A to H along the line $ADFH$. The actual total indicated work done is of course the sum of the indicated work done in the three cylinders, viz.,

Overall indicated enthalpy drop,

$$dh = dh_1 + dh_2 + dh_3 = 141.0 + 149.0 + 132.0$$
$$= 422.0 \text{ kJ/kg}$$

The overall adiabatic enthalpy drop

$$dh_s = 659.0 \text{ kJ/kg, so that the}$$

Overall indicated efficiency ratio of the engine

$$= \frac{422.0}{659.0} = 0.64$$

At this point, it should be noted that if we could design, build and operate our engine as a Rankine engine, there would be no need to adopt multiple expansion. In practice however, had we expanded steam from 14.0 bar dry saturated to 0.2 bar in a single cylinder, the large temperature range would have resulted in large heat exchange losses between the steam and the cylinder metal which would reduce the useful indicated work done, and the actual expansion line might then have been a line such as AK.

Thus by tripling the engine, we do not improve the *cycle efficiency*, but we improve the actual engine, rendering its performance nearer to that of a perfect Rankine engine working between the same limits. We improve the *efficiency ratio*.

If we increase only the *initial pressure*, the expansion line will move over to the left, the adiabatic enthalpy drop will be increased, but the steam will be considerably wetter throughout, i.e. what we gain in cycle efficiency due to increased adiabatic enthalpy drop, we may well lose again in efficiency ratio due to increased wetness losses.

If we increase only the *initial temperature*—by superheating—the expansion line will move over to the right, and not only do we gain slightly on adiabatic enthalpy drop, but also the steam remains in a superheated condition quite a considerable way down the expansion line, and is much drier at the L.P. end, thus significantly reducing wetness losses. The student should compare these conclusions with the features discussed in Chapter 9.

Judicious choice of the initial pressure and temperature is required to enable us to best exploit these features. For example, if in the previous example, we had decided to superheat the steam to an initial temperature of 320.0°C, then the higher L.P. dryness fractions would justify a somewhat higher initial pressure, say 17.0 bar. In general, *increased initial pressure* should always be accompanied by *increase of superheat*.

Engines do not normally work with initial steam temperatures in excess of 350.0°C on account of H.P. cylinder lubrication difficulties, and the corresponding maximum initial pressure is about 19.0 bar. (Turbines can work with very much higher initial steam temperatures, hence higher initial pressures are justified).

Let us now look at a triple expansion engine generally similar to that in the previous example, but having initially superheated steam. The initial steam conditions are 17.0 bar, 320.0°C and L.P. exhaust pressure 0.2 bar. From trial results, the indicated powers are H.P. 418.0 kW, I.P. 354.0 kW, L.P. 358.0 kW, the I.P. and L.P. receiver pressures are 5.0 bar and 1.4 bar respectively and the steam consumption 7000 kg/h.

The conditions are shown in Figure 12.7.

H.P. cylinder indicated enthalpy drop,

$$dh_1 = \frac{418.0 \times 3600}{7000} = 215.0 \text{ kJ/kg}$$

H.P. cylinder indicated efficiency ratio $= \dfrac{215.0}{284.0} = 0.756$

I.P. cylinder indicated enthalpy drop $= \dfrac{354.0 \times 3600}{7000}$
$= 182.0 \text{ kJ/kg}$

I.P. cylinder indicated efficiency ratio $= \dfrac{182.0}{240.0} = 0.758$

L.P. cylinder indicated enthalpy drop $= \dfrac{358.0 \times 3600}{7000}$
$= 184.0 \text{ kJ/kg}$

L.P. cylinder indicated efficiency ratio $= \dfrac{184.0}{300.0} = 0.613$

Overall indicated enthalpy drop $dh = 581.0 \text{ kJ/kg}$

Overall indicated efficiency ratio $= \dfrac{581.0}{794.0} = 0.732$

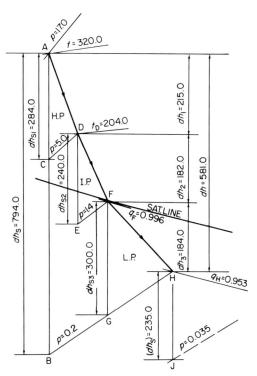

Figure 12.7 Triple expansion engine with initially superheated steam

Examination of the Mollier diagram in Figure 12.7 shows that the steam remains in a superheated condition almost down to I.P. exhaust—only the L.P. cylinder suffers from wetness losses, and its low efficiency ratio relative to the H.P. and I.P. cylinders is indicative of this. Even so, the steam throughout the L.P. cylinder is drier than in the saturated steam engine, hence the L.P. cylinder efficiency ratio is significantly higher.

Since the steam remains superheated throughout the H.P. and I.P. cylinders, condensation and re-evaporation losses cannot take place in these cylinders, and it could be argued that only one cylinder need be used instead of two. This is quite a sound argument even if some heat exchange losses remain. Indeed, after superheating was introduced and initial steam temperatures increased, the main advantage of the quadruple expansion engine disappeared, and in more recent days, the triple-expansion engine is sometimes replaced by a compound engine having two stages of expansion, but retaining four cylinders (two H.P. and two L.P.) to give a more uniform torque, better balancing and lighter rods and running gear.

Let us now examine the low pressure end of the engine expansion line. Exhaust steam leaves the L.P. cylinder at *H* (Figure 12.7) and passes into the condenser in which it is condensed, and its latent heat thrown away in the overboard discharge. If the condensing plant can be improved (see Chapter 6) so as to give a lower condenser pressure, further work may be extracted from the L.P. exhaust steam before it passes to the condenser. Reference to the Mollier diagram in Figure 12.7 will show that if the condenser pressure could be lowered to 0.035 bar, then a further adiabatic enthalpy drop of 235.0 kJ/kg immediately becomes available (from *H* to *J*).

This additional enthalpy drop could not be used efficiently in an additional engine cyclinder unless the latter were of prohibitively large dimensions, but it may readily be exploited by an *exhaust turbine*. As the exhaust turbine works entirely in the wet zone and in order to maintain reasonable simplicity of design, it is unlikely that the internal efficiency ratio of the exhaust turbine would exceed 0.65. Hence the turbine actual internal enthalpy drop would be $dh_4 = 0.65 \times 235.0 = 153.0$ kJ/kg, and its actual expansion line would be *HK* on the simplified diagram shown in Figure 12.8. The same steam quantity, viz. 7000 kg/h would pass through as through the

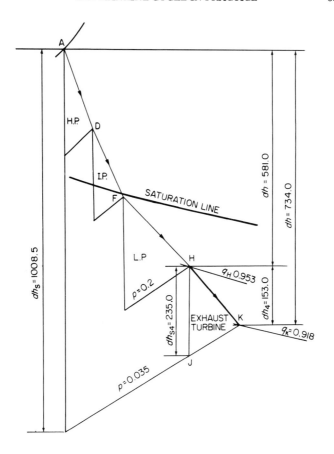

Figure 12.8 Triple expansion engine and exhaust turbine

engine, and the internal power developed by the turbine would be

$$\frac{153.0 \times 7000}{3600} = 295.0 \text{ kW}$$

Thus, for the same steam consumption, the total internal power of the engine/turbine combination is increased to

$$418.0 + 354.0 + 358.0 + 295.0 = 1425 \text{ kW}$$

an increase of 26.0 per cent compared with the straight triple.
    Alternatively, if increased power is not required, the same total power, viz. 1130 kW could be obtained with approxi-

mately 26.0 per cent less steam and therefore 26.0 per cent less fuel.

The application of the exhaust turbine means that the overall adiabatic enthalpy drop is increased to 1008.5 kJ/kg and the overall internal enthalpy drop to 734.0 kJ/kg. The overall internal efficiency ratio of the engine/turbine combination is therefore

$$\frac{734.0}{1008.5} = 0.728$$

compared with 0.732 for the straight triple.

Thus the introduction of the exhaust turbine does not materially affect the *efficiency ratio* but increases the cycle efficiency by reducing the lower cycle temperature limit (see Chapter 9).

There are several exhaust turbine systems in use. These differ only in the manner in which the exhaust turbine power is applied to the cycle.

The turbine power may be applied *mechanically* to the engine crankshaft by a reduction gear, as in the Bauer–Wach, Brown–Boveri, White, and Christiansen and Meyer systems.

Alternatively the exhaust turbine may drive a generator which supplies current to an electric motor geared to the shaft as in the former M.V. system. In this case, the turbine power could be regarded as being applied *electro-mechanically*.

Again, the turbine power may be applied not directly, but indirectly, as in the Götaverken system (see Chapter 7). The exhaust turbine drives a centrifugal compressor which is used to raise the pressure of the H.P. exhaust steam before it passes into the I.P. cylinder. Thus the turbine power could be regarded as being applied *regeneratively*, and the illustration of this system on the Mollier diagram is most interesting and instructive.

TRIPLE EXPANSION ENGINE WITH EXHAUST TURBINE AND STEAM COMPRESSOR

The skeleton diagram for the straight triple-expansion engine is shown in Figure 12.9, and the exhaust turbine and turbo-compressor lines are shown superimposed. Let the efficiency

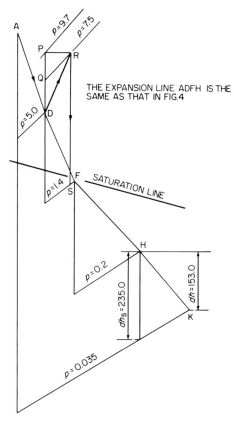

THE EXPANSION LINE ADFH IS THE
SAME AS THAT IN FIG.4

Figure 12.9 Principle of the Götaverken system of exhaust turbine and steam compressor

ratio of the exhaust turbine be 0.65 as before, so that the actual turbine heat drop is 153.0 kJ/kg.

Ideally, the turbine-driven compressor should now apply this 153.0 kJ/kg of work *adiabatically* to the H.P. exhaust steam, i.e. all of the 153.0 kJ/kg should cause a *pressure rise at constant entropy*. If this were so, the state point of the steam would move from D to P between H.P. exhaust and I.P. inlet, i.e. DP would be an *adiabatic compression*. The compressor itself, however, has a fractional efficiency ratio, say 0.6, and this means that the adiabatic increment is $0.6 \times 153.0 = 92.0$ kJ/kg, from D to Q, and the remainder $153.0 - 92.0 = 61.0$ kJ/kg is added as a temperature increment at constant pressure from Q to R (the 61.0 kJ/kg does not compress the steam, it merely "churns" it, causing temperature rise by fluid friction.)

The actual compression line is therefore DR, and the I.P. cylinder now receives steam at R instead of at D as in the straight triple.

It will be immediately evident from the Mollier diagram that if the H.P. exhaust pressure remains at 5.0 bar and the L.P. receiver pressure remains at 1.4 bar, then the adiabatic heat drop RS for the I.P. cylinder is going to be considerably larger than that for either the H.P. or the L.P. cylinder. Such a large I.P. heat drop would mean that this cylinder would develop much more power than either of the other two cylinders and such a state of affairs could be unsatisfactory, physically.

It is invariably found however that the application of the exhaust turbine and the compressor causes the following two effects:

1. Due to the suction effect of the compressor, the H.P. exhaust pressure falls by $0.7 - 0.9$ bar.
2. Due to the restriction of the exhaust turbine, the L.P. exhaust pressure rises by 0.07 to 0.11 bar.

The combined effect of these two features materially assists in a more equitable distribution of power among the three cylinders, and if in addition, the L.P. cut-off can be made somewhat earlier, it is possible to achieve practically equal powers.

The recompression and reheat of the H.P. exhaust steam mean that both the I.P. and L.P. cylinders receive more highly superheated steam, thus reducing wetness losses. In consequence, their efficiency ratios may be expected to be higher than when working straight triple.

Figure 12.10 shows the conditions obtained from a typical installation of this type. All three engine cylinders work in the superheat zone, hence only the exhaust turbine suffers from wetness losses. The internal efficiency ratios are

H.P.	0.71
I.P.	0.75
L.P.	0.7
Exhaust turbine	0.64

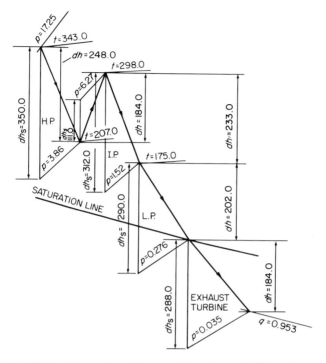

Figure 12.10 Mollier diagram for triple expansion engine with Götaverken exhaust turbine and compressor

The total actual indicated enthalpy drop for the engine is

$$248.0 + 233.0 + 202.0 = 683.0 \text{ kJ/kg}$$

The straight triple in Figure 12.4, with slightly lower initial steam conditions, had $dh = 581.0$ kJ/kg, hence the present system shows a saving of 17.55 per cent over the straight triple.

The student should note that the Götaverken system:

1. Increases the *cycle efficiency* since it lowers the lower cycle temperature limit and raises the potential (the temperature level) of the exhaust turbine work before the latter is applied to the cycle.
2. Increases the *efficiency ratios* of the I.P. and L.P. cylinders by providing them with more highly superheated steam thus reducing wetness losses.

This system, the practical details of which have been discussed in Chapter 2, may be further exploited by the application of regenerative feed heating (see Chapter 11), and by using the exhaust turbine to drive a centrifugal boiler feed pump as well as the steam compressor.

Triple expansion engine with steam reheater

A typical example of this type is the North Eastern reheater engine. Steam is initially superheated to 400-410°C total temperature in the combustion chamber superheater. Before admission to the H.P. cylinder, the steam is passed through the tubes of the reheater in which its temperature is reduced to 330-340°C by giving up heat to the H.P. exhaust steam—the latter being passed over the outsides of the reheater tubes on its way to the I.P. cylinder.

In this way, the H.P. exhaust steam is reheated—nominally at constant pressure—before passing into the I.P. cylinder.

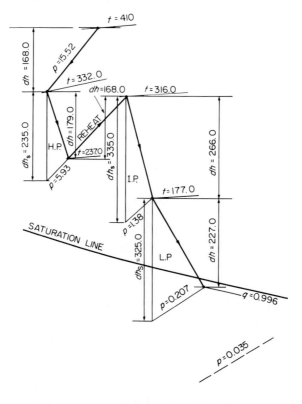

Figure 12.11 Mollier diagram for triple expansion engine with steam reheater between H.P. and I.P. cylinders

The I.P. and L.P. cylinders therefore receive more highly superheated steam and their efficiency ratios are improved accordingly.

In practice there is some *pressure drop* across both the main steam and H.P. exhaust steam sides of the reheater, but for clarity these have been ignored in Figure 12.11. The conditions shown are typical of what might be expected from an engine of this type. The power developed by the H.P. cylinder is low by comparison with the I.P. and L.P., but if it were attempted to correct this by lowering the reheat pressure, the cycle efficiency would be reduced. The reheater temperature difference would be increased, but this could be offset by the increased steam volume (see Chapter 9).

The student should note that the principle of reheating at constant pressure is *irreversible*, as explained in Chapter 9. Such reheating therefore only slightly increases the cycle efficiency, but significantly increases the *efficiency ratio* by improving the performance of the I.P. and L.P. cylinders. Although the main steam temperature has been raised to 410°C, heat is not exploited in the cycle at this temperature. The heat is *degraded* from 410/332°C to 316/237°C before being applied to the cycle.

The steam remains in a superheated condition practically right down to L.P. exhaust.

The efficiency ratios of the three cylinders are

H.P. 0.76   I.P. 0.79   L.P. 0.7

The potential enthalpy drop for an exhaust turbine between 0.207 bar and 0.035 bar should be noted.

There also exists the possibility of improving the cycle efficiency by the application of regenerative feed heating (see Chapter 11).

Four-cylinder compound engine and exhaust turbine with two steam reheaters

This section refers to the White combination engine as described in Chapter 7.

The Mollier diagram for a typical installation is illustrated in Figure 12.12. The H.P. exhaust steam is reheated by the main steam passing to the H.P. cylinders and the L.P. exhaust steam is reheated by the main steam passing to the steam-driven auxiliaries.

This engine has two outstanding advantages—superheated steam to both cylinders and relatively high running speed, 4.5–5.0 rev/s. Thus, wetness losses are reduced by the superheat, and the heat exchanged between the steam and the cylinder metal is reduced by the high speed reducing the time available for such heat exchange. Thus the two cylinders of this engine have very high efficiency ratios—of the order of 0.85 and 0.9. These are good—very good, and it is doubtful if any better efficiency ratios could be obtained from any steam plant—whether engine or turbine.

The engine develops 54.0 per cent of the total power, i.e.

$$\text{Engine} \; = 212.0 + 229.5 = 441.5 \text{ kJ/kg}$$
$$\text{Turbine} = \qquad\qquad = 382 \text{ kJ/kg}$$

The efficiency ratio of the exhaust turbine is low compared with that of the engine cylinders, and it is possible that the overall efficiency could be increased somewhat by increasing the proportion of power developed by the engine. Any attempt to do so within the given steam conditions, however, would adversely affect some of those very features which render the engine efficiency ratio so good. To make the engine develop a greater proportion of the total power while still retaining the high efficiency ratios of both engine cylinders, we would have to increase the initial steam conditions at the engine to the limit for reciprocating engines and increase the steam temperature at the superheater outlet to give a higher reheat temperature at the L.P. cylinder and at the exhaust turbine.

This system could be further exploited by adding at least one more stage of regenerative feed heating (Chapter 11).

The student should note that it does not matter that this engine has two H.P. and two L.P. cylinders. So far as the Mollier diagram is concerned, we deal only with the changes taking place in each 1.0 kg of steam as it passes through the engine and turbine, and the fact of there being two compound engines *in parallel* as it were, does not affect the diagram in any way.

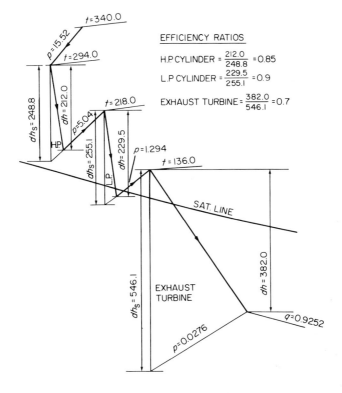

EFFICIENCY RATIOS

H.P. CYLINDER $= \dfrac{212.0}{248.8} = 0.85$

L.P CYLINDER $= \dfrac{229.5}{255.1} = 0.9$

EXHAUST TURBINE $= \dfrac{382.0}{546.1} = 0.7$

Figure 12.12 Four-cylinder compound engine and exhaust turbine with two steam reheaters

REPRESENTATIVE MODERN STEAM TURBINE CYCLES

As discussed in Chapter 9, the choice of cycle for steam turbines is influenced by many factors, and the cycle finally adopted for any particular application is the result of an optimisation of these factors. While detailed overall economics is outside the scope of this book, there are certain points worthy of note, so that the student may appreciate why we do not always adopt the plant and conditions which will give the highest efficiency.

During the past twenty years marine-steam-turbine develop-ment has been characterised firstly by a very significant increase in unit size and power, and secondly, by the use of higher initial steam pressures and temperatures. At the present time turbine steamers of 15 000–26 000 kW on one shaft are becoming commonplace. The advantages of large unit size (that is, large power developed on one shaft) are:

(i) Reduced first cost.
(ii) Reduced weight and reduced space occupied.
(iii) Reduced fuel cost.
(iv) Reduced number of running units, resulting in reduced maintenance and reduced number of spare parts carried.
(v) Reduced crew requirement.

(i), (ii) and (iii) may be more readily appreciated after reading Chapter 10, from which it will be evident that a turbine unit for twice the power is much less than twice the size, weight and cost. Further, the parasite losses in a large turbine unit are a smaller percentage of the heat available for doing work, resulting in increased efficiency.

A possible disadvantage of large turbine units is the consequences of major breakdown, but experience in general has indicated that such breakdown is most unlikely. Nevertheless, this feature must be borne in mind when selecting plant and conditions to ensure that reliability is not sacrificed for efficiency alone. Chapter 10 discussed, in general terms, the theoretical and practical benefits on efficiency by adopting high initial steam pressures and temperatures and by the application of reheat, and we restate the conclusions here:

(i) Increasing only the initial pressure increases the *cycle efficiency* by a very significant amount.
(ii) Increasing only the initial pressure reduces the final dryness fraction by a very significant amount, and the corresponding adverse effect of wetness losses on the *efficiency ratio* will considerably reduce the benefit from the increased cycle efficiency. Further, excessive wetness towards the exhaust end can cause erosion damage to the blades of the last stages.
(iii) Increasing the initial temperature increases the cycle efficiency by a moderate amount, but raises considerably the final dryness fraction, thus reducing wetness losses and significantly raising the efficiency ratio. The combined effect of these is a very considerable improvement in economy.

(iv) If reheating, at the optimum reheat pressure, is applied, a further moderate gain in cycle efficiency is obtained. Also, the steam dryness fraction in the L.P. stages is further raised, giving another improvement in efficiency ratio, and reducing the severity of exhaust end blade erosion.

Obviously, for maximum efficiency, the initial steam conditions should be as high as possible, with reheating at the optimum reheat pressure to a temperature equal to the initial temperature. Higher initial pressures, however, require thicker, stronger, heavier and more expensive turbine casings, valves and piping. High steam temperatures require the use of special materials, and the turbine design should be such as will reduce the amount of these materials to a minimum, and also reduce the risk of casing distortion and rotor instability. To this end, H.P. turbines are now often made with double casings, see Chapter 3. The smaller pressure and temperature differences across the cylinder walls and flanges means that the latter can be made thinner and of more uniform shape, thus minimising the risk of thermal distortion.

High steam pressures and temperatures impose more severe conditions on joints, valves, glands, etc., which if not adequately designed and maintained can result in reduced availability and consequent loss. If reheat is used a significant quantity of additional piping and equipment must be provided, paid for and maintained. Special materials and double casings

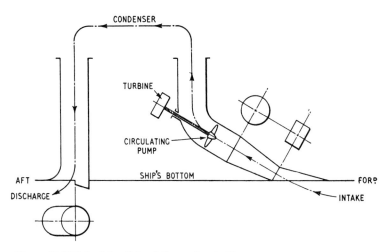

Figure 12.13 Principle of circulating water scoop

may be required in the I.P. as well as in the H.P. turbine. We should, theoretically, reheat at the optimum reheat pressure. However, if we reheat at a pressure less than the optimum the reheater tubes and steam pipes can be made thinner, lighter and less expensive. On the other hand, the specific volume of steam is greater at lower pressures, and the internal area of the tubes and pipes may have to be increased if the steam velocities, and hence pressure drops, are to be kept reasonable. If we reheat at a pressure higher than the optimum the same argument could be used, but in reverse.

In deciding the steam conditions to be adopted for any particular installation, all such features have to be carefully considered and optimised. The latter process simply means finding a compromise among all the conflicting features which will give the best return. For instance, raising the initial steam pressure and temperature will certainly reduce the fuel consumption significantly at full power. What is the cost of the oil fuel now? What will it be in ten or fifteen years' time? How many days of its life will the ship steam at full power? Will the higher steam conditions cause any running and maintenance problems which will lead to reduced availability and consequent loss? Will the additional first cost outweigh the saving in fuel cost? Will increased engine-room staff be required?

Each feature and each item of plant must be considered not only in isolation but for the entire integrated installation. In general, if the saving taken over the life of the ship is not significantly more than the sum of the additional capital cost, maintenance cost, availability cost, etc., then there is no case for the higher steam conditions. It will immediately be obvious that an important point is the quality of the ship's engineers in running and maintaining the job.

Modern turbine steamers work with initial steam conditions from 40.0 bar, 425°C up to 60.0 bar, 510°C, and it is quite possible that 105.0 bar, 540°C or even 565°C may be used in the near future. Whatever the steam conditions, there are many variations which may be applied to the basic Rankine Cycle. Over 60.0 bar the application of reheat may be attractive. We may apply three, four, five or more stages of regenerative feed heating with or without stage desuperheating and drain cooling. We may drive the major auxiliaries by separate engines or turbines, the latter taking steam from the main boiler, or bled from the main turbines. Alternatively, we may drive these auxiliaries by electric motors or from the main turbines. Auxiliary drives obviously raise the question of port working when the main turbines, and probably the main boiler, are not in use. The main circulating-water system may be arranged to take advantage of the "scoop" action of the forward way of the ship (Figure 12.13), so that when under way the condenser is virtually circulated by power developed by the main engines. Even so, an independent circulating pump is required for port working, slow and astern.

The final choice of system is dictated by what is most economic *overall*, rather than merely by what is most efficient in theory. The following examples are chosen to illustrate some modern steam-turbine cycles, and illustrate the manner in which thermodynamic theory is exploited in practice up to present-day limits.

Non-reheat steam turbine cycles

Figure 12.14 shows the comprehensive heat balance diagram and Figure 12.15 shows the Mollier diagram for a single-screw steam turbine installation, to develop 14920 kW at the shaft and having initial steam conditions 50.0 bar, $510°C$. This is typical of the more moderate of the range of initial steam conditions used in modern practice. The condenser pressure is 0.05 bar, and there are four stages of regenerative feed heating, the second stage being a direct-contact deaerating heater. The main boiler feed pump is driven from the H.P. turbine pinion shaft, and the main electric generator is driven from the reduction gear.

The H.P. turbine has one two-row Curtis stage, followed by seven single-row pressure stages. The H.P. turbine stages are of the impulse type, each having a suitable degree of re-action (as explained in Chapter 10).

The L.P. turbine has seven stages, in which the degree of reaction increases progressively such that the last three are reaction stages (i.e. 50 per cent reaction as explained in Chapter 10).

For clarity, the expansion line in Figure 12.15 indicates only the state points of those turbine stages from which steam is extracted for feed heating. There are two extraction points (or "bleed" points) in the H.P. turbine, one at the H.P. turbine exhaust and one in the L.P. turbine. Note that the turbine expansion line does not begin at the initial state point, but at a point slightly to the right. This small horizontal part of the expansion line indicates the throttling loss (pressure drop at constant enthalpy) through the fully open ahead steam valve. The first bleed point (18.5 bar, $400.3°C$) is after

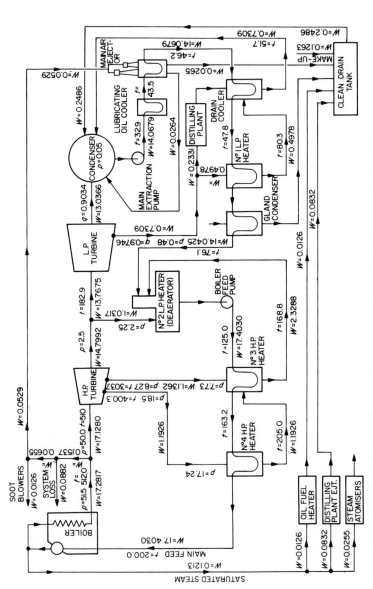

Figure 12.14 Heat balance diagram for non-reheat steam turbine cycle for 14 920 kW with initial steam conditions 50.0 bar, 510° C and with condenser pressure 0.05 bar

W = quantity, kg/s
p = pressure, bar
t = temperature, °C

Turbine gland steam flows omitted. Pressure drop, turbine stage to L.P. heater = 10 per cent
Pressure drop, turbine stage to H.P. heater = 6.5 per cent

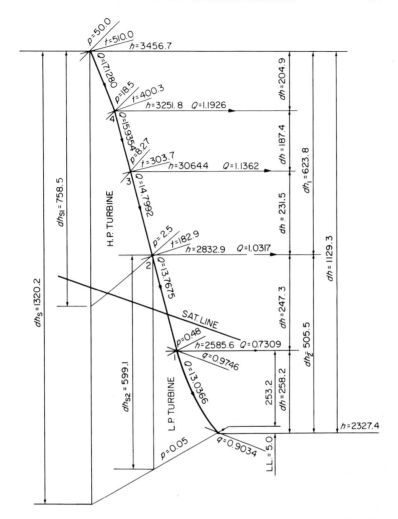

Figure 12.15 Mollier diagram for non-reheat steam turbine cycle for 14 920 kW with initial steam conditions 50.0 bar, 510° C and condenser pressure 0.05 bar

the Curtis stage. Note that the slope of the expansion line for the Curtis stage is less than that for the single-row stages. This is because of the multiplication of blade, etc., losses in the Curtis stage which renders its stage efficiency less than that of a single-row stage. Note also the progressive worsening of the stage efficiency after the expansion line crosses the saturation line, due to increasing wetness loss.

Steam at the rate of 17.128 kg/s passes through the Curtis stage and does 204.9 kJ/kg of useful work internally, hence the Curtis stage internal work is $17.128 \times 204.9 = 3509.4$ kJ/s, and since 1 W = 1 J/s, we can say that the power developed internally by the Curtis stage is 3509.4 kW.

The last stage of the L.P. turbine is a reaction stage having a mean diameter of 1.07 m running at 50.0 rev/s and having $u/c_0 = 0.7$ and $\alpha = 30.0°$. Hence $u = \pi \times 1.07 \times 50.0 = 168.0$ m/s, and $c_0 = 168.0/0.7 = 240.0$ m/s, and from the velocity diagrams $c_2 = 100.0$ m/s, i.e. leaving loss $= (100.0/44.725)^2 \doteqdot 5.0$ kJ/kg.

The steam quantities through the various sections of the two turbines, and the appropriate internal work are shown on the Mollier diagram in Figure 12.15, and these may be summarised as follows:

$$\text{H.P. turbine } 9921.5 \text{ kW} = 59.67 \text{ per cent} \begin{cases} 17.128 \times 204.9 & = 3509.4 \text{ kW} \\ 15.9354 \times 187.4 = 2986.2 \text{ kW} \\ 14.7992 \times 231.5 = 3425.9 \text{ kW} \end{cases}$$

$$\text{L.P. turbine } 6705.3 \text{ kW} = 40.33 \text{ per cent} \begin{cases} 13.7675 \times 247.3 = 3404.8 \text{ kW} \\ 13.0366 \times 253.2 = 3300.5 \text{ kW} \end{cases}$$

$$\text{Total} \qquad = \underline{16\,626.8 \text{ kW}}$$

(Note that for clarity, the gland steam flows have been omitted).

The total power developed *internally* at the turbine shafts is thus 16 626.8 kW. To obtain the power delivered at the propeller, we must subtract the power consumed by external mechanical losses (e.g. thrust and journal bearing loss, flexible coupling loss, gear loss, main engine-driven oil pump power, etc.), the power required to drive the feed pump and the power to drive the main generator. Strictly speaking, the power delivered to the propeller should exceed the contract 14 920 kW by the amount of power required to operate the condenser circulating water scoop. Let us make an estimate of to what the major items might amount.

The condenser circulating system is inherently a low head system—possibly having a total system head of 4.5 m—and the condenser might require 75.0 kg of water per 1.0 kg of steam condensed, hence

C.W. quantity $= 13.0366 \times 75.0 = 978.0$ kg/s

$\therefore$ Work done on C.W. $= 978.0 \times 9.80665 \times 4.5$

$= 43\,150$ Nm/s, and since

1.0 Nm = 1.0 J, and 1.0 J/s = 1.0 W

$$\text{Power developed on C.W.} = \frac{43\,150}{1000} = 43.15 \text{ kW}$$

If the efficiency of the scoop system is taken as 0.6, then

$$\text{Power input to C.W. scoop} = \frac{43.15}{0.6} = 72.0 \text{ kW}$$

Hence, actual power required at propeller

$$= 14\,920.0 + 72.0 = \underline{14\,992.0 \text{ kW}}$$

The main generator output is 700.0 kW and if we take the generator efficiency as 0.93, then

$$\text{Power input to main generator} = \frac{700.0}{0.93} = \underline{\underline{753.0 \text{ kW}}}$$

The power required to drive the feed pump might be estimated as follows: To obtain the feed pressure at the pump discharge, we must add to the superheater outlet pressure (51.5 bar) the pressure drops through the superheater, economiser, H.P. heaters and piping, and through the feed regulator. Further, the boiler drum will be located considerably higher than the feed pump, hence this static lift also will have to be included. Investigation of all these factors is not within the scope of this book, and for our purpose we will assume that the feed pump discharge pressure is 1.3 times the superheater output pressure, i.e.

Feed pump discharge pressure = 1.3 × 51.5 = <u>67.0 bar</u>

The pressure on the suction side of the feed pump is the deaerator pressure plus the static height of the deaerator less the hydraulic friction loss in the suction pipe between the deaerator and the pump.

The deaerator pressure is 2.25 bar.

The deaerator might be located about 18.0 m above the pump, and if the water was cold, 1.0 m of water $\equiv 10^3$ kg/m$^2 \equiv$ 9.80665 × 10^3 N/m^2, hence 1.0 m height of cold water $\equiv$ 9.80665 × 10^3/10^5 = 0.0980665 bar, so that if the water were cold, deaerator static pressure = 18.0 × 0.0980665 = 1.7652 bar.

Since however the deaerator water is at 124.0°C (the saturation temperature corresponding to the deaerator pressure of 2.25 bar), its specific volume is 1.0643 dm³/kg, compared with 1.0 dm³/kg for cold water, and the mass of a given height of hot water will therefore be *less* than the same height of cold water.

Hence for hot water,

$$\text{Deaerator static pressure} = 1.7652 \times \frac{1.0}{1.0643} = 1.659 \text{ bar}$$

and if we assume 0.4 bar for pipe friction,

$$\textit{Feed pump suction pressure} = 2.25 + 1.659 - 0.4$$
$$= \underline{3.509 \text{ bar}}$$

The feed pump therefore has to raise the pressure of 17.403 kg/s from 3.509 bar to 67.0 bar, hence

$$\text{Useful work done on feed water} \doteqdot 1.0643(67.0 - 3.509)$$
$$= 67.57 \text{ bar dm}^3/\text{kg}$$

and since 1.0 bar dm³ = 0.1 kJ

$$\text{Useful work done on feed water} = 67.57 \times 0.1$$
$$= 6.76 \text{ kJ/kg}$$

and since 1.0 kW = 1.0 kJ/s,

$$\text{Useful power developed on feed water} = 6.76 \times 17.403$$
$$= 117.63 \text{ kW}$$

If the pump efficiency is 0.8, then

$$\textit{Power input to feed pump} = \frac{117.63}{0.8} = \underline{147.0 \text{ kW}}$$

Thus the propeller requires 14 992 kW, the main generator requires 753.0 kW, and the main feed pump requires 147.0 kW, a total of 15 892 kW. The difference between this power and the power developed internally in the turbines is the power required for external mechanical losses, viz.

$$\text{External mechanical loss} = 16\,626.8 - 15\,892.0$$
$$= 734.8 \text{ kW}$$

Note that this is approximately 4.5 per cent of the turbine internal power.

From the Mollier diagram in Figure 12.15.

$$\text{Internal efficiency ratio of H.P. turbine} = \frac{Dh_1}{Dh_{s1}}$$
$$= \frac{623.8}{758.5} = 0.822$$

$$\text{Internal efficiency ratio of L.P. turbine} = \frac{Dh_2}{Dh_{s2}}$$
$$= \frac{505.5}{599.1} = 0.8438$$

Overall internal efficiency ratio of H.P. and L.P. turbines

$$= \frac{Dh}{Dh_s} = \frac{1129.3}{1320.2} = 0.8554$$

The steam consumption rate of the main turbines alone at full power when feed heating is

$$\frac{17.128}{14\,920.0} \times 3600 = 4.133 \text{ kg/kWh}$$

(based on the propulsion power.)

The criterion, of course, is not the performance of the main turbines alone, but is the combined performance of the boiler, the turbines, the auxiliaries and the ship services. The heat balance diagram shows that the total "all purposes" steam requirement is 17.403 kg/s, hence the steam consumption rate

$$= \frac{17.403}{14\,920.0} \times 3600 = 4.199 \text{ kg/kWh}$$

for all purposes.

The boiler delivers 17.2817 kg/s of superheated steam at 51.5 bar, 512.0°C having enthalpy 3459.7 kJ/kg and 0.1213 kg/s of saturated steam at the boiler drum pressure of about 56.0 bar, having enthalpy 2789.0 kJ/kg. The average enthalpy of the steam from the boiler is therefore

$$\frac{(17.2817 \times 3459.7) + (0.1213 \times 2789.0)}{17.2817 + 0.1213} = 3454.9 \text{ kJ/kg}$$

The feed water to the boiler at 200°C has liquid enthalpy 852.4 kJ/kg. Hence nett heat received in boiler = 3454.9 − 852.4 = 2602.5 kJ/kg, and the all purposes heat consumption rate of the turbines and auxiliaries is

$$2602.5 \times 4.199 = 10\,928 \text{ kJ/kWh}$$

The boiler efficiency would probably be about 0.88, hence the fuel heat consumption rate for all purposes = 10 928/0.88 = 12 419 kJ/kWh, and since 1.0 kW = 1.0 kJ/s, then 1.0 kWh = 3600 kJ/h, and the overall all-purpose thermal efficiency = 3600/12 419 = 0.2899 or 28.99 per cent.

Standard boiler fuel oil has a calorific value of 43 032 kJ/kg, hence

$$\textit{Fuel oil consumption rate for all purposes} = \frac{12\,419}{43\,032}$$

$$= \underline{0.2886 \text{ kg/kWh}}$$

Pumps, generators and boilers are introduced herein only in so far as they affect the steam turbine cycle and the heat balance diagram. They are fully dealt with in detail in the companion volumes of the Marine Engineering Series.

Figures 12.16 and 12.17 show the heat balance diagram and the Mollier diagram for the same type of cycle, but with initial steam conditions 63.0 bar, 510°C, and for a much larger power—23 882.0 kW. The condenser pressure is 0.05 bar as before, but the feed temperature has been increased from 200°C to 213°C, still using four stages of feed heating. The H.P. turbine does not have a Curtis stage, but consists of nine single-row pressure stages, giving a higher H.P. turbine efficiency ratio than in our last example. The

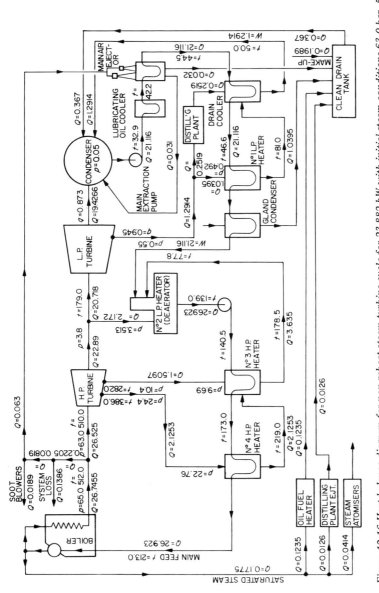

Figure 12.16 Heat balance diagram for non-reheat steam turbine cycle for 23 882 kW with initial steam conditions 63.0 bar, 510°C, and condenser pressure 0.05 bar

p = pressure, bar   t = temperature, °C   Q = quantity, kg/s   q = dryness fraction

Turbine gland steam flows omitted

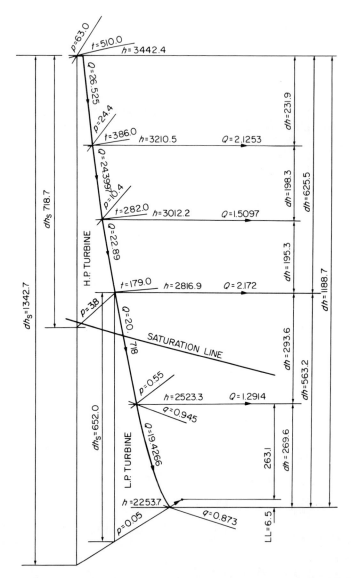

Figure 12.17 Mollier diagram for non-reheat steam turbine cycle for 23 882 kW with initial steam conditions 63.0 bar, 510° C and condenser pressure 0.05 bar

L.P. turbine has eight stages—one more than in the previous example—hence even although the higher initial pressure without increase of initial temperature causes the expansion line to proceed further into the wet zone and therefore causes increased wetness losses, this is compensated for by the extra stage, the L.P. turbine efficiency ratio being actually higher than before.

The leaving loss is 6.5 kJ/kg, and the distribution of the internal power developed is

$$
\text{H.P. turbine 15 460 kW = 58.0 per cent} \begin{cases} 26.525 \times 231.9 & = 6151.7 \,\text{kW} \\ 24.3997 \times 198.3 & = 4838.0 \,\text{kW} \\ 22.890 \times 195.3 & = 4470.3 \,\text{kW} \end{cases}
$$

$$
\text{L.P. turbine 11 193.7 kW = 42.0 per cent} \begin{cases} 20.718 \times 293.6 & = 6082.5 \,\text{kW} \\ 19.4266 \times 263.1 & = 5111.2 \,\text{kW} \end{cases}
$$

$$
\text{Total} \qquad \underline{26\,653.7 \,\text{kW}}
$$

We may assess the main engine-driven auxiliary power by the same methods as before, viz.

$$
\text{C.W. scoop} = \frac{19.4266 \times 75.0 \times 4.5 \times 9.80665}{1000 \times 0.6} = 107.2 \,\text{kW}
$$

$$
\therefore \text{Total power required at propeller} = 23\,882 + 107.2
$$
$$
= 23\,989.2 \,\text{kW}
$$

$$
\text{Main generator (750 kW)} = \frac{750.0}{0.93} = 806.4 \,\text{kW}
$$

Main feed pump

Discharge pressure = $1.3 \times 65.0 = 84.5$ bar

$$
\text{Suction pressure} = 3.513 + \frac{18.0 \times 0.098\,0665}{1.0783}
$$
$$
- 0.35 = 4.803 \,\text{bar}
$$

Feed pressure rise = $84.5 - 4.803 = 79.697$ bar

$$
\text{Input power} = \frac{1.079 \times 79.697 \times 0.1 \times 26.923}{0.8}
$$
$$
= 289.4 \,\text{kW}
$$

External mechanical loss = $26\,653.7 - 23\,989.2 - 806.4$
$$
- 289.4 = 1568.7 \,\text{kW}
$$

i.e. about 5.89 per cent of the turbine internal power.

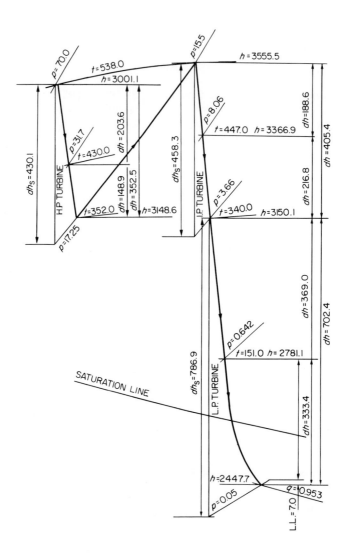

Figure 12.18 Mollier diagram for reheat regenerative cycle for 22 380 kW with initial conditions 70.0 bar, 538° C, reheating at 17.25 bar to 538.0° C, and with condenser pressure 0.05 bar

From the Mollier diagram, Figure 12.17,

Internal efficiency ratio of H.P. turbine $= \dfrac{Dh_1}{Dh_{s1}} = \dfrac{625.5}{718.7}$

$$= 0.8702$$

Internal efficiency ratio of L.P. turbine $= \dfrac{Dh_2}{Dh_{s2}} = \dfrac{563.2}{652.0}$

$$= 0.8638$$

Overall internal efficiency ratio of H.P. and L.P. turbines

$$= \frac{Dh}{Dh_s} = \frac{1188.7}{1342.7} = 0.8852$$

Average enthalpy of steam from boiler

$$= \frac{(26.7455 \times 3444.8) + (0.1775 \times 2777.0)}{26.7455 + 0.1775} = 3440.0 \text{ kJ/kg}$$

Liquid enthalpy of feed at $213.0°C = 911.5$ kJ/kg

Net heat received in boiler $= 3440.0 - 911.5$
$$= 2528.5 \text{ kJ/kg}$$

Steam consumption rate $= \dfrac{26.923}{23\,882.0} \times 3600$

$$= 4.058 \text{ kg/kWh, for all purposes}$$

Turbine plant heat consumption rate $= 4.058 \times 2528.5$
$$= 10\,261 \text{ kJ/kWh,}$$

and again assuming a boiler efficiency of 0.88

Fuel heat consumption rate $= \dfrac{10\,261}{0.88} = 11\,660$ kJ/kWh

for all purposes.

This gives an overall thermal efficiency $\dfrac{3600}{11\,660} = 0.3087$ or

30.87 per cent

and oil fuel consumption rate $\dfrac{11\,660}{43\,032} = 0.271$ kg/kWh

for all purposes.

This is a saving in fuel consumption rate of 0.2868 − 0.271/0.2886 × 100 = 6.1 per cent over the 50.0 bar cycle with the less efficient turbines.

Let us consider what modifications we have made to obtain this saving in fuel, and what these modifications could cost us in other ways.

1. We have increased the initial pressure, so increasing the average temperature of cycle heat reception and therefore *increasing the cycle efficiency*. The increased pressure means that the pressure parts of the boiler, the main steam pipes and valves, and the steam end of the H.P. turbine will have to be stronger and heavier and therefore more expensive.

2. By restaging the turbines we have increased the *efficiency ratio*. The restaging means that the turbine lengths, and possibly the mean diameters may have to be increased. The turbines may therefore be more expensive, and occupy more space.

3. By raising the feed temperature while retaining the same number of feed heating stages, we have only just compensated for the increased range of feed heating (due to the higher boiler pressure), hence the contribution made by the feed heating is about the same for each cycle.

However, neither of these modifications is of large magnitude. The modifications—and hence the penalties—are quite moderate, and the 63.0 bar 510°C cycle may be regarded as a reasonable compromise between efficiency on the one hand and moderate first cost on the other. The initial steam temperature has been maintained at 510°C, and the initial pressure raised only to that which will ensure that the turbine exhaust end wetness does not exceed the acceptable maximum of 12.0 − 13.0 per cent. The turbine plant is not over-complicated, thus problems with operation, reliability and maintenance should be minimal.

Note that by shutting off the bled steam to No. 4, or to Nos. 3 and 4 H.P. heaters, more steam may be passed through a large proportion of the main turbine stages, and increased power may therefore be developed. This feature might be of benefit temporarily in an emergency, but the overall efficiency of the plant is, of course, lowered. Further, before operating in this manner, it must be established that the turbine stages

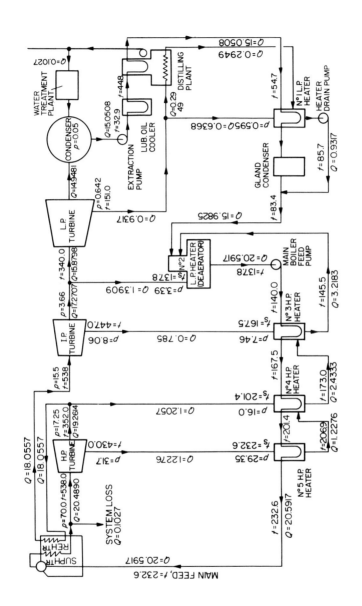

Figure 12.19 Simplified heat balance diagram for reheat regenerative cycle for 22 380 kW with initial steam conditions 70.0 bar, 538°C, reheating at 17.25 bar to 538°C, and with condenser pressure 0.05 bar

are capable of withstanding the resulting increased pressures, that the shafts, couplings, gearing, etc., are capable of transmitting the increased power, that the main extraction pump and the L.P. heater drain system will not be overloaded, and that the boiler will not be adversely affected by the reduced feed temperature. These matters are normally dealt with in the engine builder's and boilermaker's operating instructions.

Reheat steam turbine cycles

Figure 12.18 shows the Mollier diagram and Figure 12.19 the heat balance diagram for a 22 380.0 kW single-screw steam turbine installation having initial steam conditions 70.0 bar, 538°C, and having one reheat at 17.25 bar to 538°C. The condenser pressure is 0.05 bar, and there are five stages of feed heating, the second stage being a direct-contact deaerating heater.

The main boiler feed pump is driven from the forward end of the H.P. turbine rotor and the main generator from the forward end of the L.P. turbine. The condenser air pump is electric motor-driven and the distilling plant is condensate circulated. The drain from No. 1 L.P. heater is not passed through a drain cooler and thence to the condenser, but is pumped forward into the condensate main by a heater drain pump.

The H.P. and I.P. turbines each have eight single-row impulse stages, and the L.P. turbine has six impulse stages followed by four reaction stages. The H.P. turbine exhausts at 17.25 bar, some of the exhaust steam being bled off for feed heating, and the remainder being passed though the boiler reheater before passing to the I.P. turbine. In passing through the reheater system there is a pressure drop of 1.75 bar, hence the reheat line in Figure 12.14 is not a line of constant pressure. Note that the reheat has the effect of displacing the I.P. and L.P. turbine expansion lines upwards and to the right, so that only the last few L.P. turbine stages work in the wet zone. Consequently, only those few stages suffer wetness loss, and the steam is much drier towards exhaust than would be the case with no reheat. Reduced wetness loss improves the efficiency ratio, and drier steam reduces exhaust end blade erosion. The leaving loss is 7.0 kJ/kg.

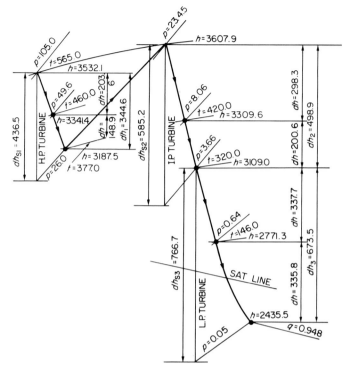

Figure 12.20 Mollier diagram for reheat-regenerative cycle for 26 000 kW, with initial steam conditions 105.0 bar, 565.0° C, reheating at 26.0 bar to 565.0° C with condenser pressure 0.05 bar

For clarity, the steam quantities have been omitted from the Mollier diagram in Figure 12.18. These of course can be readily obtained from the heat balance diagram in Figure 12.19.

Using the same methods as before, the turbine internal power is

H.P. turbine 7040 kW = 28.24 per cent $\begin{cases} 20.489 \times 203.6 = 4172.0 \text{ kW} \\ 19.2614 \times 148.9 = 2868.0 \text{ kW} \end{cases}$

I.P. turbine 7149.7 kW = 28.68 per cent $\begin{cases} 18.0557 \times 188.6 = 3405.4 \text{ kW} \\ 17.2707 \times 216.8 = 3744.3 \text{ kW} \end{cases}$

L.P. turbine 10738.3 kW = 43.08 per cent $\begin{cases} 15.8798 \times 369.0. = 5859.4 \text{ kW} \\ 14.9481 \times 326.4 = 4878.9 \text{ kW} \end{cases}$

Total   = 24 928.0 kW

The turbine internal power is distributed as follows

Main feed pump	350.6 kW
Main generator	618.4 kW
C.W. scoop	85.8 kW
External mechanical loss	1493.2 kW
Propulsion	22380.0 kW
Total internal power	24928.0 kW

The external losses amount to 6.0 per cent of the turbine internal power

The efficiency ratios are

$$\text{H.P. turbine} = \frac{352.5}{430.1} = 0.82$$

$$\text{I.P. turbine} = \frac{405.4}{458.3} = 0.885$$

$$\text{L.P. turbine} = \frac{702.4}{786.9} = 0.89$$

The total steam consumption rate is

$$\frac{20.5917}{22\,380} \times 3600 = 3.3122 \text{ kg/kWh for all purposes}$$

Net heat received in boiler and superheater
$$= 20.5917(3501.1 - 1002.6) = 20.5917 \times 2498.5$$
$$= 51\,454 \text{ kJ/s}$$

Net heat received in reheater
$$= 18.0557(3555.5 - 3148.6) = 18.0557 \times 406.9$$
$$= 7347.7 \text{ kJ/s}$$

Total net heat received
$$= 51454 + 7347.7 = 58\,801.7 \text{ kJ/s}$$

Turbine plant heat consumption rate
$$= \frac{58\,801.7}{22\,380} \times 3600 = 9459 \text{ kJ/kWh}$$

Assuming a boiler efficiency of 0.88 gives fuel heat consumption rate for all purposes = 9459/0.88 = 10 748 kJ/kWh, corresponding to an all-purposes thermal efficiency of 3600/10 748 = 0.3349. If the calorific value of oil fuel is 43 032 kJ/kg, then oil fuel consumption rate for all purposes = 10 748/43 032 = 0.2498 kg/kWh. This is an improvement of

$$\frac{0.271 - 0.2498}{0.271} \times 100 = 7.83 \text{ per cent}$$

over the 63.0 bar 510.0°C non-reheat cycle. It is interesting to examine the reasons for this significant gain.

1. The initial steam pressure and temperature are higher.
2. The reheat is carried out at the optimum pressure, hence the maximum theoretical improvement in cycle efficiency due to reheating is to be expected.
3. High turbine stage efficiency is consistent throughout the three main turbines. This implies judicious staging, selection of u/C_0, and degrees of reaction.
4. The efficiency ratio of the L.P. turbine is improved by the suppression of some of the wetness losses. This is due to the reheat.
5. There is an additional stage of feed heating and a higher final feed temperature.
6. The H.P. feed heaters have desuperheating and drain cooling sections, giving zero terminal temperature difference, and 5.5°C approach temperature difference.
7. The heat rejected by the distilling plant has been recovered in the feed heating system.
8. The No. 1 L.P. heater drain is pumped forward instead of being discharged to the condenser.

The theoretical aspects of 1 and 2 are discussed in Chapter 9, of 3 in Chapter 10, and of 5, 6, 7 and 8 in Chapter 11.

For the sake of clarity, the turbine gland steam flows have been omitted from these explanations. Reference to Chapter 3 will show that high pressure gland steam leak-offs are normally used to pack lower pressure glands, a gland steam collector being provided to act as a "buffer". Excess steam from the gland steam collector is discharged to a feed heater, and low pressure gland leak-offs to a gland condenser, the latter acting virtually as an additional heater in the feed heating system. The various quantities involved can be quite considerable and have of course, in practice, to be taken into consideration when calculating the heat balance. The effect would be to alter somewhat the quantities of steam passing through the various sections of the turbines and to the heaters from those shown on our rather simplified heat balance diagram.

Another interesting feature of this system is the substitution of a motor-driven air pump for the customary steam jet air ejector. This shows a small gain in efficiency in the present case, although this does not necessarily follow for all other cases.

Figure 12.20 shows the Mollier diagram for the same type of cycle but having what may be regarded as the most advanced steam conditions which would be contemplated for marine application at the present day.

This is again a single-screw steam turbine installation for 26 000 kW having initial steam conditions 105.0 bar, 565°C with one reheat at 26.0 bar to 565°C, and condenser pressure 0.05 bar. There are again five stages of feed heating, but the final feed temperature has been raised to 259°C. The power for the main generator is 615.0 kW and for the main feed pump 485.0 kW.

The oil fuel consumption rate is of the order of 0.237 kg/kWh for all purposes, which is an improvement of 5.1 per cent over the 70.0 bar 538°C reheat cycle.

This order of fuel consumption rate is some 20.0–25.0 per cent lower than that of the then large turbine steamers of twenty five years ago.

13 Future possibilities

In attempting—with no little caution—to offer the author's opinions on the possible future of marine steam machinery, it seem prudent, although perhaps somewhat paradoxical, to begin by looking backwards.

During the quarter of a century which has passed since this book was first published, marine engines and engineering have undergone certain changes which we may summarise quite briefly as follows.

Although there are many steam engine and steam turbine-driven ships at sea, interest in new steam machinery has now become limited practically solely to large-power turbines, i.e. to that category in which steam turbines can—on a thermal efficiency basis—compete more effectively with diesel engines.

Interest in new steam reciprocating engines appears to have waned in the 1950s and 1960s, until at the present moment it is practically non-existent. There can be little doubt that the sole reason for this is that the difficulties of H.P. cylinder lubrication limits the initial steam conditions which can be used, and hence limits the cycle efficiency to a level which is well below that of diesel engines or of high-pressure high-temperature steam turbines.

Gas turbines have continued to develop, and there are now a number of ships at sea with gas turbine main engines, although in general their thermal efficiency appears as yet to be lower than that of diesel engines or steam turbines.

Finally, for all marine engines, the use of oil fuel has become practically universal.

If the orthodox view is taken, these changes would be regarded simply as developing technique in the face of economic necessity.

Within the last five years however, there has occurred a revolutionary change in oil fuel economics which virtually amounts to a pre-warning that the world's oil resources are not inexhaustible.

The immediate consequence of this is that the thermal efficiency of a ship's engines—whatever type they may be—

will have a much greater influence on the overall economics of the ship than formerly, hence it seems likely that in the immediate future, the present emphasis on diesel engines and on high-pressure high-temperature steam turbines will continue, since in the present conditions and in the present state of knowledge, these offer the highest thermal efficiency, and therefore the lowest oil fuel consumption rate.

In the longer-term view however, it seems likely that this situation cannot continue. The consumption of oil fuel at the present rate—not only by merchant shipping, but by a very large proportion of the world's industry and other forms of transport—can only mean rapid depletion of known resources, and therefore rapid and continuous rise in price. The high thermal efficiency of diesel engines and of oil-burning turbines is of little value if the price of oil fuel is high compared with that of other fuels, or if oil fuel is unobtainable.

There is as yet no new "miracle" technology which would suggest any radical departure from the already well-known and well-proven types of marine engines—whether steam or internal combustion—and whatever be the future of oil, there can be little doubt that the search for economic and readily available alternative fuels will become an urgent priority. From this aspect, steam-driven machinery is likely to become dominant, since not the least of its advantages is its ability to burn any type of fuel.

Even given such alternative fuels, the need for conservation, and for economic operating fuel cost will remain, hence the quest for high thermal efficiency—commensurate with the type and the price of the fuel—will continue. With this greater emphasis on operating efficiency, it is possible that the tendency to consider first cost as the major item in machinery selection will no longer be justified, but it is important that any efforts to increase efficiency must not prejudice safety or reliability, or place any additional or undue responsibilities on the engine room staff.

The thermal efficiency is the product of the *cycle efficiency* and the *overall efficiency ratio*. Broadly speaking, the cycle efficiency depends largely on the initial steam conditions and on the condenser pressure, and the efficiency ratio depends largely on judicious staging, and on meticulous attention to detail design.

Although the steam turbine is already a highly developed, efficient and reliable power unit, there exists some scope for further improving the thermal efficiency. Even within the currently accepted limits of initial steam conditions, modifications to the cycle, e.g. reheating, feed heating, optimum use of auxiliary exhaust steam, etc., could give worthwhile improvements.

A reappraisal of the turbine exhaust end design may show that condenser pressures as low as 0.035 bar could sometimes be justified, even accepting that the increased erosion could necessitate replacing the last stage blades possibly every two years. There is already considerable land experience with initial steam conditions considerably higher than the present accepted limits for marine practice, and as appropriate materials are developed and proved, it is possible that this means of increasing the cycle efficiency could be further exploited.

For low powers—i.e. less than about 3000 kW—the author believes that steam reciprocating engines could again become quite attractive. Steam engine cylinders using superheated steam have already shown high efficiency ratios, and if determined research could solve the problem of high temperature cylinder lubrication, higher initial steam conditions could be applied immediately and a much higher cycle efficiency so obtained.

This concept is not new—it was recognised almost fifty years ago, when several high-pressure, high-temperature engines were put into service, some of which achieved thermal efficiencies comparable with diesel engines.

It appears that these types of steam engines failed to survive only because of H.P. cylinder lubrication problems, and it may well be that the time as now come for modern methods of research to be applied to their solution. Given such a solution, a high-pressure, high-temperature reciprocating engine, with or without an exhaust turbine, could well become attractive for low-power steam machinery.

Some other possibilities involving steam machinery are briefly reviewed below.

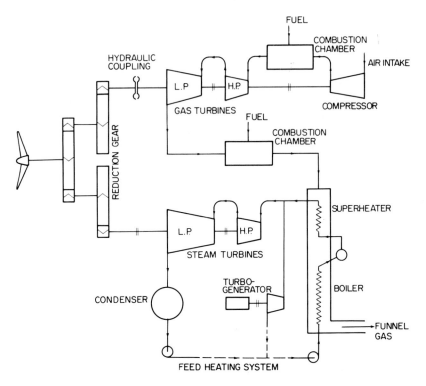

Figure 13.1 Principle of combined steam and gas turbine cycle

Combined steam and gas turbine cycles

Gas turbines exhaust at quite high temperature—of the order
of 450°C—and the combined cycle makes use of the high-
temperature exhaust from the gas turbine unit in generating
steam for the steam turbine unit. The latter exhausts at the
low temperature corresponding to its condenser pressure,
hence if judiciously designed, the combined cycle efficiency
is higher than the cycle efficiency of the gas turbine alone.

The steam generating equipment may be either a simple
"waste heat" boiler, or it may have supplementary firing. The
latter, rendered possible by the fact that there is sufficient
free oxygen in the gas turbine exhaust to support combustion
up to temperatures of the order of 1750°C, gives higher initial
steam conditions, increased steam generation, and hence
increased steam turbine power. Also from the practical aspect,
operation is rendered much more flexible, e.g. the total power
can be varied by varying the boiler firing rate without change

to the gas turbine operating conditions; steam can be raised without the gas turbine being in operation, and the combined plant started up without electrical or pneumatic systems. The gas turbine and the steam turbine may be operated independently of one another, hence "get home" or "carry on" power is available in the event of major breakdown of either unit; reversal can be obtained by providing the usual simple astern stages in the steam turbine, so avoiding the need for the more complicated means, i.e. controllable pitch propeller or reversing gear, which is normally required for gas turbines on account of the impracticability of using astern stages in the latter.

Although the features of the gas turbines are not within the scope of this book, Figure 13.1 shows the principle of such a combined system. The steam turbines develop about 80.0 per cent of the total power, with initial steam conditions 63.0 bar, 480°C, and condenser pressure 0.05 bar, and the overall thermal efficiency is of the order of 33.0 per cent. The features of the steam turbines do not differ in any way from those described in earlier chapters.

Nuclear power for marine propulsion

The term "nuclear power" continues to mean simply a steam-turbine installation whose boilers are fired by nuclear fission. Although a nuclear boiler is quite different from a conventional boiler, its application does not demand any radical departures from more or less conventional turbine designs. Depending on the type of nuclear reactor used, a wide range of initial steam conditions is available, and in some cases special protection against wetness in the turbines is required. In many cases a by-pass system is necessary to enable steam to be "dumped" direct to the condenser from the boiler. The by-pass is used at reactor start-up, when the steam quality may be poor, and probably at sudden turbine power reduction until followed up by reactor power reduction.

The following notes are based largely on a paper by Messrs. Gaunt and Wilkinson, read to the Manchester Association of Engineers, and are included by kind permission of the Association.

Up until about 10 years ago, the use of nuclear boilers could not be shown to be economic by comparison with conventional steam-turbine installations or with diesel engines. The advent of the large container ship, however, prompted further studies, which indicated that nuclear-fuelled steam-turbine installations could become economically competitive at about 30 000 kW and could become very attractive in the power range 45 000–75 000 kW. The recent revolutionary change in oil fuel economics and availability is likely to intensify interest in nuclear boilers, and to influence the range of powers in which they are attractive. The first cost of a nuclear boiler is high, but nuclear fuel cost is relatively low, and this fuel-cost advantage could be very significant for large powers and high utilisation. Nuclear fuel is of small dimensions, hence for any given size of ship the dead weight carrying capacity is increased. The nature of nuclear fuel is such that refuelling need be carried out only at long intervals, thus eliminating refuelling delays. The main disadvantages are environmental, i.e. the possibility of release of dangerous products resulting from damage caused by collision, etc., and the safe disposal of long-lived radioactive waste, neither of which can be treated lightly.

The turbine machinery visualised is a single-screw, two-cylinder, cross-compound, double-reduction geared installation developing 30 000 kW and taking steam at 40.5 bar, 300°C. The L.P. turbine would have an integral centrifugal water separator to limit the steam dryness fraction in the lower L.P. stages. For the special boiler, a very high standard of feed-water purity is essential, and because of this the condenser would have double tube plates, and a full-flow demineralising plant would be provided in the feed system immediately upstream of the first L.P. heater. Due to the relatively low steam conditions, the steam- and water-flow quantities would be greater than usual, and the condenser heat load would be higher. A 15 per cent steam-dumping equipment would be provided for start-up and to maintain minimum reactor load.

The reactor core could be designed to give a life of 1200 days at full power, corresponding to a refit period of about four years. The expendable parts of the demineralising plant could be designed to last for a complete voyage.

Other than the special features mentioned, the engine-room would have standard marine equipment, and emergency "get home" power could be provided either by an auxiliary oil-fired boiler or by an emergency electric motor operated from diesel generators.

The supercritical steam cycle

Although there are, in different parts of the world, a number of supercritical land steam turbine installations which have been in successful operation for a number of years, it is difficult—and certainly too early—to speculate whether the benefit of increased efficiency which it offers could be consistently associated with the high standards of flexibility and reliability demanded of marine installations, or whether the more complicated plant could be justified. Nevertheless, with the recent metamorphic change in the economics and the availability of oil fuel, the steam turbine seems likely to remain a powerful competitor in the field of marine propulsion, and there remains the possibility that the supercritical steam cycle could one day be adopted. The following brief notes may therefore not be amiss while we are dealing with future possibilities.

In Chapter 9, it was demonstrated that the higher the *average* temperature of cycle heat reception, then the higher is the cycle efficiency. It was also shown that one method of raising the average temperature of heat reception is to raise the initial pressure, and we established that the best cycle efficiency on present-day limits of initial steam conditions is that illustrated in Figure 9.18.

If however, the initial pressure is raised up to the critical pressure (221.2 bar) or above, the horizontal evaporation line on the *Ts* diagram disappears, and a significant increase in the average temperature of heat reception—and therefore in cycle efficiency—is achieved. This is illustrated in Figure 13.2, in which diagram (a) is the same cycle as in Figure 9.18 (Chapter 9). Diagram (b) shows the effect of increasing the initial pressure up to 221.2 bar, and diagram (c) up to 240.0 bar, while still retaining the present-day limit of initial steam temperature, 520°C (793.15 K). We may ponder for a moment on the ultimate theoretical extremes of this. As the pressure is raised, the final dryness fraction diminishes, and increased initial steam temperature and multiple reheat are required to limit the final wetness. If, for the initial steam conditions, we take a notional excursion to the extreme upper end of the steam tables (1000 bar, 800°C), and apply two reheats, this would result in diagram (d) in Figure 13.2, which is clearly tending towards a tall Carnot rectangle. Thus in Figure 13.2:

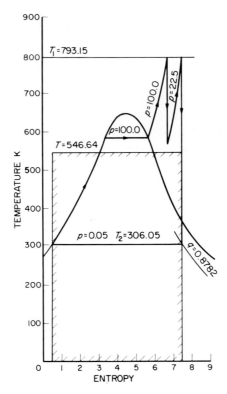

Figure 13.2 The supercritical steam cycle
(a) Subcritical pressure: cycle efficiency = 0.4404 gross, 0.4378 nett

Diagram (a) shows approximately the best subcritical cycle which can be used within present-day limitations on materials etc.

Diagram (c) shows approximately the improvement by going supercritical to the highest initial pressure which is likely to be acceptable in the foreseeable future.

Diagram (d) shows what could be done if there were no material limitations, the initial pressure and temperature being limited only by the limits of our knowledge of the properties of steam. As the initial pressure is raised, the feed pump work increases, and at the higher pressures, this causes a significant reduction in the available cycle work. In Figure 13.2 the net cycle efficiency has been obtained by correcting the gross cycle efficiency to allow for the feed pump work (see Chapter 9, page 361).

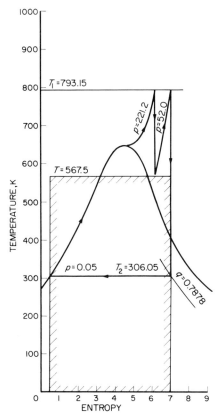

Figure 13.2(b) Critical pressure: cycle efficiency = 0.461 gross, 0.455 net

To return to practicalities, however, the behaviour of water and steam at and above the critical pressure is quite different from that of water and steam at pressures below the critical pressure. There is no constant temperature "boiling" phase while the steam receives latent heat. The reception of the total heat of the steam is a continuous process at varying temperature from A to B, Figure 13.2(c), during which there is a "transition" period when the water changes to steam. There is therefore no boiler drum, the boiler consisting of, in simple terms, a number of tubes in parallel, into one end of which the feed pump forces water at the supercritical pressure, and out of the other end issues superheated steam at the supercritical pressure. Such a boiler is called a "once-through" boiler, and obviously cannot be fired until an adequate circu-

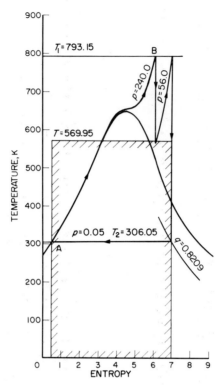

Figure 13.2(c) Supercritical pressure: cycle efficiency = 0.463 gross, 0.456 net

lation through the tubes is established and maintained. This circulation is at first cold water, then hot water, then steam and finally highly superheated steam. During the periods of circulation of water and low-quality steam, the boiler cannot of course be connected to the turbines, and a starting bypass system with flash vessel and with pressure-reducing and desuperheating equipment is required to "dump" the water and steam to the condenser. Figure 13.3 shows a simplified diagram of such a system.

When suitable steam condition is attained, the steam flow is transferred from the bypass to the turbines as required. The bypass system should always be available and kept warmed through to anticipate sudden power reductions, e.g. when manoeuvring. The boiler cannot be blow-down hence extreme water purity is essential.

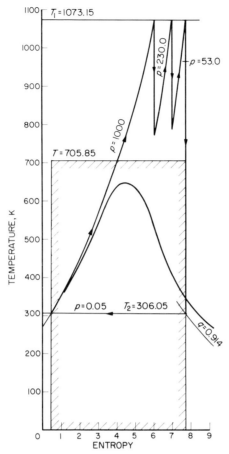

Figure 13.2(d) Extreme supercritical pressure: cycle efficiency = 0.5665 gross, 0.5467 net

The binary vapour cycle

Water/steam as a working substance has many advantages. Water is readily available in any quantities, and even allowing the need for evaporators, and more recently, water treatment, it is relatively cheap. It is chemically stable, non-inflammable and non-toxic. Although water is corrosive in the presence of oxygen, it is not aggressively so. Steam condenses at low pressure with ordinary circulating water temperatures. Practically all aspects of steam technology are well known, and have been well proven over a period of a hundred and fifty years.

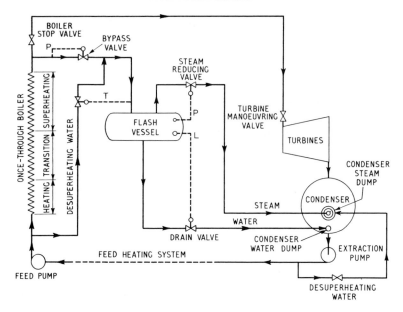

Figure 13.3 Simplified diagram of starting bypass system for once-through boiler
P. Pressure control
T. Temperature control
L. Level control

There are however, two features of the water/steam working substance, which, in view of past history and of present-
day research, merit some consideration while we are dealing
with future possibilities.

1. If on the basis of a constant initial steam temperature of
   570°C (i.e. the maximum which, from the materials
   viewpoint, would be contemplated in the foreseeable
   future), and with a constant exhaust pressure of say
   0.05 bar, we calculate the Rankine cycle efficiency for
   various initial steam pressures (using the methods as for
   the cycle in Figure 9.9 (Chapter 9)), we obtain the
   curve of gross cycle efficiency shown in Figure 13.4. As
   the initial pressure is increased however, the feed pump
   work increases and becomes quite significant at the
   higher pressures, and to obtain a true picture, the feed
   pump work must be deducted from the cycle work. This
   results in the curve of net cycle efficiency, which it will
   be observed reaches a maximum at about 350.0 bar.

This means that to obtain the maximum advantage from the given initial steam temperature, *the initial pressure must be high*—in this case about 350.0 bar.

2. If with these initial steam conditions, 350.0 bar, 570°C, we regard 0.05 bar as the lowest practicable exhaust pressure, then the initial specific volume of the steam is 8.8341 dm³/kg, and the final specific volume after adiabatic expansion is 19 656 dm³/kg, i.e. an increase of 2225 times. In practice, the expansion is not adiabatic, and depending on the value of the internal efficiency ratio, the specific volume at the end of actual expansion is even greater—possibly 2500 or 3000 times the initial specific volume. This means that towards the exhaust end, *large blade discharge areas are required*, leading to the well known turbine problems of large mean diameters, large blade heights and increased blade erosion.

Recognition of these two features is not new—they were identified a long time ago—and it is true to say that the search for a suitable alternative working substance (i.e. one which does not evince these two features), has gone on for many years, the impetus of the search being influenced from time to time as the prodigious efforts of the metallurgists and the turbine designers produced materials capable of withstanding higher temperatures and pressures, and efficient, reliable turbine exhaust ends to deal with the large volumes of steam at low pressure.

Regarded solely from the aspect of the above two features, an ideal working substance would be one which would (a) enable the average temperature of cycle heat reception to be raised to the maximum associated with the highest acceptable initial temperature without requiring a high initial pressure, and (b) have much smaller specific volumes than steam at the low pressure end of the cycle.

Of all the working substances which have been tried or proposed, it is fortunate that steam/water is the one which best satisfies these two requirements simultaneously. There are some alternative working substances which are better than steam/water at the high-temperature end of the cycle but are very much worse at the low-temperature end, and vice versa. Steam/water is the *single* working substance which imposes the least restriction in this respect.

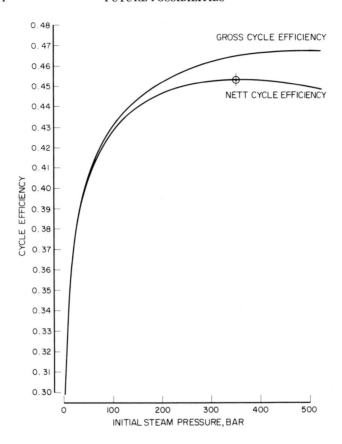

Figure 13.4 Non-reheat cycle efficiency for constant initial steam temperature 570.0° C, constant exhaust pressure 0.05 bar, and with varying initial steam pressure

$$\text{Gross cycle efficiency} = \frac{Cycle\ work}{Cycle\ heat}$$

$$\text{Net cycle efficiency} = \frac{cycle\ work\ -\ feed\ pump\ work}{cycle\ heat}$$

By using an appropriate alternative working substance to replace steam/water either at the high-temperature end or at the low-temperature end of the cycle we have a *binary vapour cycle*. The simplest way to visualise a binary vapour cycle is to imagine it as two Rankine cycles in which the condenser of the primary cycle is virtually the boiler of the secondary cycle (see Figure 13.7).

If the object is to minimise the primary boiler pressure, then an appropriate alternative working substance would be

used in the primary cycle, and steam/water in the secondary
cycle. If the object is to reduce the physical dimensions of
the secondary exhaust end, then the primary cycle would use
steam/water, and the secondary cycle would use an appropriate alternative working substance.

The earliest practical application of the binary vapour
cycle was made with the object of utilising the heat energy
in low pressure steam which could not be utilised in steam
reciprocating engines because of the prohibitively large L.P.
cylinder volumes required. The primary working substance
was steam/water and the secondary working substance was
sulphur dioxide. The development of the exhaust steam turbine, however, provided a simpler and more ready means of
utilising low-pressure steam, and in consequence, active
interest in the binary vapour engine ceased for quite a long
time. In recent years, however, the principle has again been
receiving a great deal of serious attention, mainly for
turbines, as it offers the possibility of considerably reducing
the dimensions, problems and costs of L.P. turbines, particularly where large powers and low exhaust steam pressures are
involved.

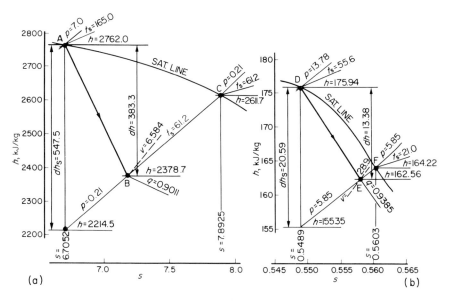

*Figure 13.5 Mollier diagrams for primary and secondary sections of binary vapour
cycle*
(a) Primary—drawn for 1.0 kg of steam
(b) Secondary—drawn for 1.0 kg of dichlorodifluoromethane

Sulphur dioxide of course would not be used nowadays, as not the least of its disadvantages are that it is poisonous and incipiently corrosive. Many secondary working substances have been considered already, and it is possible that many more will be investigated. It is much too early to make any statement as to what is the best secondary working substance, but the most favoured at present is one bearing the somewhat cumbersome name of dichlorodifluoromethane (probably better known by its original trade name of Freon 12). For brevity, we will call it dichloro.

A simple example will illustrate the features of such a binary vapour cycle. In Figure 13.5(a), AB is the expansion line for the primary engine receiving steam at 7.0 bar, dry saturated, and exhausting at 0.21 bar with an efficiency ratio of 0.7. In Figure 13.5(b), DE is the expansion line for the secondary engine receiving dichloro vapour at a pressure of 13.78 bar, dry saturated, and exhausting at 5.85 bar with an efficiency ratio of 0.65. The coordinates of the points D and F in Figure 13.5(b) are obtained from tables of the properties of dichloro. in just the same way as the coordinates of the points A and C in Figure 13.5(a) are obtained from the Steam Tables. For reference, the appropriate properties are as follows:

Steam (above $0°C$)

p, bar	t_s, °C	h_f, kJ/kg	h_{fg}, kJ/kg	h_g, kJ/kg	s_f	s_{fg}	s_g	v_g, dm³/kg
7.0	165.0	697.1	2064.9	2762.0	1.9918	4.7134	6.7052	272.68
0.21	61.2	255.9	2355.8	2611.7	0.8454	7.0471	7.8925	7306.8

Dichlorodifluoromethane (above $0°C$)

p, bar	t_s, °C	h_f, kJ/kg	h_{fg}, kJ/kg	h_g, kJ/kg	s_f	s_{fg}	s_g	v_g, dm³/kg
13.78	55.6	55.78	120.16	175.94	0.1830	0.3659	0.5489	12.61
5.85	21.0	20.21	144.01	164.22	0.0708	0.4895	0.5603	30.775

Now every 1.0 kg of steam condensed in the primary condenser gives up $(2378.7 - 255.9) = 2122.8$ kJ, and every 1.0 kg of dichloro evaporated in the primary condenser takes in $(175.94 - 20.21) = 155.73$ kJ.

Hence to condense 1.0 kg of steam requires 2122.8/ 155.73 = 13.63 kg of dichloro.

This means that for every 1.0 kg of steam applied to the primary cycle, we must apply 13.63 kg of dichloro to the secondary cycle.

If therefore, we multiply the *specific* properties of Figure 13.5(b) by 13.63, we can superpose it on Figure 13.5(a), giving the composite Mollier diagram shown in Figure 13.6, in which the secondary enthalpies (h'), the secondary entropies (s'), and the secondary specific volumes (v') are each 13.63 times h, s and v of Figure 13.5(b).

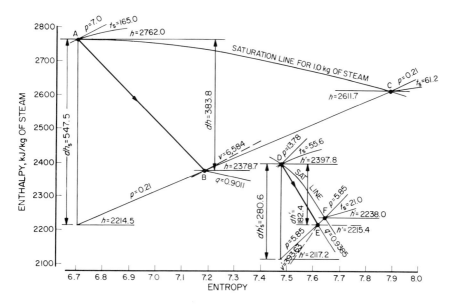

Figure 13.6 Composite Mollier diagram for binary vapour cycle. Note: the saturation line DF is drawn for 13.63 kg of dichlorodifluoromethane

Figure 13.7 shows the system diagram, illustrating the conditions at the various points in the cycle.

θ_1 and θ_2 are the approach and terminal temperature differences for the primary condenser (see Chapter 8).

Had we attempted to use the steam engine alone to expand steam right down to the lower cycle temperature limit of 21°C, the final steam pressure would have been 0.024 bar, and with the efficiency ratio of 0.7, the final specific volume would have been 48 705 dm³/kg. By using dichlorodifluoromethane instead of steam at the low-temperature end

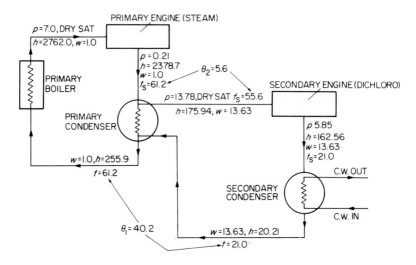

Figure 13.7 Simplified system diagram for steam/dichloro binary vapour cycle

of the cycle, the final specific volume = 28.88 dm³/kg, which for 13.63 kg gives a final volume of 28.88 × 13.63 = 393.63 dm³, compared with 48 705 dm³/kg for steam. This means that even with a mass flow of dichloro 13.63 times that of the steam, the exhaust end of the secondary engine has to accommodate a volume which is less than 1.0 per cent of that required by a single steam cycle. Because of the small specific volume, however, the secondary fluid density is much greater than that of low pressure steam, and to prevent pressure drop losses, the acceptable velocities are only about one third of those normally used for steam. Even so, the exhaust end flow areas of a dichloro secondary turbine would be of the order of only 3.0 per cent of the area required at the L.P. exhaust end of a single cycle steam turbine.

By optimum matching of the primary and secondary cycles, and by judiciously applying regenerative feed heating, it is possible to achieve worthwhile gains in thermal efficiency.

The general principles, and the methods of calculation for the primary and for the secondary cycle do not differ from those previously described for single steam cycles.

There have also been in the past, practical applications of the binary vapour cycle in which an alternative working substance was used at the high temperature end of the cycle. One such binary vapour cycle—designed and built almost

50 years ago—used mercury as the primary working substance and steam as the secondary. Again we may use a simplified example to illustrate the features.

If we take 520°C (793.15 K) as the maximum initial temperature which can be safely tolerated by present-day materials, and if we take 0.05 bar as the lowest practical exhaust pressure which can be maintained, then in order to achieve a high average temperature of heat reception with a single steam cycle, we must use a high initial pressure, e.g. 240.0 bar as shown in Figure 13.2(c). For convenience, this Ts diagram is repeated in Figure 13.8(a).

If with the same initial temperature and the same final pressure, we use mercury as the working substance in a single cycle, then the Ts diagram would be as shown in Figure 13.8(b). A table of the properties of mercury vapour shows that 793.15 K is the saturation temperature corresponding to a pressure of 10.276 bar, hence a high average temperature of heat reception (765.6 K) can be achieved with quite a low

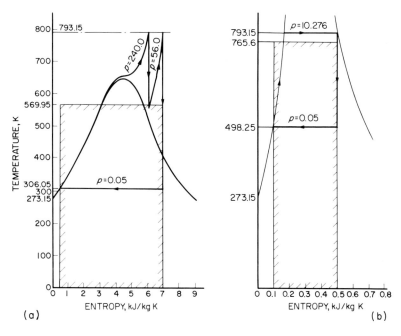

Figure 13.8 Comparative Ts diagrams for steam and mercury, with upper cycle temperature limit 793.15 K and lower cycle pressure limit 0.05 bar
(a) Drawn for 1 kg steam. Gross cycle efficiency = 0.463
(b) Drawn for 1.0 kg of mercury. Gross cycle efficiency = 0.3491

initial pressure (10.276 bar). The single steam cycle gives only 569.95 K with initial pressure 240.0 bar, with superheat, and with one reheat. From this aspect therefore, mercury is superior to steam as a working substance.

At the low temperature end of the cycle however, mercury vapour condensing at 0.05 bar has a saturation temperature of 498.25 K, compared with 306.05 K for the single steam cycle. From this aspect therefore, mercury is inferior to steam since the lower cycle temperature limit for the former is much higher.

The adverse effect at the low temperature end of the single mercury cycle is greater than the beneficial effect at the high temperature end, resulting in a lower cycle efficiency than the single steam cycle.

By using a mercury–steam binary vapour cycle, we combine the advantage of mercury at the high temperature end with the advantage of steam at the low temperature end. Suppose that for the primary cycle, we retain the upper and lower limits shown in Figure 13.8(b).

The properties of mercury vapour relevant to the example are as follows:

p, bar	T_s, K	h_f, kJ/kg	h_g, kJ/kg	s_f, kJ/kg K	s_g, kJ/kg K	v_g, dm^3/kg
10.726	793.15	81.3	350.3	0.1667	0.5054	29.676
0.05	498.25	35.15	331.4	0.0938	0.6859	4158.6

Suppose we allow a terminal temperature difference of 50.0 K for the primary condenser; this fixes the upper temperature limit for the secondary (steam) cycle as 498.25 − 50.0 = 448.25 K, corresponding to a steam pressure of 8.92 bar. The secondary cycle exhaust pressure we can again make 0.05 bar, corresponding to a lower cycle temperature limit of 306.05 K.

Referring to Figure 13.8(b) each 1.0 kg of mercury condensed in the primary condenser rejects enthalpy 498.25 (0.5054 − 0.0938) = 498.25 × 0.4116 = 205.09 kJ, and each 1.0 kg of steam generated in the primary condenser requires enthalpy 2771.8 − 137.8 = 2634 kJ, hence the quantity of mercury required is

$$\frac{2634}{205.09} = 12.845 \text{ kg/kg of steam}$$

Thus if we multiply the entropies of Figure 13.8(b) by 12.845, we can draw the combined Ts diagram for the binary vapour cycle on common coordinates as shown in Figure 13.9. The cycle heat is the heat received in the primary cycle, viz. $12.845 \ (350.3 \ - \ 35.15) \ = \ 12.845 \times 315.15 \ = \ 4048.2$

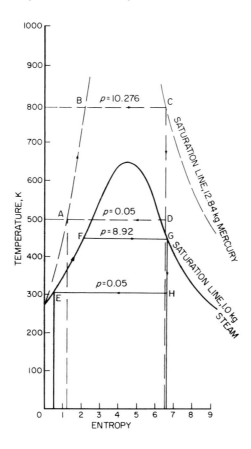

Figure 13.9 Combined Ts diagram for mercury/steam binary vapour cycle

kJ/kg of steam. The total cycle work is the sum of the primary and secondary cycle work, viz.

Primary cycle work =
$12.845 (h_C - h_D) = 12.845(350.3 - 234.13) = 1488.3$ kJ/kg of steam

Secondary cycle work =
$h_G - h_H = 2771.8 - 2018.6$ $= 753.2$ kJ/kg of steam

Total cycle work = 1488.3 + 753.2 = 2241.5 kJ/kg of steam

$$\text{Binary vapour cycle efficiency} = \frac{2241.5}{4048.2} = 0.5537$$

If we compare this cycle efficiency with that of the single steam cycle between the same temperature limits (Figure 13.8(a)), it will be immediately obvious why this type of binary vapour cycle is again receiving serious consideration. As mercury is very expensive, and its vapour very poisonous, it would not now be used, and the immediate need is for some other primary working substance which has approximately the same physical properties as mercury but which is non-toxic and is much less expensive.

14 Going to sea; setting watches; engine room procedure

An engineer, having applied for and obtained a situation as sea-going engineer with a shipping company, will be instructed when and where to join the steamship to which he has been appointed.

On arrival at the vessel he should inquire the whereabouts of the chief engineer's cabin and duly report to him. The chief engineer will, after an interview, hand him over to the second engineer. In future it is the second engineer from whom he will receive his orders. The chief engineer does not generally deal with junior engineers except through the second engineer.

First days on board

Having been shown to his cabin, and depending on instructions from the second engineer, he will probabily change into a boiler-suit or patrol-suit and go down into the engine-room. There he will be shown round, after having been introduced to the other engineers.

The first survey of the engine-room and boiler-room will be rather bewildering if the engineer has had no previous experience of ships; the other engineers, however, know the position, and make allowances. Too much is not expected of a new engineer, as it is to the advantage of everyone that he should not be given responsibility until he has mastered the construction, running and routine of all things in the machinery space. This does not mean that he will be idle. Supposing the vessel to be in port for a few days, there will be many jobs of overhaul going on, and the engineer may find himself sent to help the fourth engineer to overhaul a feed pump. In this way he begins to become acquainted with the construction of at least one of the auxiliaries, and he must be content with slow progress in this direction, or he may find that he is working alone for a period, having been sent to overhaul one or more of the multitude of valves which are located in every ship's machinery spaces. This is a job with which we may assume he is quite conversant.

The new engineer

Being now a ship's engineer, he will soon learn that when a job is done it is expected to be well done, because there is no time to spare in doing work twice over. He will be very fortunate if he does not make a bad blunder within the first few weeks. A badly made steam-pipe or valve-cover joint which blows out just before the ship is ready to sail is an experience he will not easily forget. In fact, the sense of responsibility grows, and he is conscious that any neglect of his will react on the other engineers.

If there is a workshop on board he may find that he is working in much the same way as he did ashore. Many vessels now have a fully equipped workshop with lathe, boring machine, grinder, etc., and many small parts are now made on board which would otherwise have to be ordered ashore. Deck-winches often come to grief during working of cargo, and the new engineer may find himself called upon to make a repair.

While on his way round he will have noticed the variety of tools in the store-room. It is generally well equipped with all the tools found to be necessary by the company during years of experience. Nevertheless, the engineer will find it a great advantage to carry his own kit of small tools.

Preparation for going to sea

Eventually he sees the various parts of the machinery being *boxed-up*. Steam is being raised in the boilers, and the engine-room floor-plates cleared and cleaned. He realizes his inexperience at this stage, when the engines are being prepared for going to sea, and is glad when he merely has to assist in opening up the main boiler stop-valves or told to keep his eye on the water-level.

About this time he may also learn that all the double-bottom tanks and cargo-hold bilges are controlled from the engine-room, and that one of his duties will be to know where all the valves are situated and which pumps can be used for pumping the various compartments.

From *Stand-by* to *Full Away*

The auxiliary machinery is started up, the main engines are warmed through and eventually *stand-by* is rung on the engine-room telegraph. The engineer feels the tenseness, as everything is kept in readiness for the first movement of the engines. All engineers are down below, and each has his duties to perform. The duties vary according to the size of the vessel and whether fitted with single, twin or more screws. During the period of manoeuvring out of port the second engineer may be in control of the main engines, and it will be noticed how the other engineers are kept informed of all that is going on. They sense a fault quickly, and act smartly at the need or order of the second engineer.

Once *full away* is rung on the telegraph, drains are closed and the engines are tuned to full power. It is then that the engine-room staff, and indeed the whole crew, settle down to sea-going routine.

If the vessel is a *single screw*, carrying five or six engineers, the new engineer will probably find he is to be on watch with the second engineer. In this way he is under supervision while learning how a "watch" should be kept. He is given the opportunity of asking questions as difficulties arise. He has time to trace pipe-lines, and gradually begins to know the steam, exhaust, feed and other valves so well that he does not require to read the name-plate every time he is opening the valve. A new engineer should make sketches of all pipelines as soon as possible, if he is to feel confident while on watch.

A large modern turbine steamer will probably have centralised control, involving some form of turbine supervisory equipment. The new engineer should again, as soon as possible, endeavour to familiarise himself with the principles of the turbine supervisory, so that ultimately, he will quickly appreciate the meaning of the various indications and alarms, and the action which it is necessary to take to correct a fault.

Duties of the engineers

In all ships the various items comprising the whole of the power unit are the responsibility of the chief engineer, whose duties are generally supervisory and consultant. He enters information on the running of the machinery in the official log book, and makes important tests, such as may be carried out daily on a sample of lubricating oil or the boiler water. On receiving new fuel oil he will test it for viscosity, flash point and settling point.

The second engineer is in charge of all engine-room personnel. He plans the work of the engine-room and sees that routine overhauling is carried out. At sea he is in charge of the four to eight watch.

The third engineer's duties are to inspect and overhaul as required the main engines and main gearing, all electrical equipment running and repair, and sometimes he is also in charge of the domestic refrigerator. At sea he is in charge of the twelve to four watch.

The fourth engineer overhauls all pumps and forced-draught fans and their engines, if so driven. At sea he is in charge of the eight to twelve watch.

The fifth engineer overhauls all boiler valves as required in port and deck-winches at sea, when not keeping a watch. He probably keeps the night-watch while in port.

In a large vessel with, say, three propeller shafts, there will be three engineers on watch at one time, viz:

4–8 Watch	Second, Fifth, Eighth Engineers
8–12 Watch	Fourth, Seventh, Tenth Engineers
12–4 Watch	Third, Sixth, Ninth Engineers

The sixth, seventh and eighth engineers are on stokehold watch. In addition, there may be first and second refrigerator engineers and first and second electricians.

The chief engineer's duites are as before. He is in complete charge of the engine-room machinery, and responsible to the superintendent engineer ashore for its efficient and economical running.

The second engineer, again, besides keeping his watch, is in charge of all work going on in the engine-room at any time. He may also keep a check on the quality of the boiler water.

The third engineer may have the port and centre main engines under his special care as regards condition and repair, the steam side of the electrical generators and the ship's emergency set.

The fourth engineer attends to the starboard main engine. He is made responsible to the chief for taking aboard fuel, and at sea he prepares the *scrap* or working log book with pressures, temperatures and revolutions for the chief.

The fifth engineer is responsible for the overhaul and running of all main feed pumps.

Other duties are as follows:

Sixth engineer: oil-fuel transfer pumps.

Seventh, eighth and ninth engineers: general boiler overhauling.

Tenth engineer: boiler work and spare refrigerator engineer.

Large modern turbine steamers may also carry a specialist engineer, who by reason of his previous training and experience, is intimately familiar with all aspects of the turbine control and supervisory equipment, involving as it does, a detailed knowledge of instrumentation, electrical circuits and electronic equipment. He is responsible for the correct functioning of the control and supervisory equipment, so that it continues to give accurate and reliable information on which the other engineers can take action to ensure the safe and efficient operation of the turbine machinery.

Index